02

Despite the significance and enduring place of nationalism in the history of Ireland, there is still no comprehensive analytical treatment of the nationalist tradition. This book fills that gap, analysing the political ideology of Irish nationalism and tracing its implementation into political action from its origins to modern times.

Boyce rejects the idea that Irish nationalism, or any other kind, simply 'happened' at a particular time. He argues that it was the result of a long and gradually developing tradition that owed much to many diverse groups in Irish society. Boyce identifies the chief characteristics of Irish nationalism as a sense of race, religion, and territorial integrity, all of which were influenced profoundly by the power of England. The book explains how Irish nationalists had to struggle to overcome regionalism, passivity, rural backwardness, limited horizons, class differences and religious conflict, and how, in seeking for a common denominator that would enable them to mobilize the 'nation', nationalist leaders sacrificed their fundamental goal – the creation of a comprehensive Irish nation, embracing all classes and creeds of Irishmen.

Describing the triumph of nationalism in twentieth-century Ireland, the book shows how this was simply a veneer on the politics of a deeply divided people. It explains how the experience of statehood in both Northern and Southern Ireland has shaped the political, social and cultural outlook of the people.

Nationalism in Ireland

D. GEORGE BOYCE

London and New York

First edition published in 1982
by Croom Helm Ltd

Second edition published in 1991
by Routledge

Third edition published in 1995
by Routledge
11 New Fetter Lane, London EC4P 4EE

Simultaneously published in the USA and Canada
by Routledge
29 West 35th Street, New York, NY 10001

© 1982, 1991, 1995, D. George Boyce

Printed and bound in Great Britain by
TJ Press (Padstow) Ltd, Padstow, Cornwall

British Library Cataloguing in Publication Data
A catalogue record for this book is available from the British Library

Library of Congress Cataloguing in Publication Data
A catalogue record for this book has been requested

ISBN 0 415 12776 9

To the memory of my mother and father

CONTENTS

PREFACE TO THE THIRD EDITION

When this book was first published in 1982, nationalism seemed to be a political anachronism as far as Western Europe was concerned; since 1989 we have seen, to coin a phrase, the 'Ulsterisation of the world', as the collapse of communism led to intense and often violent national conflict, with Bosnia held up as the cracked mirror in which the North of Ireland beheld its real face.

The return of nationalism to the political agenda has been followed by a new scholarly interest in the subject, building upon the pioneering work of A. D. Smith, Ernest Gellner and others. The study of nationalism has been approached from various directions: as an analysis of texts; as an aspect of social and political mobilisation; and as the work of élites who 'invent' traditions. At the heart of the debate about nationalism is the recognition that its development is inseparable from the quest for political power, and that nationalism and the state need to be studied together. Even cultural nationalists need to capture, or create, a state that will be sympathetic to their needs. This recognition has helped divest nationalism of the sense of mystery that seemed to surround it – the sense that it was in some way the natural and God-given destiny of self-evident nations. But if nationalists 'invent' traditions, they cannot invent just any tradition; they must draw upon the wells of history. Ireland has drawn upon these wells, in the creation of the modern Irish state, and in the conflict between nationalist and unionist in modern Ulster. Political élites and their followers must appreciate each other's codes if they are to create a sense of community based upon a shared view of the past.

The success or failure of this process depends upon political circumstances; the historian of ideas must attend to this aspect of the subject, if the texts involved are not to appear as 'eternal' or 'classical', divorced from their social and political context. For example, Irish republicanism, virtually extinct in the north of Ireland by the 1960s, gained a new lease of life in the 1970s and 1980s; but the south of Ireland witnessed no new republican political dynamic in these decades. Its nationalism did not die out, but rather renewed itself in ways that seemed to reflect the community's changing needs, as a would-be modern state in a would-be European Union.

Nationalism and unionism continue to set the broad parameters of Irish political life. Unionists distrust the 'soft' nationalism, perhaps even the post-nationalism, of the south as much as they fear the harder nationalism in the north. And it may be that the Republic of Ireland's political élite is reformulating its political goals in subtle, but ominous, ways as far as unionists are concerned. But it seems certain that all political élites need to prepare their followers for a partial surrender of their position, if the present truce is to turn out not merely an interlude between wars. All need to recognise that Ireland has not one but many histories; and a long study of nationalism in Ireland suggests that the outcome of the political process is not only unpredictable, but also unlikely to satisfy all those who wish to see Ireland as 'a nation once again'.

D. G. Boyce
January 1995

PREFACE TO THE SECOND EDITION

I am grateful to Routledge for giving me the opportunity to correct errors in the original edition of this book. I have added a new chapter reflecting on my analysis of nationalism in Ireland and discussing the advances made in the subject since the book was first published in 1982. I have also taken the opportunity to consider the current historiographical controversy and, finally, to comment on Irish nationalism in the last decade.

I have also included an updated bibliography.

D.G. Boyce
September 1990

PREFACE

This book is mainly about Irishmen thinking aloud about their politics: a disagreeable habit, but one which they share with other nations. The material consists largely of 'public' sources: newspapers, pamphlets, poems, popular literature and speeches and declarations of various sorts.

In an age when historical research has developed in two divergent directions — the statistical analysis of party machines and electoral politics on the one hand, and the patient reconstruction of episodes in 'high politics' on the other — such an approach needs accounting for. Irish politics cannot be explained without reference to beliefs[1] as well as machinery; nor are they containable within the 'charmed circle' of the high political world.[2] For example: the rise of labour in Britain has been described in terms of pressure groups and vested interests, with ideology set aside;[3] but in 1918 the recently established Irish Labour party was obliged to issue a carefully worded manifesto supporting self-determination for all peoples, but declining to say whether or not the party favoured Irish independence: the distinction between Labour's claim that it would win 'for Ireland freedom', rather than 'freedom for Ireland' was a subtle but significant one.[4] And while its shade of meaning might escape English observers, it did not escape observers in Ireland. The necessity to choose words carefully in the context of Irish politics has been succinctly put by the Ulster poet, Seamus Heaney: 'whatever you say, say nothing.'[5]

This is perhaps for Irishmen a wise piece of advice, but one that the national character seems to render them incapable of following. I am here concerned with them when they are in their more customary mood of saying something, and saying something about their nationality, and their nationalism. I have not analysed their sayings philosophically: even if they were susceptible to such a method — and most of the material is far from philosophical in content — I am not competent to undertake a systematic analysis of this kind. Nor have I adopted the statistical approach to Irish nationalism; here again my material and my academic shortcomings happily coincide. I have, however, tried to trace the relationship between nationalism and social and economic change in Ireland, and thus to explain why Irish nationalist ideology has failed to realise one of its most persistent goals: the creation of a comprehensive

Irish nation embracing all creeds and classes of Irishmen.

In writing a synthesis of this kind, I have inevitably relied heavily on specialist works, especially those of the younger generation of Irish historians. These able and enthusiastic scholars will be painfully aware of the use to which I have put their work; they will be even more painfully aware of the way in which I have tried to put my own interpretation on it. I am indebted to them; and I only hope that my broad generalisations on the fascinating subject of nationalism will not strike them as too far-fetched.

I should like to thank the various libraries in which I have worked: the British Library and the British Library Newspaper Library; the Bodleian Library; the Queen's University Library; the Linen Hall Library; the National Library of Ireland; The State Paper Office, Dublin; and the library here in University College, Swansea, and above all the inter-library loan section, whose staff have been indefatigable in meeting my many and varied requests for books.

I am grateful also to the British Academy and the Nuffield Foundation for generous grants in aid of this research. The Nuffield Trust also helped with the cost of typing the manuscript.

I should like to thank also Professor W.H. Greenleaf and my colleagues in the Department of Political Theory and Government, and the University College of Swansea for their generosity in allowing me a sabbatical year in a time of diminishing staff resources. I am grateful to Mrs Pat Rees for typing the manuscript at a very busy time, and to Mrs Eileen Wimmers for rallying round at the last stages.

My wife Kathleen has encouraged me all along, and carried the main burden of the somewhat uneven tenor of the life of a young family. Barbara and Paul Lintzgy and their family helped us with the children in a way that cannot be acknowledged by a mere expression of thanks. My former teacher, Professor J.C. Beckett, was, as always enthusiastic, encouraging, and full of inspiration. He taught me to try to take the long view of Irish history. He has of course no responsibility for this particular example of it for, as he has himself remarked, following Dr Johnson, 'All claret would be port if it could'.[6]

Notes

1. See review by Iain McLean of P.M. Sacks, *The Donegal Mafia: an Irish Political Machine* (*Political Studies*, Vol. XXVI, No. 1 (March 1978), p. 160).

2. R.F. Foster, 'To the Northern Counties station: Lord Randolph Churchill and the prelude to the orange card', in F.S.L. Lyons and R.A.J. Hawkins (eds), *Ireland under the Union: Varieties of Tension* (Oxford, 1980), p. 287.

3. Ross McKibben, *The Evolution of the Labour party, 1910-1924* (London, 1974).

4. A. Mitchell, *Labour in Irish politics, 1890-1930: the Irish labour Movement in an Age of Revolution* (Dublin, 1974), pp. 94-5; for another example see the Gaelic League resolution of 1915, when a 'free' was substituted for an 'independent' Ireland (D. Coffey, *Douglas Hyde, President of Ireland* (Dublin, 1938), pp. 122-3).

5. S. Heaney, *North* (London, 1975), p. 57.

6. J.C. Beckett, *A short history of Ireland* (London, 1961 ed.), p. vii.

ABBREVIATIONS

EHR	English Historical Review
HJ	Historical Journal
IHS	Irish Historical Studies
IRHS	International Review of Social History
JCHAS	Journal of the Cork Historical and Archaeological Society
P. and P.	Past and Present
SPOI	State Paper Office of Ireland
TRHS	Transactions of the Royal Historical Society

Lord, how quickly doth that country alter men's natures

Eudoxus, in Edmund Spenser, 'A view of the state of Ireland', (Henry Morley (ed.)), *Ireland under Elizabeth and James the First Described by Edmund Spenser, by Sir John Davies and by Fynes Moryson* (London, 1890), p. 192.

INTRODUCTION: NATIONALISM AND IRELAND

In 1904 Eoin MacNeill, later to become Ireland's foremost 'scholar revolutionary',[1] delivered a lecture in University College, Dublin, entitled 'Where does Irish History begin?'[2] For the student of Irish nationalism, the question is an equally pertinent one. Does he begin his exploration in the Gaelic period of Irish history, in the pre-Norman Ireland that is so often regarded as the custodian of the real Irish tradition? Or must he look to the revolts of the Geraldines or the Gaelic chieftains in the sixteenth century? Did the confederate Catholics of the 1640s, with their motto *'pro Deo, pro rege, pro patria Hibernia unanimis'* lay the foundations? Or — in quite the opposite camp — were the Protestant patriots of the eighteenth century — Swift, Grattan, and, in his very different way, Tone — the forerunners? Or is Irish nationalism essentially a modern phenomenon, the product of social and economic change in the nineteenth century, the child of 'modernization' (however that currently popular phrase is understood), the rationalization of the urban and agrarian middle classes' perception of what side their bread was buttered on — or, conversely, the romantic reaction in the early twentieth century against that bourgeois mentality? The historian of Irish nationalism thus finds himself poised between two contrasting but equally hazardous paths: either he can search the more remote past for 'trace elements' of his subject, and run the risk of writing history teleologically; or he can begin his analysis in the modern period, at the time of the French Revolution perhaps, and accept an unsatisfactory, and equally unhistorical, discontinuity between traditionalist and modern phases:[3] nationalism, like rugby football, begins when somebody suddenly decided to pick up the ball and run with it. But historical phenomena do not begin in that way; and neither, possibly, did rugby football.

The difficulties surrounding the attempt to locate the origins of Irish nationalism, or of any country's nationalism, are reinforced by the wider question of what the term nationalism means anyway. To Professor Hugh Seton-Watson nationalism 'is a phenomenon less than two hundred years old, essentially subsequent to the French Revolution'.[4] John Plamenatz agrees that 'there was little or none of it in the world until the end of the 18th century'.[5] Eugene Kamenka, while agreeing that nationalism 'is a modern and initially a European phenomenon,

15

best understood in relation to the developments that produced, and were symbolized by, the French Revolution', none the less adds the rider, 'this is not to say that the rise of political nationalism as a modern phenomenon has no preconditions'; and he goes on to argue that the 'concept of the nation and the nation-state as the *ideal*, or *normal* form of international political organization . . . emerged – slowly – in Europe out of the ruins of the Roman Empire'.[6] Some medievalists are willing to apply the term 'nationalism' to their period; others have declared openly that nationalism had become a basic political fact in western European history by the fourteenth century.[7] But one authority has strenuously denied that there is any such thing before the rise of modern states in the 16th-18th centuries.[8]

The difficulty in knowing when one is talking about nationalism and when one is talking about something else arises, mainly, from the problems encountered in defining the content or substance of nationalism, in delineating its essential characteristics. The most obvious and easily grasped test of nationalism is language, that most distinctive mark of a nation, embodying its history and its literature; but Switzerland, with its variety of languages, or Israel, where a national language had virtually to be invented for the purposes of modern secular use,[9] are obvious exceptions to that obvious rule. If the basis of nationalism is ethnic, the existence of a distinct racial type, then not only the United States but also some of the most ancient European nations can be cited as lacking national characteristic: as Ernest Renan remarked in 1882, 'France is Celtic, Iberian, Teutonic, and Germany is Teutonic, Celtic and Slavonic.'[10] Religion is a badge of nationality in some cases, but in Third World countries of the post-war era self-styled Marxist movements have combined their Marxism with nationalism,[11] and sometimes with religion as well; indeed, Ireland has her own example in the writings of James Connolly. Common traditions and customs, social manners and public institutions may be taken as the moulder of nationalism; but despite sharing many, perhaps all of these, the nations of the United Kingdom have not lost their identity, nor has Welsh, Scottish, or English nationalism lost its potency.

Given the disagreement over the chronology of nationalism, and its nature, it is hardly surprising that attempts to explain why it arises are equally fraught with contradictions. Nationalism might be considered a kind of modern substitute for religion, gaining in strength as religious faith declines; but the examples of Ireland, Wales, Brittany, the Basque country, South Africa and Scandinavia, where the nationalist movements enjoyed the support and leadership of the clergy, and were nowhere in serious conflict with religion, defeat the generalization.[12] Some nations grew out of the expansion of one dynasty, such as France and England; in other cases, such as Italy, the external assistance of France, Prussia and the United Kingdom were necessary, even though the nation had a strong cultural unity. Many modern nations arose from the collapse of empires: the Austro-Hungarian, the Turkish empires, the British empire; but the policy of 'national self-determination' left minorities bitterly resentful of their inclusion in the 'natural' national units; and, in the case of Britain imperialism – by carving lumps of territory in Africa into political and administrative units – created the entities which became states and in most cases nations when the ruling power receded. Nationalism might have been 'caused' by the rise of the bourgeoisie in capitalist Europe; but nationalism is not confined to the bourgeois epoch, for it has split the international communist movement too often to be dismissed as a mere petite-bourgeoisie survival.[13]

There has never been agreement about what constitutes a nation;[14] hence the plethora of 'definitions' ranging from the complex and solemn to the simple and facetious (though by no means inappropriate). There is Ernest Barker's definition:

A nation is a society or community of persons, whose unity is based (i) primarily on space, or neighbourhood, issuing in the feeling of neighbourliness, and in that common love of the natal soil or *patria* which is called patriotism; (ii) secondly on time, or the common tradition of centuries, issuing in the sense of a common participation in an inherited way of life, and in that common love for the inherit- ance which is called nationalism.

And, by contrast, that of H.G. Wells:

A nation is in effect any assembly, mixture or confusion of peoples which is either afflicted by, or wishes to be afflicted by a foreign office of its own, in order that it should behave collectively as if it alone constituted humanity.[15]

Little wonder that the historian retreats hurriedly into the last refuge of the non-social scientist: the definition of a nation as a group of people who consider themselves to be a nation.[16]

This offers an avenue of escape to the historian: he can take comfort in the reflection that nationalism is something that he recognizes when he sees it; that nationalism is the ideas deployed by people who are called, or who call themselves, nationalists, and who belong to a nation — which, in turn, is an entity that the historian recognizes when he sees it. Thus he can get on with the business of writing his history of German, Italian, Irish, French or whatever nationalism or nation he is interested in, without bothering about definitions which seem to confuse rather than elucidate. And, after all, one philosopher has appeared for the historian's defence: 'definitions', Eugene Kamenka has written, 'if they are useful at all, come at the end of an inquiry and not at the beginning. In the study of history and society they provide no substitute for grasping a phenomenon in all the complexity of its historical and social development.'[17] But this still leaves the primary problem unsolved: in dealing with a complex historical and social phenomenon like Irish nationalism it is important to know where to begin; and, before deciding where to begin, it is necessary to establish some framework, some points of reference, some boundaries for the subject matter, however historical the subject matter may be. It would be confusing, for example, if, in a geographical treatise the author referred to the weather of the British Isles when he meant to talk about the climate.

The analysis here presented employs four distinct, but closely related, concepts: cultural identity; national identity; colonial identity; and nationalism. And it uses them in the following senses.

Cultural Identity

This is felt by members of a group who either have or have had a distinct or relatively autonomous existence, and who have shared a recognizably common way of life.[18]

National Identity

This is felt by members of a group who define their culture as the national one, and their group as the true legitimate inheritors of the national territory, of the homeland.

Colonial Identity

This lies somewhere between the first two, and is felt by members of a group whose national identity takes its origins in the mother country, but whose cultural identity has been shaped by their new environment.

Nationalism

This is the assertion by members of a group of autonomy and self-government for the group (often, but not invariably, in a soverign state), of its soldiarity and fraternity in the homeland, and of its distinctive history and culture.[19]

The chief characteristics of nationalism in Ireland have been race, religion, and a strong sense of territorial unity and integrity; and in all its modes it had been profoundly influenced by the power and proximity of Britain. Its demands have ranged across the whole spectrum of constitutional relations, from the idea of a kingdom of Ireland, subordinate to the British crown but not to the British parliament, to outright separation; but it has consistently emphasized the importance of parliamentary independence and parliamentary government, with cultural themes playing a significant, but essentially subordinate, role. It will here be argued that the Gaels possessed a strong sense of cultural identity, which, under the impact of colonization, was transformed into a sense of national identity, and by the end of the Tudor period into embryonic ethnic nationalism. Or that the Anglo-Irish, or Old English, of the medieval colony were by the sixteenth century evolving the idea of a national identity based on religion and love of the *patria*, which, under pressure from the English government, became the ideology of the 'Irish nation' of the seventeenth century, an ideology accompanied by intimations of nationalism. Or that the new settlers of the seventeenth century developed, after the Williamite wars, a sense of national identity that was always implicit in colonial identity, based on religion and love of country. And that nationalism became a fully formed and articulate sentiment in the Ireland of the protestant ascendancy in the last quarter of the eighteenth century.* After the union with Britain in 1800 Catholic national identity was revived, and given a new political direction: the nationalism of the Catholic democracy, influenced by Protestant and revolutionary traditions, and by the resurgence of Gaelic ethnic nationalism in the late nineteenth century, but able to defend its character against all comers. Each of these phases played a part in the

---

*In arguing this I find myself at one with the Dublin committee of the United Irishmen; see Liam de Paor, 'Cultural pluralism', in *Studies*, Vol. 67 (Spring-Summer, 1978), p. 82.

evolution of modern Irish nationalism; each innovation received inspiration from something that had gone before.

It is therefore necessary to make an early start in the study of Irish nationalism. For, whatever their motives or special characteristics, Irishmen used prescriptive arguments in their politics: the language of Irish politics, and especially of Irish nationalist politics, was a conservative one, searching for precedents, seeking to find the justification for their political behaviour in Ireland's past, Gaelic and Anglo-Irish, native and colonial. Only very rarely were fundamental or abstract rights emphasized; and, when they were – by, for example, the United Irishmen – they derived their support from a more deep-seated sense of historical grievance: it has been truly said that 'nationalism in Ireland has been reared less on the rights of man than on historical wrongs'.[21] But this sense of historical wrong was felt as much by eighteenth-century Protestants as by nineteenth-century Catholics, though for very different reasons: each nationality incorporated some at least of the ideas of its predecessor, and then added its own contribution to the dialogue.[22] Hence the study of Irish nationalism involves the student, not in tracing the history of one 'indestructible nation', but in examining certain aspects of the history of what one historian has described as that 'element of instability', the people of Ireland.[23]

For Ireland's nationalist traditions developed in a land peopled by what George Bernard Shaw described as 'that hackneyed myth, the Irish race'. 'We are a parcel of mongrels', Shaw snorted. 'Spanish, Scottish, Welsh, English, and even a Jew or two'.[24] The mongrels who constitute the people of Ireland are the result of several hundred years of settlement and conquest, beginning with the Gaels and ending with the 'New English' and Scottish settlers of the seventeenth century. The racial difference between these groups was soon blurred and was eventually replaced by the politico-religious distinction between Catholic and Protestant; but these convenient labels must not be allowed to obscure the contrasts in outlook *within* as well as between such broad distinctions: between Catholic native Irish and Catholic Anglo-Irish; between Protestant New English and Protestant Ulster Scot. And, within each 'sub-group' were to be found various layers of society: Gaelic aristocratic chiefs and their followers, and their toilers on the soil; Anglo-Irish Catholic landowners and their economic dependants; Protestant landlords and Protestant tenants in Ulster; Catholic large farmers and Catholic landless labourers in the south of Ireland; small-town middle classes and the workers of Dublin city.

Irish nationalist leaders, therefore, had to mobilize very different kinds of people to break into the routine that dominates most men's lives, to attack passivity, tradition, rural backwardness and limited horizons.[25] And all Irish nationalists − whether they were eighteenth century Protestant gentlemen, or twentieth century intellectuals − had to search for issues which would give at least some semblance of reality to their claims that the nation, or the people was united behind them. Regionalism in nineteenth century Ireland had to be overcome; and the nationalist movements of Daniel O'Connell and Charles Stewart Parnell − and, in the twentieth century, Sinn Féin − stand as commanding peaks in an otherwise rough and broken political landscape.

The student of Irish nationalism is therefore obliged to spend much of his time and effort analyzing nationalist political ideas, nationalist rhetoric and nationalist language. But this does not in any sense divert him from the true nature of his subject. While he must not, of course, take this political language at its face value, its shape at any particular time or circumstance throws light on the character of the nationalist movement with which he is concerned. Even if nationalist language were no more than a rationalization for ambitions or social aspirations − and it was certainly much more than this − it raises the question of why certain ideas or appeals were regarded as more likely to produce the desired result than others. Politicians, seeking to legitimize their behaviour in the eyes of their doubting contemporaries, adopt a language likely to be accepted and approved by the social groups whose support they hope to acquire.[26] And whether it was Henry Grattan telling Irish Protestants that they were defending the ancient liberties of Ireland, or Daniel O'Connell assuring his mass meetings that the Irish peasantry was the finest in Europe, or Charles Stewart Parnell presenting home rule as a panacea for agrarian ills, or Eamon de Valera describing his constituents as descendants of Brian Boru, they were appealing to ideas which their contemporaries were prepared to admire and approve of.

In their proselytising missions, Irish nationalists were obliged to search for a common denominator, a unifying principle or set of principles; and, given the varied nature of Irish society, this meant that some members of the nation did rather better out of the fight for freedom than others. For eighteenth century Irish Protestant nationalists their common bond was their religion and their social position: when the question of Catholic political rights and Protestant radical reform demands were presented to them, they found that their 'national solidarity' was torn asunder. For nineteenth century nationalists, whether Catholic or Protestant, the choice was again an unenviable one: to seek to widen the religious basis of Catholic national identity might threaten national solidarity with no obvious political advantage. To aspire to include landlords in the nationalist movement — and Protestant nationalists like Thomas Davis and Parnell certainly hoped that the natural leaders of society could be thus attracted — might jeopardise the driving force of the movement, the aspirations of the tenant farmer. And even within the farming classes there was a wide variety of people, ranging from the small farmers eking out a living in the west to the cattle ranchers and the prosperous farmers of the midlands and the east. Irish nationalist leaders were remarkable successful in promoting the idea of unity and fraternity in the nation. That they were successful was partly because of their own political skills, but mainly because economic and social pressures fell on an already well-defined set of cultural relationships,[27] relationships shaped by the political and religious history of Ireland. The relationship between landlord and tenant was presented, and easily accepted, as one between Saxon interloper and native owners of the soil; Irish socialism became quickly identified with the age-long struggle between the Gael and the Gall.

The early twentieth century saw the triumph of nationalism in twenty-six counties of Ireland, an event celebrated in a derisory fashion by republicans in their song:

God save the southern part of Ireland
Three quarters of a nation once again.

In fact the Ireland that won independence in 1922 was not even a united, three-quarter nation: it was divided between sea-green incorruptible republicans and those who accepted dominion status as the best that could be wrung from Britain; it contained a middle class of large farmers, shopkeepers and businessmen who feared that the revolution might lead to the breakdown of public order and the destruction of their way of life; it had to contend with a Protestant and Unionist minority, small in numbers but influential in position, which might prove resentful and hostile to the new state; it numbered among its ranks Gaelic cultural enthusiasts who wanted to make Ireland not only free but Gaelic as well, to the exclusion of nearly everything else. The way in which the divisions left behind by the destruction of the Union, the revolution and the civil war were healed and a homogeneous twenty-six county Ireland created is the concluding theme of this book.

In this state there gradually emerged something that had never existed in Ireland at any time in her history: a single nation, in a nation state, sharing a common view of their history and untroubled by any irreconcilable political divisions. The contrast with Northern Ireland hardly needs remarking; for the creation of the state of Northern Ireland exacerbated already existing cultural and political frictions, and exposed them to the vagaries of Dublin politics, since one of the most important unifying themes of southern politics after the 1920s was *Hibernia Irredenta*. No historian writing about Irish nationalism can exclude from his mind the contemporary scene in Northern Ireland. In particular the record of the Provisional IRA has, in the eyes of many, discredited nationalism, and especially republicanism.[28] But my concern is not to expose or condemn, but simply to seek to understand, amongst other things, why the pluralist origins of the Irish people have failed to find adequate expression in their dominant political tradition.

Notes

1. Eoin MacNeill (1867-1945), leading advocate of the Gaelic movement in Ireland, Professor of early (including medieval) Irish history in University College Dublin, 1909, first president of the Irish Volunteers, 1913, court-martialled and sentenced to life imprisonment by the British in 1916, released 1917, M.P. (Sinn Féin) for Derry city and the National University of Ireland, 1918, Minister of Education in the Free State executive, 1922.

2. F.X. Martin and F.J. Byrne (eds.), *The Scholar Revolutionary: Eoin MacNeill 1867-1945 and the Making of the New Ireland* (Shannon, 1973), p. 17.

3. E. Stokes, 'Traditional resistance movements and Afro-Asian nationalism: the context of the 1857 mutiny rebellion in India', *Past and Present*, No. 48 (1973), pp. 100-118.

4. H. Seton-Watson, *Nationalism Old and New* (Sydney, 1965), p. 3.

5. J. Plamenatz, 'Two types of nationalism', in E. Kamenka (ed.), *Nationalism: the Nature and Evolution of an Idea* (Canberra, 1974), p. 23.

6. Kamenka, op. cit., pp. 3, 6.

7. D. Obolensky 'Nationalism in eastern Europe in the middle ages', *TRHS*, vol. *27* (1972), pp. 1-16.

8. H. Kohn, *The Idea of Nationalism: a Study in its Origins and Background* (New York, 1951).

9. E. Hobsbawm, 'Some reflections on nationalism' in T.J. Nossiter, A.H. Hanson and S. Rokkan (eds.), *Imagination and Precision in the Social Sciences* (London, 1972), pp. 385-406.

10. E. Renan, 'What is a nation?' in *The Poetry of the Celtic Races and other Studies by Ernest Renan*, translated with an introduction and notes by William G. Hutchinson (London, n.d. [1896?]), pp. 61-83.

11. A.D. Smith, *Nationalism in the Twentieth Century* (London, 1979), Chap. 5.

12. A. Butt Philip, *The Welsh question: Nationalism in Welsh Politics, 1945-1970* (Cardiff, 1975), p. 328.

13. Hobsbawm, op cit. For a convenient survey of these various factors see H. Seton-Watson, *Nationalism old and new*, passim.

14. Smith, op. cit., pp. 12-13.

15. M. Ginsberg, *Nationalism: A Reappraisal* (Leeds, 1961), p. 2.

16. And not only the historian. See G.C. Field, *Political theory* (London, 1965 edn.), p. 242. 'We cannot, in general, say much more than that people are of one nationality when they believe themselves to be so'.

17. Kamenka, 'Political nationalism: the evolution of an idea', op. cit., pp. 3-20.

18. I take this definition of cultural identity from F.S.L. Lyons, *Culture and anarchy in Ireland, 1890-1939* (Oxford, 1979), p. 3.

19. I am obliged for the substance of this definition to A.D.S. Smith (ed.), *Nationalist movements* (London, 1976), pp. 1-2.

20. The comparison with Ancient Greece is instructive; see Kohn, op. cit., pp. 50-60.

21. K.H. Connell, 'The potato in Ireland', in *Past and Present*, No. 23 (1962), p. 65.

22. For the idea of nationalism as a species of 'Platonic dialogue' see Stokes, op. cit., p. 101.

23. J.C Beckett, *Confrontations: Studies in Irish History* (London, 1972), p. 23.

24. D.H. Greene and D. H. Lawrence, *The Matter with Ireland* (London, 1962), p. 294.

25. A.D. Smith, *Nationalist Movements*, p. 7.

26. I have been guided in my approach to this problem by H.T. Dickinson, *Liberty and Property: Political Ideology in Eighteenth Century Britain* (London, 1977).

27. L.M. Cullen, 'The cultural basis of Irish nationalism', unpublished paper delivered at a seminar on nationalism in Britain and Scandinavia in the nineteenth century, Gregynog Hall, Wales, September 1979, p. 17. See also A.D. Smith, *Nationalism in the Twentieth Century* (London, 1979), p. 160.

28. The most prominent example is Dr C.C. O'Brien; see especially his *Herod: Reflections on Political Violence* (London, 1978).

1 COLONY AND NATION

Modern Irish nationalists would perhaps be surprised to learn that they had anything in common with Cromwellian Englishmen; but, like the radical thinkers of the English Revolution, they believed that 'our very laws were made by our conquerors'.[1] And, just as those Englishmen appealed to Anglo-Saxon rights against seventeenth century encroachment, so did Irish nationalists appeal to Gaelic tradition against foreign innovation. 'Foreign' applied to anything which followed the Normans in 1169; and the Gaelic dispossession of the earlier inhabitants of Ireland was conveniently forgotten. The Gaels have been described as 'conquering castes' with camp followers of 'various breeds',[2] and their shaky title to Ireland is further vitiated by their failure to retain any significant degree of racial purity. Indeed, it was impossible for them to do so: they would have had to exterminate a native population which had been established for over five thousand years, and they would have had to resist any intermarriage with the Scandinavian seafarers who came to Ireland in the ninth century, first to raid and then to settle.[3] Nevertheless, later generations of Irishmen, whatever their political or religious complexion, have all found it necessary to come to terms with the belief that the Gaels in some sense represent 'the Irish in the infancy of their race'.[4]

The Goidelic Celts were comparatively recent invaders of Ireland. They entered Ireland between 500 and 300 BC as a war-like race of conquerors;[5] and it may well be that the tacit assumption by many nationalist historians that this last Celtic invasion was 'good', and all post-Celtic incursions and invasions 'bad' was because the later invaders were unfortunate enough to have their misdeeds chronicled,[6] while the Gaels were able to compose their own, more flattering, version of their history. They were also able to claim that the Gael had been in occupation of Ireland since time immemorial, and that all Irish families of any importance were of Goidelic origin.[7] It might seem, however, that any investigation into the nature of pre-Norman Ireland is superfluous: if the Gaels were but one wave of successive invaders of Ireland, then to the historian, as distinct from the politician, Gaelic Ireland has no special significance. Moreover, if it is also bad history to regard the modern Irish nation, or what is usually considered the Irish nation, as in any real sense the direct descendants of the Gaels,[8] then there scarcely seems any point in examining the Gaelic political and social system. But this is to carry historical revisionism too far. The nature of Gaelic Ireland has exerted not only a fascination in the minds of later genera-tions of Irishmen (Catholic and Protestant), but also an influence on the history of Ireland.

That Gaelic Ireland has been endowed with certain myths hardly needs stating. The Gaels were invaders of Ireland and therefore had no more title to 'originality' than the Normans or the English settlers of the seventeenth century. Moreover, their coming did not mark a com-plete break with the past: Gaelic culture, like Norman and English culture, was 'poured into an Irish mould'.[9] Ireland influenced the Gaels as much as the Gaels influenced Ireland. The high kingship of Ireland claimed by the O'Neills in the seventh century, which had its sacred centre at Tara, recalled the pagan age, for the newcomers, in selecting Tara, selected a site held to be sacred since the Bronze Age;[10] and kingship itself as an archaic institution, a part of the heritage of earlier institutions.[11] The Gaels were also obliged to adjust their ways to the invaders who followed them: in choosing their sites for provincial capitals, the Gaelic kings of the twelfth century proved their adapt-ability by moving into the Norse cities of Dublin, Cork and Limerick.[12]

The existence of these 'province kings' is itself another contradiction of the nationalist concept of Gaelic Ireland: that a nationally united Ireland had existed from the arrival of the Gaels. Thus the twentieth century scholar, Eoin MacNeill, sought to prove that there was a high-kingship of Ireland, an Irish law of a national extent, and a king who was supreme judge and law-giver.[13] This contrasted with the view of G.O. Orpen, who set down his own version of an anarchic Ireland in a 'tribal state', possessing an *ard rí* with no political power but only nominal authority. Ireland, unlike most other European countries, was free from external threat, and had every opportunity to construct some kind of political unity; but, Orpen argued, this very absence of threat from Roman or Barbarian invasion meant that Ireland could remain in happy oblivion, free from any danger that might have 'roused the Gael from his slumbers'.[14]

This picture of a country marked out from contemporary Europe by its failure to build up national institutions has been accepted by many modern historians, and it is an amusing paradox that a country which prided itself on its strong sense of nationalism, that sought statehood and emphasized unity, should in its infant days have been totally devoid of all these characteristics. The nations of Europe assumed their shape gradually in the middle ages, and most successfully where they had the advantage of a definite and defensible core such as the *Ile de France*; from such a heartland regions could be absorbed, and larger political units emerge.[15] And when political structures widened and developed beyond the local community, then the number of people participating in these political structures grew and so a process of nation building quickened and developed.[16] But Ireland, with its conglomeration of independent kingships, its local rivalries and patriotisms (which often degenerated into warfare[17]), its lack of a national heartland, its alien capital of Dublin and its topographical fragmentation, easily drew the comment that 'the Irish are a byword for their prolonged failure to create an effective united Irish state'.[18]

Ireland, however, may not have been so far outside the mainstream of European life as Orpen and later authorities have asserted.[19] The 'patch-work quilt' of Irish political institutions, the dynastic subkingdoms, the fluid network of local supremacies were altering by the twelfth century. Before the Viking incursions there were two outstanding overkings: O'Neill, dominating the north and the eastern midlands, and Eoganacht of Munster, dominating the southern part of Ireland. There was no national monarch or king of all Ireland; but there was a breakdown of localized petty kingdoms, the emergence of more extensive power blocs, and the growth in both the powers and ambitions of kings. The poet-historians of eleventh and twelfth century Ireland elaborated and embroidered the concept of a monarchy of all-Ireland, and dynasties such as the O'Brien sought to assert that they were the chosen dynasty, 'the sons of Israel of Ireland', who would extend their rule over all Ireland as the Normans had done in England. Before the Norman invasion the focus of political life in Ireland was a struggle for the kingship of Ireland, with rival provincial kings fighting for the title. By the beginning of the eleventh century Brian Boru had enforced his authority over the whole of Ireland, but he did not succeed in establishing an effective government of the country to match his title, and the high kingship had no rule of primogeniture to give it a lasting stability. Decentralized independence remained the essentially Irish way of life; and the high kings were not strong enough to resist external threat or the resurgence of localism in Ireland itself.

Nevertheless, the Irish high-kingship's importance must not be overlooked: for its significance lay less in the thing itself than in the underlying trends which it revealed. And it is the nature of political society in Ireland, rather than the fragile institutions which rested upon that society, that the Gaelic contribution to Irish political tradition is to be found. For the Gaels were developing a sense of belonging to a larger community or *natio*, a sense of their past, or at least of their imagined past. The phrase 'men of Ireland' was used of the followers of the greatest kings, and of the lesser kings and nobles under their sway; and as early as the seventh century the Gaels had begun to create an elaborate legend of their origins embracing all the tribes and dynasties of the country, and treating the principal elements of the ancient population, Celtic and pre-Celtic, as offshoots of one stock, united in ancestry. 'The shades of the ancestors hung heavy over Gaelic Ireland and claims derived from them were not forgotten'.[20] The Gaels may not have enjoyed the institutional framework of the Anglo-Saxon kind from which national consciousness could emerge; but they jealously guarded their own cultural, social and linguistic peculiarities, and, like medieval Wales, Ireland was a country of local loyalties whose sense of 'otherness' was found by looking to the past.

It has been suggested, in the Welsh context, that the practice of writing down old traditions is a sign of growing self-consciousness;[21] and, if this be so, then the Gaels were moving towards a growing awareness of their *'natio'* or community. Ireland had a class of poets (file) whose place in early Irish society was similar to that of the druid in ancient Gaul, that of the omnipotent man of learning, the seer. These poets preserved a kind of history compounded of folklore, racial memories, mythology, dynastic propaganda, genealogy, and they were the guardians and expounders of traditional law — law that was held to be good for the whole of Ireland. From such materials grew the saga literature of Ireland, preserved in manuscript from the twelfth century, but often embodying much earlier ideas; and one of the most famous 'cycles of the kings' which they preserved was a biography of Brian Boru, written in the twelfth century in support of the pretensions of his descendants, the O Brien kings of Ireland, and entitled 'The war of the Gaedhil (Gael) with the Gall (foreigner)'.[22] In it Irish history was depicted — not for the last time — as a struggle against foreigners (in this case the Norsemen) which reached a triumphal climax with the rise of the royal house of Dal Cas and the career of Brian.[23]

The historians of pre-Norman Ireland created and circulated a legend of Irish history, of Irish unity and of Irish antiquity going back to ancient times, to the Flood, and to the coming of the first ancestor of the Gaels, Milesius of Spain. It was the impact of invaders that helped the Gaels towards their concept of one nation, united in their veneration of their ancient customs and of the land that bore them.[24] The *Leabhar Gabhala* (Book of Invasions), put into writing in about 1050, gathered the fictions, traditions and facts collected by the poet-historians, and their version of events was fully accepted by the Gaels before the Normans came to Ireland, and was still believed in the seventeenth century. The poets cultivated a concept of Ireland symbolized – again, not for the last time – as a woman, Eire, Fodhla or Banba, reigning over the men of Ireland. Thus the Gaels had developed a notion of their ancient pedigree and of their sole legitimate claim to the land of Ireland, and a strong sense of race and of pride in Gaelic culture, a sense of pride and race which all Gaelic princes held, no matter how much they allied with the foreigner when it suited their political purposes.[25] And such alliances could in any case be fitted into, and reconciled with, Gaelic tradition. Norse-Irish alliances were a familiar aspect of pre-Norman Ireland in the incessant squabbling for paramountcy among the Irish kings, and such activities were not, of course, regarded as in any sense 'unpatriotic'.[26] But the poets and their patrons felt it useful at least to portray them in a particular light: the battle of Clontarf in 1014, which was essentially part of the revolt of the men of Leinster against the dominance of the upstart Brian Boru, a revolt in which the Leinstermen's Norse allies played an important role, but a secondary one, was subsequently elevated into a heroic saga of a sovereign of Ireland who led the forces of the nation to victory over the foreigners.[27] And when Dermot MacMurrough, King of Leinster, invited the Normans into Ireland in 1169 to help him against his rebellious subjects, he may have been inspired by the example of his mythical ancestor, Labraid Loingsech, who as an exiled prince recovered his patrimony with the aid of foreign troops.[28]

The Norman 'invasion' of Ireland was, therefore, more in the nature of a response to an invitation; but it was bound to attract the attention of the king of England, Henry II, who could not tolerate the possibility of an independent Norman state on his western flank, and who, in 1171, came to Ireland to accept the surrender of Waterford and establish an English royal presence in Ireland. Because Henry came to curb the activities of his barons in Ireland, he was, naturally enough, made welcome by the Irish princes. The Irish clergy were his firm supporters also. And the high king, Rory O'Connor, made a treaty with Henry in 1171 recognizing him as 'lord of Ireland', and in turn receiving confirmation of his title as king of Connaught and high king of Ireland.[29]

Had the Normans not come to Ireland, Rory O'Connor might have forged some kind of national monarchy of the kind that had already been created in neighbouring countries;[30] but the Norman intervention introduced the first of those breaks in a pattern of development which one Irish historian has drawn attention to.[31] A genuine national monarchy did not emerge; but neither did the kings of Ireland unite to check and expel the invader. Instead each ruler fought for himself, now allied with, now against, the newcomers.[32] Nevertheless, the events of the twelfth century were significant for the nationalist tradition in Ireland, though not in the way that they have often been portrayed. They were not the beginning of a process of 'Irish' resistance to the English which lasted unbroken from 1171 to 1921: there never were two 'sides' in Ireland whose struggle can be reduced to such simple proportions. But the Normans were the forerunners of the English colony in Ireland, and the presence of that colony was to have a profound effect on the nature of national identity in Ireland, and on the expression of the political rights of the country.

Now that Ireland was no longer an isolated land, contact with the foreigner gave a strength and meaning to the cultural and linguistic unity of the Gaels. The lordship of Ireland in theory covered the whole country; but in fact Ireland was governed under two systems, that of the native kings and that of feudal law in the Norman-occupied territory. This division between 'native' and 'colonist', this distinction between the 'foreigners of Ireland' and the Gaels, dominated the course of Irish history and has not altogether been eradicated even today. It was not always a rigid division, for at different times, and in different parts of the country, it seemed on the point of disappearing or of becoming politically meaningless. Nor was it a racial one, for intermarriage between 'settler' and 'native', and the adoption of each other's ways made Irish society much more complex than the division would suggest. But it survived and outlived local peculiarities, the lack of political unity among the Irish, and their failure to see far beyond their own regions. The Irish experience of post-12th century colonization paralleled that of Wales: in both cases the settler/native dichotomy came to correspond to identifiable national groups, Welsh and English, Irish and English, and, in seventeenth century Ireland, Irish, Old English and New English.

The medieval period of Irish history saw cultural intercourse between colonist and native, and a growing fear amongst English administrators concerning the dangerous consequence of Hibernicisation of the 'English by blood'.[33] From at least 1297 statutes were passed providing that Englishmen 'should relinquish the Irish dress, at least in head or hair', or that 'no mere Irishman, being of the Irish race' should be appointed to municipal office, or, in that most famous of all statutes, the Statute of Kilkenny in 1366, forbidding any alliance of marriage, fostering of children, or concubinage, and deploring the behaviour of the English who 'forsaking the English language, fashion, manner of riding laws and usages, live and govern themselves by the manners, fashion, and language of the Irish enemies, and have made divers marriages and alliances between themselves and the Irish enemies, by which the said land and its liege people, the English language, the allegiance due to our lord the king, and the English laws are put in subjection and decayed'. The Statute of Kilkenny was the product, not of English domination, but of English fear that the tide of their power was ebbing, and of the recognition that the division based on descent was in danger of obliteration.[34] But, however real that danger appeared to be, the distinction between 'native' and 'colonist' proved a lasting one, and one of which the native Irish were only too well aware. Domnall O'Neill, king of Tir Eoghain, describing himself as king of Ulster and heir to the high kingship of Ireland, and speaking (somewhat optimistically) in the name of the Irish people, remonstrated with the pope in 1318 about 'English inhabiting our land, who call themselves of the middle nation':

> For such is their arrogance and excessive lust to loor it over us and so great is our due and natural desire to throw off the unbearable yoke of slavery under them and to recover the inheritance so wickedly seized by them that as there has not been in the past, there cannot be in the present or in the future, any sincere goodwill between them and us.[35]

And, as far as the Irish annalists were concerned, the Anglo-Irish remained foreigners, even while they distinguished between them and the English.[36] Of course, the friction between the two nations of medieval Ireland was exaggerated by English governors and ambitious Irish kings alike: but it was firmly rooted in cultural identity.

In Ireland, as in Wales, it was the governance of the areas of the country where the colonists settled that made for the chief distinction between native and foreigner and helped carry that distinction into the early modern period. For the English presence in Ireland, like that in Wales, was not merely a military one, nor was it an act of territorial annexation. It was accompanied by administrative, governmental and legal innovations[37] which were to shape the country's development, and give it a focus around which Irish political ambitions could gather.

This was a slow development. Henry II did little to establish English governmental structures in Ireland, beyond appointing a few officials; he was content to create a balance of power between the various factions that vied for power and position. Three of the Irish province kingdoms were left in the hands of the native rulers; two in Norman hands (de la Clare in Leinster and de Courcy in Meath); and in 1175 an informal agreement known as the treaty of Windsor left Rory O'Connor as high king over the Irish provinces. In 1183 O'Connor voluntarily retired from the high kingship and ended the 1175 agreement. Henry had now no high king with which to negotiate, and he decided to replace a *modus vivendi* with a system – a new monarchy of all Ireland, embracing all the diverse elements, distinct from the monarchy of England, and similar to the kingdom of Scotland. He applied to the pope for recognition of Ireland as a kingdom for his son John, and for a crown. His request was granted; but Henry subsequently thought better of the scheme, and instead granted John the title of 'lord of Ireland', *Dominus Hiberniae*, not *Rex Hiberniae*.[38]

When John succeeded to the throne in 1199, the lordship of Ireland was annexed to the kingdom of England. His policy was three-fold: to reduce the power of the older baronage in Ireland; to favour the Irish chiefs for policy's sake; and to build up a central government strong enough to override both. But this ambitious scheme failed to live up to expectations, and in the late thirteenth century the lordship of Ireland was 'less a lordship than a patchwork of lordships'.[39] John at least built up the fabric of legal monarchy in Ireland; but 'government by Dublin castle'[40] did not, in any real sense, begin. He introduced a judicial code, 'The customs of Ireland' and established an Irish currency. But the extent of English governmental power in Ireland varied, and Ireland remained an intensely regional country, with a marked absence of governmental institutions and a thin veneer of English central and local administrative practices overlaying non-English social and political arrangements: some lords assented to the Statute of Kilkenny, but adopted practices at variance with them.[41]

Nevertheless, by the end of the thirteenth century the English kings had given Ireland what she had never possessed before: a parliament.[42] The first known Irish parliament met in Castledermot in 1264 and, like its counterpart in England, it had judicial, consultative and legislative functions. Most of its legislation was of an ephemeral nature; and the commons did not come to parliament until the late thirteenth century, and only very gradually did they establish themselves as a permanent feature of the assembly. The franchise was restricted to the knights of the countryside and the burgesses of the towns, and Gaelic Ireland was excluded from representation until the time of Henry VIII, and then only represented by Gaelic lords who had been raised to the rank of the peerage. The areas represented were similarly restricted: only the counties of Dublin, Kildare, Louth and Meath were regularly represented, and the town of Waterford; by the early fifteenth century there were only 44 members in the commons. In the upper house only a small number of spiritual peers sat with the temporal peers; and both categories were, like the commons, regional in character. Lords, commons and lesser clergy were drawn mainly from areas where the great lords, who dominated the council, could control and influence them.[43]

Not only was this a regional parliament; its legislation often displayed the anti-Gaelic spirit of much government legislation in the middle ages. One of the acts of the parliament of 1297 declared that colonists who did not wish to be treated as Irish must refrain from wearing Irish garb or hair style otherwise they would be regarded as Irish and suffer the consequences. In 1310 it was enacted that 'no mere Irishman (*nullus merus Hibernicus*) should be received into a religious order among the English in the land of peace in any part of Ireland'.[44] This decree was speedily revoked; but its enactment revealed that even within the church the two nations were far from forming an integrated whole.[45]

Nevertheless the Norman – or, as they may now more properly be called, the Anglo-Irish – colony soon began to make the English government realize that its position of dependence on England did not mean that its loyalty could be taken for granted. In the 1330s disagreements arose over the mother country's attempt to enlist colonial aid in the Scots wars, and over colonial objection to English-born men holding legal offices. The crisis came to a head in 1341 when the justiciar, Sir John Darcy, named as his deputy Sir John Morice, 'a plain English knight', on whose advice Edward III had relied when framing his policy on grants made in Ireland during his minority. Morice was instructed to enforce an edict ordering that all officers within the land of Ireland who held estates or were married in the country should be replaced by Englishmen whose estates were altogether in England 'by whom we think to be better served'. Morice dismissed his old officers and summoned parliament to Dublin for October 1341. Desmond and Kildare, the great Anglo-Irish lords, appealed to the whole colony and summoned a rival Parliament to Kilkenny in November. 'Never', wrote the Anglo-Irish Annalist, 'before had there been so marked a rift between the English of England and the English of Ireland'.[46]

Desmond's parliament appealed to the king and sent two envoys with an indictment of the English Government, past and present. The difficulties confronting the realm – the loss of a third of Ireland to the

Irish and the fall of certain castles — lay in the failure of the king's ministers, for these officials constantly overrode the rights and laws of the king's Irish subjects. Cases were settled in English courts which could be settled in Ireland; the land was being ruined by the neglect of absentees. The colonists stressed their loyalty to the crown, contrasting it with that of the 'Scots, Gascons and Welsh' who had often levied war against the crown. The Act of Resumption which had been threatened under Morice was an injustice, for, according to Magna Carta (which had been extended to Ireland in 1217) no man could be deprived of his freehold without due process of law.

These demands were, of course, the demands of an Anglo-Irish vested interest who had little time for the Gaelic population. They did not speak for Ireland, nor did they claim to do so, but only for their part of Ireland — and only then for their own possessions in their own part of Ireland. Their struggle to defend their rights was assisted by the king's preoccupations in the French wars, and in 1343 he was obliged to repeal the statute which excluded the Irish-born from office. But in 1344 another pure Englishman, Sir Ralph d'Ufford, became justiciar. He entered Ireland with a strong army, determined to be severe on the Earl of Desmond, and when Desmond again rebelled he was outlawed and his earldom forfeited. His supporters wavered, for loyalty to the crown was, as it remained, central to Anglo-Irish politics. But when d'Ufford died in April 1346 his replacement, Roger Darcy, was a man of lesser mettle. Desmond was exempted from the general pardon of 1346 but was allowed to state his case to the king and was taken into favour again. In 1351 Magna Carta was confirmed; and in 1355 Desmond's triumph was made complete when he was appointed justiciar.[47]

Desmond was no selfless Anglo-Irish patriot; still less was he a friend to the native Irish: and his last act as justiciar in November 1355 was to mount an expedition against them. He was an ambitious lord whose support was very localized; but the language he used to advance his self-ish concerns represented that mixture of pride and insecurity that was to become typical of the Anglo-Irish colony, especially when it believed that its Englishmen's rights were in danger of being slighted. In particular, the Anglo-Irish parliament was quick to sense any impugnment of its rights and liberties. In 1375 it was requested to send representatives to appear before the council of England to treat with it on the affairs of Ireland; and it replied that 'according to the rights and liberties enjoyed from the time of the Conquest and before' it was not bound to send representatives, and although it now elected them, it reserved the right to assent to any subsidies made in its name. Compliance in the present request was not to be taken as prejudicing the rights, laws and customs which parliament had enjoyed since the conquest and before.[48] During the York and Lancaster conflicts of the fourteenth century the Anglo-Irish parliament found itself drawn into the political arena when Richard, Duke of York, the lieutenant of Ireland, fled there in 1459 after his defeat at Ludlow. In 1460 he summoned a parliament to Drogheda to drum up support. The parliament ratified his appointment as lieutenant for the term indicated in the letters patent of March 1457 and declared that to plot against the lieutenant was to plot against the king. It went on to assert that no Irish resident ought to obey any direction, given under any other seal than the Irish great seal, requiring him to answer outside Ireland, and that:

the land of Ireland is and at all times has been corporate of itself by the ancient laws and customs used in the same, freed of the burden of any special law of the realm of England, save only for such laws as by the lords spiritual and temporal and the commons of the said land shall have been in great council or parliament there held admitted, accepted, affirmed and proclaimed.[49]

This declaration was little more than a device used by the duke of York to protect himself from the Lancastrians; but its ready acceptance by the Anglo-Irish parliament was based on a long-standing grievance among the colony concerning the competence of the Irish courts – chancery, king's bench, common bench, exchequer, parliaments and great councils – to determine all manner of pleas and plaints arising in Ireland, as well as touching the king and other persons, and the claim that it had not been the practice for Irish residents to plead or to be impleaded in such causes outside Ireland by means of writs and privy seals from England. The other claim asserted in 1460, that only those English laws were in operation in Ireland that were admitted, accepted, approved and proclaimed in Irish parliaments and great councils, may have had no basis in history;[50] but it was one that the colony was to resurrect again and again in its future dealings with the mother country, and, indeed, it became the legal basis of the Irish nationalist claim up to the eighteenth century and beyond.

It would be highly misleading to suggest, however, that it is possible to speak of a single Anglo-Irish political entity, jealously guarding the welfare of its country. Disputes and disagreements between the great Anglo-Irish lords were endemic, and the feud between the Butlers and the Geraldines was one that disturbed the peace of Ireland from the later fourteenth century until the end of the fifteenth. When Thomas, seventh earl of Kildare, was made justiciar in 1478, and was then succeeded by his son, Gerald, the Anglo-Irish parliament became the instrument through which they could cloak their actions in legality. Parliament still represented little more than a few towns of Leinster and Munster and the commons of four shires, Dublin, Meath, Kildare and Louth, and such bishops and lords of parliament as still performed their parliamentary duties; but, like its predecessors, it defended the principle that English Acts could bind Ireland only when accepted by the Irish legislature; and, like the parliaments of the thirteenth century, it held the theory of *plena potestas*, and the fiction that the statutes of the king and his Parliament of Ireland were binding over the whole island, and on the native Irish also as far as and when they could be enforced. That this was far from true was shown in 1472 when bitter complaint was made that neither 'the writs of the king nor the law of the king nor his court is . . . used betwixt the people of the king of Ulster'.[51] Nevertheless this colonial Parliament, with its official language French or Latin, its language of debate French or English — but never Gaelic — and its sturdy defence of the self-interest of the Anglo-Irish, gave some institutional framework to the idea of a unitary Irish state,[52] whose laws were applicable to the whole people of Ireland, a political concept that had taken but shallow roots in pre-Norman Ireland.

These tentative developments were swept away in 1494 when Kildare was arrested and English sovereignty re-asserted by Acts of Parliament. The crown resumed the judgement of treason and rebellion, the command of royal castles, the choice of officials and the control of the Irish legislative body. In future no parliament was to meet in Ireland without express licence under the great seal of England, and no Act was to be passed in any such parliament unless it had first been sanctioned by the Deputy and council, and approved by the king and council in England. Henry VII's immediate concern was to protect himself from the possibility of a pretender to the throne possessing himself of Ireland and performing any acts of sovereignty; Kildare was restored to the deputyship in 1496, and control of the Irish Parliament was soon abandoned.[53] But Poynings Acts and the political and constitutional tendencies which they were designed to check were to become the stuff of Protestant patriotic debate two centuries later.

The Irish medieval Parliament was an institution representing only one of the two *natios* in the country; and the colony's unease, occasionally breaking out into hostility, about its Irish neighbours found legislative expression in the numerous statutes which sought to restrain any too close intermingling of the communities. Inevitably, these statutes were rendered less effective by the natural intermingling of the *natios*, and the Anglo-Irish and native Irish did not form two distinct racial types. For an Anglo-Irishman to cease speaking Norman French or English and begin speaking Gaelic did not alter his physique; but it did alter his political interest, and his allegiance to the particular political nation in which his aspirations, his daily concerns, his family's future prospects lay.

There were, perhaps, several occasions when the divisions between the nations of medieval Ireland might have been broken down, and a unity of all Irishmen – or, rather, of that proportion of Irishmen which constituted the politically active groups of society – achieved. In the early fourteenth century Edward the Bruce of Scotland invaded Ireland, sending messengers to 'each and every king of Ireland, the prelates too, the clergy and inhabitants of all Ireland, our friends' to 'treat with each and every one of you, in our name, about a perpetual confederation of special friendship between us and you . . . by which, God willing, our nation (i.e. the Scots and the Irish) may be restored to its ancient liberty'. But no more than a handful of kings adhered to Bruce's appeal, or proved themselves willing to accept his sovereignty; and those among the Anglo-Irish who associated themselves with Bruce did so in the same spirit as the native Irish, seeing the invasion as an opportunity to settle old scores, to claim rights denied to them, or to better their position by the use of force. These 'English rebels' were a common preoccupation of the Government of Ireland, and they were themselves at odds with some of the great Anglo-Irish magnates. The Bruce invasion failed to provide Ireland – Gaelic or Anglo-Irish – with a liberator or a national monarch simply because this was not what Irishmen wanted; and never again, while the medieval lordship of Ireland lasted, was an attempt made to unite the Gael and the Gall.[54]

If the political division of Ireland could not be undermined by unity, then it could perhaps be destroyed by the complete victory of one or other of the nations. Such a victory seemed possible, for wherever the Normans went after 1169 – into Thomond, Desmond or the Decies – there was always to be found some Gaelic family willing to co-operate with them in their enterprise.[55] In the thirteenth century the colony grew and the area of direct royal government increased. But the extent of Anglicization of the lordship varied from one area to another, and in some places was extremely superficial; and the Bruce invasion of 1316 revealed how weak the power of the central administration really was.

The fact that many of the Anglo-Irish in Ulster and elsewhere supported the Bruce was symptomatic of the general instability of English
government in Ireland; and many of the Gaelic Irish made good use of
the opportunity to regain their lands. The Government, already financially shaky, was not capable of maintaining the degree of control
which it had achieved in the thirteenth century;[56] and the two centuries which followed saw something of a 'Gaelic revival' in Ireland, and
the possibility of an entirely different pattern of development.

This revival took several forms: the recovery of lost lands; military
reconquest; and cultural revival. The poets wrote of Ireland as 'a
'woman who has risen again from the horrors of reproach' and now
belonged to Irishmen once more.[57] By the late fourteenth century
many Gaelic lords were showing a dangerous tendency to confederate,
in Leinster and in Munster.[58] Richard II's expedition to Ireland in 1394
checked the Gaelic menace, for his strong military force and his political skills enabled him to regain possession of Leinster and the submis-
sion of the Gaelic lords, MacMurrough, O'Neill, O'Connor and O'Brien,
who swore fealty and restored the occupied lands. The king's return to
England early in 1395 was quickly followed by a collapse of his settlement, and a second expedition in 1399 proved no more permanently
successful. Once Richard left, Ireland was consigned to her own devices,
and 'the Irish enemies' proved 'strong and arrogant and of great power,
and there is neither rule nor power to resist them'.[59]

But, once again, a possible pattern of political development did not
fulfil itself. The very lack of a Gaelic ruling dynasty, possessing wide
authority, was both a strength and a weakness to English rule in
Ireland. A strength, in that Gaelic Ireland continued as a congeries of
ententes and alliances, with no central directing power, no institutional
body to give political purpose to Gaelic cultural and national identity.
A weakness, in that the English Government, unable to single out one
king with whom to deal, one man who could 'deliver the goods', was
obliged to adopt a defensive posture and maintain the frontiers of
English power as best it could. Before the mid-fifteenth century an area
identified as the 'pale' around Dublin and closely associated with the
English parts of counties Dublin, Meath, Kildare and Louth, marked the
boundary of English power.[60] But the Anglo-Irish, for their part, were
not absorbed or conquered by the Gaels; they organized their territories
to be as self-sufficient and as autonomous as possible: living in frontier
conditions, they developed frontier virtues.

Still, there were signs that some kind of cultural assimilation of the
Anglo-Irish with the Gaelic Irish seemed possible. The notorious first

earl of Desmond got on well with the Irish, admiring their carefree gaiety, their hospitality, their good conversation and their songs;[61] and the third earl was an accomplished composer of Irish poetry and had a keen interest in Irish learning.[62] This kind of cultural bond, found in a leading representative of a people who had thrown their lot in with Ireland, and who by 1317 spoke of themselves as a 'middle nation', neither English nor Irish, or perhaps both English and Irish,[63] might seem a prelude to a blending of the different Irish traditions.

But the Desmonds and their like simply showed, as generations of Anglo-Irishmen were to show, that it was possible to embrace Irish cultural values enthusiastically while rejecting Irish politics; similarly, later generations of Irish nationalists could reject emphatically Anglo-Irish culture while eagerly seeking to assert the political and consti-tutional values of the Anglo-Irish Parliament. The Anglo-Irish were conscious of themselves as a 'middle nation', mingling with the native Irish, but never of native Irish stock. This distinction was found even in the church, where dioceses were split into two cultural regions, and attempts were made to keep certain offices or areas or monastic houses and friaries exclusive to one or other of the nations. Bishops, abbots and other clergy who attended parliaments or councils were nearly always of English birth or descent, having little fellow-feeling with their Irish counterparts. Appeals to charity, such as that of a thirteenth century archbishop (who happened to be German) praising the work of the community of the priory of Clanthory, Co. Meath 'situated as you are in the borders of Ulster and Leinster, between two nations which persecute each other'[64] had little effect, especially in the monastic orders.

The decline of English power in the second half of the fourteenth century made the problem of the church more pressing. The Statute of Kilkenny enacted that beneficed clergy living among the English should learn English; that no Irishman 'of the nations of the Irish' should be admitted by provision, collation, or presentation into any cathedral, collegiate church, or benefice among the English of the land; and that no religious house among the English should in future admit Irishmen. To some extent these provisions were a matter of common sense: it was desirable that clergy should know English when adminis-tering the English and dealing with an English-speaking Government; and they were approved by the archbishops of Cashel and Tuam and the bishop of Killaloe, who were all Irishmen.[65] But national distinc-tions were never very far below the surface, and were apt to sour relations between the English and the Irish in the church. In 1421 the archbishop of Cashel was accused by the bishop of Waterford and Lismore of a wide variety of offences, including making very much of the Irish, loving none of the English nation, bestowing no benefice upon any Englishman and counselling other bishops not to give the least benefice to any of them.[66]

Anglo-Irish self-consciousness, which prevented their assimilation into the Gaelic political world, was reinforced by the special position which they came to hold in fifteenth century Ireland. With the decline of English power and its shrinking to the pale, the English Government was forced to rely more and more on the great Anglo-Irish families to maintain some kind of order and political stability within the pale and beyond it. The Anglo-Irish lordships were a mixture of Gaelic and English customs, institutions, language and manners, scarcely distinguishable in their mongrel appearance from their Gaelic neighbouring power blocs; but their political complexion was a very different matter: for they could aspire to rule their neighbouring areas on behalf of the English Government.

From the 1470s the Kildares were the masters of their world, controlling the Government with few interruptions until the reign of Henry VIII. The other Anglo-Irish families who had competed, or might compete, were eclipsed, either because of political miscalculation, as in the case of the Butlers, or by a combination of their rivals, as in that of the Desmonds. The power of the Kildares was based on their landed wealth, control of parliamentary institutions, patronage, marriage alliances, military strength, and, crowning all this, their ability to dominate the Irish council.[67] Gaelic lords, under the shadow of this great dynasty, paid dues, mainly in kind, for Kildare 'protection'. And so tenacious was the Kildare grip on Irish politics that when the great earl died in 1513 his son, Garret Og (Young Gerald) succeeded him to the deputyship of Ireland as naturally as he succeeded to his father's earldom.

It might be argued that the Kildares could have built up some kind of Irish nation, uniting the Gaelic and Anglo-Irish traditions under their personal dynasty. But their rise to power was based on that very lack of national unity among the Irish and the Anglo-Irish which enabled them to climb the greasy pole. The native Irish had no share in the government of the lordship, and it was to the king of England that Kildare looked for his honours, his rewards, his advancement. Political power, as much as a sense of national distinction, separated the Anglo-Irish from the Gaelic Irish, and from the 'English by birth' of the pale, whose interests cut them off from the Anglo-Irish and Gaelic peoples alike.

Later Irish nationalists have come to see the Kildares as exponents of the national cause, with Garret Og standing for 'Ireland for the Ireland men' and thus supplying the 'lasting argument for self-government as against rule from over-sea'.[68] But such an ideal would have spelt, not the making of the Kildare ascendancy, but its ruination.

The contribution of medieval Ireland to the Irish nationalist tradition was not the clear-cut, unambiguous one that nationalist historiography depicted; nevertheless, there was a significant contribution, but one of a dual, almost contradictory nature. There was what might be called a negative influence: the failure of the two nations, Gaelic and Anglo-Irish, who dominated medieval Irish politics and society, to find some kind of ground for common action, and, more important, to create a sense of national unity to match their racial and cultural intermingling. The myth of the Gaelic Irish remained what it had been since at least the time of the Viking invasions: that of the native Irish fighting to throw off the foreign oppressor. Men whose aims were particularist, personally ambitious or downright predatory cloaked their actions in appeals to national sentiment and racial exclusiveness; for it was thus that they sought to legitimize their behaviour. There never was a state of 'racial war' in medieval Ireland to match this myth; but a sense of cultural distinctiveness persisted which made any concerted political policy on the part of Gaelic and Anglo-Irish difficult, but not, of course, impossible.

What Ireland lacked was the kind of myth propagated by Geofrei Gaimar, whose *L'Estoire des Engleis* was written in the twelfth century. Gaimar had lived in England, probably in East Yorkshire, and his history of the English provided a neat blend of the traditions of both native and conqueror. He even succeeded in telling the story of Hereward the Wake without creating either an anti-Norman or anti-English impression; and he adapted Geoffrey of Monmouth's tale about the ending of the struggle between Saxon and Briton with the coming of a people 'dressed in wood and in iron corselets' who would 'give their dwellings back to the earlier inhabitants' (the British). Gaimar neatly altered this story to fit his audience, treating the English as the Britons, and substituting the Danes for the English. Thus the Normans became not conquerors but liberators. If the Normans could not suppress the English tradition then they could at least reconcile it with their own.[69]

The Anglo-Irish came nearest to this kind of myth in their parliamentary tradition. Here they found it expedient to adopt the idea of a legal — but not racial or national — continuity, stressing that the land of

Ireland had always been 'corporate of itself by the ancient laws and customs used in the same, freed of the burden of any special law of the realm of England save only such laws as by the lords spiritual and temporal and commons of the said land had been in great council or parliament there held, admitted, accepted, affirmed and proclaimed according to sundry ancient statutes thereof made'.[70] But the idea that they were in any national sense the descendants of the Gaels, of the 'original people' of Ireland, was not one they could safely adopt while the Gaels were still in control of much of the island of Ireland, and were in a position to defend strongly their local particularisms. The kind of myth constructed by the Normans was one that could be created only from a position of complete domination, for it was similar to that of the Gaels themselves, who had evolved their racial myth not only from colonization, but from conquest. The Anglo-Irish positive contribution to the nationalist tradition – the assertion of the legal continuity of the rights of the Irish parliament – was not accompanied by a positive assertion of the blended nation, such as that given to the Normans by Geofrei Gaimar or William of Malmesbury.[71] No Anglo-Irish chronicler hit on the idea of claiming that the colonists had come to liberate the original inhabitants of Ireland from the Gaels, though such a claim would have had no less authenticity than the Norman myth. The Anglo-Irish, heirs to an incomplete conquest, sought to prove a descent from the 'blood of the first conquest';[72] it was as far as they dared, or needed, or desired to go.

It would be an oversimplification, but a pardonable one, to suggest that whereas the Gaelic Irish saw themselves as the Irish nation, they lacked a centralized political institution in which they could build up a habit of concerted political behaviour; and that whereas the Anglo-Irish possessed such an institution, their Parliament, they lacked a sense of themselves as the Irish nation (seeing themselves merely as *a* nation *in* Ireland) to match their Parliament's formal claim to legislate for the whole country. When a later and very different generation of Anglo-Irishmen made good their claim to be the Irish people, and also eagerly asserted the political and constitutional rights claimed by the medieval colonists, Irish nationalism at last became a political reality.

But all this was in the future; and Ireland emerged from the middle ages without a central unifying myth, and with the distinction between native and colonist, Gael and Gall, still strong and thriving: cultural exchange, intermarriage, temporary alliances for political convenience, modified, but could not destroy, this distinction. In England, despite the harshness and cruelty of the Norman conquest, the conquerors succeeded in creating such a myth; and the appearance of the idea of the 'Norman Yoke' in the seventeenth century, though it provided a stimulus to radical thinkers of that and later ages,[73] did not perpetuate the notion of racial distinctiveness, of a colonial layer of people who took the land from its rightful owners.[74] In England in 1966 the Norman conquest was regarded as a cause for national celebration; in Ireland in 1969 official bodies were adamant in their refusal to commemorate the coming of the Normans eight centuries before.[75] The contribution of the colonial presence in Ireland, that dynamic force in the making of Ireland's nationalist tradition, was thus formally and publicly repudiated.

Notes

1. C. Hill, *The Century of Revolution, 1603-1714* (London, 1972 edn.), p. 177.

2. E.E. Evans, *The Personality of Ireland* (C.U.P., 1973), pp. 43-5.

3. A.T.Q. Stewart, *The Narrow Ground: Aspects of Ulster, 1603-1969* (London, 1977), pp. 27-9.

4. S. O Faolain, *The Irish* (London, 1947), p. 11.

5. E. Curtis, *A History of Medieval Ireland from 1086 to 1513* (London, 1978 edn.), p. xix; M. Dillon and N.K. Chadwick, *The Celtic Realms* (London, 1973 edn.), pp. 18-20. The term 'Goidelic' refers to the group of Celtic languages which these latest immigrants spoke. (Ibid., pp. 56-7).

6. E.E. Evans, op. cit., p. 46.

7. M.A. O'Brien, 'Irish origin legends', in M. Dillon (ed.), *Early Irish Society* (Dublin, 1963 edn.), pp. 36-51.

8. E.E. Evans, op. cit., pp. 44-5, 58-9; P. Wilson, *The Beginnings of Modern Ireland* (London, 1912), p. 7.

9. Evans, p. 47.

10. Curtis, op. cit., p. xxi; F.J. Byrne, *Irish Kings and High Kings* (London, 1973), pp. 53-62.

11. D.O Corrain, *Ireland before the Normans* (Dublin, 1972), p. 32.

12. Curtis, op. cit., p. xxi.

13. F.X. Martin and F.J. Byrne, *The Scholar Revolutionary: Eoin MacNeill, 1667-1945, and The Making of the New Ireland* (I.U.P., Shannon, 1973), pp. 32-33.

14. D. O Corrain, 'Nationality and kingship in pre-Norman Ireland', in T.W. Moody (ed.), *Nationality and the Pursuit of National Independence* (Belfast, 1978), pp. 1-35; G.H. Orpen, *Ireland under the Normans* (4 vols: vols. I and II, Oxford, 1911; vols. III and IV, Oxford, 1920), vol. I, pp. 20-28.

15. E.E. Evans, op. cit., pp. 24-5.

16. M. Richter, 'The political and institutional background to national consciousness in medieval Wales', in Moody, op. cit., pp. 37-55.

17. F.J. Byrne, *Irish Kings and High-Kings*, p. 27.

18. E.E. Evans, op. cit., p. 68.

19. The following paragraphs are based on O Corrain in Moody, op. cit.; O Corrain, *Ireland Before the Normans*, Chap. 2, pp. 96-7, 120-31; J. Otway-Ruthven, *A History of Medieval Ireland* (London, 1968), pp. 28-36; and

F.J. Byrne, op. cit., Chap. 12.

20. Curtis, *Medieval Ireland*, p. 5.

21. Richter, op. cit., p. 38.

22. O Corrain, *Ireland before the Normans*, p. 78.

23. Otway-Ruthven, *Medieval Ireland*, pp. 24-5.

24. M. Sheehy, *When the Normans came to Ireland* (Cork, 1975), pp. 36, 88.
Indeed, the Irish had no common word for themselves until they came into contact with foreigners: the expressions 'The Gaels' is a borrowing from the Welsh
word Gwyddyl (F.J. Byrne, *Irish Kings and High Kings*, p. 8).

25. Curtis, *Medieval Ireland*, p. xix.

26. O Corrain, *Ireland before the Normans*, pp. 92-3.

27. Ibid., pp. 130-31.

28. Byrne, *Irish Kings and High Kings*, p. 11.

29. J.F. O'Doherty, 'The Anglo-Norman Invasion' in *Irish Historical Studies*,
vol. I, (Sept. 1938), pp. 154-7.

30. D.A. Binchy, *Celtic and Anglo-Saxon Kingship* (Oxford, 1970), p. 45.

31. J.C. Beckett, 'The study of Irish history', in *Confrontations* (London,
1972), pp. 11-25.

32. L. de Paor, *Early Christian Ireland*, (London, 1960), p. 183.

33. J.A. Watt's phrase; see *The Church and the Two Nations in Medieval
Ireland* (Cambridge, 1970), p. 173.

34. J. Otway-Ruthven, *Medieval Ireland*, pp. 291-5; G.J. Hand, 'The statutes
of the native Irish in the lordship of Ireland, 1272-1331' in *The Irish Jurist*,
vol. I (1966), pp. 93-115, and 'The forgotten statutes of Kilkenny: a brief
survey', op. cit., pp. 299-312.

35. Watt, op. cit., pp. 186-7.

36. A. Cosgrove, 'Hiberniores Ipsis Hibernis', pp. 12-13.

37. There were, however, significant differences between the legal systems
used in Ireland and Wales. The Statute of Wales integrated much native law and
custom in a uniform code; in Ireland native law retained no significant foothold
in areas where the Normans prevailed. Thus the native Irish in such areas became
unfree in law (Hand, op. cit., pp. 93-4); Otway-Ruthven, 'The native Irish and
English law in medieval Ireland' in *Irish Historical Studies*, vol. VII, (March
1950), pp. 1-16.

38. W.L. Warren, 'John in Ireland, 1185' in P.J. Jupp and J. Bossy (eds.),
Essays presented to Michael Roberts (Belfast, 1976), pp. 11-23.

39. R. Frame, 'Power and society in the lordship of Ireland, 1272-1377', in
Past and Present, No. 76 (August 1977), p. 3.

40. Curtis, *Medieval Ireland*, p. 100.

41. Frame, op. cit., p. 26.

42. H.G. Richardson and G.O. Sayles, *The Irish Parliament in the Middle Ages*
(Philadelphia, 1964 edn.), Chap. 5.

43. J. Lydon, *Ireland in the later middle ages* (Dublin, 1973), pp. 31-6.

44. Curtis, *Medieval Ireland*, pp. 173-5, 332.

45. J.A. Watt, op. cit., p. 183.

46. G.O. Sayles, 'The rebellious first earl of Desmond' in J.A. Watt, J.B.
Morrall and F.X. Martin (eds.), *Medieval Studies Presented to Aubrey Gwynn,
S.J.* (Dublin, 1961), pp. 203-227.

47. Curtis, op. cit., pp. 206-226; Sayles, op. cit., pp. 219-225.

48. Curtis, op. cit., pp. 248-9.

49. Ibid., pp. 321-3.

50. Richardson and Sayles, op. cit., pp. 260-62.

51. Curtis, op. cit., pp. 252-3, 334-5.

52. For the applicability of the expression 'state' to the middle ages see Sidney
Z. Ehler in J.A. Watt, J.B. Morrall and F.X. Martin (eds.), *Medieval studies
presented to Aubrey Gwynn*, S.J. pp. 492-501. Ehler argues that when a vassal

county satisfied the requirements of having their territories, their populations and their established governments, they justify the appellation of 'state'. Ireland, unlike Wales, had its own parliamentary institutions and was not fully incorporated into England, it was not, of course, sovereign in the modern sense, but then no medieval state was.

53. Richardson and Sayles, op. cit., Chap. 17; Otway-Ruthven, *Medieval Ireland*, p. 408.

54. J.F. Lydon, 'The Bruce invasion of Ireland', in *Historical Studies*, IV (A.A. Hayes McCoy (ed.), London, 1963), pp. 111-25; see also J. Lydon, *Ireland in the Later Middle Ages* (prologue) and J. Otway-Ruthven, *Medieval Ireland*, pp. 224-38.

55. F.X. Martin, 'The first Normans in Munster' in *JCHAS*, vol. *lxxvi* (Jan.-June 1971), pp. 48-71.

56. J.F. Lydon, in Hayes-McCoy, op. cit., p. 122; Otway-Ruthven, op. cit., Chaps. vi and vii.

57. Lydon, *Ireland in the Later Middle Ages*, p. 61.

58. Ibid., p. 106.

59. Ibid, pp. 109-25. K. Nicholls, *Gaelic and Gaelicised Ireland in the Middle Ages* (Dublin, 1972), pp. 17-20.

60. Lydon, *Ireland in the Later Middle Ages*, pp. 130-39.

61. G.O. Sayles, 'The rebellious first earl of Desmond', op. cit., p. 226.

62. J.F. Lydon, *The Lordship of Ireland in the Middle Ages*, p. 184.

63. Ibid., p. 291; B. Fitzgerald, *The Geraldines* (London, 1951), pp. 105-16.

64. Lydon, *Lordship of Ireland in the Middle Ages*, pp. 285-88.

65. Otway-Ruthven, *Medieval Ireland*, p. 139.

66. Ibid., p. 360.

67. Lydon, *Lordship of Ireland in the Middle Ages*, pp. 268-72; J. Lydon, *Ireland in the Later Middle Ages*, pp. 154-63.

68. A. Stopford Green, *Irish Nationality* (London, 1929 edn.), pp. 118-19.

69. R.H.C. Davis, *The Normans and their Myth* (London, 1976), pp. 126-8.

70. Lydon, *The Lordship of Ireland in the Middle Ages*, p. 263.

71. Davis, op. cit., pp. 128-30.

72. Curtis, op. cit., p. 235.

73. C. Hill, 'The Norman yoke', in *Puritanism and Revolution* (London, 1965 edn.), pp. 50-122.

74. Brian O Cuiv, 'Literary Creation and Irish historical tradition', in *Proceedings of the British Academy*, vol. XLIX (1963), pp. 233-62.

75. F.X. Martin draws attention to this contrast in his article, 'The first Normans in Munster', op. cit., p. 54.

2 INTIMATIONS OF NATIONALISM IN TUDOR IRELAND

'The blood of the First Conquest has in a manner failed'.[1] So wrote a Tudor official at the beginning of the sixteenth century. On the accession of Henry VIII in 1509 the earl of Kildare ruled in Dublin as deputy of the king. Only within the area of the Pale was English government a direct and constant experience; here the inhabitants of the most English part of Ireland looked to their government to protect them from oppression by Gaelic and Anglo-Irish alike. Tudor monarchs, for their part, were understandably reluctant to intervene too directly or vigorously in Ireland, or to undertake the task of disarming 'so warlike a country' and reducing 'so great and privileged a nobility'.[2] English involvement in Irish affairs was a slow, piecemeal and largely uncoordinated effort, at least until the end of the sixteenth century. But that involvement, however faltering at first, was to have important consequences for the relationship between the different cultural traditions within Ireland, and on the constitutional and political connection between Great Britain and Ireland.

It is tempting to single out religion as the single most important factor in Tudor Ireland, one that was bound to create a division between the English Government and its Irish subjects. Religion is certainly a major determinant of Irish nationality; but, until the mid-seventeenth century, religion was not a unifying political force among Irishmen, though attempts were certainly made to make it so. In 1614 George Carew predicted that the interests which separated the Old English (as he called the Anglo-Irish colony) from the Irish would prove weaker than the cohesive force of their common religion, and that before long they would find themselves in union against the English.[3] But the sixteenth century, though harbouring the seeds of this alliance, has a special interest of its own for the historian of Irish nationalism; and its significance is best understood by turning to that frequent source of social and political change in Ireland, the English Government.

Social and political change could hardly be expected to come from anywhere within Ireland.[4] Ireland was divided into a network of small units, some ruled after the Gaelic manner, some under feudal control, but all jealous of their independence both from Dublin and from local magnates.[5] It was, like many European countries of the time, a society where warfare was considered a proud and glorious occupation; it had the characteristics of an incomplete colonial adventure: a land in turmoil, a 'frontier' atmosphere, offering opportunities to men of skill and initiative to carve out a rich future for themselves and their offspring.[6] It was also a possible source of danger to the mother country, however, and Irish support for the Yorkist cause was a timely demonstration to the Tudors of the dangers inherent in leaving Ireland too much to its own devices, especially when England might have enemies on the continent. Any attempt to revive the flagging authority of the Pale posed important questions for the Anglo-Irish and the Gaelic Irish alike. If the interest of England was identified with the English interest in Ireland, then the Anglo-Irish stood to gain from any new departure in Tudor policy. If, however, the English interest was not thus identified, then any vigorous change of direction in Dublin had serious implications for them, for their services as a governing élite might be dispensed with, and the fate which they sought most of all to avoid – identification with the native Irish – might eventually befall them. For the native Irish, any renewed attempt at conquest and colonization was a threat to their strongly defended local power and a menace to their conservative instincts.

During the reign of the first two Tudors these threats seemed more apparent than real. The object of Tudor policy was to govern Ireland, but to govern it in the least expensive and least demanding way possible. During the 1520s and 1530s experiments were made with the government of Ireland, and some nine changes of governor took place within the space of 14 years.[7] But experiments in administration of such frequency are very often more a symptom of failure than of success; and, in the end Henry VIII returned to the point from which he had departed: whatever the abuses or dangers inherent in the method of 'aristocratic delegation' of power to the great Anglo-Irish families, they paled beside the alarming financial, military and political implications of any vigorous alternative policy.

But the last two years of Kildare's rule in Ireland saw an increasing control and closer supervision of the deputy by Thomas Cromwell. Cromwell was disposed to encourage direct communication to himself, instead of through the deputy, and to circumvent Kildare by bringing patronage more fully under royal control. He was also quick to investigate complaints about Kildare's alleged mis-government. Kildare became uneasy: he seemed to be caught up in Cromwellian intrigue, and his prospects looked more alarming when Cromwell promoted officials who were ill-disposed towards him.[8] His response was the last resort of the member of an élite whose status and power is threatened by a new order: he rose in rebellion to demonstrate to the king that the crown could not rule Ireland without his assistance, and that exclusion from government would result in political chaos in Ireland. Kildare chose his moment well, for Henry's deteriorating relations with the papacy over his divorce suit, filed in 1527, tempted the Emperor Charles V to look towards Ireland as a means of bringing pressure to bear on the English king. This coincidence of Kildare tactics with Imperial strategy served to give Kildare's rebellion something of a religious flavour, and, superficially, to link it with later uprisings like 1641 or even 1798. But, although Kildare's son, Thomas, Lord Offaly, denounced Henry as a heretic, and required an oath of allegiance to himself, the pope and the emperor, the rebellion failed to catch fire as any kind of religious crusade. Quite simply, relations between the English Government and the leading Anglo-Irish dynasty had broken down, and the Kildares hoped that normal relations would be resumed as soon as possible, on terms favourable to themselves.[9]

The king did not play his hoped-for part in this armed negotiation with the Kildares, except for a brief period in the summer of 1534 when he was still in a weak position militarily. His counter-thrust was the more ambitious one of putting down the rebellion, and Kildare and his leading supporters were attainted in 1534-6. The inevitable sequel to such a move was the search for some new ways of governing Ireland, and new ways of governing necessarily involved the king in establishing a permanent garrison there, and in negotiating directly with the Irish chiefs whose only previous contact with the king had been through the medium of the Kildares. The overthrow of the Kildares meant that from now on Englishmen served as governors of Ireland; and Kildare's clients, as well as those who had remained loyal to the government, were confronted with the inescapable fact of a permanent English-run administration controlled from Westminster and backed by an army.

The Kildare rebellion was the first serious challenge to Tudor rule in the sixteenth century, and it inaugurated a series of major movements of disaffection, in the 1550s, the 1560s, the 1580s and the 'nine years war' of the 1590s. But these were rebellions, not revolutions; they were not attempts to inaugurate changes in Irish society and politics, but to prevent such changes, to keep things as they were. The 'Irish revolution' of the sixteenth century was the work, not of Anglo-Irish or native Irish rebels, but of the English Government. It was the English Government that sought to re-model Irish society, to make it more amenable to English rule, and, if all else failed, to replace its governing élites with a new one. And, even though the practice of this new departure did not live up to its promise, its threat held dangerous implications for the Anglo-Irish and native Irish alike.

This first sign of the English revolution in Ireland was seen in the Irish parliament of 1541-43 which elevated Henry from lord of Ireland to king of Ireland, a move which was a kind of declaration of intent, but one from which no Tudor or Stuart monarch found it possible to retreat. The kingship of Ireland was a promise of the political unification of the country under the crown's jurisdiction;[10] and in order to give this policy some meaning it was necessary for Henry to seek a new relationship with the Anglo-Irish and native Irish, and to make them dependent on the king. This would require little alteration for the Anglo-Irish to whom it meant not much more than the application of existing law; for the native Irish it involved a more substantial re-orientation. The method used to encourage the Gaelic lords to exchange old ways for new was that of 'surrender and re-grant': ruling lords would surrender their lands to the king and receive them back as a fief from the crown. Their fiefs would thus pass to the eldest son, by English, not Gaelic custom; and chiefs would pay due obedience to the king. Most Gaelic chieftains were content to adopt this practice, the more powerful of them receiving English titles; and, once again, there seemed on the surface to be some opportunity of creating some common ground between the Anglo-Irish and the native Irish. But the two nations of medieval Ireland were not so easily transformed by legislation into one. The Anglo-Irish were as anxious as ever to stress their loyalty to English culture, to play the role of a ruling class in Ireland, to portray the Gaels as incorrigibly subversive. The Gaels had difficulties of their own. Gaelic septs who had been excluded from succession by the new law sought to overthrow the chieftains who had submitted to it; and, in any event, the task of subduing 'so warlike a country' was likely to prove a long haul. The continuing disorder in Tudor Ireland was soon reflected in the building of fortifications in Gaelic areas, in the sealing off of the Pale from the rest of the country, in the use of 'soldier-cultivators' to populate the vulnerable areas around the Pale.[11]

The fusion of the Anglo-Irish with the native Irish might be anticipated on other grounds; and, in particular, their possession of a common religion in the age of reformation;[12] and the fact that the Kildares had appealed to religious sympathies would seem to indicate that there were such sympathies to appeal to. Certainly the reformation came to Ireland as an alien movement, but it probably came to England in this way as well. There was nothing in the Irish character predisposing it towards clinging to the old faith any more than there was in the English or German character: from 1530 to 1560 England passed from Roman Catholicism to English Catholicism, to moderate Protestantism, to radical Protestantism, to Roman Catholicism, and back to moderate Protestantism again.[13] Of course, this could be cited as a classic revelation of the English character, a justification of the title 'perfidious Albion'. But practical politics rather than national susceptibilities are the key to the fate of the reformation in both England and Ireland.

It is true, none the less, that Ireland had certain features marking her off from England before the reformation: Ireland had no long-standing tradition of anti-clericalism, no tradition of critical inquiry or questioning at an intellectual level; few ideas of the new learning reached the Anglo-Irish towns, and fewer still the Gaelic countryside. Despite the fact that the English monarchs and the pope were natural allies in securing the legal title of English kings in Ireland, embodied in the Bull Laudabiliter, protests against the yoke of the foreigner never took on an anti-papal colour, but, on the contrary, were expressed in complaints to the pope that English kings were failing to keep their part of the contract, and were encroaching on the rights of the church. Indeed, the practice of appealing directly to the pope ('Rome-running') for intervention on their behalf was so rife amongst the Gaelic Irish that it aroused complaint from English officials in Ireland.[14]

It is also true that while the Irish 'reformation parliament' accepted Henry's legislation in 1536 without serious resistance, there was resistance to the principle of royal supremacy over the church, and opposition to 'Catholicism without the pope' from local inhabitants and some clergy.[15] But the decisive influence on Irish and Anglo-Irish Catholic reaction to English ecclesiastical policy depended largely on the political conditions prevailing at any time. There was no 'national alliance' between palesman and Gaels, but occasional alliances, or attempted alliances, of convenience, made and broken depending on how each group, and in particular the Anglo-Irish, perceived their interests to stand in relation to the government. This did not prevent the leaders of each group calling upon their Catholic faith as some kind of potentially unifying principle; but they did this because there was no other unifying principle on which they could call, given their traditional native/colonist relationship; and the principle of religion, in the event, did not prove a sufficiently unifying bond in the divided Ireland of the sixteenth century.

The Irish parliament accepted with little demur the king's ecclesiastical legislation of 1536 and 1537. Some assiduous preaching by friars and priests encouraged an invasion of the Pale by O'Neill and O'Donnell of Ulster in support of the young Gerald Fitzgerald of Kildare, half-brother of Silken Thomas; but immediate political considerations surfaced again; and the failure of the Jesuit missionaries who arrived in Ulster in 1542 with letters from the pope and Ignatius Loyola, only to be given short shrift by the northern chiefs, showed that the royal supremacy over the Irish church was at least acceptable. Quite simply, neither the Gaelic chiefs nor the Anglo-Irish lords were in a position to resist the king, and appeals by 'friars and priests of all the Irishry . . . that every man ought, for the salvation of his soul, (to) fight and make war against our sovereign lord the king's majesty' on promise that 'if any of them die in the quarrel, his soul, that so shall be dead, shall go to heaven'[16] made little impression in this world, however much they might have availed the Irishry in the next.

Henry was now supreme head of the Irish church in its entirety; but the ease with which this was accomplished must not obscure the underlying difficulties of the crown. Politically, Ireland was still in an unstable condition, and law and order was a shaky affair. And, although the Anglo-Irish had loyally accepted the king's reformation legislation, they disliked the idea of an ecclesiastical structure without the pope. However, they knew full well that they relied upon the crown for their position, their rights and their customs, and, above all, their superior status over the Irish. It would be wrong to doubt the sincerity of their faith, and when it came to accepting the implications of their parliamentary actions their position was, to say the least, uncomfortable.[17] They disliked the doctrinal and liturgical changes which took place under Edward VI: the new communion service of 1548, which replaced the mass; the removal of surviving religious images; the new service book, the Book of Common Prayer.[18] The succession of Mary in 1553, and the attempt to reverse the religious policy of the last two monarchs, was met with enthusiasm in Ireland.[19] But politics rather than religion was still the dominant theme in Irish life, especially the politics of colonization. The attempted plantation of Leix and Offaly (renamed Queen's county and King's county respectively) begun under Edward VI and revived in Mary's reign, provoked strenuous efforts by the dispossessed to eject the newcomers. And the Anglo-Irish lords for their part, could hardly forget that Gaelic chieftains, whatever their common religious beliefs, were their traditional foes. Thus both Catholic nations in Ireland had much better things to do with their time than burn heretics and persecute Protestants.

Ireland, therefore, might have been brought over to the reformed faith by the same means that brought over the recalcitrant areas of England: propaganda, painstaking policy, and, as a last resort, the use of force. Force there was to be in plenty during the reign of Elizabeth; but propaganda and policy were lacking. They were lacking from the beginning, when, at the dissolution of the religious orders in Ireland, the new English arrivals in Ireland benefited as much as the Anglo-Irish, who had a long-standing presence in the country.[20] The Anglo-Irish faced the problem which had always been implicit in Tudor policy: if the Government failed to regard them as an essential part of its 'forward' policy, then they would find it more difficult to retain the English part of their political and cultural identity. The Government faced the consequences of its attitude to the Anglo-Irish: if it no longer perceived them as the essential ruling colonial élite, then what was the point in spending time and money attempting to convert them to the new religion? Thus it became more difficult for the English to see the 'Englishness' of the Anglo-Irish, and more tempting to stress their essentially Irish character, or at least the worst parts of it: and when to this racial antipathy was added the immense difficulties of enforcing reformation legislation, the lack of missionary zeal among the Protestant clergy, the tardy establishment in 1592 of Trinity College Dublin to train Protestant missionaries and equip them with Irish,[21] it seemed easier to displace the Anglo-Irish ruling élite, and the Gaelic chieftains, than to convert them. Indeed, to many Englishmen, it seemed that the Irish and the Anglo-Irish were so far beyond the hope of civilization that conversion was an impossibility.

All this is not to reduce or denigrate the contribution of the papacy, and especially of its commissary in Ireland, David Wolfe, SJ, to the religious conservatism of Ireland. Wolfe, a Limerick man, was given the brief of making contact with the main Irish chieftains, ascertaining their attitude towards religion, and encouraging them in their fidelity. His aim was also to give some administrative shape to the Catholic church in Ireland, to see if bishops resided in their dioceses, instructed their flocks and carried out all their duties. He also inquired into the clergy's manner of administering the sacraments, and sought to establish schools, staff them with Catholic teachers, and send to Rome a list of ecclesiastics suitable for the episcopacy. Wolfe's was not a political mission, but a spiritual one on the lines laid down by the Council of Trent. He had no intention of inspiring a papal war against Queen Elizabeth, whose Irish parliament had in 1560 passed her reformation legislation with almost bewildering speed. Wolfe did not spearhead an anti-Protestant or anti-English crusade, but set himself to the more fruitful task of hard work, organization, and attention to detail in matters of church organization and instruction.[22]

The political importance of religious change, or the lack of religious change, is, perhaps, more obvious to later observers than to contemporaries. The failure of the reformation in Ireland certainly posed vexatious problems for the English crown; but it was not yet a political threat, especially since the papacy, until 1570, was still working on the assumption that the English Queen could be won back to the Catholic faith, and that Ireland was, in the natural order of things, subject to England and would continue to be governed by her. Of more immediate importance for the crown was the question of asserting political authority in Ireland, especially in the Gaelic areas. The chief problem was Ulster, and particularly the rise to power of Shane O'Neill who was elected as 'The O'Neill' in 1559 in defiance of the English law of succession and the English title. Shane O'Neill was persuaded to visit England and given a vague assurance that he would be created Earl of Tyrone; but his ambitions grew, and the crown felt obliged to take some action against him. But the old Tudor dilemma of combining parsimony with political action frustrated any attempt to put an end to O'Neill's ambitions. Various schemes were canvassed, not only for the subjugation of O'Neill, but for the resolution of the whole Irish problem. Sir Henry Sidney, former president of Wales and Lord deputy of Ireland in 1565, produced a comprehensive plan for the government of Ireland. There were three areas to be considered: the Gaelic areas of Leinster; the feudal lordships; and the Gaelic areas of Ulster, and of South West Munster.

Sidney's plan was to establish regional organs of government in the south and west, and to seek to overthrow the O'Neill in Ulster and divide his lands among his family and the subservient septs, with the remainder given over to military governors and English colonists. Provincial presidencies in Munster and Connaught would bring local independence and palatinate jurisdiction to an end, and would be a more forceful instrument of government than the councils of Wales and the North. Presidents were given wide discretionary powers, and instructed to secure whatever land could be shown to be crown property. Here was a step towards colonization; but the Government was by no means anxious to drive the Irish into revolt, and it was Queen Elizabeth's instinct to defer, for as long as possible, fundamental choices of policy. Hence, when The O'Neill was overthrown by his enemies, the O'Donnells in 1567, she authorized the break-up of the O'Neill lordship, with some fortifications in Carrickfergus, Armagh and Oldfleet (Larne), and measures to implement plantation. But the enterprise in 1571 to plant the area around the coast of Belfast, from the Ards peninsula to Lough Neagh, and almost the whole of Antrim, proved abortive; and in 1575, in the interests of economy, a third of the Queen's forces in Ireland was disbanded. Nevertheless, another step towards colonization had been taken; and, more important, the new English colonists had come face to face with the Gaelic Irish, and had found them to be unreasonable, barbarous people, with whom no compromise was possible to redeem their lack of civility.[23]

It was the impact of English colonization rather than the impact of the reformation that was a decisive event in establishing the relationship between England and Ireland in the sixteenth and seventeenth centuries. Ireland under the Tudors was considered part of an 'empire', that is a heterogeneous collection of people (Irish, Welsh, English) living under the rule of a single monarch; and there was nothing unusual about a set of people with a different culture or language living under such a system providing there was a mutual recognition of the rights of the ruling élite on the one hand, and those of the king on the other.[24] And not only ruling élites were to be cared for. Elizabeth recognized that the native Irish were subjects of the crown, and should be 'well used': the Scots in Ulster, by contrast, were interlopers.[25]

It is all the more surprising, therefore, that with a few notable exceptions, such as Archbishop Long of Armagh, and Sir William Herbert, one of the major planters in Munster,[26] the new officials, churchmen and colonists should have regarded the Irish — native and Anglo-Irish — as a barbarous and uncivilized people. For, setting aside questions of racial prejudice, such an outlook was likely to prove an expensive one for the Tudors. It meant finally jettisoning the Anglo-Irish, whose advantage was that they could provide a sufficient administrative framework by keeping the Irish and 'debased' Anglo-Irish obedient, and forcing them to submit to English law; thus Ireland could be governed by its colonial class with a minimum of government troops. Yet the last quarter of the sixteenth century saw the gradual abandonment of this ruling élite as a primary means of governing Ireland, despite its professions of loyalty and despite the obvious advantages of avoiding any major commitment of men and money to Ireland.

The Anglo-Irish were perhaps the victims of their own failure to conquer Ireland and thus make their position of governing the country indispensable.[27] But the dislike they inspired in the new English officials

and settlers is harder to explain. Sidney referred to the Irish habits of
the Anglo-Irish, their 'delight' in speaking the Irish language, their
manners, habits and conditions spotted with Irish stains.[28] Edmund
Spenser, writing in 1594-1596, constructed a dialogue between Ireneus
and Eudoxes, in which Ireneus referred to the 'chiefest abuses' in
Ireland which were 'grown from the English' some of whom 'are now
much more barbarous and licentious than the very wild Irish'. When
Eudoxes referred to the unusual phenomenon of the English adopting
the Irish tongue ('for it hath ever been the use of the conqueror to
despise the language of the conquered and to force him by all means to
learn his'), Ireneus replied that 'the chief cause of bringing in the Irish
language' was 'the fostering and marrying with the Irish, the which are
two most dangerous infections'. The 'degenerate English' were one
thing; the English of the Pale had preserved themselves in reasonable
civility. But when it came to religion, the faults found here were one
and the same: 'That is, that they be all Papists by their profession, but
in the same so blindly and brutishly informed, for the most part, that
not one amongst a hundred knoweth any ground of religion or any
article of his faith, but can perhaps say his Paternoster or his Ave Maria,
without any knowledge or understanding what one word meaneth
thereof.' The remedy which Ireneus prescribed for this held ominous
implications for the Anglo-Irish and the native Irish. It was vain to
prescribe laws where no man cared for the keeping of them: 'Evils
must first be cut away by a strong hand before any good can be planted.' And the Anglo-Irish needed a 'sharper reformation than the Irish;
for they are more stubborn and disobedient to law and government
than the Irish be'.[29]

Religion to the new English was not the primary fault of the Anglo-
Irish and the native Irish; rather it was — in its debased Irish form — a
symptom of the general lack of 'civility', of their inferiority as a race.
And this lack of civility provided a reason for the efforts of officials
and colonists to reduce the country to civility. The argument was,
undoubtedly, a circular and self-justifying one: colonization and conquest of a barbarous country and people could be justified on the
grounds that if the country were not barbarous, then it would not need
colonization; the very fact that it was being colonized was proof of its
barbarity; and its barbarity was further proof of the need to colonize
it. But there were many aspects of Irish society — the prevalence of the
feud, the disorder, the unorthodox religious practice, even the dress
and appearance of the people[30] — which bore genuine witness of a
country in a lesser stage of civilization. The 'image' of Ireland was by

no means divorced from reality: a Jesuit mission in 1660 found an antipathy between a society so constituted and the form of Christian life they were seeking to diffuse.[31]

The English, therefore, could set aside moral restraints, since such restraints, reasonable enough in the relations between two civil and Christian peoples, only stood in the way of a secular ruler whose sword could be used to promote social order and progress against the anarchic desires of the natives. English adventurers in the remoter parts of Ireland found Christianity totally lacking: as Sidney put it, the Irish were like 'atheists and infidels'. To Sir John Davies, the way ahead was clear: 'A barbarous country must first be broken by a war before it will be capable of good government; and when it is fully subdued and conquered if it be not well planted and governed after the conquest it will oft soon return to the former barbarism'.[32] Catholicism in its Irish form was the badge of the inferior race; it followed naturally that Protestantism was the mark of the superior, civilizing and colonizing race. And, since the whole enterprise was seen in racial terms, it followed that the Anglo-Irish, marked with the brand of inferior Irish Catholicism, were easily lumped with the native Irish as part of the inferior Irish race.

In sixteenth century Britain religion and nationality were identical; indeed, one of the reasons for the easy success of the reformation was its shrewd identification with the ancient and true religion of the British people.[33] It was natural enough therefore for the new colonists to assume that the same applied in Ireland, and to regard all Irish as Catholics, and all Catholics as Irish. The deep distinction between themselves and the natives which the Anglo-Irish insisted upon was not so evident to the adventurers.

To this ideology of colonization was added the inevitable excesses of an ill-disciplined sixteenth century army, let loose in a country with few legal or political restraints. Munster and Connaught felt the 'fire and sword'[34] of the English armies as they burned and devastated their way through the countryside between 1565 and 1575. They were no worse than those of the Spanish conquistadors in the New World as they too set about the task of reducing a barbarous and infidel people to civility; but they introduced a new element of violence and ruthlessness that characterized the confrontation between native and settler; and, more significant, they were accepted and even approved of by the Queen, whose early instructions to her officials and soldiers had been to shed no more blood than was necessary.[35]

For the Anglo-Irish the new and ruthless colonial policy posed a

particularly acute and distressing dilemma. Their role as a loyal mediator between native Irish and new English was crumbling; yet, if they
choose to assert themselves by the same method that Kildare had used
in the reign of Henry VIII, they could hardly hope for aid from the
native Irish from whom they still distanced themselves nationally.
Where, then, could they look for common ground if it came to forging
a political alliance with those of the Irish who could be persuaded to
help them? Here religion provided a possible bond, indeed the only
possible bond, given the Anglo-Irish desire to retain their identity of
'English by blood'.

The test of this bond's effectiveness came between 1569 and 1579
when the Anglo-Irish lord, James Fitzmaurice Fitzgerald rose in revolt
in Munster. His revolt was a defence of his vested interests in an area
which was particularly sensitive because of its proximity to Europe
through its southern ports, and its possible access to England's continental enemies. Fitzgerald directed the mayor of Cork to abolish the
heresy of the Huguenots and to set up Catholicism, stating in his proclamation that the Queen:

> ys not contented to dispose all our wordly goods, our bodys and our
> lyves as she lyst, butt must also compell us to forgoo the Cathlych
> faith by God into His Church given and by the see of Rome hitherto
> preserved to all Christian men.[36]

But this appeal seems to have met with little response from the townsmen of Cork; and it was too ambitious for most landowners in Munster.
Fitzmaurice's support withered away and in 1575 he fled to the continent.

His return in 1579 saw a revival of the idea of a Catholic crusade
against the heretics, in which he was encouraged by Pope Gregory XIII,
offered a small papal force, and accompanied by Dr Nicholas Sanders, a
papal comissary. Fitzmaurice appealed to all to 'keep to the Catholic
faith, and forthwith to expel all heresies and schismatical services'
which would 'not only deliver your country from heresy and tyranny,
but also do that most Godly and noble act without any danger at all,
because there is no foreign power that would or durst go about to
assault so universal a consent of this country'.[37] The Catholic crusade
quickly faltered with the death of Fitzmaurice within a month of his
landing in Ireland, killed in a chance encounter with another Anglo-
Irish family, the Burkes of Limerick. The earl of Desmond took up the
cause, appealing to his countrymen to 'join in the defence of our

Catholic faith against Englishmen which have overrun our country';[38] but this desperate course was forced on him by his proclamation as a traitor. His appeal met with some response in Leinster, where Lord Baltinglass and Feach More Hugh O'Byrne rebelled, but there was no widespread revolt of Anglo-Irish and Gaelic Irish against the crown, and disturbances in Ulster, Connaught and the midlands were local in character.[39] The Butlers in Munster and many of the native Irish remained loyal to the crown, and loyalty prevailed in the Pale and in most of the Anglo-Irish towns. Where rebellion did occur, as in Ulster where Turlough Luineach O'Neill avowed himself a Catholic champion, the internal struggle between Turlough and Hugh O'Neill, the baron of Dungannon, was the real issue at stake.[40] Religion could not unite the Anglo-Irish in a common cause, let alone the Anglo-Irish and the Gaelic Irish.

The Anglo-Irish, having refused for the most part to take the path of rebellion, were still confronted with the alternative, and equally distasteful path of acquiescence in an increasingly hostile government policy. After the defeat of Desmond in Munster his property was declared confiscated to the crown, a traditional reaction to the defeat of a Gaelic chieftain, but now extended to the Anglo-Irish. The land thus confiscated was to be divided into 'seignories', varying in size from 4000 to 12,000 acres, to be granted to English 'undertakers' who were to plant them with English-born families. The plan was less effective in execution, for it was beyond the powers of the undertakers to secure a settlement on the necessary scale; but the movement of population, though less than that involved in seventeenth century plantations, was impressive by Elizabethan standards: perhaps some 12,000 colonists were settled in Munster by 1598, when renewed rebellion swept them away.[41]

More important than this confiscation of a rebel Anglo-Irishman's lands was the attitude of the English Government to the most loyal of all the Old colonists, those settled in the Pale. The parliament of 1569-71 bore witness to the increasing disenchantment of the Anglo-Irish and their growing alienation from the crown. There was no parallel to this in England, however many difficulties her parliament might pose for the queen; for the English parliament was genuinely based on the nation, or at least on the political nation, whereas the Irish parliament, though it now had a small Gaelic representation because of the shiring of Ireland, was becoming an arena of conflict between the Anglo-Irish and the new English. And when the last Tudor parliament met in 1585-6 the political alignment of the crown with the new colonists against the Anglo-Irish and the native Irish became more pronounced. Most of the measures put forward by the Government were passed, including the acts of attainder against the leaders of the late rebellion. But some government legislation was deferred — for example, the legislation against the Jesuits — and the speaker of the House, Justice Walsh, in his concluding address warned against the dangers presented to the constitution by autocratic power: a shot aimed at the new English who sought to appeal to the Crown directly to overcome Anglo-Irish delaying tactics.[42]

If the Anglo-Irish were to be treated as mere Irish by the Government, and alienated from it by the Government's centralizing policy, then they might possibly manoeuvre for power by threatening to take the Government at its word. Some Anglo-Irish rebels in the 1560s and 1570s had anticipated this by discarding English ways in favour of Gaelic practices, and assuming Irish titles instead of English ones in an attempt to gain support from Gaelic chieftains. Their threat to 'turn Irish every one'[43] was now revived, and the Anglo-Irish sent out signals to their new English masters by wearing Irish apparrel.[44] The important question — and one which would have a profound influence on the development of the nationalist tradition in Ireland — was whether the Anglo-Irish, in their extremity, would go further than mere threats of changes in title and dress, and establish some kind of political relationship with the Gaelic Irish that might lead to a comprehensive national identity, and, possibly, the check, if not defeat, of Elizabethan colonization.

To seek to explore the attitudes of the Gaelic Irish might at first sight appear unprofitable. The Gaelic penchant for local independence, and limited social and political horizons, might appear to hold more interest for the anthropologist than for the historian, let alone the historian of nationalist ideas. But local horizons and a political ideology are not necessary incompatibles, as the medieval Gaelic tradition revealed. Indeed, the very localized nature of Gaelic politics made it all the more essential for the Gaelic poets to attempt to offer some more idealistic and high-principled explanation of their patrons' behaviour when the chieftains sought to realize their ambitions, or quite simply to defend themselves against colonial encroachment. The Gaelic chieftains who took up the Geraldine cause after the overthrow of its Anglo-Irish leaders in 1539 did so out of fear of English conquest and colonization; but their alliance included some of the most powerful and prestigious dynastic families — the O'Donnell's of Tyrconnell, the O'Neills of Tyrone — and the idea of concerted action to restore the

Irish high-kingship, or to transfer allegiance to the king of Scotland, was mooted.[45]

This kind of perspective was more quickly and easily acquired in the decades of Elizabethan advance into Gaelic Ireland; even the Gael's political complacency was shaken by Tudor imperialism. The Gaelic bards sought to elicit from their lords something over and above their traditional role as defenders of the local patrimony. One or two pieces written for Hugh McShane of south Leinster placed Gaelic politics in a wider national dimension, admonishing him not to neglect his lover, Ireland, and extolling Hugh as the banisher of foreign troops. The themes of national rebellion and cultural decay were linked, and a Gaelic dynast presented as a national leader. Hugh's son, Feagh, would fulfil the prophecy of the victory of the Gael over the Gall; and the land of Ireland was described as the land of the Gaels, who must combine in concerted resistance to the foreign enslaver. The dynasty was no longer to be concerned merely with self-aggrandizement, but with the struggle for national existence being waged by the Irish nation. Booty and plunder no longer provided a prime cause for celebration; the event which brought most warmth to the bard's heart was the prospective slaughter of the foreign foe; and poetry reflected the savage character of the racial war waged between the Gael and the English in the late Tudor period.[46]

The political poetry of the Gaelic bards and the political motivation of the Gaelic chieftains were not, of course, in harmony; praise, flattery and counsel were all very well in their place, but it was a wise Gaelic lord who tempered ideological considerations with practical common sense. Nevertheless, the last decade of the 16th century witnessed a Gaelic rebellion of national dimensions that threatened to overturn the Tudor conquest, and which presented some sort of united front to the English monarchy. Its leader, Hugh O'Neill, was, on the face of it, an unlikely candidate for such a role; when he succeeded to the title of The O'Neill in September 1595 he was well disposed to the English state and indeed his position in Ulster depended initially on English support. But his desire to assert the historic O'Neill claim to the overlordship of Ulster caused friction with English officials and their armed forces, despite Hugh's hope of maintaining the dual position of ruler of the Ulstermen and peer of the realm. The Government was aware by 1595 that the Ulster lords were in communication with Phillip II of Spain with a view to securing his support against Elizabeth.[47] Both sides were motivated as much by fear as by aggression; and at first Hugh's rebellion was a discrete affair, made in defence of his liberties against the Queen's government.

But as the rebellion gathered momentum, it developed two significant ideological themes: a national call to the 'whole Irish nobility' and an offer to 'right (the people) in their supposed Irish claims and titles to land and countries';[48] and the championing of the old religion against Protestantism. O'Neill told Ormond that 'they that are joined with me fight for the Catholic religion and liberties of our country';[49] but religion sat uneasily on the shoulders of the Gael. More convincing was O'Neill's identification with Gaelic history and Gaelic culture, and his appeal to the Munster lords to look forward to a time when 'this island of Ireland shall be at our direction and counsel'.[50] Certainly the Catholic world, in Ireland and outside, was suspicious of O'Neill's professions as defender of the faith: many Catholics in Ireland, especially in the towns, remained neutral, and Catholic lords like Barrymore stood out against him and insisted that the Queen had never refused liberty of conscience to them. The pope, for his part, resisted pressure from O'Neill to excommunicate those who fought for Elizabeth against the Irish rebel leaders;[51] and the Jesuits of the Pale seriously impugned the motives of the Irish chieftains in the O'Neill rebellion.[52]

For O'Neill's rebellion, despite its tendency to assume the tone of a Catholic crusade, was a last stand of Gaelic Ireland against Tudor encroachment, a last stand of those who still retained 'in memory that their ancestors have been monarchs and provincial kings'.[53] It also brought about a conclusion of the Tudor conquest, when Elizabeth's forces, under an energetic new deputy, Lord Mountjoy, took the military steps necessary to effect the final downfall of the Gaelic order. O'Neill's surrender in 1603 did not immediately destroy his power; indeed, he was received courteously in England and was recognized as the absolute owner of his lordship, and formally pardoned by King James. Gaelic Ulster was not destroyed; and the English policy of relying on Irish lords to govern the country on the state's behalf, used since the early sixteenth century, was continued in preference to Mountjoy's scheme for the establishment of a provincial presidency in Ulster.[54] But changes were on the way which, as Hugh O'Neill recognized, posed a grave threat to the way of life that he sought to defend; in the words of Sir John Davies, the idea of Jacobean Government was that 'there will be no difference or distinction but the Irish sea betwixt us', for 'heretofore the neglect of the law made the English degenerate and become Irish; and now, on the other side, the execution of the law doth make the Irish grow civil and become English'.[55] This process of Anglicization was to be pushed forward at every level:

central government, jurisdiction, economy and society. Hugh O'Neill recognized that the conservatism of the old Irish way of life was power-less against this threat; and he continued as an innovating and powerful lord until a temporary loss of nerve caused him to flee to the continent with the Earl of Tyrconnell in 1607. The English Government was quick to respond to this opportunity, unexpected though it was; and official propaganda gave out that the Ulster earls, having conspired against the king abroad, and oppressed his subjects at home, had fled to escape the consequences.[56] The way was now open for the Government to restore 'true civility' to Ulster; the method of so doing was not to be the slow process of Anglicizing the native population, but to establish 'a mixed plantation of British and Irish, that they might grow up together in one nation'.[57]

The romantic episode of the 'flight of the earls' has its own special place in Irish nationalist imagery; and it concludes a century in which those potent elements in Irish nationalism — race, religion and rebel-lions — jostled each other on the Irish political stage. It is tempting to select any one of these elements — especially the religious one — and identify it as the central characteristic of the Tudor age, as the turning point in Anglo-Irish relations.[58] But the evidence does not admit such a clear-cut choice; for example, Tudor distrust of the Kildares pre-dated the reformation in Ireland; and the Anglo-Irish regarded religion as a purely personal affair which did not stand in the way of their accept-ance of the implications of their descent; as the 'English by blood', whose status as a middle nation did not, they maintained, compromise their loyalty to the crown. Fitzmaurice was perhaps an exception; David Wolfe, the papal emissary, described him in 1574 as:

A young man, but a good Catholic and a brave captain. He was minded to enter some religious order, or to quit Ireland to live in some Catholic country, but by the advice of the good prelates and Catholic religious he stayed where he was for the good of the coun-try.[59]

Against this must be set the recent re-assessment of Fitzmaurice as an opportunist seeking to usurp the power of Desmond, and thus attempt-ing to widen the scope of his personally ambitious rebellion.[60] Shane O'Neill, who rebelled in 1559-67, and whose emissaries to France spoke of 'the English heretics, enemies of God and the Roman church'[61] was described by Wolfe as a cruel and impious heretical tyrant.[62] And although Hugh O'Neill also posed as a Catholic champion, his rebellion was essentially a defence of his Gaelic way of life. It would seem, in short, that official Catholic suspicion of the sincerity of its Gaelic, and even its Anglo-Irish crusaders, was justified.

Religion was but one aspect of the changing attitude of Tudor government to Ireland and the people of Ireland. This changing attitude was partly dictated by strategic concerns in an age when England often felt threatened by continental enemies; partly it was motivated by a concern to bring civility to what was, after all, an integral part of the crown's dominions; partly it was the product of an uneven, often faltering, but never abandoned administrative momentum, as English officials sought to remedy the defects, the inconsistencies, the irrationalities of frontier administration. Hence Gaelic and Anglo-Irish alike found themselves under increasing pressure, political, legal and economic, living in an uncertain and turbulent time: their titles and rank challenged, their liberties and their ancient political heritage undermined by centralized government, and their religion regarded with growing dislike and suspicion by the new officials and settlers precisely because it was *their* religion, and not the religion of the New English.

It was typical of the outsider to see a religious unity among his enemies where none existed, or at least to exaggerate this unity. The Irish church itself was partitioned on an ethnic organizational basis, a cleavage which was reflected in the division of the diocese of Armagh into two sections (with the Archbishop of Armagh nominally English or Anglo-Irish, and the dean of Irish descent).[63] The religious orders were similarly divided: the Jesuits' main sphere of influence was in the Pale districts and among the principal Anglo-Irish families, and their sympathies were never with the Gaelic chieftains in their war against Elizabeth; the Observantine Franciscans and the Dominicans had close links with the Irish.[64] For almost every Catholic Irishman or Anglo-Irishman in arms against the state, there was at least one in arms in its defence, and another waiting in a kind of watchful neutrality.

The lack of unity within the political nations of Ireland frustrates any attempt to find a common theme — religious or otherwise — in the rebellions against the crown that characterized Tudor Ireland. The Kildare rising that began the age of rebellions was very different in its motivation and composition from that of Hugh O'Neill which marked its end. The fact that both had religious connotations must not obscure the vital difference between the protest in arms of a slighted Anglo-Irish nobleman, and the defence of the Gaelic tradition made by a chieftain who was feeling his way towards a species of ethnic nationalism.

By the end of the sixteenth century, several different, and in some respects contradictory, trends can be discerned in the evolution of Ireland's nationalist traditions. Religion — although it was not the whole story — was certainly used as a rallying cry, however unsuccessfully for Anglo-Irish and Gaelic rebels. Gaelic racial sentiment, and the assertion of the historic rights of the Irish chieftains, had become more fully articulated, particularly in the nine years war waged by Hugh O'Neill. Rebellion, hitherto the prerogative of the Gaels, had now become a part, albeit a small one, of Anglo-Irish political behaviour: the Anglo-Irishman who was prepared, whatever his motives, to abandon his normal condition of loyalty to the crown and declare himself a rebel was to become an enduring and potent part of the Irish nationalist tradition. Indeed the whole notion of a national rebellion against English rule, inconceivable before the Tudor age, had become an almost normal aspect of Irish politics.

A truly national rebellion, however, remained more of a notion than a reality. No Tudor rebellion ever included the whole political nation of Ireland; nor, of course, did it have much to offer the common people, who were referred to by their betters as peasants, churls or even slaves. Their lives were those of hardship punctuated by repression, war, exploitation, and, under Shane and Hugh O'Neill, a form of military conscription which few of them must have found in any way to their liking.[65] The Connaughtmen who resisted Sir Henry Sidney's attempt to introduce the English order in that province in 1576 did so because it would make 'the churl as good as a gentleman'.[66] Caught up in the wars and rebellions of their time, they were the innocent victims of political change over which they had no control and with which they had little desire to associate. Had the nine years war been successful for the Gaels, it would have preserved an Ireland not only free and Gaelic, but aristocratic as well.

The Tudor period was not, of course, one of unrelieved war and rebellion; and it saw a constitutional change in Ireland's status that was to have great significance in the future. When Henry VIII assumed the title of king of Ireland in the Irish Parliament of 1541-3 it made little or no practical difference to Anglo-Irish relations. But the idea of a kingdom of Ireland, a community of subjects under the sovereign jurisdiction of the crown, but with certain inherent rights which could be asserted against English institutions of government became, in the seventeenth century, an integral part of Anglo-Irish political thinking; and it also foreshadowed the idea of a united Catholic Irish nation, based on a common faith and a common allegiance to the English crown.

These ideas were first aired by representatives of the Anglo-Irish in the last decades of the sixteenth century. In the parliament of 1585-6 the speaker, Justice Walsh, affirmed that Ireland was one body politic, and that the queen was head of this body politic, and in that respect allied to all; therefore the crown's deputy in Ireland should 'accept in the same sort of us, without any differences or distinctions of persons'.[67] Another Anglo-Irishman, Richard Stanihurst, aware of the growing rift between government policy and the loyalty of the Anglo-Irish, sought to give a more favourable picture of Gaelic social and religious behaviour than that usually drawn by his nation; and, although he remained strongly aware of his Anglo-Irish identity, his enthusiasm for the counter-reformation inspired him to emphasize the common religious faith of the Gaels and the Anglo-Irish, and to play down their political differences.[68] But this kind of comprehensive ideology failed to permeate the sixteenth century Anglo-Irish community just as the comprehensive ideology of Thomas Davis failed to permeate the Anglo-Irish (and the Roman Catholic) people 300 years later; the generality of the Anglo-Irish behaved like the Burkes of Connaught, who readily accepted English titles to their land which were good in English law, and who cared little for the fate of the 'Macs and Oes' of the native Irish.[69] Only the momentous political and social changes of the seventeenth century accomplished the fusion, even then incomplete, of the older inhabitants of Ireland, with all its implications for Irish identity and for Irish nationalism.

Notes

1. E. Curtis, *History of Medieval Ireland*, p. 364.

2. Ibid., p. 375.

3. A. Clarke, 'Colonial identity in early 17th century Ireland' in T.W. Moody (ed.) *Historical Studies* XI (Belfast, 1978), pp. 57-71.

4. But see B. Bradshaw, *The Irish Constitutional revolution of the sixteenth century* (Cambridge, 1974), pp. 32-57.

5. N.P. Canny, *The Elizabethan Conquest of Ireland: A Pattern Established* (London, 1976), Chap. 1.

6. K.S. Bottigheimer, 'Kingdom and colony: Ireland in the westward enterprise, 1536-1660' in K.R. Andrews, N.P. Canny and P.E.H. Hair (eds.), *The Westward Enterprise: English Activities in Ireland, the Atlantic and America, 1480-1650* (Liverpool, 1978), Chap. 3.

7. Canny, op. cit., p. 31.

8. S.G. Ellis, 'Tudor policy and the Kildare ascendancy in the lordship of Ireland, 1496-1534', *Irish Historical Studies*, vol. *xx*, No. 79 (March 1977), pp. 235-71.

9. Ellis, op. cit., pp. 260-61; B. Bradshaw, 'Cromwellian reform and the origins of the Kildare rebellion, 1533-34' in *TRHS*, 5th series, vol. *27*, pp. 69-93.

10. B. Bradshaw, 'The beginnings of modern Ireland' in B. Farrell (ed.), *The Irish Parliamentary Tradition* (Dublin, 1973), pp. 68-87.

11. Canny, *Elizabethan Conquest*, pp. 32-6.

12. P. O'Farrell, *Ireland's English question: Anglo-Irish relations, 1534-1970* (London, 1971), pp. 20-21.

13. J.H. Hexter, *Reappraisals in history* (London, 1967 edn.), p. 30.

14. C. Mooney, 'The first impact of the reformation' in *A History of Irish Catholicism*, vol. *III*, Parts 2 and 3, pp. 1-53.

15. B. Bradshaw, 'The opposition to ecclesiastical legislation in the Irish parliament', *Irish Historical Studies* vol. *16* (1968-9), pp. 285-303.

16. G.A. Hayes-McCoy, 'The ecclesiastical revolution 1534-47', in T.W. Moody, F.X. Martin and F.J. Byrne (eds.), *A New History of Ireland*, vol. *III Early Modern Ireland* (Oxford, 1976), pp. 66-67; R. Bagwell, *Ireland under the Tudors*, vol. *III* (London, 1963 edn.), pp. 239-40.

17. Bradshaw, 'The opposition to ecclesiastical legislation . . .', op. cit., pp. 302-3.

18. R. Dudley Edwards, *Ireland in the Age of the Tudors* (London, 1977), p. 64, Bagwell, op. cit., p. 341.

19. Hayes-McCoy, op. cit., p. 75.

20. Bottigheimer, op. cit., pp. 46-7.

21. Dudley Edwards, op. cit., pp. 95-6; Bagwell, op. cit., pp. 470-73.

22. F.M. Jones, 'The counter-reformation' in *A History of Irish Catholicism* vol. *III* (1967), parts 2 and 3, pp. 8-12.

23. Canny, *Elizabethan Conquest*, pp. 58-91; Hayes-McCoy, 'The ecclesiastical revolution', in *New History of Ireland*, pp. 94-99.

24. Bottigheimer, op. cit., p. 47.

25. Canny, op. cit., p. 120.

26. B. Bradshaw, 'The Elizabethans and the Irish' in *Studies*, vol. *66* (1977), pp. 38-50.

27. Bottigheimer, op. cit., pp. 46-8.

28. Ibid., p. 50.

29. H. Morley (ed.), *Ireland under Elizabeth and James the First* (London, 1890), pp. 101-203.

30. A.C. Judson, *The Life of Edmund Spenser* (Baltimore, 1945), pp. 74-83.

31. J. Bossy, 'The counter-reformation and the people of Catholic Ireland, 1596-1641', in *Historical Studies*, VIII (Dublin, 1971), pp. 155-69.

32. Canny, op. cit., p. 135. See also D.B. Quinn, 'Edward Walshe's 'conjectures' concerning the state of Ireland (1552)', in *Irish Historical Studies*, vol. *5*, No. 20 (Sept. 1947), pp. 303-22.

33. G. Williams, 'Some Protestant views of early British church history' in *Welsh reformation essays* (Cardiff, 1967), pp. 207-19.

34. The words of one of Sidney's officials in Connaught (B. Bradshaw 'The Elizabethans and the Irish', op. cit., p. 47).

35. N.P. Canny, 'The ideology of English colonization: From Ireland to America' in *William and Mary Quarterly*, vol. *30* (1973), pp. 575-598.

36. Canny, *Elizabethan Conquest*, p. 147.

37. Bagwell, *Ireland under the Tudors*, vol. *III*, pp. 13-15.

38. M. MacCurtain, *Tudor and Stuart Ireland* (Dublin, 1972), p. 79.

39. Hayes-McCoy, op. cit., p. 107.

40. R. Dudley Edwards, *Ireland in the Age of the Tudors*, pp. 142-3.

41. Hayes-McCoy, op. cit., pp. 113-15; D.B. Quinn, 'The Munster plantation: problems and opportunities' in *JCHAS*, vol. *71* (1966), pp. 19-40.

42. Bradshaw, 'The beginnings of modern Ireland', op. cit., pp. 80-87.

43. Canny, *Elizabethan Conquest*, pp. 142-6.

44. Ibid., pp. 149-50, 153.

45 Bradshaw, *The Irish Constitutional Revolution*, pp. 177-80.

46. B. Bradshaw, 'Native reaction to the westward enterprise: a case-study in Gaelic ideology' in Andrews *et al.*, op. cit., pp. 65-80; Shane O'Neill, in 1566, also declared that the time had come to banish the Sassenach from the land (M.V. Ronan, *The Reformation in Ireland under Elizabeth, 1558-1580* (London, 1930), pp. 219-220.

47. Hayes-McCoy, 'The completion of the Tudor conquest, and the advance of the counter-reformation, 1571-1603' in *New History of Ireland*, pp. 117-22; F.M. Jones, 'The counter-reformation', op. cit., pp. 48-9.

48. Hayes-McCoy, 'Gaelic society in late 16th century Ireland' in G.A. Hayes-McCoy (ed.) *Historical Studies* IV (London, 1963), p. 58.

49. Hayes-McCoy, in *New History of Ireland*, p. 127.

50. Ibid.

51. R. Dudley Edwards, 'Ireland, Elizabeth I and the Counter-Reformation' in S.T. Bindoff, J. Hurstfield and C.H. Williams (eds.) *Elizabethan Government and Society* (London, 1961), pp. 315-339.

52. Jones, op. cit., p. 44.

53. Hayes-McCoy, in *Historical Studies*, IV, p. 58.

54. N.P. Canny, 'Hugh O'Neill, Earl of Tyrone, and the changing face of Gaelic Ulster', in *Studia Hibernica*, vol. *10* (1970), pp. 7-35.

55. H. Morley (ed.), *Ireland under Elizabeth*, pp. 339-40.

56. A. Clarke, 'Plantation and the Catholic question', in *New History of Ireland*, pp. 193-7.

57. Morley, op. cit., pp. 339-40.

58. O'Farrell, *Ireland's English question*, p. 31.

59. P.J. Corish, 'The origins of Catholic nationalism' in *A History of Irish Catholicism*, vol. *III*, parts 7 and 8 (Dublin, 1968), p. 11.

60. Canny, *Elizabethan Conquest*, p. 147.

61. MacCurtain, *Tudor and Stuart Ireland*, p. 73.

62. Ronan, *Reformation in Ireland*, p. 220.

63. MacCurtain, op. cit., pp. 22-8.

64. F.M. Jones, 'The counter-reformation', op. cit., pp. 37-8; A. Clarke, 'Colonial identity in early 17th century Ireland' in *Historical Studies*, XI, p. 68.

65. Canny, *Elizabethan Conquest*, pp. 21-6; 'Hugh O'Neill', op. cit., pp. 29-30.

66. Hayes-McCoy, 'Gaelic society in the late 16th century', op. cit., p. 50.

67. B. Bradshaw, 'The beginnings of modern Ireland' in B. Farrell (ed.), *The Irish Parliamentary Tradition*, pp. 68-87; *The Irish Constitutional Revolution of the Sixteenth Century*, pp. 276-88.

68. C. Lennon, 'Richard Stanihurst (1547-1618) and Old English identity', *Irish Historical Studies*, vol. *XXI*, (1978), pp. 121-43.

69. Hayes-McCoy, 'Gaelic society in late 16th century Ireland', op. cit., p. 55.

3 FOR GOD, KING AND COUNTRY

The Tudor conquest of Ireland was never at any time a simple affair of 'Ireland versus England', for Irish society was too complex and too divided to react with one hand or one voice to English policy. Each group's response was influenced by its political traditions: the loyal Anglo-Irish of the Pale and the towns stressed the ancient liberties and constitutional rights of Ireland; the native Irish transferred their dislike of foreigners to the New English, whom they dubbed 'foreign wolves';[1] and the rebellious Anglo-Irish and Gaelic Irish both paraded their Catholicity with varying degrees of conviction and sincerity. The final collapse of Hugh O'Neill's rebellion, although it ended any ideas of Irish separation from the English crown, did not resolve the problems posed to the Anglo-Irish and Gaelic Irish by the crown's new attitude to them. On the contrary, Irish anxieties about their future were given a sharper edge by two major developments under the early Stuarts; the arrival in force of new British and Protestant settlers; and the accelerating pace of religious discrimination in the face of what was increasingly regarded as the doubtful loyalty of even the Anglo-Irish. Out of the tension thus generated there evolved a response that has exerted a lasting influence on Irish nationalism and indeed on all aspects of Irish life: the formal identification of the Irish nation with the Roman Catholic people of Ireland.

The Anglo-Irish, unlike the Gaelic Irish, had throughout their history enjoyed the fruits of active participation in the administration of Ireland, or, rather, of those parts of Ireland which could be administered. They had enjoyed positions of trust and influence; and, in general, they had proved themselves willing to assist the Government, as they did in the reformation parliament of 1536, however quick they might be to demonstrate their self-assertiveness should the need arise. But from the late sixteenth century there were ominous signs that the exclusion of an Anglo-Irish influence at governmental level was becoming an axiom of English policy. With the accession of James I, from whom much had been expected by Catholics, the grounds for this exclusion became more overtly religious: the acts of Supremacy and Uniformity were enforced, and fines and forfeitures imposed on nonconforming office holders. The services of Catholics in the administration began to be dispensed with; and a large measure of power, including the post of Lord Deputy, was entrusted to locally based Protestants.[2]

The presence of locally based Protestants was the most disturbing threat to the Anglo-Irish, or, as they may now be called, 'Old English'. Hitherto they had maintained, to themselves and to the world, that Catholicism and loyalty were perfectly compatible. The fact that the 'New English' (as the Gaels, with their characteristic readiness to classify intruders in a corporate, and usually derogatory, sense, dubbed them)[3] were Protestant and loyal eased the process by which the Government could transfer authority, confidence and influence to the settlers. But this was still a vexing and complex problem for the authorities; for the question of in whose interest the Tudor conquest had been made was confused by the attitude of the Old English, who quite simply persisted in ignoring the possibility that they were to be numbered amongst the defeated. Theirs was a perfectly tenable position. If the conquest was in the interests of England, then the Old English were among the victors, for they were 'English by blood'. But if the process of the Anglicization of Ireland was to be closely linked with the making of a Protestant Ireland then their position was much less secure. Thus the next 40 years were spent by the Old English in trying to work within the colonial system to defend their rights, and by the New English in seeking to advance theirs.

The Government was therefore confronted with a set of claims and counter-claims when it came to assess the role of the Old English in the post conquest decade. The religious restrictions on Roman Catholics did not amount to very much; they had to acknowledge the royal supremacy in church and state, and more or less regularly attend divine service.[4] The real danger to them was not purely nor perhaps even primarily religious, but arose from the possibility that their special nationality might not get the recognition it deserved; that they might be lumped together with the 'degenerate English', and possibly even the Gaelic Irish, in one disloyal band. The nomenclature of one family, the Stauntons of Mayo, served to illustrate the point. They were originally thirteenth century settlers, who had become so Gaelicized by the end of the fourteenth century that they had adopted an Irish surname; but by the end of the sixteenth century they found it expedient to resume their original name.[5]

The Old English developed their political thinking to accommodate themselves to the trends of government policy. The Old English Primate of Ireland, Peter Lombard, maintained that the interests of the Roman Catholic church in Ireland could best be served by the political support of the king. This implied that the subjects of a prince need not profess the same religion as the prince himself, and ran counter to contemporary European thought, which held that temporal and spiritual allegiances could not be separated. The Old English maintained that a community of secular interests between subject and prince was a sufficient guarantee of loyalty without the additional bond (or more accurately in contemporary terms, the essential bond) of religious conformity.[6]

This attempt to reconcile the Pope's spiritual primacy with the subject's loyal duty to uphold the political authority of the English king must have appeared an admirable compromise to the Old English; but, in its European context, it was a unique and shaky claim. Protestants believed that Roman Catholic christianity was an erroneous and idolatrous form of worship, and one that aimed at earthly domination by forbidding its adherents to surrender their loyalty to a temporal prince. The recent history of England, especially the excommunication of Elizabeth by Pius V, and the Spanish armada, seemed to give substance to that opinion. And, in any case, it was an opinion with a substance of its own: for the question remained whether the crown's Catholic subjects could give their loyalty to the prince, and were free to do so. Rome claimed the authority to depose rulers for offences against religion and the natural law; and the Pope was, ultimately, the sole judge of anyone's professions of loyalty. Since ultimate spiritual authority lay with the Pope, an oath of allegiance or a promise to yield temporal obedience could prove doctrinally invalid.[7]

James's personal instinct was for a compromise, whereby Roman Catholics could be won over to the reformed religion, but not compelled to attend state worship; but he was driven by English suspicion to adopt a sterner line; and in July 1605 he proclaimed an anti-Catholic policy, disavowing toleration, ordering Catholic clergy to leave the realm, and instructing the laity to attend divine service.[8] In an overwhelmingly Catholic country like Ireland, however, such a policy could not be pushed to its logical extreme; and, indeed, it was pushed to what might be called its illogical extreme, in that it bore most heavily on the Catholics of the Pale, who were governable enough to make its application practicable. Once again the gulf between the native Irish and the Old English widened; and the Old English of the Pale were distinguished from those outside it since they were being singled out for special discriminatory treatment. The Gaelic Irish, whose loyalty was most suspect, were now being left largely alone. To this was added the continuing division between the colonial and native Irish Roman

Catholic traditions, with the Old English adopting the modern, triden-
tine Catholicism, and the native Irish holding fast to their more old
fashioned brand of religion. To the Old English their new style Catholicism spelt modernity, civility, a more advanced civilization appropriate
to their status, and one which put them on a par with English Protestantism. The native Irish, on the other hand, were proud of their
religion which was firmly rooted in Celtic Christianity.[9] A union of
hearts between Old English and native Irish, based on their common
Catholicism, was unlikely in these conditions; a union of convenience
and expediency perhaps hardly more so. But English Government
policy, against all the odds, produced the latter by 1641; the former
was never achieved, even after 1641.

The Old English sought to avoid any such identification with 'Irish
Catholicism'. They sought to defend themselves against accusation of
disloyalty by offering their temporal loyalty to the king; and they used
their idea of this special relationship to the crown as an argument for
their inclusion in the powers and privileges of office and trust. Their
sense of separation from the Gaelic Irish and degenerate English was
reinforced by their different experience of the Government's Anglicization policy: although the New English were able to dominate regional
government, and even introduce English gaming laws, the Old English
share of the land of Ireland remained little altered since Tudor times.
This did not, of course exempt them from the danger inherent in the
crown's anti-Catholic policy, since the crown might challenge their
titles to their land by resurrecting its hereditary claims. But it meant
the old English strategy was a conservative one: either to maintain the
status quo, or to restore it if necessary.[10]

For the native Irish of Ulster, maintaining or restoring the status
quo was necessarily a more far-reaching affair. For here the Government had decided that the flight of the earls in 1607 offered an
opportunity that could not be missed of binding Ulster firmly to the
British crown, not by Anglicizing her population, but by establishing
there a new, loyal, British people. An official survey was made in 1608,
plans drawn up, and the scheme set afoot. Not only would landowners
change, but tenants also would be settled on land which had been
cleared of its native inhabitants. Some provision, however, was to be
made for the 'deserving Irish'; and the nine counties of Ulster, with the
exception of Antrim, Down and Monaghan, were to be planted. In
practice, the scheme was modified in several important respects, for in
the end the Gaelic landowners fared less well than the tenants. The
'deserving Irish' were seldom granted lands that they already occupied,

or received as much as they believed themselves entitled to; and the native Irish tenants were not removed from the soil, since, with a few exceptions, it suited the economic interests of the settlers to retain their services.[11]

Scottish migration to Ulster and Ulster migration to Scotland had been going on since Celtic times, and the very survival of the Gaelic areas of Ulster was due in no small part to their reinforcement from the western highlands and islands of Scotland. But the plantation of Ulster brought not soldiers and Islanders, but settlers and landlords, and the planting of a new population whose need to defend its territory gave it a sense of solidarity, and whose dissenting religion made it stand apart from the rest of Ireland.[12] Moreover, the union of the three kingdoms with the accession of James I gave a political shape to the demographic fact, in that it placed at James's disposal a loyal population, and one, what was more, that thought of itself, not as a separate colony, but as an extension of Scotland itself. The Ulster Scots were, in short, the Scots in Ulster. They had none of the airs and graces of the Old English; they did not see themselves as any species of 'middle nation', and they had no special political stance.[13] However, that they were in the process of displacing the old landowners could not be disputed; and the system of short leases and high rents ensured that the Irish tenants gained little from their new masters. One Fermanagh undertaker spoke vividly of his sense of unease: 'Although there be no apparent enemy, nor any visible main force, yet the wood-kern and many other (who have now put on the smiling countenance of contentment) do threaten every house, if opportunity of time and place doth serve.'[14]

The Irish landowners elsewhere fared little better than they did in Ulster. They were now subject to English property law, which rendered their titles of uncertain validity; and the land-hungry New English were bent on a widespread and relentless pursuit of property. Royal officials in Dublin were only too willing to assist them in their quest, by confirming doubtful titles, or offering them land from the crown on highly favourable terms. The native Irish landowners were constantly aware of the threat posed by the new men who they believed meant 'little by little to root them out utterly'. The practice of investigating land titles, pursued vigorously by the commission for defective titles, also threatened the old English. Past failures on the part of royal tenants to meet the full measure of their legal obligations to the crown could be uncovered by prying investigators who might profit from their discoveries, perhaps by gaining a lease of property with a flaw in the title on favourable terms and collecting rent from the occupiers.[15]

Little wonder, then, that when in 1610 the Government decided to call the Irish Parliament, partly to give statutory confirmation to forfeitures, partly to pass laws regulating religious conformity, and generally to handle the backlog of business accumulated since the completion of the Tudor conquest, it was anxious to ensure that it could overcome Catholic opposition from whatever quarter. This it sought to do by the expedient of creating more parliamentary boroughs with a Protestant character; and the result was a parliament which met in 1613 with a Protestant majority in the commons of thirty-two, and a majority in the lords secured through the twenty members of the episcopate, who outnumbered the twelve Protestant and four Catholic peers who attended.[16] Protestant domination of the Parliament might seem to be tempered by the presence in the commons of a small native Irish representation; and indeed Sir John Davies, as Speaker of the House of Commons on 2 May 1613, referred to the unique composition of the Parliament 'When all the inhabitants of the Kingdom, English by birth, English by blood, the new British colony, and the old Irish natives, do all meet together to make laws for the common good of themselves and their posterities'.[17]

Behind this pleasing rhetoric, however, there lurked the hard reality of English Government policy, determined to probe the power and position of the Old English. Indeed, the seating of Davies as speaker provoked a row with the Old English who had their own candidate for the chair, and parliament was prorogued for a year. Their attempt to convince James that they were, none the less, loyal to his crown drew from him the rebuke that 'you are only half-subjects of mine. For you give your soul to the pope, and to me only the body and even it, your bodily strength, you divide between me and the King of Spain'.[18]

Such accusations of disloyalty could not but have an impact on the native Irish. The Old English stress on their loyalty was coloured by their insistence on its special quality, a quality which the Irish did not possess, or so the Old English alleged. If Catholicism was compatible with loyalty, as the Old English political thinker Peter Lombard, maintained, then, as he suggested, native Irish and Old English could combine in their common religion and their common allegiance to the king. But it did not suit the Old English political tactics to allow that such was the case; and they stressed both their loyalty and native Irish disloyalty, claiming that 'Irish' was synonymous with rebelliousness. They were not Catholic nationalists, but conservative traditionalists in opposition to the English state and its adventurers.[19]

The Old English assertion of loyalty and of Irish disloyalty was not

entirely without justification: many of the Gaelic Irish who went to
the armies of Spain and other foreign countries still favoured armed
resistance to England. But some of the native Irish, a contemporary
noted, had settled 'into a fair and honest course of life, and are doubtless well-affected to the English monarchy'. The native Irish might also
hope for something from the king if they too adopted a loyal stance:
and they abandoned any schemes of foreign intervention or the return
of the Gaelic earls. The problem was that the government's intentions,
and the presence of the New English settlers, rendered this a difficult
game to play. The essence of Irish political life in the early seventeenth
century was its fluidity.[20]

After the troubles of the parliament of 1613-14 the government
adopted a reserved attitude towards the Old English, postponing any
kind of firm decision. Pressure on recusancy in the shape of fines was
kept up until 1623, when a Spanish marriage for James's son Charles
was being negotiated. But for the Old English the most disconcerting
development in government policy was the establishment of the court
of wards and liveries which replaced a temporary commission. In this
court, discrimination against the Old English was practised in a particularly distressing manner. The crown often used its right of wardship to
have recusant minors brought up in the Protestant faith; and an heir,
suing out his livery, was required by law to take the oath of supremacy,
a requirement which was, after 1622, more strictly enforced. When in
1624 the possibility of a Spanish marriage for Charles fell through, and
war with Spain seemed likely, pressure on the Irish recusants grew. But
the Old English were placed in a better bargaining position by the
accession of Charles I in 1628; for the king needed money, and his lord
deputy was authorized to negotiate with the lords and gentry of the
Pale to see if it could be got.[21]

There followed a decade of uncertainty in English policy towards
Ireland. Now the Old English were to be trusted to form trained bands
for the protection of the county in the event of war with Spain; now
they were not to be trusted. In 1628 a bargain was struck between the
king and a representative group of Old and New English, and a set of
reforms agreed, ranging from administrative tinkering to radical policy
alterations; the working rules of the court of wards were amended, and
− a large concession to the recusants − an oath of allegiance was substituted for the oath of supremacy. In return the king received successive annual subsidies of £40,000; and all these agreements were to be
confirmed in parliament. In the event no such confirmation took place;
and the 'instructions and graces' were held entirely at the king's will,

with no legal sanction.[22]

The position of recusants did improve, however; but this was not a lasting victory for the Old English interest. The original offer to suspend recusancy fines was dropped; and proposals to secure for Catholics the right to hold public office were rebuffed. The deal — for such it was — of the Graces marked no significant change in government policy towards Roman Catholics in Ireland. This was shown in the more advanced anti-Catholic policy pursued under Falkland's successors, the Lords justices Richard Boyle, Earl of Cork, and Adam Loftus, Viscount Loftus of Ely. These men were members of the New English interest, and they sought to ignore or belittle the Old English demand for observation of the various articles of the Graces. In 1630 another blow was struck against Old English confidence in the mother country. The policy of plantation was resumed in the baronies of upper and lower Ormond in County Tipperary. This was a threat to Old English, not native Irish, property; and the earl of Ormond, Walter Butler, displayed all the Old English incomprehension and resentment of the slighted colonist when he protested that he was the first Englishman who had been treated as if he were Irish. As it happened, an investigation proved that land titles in the areas under consideration were sound; but another project for planting Mayo, Sligo and Roscommon, though once more abortive, revealed that the Government had determined in principle on planting parts of Connaught. In 1632 juries were empanelled and directed to compile lists of Roman Catholics to enable recusancy fines to be levied as soon as the last of the subsidies expired in the autumn.[23]

The arrival of Thomas Wentworth, Earl of Strafford, as lord deputy in 1632 seemed to hold out more hope for the Old English. Strafford's policy was 'to bow and govern the native by the planter, and the planter by the native';[24] and it brought much success to Wentworth who, on his departure in 1640, left economic prosperity, a reformed church, a more stable revenue, and a properly equipped and paid army. But his means were inimical to the peace of Ireland, even though his ends were, in many respects, to her advantage. For the policy of raising the hopes, now of one section of the Irish people, now of another, only to dash them contributed to the general unease of the country. Despite the idea of a firm and thorough approach to the problems of Irish administration, no-one knew where he stood. Wentworth's proposal to revive plantation policies by exploiting widespread uncertainty about property rights alarmed the Old English; but Protestants had no cause to love him either. The establishment of a court of high commission as an instrument of religious policy seemed to them to promise a new standard of uniformity and orthodoxy at variance with the heterogenous and Calvinist nature of Irish Protestantism. And his willingness to allow Catholics to raise their heads — with Catholic bishops taking up residence in most dioceses, the number of priests increasing, religious houses proliferating — alarmed Protestants and allowed the Old English and native Irish to feel some hope of bettering their status.[25] He even managed to offend the New English official class by his attempt to recover church lands.[26]

Political instability within Ireland was parallelled by the mounting political crisis in the British Isles as a whole. Charles I, embroiled with the Scottish presbyterians, saw Ireland as a possible source both of danger and of support. Ulster, with its Scottish population, might prove a dangerous breeding ground for the king; but the Ulster native Irish were well poised for an attack on the west coast of Scotland; and in 1639 Charles's renewed conflict with the Scots caused a revival of the possibility of an Irish army that could be used in Scotland, an army, moreover, that might be financed from moneys supplied by an Irish Parliament.[27] Parliament at first seemed pliable, and subsidies were granted; but when it reassembled on 1 June 1640 a new and unlikely alliance emerged: that of the Old and New English, based on their common hostility to Wentworth. This common attack on the lord deputy, however, could not obliterate the deep-rooted differences between the two groups. The Old English were still in a minority in the house of commons, and their influence could not be exerted without protestant support. This was forthcoming: because of the need to bury the differences between the Old and New English, religious grievances were set aside, and the paliamentary opposition concentrated on the constitutional arguments against Wentworth's administration.

In October 1640 the second session of the Irish Parliament opened, and preparations were made for a concerted attack on the lord deputy. The petition presented against him, like all the constitutional statements made during the course of the seventeenth century crisis in Ireland, drew its inspiration from Old English theory. The Old English alone had the experience, the traditions, to give a convincing legal form to Irish grievances; and the petition claimed that the crown's 'legal and dutiful people of this land of Ireland, being now for the most part derived from British ancestors, should be governed according to the municipal and fundamental laws of England'. The grievances listed included such matters as high customs rates and monopolies; and the demand for redress was based on the Irish people's entitlement to the rights of Englishmen. A committee of thirteen including seven Old English members was appointed to take the grievances to England, but Wentworth's deputy Wandesford refused to allow it to leave; and the opposition responded by authorizing three peers (Gormanston, Kilmallock and Muskerry) to 'repair to his Majesty to complain of grievances'. This demonstration was supported by some eighty-four members of the House of Commons who wrote to the speaker of the English commons requesting leave to present the petition of remonstrance to the king, and calling to mind 'the near links and great ties of blood and afinity betwixt the people of this kingdom and the famous people of England from whose loins we have descended . . . being therefore flesh of their flesh and bone of their bone subjects to one gracious sovereign and governed by the same laws'.[28]

This joint action disguised a difference of purpose between the Old and New English. The Protestants wanted to aid the parliamentary opposition in London led by Pym; the Old English still hoped to negotiate the Graces with the king. But any concessions thus secured could only be protected by the reassertion of parliamentary sovereignty, which Wentworth had in fact, if not in law, denied. In January 1641 the commons committee in Ireland was instructed to petition for an act of explanation of Poyning's law to clarify the legal procedure of the Irish parliament; and in February a committee was set up to consider a series of questions about the legality of various administrative practices. A number of 'queries' was drawn up by Patrick Darcy, an Old English recusant from County Galway. The judges failed to give the commons a satisfactory answer; but the significance of the queries did not rest upon the judges' response to them. It rested upon Darcy's need to elaborate the exact nature of lawful authority in Ireland so that he could curb the abuses of executive government there. The first query asked 'whether the subjects of this kingdom be a free people, and to be governed, only, by the Common Lawes of England, and Statutes of force in this kingdome?'; and in the preamble stress was put on the protestation as 'their birth-right and best inheritance'. The judges agreed that the subjects in Ireland were indeed a free people and to be thus governed.[29]

Part of the arguments put forward by Darcy concerned the rights of the Irish Parliament. Later generations were to select this as the core of the petition, although at the time it was only one aspect of the general attack on arbitrary government; nevertheless, it was a bold statement of Old English constitutional thinking. The making of laws was the prerogative of the king, lords and commons in Parliament. Ireland was 'annexed' to the crown of England, hence it was to be governed by the laws of England, but only after these had been 'received and enacted in parliament in this kingdom'. With this claim for the rights of Irishmen to be governed on the same footing as Englishmen was coupled a firm declaration of loyalty to the crown;[30] but these ringing declarations marked the end of the Old and New English parliamentary alliance. The fall of Wentworth, and his execution on 12 May 1641, and the disband-ment of the Irish army meant that the English parliamentary opposition no longer needed the co-operation of the Irish parliament; and the New English had no sense of coherence, no corporate identity, to sustain the momentum. Nor had they any reason to do so; the victory of the oppo-sition in the English Parliament was enough for them, and they had every hope of securing control over the authority formerly wielded by the lord deputy. But the Old English still found themselves at the mercy of the king's Government, now a doubtful prospect, and at the mercy also of the English Parliament's ill-will, of which there could be no doubt. The Old English needed a king who would maintain his prerogative powers for the protection of recusants and their lands, and yet a king whose powers would not be such as to restore the policies of the hated Wentworth. Theory and practice both urged the Old English to support the king in his attempt to regain the initiative in England and confound his English and Scottish enemies. When it was discovered that the king was hoping to use disbanded soldiers of Wentworth's army for his own ends, there were elements in Ireland ready to adopt this as their cue to resort to the argument which Charles was, evidently, planning to employ: the argument of armed force.

In October 1641 the native Irish rose in revolt, and within a short time the whole English grip on Ireland seemed to be threatened. This rebellion was to have profound consequences for Anglo-Irish relations and for relations between the various political groups within Ireland; but it was not simply a blind revolt of an oppressed people against their English and Scottish enemies, a 'rising of despair against . . . the bru-tality of alien colonists'.[31] The complex nature of the rebellion is seen in the character of its leaders; in their declared aims; and in the fact that it was eventually joined by that most conservative or Irish political groups, the lords and gentry of the Pale.

The original leaders of the 1641 rebellion were, certainly, native Irish; and the rebellion was most serious and most bloody in Ulster, that part of Ireland which had been the last to lose its Gaelic social and political identity. But its leader, Rory O'More, was no Gaelic hero of the stamp of Hugh O'Neill. Before he rose to fame as the 'leader' of 'Ireland' he was commonly known as Roger Moore, a landowner with property in counties Armagh and Kildare, and a man who had political and family connections with the Old English. Connor, Lord Maguire, was Fermanagh Irish with Old English family connections and an Oxford education; Phelim O'Neill was Ulster Irish, but reckoned good for a loan of £6,000 in the 1630s, much of it raised in London. Most of the leaders were of this stamp:[32] members of a socially notable propertied class, who had, on the accession of Charles I, been quick to declare their loyalty to the crown.[33] They were certainly not 'wild Irish', even though their rank and file might conform, to some extent at least, to that stereotype. Even the great Owen Roe O'Neill was a royalist, and conceived no idea of political separation from England.[34]

Such men, from the landed class, were hardly likely to prove political or social radicals; and their aims in 1641 were conservative and old fashioned. They amounted to an attempt to ward off the consequences of the change in the distribution of political power that was taking place in England: the increasing authority of the English parliament, and the correspondingly weakening authority of the king. The native Irish were, in short, king's rebels, seeking to exploit the king's predicament as a means of defending themselves against further encroachment by the parliament of England.

Their aims were clearly stated in Sir Phelim O'Neill's proclamation, made at Dungannon on 24 October 1641. The 'meeting and assembly of the Irish' was 'in no way intended against the king, or to hurt any of his subjects either of the English or Scottish nation; but only for the defence and liberty of ourselves and natives of the Irish nation'.[35] A 'general remonstrance or declaration of the Catholics of Ireland' in December 1641 maintained that the rebels had 'taken arms and seized the best forts in the kingdom, in order to hold them in the king's name'.[36] And the defensive nature of the rebellion was revealed in a general remonstrance of 23 October 1641 which alleged that the English parliament, 'maligning and enquiring any graces received from His Majesty by our nation . . . drew His Majesty's prerogative out of his hands'. Parliament threatened the Roman Catholic religion and even considered sending over the Scots 'with the sword' against the Irish 'to supplant us and raze the name of Catholicke and Irish out of the whole kingdom'.[37]

Not all parts of Ireland rose with the speed and ferocity of Ulster; Munster, for example, was a tardy and reluctant recruit to the rebellion. But the choice facing the native Irish, and the Old English, was exceedingly limited: the parliamentary game played by the latter in 1640-41 was now played out, at least for the time being. Moreover, the Old English were now in a vulnerable position, militarily as well as politically. The government in the Pale was profoundly suspicious of papists, and unwilling to place arms in Old English hands, despite the perfect sincerity of their professions of loyalty, and yet unable to defend them against the rebels. The Pale was soon under threat; a Government army was defeated on 29 November; and there was no sign of reinforcements from England. This imminent threat, and the fact that the rebel leaders were, socially, comparable to the Old English ('discontented gentlemen', as the Old English called them in a brief meeting of the Irish Parliament in November)[38] made a juncture of causes more easy; and once the Old English had assured themselves that the Irish rebels were indeed loyal to the king, they were persuaded that the only hope of a successful resolution of their grievances was to continue in arms the conservative and limited aims that they had asserted constitutionally in parliament.

From the moment the Old English participated in the rebellion it became theirs. Their constitutional theory became the dominant one, and the 'confederation of Kilkenny', as later historians called it, sought a *rapprochement* with the crown and an independent parliament. In retrospect, these might seem contradictory aims: but they were to the confederates complementary. The dependence of the confederates on the crown caused them to emphasize the independence of the legislature, since the confederates' aims could best be pursued by preserving the authority of the king through the exclusion of that of the English Parliament. The confederates stated their position to Clanricarde in February 1642, when they declared that they were fighting for 'the liberty of this our country, which the parliament of England (our fellow subjects) seeketh to captivate and enthral to themselves'.[39] And Charles I in his negotiations with the confederates in January 1643 took their claims seriously enough to defend the operation of Poynings' Law. If it were repealed under pretence that it was made 'when a great part of Ireland had none to answer for them in that Parliament there' . . . 'the whole frame of government of that kingdom will be shaken'. And for the Irish Parliament to have a power to propose legislation without the approbation of the king and his privy council in Ireland would have consequences 'far greater than may appear *prima facie*'.[40]

However expedient the confederates' claim might be in the context of Irish politics in the early 1640s, it was firmly rooted in the Old English tradition, and based, not on Gaelic ideas, nor on any abstract principle of right, but on the (admittedly somewhat imaginary) rights of Englishmen in Ireland: 'This your majesty's kingdom of Ireland in all secessions of ages since the reign of King Henry II . . . had parliaments of their own, composed of lords and commons, qualified with equal liberties, powers, privileges and imunities with the parliament of England, and only dependent on the crown of England and Ireland'.[41] Paradoxically, this tradition of parliamentary independence was asserted by an assembly at Kilkenny that, the confederates freely admitted, was no parliament, in that the king was not present; but as the earl of Castlehaven put it, 'we hope, in time, the storm being passed, to return to our old Government under the King'.[42]

The acceptance of the Old English constitutional position by the native Irish did not obliterate the historical differences between the communities; and, in order to ease the uncomfortable feelings of the Old English rebels in 1641, Rory O'More addressed them as the 'new Irish'.[43] This was not entirely welcome to the Old English, for it undermined their colonial status; and in order to keep some kind of united front the confederate leaders were at pains to emphasize the connection between religion and nationality in Ireland. When Rory O'More met the Old English at the hill of Crofty in the Pale in 1641 he declared publicly that 'we are of the same religion, and the same nation; our interests and sufferings are the same';[44] and the oath of association to the confederacy was altered to accommodate this sense of common identity: 'There shall be no difference between the ancient and mere Irish and the successors of English, moderne or ancient' so long as 'they be professors of the holy church and maintainers of the country's liberties'.[45] In October 1642 the confederates made it clear that they identified the Irish Roman Catholics with the Irish nation. They had assembled, they declared, to decide what to do 'for the exhaltation of their religion, the defence of the King and the Royal House, the protection of their own properties, liberties and lives against the attention of the enemy' who intended amongst other things to 'extinguish the Irish nation and its liberties'.[46] All this was summed up in the confederate motto: '*Pro Deo, pro rege, pro patria*'.[47]

This concept of a united, Catholic Irish nation was not of course invented in 1641, though the events of that year gave it a special strength; it was postulated by some members of the Old English community in the sixteenth century, and David Rothe, in his history of the Catholic persecution in Ireland, gave special attention to the parliamentary struggle against the implementation of Protestantism in the reign of Elizabeth.[48] Many of the clergy in the Catholic college abroad, Old English and native Irish, identified the Catholic religion with the Irish heritage, seeing the Protestants as a common calamity for the nation. Hence John Roche in 1625 quoted in support of this view a Protestant source:

> the very ground the Irish tread, the air they breathe, the climate they share, the very sky above them, all seem to drawn them to the religion of Rome, so much that if one of them appears to abandon it the very enemies of the Catholic faith doubt his sincerity.[49]

Roche's point was confirmed, somewhat crudely, by the tendency of English officials to regard all Catholics in Ireland as the same under the skin, as 'Irish papists' without distinction.[50] The distinctions, however, remained, and were soon to be revealed; but the theoretical fusion of the Old English and native Irish in one Catholic Irish nation was to have profound consequences for concepts of nationality in Ireland. The emotional tones in which Captain Oliver French addressed the States General of the United Provinces in May 1648, when the confederate cause was in serious danger of defeat, revealed the extent to which the colonial status of the Old English had been eroded:

> Wee are a nation that was never conquered nor subdued by any forraigne force, but by arguments amongst ourselves, by our respects and abundant affections to the crowne, and great monarchy of England, continued by us from age to age, for uppwards of five hundred years, in despyght of all oppressions of our persons, suppressions of our rights, usurpations of our birth-rights, . . . by our fellow subjects and neighbouring Christians of England, every day more and more encreased. (until we took up) defensive armes against the said oppressions and tyrannies in and for the interests of our fayth, king and country . . .[51]

The 'arguments amongst ourselves' to which French referred were a feature of the confederacy throughout its existence. The Old English were particularly anxious to secure their lands against further encroachment by the Government; those of the Irish who had lost their lands in earlier confiscations were unwilling to accept a settlement with the king that did not go some way towards restoring their economic fortunes.[52] The Old English had no intention of negotiating a settlement with Charles that would confer equal power on the church and the native

Irish, and, while they were willing to demand the abrogation of penal laws, they were opposed to placing religion in the forefront of the confederate programme, and utterly set against the restoration of the church as an independent institution exercising authority in its own right. Many of the Old English had, after all, recently acquired church lands and had no wish to have their acquisitions questioned. Indeed, it appeared that the Old English, in their negotiations with the king, had taken over the rebellion for their own ends, for scarcely any grievances of the native Irish were mentioned in the lists of demands presented to Charles. And only the arrival in Ireland of the formidable papal nuncio, Rinuccini, in October 1645, prevented the Old English from making peace with the king on their own terms.[53] Disagreements over aims caused a rupture between the central council of the confederates and the military council which was dominated by the native Irish; but the 'fusion' of Old English and native Irish, now seriously impaired, was soon to be sealed by an external force: the Cromwellian conquest of Ireland.

It is easy to exaggerate the hostility between the Old English and native Irish on the one hand, and the New English on the other; the reluctance of the Munster Irish to rise in 1641 compares with their onslaught on the small English colony in 1598. But any possibility of good relations between Protestants and Catholics in Ireland was grievously weakened by the massacres and brutality committed by the Irish rebels in 1641, especially in Ulster, atrocities which, though undoubtedly exaggerated for propaganda purposes in Britain, so alarmed the Old English of the Pale that they protested in 1642 that 'what murders, robberies, or other outrages were lately committed upon the British Protestants were done by the meaner sort of people, without allowance or privity of their commanders'.[54] There was a good deal of truth in this assertion;[55] but the events, real and imagined, of 1641 so outraged and inflamed British Protestant opinion that there was a general demand for retribution to be visited upon those 'barbarous wretches who have imbrued their hands in so much innocent blood'.[56] A Cromwellian army, backed by an incensed Protestant public was in no mood to distinguish between one kind of Catholic or another, or between those innocent of massacre and those who were guilty.[57] The Munster Protestants, for example, were now obsessed with one ambition: to crush the rebellion and to make no concession to the confederates.[58] And not only the confederates: anyone who happened to be on their side was included in the general censure. It is significant that the storming of Drogheda, and the slaughter of its garrison and many of its civilians in 1649, numbered among the victims many English royal-ists;[59] and it is even more significant that, when he turned his attention to Cork, Kinsale and Bandon, the Protestant royalist garrison joined Cromwell of its own free will.[60] The boundaries of sectarian politics, which were always blurred and confused even up to 1640, had now become clear: loyalty to king or parliament had been exchanged for loyalty to Catholicism or Protestantism.

Sectarian politics were now the style; and their influence was expres-sed in a Gaelic poem on the condition of the Irish written in 1650, whose identification of faith and fatherland contrasts sharply with the secular political Gaelic poetry of the Elizabethan age:

Wilt thou not listen?
Or is it thy will never again to look upon us?
Upon us, who have always adored thee,
Now punished unjustly under the Saxons . . .

Soon will the heroes combine;
And, united hand in hand,
They will vanquish the strangers at Saingel
And rout the foreigners at Mullaghmaistin.

Then none shall league with the Saxon,
Nor with the half-naked Scot.
Then shall Erin be freed from settlers,
Then shall perish the Saxon tongue.

The Gaels in arms shall triumph
Ove the crafty, thieving, false sect of Calvin.[61]

When the native Irish and Old English made their last stand in 1688-9 it was under a Catholic king against a Protestant one. And William King, writing in 1691 to justify the Protestant rebellion against the Catholic king James, readily identified the 'popish Irish interest in Ireland', citing a letter from one Catholic bishop to another, written in 1689, which picked out two parties in Ireland 'to wit, the Protestant. New-comers and usupers', and 'the Catholics of Ireland'.[62] This schematic diagram was still an oversimplification, for there was by no means an identity of interest between the Presbyterians of Ulster and the New English members of the episcopal church; but it was accurate enough in times of political crisis in the seventeenth century. The fusion of

'Catholic' and 'Irish' was so complete that later Irish nationalists could lament the fall of the Geraldines in the 1530s, or the Old English rebels in 1650 at the hands of Oliver Cromwell, without acknowledging or even realizing that they were lamenting, not the collapse of 'Irish', but rather of Old English identity and power: and it was with some justification that Sir Richard Cox, in his *Hibernia Anglicana*, published in 1689-90, complained that:

> if the most ancient Natural Irish-Man be a Protestant, no man takes him for other than an English-Man; and if a Cockny be a Papist, he is reckoned in Ireland as much an Irish-Man as if he was born on Slevelogher.[63]

Protestants, perhaps, had only themselves to blame for this. Official reluctance to take the strong intellectual and coercive measures necessary to give the reformation in Ireland a chance of success in the sixteenth century[64] was now compounded by another lost opportunity under the Cromwellian regime. The conquest of Ireland by Cromwell offered a second chance to eradicate religious differences, a line of action that had earlier been proposed by Edmund Spenser who wanted 'some discreet ministers of their (the Irish) own countrymen' to be sent over, and who contrasted the zeal of the 'Popish priests' with the lassitude of those ministers of the gospel who could not be 'drawn forth from their warm nests to look out into God's harvest'. Protestant evangelism and education, the introduction of English customs, language, and dress, the establishment of English law, could now be pressed forward, and a drive made against Catholic worship. But this faltered during the Interregnum: too few preachers were sent; the Roman Catholic church responded vigorously; and the number of converts, although not inconsiderable, was insufficient and transient.[65] It no longer seemed worthwhile to undertake a mass conversion of the Catholics anyway, since the Protestant religion was the badge of a superior political and social status.

Moreover, Englishmen were obsessed with the idea of the collective guilt of the Irish for the atrocities of the 1641 rebellion: it made more sense to punish the guilty than waste time converting them to the true religion.[66] And it was important to retain a distinction between Protestants and Catholics, since the increasing proportion of land held by Protestants after 1650 meant that the Catholics' material interests must clash with those of the new owners of the land. In 1652 the English Parliament passed an Act of settlement which, in effect, divided the people of Ireland into 'English Protestants' and 'Irish Papists'. The lands of Papists were declared forfeit, except for the province of Connaught; and the forfeited lands were to be divided between the Government; the 'adventurers' who had advanced money for the conquest of Ireland; and soldiers, to discharge the arrears of pay. The broad category of 'Irish Papist' embraced many diverse groups: Old English, native Irish, and even some of the New English who were of the Roman Catholic faith. If 'Catholic' and 'Irish' were synonymous, it was at least partly because it suited the Government and the Protestant New English to regard them as such; quite apart from the emotional desire to punish Catholics for their treachery in 1641, there was the simple economic fact that only by confiscation and the appropriation of papists's land could Parliament foot the bill for the conquest of Ireland. To use a modern expression, only thus could Cromwell's military campaigns be self-financing.[67]

Applying the confiscation policy proved a complex and lengthy business. There were no adequate surveys of the country; there was not even enough land to go round, and some land in Connaught, originally allocated to the Irish, had to be reallocated to Cromwellian soldiers, and the people already settled there had to be transplanted again. In some areas, however, such as Wicklow, the absence of a yeoman Protestant class made it imperative for the planters to retain Irish labour, including some of the old proprietors.[68] Most important for the Protestants, the core of their interest was not the new Cromwellians but the 'old' Protestants established in Ireland before 1649. No more than a quarter of the soldiers remained, and those who did came largely from the officers; of the adventurers, only some 500 had been confirmed in their estates by the mid 1660s. This enabled the Protestant interest to escape any taint of Cromwellianism when the Interregnum was succeeded by the restoration of Charles II in 1660, and Catholic hopes of a division in the Protestant ranks, by which they might recover their lost lands, were quickly dashed: the English interest was firmly settled in Ireland and determined to remain where it stood.[69] And while the Protestants could suffer the concession of a measure of religious toleration to their enemies, they were certainly not prepared to see that 'which they had gotten with their lives' filched from them 'with ayes and noes'.[70] The Catholic share of land, which was about 60 per cent in 1641, dropped to between 8 and 9 per cent (almost all of it in Connaught or Clare) by 1660, and was little over 20 per cent in 1685.[71] And not only were the Protestants secure on the land; the towns and cities of Ireland, formerly a stronghold of Old English influence, were now placed firmly in Protestant hands: Catholics lost control of town corporations and were not permitted to engage in trade.[72]

But there were still enough Catholic landed proprietors to take advantage of the accession of King James in 1685; and dispossessed Catholics were not prepared to accept the disappointments of the restoration as final.[73] The accession of James saw the climax of the dispute between the Irish Catholics and the English Protestants for possession of Ireland. From January 1686 to February 1687 the Irish Government was dominated by Richard Talbot, earl of Tyrconnell, a Catholic descendant of a Norman family, who soon alarmed the Protestants by his policy of granting commissions in the Irish army to Catholics. Protestant fears were fanned when Tyrconnell at last managed to gain formal control when he was appointed lord deputy in February 1687; and soon the majority of judges and privy councillors were Catholics. But even more alarming was the prospect of an attack on the land settlement, an attack which Catholics pressed the lord deputy to pursue. James was aware of the need for caution on such a dangerous course, and in the Spring of 1688 a compromise was worked out whereby Cromwellians should be left in possession of half their estates, with the other half restored to their former proprietors.[74] But this compromise completely misunderstood the attitude of the New English interest, one of whom, the chief justice John Keating, in an address to James on behalf of the purchasers under the Act of Settlement, declared that:

> We sold our estates in *England*, transported us and our families into Ireland, to purchase, improve and plant there. We acquired lands as secure titles as Acts of Parliament . . . could make them. Our conveyances both by Deeds and matters of Record are allowed good, firm and unquestioned by any Law in force at the time of the Purchase. We have had our possession 10, 12 or 15 years, and are grown old upon them. We have clearly drawn our effects from *England* and settled here, not doubting but our posterity may be so likewise. Now old proprietors . . . would have a new law to dispossess us of our estates and improvements made as aforesaid.[75]

Keating was a moderate who sought to come to terms with James and who even excused Tyrconnell;[76] more resolute men were hardly likely to demand less than he did.

The last year of James' brief reign, however, promised that the New English would have to accept considerably less than a compromise solution of the land question. According to Sir William Petty the priests comforted their flocks 'partly by prophecies of their restoration to their ancient estates and liberties, which the abler sort of them fetch from what the Prophets of the Old Testament have delivered by way of God's Promise to restore the Jews to the Kingdom of Israel'.[77] These exciting prophecies seemed nearer realization when the English revolution compelled James to rely on Irish support to regain his throne; and on his arrival in Ireland in March 1689 he issued a proclamation summoning a parliament for May. This was the first Parliament in Ireland in which Catholics had been predominant since the beginning of the seventeenth century; and it was the last Irish Parliament which they were to dominate until the establishment of Dáil Eireann in 1919. Not surprisingly, it has attracted much attention and admiration from nationalists, in particular because of the constitutional arguments advanced there, and its (unsuccessful) attempt to secure the repeal of Poyning's Law. James did agree reluctantly to an act declaring that the English Parliament had no right to legislate for Ireland: Ireland had always been a kingdom distinct from that of England; and claims of the English Parliament to legislate for Ireland were 'against justice, and natural equity, offensive to the people and destructive of the constitution'. English appellate jurisdiction was also denied, and an Irish appellate court substituted for an English one.[78]

All this was done with a purpose. As one contemporary noted, it would 'render the Irish Catholics effectually potent . . . to make the Parliament of Ireland absolute in enacting lawes, without being obliged to send beforehand the prepared bills'.[79] The purpose of the laws thus passed, however, was to overturn the verdict of the Cromwellian conquest and of the Stuart restoration. This raised problems, for some of James's Catholic supporters had bought land, and the title to it was based on the land settlement of King Charles's reign. James was persuaded against his will to accept total repeal; and the acts of Settlement and Explanation were annulled, as were all titles derived from them. The landowners of 1641 were authorized to take steps to recover their property, and all rebels against James — that was, in effect, all Protestants — were to forfeit their lands. But in landed matters, as in constitutional, the Old English domination of the political life of Ireland was asserted for the last time. Those dispossessed before 1641, notably the Ulster Irish, were not specifically provided for; the Old English would benefit most from the proceedings of the 'Patriot parliament', if these proceedings were ever made effective.[80]

Had James succeeded in Ireland his success would not have been followed by the restoration of Gaelic rule, or the undoing of the English conquest. Economically, England and Ireland were to be bound closely together; and although the patriot parliament's legislation would have wrought great changes in Ireland, it would not have turned the clock back to pre-1169 days. Ireland would have been an English dependency under a Catholic oligarchy — the kind of Ireland in which the Old English had flourished and could, perhaps, flourish again.[81]

Nevertheless, the myth of James's brief reign was a powerful and enduring one; and the verse of the contemporary Gaelic poet, David O Bruadair, reflected the impression that the confederate watchwords of God, king and country had wrought upon Gaelic political ideas. In his 'Summary of the purgatory of the men of Ireland' O Bruadair execrated the 'gang who betrayed King Charles'. And in his long eulogy on the 'Triumph of James I', composed in October 1687, he avowed:

> That it is not Elizabeth I magnify,
> But the Stuart King James, bright star of royalty,
> That hath risen under God to succour us.

'A prop of the right-roaded faith' was he; and O Bruadair linked the English king not only with the true faith, but with the ancient royal history of pre-Norman Ireland:

> Welcome his coming, rejoice, and raise cheers for
> The High King, beloved and golden-lawed,
> Who comes of the true blood of Corc the renowned king
> Of the fort of this province's capital.

'Glory on high', he concluded, 'free from straits is my plight . . . Since the hosts of Fal's men are now serving the king'; a king, he maintained in his poem 'The triumph of Tadhg', composed in 1690, who was a 'true-blooded Gael of our own Caiseal's royal stem, And also a Frenchman descended from Pharamond'.[82]

The overthrow of the patriot Parliament's programme for an old Ireland by the Williamite military victories of 1689-91 was important, therefore, not only for the Old English, but for the Irish nationalist tradition. The final downfall of the old order, the loss of political influence by the Old English and Gaelic Irish, meant that the Catholics of Ireland — whatever their diverse origin — soon came to regard themselves as heirs to a common tradition; a tradition of spoilation, persecution, and defeat. Land and religion became central to this experience, and were resurrected to become the driving force of the resurgent nationalism of the nineteenth century. Sir Audley Mervyn had predicted in 1663 that Irish claims to land would still be made, whatever law or lawyers might say. 'Sir,' he wrote:

> in the North of Ireland, the Irish have a custom in the winter, when milk is scarce, to kill the calf and preserve the skin, and stuffing it with straw they set it upon four wooden feet which they call a *puckan*, and the cow will be as fond of this as she was of the living calf; she will low after it and lick it and give her milk down, so it stands but by her. Sir, these writings will have the operation of this puckan, for wanting the land to which they relate they are but stuffed with straw, yet, sir, they will low after them, lick them over and over in their thoughts, and teach their children to read by them instead of horn-books. And if any venom be left they will give it down upon the right of these puckan writings, and entail a memory of revenge, though the estate tail be cut off.[83]

Above all, the events of the seventeenth century provided a series of colourful and emotional images, of battles, sieges, massacres, of promises made and promises broken. The Old English, that 'middle nation' who contributed so much to Irish constitutional theory, to Irish parliamentary government, and to the whole question of what constituted 'Irishness' anyway, lost its distinctive position in this Irish legend. It is significant that nationalists' most admired and loved hero of the Williamite wars, Patrick Sarsfield, was Old English on his father's side, and Gaelic on his mother's,[84] thus giving a neat symbolic finale to the Catholic Irish version of the history of Ireland in the seventeenth century.[85]

But the defeat of King James by King William did not break the continuity of the Irish nationalist tradition in its constitutional character. Generations of Protestants, from William Molyneux in the late seventeenth century to Henry Grattan in the eighteenth, asserted the Protestant ascendancy's right to rule Ireland in its own way, and based their case on the writings, speeches and claims of the Old English. The ascendancy's hostility to the Catholic and Gaelic tradition did not prevent them from raising the confederate cry of 'God, king and country' even though the king (and probably also the God) differed substantially from those of the men who first coined the slogan. The Protestant victory at the battle of the Boyne has some claim to be regarded as a highly significant date in the calendar of Irish nationalism.

Notes

1. N.P. Canny, *Elizabethan Conquest*, p. 139.

2. A. Clarke, 'Colonial identity in early 17th century Ireland' in *Historical Studies*, XI, pp. 57-9; N. Canny, 'Dominant minorities: English settlers in Ireland and Virginia, 1554-1650' in A.C. Hepburn (ed.) *Minorities in History* (London, 1978), pp. 51-69.

3. M. MacCurtain, *Tudor and Stuart Ireland*, p. 124.

4. A. Clarke, in *New History of Ireland*, vol. *III*, pp. 188-9.

5. A. Clarke, *The Old English in Ireland*, 1625-42 (London, 1966), p. 6. The layers of Old English society have been classified as follows: an 'outer rim' of (1) families of 'degenerate English', now almost wholly Gaelicized; (2) those of Old English stock who had adopted the protestant religion without acquiring correspondingly protestant interests and outlook; (3) those of Irish extraction who associated themselves with Old English sentiments and who 'have land, settle into an honest and fair course of life, and doubtless are well-affected to the English monarchy'. This outer rim shaded into the inner core of the Old English whose identification with the political and social ethos of the group was complete (A. Clarke, op. cit., p. 14).

6. Ibid., pp. 21-22.

7. Clarke, in *New History of Ireland*, p. 190.

8. R. Bagwell, *Ireland under the Stuarts*, vol. *I* (London, 1963 edn.), pp. 19-20.

9. A. Clarke, 'Colonial identity', pp. 62-71.

10. Clarke, *Old English in Ireland*, pp. 25-6.

11. T.W. Moody, 'The treatment of the native population under the scheme for the plantation in Ulster' in *Irish Historical Studies*, vol. *I*, (March, 1938) pp. 59-63. See also Stewart, *The narrow ground*, pp. 34-41.

12. J.C. Beckett, 'Irish-Scottish relations in the seventeenth century', in *Confrontations*, pp. 26-45; M. Perceval-Maxwell, *The Scottish Migration to Ulster in the Reign of James I* (London, 1973), pp. 10-11, 309-11, 316.

13. Bottigheimer, in K.R. Andrews, *et al* (eds.) *The Western enterprise*,,p. 57.

14. Clarke, in *New History of Ireland*, pp. 196-205; see also Bagwell, op. cit., pp. 82-3; Thomas Blenerhasset in 1610 spoke of the need to guard against 'the crueal wood-kerne, the devouring wolf, and other suspicious Irish'.

15. Clarke, in *New History of Ireland*, pp. 206-8.

16. The house of commons contained 132 Protestants and 100 Roman Catholics; of the latter, some 18 were native Irish. In the lords the Protestant majority was 24 to 12 (MacCurtain, op. cit., pp. 120-21).

17. H. Morley (ed.) *Ireland under Elizabeth and James I*, p. 403.

18. Clarke, *New History of Ireland*, pp. 214-9; see also Bagwell, *Ireland under the Stuarts*, I, p. 131.

19. R. Dudley Edwards, 'Ireland, Elizabeth and the counter-reformation', in S.T. Bindoff *et al* (eds.) *Elizabethan Government and Society*, pp. 336-7.

20. A. Clarke, 'Ireland and the general crisis', *Past and Present*, No. 48, (1970) pp. 79-99.

21. Clarke, *New History of Ireland*, pp. 230-32.

22. Ibid., Chap. VIII.

23. Ibid., pp. 240-42.

24. J.C. Beckett, *The Making of Modern Ireland* (London, 1966 edn.), p. 65.

25. H. Kearney, *Strafford in Ireland* (Manchester, 1959), Chap. X; Clarke, *New History of Ireland*, p. 264.

26. Ibid., p. 126.

27. Ibid., pp. 185-88.

28. Clarke, *Old English in Ireland*, pp. 134-5.

29. *An Argument Delivered by Patrick Darcy, Esquire.* (Dublin, 1764 edn.), passim.

30. Ibid; see also A. Clarke, 'The policies of the Old English in parliament, 1640-1641' in *Historical Studies*, V (London, 1963), pp. 85-100, and B. Corish, 'The rising of 1641 and the Catholic Confederacy', in *New History of Ireland*, p. 300.

31. A. Stopford Green, *Irish Nationality*, p. 160.

32. Clarke, 'Ireland and the general crisis', op. cit., pp. 88-9.

33. W.A. Phillips (ed.) *The History of the Church of Ireland: from the earliest Times to the Present Day*, vol. *III*, *The Modern Church* (London, 1933), p. 2.

34. R. Bagwell, *Ireland under the Stuarts*, vol. *II* (London, 1963 edn.), p. 198.

35. *Calendar of State Papers Irish*, 1633-47 (London, 1901), p. 342.

36. Ibid., p. 355.

37. Sir J.T. Gilbert, *A Contemporary History of Affairs in Ireland, 1641-52*, vol. *I*, part i (Dublin, 1879), pp. 360-61.

38. A. Clarke, 'Ireland and the general crisis', op. cit., p. 98.

39. J.C. Beckett, 'The confederation of Kilkenny reviewed' in *Confrontations*, pp. 54-5.

40. J.T. Gilbert, *History of the Irish confederation*, vol. *II* (Dublin, 1882), pp. 141-3; see also ibid., vol. *III*, pp. 128-33, 175-8, 278-93, 305-12.

41. Beckett, op. cit., p. 56.

42. Gilbert, *History of the Irish confederation*, vol. *I*, p. lxii.

43. Clarke, 'Ireland and the general crisis', op. cit., p. 81.P.F. Moran, (ed.), *Spicilegium Ossoriense*, 2nd series (Dublin, 1878), p. 42.

44. Gilbert, *History of the Irish Confederation*, vol. *I*, p. 37.

45. Clarke, *Old English in Ireland*, p. 182, fn. 1; P.F. Moran (ed.), *Spicilegium Ossoriense*, p. 13.

46. Gilbert, *History of the Irish Confederation*, vol. I, p. lx.

47. Beckett, op. cit., p. 53.

48. Dudley Edwards, 'Ireland, Elizabeth I and the counter reformation', op. cit., pp. 336-7.

49. P.J. Corish, 'The origins of Catholic nationalism', in *History of Irish Catholicism*, vol. *VIII*, part iii, pp. 27-31. See also *New History of Ireland* pp. lvi, 632.

50. Gilbert, *Contemporary History*, pp. 383-93.

51. Gilbert, *History of the Irish Confederation*, vol. *VI*, pp. 232-5.

52. Gilbert, *Contemporary History*, pp. 282-3.

53. J. Lowe, 'Charles I and the confederation of Kilkenny, 1643-9' in *Irish Historical Studies*, vol. *XIV*, (March, 1964), pp. 1-19; Corish, 'Origins of Catholic nationalism', pp. 36-7, 40-56: Dudley Edwards, op. cit., pp. 338; M.J. Hynes, *The mission of Rinuccini, nuncio extraordinary to Ireland* (Dublin, 1932), pp. 38-9, 42-3.

54. W.A. Phillips, *History of the Church of Ireland*, vol. *III*, (London, 1934), pp. 72-3.

55. For a modern assessment of the 1641 rising in Ulster see M. Perceval-Maxwell, 'The Ulster rising of 1641, and the depositions', in *Irish Historical Studies*, vol. *XXI* (Sept. 1978), pp. 144-67.

56. Bagwell, *Ireland under the Stuarts*, II, p. 194.

57. See the phraseology of the lords justices' proclamation of 23 October 1641 (Bagwell, op. cit., II, pp. 320-21). An amended, toned-down proclamation was issued on 29 October (Ibid., p. 324).

58. J.A. Murphy, 'The politics of the Munster protestants, 1641-49', in *JCHAS*, vol. LXXVI, No. 223 (Jan.-June 1971), pp. 1-20. For the reaction of one

'papist' see Murphy, p. 3, fn. 6: 'at the reading of the words "ill-affected Irish papist", to one Domhnall O'Sullivan, St. Leger, the lord president of Munster noted "I did never in my life observe more venomous rancour in any man's face than was in his".'
    59. Bagwell, *II*, p. 195.
    60. Ibid., pp. 208-9.
    61. J.T. Gilbert, *A Contemporary History of Affairs in Ireland*, vol. *III*, part ii, (Dublin 1880), pp. 190-96.
    62. W. King, *The State of the Protestants of Ireland under the Late King James's Government* (Dublin, 1730 edn.), pp. 61, 81.
    63. W.A. Phillips (ed.) *History of the Church of Ireland*, vol. *III*, p. 535. For the Catholic explanation of this kind of sentiment see J.T. Gilbert, *A Jacobite Narrative of the War in Ireland, 1688-91* (Dublin, 1971 edn.) pp. 55-6.
    64. B. Bradshaw, 'Sword, word and strategy in the reformation in Ireland', *Historical Journal*, vol. *21*, No. 3 (1978), pp. 475-502.
    65. T.C. Barnard, *Cromwellian Ireland: English Government and Reform in Ireland, 1649-1660* (London, 1975), Chaps. 1, 5.
    66. Ibid., p. 297. K. Lindley, 'The impact of the 1641 rebellion upon England and Wales, 1641-5', *I.H.S.*, vol. *XVIII* (1972), pp. 143-76.
    67. P.J. Corish, 'The Cromwellian regime, 1650-60', in *New History of Ireland*, pp. 357-62.
    68. Ibid., pp. 364-74.
    69. Bottigheimer, *The Westward Enterprise*, pp. 62-3; Barnard, op. cit., p. 304.
    70. Beckett, *Making of Modern Ireland*, pp. 120, 126; for an expression of Catholic hopes at the restoration see J. Lynch, *Cambrensis Eversus* (1662; 3 vols., Dublin 1848-51), I, Dedication.
    71. J.G. Simms, *Jacobite Ireland* (London, 1969), p. 4.
    72. Corish, *New History of Ireland*, p. 373.
    73. See e.g., Address from the Roman Catholic Bishops of Ireland to the king, 24 July 1685 (P.F. Moran, *Spicilegium Ossoriense*, p. 270).
    74. J.G. Simms, 'The war of the two kings, 1685-91', in *New History of Ireland*, pp. 478-81.
    75. King, *State of the Protestants*, pp. 99-100.
    76. Bagwell, *Ireland under the Stuarts*, vol. *III*, p. 230, fn. 1.
    77. W. Petty, *Political Anatomy of Ireland* (Irish University Press, 1970 edn.) pp. 95 ff.
    78. Simms, *Jacobite Ireland*, pp. 77-81.
    79. R.H. Murray, *Revolutionary Ireland and its Settlement* (London, 1911), p. 123, fn. 2.
    80. For the proceedings of the 'patriot parliament' see Bagwell, op. cit., Chap. li.
    81. Simms, *Jacobite Ireland*, pp. 81-94.
    82. Revd. John C. MacErlean (ed.), *The poems of David O Bruadair* (3 vols., London, 1910-17), *III*, pp. 13, 79, 81, 87, 139. Pharamond was said to have been the first king of the Franks.
    83. Bagwell, op. cit., pp. 32-33. Mervyn's letter was to Ormonde in Dublin Castle, 13 Feb. 1662/3.
    84. Sarsfield's mother was the daughter of Rory O'More. His family came to Ireland in the reign of Henry II, and settled as members of the Anglo-Norman gentry of the Pale (J. Todhunter, *Sarsfield* (London, 1895) p. 3).
    85. For O Bruadair's eulogy of Sarsfield see MacErlean, op. cit., pp. 143-57.

4 FROM ENGLISH COLONY TO IRISH NATION: THE PROTESTANT EXPERIENCE

The spectacle of the New English interest assuming the mantle of the Irish nation is one more liable to excite contempt than admiration. Even P.S. O'Hegarty, who strongly disapproved of the use of the term 'Anglo-Irish' to single out the protestant Anglican inhabitants of his country,[1] and who conceded that the eighteenth century Irish Parliament, whatever its faults, provided 'the nucleus of a National Parliament', condemned the Protestant 'garrison' who had usurped 'the name of the People of Ireland'.[2] The way in which the Protestant ascendancy rose to power was hardly likely to receive approbation from Irish Roman Catholics, or, for that matter, Irish Protestant Dissenters. The shrill appeals of the New English for government help to buttress their political ambitions in the early seventeenth century; their opportunism and their undignified scramble for land; their hatred of the Catholic religion; their flight from Ireland in king James's reign followed by their triumphant return in the pockets of king William's army; their enactment of the penal laws against Catholic and Dissenter: all these betokened a band of mercenary adventurers, 'cheese eating bodachs',[3] out for what they could get, rather than a people who cared for the country they had settled in and won. When to this catalogue of human failings is added the contemporary sneer that attaches to the epithet 'colonial',[4] it is understandable that critics have seized on the term colonial rather than the term national to describe the eighteenth century ascendancy.

Hostility to the Protestant ascendancy is based on a number of counts, ranging from their absenteeism to their xenophobia; but perhaps two grievances have been especially emphasized: the penal laws, and the corrupt and unrepresentative nature of the eighteenth century Irish Parliament. The former have been denounced by generations of Irishmen and, it must be noted, not only by Irish Roman Catholics and nationalists, as amounting to a system akin to South African apartheid;[5] the latter has been described as a venal and oppressive institution representing only the interests of a selfish caste.[6] But, whatever the justification for these strictures, one thing is clear: it was upon the penal laws, that comprehensive system of legal discrimination, and the Irish parliament, that the ascendancy's power rested. It is time to examine those twin pillars of Protestant oppression and Protestant freedom.

On 13 September 1692 the secretary of state, the earl of Nottingham, wrote to the lord deputy, Sidney, that he 'did not know that any favour was intended to the Papists of Ireland more than their Majesties are obliged, in justice, to allow them and is necessary for the peace of that country'.[7] The desire to reconcile justice with security was a difficult one to accomplish in the atmosphere of post-revolutionary Ireland. Not only had Irish Protestants escaped destruction by what seemed an uncomfortably close margin; the country was still in a far from settled condition, with bands of 'rapparees' − armed gangs consisting mainly of Jacobite ex-soldiers − on the loose and with the very real danger of another French invasion. Then there was the fear aroused by the possibility of Papal support for the Stuart cause, which found expression in an oath administered to those Huguenot refugees from France who were in receipt of a grant of land, by which they must 'abhor, detest and abjure as impious and heretical, that damnable doctrine and position that princes excommunicated or deprived by the pope or any authority of the see of Rome, may be deposed and murdered by their subjects, or any other whatsoever'.[8] The belief that the deposing power of the pope was accepted by every Roman Catholic was axiomatic to Irish Protestants; and any Catholic priest, or member of the landed gentry − and there were still some of the latter around − were regarded as potential Jacobites.

All these fears coloured Irish Protestant political attitudes for more than 20 years after their victory in 1690-91; and they were expressed in the strong opposition to the treaty which William concluded with the beaten Jacobites at Limerick in October 1691. The civil articles of the treaty guaranteed religious toleration for the Roman Catholics 'consistent with the laws of Ireland, or as they did enjoy in the reign of King Charles II'; security of life and property for Jacobite officers and soldiers remaining in Ireland; and security for the civil inhabitants of Limerick and other places held by the Jacobites and of areas under their protection.[9] These terms were generous, and they did not seem to Protestants to hold out sufficient guarantee of their safety in the face of a possible Catholic revival, nor to constitute a sufficient punishment of the Catholic enemy. The Irish Protestants did not ratify the treaty until 1697, and only then in a form that ignored or set aside its most important provisions for civil and religious liberty.

The Irish Parliament which broke the treaty of Limerick was an exclusively Protestant body,[10] and it was necessary for William to meet

its prejudices in order to win sufficient support for the tranquil government of the country. When the Irish Parliament pressed for penal legislation against Roman Catholics, the English Government felt that it had
little choice but to yield; and in 1695 a new Irish parliament was
presented with measures calculated to assuage Protestant fears. Laws
were passed for disarming Papists and for restaining their resort to
foreign seats of learning. Among those sections of the laws relating to
arms was one enacting that, except in the time of invasion, no Papist
could keep a horse of more than £5 value; and if a Protestant
discovered a breach of this law, no matter what the value of the horse
concerned, it became his property on paying five guineas to the
owner.[11]

This was a foretaste of future penal legislation. In 1697 the same
Parliament passed an act banishing all Roman Catholic bishops and
regular clergy, and the preamble to the act again epitomized Protestant determination to be rid of the menace of popery for ever: priests,
it alleged, 'do not only endeavour to withdraw his Majesty's subjects
from their obedience, but do daily stir up, and move sedition and
rebellion to the great hazard of the ruin and desolation of this kingdom'. Matrimonial laws were enacted to ensure that if man or woman
should persist in intermarrying with a Catholic, he or she would pay the
forfeit of their property rights of inheritance.[12] But these laws were
more severe in intention than in practice; and in 1704 parliament felt
it necessary to pass an act 'to prevent the further growth of popery'.
Before this the penal code relating to property was more draconian
in England than in Ireland, since in England Roman Catholics were
forbidden to buy or inherit real estate whereas in Ireland they had
merely been forbidden to purchase forfeited property. Now the ban
was extended to all property; and Catholic landed families were faced
with the stark choice of conforming to the Church of Ireland or seeing
their estates sub-divided and themselves sinking lower and lower in the
social scale. The education of Irish Catholics abroad was proceeded
against; and Catholics were forbidden to act as guardians to children
under age. A sacramental test was imposed on anyone seeking public
employment; and an oath of allegiance and an oath abjuring the pretender were to be taken by all those seeking election to parliament. The
seal was set on the penal code by the Act of 1728 which deprived
papists of the vote at parliamentary elections.[13]

This detailed catalogue reveals that the main purpose of the legislation was political. It was not meant primarily to extinguish popery
from Ireland (though that would have been a welcome bonus to the

Protestants). An Act for registering the popish clergy was passed, requiring priests to send in returns of their name, abode, age, time and place of receiving holy orders, and giving security for good behaviour. Roman Catholic worship was not prohibited, and 'mass houses' were common. Land, not theological abstractions, was the object of the code; political power had to be monopolized by the Protestants, more particularly by the Anglicans, if they were never again to run the risks that they had run in James's reign.[14]

The penal laws therefore require neither historical justification nor condemnation, but historical explanation. They were the kind of legislation that was enacted in many European countries, in France, in the Empire, and in England itself, to curb political/religious minorities. The important difference was that in Ireland the people against whom the code was enacted were not a minority but a majority. Thus the danger to the state was all the more acute: in 1707, for example, Archbishop King reported that a French invasion scare, which he had earlier dismissed, had now frightened the people 'almost . . . out of their wits'.[15] Irish Dissenters, for their part, were not free from taint in Anglican eyes; and the sacramental test added to the popery act of 1704 was mainly injurious to the Presbyterians who had hitherto been free to enter all civil and military employments.[16] The political, rather than religious motives, of the penal code were seen in the Anglican church's lack of interest in converting the Roman Catholics. The Church of Ireland often toyed with proselytizing schemes, and considered establishing schools where Catholic children would be taught the Protestant faith and the English language, but nothing ever came of this.[17] And the tradition, reaching back to the seventeenth century, of allowing Catholics to go to hell in their own way[18] provided they presented no political threat was continued.

Nevertheless, it is not difficult to understand why nationalists have found the penal code at odds with the Ascendancy's claim that it represented the Irish nation. Certainly, the code offers a stark contrast to the patriot Parliament's law removing all civil disabilities on account of religion and guaranteeing freedom of worship. But that same Parliament's act of attainder, although it included Catholics who had placed themselves under William, was, in effect, an anti-Protestant measure, and one that would have destroyed Protestant power: the property of over 2,400 Protestants would have been forfeited.[19] The fact was that by 1688, as archbishop King put it, 'there was no medium, but that we or they must be undone'.[20] No political group could have dominated in Ireland without the complete political, social and economic subjection of its rivals, and for the Anglicans those rivals numbered amongst their ranks the Presbyterians of Ulster. In Protestant eyes the penal code was justified by its success. The Presbyterians might grouse and grumble after their cantankerous fashion,[21] but they kept themselves out of dangerous company, for most of the eighteenth century at least. The Catholics did not even grumble: and in 1715 and 1745, when Jacobitism threatened the peace of the British crown, Ireland remained tranquil.

The political stability of Ireland enabled the Irish Parliament, after the vicissitudes of the seventeenth century, to establish itself as a permanent part of the Irish system of government. This bulwark of the Ascendancy had all the characteristic features of an eighteenth century legislature: it was dominated by landlords; it was the field on which personal rivalries between the political families and their groups could be fought out; it was seldom responsive to public opinion. Indeed, except for a few brief outbursts, there was in the early part of the century little in the way of public opinion for Parliament to be responsive to. General elections were held very infrequently, since there was in Ireland no Septennial Act to force a dissolution of Parliament before the demise of the monarch. Moreover parliament had no continuous control over the Irish executive, and no share in the formation of ministries which were made in England: the lord lieutenant was simply a member of the British cabinet charged with executing its policy. Above all, while Parliament might be touchy on certain sensitive issues affecting Ireland – for example the grant of a patent in 1722 to William Wood, a Wolverhampton ironmaster, empowering him to coin money for Ireland – it had no central political purpose beyond the perfectly normal eighteenth century practice of enabling the executive to carry on the king's government. The smoothest way to do this was to hand the management of the Irish Parliament over to Irish politicians, men who undertook to provide the Government with a majority in the House of Commons; in return these 'undertakers' received a substantial share of official patronage and some say in policy making, such as it was. Once the Whig versus Tory conflict of Queen Anne's reign ended, there was little in the way of principle to divide Irish politicians, and much in the way of patronage for them to fall out over. It proved simpler for the lord lieutenant to rely on one powerful parliamentary manager to do the business, instead of a myriad of lesser men; and, inevitably, the manager escaped the dominance of the lord lieutenant, becoming a powerful and independent figure.[22]

Since the main business of the Irish Parliament was to enable the king's Government to be carried on, it was necessary for the executive to establish some kind of working arrangement with parliament in passing legislation. Under Poynings' Law bills were framed by the Government and presented to the Irish Parliament for acceptance or rejection, but not amendment; and, even though Parliament established a convention whereby its desired legislation was embodied, not in bills but in 'heads of bills' − that is, a brief outline of bills − which were then 'drawn into form' and sent to England, these heads of bills could still be altered or suppressed in the Irish or English council, and when returned to Ireland could not be amended, but only accepted or rejected as they stood. The house of commons, however, acquired the right of initiating all money bills, in the form of heads of bills, and the lord lieutenant always watched anxiously when these items were being discussed in the House. The Irish Parliament, or rather, the Irish house of commons, was not a mere mouthpiece of the lord lieutenant or of his 'undertaker'; it required care and attention in management, and the managers themselves could use their power to give the lord lieutenant a difficult time, if they so wished.[23]

Still, the sight of an Irish legislature in the hands of great magnates was hardly an edifying one to nineteenth century nationalists, even though some of them preferred any Irish Parliament to no Irish Parliament at all. And the fact that such a Parliament, composed of personal and family groups, managed by undertakers, and with its legislative powers circumscribed, could come to assume a central place in Irish political life in the eighteenth century requires explanation. If Parliament was merely the tool of the Protestant 'garrison', then it would hardly have progressed beyond its generally humdrum early eighteenth century existence: 'garrisons' breed siege mentalities, not the kind of positive attitudes found among the many Protestant Irishmen who made their mark in the Irish Parliament. Nor were Protestant attitudes simply the product of the stability of Ireland after the alarms of the late seventeenth century, although this stability was an important contributing factor.[24] In order to understand fully the Protestant contribution to the Irish nationalist tradition it is necessary to examine that complex process by which the colonists came to regard themselves as the Irish people.

The Irish Parliament and its penal code were the products of their own age and cannot usefully be judged by any other standard; nevertheless, it is to be wondered at that a set of men, thus circumstanced, could bring themselves to assert the rights of Ireland against England when it was upon England that they had depended for their very

survival, and for their victory over the Roman Catholic majority in
1689-91. And more surprising is the way in which they could reconcile
their system of legal discrimination against the majority of Ireland's
inhabitants with their claim to represent the Irish nation. The answer to
the first problem is to be found in the Irish Protestant version of the
Williamite wars. The Protestant story was one of brave defiance of king
James and his Catholic hordes; of sieges at Derry and Enniskillen; of
victory at the Boyne and Aughrim, victory aided, they admitted, by the
armies of England, but not won by those armies.[25] Without the strong
right arm of the Irish Protestants, there would have been no Williamite
conquest of Ireland; if anything, England was in *their* debt, rather than
the other way round. The answer to the second question — how the
Protestants came to identify themselves with Ireland in such a profound
way — is a more elusive matter.

It is more elusive because it encompasses a long and gradual process
by which outsiders, newcomers, colonists, adapt themselves to a new
environment and develop a particular relationship to it. Whether this
identification is complete, so that the colonists cease to be regarded as
colonists and become the natural inhabitants of a country, is, partly, a
matter of chance: Americans and Australians were as much colonial as
the New English in Ireland; but, over a period of time, they have shed
the epithet 'colonial', even though the people from whom they wrested
the land were as harshly and as summarily dealt with as the Roman
Catholics of Ireland. Indeed, the cynic might observe that, since
modern Americans are not regarded as colonists, the mistake made by
the English in Ireland was that they were not successful enough — that,
unlike Americans, they did not succeed in almost exterminating their
indigenous population. To some, the English in Ireland resemble the
white Rhodesians rather than modern Australians or Americans. Superficially, the comparison appears appropriate: a minority élite seized the
land belonging to the indigenous majority, established political and
administrative superstructures on the model of the mother country, but
entirely in their own interests and worked entirely by themselves, and
proceeded to defy the mother country and assert their colonial rights
against the British and the indigenous majority.

But the comparison, though tempting, is essentially a misleading
one. For the 'white' Irishmen, unlike the white Rhodesians, were
profoundly influenced by Ireland, by the country and the traditions
which they found there. It might be argued that Rhodesia was 'independent' before the coming of British settlers; but there was no legal or
constitutional evidence for this, no already existing political institutions,

nothing which the colonists could appeal to or believe in. And the same applied to the early American colonists. Virginia was a new country in a way that Ireland, already cluttered with layers of early, and politically conscious, settlers, was not. The New English, like the Old English before them found it impossible to resist Irish influences and Irish ways, and they were quick to resent the assumptions of outsiders: as early as 1641 Audley Mervyn, a native of Hampshire who had recently acquired lands in Ulster, spoke of Ireland as 'a mother to most of us, yet certainly a nurse unto all of us';[26] and in the 1640s the Old Protestants of the Munster area showed resentment at the New Protestants of the Cromwellian army, and especially their officers, whose arrogant behaviour displeased them.[27] It was true that in 1692 James Bonnell, secretary to the forfeiture commissioners dealing with the appropriation of land, likened the Protestants to colonists in New England 'among the natives of whom they are always in danger';[28] but Protestant behaviour in the parliament of 1692, when the Lord Lieutenant, Sidney, found himself embattled with Irish members indignant at what they regarded as his high-handed attitudes, revealed that Protestants could stand up for themselves. Moreover, the Protestants had one great advantage which was denied to the Old English. Unlike the Old English they had, with government help, conquered the whole of Ireland; and they had succeeded in making themselves an indispensable political nation, fully possessed of the will to rule the country.

Because Ireland, unlike Virginia, was a country with a long history of settlement, and a whole set of rules and practices accumulated or claimed by past generations, it was easier for Protestants to advance the rights of their country against the British Government. The Irish Parliament of 1692 had no experience of procedure; but it readily turned to the records of earlier parliaments for precedents. Bishop Anthony Dopping of Meath published the *Modus Tenendi Parliamenta in Hibernia* shortly before Parliament convened.[29] And in October 1692 Sidney complained disbelievingly that the Irish Commons talked 'of freeing themselves from the yoke of England, of taking away Poynings' Law, of making an address to have a habeas corpus bill and twenty other extravagant discourses have been amongst them'.[30] All this was an exaggeration; the Commons was mainly concerned with securing the interests of Protestants against lenient treatment of Catholics by the English Government; but to do so they put forward constitutional claims concerning supply, declaring the Commons 'sole right' to decide the ways and means of raising money, and to prepare heads of bills for raising supply.[31] The Irish Protestants were seeking a parliamentary constitution: and their search was made easier by the precedents already firmly embedded in the constitutional history — some of it real, some imagined — of Ireland.

In 1698 William Molyneux, M.P. for Dublin University, investigated *The case of Ireland's being bound by Acts of Parliament in England*. He was inspired to do so by the English Parliament's promise to linen manufacturers in England that it would consider passing legislation prohibiting altogether the export of woollen goods from Ireland to any foreign country; but he based this particular case on a general statement of the kingdom of Ireland's constitutional rights, tracing how Ireland became a kingdom annexed to the crown of England, denying that Ireland was ever a conquered country (and thus a country that could be said to have forfeited the right to the English parliament to exercise jurisdiction over her), and describing the 'original compact' between Henry II and the people of Ireland 'that they should enjoy the like liberties and immunities, and be governed by the same . . . laws, both civil and ecclesiastical, as the people of England'. Molyneux was anxious to emphasize that the kingdom of Ireland *was* annexed to the imperial crown of England, and he acknowledged that 'we must ever own it our happiness' that this was so; yet, even so, Ireland had always enacted statutes relating to the succession 'by which it appears that Ireland, tho annexed to the Crown of England has always been looked upon to be a Kingdom complete within itself, and to have all jurisdiction to an absolute kingdom belonging, and subordinate to no legislative authority on earth'.[32]

Jonathan Swift, when stating Ireland's case during the controversy over Wood's halfpence in 1724, took up Molyneux's theme. He discussed the ideas of those who declared that Ireland was a dependent kingdom 'as if they would seem, by this Phrase, to intend, that the People of Ireland is in some State of Slavery or Dependence, different from those of England; Whereas a *dependency Kingdom* is a modern Term of Art; unknown, as I have heard, to all ancient civilians, and *Writers upon Government*; and Ireland is, on the contrary, called in some Statutes an *Imperial Crown*, as held only from God; which is as high a Style, as any Kingdom is capable of receiving'. He had, he added, looked on all English and Irish statutes without finding any law that made Ireland dependent upon England, any more than England depended upon Ireland: for England and Ireland shared the same king: and Swift depended 'only on the King, my sovereign, and on the Law of my own country'.[33]

Both Swift and Molyneux drew heavily on earlier material. Patrick

Darcy, when delivering Ireland's case against the arbitrary practices of the lord lieutenant, Strafford, in 1641, had used the idea of an ancestral constitution; and Molyneux, like Darcy, claimed that Henry II and his successors had guaranteed that Ireland should be governed by the laws of England, with new laws made only by consent of the Irish Parliament. In 1643 the Confederate Catholics asserted that the kingdom of Ireland had long had a Parliament of its own, and that no English statute was binding on Ireland until accepted by the Irish Parliament; some of the medieval laws and cases which they cited in support of this contention were used by Molyneux in his tract.[34] Molyneux also cited a manuscript drawn up for the use of James, duke of Ormond, by his father in law, Sir William Domville, in July 1660, in which Domville observed that the independency of Ireland was established by common law, statute law, the practice of former ages, and by royal recognition shown by titles and by prerogative act.[35]

Molyneux, like Darcy, extolled Magna Carta as the palladium of Englishmen's liberties, and asked how Ireland could 'receive these charters of Liberties' and yet 'be no Partakers of the *Freedoms* therein contained?'[36] But such claims did not account to an acknowledgement of the colonial status of the Protestants of Ireland; they were not the usual claims of Englishmen abroad, of Uitlanders who demanded the exercise of the laws of the mother country for their defence and protection in an alien land. Molyneux made it clear that such liberties could be claimed, not because Ireland was a colony, but – on the contrary – because Ireland was *not* a colony. He examined the proposition that Ireland's status was like that of the Roman colonies, subject to and bound by, the laws made by the senate in Rome, or in Ireland's case, those made by the great council at Westminster. This, he declared, was the 'most extravagant' objection raised against Ireland; and it had no foundation in reason or record:

> Does it not manifestly appear by the constitution of *Ireland*, that 'tis a *Compleat Kingdom* within itself? Do not the Kings of England bear, the Stile of Ireland, amongst the rest of their kingdoms? Is this agreeable to the nature of a *Colony*? Do they use the title of Kings of *Virginia*, New *England*, or Mary-land?

Ireland was given by Henry II to John in parliament at Oxford 'and made thereby an *absolute Kingdom*, separate and wholly Independent on England, till they both came united again in him, after the death of his brother Richard, without issue. Have not multitudes of Acts of of Parliament both in England and Ireland, declared *Ireland a compleat Kingdom?* Is not *Ireland* stiled in them all, the *Kingdom*, or *Realm* of *Ireland*? Do these names agree to a *Colony*?[37]

Ireland had a parliament and courts of justice,[38] unlike a colony; and if the claim of the New English for the rights of Magna Carta was a colonial one, then it must be conceded that the like claim by the confederate Catholics was a colonial one also. But the Protestants entertained no doubts about the fact that Ireland, among the nations of Europe 'had . . . all the weight and dignity of a respectable and free nation, long before its connection with England',[39] and that any attempt to 'bind this ancient kingdom, by laws to which it has not given consent' was 'an innovation on the constitution, an infringement of royal prerogative, and an invasion of those rights to which we are entitled by the laws of God, of nature and of nations'.[40] There remained, however, one great central problem for the Protestant nationalists: it was all very well to claim that Irish constitutional theory could be inherited by the Protestants; but how could they regard them-selves as the legitimate heirs to that 'respectable and free nation' that enjoyed the benefits of freedom before the coming of the English? How could they claim any kind of real or legal descent from the Native Irish and Old English whose power they had destroyed and whose property they had taken? How, in short, could they call themselves the Irish nation?

The question of who constitutes 'the people' of a country which had undergone layers of settlement, from the Gaels to the New English, is not an easy one to answer. In the twentieth century, the definition would undoubtedly give pride of place to whichever of the people were considered to be the 'original inhabitants'. In Kenya in the 1920s, for example, the colonists claimed that 'we, the people of Kenya, demand our inalienable rights of self-government'; but the majority report of the Hilton Young Commission in 1929 declared that the European settlers were not the people of Kenya. The people of Kenya, it stated, had not yet formed itself; but the paramount element in the formation must be the native African element.[41]

If this is taken as the criterion, then the Irish protestants could make no legitimate claim to be the Irish nation. But for most of the eight-eenth century no-one thought of distinguishing between 'natives' and settlers in this way. Since Ireland was not a colony anyway, but an ancient kingdom, it was meaningless to talk in such terms: the only 'natives' were the protestants.[42] What, then, had happened to the Catholic majority? According to Molyneux, it was manifest that the greatest body of the present people of Ireland, are the progeny of the English and Britons, that from time to time have come over into this Kingdom; and there remaining but a mere handful of the Ancient Irish at this day; I may say, not one in a thousand. So that if I, or any body else, claim the like Freedoms with the Natural Born subjects of England, as being descended from them, it will be impossible to prove the contrary.[43]

Swift also took comfort in the reflection that the number of papists was dwindling; some had turned Protestant, and more would do so.[44] And this fiction — that the Roman Catholics were ceasing to exist — could be maintained because of the effectiveness of the penal laws. Since the Catholics were obliterated politically, they could also be obliterated from the minds of most Irish Protestants. And in another place in his argument Molyneux clearly identified himself with the 'People of Ireland' to whom 'the laws and liberties of England were granted above 500 years ago',[45] conveniently ignoring the implications of his argument if the people of Ireland were taken to be the Roman Catholics. Some Protestants went further. The nationalist leader, Henry Grattan, maintained in parliament that some of the 'gentlemen whom I now see in their place are the descendants of Kings', thus establishing a direct line of descent from the native Irish.[46]

This line of argument was, however, very rare; on the whole the Anglo-Irish wisely avoided any attempt to deal in racial terms; indeed, they felt no compulsion to do so. Their patriotism was one of place, not of race. And the M.P. and patriot, Sir Jonah Barrington, explained that the British settlers of the seventeenth century 'evinced a more than ordinary attachment to the place of their settlement, and vied with the Irish (sic) in an inveterate hostility to the domination of their own compatriots; and in the direct descendants of those British colonists, England has since found many of the most able, distinguished, and persevering of her political opponents'.[47] 'I am an Irishman', declared the earl of Charlemont, 'I pride myself in that appellation'.[48] Barrington even took pride in the attempts by Catholics in the seventeenth century to resist that very monarch to whom he owed his present security. Ireland was loyal to James, but England negotiated with a foreign prince to invade their country and overthrow their monarch: 'at the head of his foreign guards, William, unequivocally an usurper, marched into the metropolis of Great Britain, seized on the throne'; but Ireland defended her legitimate monarch against 'the usurpation of a foreigner'.[49]

It is tempting to assert that the Anglo-Irish developed the theory that to be born in Ireland made one an Irishman, thus standing as an exception to the exclusiveness of later Irish nationalists; but there was one, very important, qualification which the vast majority of Protestants made: one had not only to be born in Ireland, but also to be born an Anglican. Protestant nationalism was not only one of place; it was also a nationalism of faith. Because the nation was Protestant, the Anglican church constituted a kind of national church. Swift was perhaps the strongest exponent of this point of view. 'We of this kingdom', he wrote in 1709, 'Believe the Church of *Ireland* to be the National Church, and the only one established by law'. It was on these grounds that Swift opposed a repeal of the sacramental test: 'if once we repeal our *Sacramental Test*, and grant a Toleration, or suspend the Execution of the Penal Laws, I do not see how we can be said to have any Established Church remaining; or rather why there would not be as many Established Churches as there are Sects of Dissenters.' Once admit Dissenters to public employment, and they would in a few years grow to be a majority in the house of commons and make themselves the 'National Religion'.[50] Not all Anglicans felt as strongly on this issue as Swift; but even the more liberal minded Henry Grattan consoled himself with the thought that to give indulgence to Roman Catholics could never be injurious to the Protestant religion, for 'that religion is the religion of the state, and will become the religion of Catholics if severity does not prevent them'.[51]

One final characteristic of Protestant nationalism may be singled out; the resentment occasioned to the 'people of Ireland' by slights and indignities heaped on them by the English. This would appear to be a more typically 'colonial' sentiment, the reaction of the colonist when confronted with the assumptions of superiority held by the inhabitants of the mother country; and, undoubtedly, it was focused on the operation of the navigation Acts of 1660 and 1671, and the cattle Acts of 1663 and 1667, which regulated Irish trade in the colonial manner, so that it did not compete with the mother country.[52] Swift satirised the mercantile system in his tract 'The injured lady', when the 'lady', Ireland, was reminded by her suitor, England 'of the vast obligations I lay under to him, in sending me so many of his People for my own good, and to teach me manners . . . that from henceforward he expected his Word should be a Law to me in all things'. But 'because we were a nasty sort of people, and that he could not endure to touch any thing we had a hand in, and likewise, because he wanted work to employ his own Folks, therefore we must send all our goods to his Market just in their Naturals'.[53]

But it was because Swift and his like were profoundly convinced that they were, not colonials, but true Irishmen, that they so smarted under English assumptions that they were just like the inhabitants of any other part of the empire. Because they were Irish did not mean that they need daub themselves in paint, or wear skins any more than the modern British should display their nationality by dressing as they did in Caesar's time 'when they painted their Bodies or cloathed themselves with the skins of beasts'. Swift complained about the behaviour of 'some Ministers' who 'were apt, from their very high Elevation, to look *down* upon this Kingdom, as if it had been one of their *colonies* of *out-casts* in America'.[54] But Ireland was not a colony, and Irishmen were not rude colonials; and they had the right to be addressed and treated in the same way as the inhabitants of the sister-kingdom of England. What Protestants suffered from was not a sense of colonial inferiority, but the (more usual) Irish sense of superiority, a sense of superiority bruised and battered by the mistaken assumption common in England that they were on a par with Americans, whereas they were really on a par with Englishmen − at least. When William Nicholson, an Englishman, appeared in Dublin to take his seat in the house of lords, he found that William King, archbishop of Dublin, expected him, as the most recent appointment to the Irish Bench, to sit in the lowest place despite his English service.[55]

It is misleading, therefore, to refer to Protestants' sentiment as 'colonial nationalism', as if it were in some way to be distinguished from the mainstream of the Irish nationalist tradition. If the term is taken to mean 'the demand for domestic self-government within an imperial framework'[56] then the same could be applied to the demand for repeal of the union, or for home rule, and possibly even to dominion status in the early twentieth century. If it is applied because it was the nationalism felt by the Irish Protestants, a 'colony', then it is unhistorical, since it ignores the fact that Anglo-Irish political thinking held no brief for the idea that they were colonists, or that Ireland was in any respect like Virginia or Maryland. Ireland was a 'free and perfect state or commonwealth, annexed to the crown of England, but under a *separate and distinct* government, upon the like foundation, and after the same modell, with that of England', claimed the Dublin patriot Charles Lucas.[57] What is commonly called 'colonial nationalism' is really an important strand in the complicated skein of Irish national-ism,[58] a sentiment felt by Protestant Irishmen at a time when they could and did claim to be the people of Ireland.

For it was this sentiment, however absurd or contradictory to the modern observer, that accounts for the sudden surge of national indignation which took English officials by surprise in eighteenth century Ireland. In 1719 an appeal from a disputant in a law suit (Sherlock versus Annesley) was successful in the Irish House of Lords, whereupon the other party to the dispute appealed over the Irish lords to the lords in Westminster, who decided in his favour. The Irish lords protested that appeals could be made only to them; and a statute asserting the dependency of the kingdom of Ireland was promptly passed in London to remove all possible doubts about the powers and pretensions of England over Ireland.[59] This was quickly followed by the case of Wood's halfpence, which provoked the most celebrated of Swift's 'Drapier's letters'. 'Were not the people of Ireland born as free as those of England' he demanded? 'How have they forfeited their freedom?'. Ireland had not been consulted at all in this matter; yet the people of Ireland had remained loyal even in the face of the Sherlock versus Annesley judgement and the hardship of the navigation acts newly enforced.[60]

There was, however, an obvious contrast between such fine sentiments and the everyday stuff of politics in the Irish Parliament; and Henry Boyle's management of the Irish house of commons for the 20 years after 1730 seem to establish the Namierite concept of the eighteenth century political world, with the spoils of office constituting all that had to be played for. There was indeed a 'patriot' group in the house, with support among the middle and lower orders in the country, which had as its watchword suspicion of English influence in Ireland; but it was small in numbers, even though its potential for gadfly behaviour was aptly summed up by Horace Walpole in his description of them as a 'flying squadron'.[61] The flying squadron was always watchful for an opportunity to use its influence; and a crisis in Irish high politics in 1753 offered precisely the kind of opportunity they could exploit. It arose from a clash between Boyle and his rivals, George Stone, archbishop of Armagh, and John Ponsonby, Lord Bessborough. Stone and Ponsonby, in alliance with the newly appointed lord lieutenant, Dorset, sought to challenge Boyle's control of the Commons. Boyle resolved to fight; and the ground which he chose was the constitutional one of Irish parliamentary control over finance. The years 1749, 1751 and 1753 produced a surplus in the Irish treasury, and the issue on which battle was joined concerned the legal right to dispose of the surplus (not the usual supply bill which enabled the Government to operate). In November 1753 a commons committee drafted heads of a bill for appropriating part of the surplus to the redemption of the Irish national debt, omitting any reference to the king's 'gracious intentions' or 'previous consent' to this step. The English privy council inserted the words acknowledging the king's previous consent; the Irish commons could only exercise the option of accepting or rejecting, but not amending the bill, and on 17 December they rejected it.[62]

Boyle was an unlikely ally of the patriot group; but they took their chances well, and played a leading part in his tactics over the money bill, and in the blaze of publicity which followed its rejection. Moreover, the crisis had come at an opportune moment, when there was widespread dissatisfaction with the government in the country.[63] Boyle had joined the patriotic group only out of necessity; but the language which he chose to argue his case is significant, for it was an acknowledgement of the 'actions which the age is prepared to admire'.[64] Boyle and his followers were seeking to legitimize their behaviour, and to do so they adapted themselves to the prevailing mood which saw political choice, not as one between ins and outs, but between English and Irish national interests, with the 'true question . . . whether they shall be governed by the Primate and an English party'.[65] The English government was held to be bent on drawing huge sums of money from an already financially and economically shaken Ireland. Dorset and Stone, for their part, represented the struggle as one merely for power among ambitious politicians.[66] There was much truth in this, as Boyle's eventual compromise, by which he exchanged his speakership of the commons for a pension and an earldom, demonstrated;[67] but it was not the whole story. Irish politics were no longer the affair of an oligarchy — or, more exactly, an undertaker monarchy — that they had been in previous decades. The growth in size and confidence of a commercial middle class, with aspirations to make its influence on government felt, was accompanied by the development of the Irish newspaper press.[68] The temper of the country was shown in the important role played by constitutional issues in the general election of 1761. Meetings of associations formed demanding septennial parliaments; a reduction of the pension list; the immovability of judges; a habeas corpus Bill; and the independence of the Irish Parliament. These had little effect on the composition of the new Irish House of Commons; but they indicated that public opinion was aware that Ireland was becoming increasingly regarded by England in a colonial light, and that the only response was to make the cause of liberty the cause of Ireland.[69]

From 1759 the patriot group in the House of Commons was led by a formidable pair: Henry Flood, the member for Kilkenny, and Charles Lucas, the member for Dublin; but patriotic opposition was still a frustrating experience, and it was not until the late 1760s that a major change in the working of Anglo-Irish relations gave the opposition an opportunity to launch an onslaught on the administration. After some short-lived appointments, the British Government dispatched Lord Townshend to Ireland as lord lieutenant in August 1767.[70] The Cabinet of Lord Grenville had in 1765 recommended that the lord lieutenant should reside constantly in Ireland, and not be content to leave matters almost entirely in the hands of the undertakers; and Lord Townshend quickly came to the conclusion that a reform of Irish government was needed, and that he should be the man to effect it. When, in November 1769, the Irish Commons rejected a money bill on the grounds that it did not take its rise in the House, the British Cabinet decided to back the lord lieutenant in his desire to bring about a better management of Parliament. The Irish managers of the House, Ponsonby, Shannon and Hely Hutchinson, had hoped to use the defeat of the money Bill to demonstrate their power; but they had misjudged their man; and in December Townshend registered a formal protest, prorogued the House, and dismissed Ponsonby and Shannon from their lucrative official posts. The offices thus vacated were offered to friends of the Government. Since Townshend was now the chief undertaker, it followed that the various groups in the Irish Parliament who had looked to the great Irish magnates would now look to the great English lord lieutenant; and between 1769 and the recall of parliament in 1771 Townshend built up his castle party. This proved more difficult than he had anticipated, for the lesser men on whom Townshend was relying revealed that they too could demonstrate their indispensability by lack of co-operation in the House. Nevertheless, although Townshend was obliged to re-open negotiations with Shannon to stablize affairs in the Commons, it was clear that the great undertaker was no longer master of his fate, but a subordinate of the lord lieutenant. The Castle and the patriots now stood face to face.

The patriots sought with all their might to exploit this and to portray Townshend's administration as one of 'Ireland versus England'. Townshend was dubbed the 'miserable instrument of English tyranny', playing upon 'our constitution' and showing hostility towards every man who 'did but assume the name of a friend to his country'.[71] 'We are told that we have a British constitution', declared Henry Grattan, 'but we must not aspire to the spirit of it'.[72] Irish loyalty to the king was still as firm and heartfelt as ever: and Townshend should tell the king that 'your majesty cannot detach them from your family, and neglect has not chilled the glow of their loyalty'.[73] The practice of the appointment of a non-resident lord lieutenant, and the use of deputies, was the proper way to conduct the affairs of the two kingdoms, for the deputies were 'natives of this country', and 'this gave all due pre-eminence and authority to England, without stripping this kingdom of all national weight'. Seen in this light, the undertakers were a sort of native representation; and Townshend, by seeking to destroy them, had 'made their party the party of the nation'.[74]

All this, however, was rather premature; for, despite all their efforts, the opposition could not arouse nationalist feelings in the public: the dismissed undertakers could not convincingly be portrayed as lovers of their country.[75] Worse was to come; for in October 1775 Townshend's successor, Lord Harcourt, brought off his finest coup when the patriot leader, Henry Flood, wearied by years of futile opposition, and believing that he could do more for reform from within the administration, accepted the post of vice-treasurer.[76] But, not for the last time, Irish nationalism was given a new lease of life by events in the wider world; the revolt of the American colonists against the legislation of the British Parliament.

The political crisis in North America was fully reported in the Irish newspapers, and the major documents of the American revolution were printed for public consumption. Irish nationalists did not see their case as exactly paralleling that of the Americans, however, for the Americans were colonists, whereas Ireland, Sir Hercules Langrishe noted, was 'an ancient kingdom, great in its own growth, entrenched behind an ancient constitution, co-equal and co-eval with England'.[77] Irish nationalists did not emphasize constitutional theory, and rarely used American material.[78] To Henry Grattan, now the leader of the nationalists in Parliament, the question of independence was not one of asserting new rights, based on some general principles, as the Americans must do, but the recovery of that legislative power which, for centuries, Ireland had been unjustly deprived of. These prescriptive rights had been invaded by various Acts of Parliament and judicial decisions. Deprived thus of her liberties, Grattan asserted in 1780, Ireland was indeed a 'colony without the benefit of a charter, and you are a provincial synod without the privileges of a Parliament'. England must be made to restore lost liberties, not grant new ones.[79]

The process by which the British Government 'restored' Ireland's ancient liberties, and made her a nation once again, was hastened by the course of events in America. The war was followed by economic depression in Ireland, acutely felt in Dublin by the beginning of 1778. Manufacturing workers were thrown out of employment; credit was restricted and bankruptcies widespread. The Government itself felt the double pressures of rising expenditure because of the war and falling revenue with which to pay for it.[80] To all this distress was added the danger of a French invasion; and it was to meet the threat of a French descent on a largely undefended Ireland that Volunteer companies began to spring up all over the country, eager to perform military duties until the Government could properly organize the militia.[81] The Volunteers were at first only interested in soldiering; but their political potential, as a species of armed pressure group, could hardly go long overlooked in the political excitement of 1778-79; and the parliamentary nationalists did not scruple to use them to browbeat the British Government: 'physical force' men and parliamentarians had established an undefined, but powerful, political relationship.

Nationalist fervour was encouraged by the growing belief that the Roman Catholic threat was finally laid to rest, and, more important, that any conflict of interests between Irish Protestants and Catholics could only work to the advantage of the British Government, for Catholics looked to the British, rather than to the Irish Parliament, for relief from the penal code. In 1778 most of the penal legislation of 1704 relating to the leasing and inheriting of land was abandoned. This was a Government measure; but opposition to it in the Irish Parliament was only overcome through patriot support;[82] and enthusiasts like Sir Jonah Barrington were quick to hail the dawn of a new day, when 'the people were united' and 'the Catholic for the moment forgot his claims, and the Protestant no longer recollected his ascendancy'.[83] The idea of the 'common name of Irishman' was heard in the Ireland of the ascendancy, long before Wolfe Tone and the Irish republicans coined it;[84] but events were to reveal that the foundation on which it was based was as shaky in the eighteenth century as it was in the nineteenth or twentieth centuries.

Protestant confidence that their flanks were secured from a Catholic threat encouraged them to press on with their demands for redress of grievances; but their own efforts, however impressive, could hardly have proved so successful but for the firm support of the parliamentary opposition in Britain.[85] This convinced the Government that some lessening of the restrictions on Irish trade, and some concessions on the Irish Parliament's power to regulate Irish commerce must be made. But, more important, in 1782 the Government of Lord North fell, and was replaced by Lord Rockingham's administration; and, having so far encouraged the Irish in their nationalistic claims, Rockingham could hardly stand in the way of his allies in the Irish Parliament, especially when the Volunteers were forcing the pace and arousing public opinion by passing resolutions at their Convention in Dungannon.[86] In May 1782 Charles James Fox announced his readiness to 'meet Ireland on her own terms'. Within a matter of weeks the British Parliament passed legislation establishing the right of the Irish Parliament to legislate for Ireland, and the final jurisdiction of the Irish House of Lords. Poynings' law was modified to ensure that the chief governor and council in Ireland could no longer originate or alter bills, but must transmit them to the king 'without addition, diminution, or alteration'. The king retained the power to suppress bills, but not alter them.[87]

The 'constitution of 1782' was a curious affair. It did not amount to 'self-government' in any real sense of the term, for the Irish executive was still in the hands of a lord lieutenant appointed by the British Cabinet. The Irish Parliament could not bring him down; only a change of ministry in England, forced by the British Parliament, could do that. It might perhaps be more accurately described as 'self-legislation', although even here the crown retained the power of veto on the Irish parliament's bills. It was not simply the product of a victory of 'Ireland' over 'England', for one of the keys to the Irish success lay in the change of ministry in London in March 1782. It inaugurated no change in the relationship between the Irish Parliament and the Irish people, whatever their political or religious affiliation.

But nationalists are as concerned – often more concerned – with the symbol of nationhood as with the substance. And, in any case, Grattan and his followers were conservative nationalists, seeking to restore to Ireland what was rightfully hers, and thus working within constitutional limits laid down on themselves by their forebears. Hence Grattan's panegyric in his celebrated 'declaration of right' in April 1782:

I found Ireland on her knees, I watched over her with an eternal solicitude; I have traced her progress from injuries to arms, and from arms to liberty. Spirit of Swift! spirit of Molyneux! Your genius has prevailed! Ireland is now a nation! In that new character I hail her! and bowing to her august presence, I say, *Esto perpetua*![88]

The nationhood which Grattan hailed in such stirring tones, and his confident prediction that Ireland would be no longer 'a squabbling fretful sectary', were to end in the bloodshed and sectarian violence of rebellion in 1798, and the union with Britain in 1800. The inconsistencies of the 'constitution of 1782' are glaring, at least to the modern eye. And underlying these was the problem of framing a constitution that would satisfy the conservative elements in Ireland and yet cater for an age of unprecedented social and political change. Ireland's freedom, Grattan readily admitted, had been won with the help of the Volunteers; but supposing the Volunteers sought to use their power for further demands, and perhaps even for a reform of the Irish Parliament itself? Grattan foresaw the dangers inherent in the existence of this independent body of armed men. While he was making his preroration in April 1782, and glorying in the unity of the Irish people, Protestant and Catholic, who had 'joined in one great national sacrament', he was careful to praise the order and discipline of the Volunteers who had, he remarked significantly, 'sense enough' to obey 'the upper orders, the property, and the abilities of the country'; and he asked them, now that the victory was won, now that they had 'given a parliament of the people', to 'leave the people to parliament, and thus close, specifically and majestically, a great work, which will place them above censure and above panegyric'.[89]

But the political temperature of the country, once raised, could not so easily be lowered. In June 1782 Henry Flood, anxious to make his mark on the great events of the day, supported those Volunteers who declared that the 'simple repeal' of the statute, the Sixth of George I, was an insufficient guarantee of Ireland's constitutional status; a specific renunciation act was necessary, by which Britain would explicitly yield up any right to legislate for Ireland.[90] This concession was granted by the British Parliament in 1783; but the continuing uncertainty about the working of Anglo-Irish relations inspired the Younger Pitt's scheme of an economic solution to the problem: a commercial treaty between England and Ireland, so comprehensive in scope that it would bind the two countries together and make them 'one country in effect'. But the opposition in the British House of Commons worked hard to arouse nationalist sentiment in the Irish house and Pitt's proposals were bitterly contested and the project abandoned.[91] Hard upon this came the Regency crisis of 1789 when, on the insanity of George III, Pitt proposed that Parliament should define, in advance, the powers to be exercised by the prince regent. Grattan and his followers supported Fox's demand for a full, untrammelled regency, and, supported by the borough-owners who believed they were backing a winner, called upon the prince of Wales to assume the regency of Ireland. The king's recovery averted the constitutional crisis which this course of action threatened; but the affair bore out all the forebodings of the British Government in 1782 about the 'confusion which must arise in all cases of common concern from two parliaments acting with distinct and equal powers and without any operating centre'.[92]

The constitution of 1782 was held by its admirers to redress Ireland's grievances; but there remained the question of redressing the grievances of those who held that the Irish Parliament itself was a far from perfect instrument for registering Irish public opinion. It would have been surprising if Ireland had not shared in the enthusiasm for reform of the electoral system that was flourishing in Great Britain at the same time; and the ideas of British radicals like Jebb, Cartwright and Wyvill were read and debated in Ireland.[93] But the significant difference in Ireland was that there the reform movement was taken up by the Volunteers, who, it was claimed, represented the majority of the electorate, and were public spirited; if they happened to be armed, so were the barons at Runnymede. The Volunteers were the 'first society in the kingdom' and must play their part in the reform movement.[94]

Parliamentary reformers had two goals; to abolish rotten boroughs, and to alter the franchise. In September 1783 a delegation of the Volunteers met at Dungannon and resolved to hold a national convention in Dublin to debate the whole reform issue: and the spectacle of the Volunteer convention meeting in the capital bore a strong resemblance to a kind of alternative Parliament, and, moreover, a Parliament backed by force of arms.[95] But the Volunteers were not the armed revolutionaries that their actions seemed to imply; and most of them entertained no notions of browbeating the Irish Parliament let alone assuming responsibility for the government of the country. When Parliament countered the demand for reform with an expression of their confidence in the working of the 'present happy constitution', the Volunteers fell back, not upon their weapons, but upon another reform bill, considered first by county meetings and then submitted by Flood to the Irish commons in May 1784. When this move was rejected, parliamentary reform ceased for the moment to be a vital issue in Irish politics.[96]

But the reform movement in Ireland raised questions which its counterpart in Great Britain did not raise. For it involved the whole question, not only of who constituted the political nation, but who constituted the nation as such. 'It would be the highest absurdity', wrote one Irish reformer, 'to give two million people the power to destroy the half million who had fought and bled to support the free constitution in church and state we now enjoy. Their principles and ours can never be in unison. We are for freedom, they are for despotism. They have an old claim to our estates. We give them full exercise of their religion. If they had the power we should not have a similar liberty'. There were those who pointed out that the Roman Catholics were 'our brethren and are entitled to the rights of citizens. If we refuse them this extension Ireland remains divided'; but William Drennan, Ulster's most characteristic and persistent reformer, took comfort in the reflection that the superior and middle classes of Catholics, although too small in number to instil toleration into the minds of those below them, were also too wise to wish for a complete extension of civil franchises 'to those of their own persuasion'.[97]

The united nation that Grattanites prided themselves on, and that Irish reformers aspired to create in their own image, had no more foundation in fact than the united nation that nineteenth and twentieth century republicans and home rulers harped on. It is hard to see how matters could have stood otherwise: to pretend that a nation composed of different social classes, different occupational groups and religions could think and act as one was straining credulity to the uttermost. If the Irish nation correspond to the protestant landowning classes, then its exclusiveness at least gave it a measure of homogeneity that carried it through the events of 1779-82, and saw it emerge with its parliament enhanced and its privileges undiminished. But if the nation included the kind of people who made up the rank and file of the Volunteers, the middling orders of society, then the Protestant nation could no longer claim to speak with one voice. If the Presbyterians were to be numbered among the elect, then the counsels of the nation were even more divided and splintered, for the Presbyterians themselves were stratified in their political views, ranging from the 'levellers and republicans' to the downright conservative.[98] And, finally, if the Roman Catholics were to be included, then it had to be admitted that the Protestant nationalists simply had no idea how to frame a workable system appropriate to such a heterogeneous and pluralist society.[99] Grattan and his fellow nationalists are not to be too readily condemned for this failure, for it was to test men more wise and courageous than they, and find them equally wanting, in the years to come.

But Protestant nationalists must not only be judged by their shortcomings; for their achievements were to have a profound influence on the development of Irish nationalism. Their stirring nationalist rhetoric;

their bold assertion of Ireland's historic right to independence; the willingness of their great leader, Henry Grattan, and of many of his followers to admit Catholics as their fellow-Irishmen (albeit not at the expense of Protestant power); their assertion that a self-governing Ireland would be a prosperous Ireland — these could not be dismissed as the smokescreen thrown up by an alien and predatory 'colonial' ascendancy. For in the eighteenth century Irish nationalism came of age; and its contradictions and absurdities were no more than could be expected from nationalist politics, with their emphasis upon bad history, myth, sentiment and emotion. The eighteenth century achievement became a goal and an inspiration for Irish nationalists of many breeds, including Thomas Davis, Charles Stewart Parnell, Arthur Griffith, and even republicans like Bulmer Hobson and Denis McCullough.[100] The powers enjoyed by Grattan's Parliament became the minimum demand for every Irish nationalist, and the maximum demand for many of them, a symbol of nationhood even for those whose ultimate aim was separation, and who had no time for the 'Protestant garrison' who had brought it into being. Even Theobald Wolfe Tone, the apostle of Irish republicanism, admitted that the founding fathers of Protestant Irish nationalism, Jonathan Swift and William Molyneux, had anticipated his 'great discovery' that 'the influence of England was the radical vice of our Government'.[101]

It was not only in the political sphere that eighteenth century Irish nationalism made its impact. Many Protestants took pride in their country and in its cultural traditions. Charles Lucas recalled an Ireland 'formerly famed for literature'. Henry Brooke eulogized Gaelic customs. Others studied the Irish language, edited historical manuscripts, and investigated antiquities. Henry Flood left his fortune to such pursuits; at Belfast, on Bastille day, 1792, a harpists' festival was held;[102] the Royal Irish Academy was established in 1785 under the presidency of the earl of Charlemont as a body of men 'anxious to make their labours redound to the honour and advantage of their country'.[103] Even the emotive description of Ireland as the 'emerald isle' was first coined by the Ulster Presbyterian, William Drennan.[104] All this flurry of activity did not amount to the kind of cultural nationalism promoted in the late nineteenth century by Gaelic Leaguers; Protestant Irishmen did not dare, and indeed had no desire to proclaim that the essence of Irish nationality was to be found in the Irish language and its various offshoots.[105] But their re-discovery of Ireland's cultural as well as her political heritage was to start their country off to a destination which was to prove their own undoing.

It is easy to dismiss this, the first Celtic revival in Irish history, as a mere farrago of nonsense, as a usurpation of the real Irish tradition, as part and parcel of the whole absurdity of a nation that was unable to make up its mind whether it was Irish or English. But nothing could be more mistaken. It was because the Protestants believed themselves to be the Irish nation that they involved themselves in Ireland's past, and sought to shape her political future. The contradictions of Protestant nationalism were soon to be exposed in the last decade of the eighteenth century and the early part of the nineteenth, when rhetoric and antiquarianism were to prove unequal to the dynamics of a changing society. But the last word may perhaps be left to the irrepressible Sir Jonah Barrington, whose feelings, as he rode at the head of his Volunteer company, the Cullenagh Rangers, sum up a time when bliss it was in that dawn to be alive, but to be young, Protestant and Irish was very heaven:

At the head of these few men, the Author felt prouder than an Emperor, it made an impression on his youthful mind, which even in the chill of age, is still vivid and animating, a glowing patriotism, a military feeling, and an instinctive, though a senseless lust for *actual service*, arose within him, a sensation which is certainly inherent in a great proportion of the Irish people, and which seldom forsakes them but with their lives.[106]

Notes

1. P.S. O'Hegarty, *A History of Ireland Under the Union* (London, 1952), p. 616.
2. Ibid., pp. 3, 4.
3. As the Cromwellian soldiers were nicknamed by a Gaelic poet because of their complaints about the dearth of beer and cheese in Ireland (MacErlean, op. cit., p. 99). A 'bodach' was an ignorant farmer or churl.
4. For an example of this see P. Beresford Ellis, *Hell or Connaught! The Cromwellian Colonisation of Ireland, 1652-1660* (London, 1975) and *The Boyne Water* (London, 1976).
5. See e.g. D.W. Harkness, *History and the Irish* (Queens University of Belfast, new lecture series, No. 93, 1976), p. 7.
6. See e.g. Francis Hackett, *The story of the Irish Nation* (Dublin, 1924), pp. 177-9.
7. R.H. Murray, *Revolutionary Ireland and its Settlement*, p. 283.
8. Ibid., pp. 246-7.
9. For the text of the civil articles see E. Curtis and R.B. MacDowell, *Irish Historical documents, 1172-1922* (London, 1977 edn.), pp. 171-5.
10. For the constitutional setting of the late seventeenth and early eighteenth century see J.I. McGuire, 'Politics, opinion and the Irish constitution, 1688-1707'

(M.A. thesis, University College, Dublin, 1968), and his 'The Irish parliament of 1692' in T. Bartlett and D.W. Hayton (eds.) *Penal Era and Golden Age: essays in Irish History 1690-1800* (Belfast, 1979), pp. 1-31.

11. Murray, op. cit., pp. 293-302.

12. Ibid., pp. 311-12.

13. Ibid., pp. 342-8; Curtis and MacDowell, op. cit., pp. 188-94.

14. Murray, pp. 348-9, W.A. Phillips, *History of the Church of Ireland*, vol. *III*, p. 157.

15. Murray, op. cit., pp. 353-4.

16. A.T.Q. Stewart, *The Narrow Ground*, pp. 91-2.

17. Beckett, *Making of Modern Ireland*, p. 161.

18. The expression is Fr. Bradshaw's, see *Historical Journal*, vol. *21*, p. 502.

19. Beckett, *Modern Ireland*, p. 144.

20. King, *State of the Protestants*, p. 256.

21. The Presbyterians were in receipt of a regular government grant to their clergy, known as the *regium donum*, first given in the reign of Charles II and doubled in amount by William in 1690 in recognition of their loyalty. But because the Presbyterians saw it as some kind of official recognition at a time when they were denied legal status as a church, it was as often a cause of wrangling as of gratitude (A.T.Q. Stewart, *The Narrow Ground*, pp. 92-3).

22. For the structure of Irish politics in the early 18th century see D. Hayton, 'The beginnings of the "undertaker system"' in Bartlett and Hayton, op. cit., pp. 32-54; A.P.W. Malcolmson, *John Foster: the Politics of the Anglo-Irish Ascendancy* (Oxford, 1978) passim., esp. Chap. 6.

23. Hayton, op. cit., p. 48-54.

24. M. MacCurtain, *Tudor and Stuart Ireland*, p. 196.

25. D.W. Miller, *Queen's rebels: Ulster Loyalism in Historical Perspective* (Dublin, 1978), pp. 22-4.

26. J.C. Beckett, *The Anglo-Irish Tradition* (London, 1976), p. 33.

27. J.A. Murphy, 'The politics of the Munster protestants', *JCHAS*, vol. LXXVI (1971), p. 20.

28. J.I. McGuire, 'The Irish parliament of 1692', op. cit., p. 17.

29. Ibid., p. 12, Fn. 38.

30. Ibid., p. 15.

31. Ibid., p. 16. In 1699 Lord Chancellor Methuen wrote that the Irish commons, although differing amongst themselves, were agreed 'in desiring to be independent of England, and believing themselves so in right' (McGuire, 'Politics, opinion and the Irish constitution', p. 156).

32. W. Molyneux, *The Case of Ireland's Being Bound . . .* (1698), passim., esp. pp. 38, 55, 56, 123. For a convenient summary of Molyneux and his influence see J.G. Simms, *Colonial Nationalism, 1698-1776* (Cork, 1976). Early 18th century Irish political ideas are examined in C. Robbins, *The Eighteenth Century Commonwealthman* (Harvard, 1959), Chap. V.

33. J. Swift, 'A letter to the whole people of Ireland' in H. Davis (ed.), *Prose Works of Jonathan Swift* (Oxford, 1941), pp. 53-68.

34. Simms, *Colonial Nationalism*, pp. 14-16.

35. Robbins, *Eighteenth Century Commonwealthman*, pp. 139-40.

36. Molyneux, *Case*, p. 153.

37. Ibid., pp. 144-5.

38. Molyneux was also interested in a legal case between the bishop of Derry and the Irish Society, the London companies that had been granted property in Ulster in the reign of James I. The Londoners had lost an appeal by the bishop to the Irish house of lords, but their appeal to the English lords overturned the Irish lords' judgement and declared that the Irish lords had no appellate jurisdiction.

39. H. Grattan, junior; see *Memoirs of the life and times of Henry Grattan by his son* (vol. *I*, London, 1839), p. 8.

40. Barry Yelverton in 1780; see R.J. Barrett, 'A comparative study of imperial constitutional theory in Ireland and America in the age of the American revolution' (University of Dublin, D.Phil., 1958), p. 160.

41. W. Hancock, *Survey of British commonwealth affairs: Vol. I, Problems of nationality, 1918-1936* (London, 1937), p. 232.

42. See Henry Grattan: 'she is not a colony, she is not a kind of colony . . . she was not planted by England, . . .' (Henry Grattan Jnr., *Speeches of Henry Grattan*, vol. *I* (London, 1822), p. 14).

43. Molyneux, *Case*, pp. 19-21.

44. Davis, *Prose Works of Swift*, vol. *II* (Oxford, 1939), p. 120.

45. Molyneux, *Case*, p. 169.

46. H. Grattan, *Speeches*, vol. *I*, p. 118.

47. Sir Jonah Barrington, *Rise and Fall of the Irish Nation* (Dublin, 1853 edn.), p. 121.

48. Barrett, 'Imperial constitutional theory', p. 38.

49. Barrington, op. cit., p. 129-30; see also Henry Brooke, *Essay on the ancient and modern state of Ireland* (Dublin, 1760), pp. 44-5.

50. H. Davis (ed.) *Prose Works of Swift*, vol. *II*, pp. 113-125; see also vol. *IX, Irish Tracts, 1720-23 and Sermons* (Oxford, 1948), pp. 171-9, 219-31, and *Irish Tracts, 1728-33* (Oxford, 1955), pp. 243-51, 255-60, 263-79, 285-95.

51. S. Gwynn, *Henry Grattan and his Times* (London, 1939), p. 110.

52. For the navigation acts see Murray, *Revolutionary Ireland*, Chap. x.

53. H. Davis, *Swift*, vol. *IX*, p. 6.

54. Ibid., pp. 20-21; vol. *X*, p. 64.

55. C. Robbins, op. cit., p. 145; see also Brooke, *Essay*, pp. 28-31.

56. Simms, *Colonial Nationalism*, p. 9.

57. C. Lucas, *Political constitutions*, vol. *I* (Dublin, 1751), p. 130; also *Dublin Evening Post*, 15 April 1780, where the freeholders of Cork city refer to 'the free and independent kingdoms of Great Britain and Ireland'.

58. Murray, *Revolutionary Ireland*, declared that Molyneux's *Case* 'has formed the armoury from which successive generations of advocates of Irish self-government from the days of Lucas to the days of Parnell have taken down and polished their weapons of war' (p. 327).

59. Robbins, op. cit., p. 139.

60. H. Davis, *Swift*, vol. *X*, pp. 31, 34-5, 63.

61. J.C.D. Clark, 'Whig tactics and parliamentary precedent: the English management of Irish politics, 1754-1756' in *Historical Journal*, vol. *21*, No. 2 (1978), pp. 275-301. Walpole's remark is on p. 279.

62. D. O'Donovan, 'The money bill dispute of 1753' in Bartlett and Hayton, op. cit., pp. 55-87; Clark, op. cit., pp. 279.

63. O'Donovan, op. cit., pp. 74-9.

64. H.T. Dickenson, *Liberty and Property*, p. 6.

65. Clark, op. cit., p. 280.

66. Ibid., p. 297-9; O'Donovan, op. cit., pp. 83-4.

67. J.C. Beckett, *Making of Modern Ireland*, pp. 192-5; W.E.H. Lecky, *Leaders of Public Opinion in Ireland*, vol. *I, Henry Flood and Henry Grattan* (London, 1912), pp. 30-31.

68. Lecky, op. cit., pp. 31-5; M.R. O'Connell, *Irish Politics and Social Conflict* (Philadelphia, 1965), pp. 22-4.

69. Lecky, op. cit., pp. 35-41; S. Gwynn, *Henry Grattan*, p. 37; D. O'Donovan, op. cit., pp. 84-7.

70. For a new succinct account of Townshend's viceroyalty see T. Bartlett, 'The Townshend viceroyalty, 1767-72' in Bartlett and Hayton, op. cit., pp. 88-112.

71. *Baratariana* (3rd edn, Dublin, 1977), pp. iii-vii.

72. Ibid., pp. 51-4.

73. Ibid., pp. 68-71; see also *The Proceeding of the Honourable House of Commons of Ireland in Rejecting the Altered Money Bill . . . Vindicated* (Dublin, 1754), p. 94.

74. *Baratariana*, pp. 112-13, 57.

75. Bartlett, op. cit., pp. 99-101.

76. J.C. Beckett, *Making of modern Ireland*, pp. 203-4.

77. R.B. MacDowell, *Irish Public Opinion, 1750-1800* (London, 1944), p. 48; see also *The Public Register or Freeman's Journal*, 8-10 June, 1779 ('Decius').

78. R.J. Barrett, 'A Comparative study of imperial constitutional theory', pp. 23-6.

79. H. Grattan, *Speeches of Henry Grattan*, vol. *I*, pp. 38-53. See also J.T. Ball, *Legislative systems operative in Ireland* (2nd edn. London and Dublin, 1888), pp. 85-6, 120-24.

80. M.R. O'Connell, *Irish politics and social conflict*, pp. 62-4.

81. For the Volunteers see P.D.H. Smyth, 'The Volunteers and parliament, 1779-84', in Bartlett and Hayton, op. cit., pp. 113-36, and H. Butterfield, *George III, Lord North and the People* (London, 1949), pp. 108-16, 144-5, 170-73.

82. Beckett, *Modern Ireland*, p. 214.

83. Barrington, *Rise and Fall of the Irish Nation*, p. 167.

84. MacDowell, *Irish Public Opinion*, pp. 68ff; for a vivid, but short lived, example of the new mood see Stewart, *Narrow Ground*, pp. 71-2.

85. J.C. Beckett, 'Anglo-Irish constitutional relations in the later eighteenth century', in *Confrontations*, pp. 123-41.

86. Smyth, op. cit., pp. 122-25.

87. Beckett, *Modern Ireland*, pp. 255-6.

88. H. Grattan, *Speeches of Henry Grattan*, vol. *I*, p. 123.

89. Ibid., pp. 125-7.

90. M.R. O'Connell, *Irish Politics and Social Conflict*, pp. 333-42; Bartlett, op. cit., pp. 125-6.

91. J.S. Kelly, 'British and Irish politics in 1785', *EHR*, vol. *90* (1975), pp. 536-63.

92. O'Connell, op. cit., p. 343.

93. Bartlett, op. cit., p. 130; MacDowell, *Irish public opinion*, Chap. 5.

94. MacDowell, op. cit., pp. 80, 98.

95. For some doubts on this see *Hibernian Journal*, 6-8 Jan. 1783, 28 Nov.-1 Dec. 1784.

96. Bartlett, op. cit., pp. 131-34; MacDowell, op. cit., pp. 98ff.

97. R.B. MacDowell, *Ireland in the Age of Imperialism and Revolution, 1760-1800* (Oxford, 1979), p. 302.

98. A.T.Q. Stewart, *Narrow Ground*, pp. 106-7.

99. See e.g., the Earl of Charlemont to Dr. Alexander Haliday, Nov. 1791: 'complete your plan and Ireland must become a Catholic country; but whether our masters will be as tolerant as we are may be a matter of doubt' (M.J. Craig, *The Volunteer earl* (London, 1947), p. 234)).

100. J. Lee, 'Grattan's parliament', in B. Farrell (ed.), *The Irish Parliamentary Tradition*, pp. 149-59.

101. P. Mac Aonghusa and L. O Reagain, *The Best of Tone* (Cork, 1972). pp. 28-9.

102. Much to the disgust of the rationalist Wolfe Tone: see MacDowell, op. cit., p. 370.

103. N. Vance, 'Celts, Carthaginians and Constitutions: Anglo-Irish literary relations, 1780-1820', unpublished paper delivered at the second British conference

of Irish historians, University College of Swansea, March-April, 1979; Beckett, *Anglo-Irish tradition*, Chap. IV; J. Sheehy, *The Rediscovery of Ireland's Past* (London, 1980), pp. 7-15.

104. B. O Cuiv, 'The wearing of the green', *Studia Hibernia*, vols. *17-18* (1977-8), pp. 116-17.

105. Sir L. Parsons, *Observations on the bequest of Henry Flood* (Dublin, 1795), p. 25: 'It has been said most untruly, and believed most absurdly, that it was Mr. Flood's design, in his legacy to the College of Dublin, to bring the Irish language again into general use in this country. But his will shews, that his only object was to have it studied by some men of letters . . .'; see also MacDowell, op. cit., pp. 150-51.

106. Barrington, *Rise and Fall of the Irish Nation*, p. 171.

5 'THE IRISH, PROPERLY SO CALLED'

Throughout most of its existence, the Protestant nation was secure in the knowledge that the Roman Catholic majority of Ireland was politically non-existent; and, as nightmares of a Catholic uprising faded into insignificance, Protestant willingness to acquiesce in toleration of Catholics grew.[1] But toleration was, in one important respect, more easily preached than practised; for, inevitably, it involved Protestants in what one contemporary called 'political algebra'.[2] Given the fact that Catholics were a majority, how could concessions to them be reconciled with the security of the nation? The religious indifference of the eighteenth century was not altogether without impact, even in Ireland; a preface to an edition of Molyneux's *Case*, published in 1770, noted the decline of religious bigotry, and declared that 'the two sects are insensibly gliding into the same common interests'; 'commercial and not religious interests are the object of almost every nation in Europe'.[3]

But the problem in Ireland was that religion was not merely a question of worship; it had political implications which, however much in abeyance, could not finally be set aside. Thus Flood, Charlemont and Lucas, while believing in toleration, drew the line at admitting Catholics to political power. Charlemont held that at least a century must pass before Catholics would be sufficiently assimilated by education with their Protestant fellow-countrymen to enable them safely to be granted civil rights. Flood was convinced that the existence of an independent constitution in Ireland depended upon its resting on an exclusively Protestant basis; a total convulsion must follow if the vast, anarchical Catholic element was admitted to equal power with Protestants. Even Henry Grattan, whose liberalism went so far as to espouse political rights for Catholics, and who proclaimed that 'I love the Roman Catholic; I am a friend to his liberty', assured Protestants that his friendship was conditional upon Catholic liberty proving compatible with Protestant ascendancy.[4]

The dilemma implicit in Grattan's position was concealed by the political submergence of the vast bulk of the Catholics, and the declared loyalty of those few Catholics who played any part in politics. Catholic political organization first assumed a definite shape in 1759 with the founding of the Catholic Association under the leadership of

Lord Kenmare, one of the few landed Catholic families to survive the glorious revolution with his property intact. The fervent expressions of loyalty made by the Association, and the realization in British Government circles that clerical influence might be used to promote stability and order in an age of revolution, naturally produced a mood conducive to reform; and the Roman Catholic hierarchy was quick to respond to the new atmosphere. Dr Troy, bishop of Ossary, issued a letter to his clergy in February 1778 reminding his flock of the example of the Divine Redeemer 'who commands us "to give unto Caesar what belongeth to Caesar, and unto God what belongeth to God"'. He referred to Government leniency in the application of the penal laws, and warned that a 'cheerful compliance with this important obligation' was 'particularly requisite in these days of discord and calamity, when our American fellow subjects, seduced by the specious notions of liberty and other illusive expectations of sovereignty, disclaim any dependance on Great Britain, and endeavour by force of arms to distress their mother country which has cherished and protected them'. And he called upon his people to offer 'fervent prayers' for the 'spiritual and temporal happiness of our Most Gracious Lord and Sovereign King George the third'.[5]

The loyalty of Catholic leaders, and the turbulent times, pushed the British Government into the role of supporting Catholic rights against the wishes of most of its usual followers in the Irish Parliament; and relief legislation passed in 1778 and 1782 met strong opposition from MPs. The purely religious aspects of these acts — for example the repeal in 1782 of laws requiring the registration of priests — were not the main cause of Protestant fear; more significant was their relationship to land ownership, especially that of 1782 which permitted Catholics, who had taken an oath of allegiance prescribed by the relief act of 1778, to purchase and bequeath land on the same terms as Protestants. 'We feel' wrote Roman Catholic leaders to Lord Portland in September 1782, 'with pleasure that we are allowed to have a home in our native land';[6] but supposing the increasing number of Catholics practising law should encourage them to question the present landholding system and attack Protestant privilege? It was to allay such fears that an act was also passed confirming all previous legislation on land settlement. The ghost of 1689 had not yet been laid to rest; and it was a descendant of a Roman Catholic family, which had changed its religion and therefore its politics, who offered some sobering advice to the Protestant nationalists: 'When we speak of the People of Ireland', Clare said:

it is a melancholy truth that we do not speak of the great body of
the people. This is a subject on which it is extremely painful to me
to be obliged to speak, but it is necessary to speak out. The ancient
nobility and gentry of this Kingdom have been hardly treated: that
Act by which most of us hold our estates was an act of violence ...
that gentlemen may know the extent of this summary confiscation,
I will tell them that every acre in this country which pays quit rent
to the Crown is held by title derived under the Act of Settlement,
passed immediately after the Restoration. Gentlemen upon the
opposite bench should consider how far it may be prudent to pursue the successive claims of dignified and unequivocal independence
made for Ireland by the right honourable gentlemen.[7]

The Protestant dilemma was made more cruel in the last decade of the
eighteenth century by the vexed questions of franchise and parliamentary reform. To admit Catholics to political power, and to render
Parliament more open to public pressures, could well mean the undermining of the ascendancy, if not its destruction; and this fear was
rendered acute by the active efforts of some Presbyterians in the north
of Ireland, inspired by the example of the American revolution, to put
new life into Irish radicalism. Presbyterian radicals like Dr. William
Drennan were not at first concerned with Anglo-Irish relations; parliamentary reform was their main aim, and it was Tom Paine's *Rights of
Man*, and the exciting news from France in the early years of the revolution that inspired Drennan and his friends to form a secret committee
in Belfast, to which they invited the Protestant, Wolfe Tone, in the
autumn of 1791.[8] Presbyterians felt that they had a good deal to be
radical about; but their grievances were, naturally enough, peculiar to
themselves: tithes, hearth-money, excise, county and church cess, and
tolls at fairs. These gave Presbyterian radicalism its vitality in the heart-
lands of south Antrim and North Down. In the urban centre of Belfast
with its newspapers, clubs and societies, the level of political radicalism
was much more sophisticated;[9] and it was here that Wolfe Tone and
Drennan sought, through the Society of United Irishmen, to unite
Catholic and Protestant in a great national effort for reform. The
United Irishmen publicly avowed their intention of redressing grievances, not severing the connection between England and Ireland;[10] and
Wolfe Tone, for his part, was not above shameless place-hunting if the
opportunity seemed ripe. But frustrated ambition, as much as patriotism, drove him to the conclusion that nothing was to be hoped for
from England, nor from English politicians, and helped him to over-

come his aversion to the Irish 'lower orders'.[11]

Tone's 'great discovery' of all the causes of Ireland's ills[12] coincided with a new spirit among politically articulate Roman Catholics. The Catholic gentry, who had acted as the leaders of Catholic opinion, and who had exhibited an unswerving loyalty to crown and constitution, found their pre-eminence challenged by middle-class merchants and lawyers. For the landed classes the main concern was to reconcile reform with their own position in society, and their strategy was moderate and defensive; but for the middle classes, and especially the lawyers, a more aggressive approach was necessary. Lawyers felt the penal code as a limitation on their professional prospects, especially through their exclusion from those offices of state which recruited heavily from the Bar. Catholic merchants and businessmen were on their way up in the world, but found that while their money was perfectly acceptable to all sections of the people, it could not buy their way into political power and local positions of political influence. Middle class men were on the look out for change; and Tone noted with pleasure what he called a 'new spirit' among the General Committee of the Catholics under the leadership of John Keogh, a Dublin merchant. The influence of the clergy and what Tone called the 'barons' was undermined, and the 'third estate, the commercial interest, rising in wealth and power, were preparing, by degrees, to throw off the yoke'.[13] The new Catholic mood was shown in the invitation to Tone to become secretary of the Catholic committee in 1792, and in calling of the 'Catholic Convention' in December 1792.

The Catholic Convention's tactics were symptomatic of the new mood. Now, instead of waiting patiently for relief, it decided to take its case direct to London, thus bypassing Dublin Castle altogether. It could count on Government sympathy, for the international situation rendered it imperative to prevent French mischief-making in Ireland, and in 1793 the Government steered through the Irish Parliament a bill granting Catholics the parliamentary franchise on a 40/- freehold, the municipal franchise, and access to all civil and military posts, with some exceptions. Catholics were now even to be admitted into a paid peace-keeping force, the militia. Few MPs opposed the bill: they were not prepared to defy the British Government on whose support they might depend in the uncertain state of Irish and indeed European politics; but many of them did not pretend to like the trend of events. Their fears were expressed during the parliamentary debates on a private member's Catholic Relief Bill in 1792. Catholics, once in control of the State, would soon adopt a more dictatorial tone; they were not to be trusted, whatever the British Government in London might like to think; the land settlement of the seventeenth century would be endangered.[14] Sir Boyle Roche, a frequent advocate of Catholic claims, now demanded to know how the Catholics of Ireland had come to be led by John Keogh 'a retailer of poplins in Dame Street'. The Ponsonbys, Grattan's principal allies in his campaign for moderate reform, declared that they would not 'extend the British Constitution to men who cannot speak the British language'; the Catholic Irish were 'natives' to be treated as such by their betters. Here, at last, was the voice of a fearful élite; 'I could hardly obtain a hearing', wrote Grattan to his sons.[15]

The revival of Protestant social and religious prejudice was hardly encouraging to the declared aims of the United Irishmen: 'to unite the whole people of Ireland, to abolish the memory of all past dissensions, and to substitute the common name of Irishman in place of the denominations of Protestant, Catholic, Dissenter'.[16] This is, of course, one of the most worshipped phrases in the Irish nationalist breviary; but what is not so often quoted is Tone's next comment: that 'the protestants I despaired of from the outset for obvious reasons . . . it was not to be supposed that they would ever concur in measures the certain tendency of which must be to lessen their influence as a party, how much soever the nation might gain'. And most damaging of all was his description of the Catholics 'who are the Irish, properly so called'.[17]

Both the Ponsonbys and Tone, from their very different starting points, had arrived at the same conclusion: that the Catholics were the 'natives' to whom the ascendancy would allow no political power. And, more important, the United Irishmen were themselves riven with doubts about the place of Catholics in the new Ireland of the Enlightenment. Early in 1793 the Dublin Society of United Irishmen began preparing a detailed plan of parliamentary reform, and differences quickly arose over the issue of the secret ballot. Some United Irishmen, including Drennan, preferred open voting; others pressed for secrecy, since landlords would be able to compel voters to obey their dictate. But more important was that this division of opinion reflected the Catholic/Protestant division among the United Irishmen themselves. The Catholics, anxious for political power, sought the protection of secrecy to enable them to use it; the Protestants, faced with the prospect of a Catholic majority wielding political power, and unable to overcome their fears of the consequences, sought to retain the protection offered by the social and economic status of protestant landlords.[18] On this point, at least, they found themselves in agreement with one of their most determined opponents, Lord Castlereagh, who declared that an elective franchise would 'make three-fourths of the constituency of Ireland Catholics. Can a Protestant superstructure long continue supported on such a base?'[19] Drennan's metaphor, as well as his methods, was different, but his premise was the same: when he looked into the Catholic mind, he did not like it; 'it is churlish soil, but it is the soil of Ireland and must be cultivated or we must emigrate'.[20]

Here was the Protestant dilemma, one that confronted radicals and revolutionaries just as it did the members of the ascendancy.[21] But Tone, at least, was prepared to hazard all. The 'Irish, properly so called' were, he believed, 'trained from their infancy in an hereditary hatred and abhorrence of the English name, which conveys to them no ideas but those of blood, and pillage and persecution . . . strong in numbers and in misery, which makes men bold'.[22] The United Irishmen had originated as an urban movement; now Tone proposed that they carry their message to the countryside, to the peasants and farmers, and in particular to the already existing Defender organization, a secret society which offered protection to the Irish Catholic peasant against his enemy, the Protestant. Such peasant societies had flourished before the 1790s, and were endemic in eighteenth century Ireland; and their aims were by no means political, let alone nationalist. But in the atmosphere of sectarian tension and economic dislocation existing in many parts of the Irish countryside they might provide material for revolution, as Tone perceived.[23]

But what sort of material, and for what sort of revolution? What were the aims of the 'Irish, properly so called', what kind of aspirations did the 'men of no property' harbour? The problem for the United Irishmen was that anything that remotely resembled political activity, or social unrest, could not have provided less suitable material for their nationalist and non-sectarian ideals. Agrarian secret societies were not in themselves appropriate units of political revolution; in the 1760s, for example, the Whiteboys in Munster exacted vengeance on those whom they perceived as being responsible for their hardships (including Roman Catholic priests); but the first five Whiteboys executed at Waterford declared in their last words that 'in all these tumults, it had never entered into their thoughts to do anything against the king and government'.[24] The small tenant-farmers of Ulster, who worked also as weavers in the linen industry, banded together as 'Hearts of Oak' and 'Hearts of Steel' in the 1760s and 1770s, but their combination was directed against local grievances such as the collection of county cess or the letting of land to any one but themselves. In the 1780s an outbreak of violence in mid-Ulster was provoked by competition for land, which quickly assumed a sectarian character, and conflict between Protestant 'Peep O Day Boys' and Catholic Defenders was endemic in the area between 1784 and 1795. Since the protestants were small tenant-weavers, with no leavening of substantial farmers to provide some measure of social control, the Protestant gentry tended to side with their co-religionists, and many Catholics were obliged to flee to the south and west of Ireland. And, naturally enough, they took their experience of Ulster's sectarianism with them.[25]

The United Irishmen, therefore, were confronted with two main organizations when they turned their attention to the 'men of no property': the Catholic Defenders, and the Protestant Orange Society founded in Co Armagh in 1795 after a sharp fight between Catholics and Protestants. Since the aim of the latter was to defend 'the king and his heirs as long as he or they support the protestant ascendancy',[26] they were unlikely to prove fertile ground for United Irish recruitment — indeed, the reverse was the case, for many United Irishmen enlisted in the Orange Society.[27] This left the Defenders, who were described by a committee of the house of lords in 1793 as 'all . . . of the Roman Catholic persuasion; in general, poor, ignorant labouring men, sworn to secrecy, and impressed with an opinion that they were assisting the Catholic cause'.[28] The Defenders, however, were more politically aware than this brief description implies: they also harboured plans to assist a French invasion, bring about a rebellion, and secure a redistribution of protestant lands.[29] As one United Irish leader, William James MacNevin, explained 'it has been the misfortune of this country scarcely ever to have known the English natives or settlers otherwise than enemies, and in his language the Irish peasant has but one name for Protestant and Englishman, and confounds them; he calls them both by the name of Sasanagh'.[30] If the United Irishmen were to make their revolutionary overtures to the Defenders, they might well find themselves obliged to modify their programme for achieving the 'common name of Irishman'.

United Irish ambitions were given an incentive by the political excitement generated in Ireland in 1795, when, in addition to Catholic fears of an Orange terror, Catholic hopes of an important further instalment of emancipation were raised, only to be bitterly disappointed. Catholic political activity was still marked by the loyalty of its professions and the moderation of its aims; and their prospects for a step forward in their emancipation campaign appeared favourable when Lord Fitzwilliam was appointed viceroy of Ireland. Fitzwilliam belonged to the Portland group of Whigs who had recently joined Pitt in government; and the Portland whigs were believed to be close to Grattan on the Catholic question. But Fitzwilliam's instructions were not to commit himself too deeply on reform, and to lend official support only to such proposals in the Irish parliament if there seemed to be any likelihood of their success; in any other event he was to endeavour to postpone the issue. Fitzwilliam, however, was sympathetic to Catholic claims, and believed that, as the man on the spot, he was the best judge of the necessity of reform. He made continual representations to the cabinet on behalf of the Catholics; and, further, he made an unauthorized commitment of government support for a relief bill that Grattan proposed to introduce, admitting them to parliament. At this stage the cabinet warned Fitzwilliam not to enter into an engagement on the Catholic question; and when he tried to defend his behaviour he was recalled. This blow was followed by the strengthening of the Fitzgibbon interest in the Irish parliament.[31]

Grattan told the Catholics that he trembled 'at the return to power of your old taskmasters';[32] and Fitzwilliam's recall provoked dismay in Catholic ranks.[33] The United Irishmen took it as a sign that the time was ripe for revolution and the establishment of an Irish republic; but this deprived them of much Protestant support, since well-to-do Presbyterians were able to distinguish between parliamentary reform and social upheaval.[34] Middle-class Catholics, who might have been expected to flock to the United Irishmen after their disappointment over the Fitzwilliam episode, were still reluctant to involve themselves in treasonable conspiracy, especially when the Government embarked on stern repression in 1796-7, and their support, such as it was, virtually melted away when the moment for rebellion came in 1798. The Catholic hierarchy's hostility to the French revolution and its 'licentious philosophy' and 'contempt for religion' was unabated;[35] and, in the last resort, the United Irishmen depended upon the remnants of Presbyterian radicals in Ulster, and those among the Catholic rural population who had been mobilized by the Defenders, or who lived in areas like north Wexford and Wicklow where Protestants were strong, wealthy, and in a position to pose a threat to the interests of the local Catholics.[36] Memories of seventeenth century conflicts were revived by the Defenders who assured their followers that, with French help, 'they would get the conditions of Limerick';[37] and in Co. Antrim one Larry Dempsey, a Catholic deserter from the 24th Dragoons, and adjutant of the local regiment of Presbyterian rebels, waved his rusty sword and declared in his Munster brogue, 'by J. . .s, boys, we'll pay the rascals this day for the Battle of the Boyne' – a *lapsus linguae* which, not surprisingly, occasioned an animated debate among his rank and file.[38]

It would be misleading, however, to characterize the '98 rebellion as *essentially* sectarian, or to draw too deep a distinction between the revolt of the Presbyterians in Co. Antrim and the Catholics of Kildare, Meath, Wexford and Carlow, between the enlightened Presbyterian north and the reactionary Catholic south. After all, while Presbyterians became United Irishmen in south Antrim, they became Orangemen in Armagh; local circumstances and local grievances against the establishment were as important, and perhaps more important, in bringing out the disaffected elements in the countryside in 1798; and the natural instinct to follow local leaders wherever they might lead was more significant than the teaching of Voltaire of the example of Danton.[39] Moreover, while many of the Republican leaders – merchants, clergymen, shopkeepers – in the north failed to turn out when the day came, the rebellion in the south was made possible in large part by the liberalism and political dissension of the Anglo-Irish local gentry and lawyers.[40]

The southern uprising, especially in Wexford, almost immediately assumed the character of a sectarian war, with massacre, atrocity and cruelty becoming commonplace, but some at least of the rebels believed that they died fighting for their country:[41] Wolfe Tone noted that the oath of the Defenders recited that 'they will be faithful to the united nations of France and Ireland'.[42] The symbols of French liberty were juxtaposed with those of peasant atavism;[43] but these symbols were also united, for the pike, regarded by Protestants as the weapon of peasant barbarity, was also a symbol of the French revolution.[44] Thus, from its birth, Irish republicanism was an ideology riddled with contradictions: sectarian hatred existed beside the idea of the common name of Irishman; humanitarian philosophy had as its companion racial violence; social grievances and radical thinking were to be found along with notions of national independence. Had Irish republicanism from the outset been essentially an ideology of radical freethinking, or sectarianism, or comprehensive nationalism, then it would have posed fewer problems for Roman Catholics as well as Protestants; ambiguity would have been avoided, confusion cleared up. But it was the heterogeneous and contradictory nature of the republican ideal that made it at once a volatile part of the Irish nationalist tradition, and yet an unattractive one to most Irishmen of whatever religious or political belief. If there was something in it to appeal to everyone, there was also much in it to repel everyone; few men could follow its precepts, yet none could ignore them. Thus republicanism became a gesture of protest, not a set of principles that could give life and meaning to the everyday politics and government of modern Ireland.

The '98 rebellion marked the beginning of the end of the Anglo-Irish parliament, though not of Protestant nationalism, which surfaced during the debates on the Union with Britain in 1799-1800; indeed, the strength and sincerity of so-called colonial nationalism was seen in the fact that, despite the horrors of the rising, and the almost hysterical fear of the Anglo-Irish for their safety, they mounted strong opposition to the Union, and only conceded defeat when it became clear that Pitt was in an impregnable position at Westminster, and that it would fare ill for any Irish MP who held out to the end.[45] No longer could nationalists hope, as they did in the 1780s, for a change of ministry in England and a change of fortune in Ireland; now they fought alone; and there were no Irish Volunteers to give a cutting edge to their protests and their oratory. The Union did not destroy Protestant nationalism, which remained a small but energetic part of the tradition; but it did destroy the Protestant Nation. For the claim of the Protestants to be the Irish nation was founded on their kingdom of Ireland with its parliament and its legislative independence; this institutional framework gave the Protestant nation its special identity; but once it was destroyed, and the Irish Parliament merged with that of Great Britain, the Anglo-Irish could only maintain their supremacy, their ascendancy, by coming to terms with the Catholic majority, or – as they came increasingly to perceive – by coming to terms with the reliance on British power that many of them acknowledged had saved the day in 1798.

For the early nineteenth century saw the emergence of the Irish Roman Catholics as a political entity, and the development of their political consciousness inspired by their very real and keenly felt social and economic grievances. Catholic needs and aspirations were given organization and direction by Daniel O'Connell, a lawyer from a Catholic landed family. O'Connell was no single-minded nationalist, desiring self-government above good government; on the contrary, he dreaded the separation of Great Britain and Ireland that he feared must come if the Catholics did not participate in the benefits of Union.[46] O'Connell was mainly concerned to improve the lot of his people, and to dismantle the political and social influence that lay at the disposal of the Protestant ascendancy.

But these apparently mundane aspirations, this willingness to be (in O'Connell's phrase) 'West Britons' if Ireland were well-governed under the Union,[47] must not be allowed to obscure or dilute the importance of O'Connell's contribution to Irish nationalism, a contribution more significant than republicanism and separatistism. For O'Connell's era of power saw Irish nationalism acquire its integrative character, its identification of the Irish nation with the Catholic nation. Of course, he did not pluck this idea out of thin air; it was the very existence of this identification in the seventeenth century that nourished the roots of the O'Connellite tradition, and that even Tone had recognised when he referred to the Catholics as the Irish, properly so called. But O'Connell gave it a new meaning and a new urgency by placing himself at the head of a movement for Catholic emancipation, and by enlisting the help of the Roman Catholic clergy in his emancipation and later his repeal campaigns.

Yet O'Connell's nationalism was close, in time and aspiration, to the nationalism of the eighteenth century Protestants; for, although Protestant and Catholic Irishmen differed profoundly on the great political issues of the nineteenth century, they did not inhabit separate worlds. An 'independent Ireland' had enjoyed a brief but notable existence in the era of Grattan's parliament, and its memory gave all who were discontented with the Union an ideal to strive for. 'In the year of the Union', O'Connell reminisced,

I was travelling through the mountain district from Killarney to Kildare. My heart was heavy at the loss Ireland had sustained, and the day was wild and gloomy . . . My soul felt dreary, and I had many wild and Ossianic inspirations as I traversed the bleak solitudes. It was the Union that first stirred me up to come forward in politics.[48]

Moreover, O'Connell's objections to the Union were couched in language and based on principles exactly corresponding to those of the Protestant nationalists who fought their rearguard action to save the Irish parliament in 1799-1800. William Plunket declared that 'I cannot fear that the constitution which has been formed by the wisdom of ages, and cemented by the blood of patriots and of heroes, is to be smitten to its centre by such a green and limber twig as this'; and he went on to 'deny the competency of Parliament to do this act . . . I tell you, that if, circumstanced as you are, you pass this act, it will be a mere nullity, and no man in Ireland will be bound to obey it'.[49] O'Connell, in one of his most celebrated speeches on the hill of Tara in 1843, protested:

in the name of my country and in the name of my God, against the
unfounded and unjust union. My proposition to Ireland is that the
Union is not binding on her people. It is void in conscience and in
principle, and as a matter of constitutional law I attest these facts
. . . there is no real union between the two countries, and my
proposition is that there was no authority given to anyone to pass
the Act of Union.

And, as he himself pointed out, he had only to refer to the words of
'the Tories' friend, Saurin, to prove that the Union is illegal'.[50]

The fact, too, that O'Connell identified Catholic with nationalist
did not mean that he was a bigot; in this, as in the constitutional question, O'Connell was influenced by the more liberal-minded Protestant
nationalists of his day, Grattan and Tone. It is easy to find examples
of his occasional exasperation with Protestants, the vast majority of
whom opposed and sought to frustrate every move he made throughout his political career; in the House of Commons, he once blurted out
that Protestants were 'foreigners to us since they are of a different
religion'.[51] But he was anxious to adopt the idea of the common name
of Irishman, and in 1810 in Dublin he reiterated that 'the protestant
alone could not expect to liberate his country — the Roman Catholic
alone could not do it, neither could the Presbyterian — but amalgamate
the three into the Irishman, and the Union is defeated'.[52] He even
went so far as to admit that he would prefer living under the penal
code to living under the Union, because he 'would rather confide in the
justice of his brethren, the protestants of Ireland, who had already
liberated him, than lay his country at the feet of foreigners'.[53] It must
be confessed that a restored Irish Parliament was unlikely to attempt to
resurrect the penal laws; and O'Connell and his fellow Catholics would
have little need to confide in the Protestant sense of justice alone to
protect their interests. Nevertheless, the statement was well-meant;
and O'Connell can hardly be blamed for the religious divisions of
Ireland, or the political algebra commonly practised in that country.

The problem was that nationalist politics of any kind were unlikely
to flourish in post-Union Ireland. The centre of affairs — in so far as
Irish affairs could be said to have a centre at all — had shifted to
London; and O'Connell's hopes of a restoration of Grattan's Parliament,
or an alliance of all Irishmen in a great national crusade, were not
practical politics. The peasantry were still engaged in their local battles
against the landlord, and the tithe procter, but the formidable Defender
organization was no more, and the total failure of any significant

numbers of Irishmen to rally in support of Robert Emmet's brief but violent excursion into the Dublin streets in the name of United Irish principles was symptomatic of the political torpor of the times. The Presbyterians were about to begin their rise to political and social acceptance, and to discover that the Ireland of the Union was to provide ample opportunities for their advancement.[54] Irish political divisions were not those of nationalist and unionist, but of Whig and Tory; now that Protestant nationalism was dead, Ireland had no other native political tradition strong or sophisticated enough to offer any kind of focus for political life or patriotic sentiment.

Irish Roman Catholics, in particular, were left without any clear role to play now that Ireland was integrated with Great Britain. They were no longer part of that fluctuating balance of power that enabled them to make so much ground in the last decades of the eighteenth century, when British and Irish administrators, opposition Irish MPs, and radical reformers all sought to enlist Catholic support mainly, it must be admitted, for their own ends.[55] Now that they had lost their political leverage they could expect to make little progress on the unfinished question of emancipation; and the high hopes entertained during the passing of the Union that it would be accompanied by reform in the 'dearest interests'[56] of religion were soon dashed. The United Kingdom was a Protestant state; and while Ireland remained within its boundaries, it seemed at the time that she must submit to the consequences.

Nevertheless the idea that the Catholics, and especially the bishops, could be attached to the constitution was an attractive one, and not without foundation. In 1795 the government had founded a national seminary for the education of Catholic clergy, and this gave the state some regular and institutionalized basis for claiming the loyalty of the church, a loyalty that many of its bishops felt towards England in the face of godless French revolutionary doctrine. If the state now decided to arrange some form of control over the appointment of bishops, and possibly of parish priests, and in return provided a stipend for the clergy, this claim on Catholic loyalty could be extended; and the idea of a stipend had advantages for Catholics as well as the state. The voluntary system of payment which prevailed in the eighteenth century was often a source of friction between priests and people. Catholic dues were not exorbitant; but they were drawn upon a very poor people; and the Whiteboy disturbances of 1785-6 in Munster were directed against both Catholic and Protestant parsons. In 1786 there were extraordinary scenes as Roman Catholic priests were openly defied by their congregations, chapel doors were nailed up, and some priests were assaulted; in 1806 the Thrashers in Connaught were said to have an oath with a clause conceding the payment of only certain fees to the clergy; and priests were threatened with death if they failed to lower their dues. This was not a symptom of rampant anti-clericalism; Irish Catholics, in the Gaelic way, combined an affection for their priests with a healthy independence of mind and a frank criticism of those aspects of the voluntary system of which they disapproved. But such incidents gave the church an incentive to examine positively any proposal which might end the voluntary system[57]

Yet there were pitfalls here for the unwary. Dr. Troy, archbishop of Dublin, considered them in 1793, and singled out two main dangers, one pastoral and one political. In the pastoral sphere, the difficulty was that if the sum involved were too large, the clergy might neglect their duties; if too small, the people might decline to pay enough to support the clergy adequately, since that was the job of the state. Politically, State provision might weaken, if not destroy, the people's confidence in the clergy. Troy modified his views when, in 1799, with nine other bishops, he signed a statement admitting the principle of Government interference in episcopal appointments, and agreed that state provision for the Roman Catholic clergy 'ought to be thankfully anticipated'. But this admission was made in the expectation of early emancipation and in the context of the fears aroused by the '98 rebellion;[58] and after the Union there was always a strong party, especially among the Catholic laity, that opposed any kind of Government interference or stipend as part of an emancipation arrangement.

It was to that party that Daniel O'Connell belonged, and in which he first rose to political prominence. O'Connell was the leader of the new men among the Catholics of Ireland, the professional, middle-class, educated and articulate Catholics to whom the protestant ascendancy was not only an affront to their pride but a practical obstacle to their advancement;[59] and from his involvement in the Catholic Committee after the setbacks of the 1790s he was a member of the radical group, mainly lawyers, who sought to wrest control from Keogh. Keogh was now a spent force, holding the opinion that the only course for Catholics to steer after the Union was to maintain a 'dignified silence'; O'Connell met this negative policy head on with his slogan 'agitate, agitate, agitate'.[60] In 1808 his influence was decisive in persuading the Catholic Committee and the bishops to reject Grattan's emancipation bill with its accompanying government veto on candidates for episcopal appointments who were considered politically unreliable; by 1810 anti-veto feeling among the bishops had hardened; and in 1813-14 O'Connell was able to take the bishops with him on the issue, despite the pope's favourable view of the veto proposal.[61]

The objections to the veto were not theological; and, indeed, the British government, in asking for it, was asking from the hierarchy no more than any other European state at the time.[62] The objections were political: O'Connell proclaimed that he loved his religion because it was Catholic and because it was Irish; and any veto or other arrangement was 'too gross and glaring a presumption in an administration, avowing its abhorrence for everything Irish, to expect to be allowed to interfere with the religious discipline of the Irish Catholic church'. The bishop already owed allegiance to the State through his repeated and solemn oaths; but the ministers wanted him as 'their political agent — they want to have him in the subservient management of electioneering politics'. The Irish Presbyterians loved liberty until they were misguided enough to accept a *regium donum*; after that, their clergy became familiar with the Castle, and now only their 'ancient glories' were left.[63] The freedom of the church was essential for the preservation of Irish nationality; as one contemporary remarked, 'Catholics of Ireland, you are bound to assume the national voice'.[64]

The Catholic emancipation campaign in its last stage was concerned with political power, the power of Catholics not only to influence events but to direct them; not only to establish their rightful place in the Irish nation, but to be the Irish nation. O'Connell revived the Confederate concept of the Catholic Irish nation, loyal to the king; his majesty, he declared in an address to the Prince of Wales 'through life, on every constitutional question . . . has given the nation convincing proof of the liberality of his enlightened mind'. Catholics were accused of disaffection: yet how often had these Catholics sealed their loyalty with their blood: 'Did not Vimiero — did not Talavera and Badajoz give proofs of the loyalty of Catholics? at Salamanca, was it not felt in the terrors of rout and defeat by every flying Frenchman?' Allegiance to their sovereign had long been the pride and boast of the Catholic people of Ireland — an allegiance 'not created by personal kindness, but sustained by a rigid sense of duty'. The Catholics were loyal to the 'ill-fated house of Stuart'; and:

> even amidst the crimes of that unfortunate family . . . the Irish continued faithful; and, in the season of their distress, when the Stuarts deprived themselves of all other friends, the Irish Catholics served then with a zeal and a bravery proportioned only to the wants of

their former oppressors. Allegiance then, perhaps, ceased to be a duty, and was certainly imprudent; but the Irish heart was not cold or calculating, and it cheerfully spilled its dearest blood in the protection of those very princes, who, in the hour of their prosperity, had insulted and plundered them. Carried too far, it was a mistaken and an absurd principle of action; but the spring had not lost all its elasticity, and what our fathers had been, the Catholics of the present day were inclined to be.[65]

O'Connell, however, received as much and as little comfort from his king as the Confederates had from theirs. Emancipation did not come in 1813, when O'Connell had told the Catholics of Ireland that their hour of freedom was nigh;[66] and his own domineering and bullying attitude in the Catholic Committee was resented by many. In so far as the Catholic cause was advanced at all, it was advanced in parliament where in 1821 William Plunket, member for Dublin University, introduced two bills, one for emancipation and one for a veto, which passed in the commons and were nearly successful in the Lords.[67] But Plunket was out of touch with Catholic opinion in Ireland; and it was O'Connell who took the decisive step when he broke with parliamentary pressure and legislative procedures, and not only secured the long-awaited emancipation, but also demonstrated the power of the Catholic nation on those rare occasions when it could be made to speak with one voice.

O'Connell's new departure was, perhaps, not at quite so original when seen in the context of Irish political developments in the late eighteenth century. From the time of the Volunteers, Ireland had experienced a wider public participation in politics, with a whole series of conventions, committees, delegations, clubs and corps, all seeking to bring influence to bear on the governmental process. The vacuum in political life after the Union put a temporary end to all these democratic trends; but a vacuum was capable of being filled; and when O'Connell founded a new Catholic Association in 1823 to agitate for Roman Catholic political rights and to advance the interests of Catholics on all fronts, popular participation in politics was given a renewed and dynamic existence. This, admittedly, was not immediately obvious; the forty-seven original members of the Association, who paid their annual subscription of one guinea, were anything but a spontaneous mass movement, indeed, at one meeting there was not even the requisite attendance to make a quorum, and O'Connell was obliged to drag some unsuspecting Maynooth students in from the streets.[68] 'National' political activity was as difficult to achieve in early nineteenth century Ireland as it was in England; the Irish electorate was small, fragmented, and, to some extent, unknown and possibly unknowable.[69] The Irish peasants' secret societies were more of a hindrance than a help, and anyway O'Connell regarded their leaders as 'miscreants' who endeavoured 'to obtain your confidence, that they may sell your lives.'[70]

Popular politics in Ireland did not spring spontaneously from below; they were the product of hard work, good organization, and the proper use of such resources as O'Connell had to hand. The base of the movement was broadened by allowing associate members to join on the payment of a subscription of one penny a month, 'for *palpable* and *direct* purposes'.[71] This 'Catholic rent' was first organized in the towns, then in the neighbouring parishes, and then in the remote districts of the county. Provincial meetings of the Association were arranged on appropriate days in various towns to discuss affairs;[72] and in 1828 the Munster Provincial Meeting recommended the formation of 'Liberal Clubs' in each county and city, with branches in each parish to register freeholders and to make 'constitutional and legal exertions for the freedom and happiness of Ireland'.[73] To supervize the collection of the 'rent' five inspectors were appointed for every county, with one head inspector to arrange this. The collectors not only took money, but rented rooms, held meetings and discussed public policy, discussions which invariably ended in the Catholic question.[74] 'The "Government", as it was called, was everywhere; and every man fancied himself a part of the government'.[75] O'Connell was not uniformly successful in spreading his democratic movement throughout Ireland; the towns were more active than the county parishes, and contributed more, and O'Connell never solved this problem.[76] But Ireland was politicized as never before; newspapers, pamphlets and broadsheets were eagerly awaited and as eagerly read; ballad singers performed at fairs, petty sessions, markets, weddings and wakes; special facilities were set aside for reporters.[77] And an important auxiliary in this process was the Roman Catholic priesthood whose assistance, the repeal head inspectors were advised, must be got, 'otherwise success cannot, and indeed ought not to be attained'.[78]

It was now that O'Connell's adamant stand against any government interference in clerical affairs was vindicated; for the clergy were dependent on the community for their financial maintenance, and, as one poor parish priest in the west of Ireland remarked:

The people give the fruit of their labours liberally to me and I give them my time, my care and my entire soul. I can do nothing without them and without me they will succumb under the weight of their sorrows. Between us there is a ceaseless exchange of feelings of affection. The day I received government money, the people would no longer regard me as their own. I for my part might be tempted to believe that I did not depend on them and one day perhaps we would regard each other as enemies.[79]

But it was not only, and perhaps not mainly, the spiritual bond between priest and people that mutual dependence could strengthen; this bond did not prevent Roman Catholic peasants following their own instincts in matters of drink and sexual misconduct.[80] Rather it was that the priest, as an educated member of society, could act as a political mediator, interpreting the world to his flock; and, since his flock were responsible for his financial position, they for their part expected the priest to do his social and political, as well as spiritual duty, in helping his flock cope with the world around them as well as the world to come. In short, the priest had to justify his existence.[81] But this meant that he was no spoon-feeder of ideas to a passive and gullible people; on the contrary, the priest had to work with the grain of public opinion, and that grain was fashioned, not by the Catholic church, but by O'Connell and his able and active secular, middle-class lieutenants.[82] The Catholic priest in Ireland was considered to be a good guide, but a bad driver.[83] His influence as an active, articulate, hard-working member of the community was, of course, immense; and O'Connell's use of the Catholic parish base as a political unit for his emancipation campaign gave him a solid foundation for a national Catholic movement. The experience of living as Catholics, with the whole social and religious milieu which that involved, was transformed by O'Connell into a kind of national experience;[84] and the politics of the Catholic democracy were launched as the most stable and enduring contribution to the making of modern Ireland.

The Catholic Association[85] ceased to be a mere pressure group, and became a 'fourth estate', a 'kind of Parliament' which took cognisance of all political and social grievances, and to which Catholics from all parts of the county looked for protection in the law courts.[86] But it was not only a reformist movement; and to see it as a kind of extension or local variation of British radicalism is to miss the significance of its unique local character. The issue at stake was much more than the right of Roman Catholics to sit in parliament, or to obtain equality before the law; it transcended the natural desire of the lawyers, journalists, merchants and professional men to clear away the obstacle that lay in the way of a political career. For O'Connell raised the whole question to one of national pride and self-respect, to an issue of principle: the principle that the Catholic Irish nation had the right to inherit, if not the earth, then at least the bit of it that was Ireland; he managed to create a kind of millennial feeling, to cast himself as the great leader who would take his people to the promised land.[87] The whole ideology of the emancipation campaign was to free the Irish from the English yoke, to show the Irish that they could defy their enemies, and that the great aristocrats and gentlemen who ruled in Dublin Castle and London could be put in their place.

Thus, while the core of the movement was its educated, middle-class leadership, contemporary observers were struck by its mass appeal and its emotional character. Much of this was the work of O'Connell, who combined an exceptionally fine oratorical voice with a commanding personality; but O'Connell and his lieutenants also worked hard to win the Irish peasant and farm labourer away from the dangerous influence of secret societies, which directed their attacks as much against the Catholic farmer as against the protestant tithe proctor.[88] To do this O'Connell aimed all the force of his verbal violence against the authorities, seeking to project them as the enemies of the people, and promising a time when, as one Gaelic poet put it, 'the law will once again be in our own hands, with the coming of emancipation', and the 'rabble breed' would be banished from Ireland.[89] The mass meeting amounted to a form of direct pressure on the government and on his opponents; and peasants in the south interpreted the agitation as a preparation for a rising. 'When will he call us out' was a question frequently asked in the streets of Clonmel during the great Munster provincial meeting of 26 August 1828; and the answer given was 'the finger on the mouth, and a significant wink from the bystanders'.[90] The popular feeling that a great day of deliverance was at hand may have been heightened by the influence of a prophecy, first published in 1771, that Protestantism would be extinguished for ever in 1825.[91]

O'Connell and his supporters had no intention of calling anyone out;[92] and he certainly did not intend the sudden extirpation of Protestantism from the land, envisaging, rather, that it would undergo a painless extinction.[93] O'Connell's difficulty lay in maintaining the pace of such a heterogenous movement, while preventing it from breaking the bounds of law and order, and probably contributed to his decision to accept Sir Francis Burdett's relief bill in 1825 with its 'wings': the abolition of the 40/- freehold franchise in the counties and its replacement by a £10 franchise; and the payment of Roman Catholic clergy from public funds.[94] O'Connell believed that the 40/- freeholders were too much under their landlords' influence to prove usefully independent members of his movement; but in this he was much mistaken; for in the end victory was won largely by the effect of these voters. In the general election of 1826 the Catholic Association achieved success in the four counties on which they concentrated (Louth, Monaghan, Waterford, and Westmeath); 'constitutional agitation, henceforth became the code of the great confederacy of Catholics'.[95] In July 1828, when O'Connell stood for Clare against a popular Protestant emancipationist landord, Vesey Fitzgerald, his gathering support convinced Fitzgerald that there was no point in contesting the election, and he withdrew before polling took place. The Government, already doubtful about the measure of support in the House that it could rely on to oppose emancipation, decided to yield; and in February 1829 the king's speech included a promised measure of Roman Catholic relief. Catholics were made eligible for all offices of state, except those of regent, lord lieutenant, and lord chancellor of either country; Catholic members of both houses of parliament were relieved of the obligation to take the oath of supremacy, but were to take an oath denying that the pope had any civil authority in the kingdom, undertaking to defend the existing system of property, and disavowing any intention to 'subvert' the established church. But the Government also took measures to deny some at least of the fruits of victory: the Catholic Association was suppressed, and the 40/- freehold franchise replaced by a £10 franchise.[96] Those qualifications, however much they seemed justified by the course of events in Ireland, gave the relief act an atmosphere of vindictiveness; and, added to the social trends of the 1830s – the subdivision of farms, the depression of tenants into labourers, the diminishing number of leases granted by landlords – they contributed to the decline in numbers of the Irish electorate, and offered little opportunity for steady and solid political campaigning.[97] Fortunately for O'Connell, he depended for his success on the behaviour of non-electors as well as electors; but the mass-meeting, however spectacular, could not bring the results that a hard-bargaining leader with votes at his disposal in the House might achieve – especially when the mass-meeting was met with all the coercive powers of the State.

The making of O'Connell's victory at Clare demonstrated both the strengths and weaknesses of the political movement that he led. The revolt of the 40/- freeholders against their traditional allegiance to their landlord was a remarkable achievement, but it was to prove one of those high peaks so characteristic of O'Connellite politics, one of those sporadic victories that were not followed up by the kind of solid, unbroken permeation of the country necessary if O'Connell were to lead a nationwide party to sustained success. Moreover, his movement, although it mobilized more Irishmen politically than any before him, and enjoyed the goodwill, if not the active support, of many Protestants, was by no means the comprehensive organization that O'Connell wanted it to be. O'Connell was anxious to placate all Protestants, especially those of Ulster, and on one occasion he drank the health of the glorious, pious and immortal memory of King William at a public banquet.[98] 'The assistance of Protestants generates so much good feeling', he wrote 'and such a national community of sentiment that I deem it more valuable than even emancipation itself'.[99]

But by the 1820s Irish politics were bedevilled by a surge in bitterness and intolerance between Catholics and Protestants. The last vestiges of eighteenth century indifference disappeared as a Protestant evangelical crusade made progress, based on the belief in the necessity of a personal recognition of the saving power of God. The Bible was venerated as the repository of revealed truth, and Catholicism condemned as harbouring false doctrine and encouraging scriptural neglect; thus, to save the souls of all Irishmen, the evangelicals devoted time and money to the propagation of the gospel among Catholics, setting up schools where the reading of the Bible was an integral part of the day's learning.[100] Whatever this zealous activity may have done for the souls of the nation, it earned much contempt and resentment from the Roman Catholics. The reverend S. Walsh, an Irishman, wrote from London to O'Connell in October 1824 congratulating him on 'the present posture of Catholic affairs in Ireland'. A new era had commenced for the 'people of Ireland, as I must call them emphatically'; O'Connell's example was encouraging respectable Catholics to study and know their religion, and the defence of religion, hitherto neglected, was now becoming fashionable. Walsh was delighted to 'hear of the defeat of the Bible missionaries in Ireland, and I have been more than delighted to see them defeated by the zeal and talent of the laity as well if not more than that of the clergy'. They had defended their religion against 'the unhallowed encroachments of Bible men and reformers' and, revived 'our holy religion', but they must be on their guard against the evangelicals 'deep-laid plan of circulating the Bible in the Irish language among the poorer Catholics of Ireland, for a more dangerous scheme could not be devized'. The subject, he concluded significantly, was one both 'national and religious'.[101]

Thus, for all O'Connell's concern to establish good relations with his Protestant fellow-countrymen, his political campaign was not free from the language of sectarian and national hatred. At the Clare by-election of 1828 Father Tom Maguire warned the tenants of Vesey Fitzgerald not to heed the 'tongues of the tempter and the charmer whose confederates have through all the ages joined the descendants of the Dane, the Norman and the Saxon, in burning your churches, in levelling your altars, in slaughtering your clergy, in stamping out your religion. Let every renegade to God and his country follow Vesey Fitzgerald, and every true Catholic Irishman follow me'.[102] In the same year 'Honest' Jack Lawless went to Ulster to organize matters for the next election there; he found himself the victim of a hostile Protestant reception and had to flee. Equally significant, however, was the Catholic reception in Ulster; Catholics flocked to him, convinced that his object was to drive the Orangemen out of the province; and when he arrived at the borders of Ulster he was accompanied by an 'army of people, variously armed with pistols and thick sticks concealed under their frieze coats'.[103]

The root of O'Connell's difficulty was that he never could decide whether his Protestant fellow-countrymen were indeed his fellow-countrymen; in 1813, for example, he referred to the 'Irish people', meaning the Roman Catholics, and in the next breath mentioned his 'protestant fellow-countrymen'.[104] Were they, or were they not, to be counted as an integral part of the Irish nation? O'Connell's dilemma was not a novel one; Henry Grattan had faced it when he spoke for the Protestant nation, and at the same time sought to educate Protestants to regard Roman Catholics as in some way members of the Protestant nation. Both described their nation as it was — Catholic or Protestant — and as they hoped it might be — Catholic and Protestant; neither discovered the key to this transformation, and both were left contemplating the inconsistencies of their liberal ideas. Grattan pressed the claims of the Roman Catholic majority, yet fully committed himself to maintaining the Protestant constitution of Ireland; O'Connell declared his heartfelt desire to create a nation in which Protestants would feel at home with Catholics, but his whole political career was dedicated to the undermining of Protestant power, and was based on the assumption that Catholics, being the majority, would replace Protestants in wealth, property and position in Ireland.[105]

In 1831 O'Connell wrote of his conviction that the Union with

Britain must be repealed; everybody, he declared 'Catholic, protestant and Presbyterian, was the better for the legislative independence of 1782. Everybody will be equally so by the legislative independence of 1832'.[106] His repeal campaigns of the early 1830s and 1840s were separated by some five years of co-operation with the British Whigs, for O'Connell was too pragmatic and down to earth to commit himself to only one course of action; and he never abandoned his hope that Ireland might derive real benefits from the union, a hope that was by no means unjustified.[107] But he had little confidence in Peel, who by 1840 seemed likely to succeed Melbourne; and his lack of a solid, homogenous electoral base was again proving his undoing,[108] for his appeal among the masses of the people was slipping, however much his pragmatic programme might please the bishops and the middle classes. In April 1840 O'Connell founded his Loyal National Repeal Association, and issued the first in a series of addresses to the people attacking the Union.

O'Connell was concerned in his repeal as in his emancipation campaigns to win over Protestant support for his cause. In a speech delivered in 1843 to the Dublin corporation he refused to divide Irishmen into sects, persuasions or parties; he acknowledged that 'the sovereignty of our beloved Queen is no burthern or weight to the state'; he stressed that his object was to benefit all his countrymen; he repeated his remarks made earlier in his career about confiding in the sense of justice of his brethren, the Protestants of Ireland; and he quoted Saurin and Plunket in support of his case for Ireland's right to her own parliament.[109]

But − once again − when O'Connell stood among the Catholic people, when he addressed them in his incomparable oratory, he adopted a different tone. He spoke of past conflicts between the Catholic nation and its 'Saxon' oppressors. At Mullaghmast he recalled a tragedy of Tudor times, when the chiefs of the O'Mores had been treacherously massacred by English colonists. He recalled the violation of the treaty of Limerick, and he reminded his listeners of the penal laws[110] − a contrast to his oration in the Dublin corporation when he declared his preference of living under the penal laws to living under the rule of the 'foreigner'. England was the arch-tyrant, the barbarian: on her side was 'the Saxon and guilt'.[111]

There was, perhaps, little else he could do; for the peasantry, the repeal issue was nothing in itself; it needed some immediate and urgent cause to give it some meaning, to convince them that repeal was their concern. Hence in the 1830s he stressed the importance of the struggle against the payment of tithe to the established church.[112] The Catholic Church, too, found that it must compromise on the bishop's desire to extricate the clergy from too close an alliance with the O'Connellite movement; non-intervention seemed to the public a betrayal of all that the church stood for. The popular priest was one who 'never did fail . . . To put in the boys who would vote for Repale'.[113] O'Connell both created and exploited this mood: 'The Catholic church is a national church', he declared, 'and if the people rally with me they will have a nation for that church'.[114] The ballad singers put it in a more colourful fashion:

> Since Luther lit the candle we suffered penury,
> But now it is extinguished, in spite of heresy,
> We'll have our Irish Parliament fresh laws we'll dictate
> Or we'll have satisfaction for the year of ——
>
> The labourers and tradesmen that's now in poverty
> They sit within their parlour and sing melodiously.
> They'll have mutton beef and bacon with butter eggs and tea
> And religion it will come again to welcome the repeal.
>
> Then Luther's generation must take a speedy flight
> And go to Hanover from the lands of sweet delight,
> All hereticks must cast their stricks and leave this fertile land,
> For it was decreed that Harry's breed should fall by the old
>   command.[115]

The experience of the 'national church' as O'Connell depicted it, was not one likely to prove congenial to the Protestant view of history. In his great denunciation of the Union, *A memoir on Ireland, native and Saxon*, published in 1843, O'Connell dedicated his work to 'her most gracious Majesty, the Queen of Great Britain and Ireland'; but his main concern was to expose British and Protestant 'settler' iniquities in Ireland, especially those of the 'Tory landlord class-exterminators all-prime favourites at the Castle'. He listed 'proofs' of 'the horrors inflicted on (the Irish) by the lawless power and treachery of the English settlers'. He praised the religious fidelity of the Irish, and contrasted Irish faith and Godliness with the fact that 'in all our countries into which protestantism entered, it owed its introduction to men remarkable for the badness of their character and the greatness of their vices'; Irish Protestantism was not more fortunate in this respect than any other sort. The reformation was a 'religious devastation'; the plantation of Ulster 'robbery according to law'. 'O Protestantism', he cried, when writing on the subject of Strafford and Cromwell, 'what horrors have been committed in your name in Ireland!' Their crimes contrasted with the behaviour of the Confederates who 'shed no blood, committed no crime, perpetrated no barbarity, exhibited no intolerance, exercised no persecution'. 'When, oh when', he asked, 'will justice be rendered to thy sons, O loved Fatherland?'. He listed the provisions of the penal code: there never was a faction 'so stained with blood, so blackened with crime as that Orange faction which, under the name of Protestant, seeks to retain the remnants of their abused power'. He blessed God that the persecution had failed to eradicate Catholicism in Ireland, and alleged that, although the 'form of persecution' was altered, the spirit remained the same.[116]

Even when due allowance was made for typical O'Connellite hyperbole, this was strong stuff; even W.J. O'Neill Daunt, a convert from Protestantism in his early twenties, and no lover of the 'Saxon', described the bulk of the book as 'a series of extracts from English and Protestant writers, detailing the crimes committed by the England and Protestant party against the Irish Catholics'. Whatever good the publication of the book would do, he concluded 'it won't convert the Orangemen. Its contents are too blistering'.[117]

O'Connell, like any popular leader, had to tell his audience what they wanted to hear; and, since his earnest and long-held desire was to curb the violence that he feared might break out among the peasants, he was obliged to substitute verbal violence for real blows, to threaten to shed the last drop of his blood[118] while all the time preventing his fellow countrymen from shedding theirs – or anyone else's. He was careful, for example, not to list among his venerated Irish martyrs at the hand of English tyranny the United Irishmen of 1798: they were too close in time to be held up as proper leaders of the Irish national cause.[119] His 'monster meetings' were regarded by some as a form of physical force;[120] and certainly they amounted to a defiance of the Government, especially when O'Connell dared the State, as he did at Mallow, to attack the repealers and trample on his dead body, not the living man.[121] But, given O'Connell's uncertain electoral base, they were his only means of exerting what he liked to think of as 'peaceable, rational but energetic' pressure,[122] and at the same time reducing, as the *Pilot* put it in a metaphor appropriate to the railway age, 'the "high pressure" of intense popular excitement by the salutary orifice of open and general agitation.'[123] In this way the anti-British sentiment of the multitude could be channelled away from violence.

For there could be no doubt that the multitude was anti-British, whatever O'Connell might say about the venerated Queen of England. In so far as they possessed any education, it was an education gained in the 'hedge schools', those institutions which originated in the suppression of all ordinary legitimate means of Catholic education, first under Cromwell, and then under the penal code.[124] In 1829 the hedge schools formed the majority of the schools, some 9,352 in number, which received no assistance of any kind from the various Protestant education societies working to disseminate knowledge in Ireland,[125] and some of the historical material used in them was calculated — and, apparently deliberately calculated — to arouse anti-English, if not anti-Protestant sentiment among the pupils. William Carleton, a close observer and vivid novelist of the Irish peasantry in the early nineteenth century, denounced the reading material used in the schools as 'of a most inflammatory and pernicious nature as regards politics';[126] and another observer pointed out that a book *The articles of Limerick*, together with other political pamphlets were used as reading books.[127] Carleton also criticized the teachers who were men of high social standing locally, and who, he alleged, 'industriously insinuated' disloyal principles into the minds of the children.[128] Certainly one schoolmaster in Munster, whose principles, a contemporary noted 'verge very closely indeed on the broadest republicanism', described Irish history in highly nationalist terms:

He praises the Milesians he curses 'the betrayer Dermod' — abuses 'the Saxon strangers' — lauds Brian Boru — utters one sweeping invective against the Danes, Henry VIII, Elizabeth, Cromwell, 'The Bloody', William 'of the Boyne', and Anne; he denies the legality of the criminal code; deprecates and disclaims the Union; dwells with enthusiasm on the memories of Curran, Grattan, 'Lord Edward', and young Emmet; insists on Catholic Emancipation; attacks the Peelers, horse and foot; protests against tithes, and threatens a separation of the United Kingdom! . . . before congenial spirits he talks downright treason.[129]

The eloquence and learning of the hedge schoolmasters were often used on behalf of popular candidates seeking election to Parliament; one of them, James Nash of Waterford, defied the enemies of his native land: 'Let them come on, let them come on; let them draw the sword; and then woe to the conquered! — every potato field shall be a Marathon, and every boreen a Thermopylae'. Significantly, however, Nash was a firm constitutionalist;[130] here indeed was the stuff of which O'Connell-ism was made.

Whatever the niceties and qualifications of O'Connell's constitutional ideas, their popular appeal did not lie in the restoration of Grattan's parliament; it lay in the simple, direct motto of the Repeal Association: 'Ireland for the Irish'.[131] And there could be no doubt concerning the application of the term 'Irish'; it meant the Catholics, however much O'Connell sought, sincerely, to carry the Protestants with him in his political crusade. This motto deserves closer examination; for it marked a momentous change in Irish politics in the 50 years after Grattan's celebrated 'declaration of independence' in 1782. The constitution of 1782 was the high tide of Protestant nationalism; but now O'Connell could use the expression 'Ireland for the Irish' without any ambiguity whatsoever about who the 'Irish' were. And, in case there might be any ambiguity, O'Connell himself explained in his *Memoir on Ireland* that the Union entitled the Catholics of Ireland, 'that is, emphatically the people of Ireland – to religious equality with the English and Scotch'.[132] The Protestant nation was as much the victim of the radical doctrine espoused by O'Connell that numbers, not property, entitled a section of the nation to regard itself as 'the people'[133] as it was the victim of the nationalist view that the Catholics were the Irish, properly so called. A year or so before O'Connell published his *Memoir on Ireland*, Henry Grattan Jnr. in his memoir of his illustrious father, the man who above all represented Protestant Irish nationalism at its apogee, also referred to the Catholics as 'the Irish people'.[134] It was an important admission; and its implications were to pervade Irish politics for the next century and a half.

Notes

1. W.A. Phillips, *History of the Church of Ireland*, vol. *III*, pp. 248ff.

2. R.B. MacDowell, *Irish Public Opinion*, p. 182.

3. W.E.H. Lecky, *Leaders of Public Opinion*, vol. *I*, p. 136.

4. Ibid., pp. 76, 137, 147.

5. P.F. Moran, *Spicilegium Ossoriense* (3rd series), Dublin 1884, pp. 365-6.

6. H. Grattan, *Memoirs of the Life and Times of Henry Grattan* (vol. *II*, London, 1834), pp. 308-10.

7. S. Gwynn, *Henry Grattan and his Times*, p. 228.

8. R.B. MacDowell, *Irish Public Opinion*, p. 139; M. Wall, 'The United Irish movement', in *Historical Studies*, V (London, 1965), pp. 122-36; A.T.Q. Stewart, 'A stable unseen power: William Drennan and the origins of the United Irishmen' in J. Bossy and P.J. Jupp (eds.), *Essays Presented to Michael Roberts*, pp. 80-92.

9. W.H. Crawford, 'Change in Ulster in the late eighteenth century', in Bartlet and Hayton, op. cit., pp. 186-203.

10. W.J. MacNevin, *Pieces of Irish History* (New York, 1807), pp. 17-18, 142.

11. See the astonishingly revealing memorandum in his *Autobiography* (London, 1831 ed.) pp. 113-15; see also F. MacDermot *Life of Theobald Wolfe Tone* (London, 1939), pp. 147-8; for an (equally astonishingly frank) revelation of Tone's attitude see B. Hobson (ed.) *Letters of Theobald Wolfe Tone* (Dublin, n.d.), pp. 46-7.

12. P. MacAonghusa and L.O Reagain (eds.) *The Best of Tone* (Cork, 1972), pp. 28-9.

13. Ibid., pp. 40-42.

14. MacDowell, op. cit., p. 182. For a United Irish attempt to allay Protestant fears on this point see William T. Jones, *A Letter to the Societies of United Irishmen of the Town of Belfast upon the Subject of Certain Apprehensions . . .* (Dublin, 1792), p. 16.

15. S. Gwynn, op. cit., pp. 266-7; H. Grattan, *Memoirs of Henry Grattan*, vol. *IV* (London, 1842), p. 88.

16. MacAonghusa and O Reagain, op. cit., p. 46.

17. Ibid., p. 108.

18. Wall, op. cit., p. 133-4.

19. J.W. Derry, *Castlereagh* (London, 1976), pp. 37-8.

20. Drennan to Samuel McTier, 1 Sept. 1793 (D.A. Chart, *The Drennan Letters*), Belfast, 1931, p. 171.

21. For Drennan's misgivings about the Catholics see Stewart, *Narrow ground*, pp. 108-9.

22. MacAonghusa and O Reagain, op. cit., p. 110.

23. M. Elliott, 'The origins and transformation of early Irish republicanism' in *IRSH*, vol. *XXIII* (1978), pp. 405-28.

24. G. Cornewall Lewis, *On Local Disturbances in Ireland* (London, 1836), p. 14: for a review of the Whiteboys see M. Wall's essay in T.D. Williams (ed.) *Secret Societies in Ireland* (Dublin, 1973), pp. 13-25.

25. Crawford, op. cit., pp. 190-91, 202-3.

26. G.O. Tuathaigh, *Ireland Before the Famine, 1798-1848* (Dublin, 1972), pp. 7-8.

27. Miller, *Queen's rebels*, p. 55.

28. Lewis, op. cit., p. 37.

29. M. Elliott, op. cit., pp. 417-18.

30. R.R. Madden, *The United Irishmen, Their Lives and Times*, vol. *III* (Dublin, n.d.), p. 28.

31. Beckett, *Modern Ireland*, pp. 254-6.

32. H. Grattan, *Memoirs of Henry Grattan*, vol. *IV*, pp. 217-20.

33. Madden, op. cit., p. 156.

34. O Tuathaigh, op. cit., pp. 25-7.

35. Moran, op. cit., 490-504 (pastoral address of the Archbishop of Dublin, 16 Feb. 1797). See also pp. 561-2, 572-6, 579-82.

36. L. Cullen, 'Irish nationalism', Gregynog seminar paper, pp. 13-17; McDowell, *Ireland in the age of imperialism and revolution*, p. 623; T.J. Powell, 'The background to the rebellion in Co. Wexford, 1790-98', M.A. Thesis, N.U.I. (1970), pp. 51, 130-32, 177-87. For the testimony of one member of the Wexford farming class see Thomas Clancy, *A personal narrative . . .* (Dublin, 1832), esp. pp. 10-16.

37. M. Elliott, op. cit., p. 418; see also pp. 406-7, 411-13; O Tuathaigh, op. cit., pp. 26-7, 66-7.

38. D.H. Akenson and W.H. Crawford, *Local poets and social history: James Orr, bard of Ballycarry* (Belfast, 1977), p. 41.

39. Crawford, 'Change in Ulster', op. cit., pp; 201-2; Stewart, op. cit., pp. 128-37.

40. Beckett, *Anglo-Irish tradition*, pp. 58-9; T.J. Powell, 'The background to the Wexford rebellion 1790-1798', pp. 130-31, 144-51, 194.

41. R. Kee, *The green flag: a history of Irish nationalism* (London, 1972), p. 127.

42. MacAonghusa and O Reagain, op. cit., p. 113.

43. O Tuathaigh, *Ireland before the famine*, pp. 28-9.

44. MacDowell, *Ireland in the age of imperialism and revolution*, p. 574.

45. Beckett, *Making of modern Ireland*, pp. 270-79; G.C. Bolton, *The passing of the Irish act of union* (London, 1966), passim and esp. p. 218. H.L. Calkin, 'For and against a Union', *Éire/Ireland*, vol. *XIII*, No. 4 (1978), pp. 22-33, esp. p. 29.

46. M.R. O'Connell, *The correspondence of Daniel O'Connell*, vol. *III* (Dublin, 1974), p. 345.

47. W.E.H. Lecky, *Leaders of Public Opinion in Ireland*, vol. *II* (London, 1912 edn.) p. 164.

48. O'Hegarty, *History of Ireland under the union*, p. 23.

49. H. Grattan, *Memoirs of Henry Grattan*, vol. *V* (London, 1846), pp. 18-20.

50. L. Wagner (ed.), *Modern Political orations* (London, 1896), pp. 41-50. See also K.B. Nowlan, 'The meaning of repeal in Irish history', in *Historical Studies*, IV (London, 1963), pp. 1-17. Saurin, an anti-Unionist subsequently became attorney general after the Union.

51. R.B. MacDowell, *Public Opinion and Government Policy in Ireland, 1800-1846* (London, 1952), p. 124.

52. O'Hegarty, op. cit., p. 23.

53. H. Grattan, op. cit., pp. 60-63.

54. Crawford, op. cit., p. 203; James S. Reid, *History of the presbyterian church in Ireland* (3 vols., London, 1853), III, pp. 509-12.

55. M. Wall, op. cit., p. 130.

56. P.F. Moran, op. cit., pp. 601-4; the phrase was used by the bishop of Meath in December 1798.

57. J.A. Murphy, 'The support of the Catholic clergy in Ireland, 1750-1850', in *Historical Studies*, V (London, 1965), pp. 103-119.

58. Ibid., pp. 117-18.

59. For an example of O'Connell's concern about the lack of opportunities for Catholic barristers see J.O'Connell (ed.) *The Select Speeches of Daniel O'Connell, M.P.* (2nd series, Dublin, 1865), pp. 324-7. See also D. Gwynn, *Daniel O'Connell* (1947 edn.), p. 149.

60. W.E.H. Lecky, *Leaders of Public Opinion in Ireland*, vol. *II*, p. 20.

61. O Tuathaigh, op. cit., p. 54-5; MacDowell, *Public Opinion and Government Policy*, pp. 92ff.

62. B. Ward, *The Eve of Catholic Emancipation*, vol. *I* (London, 1911), pp. 69-71.

63. O'Connell, *Select Speeches*, vol. *I* (Dublin, 1865), pp. 86, 351, 421.

64. MacDowell, op. cit., p. 94.

65. O'Connell, Select speeches, I, pp. 44, 140, 181.

66. Ibid., p. 199.

67. Beckett, *Modern Ireland*, pp. 297-8.

68. Lecky, *Leaders of Public Opinion*, II, pp. 59-60.

69. K.T. Hoppen, 'Politics, the law, and the nature of the Irish electorate, 1832-1850', *E.H.R.*, vol. *92* (1977), pp. 746-776.

70. O'Connell, *Select speeches*, I, 217; see also vol. *II*, pp. 440, and M.R. O'Connell, *Correspondence of Daniel O'Connell*, vol. *I*, p. 99; vol. *III*, 402-3,

for O'Connell's detestation of the Emmett rebellion.

71. T. Wyse, *Historical Sketch of the Late Catholic Association of Ireland* (2 vols., London, 1829), I, p. 208.

72. Ibid., *I*, p. 209, 225-8.

73. Ibid., *II*, appendix xxv.

74. Ibid., *I*, p. 209.

75. Ibid., p. 247.

76. Ibid., pp. 209-10.

77. J.A. Reynolds, *The Catholic Emancipation Crisis in Ireland, 1823-29* (New Haven, 1954), pp. 74-8.

78. Wyse, *Historical Sketch, II*, appendix xxiv.

79. Murphy, op. cit., p. 119.

80. D.W. Miller, 'Irish Catholicism and the great famine', *Journal of Social History*, vol. *IX*, No. 1 (1975), pp. 81-98.

81. W.J. Lowe, 'The Lancashire Irish and the Catholic Church, 1846-71: the social dimension', in *Irish Historical Studies*, vol. *XX*, No. 78 (Sept., 1976), pp. 129-55.

82. See, for example, J.H. Whyte, 'The influence of the Catholic clergy on elections', in *EHR*, vol. LXXV, pp. 239-59; the archbishop of Armagh warned of the dangers 'lest we offend a faithful people by an unexpected separation from them' (p. 243).

83. As Wyse put it, 'guiding the people the way they had determined to go' (op.cit., *I*, p. 289).

84. Lowe, op. cit., pp. 138-9.

85. Wyse, op. cit., *I*, p. 205.

86. Lecky, *Leaders of Public Opinion*, ixxxx, vol. *II*, p. 60.

87. Ibid., p. 5. O'Farrell, *Ireland's English Question*, pp. 82-3; T. Wyse, *Historical Sketch, II*, appendix xvii.

88. J. Lee, 'The Ribbonmen', in T.D. Williams, *Irish Secret Societies*, pp. 26-35.

89. O. Tuathaigh, 'Gaelic Ireland, popular politics, and Daniel O'Connell', in *Galway Archaelogical and Historical society journal*, vol . *34* (1972-5), pp. 21-34.

90. O'Hegarty, *Ireland Under the Union*, p. 53; see also pp. 48-9; Wyse, *Historical Sketch, I*, pp. 413-14.

91. G.C. Lewis, op. cit., p. 71.

92. For O'Connell's concern to maintain law and order see his 'address' to the men of Tipperary, 30 Sept. 1828 (Wyse, op. cit., *I*, pp. 416-19, and *II*, appendix xxvii).

93. E.D. Steele, 'Gladstone, Irish violence and conciliation', in Cosgrave and McCartney, op. cit., pp. 258-9.

94. O Tuathaigh, *Before the Famine*, p. 69.

95. Wyse, op. cit., *I*, pp. 291-2.

96. Beckett, *Modern Ireland*, pp. 302-4.

97. Hoppen, op. cit., pp. 753-5.

98. Lecky, *Leaders of Public Opinion, II*, p. 83.

99. O'Connell, *Correspondence, III*, p. 404.

100. MacDowell, *Public Opinion and Government Policy*, pp. 24-31; Beckett, *Anglo-Irish tradition*, pp. 104-8; D. Bowen, *The Protestant Crusade in Ireland, 1800-70* (Dublin, 1978), pp. 61-80, 83-123.

101. O'Connell, *Correspondence, III*, pp. 81-5.

102. O. Macdonagh, 'Irish famine emigration to the United States', in *Perspectives in American History*, X (Harvard, 1976), pp. 357-446; quotation on pp. 388-9. See also B. Ward, op. cit., vol. *III* (London, 1912), p. 225.

103. O'Hegarty, *Ireland under the Union*, p. 41; Wyse, *Historical sketch*, I, pp. 400-408.

104. O'Connell, *Select Speeches*, I, p. 199.

105. Macdonagh, op. cit., p. 376; for an appreciation of the difficulties confronting liberal protestants see Wyse, op. cit., II, pp. 4-8.

106. O'Connell, *Correspondence*, IV, p. 351.

107. MacDowell, *Public Opinion and Government Policy*, Chap. 6.

108. In the general election of 1841 O'Connell's parliamentary following was reduced from 39 to 18 (Kee, *The green flag*, p. 192).

109. O'Hegarty, op. cit., pp. 120-27. When he set off from Dublin in April 1843 on a repeal campaign he was met at Clondalkin by a band playing 'God save the queen' (*Pilot*, 21 April 1843).

110. Lecky, op. cit., pp. 250, 256; see also his speech at Tara, 1843 (L. Wagner, op. cit., p. 47); see also O'Hegarty, pp. 129-30, 144-5.

111. *Pilot*, 25 October 1843.

112. Lecky, p. 109; M. Murphy, 'Repeal, popular politics, and the Catholic clergy in Cork, 1840-50', in *JCHAS*, LXXXI (Jan-Dec., 1977), pp. 39-48.

113. J. Whyte, op. cit., pp. 241-3; Murphy, op. cit., p. 44.

114. K.B. Nowlan, The politics of repeal: a study in the relations between *Great Britain and Ireland, 1841-50* (London, 1965), p. 6.

115. Ballad 'The speedy repeal'; see also 'The ass and the orangeman's daughter', but cf. 'A new song on repeal' (British Library).

116. O'Connell, *Memoir* (1843; 1970 edn., New York), passim.

117. W.J. O'Neill Daunt, *A life spent for Ireland* (I.U.P., 1972 edn.), p. 26.

118. O'Connell, *Select Speeches*, II, p. 469.

119. Lecky, op. cit., pp. 297-8.

120. Ibid., pp. 251, 267-8.

121. Kee, op. cit., p. 206.

122. O'Connell to Thomas Attwood, 16 Feb. 1830 (*Correspondence*, IV, pp. 128-9).

123. *Pilot*, 18 Oct. 1843.

124. P.J. Dowling, *The hedge schools of Ireland* (London, 1935), Chap. 1.

125. Ibid., pp. 39-44.

126. Ibid., p. 80; see also J. Godkin, *Education in Ireland* (London and Dublin, 1862), p. 60.

127. Dowling, op. cit., pp. 84-5.

128. Ibid., p. 110. O'Connell had received his early education in a hedge school (Wise, op. cit., I, p. 15).

129. Dowling, pp. 111-12.

130. Ibid., p. 112-13.

131. R. Dudley Edwards, *Daniel O'Connell and his world* (London, 1975), p. 43. See also O'Connell's speech at Trim (*Pilot*, 22 March 1843).

132. O'Connell, *Memoir*, p. 45.

133. For O'Connell in the context of British radicalism see E. Norman, *A History of modern Ireland* (London, 1973 edn.), pp. 58-60.

134. H. Grattan, *Memoirs of Henry Grattan*, IV (1842), p. 215.

6　PATTERNS OF NATIONALISM, 1842-1870

The identification of the Irish nation with the Catholic people of Ireland did not create fully segregated political communities in Ireland, nor did it divide its inhabitants into two completely distinct groups. The Protestants, however much they protested their loyalty to the Union and the British connection, were still very conscious of themselves as Irish; they could use that term as an adjective, even if they could no longer employ it as a collective noun. Moreover, the eighteenth century tradition of Protestant nationalism did not entirely disappear; just as there had been Protestant emancipationists, so were there Protestant repealers; and out of O'Connell's thirty-nine members in the parliament of 1832 thirteen were Protestants.[1] The Protestant repealers, it is true, made no significant impact on the O'Connellite movement; but they did demonstrate that Tone's idea of the common name of Irishman was not wholly spurious. There were Protestants, however, who sought to give a new meaning to that concept by searching for some cultural ingredients that might provide the stuff of a close relationship between Irishmen of differing religious and political faiths; for, whereas O'Connell could rest content in the knowledge that the Catholics were the majority, and were therefore the Irish nation – a nation of course which non-Catholics were welcome to join, provided they accepted the Catholic nation's politics, and acknowledged its religion as a 'national church' – Protestants could feel no such sense of assurance. Protestants whose blood was still fired with nationalism could not afford to rest their ideology on the soft sands of political complacency; and in 1842, when O'Connell was pressing forward with his repeal campaign, a small but influential group of nationalists, inspired by the young Irish Protestant Thomas Davis, made a bid to recreate Irish nationalism in their own image, and thus inaugurated a debate on the character of the nation that was renewed in the closing decade of the nineteenth century, but has long since passed into oblivion.

Davis was born in 1814 at Mallow, Co. Cork. His father, of a Buckinghamshire family which originally hailed from Wales, served in the Peninsular war with the rank of inspector general of hospitals, and his mother was the descendant of a Cromwellian settler. 'I myself was brought up High Tory and Episcopalian protestant', he wrote;[2] but

Davis's true religion was nationalism. 'How long will you sin against patriotism', he once demanded, pulpit style, of an audience in Trinity College historical society; and he then asked his congregation to repent, to 'act in unison with any men, be they of what party they may, for our common country'.[3] Here was summed up Davis's political creed: a fervent love of country, a disbelief that anyone could fail to appreciate the virtues of nationalism, a search for the brotherhood of all Irishmen in the common cause, and an almost missionary — not to say messianic — enthusiasm for the conversion of his fellow-countrymen, and the leading of them towards the light.

Davis's own conversion to nationalism seems to have been a quasi-religious experience. His early political beliefs were, like those of O'Connell, utilitarian; but he fell under the influence of German romanticism,[4] and his reaction against his early beliefs bore all the enthusiasm of the convert. He fulminated against:

> Modern Anglicanism i.e. Utilitarianism, the creed of Russell and Peel, as well as of the Radicals — this thing, call it Yankeeism or Englishism, which measures prosperity by exchangeable value, measures duty by gain, and limits desire to clothes, food, and respectability; this damned thing has come into Ireland under the Whigs, and equally the favourite of the 'Peel' Tories.[5]

Bigots and utilitarians he lumped together: 'If the economists could the world would be a factory, and if the bigots could it would be a graveyard'. Thus 'where an Irish peasant is gay and gallant, an English boor is sullen and sensual. The Saxon plots a vice where the Celt only meditates a compliment'. 'You cannot have the spirit of the racer and the endurance of the noggan-horse together', he concluded; English MPs were 'trained far from us amid a methodical, callous, money-griping and animal race'. And England 'warred for gain against liberty and with all the weapons of ferocity and deceit'.[6]

A nation had a unique character, otherwise it could not claim to be a nation; it was not merely an accidental conglomeration of people who happened to be inhabiting a piece of territory. A nation was defined by its culture, by which Davis meant its literature, its history, and above all, embodying these, its language. Language was the vehicle of a nation's historical memory, not merely an accidental set of speech patterns. A nation should therefore 'guard its language more than its territories', for a people without a language of its own was 'only half a nation'.[7] Language served a two-fold purpose; it formed a practical barrier to Anglicization, 'a surer barrier, and more important frontier, than fortress or river'; and it gave the national soul its vitality, its 'vigour, health and great achievements'. It was to the Irish people their only mode of expressing their mind and imagination, for:

> The language which grows up with a people is conformed to their origins, descriptive of their climate, constitution and manners, mingled inseparably with their history and their soul, fitted beyond any other language to express their prevalent thoughts in the most national-efficient way.

To lose the native tongue and to learn that of the alien was the worst badge of conquest; therefore 'Ireland must be unsaxonized before it can be pure and strong'.[8]

Davis was not unique among the Anglo-Irish for his interest in Gaelic Ireland; the late eighteenth century had seen a flourishing literary movement marked by a strong sympathy for Gaelic language, literature and antiquities. But these cultural enthusiasts had no desire to use their discoveries for political ends, or to assert that 'Irishness' was to be found in linguistic and cultural traditions. Romantic nationalism of this kind was a new, and possibly dangerous development to the Anglo-Irish; and it was also, on the face of it, dangerous to Davis, an Anglo-Irishman himself, whose roots were anything but Gaelic, and whose mastery of the language left much to be desired. Cultural nationalism suited the book of German-speaking Germans; but how could an English-speaking Protestant reconcile it with his own background and experience?

To answer this question — a question which has confronted Protestant Irishmen since Davis's time — he evolved a second major strand in his political thinking: the idea of the essential unity of all Irishmen, of whatever creed, race or class they might be.

> What matter that at different shrines
> We pray unto one God?
> What matters that at different times
> Our fathers won this sod?
> In future and in name we're bound
> By stronger links than steel;
> And neither can be safe nor sound
> But in the other's weal.[9]

But this verse, while it swelled with lofty idealism, also burgeoned with contradictions. It was a plea to Catholic Irishmen to forgive and forget the past; yet Davis always insisted on the need for a nation to remember its past, to preserve it and keep it holy. Ireland's past could prove a divisive influence, especially if the different origins of her people were inquired into too closely. Davis therefore had to reconcile ideas of racial purity (the 'Saxon boor' versus the gallant Irish peasant) with the pluralist origins of Irish society; hence his admiration of the Geraldines, who 'in Strongbow's van, By lawless force, as conquerors, their Irish reign began' but who quickly became assimilated into 'Irishness':

> not long our air they breathed;
> Not long they fed on venison, in Irish water seethed;
> Not often had their children been by Irish mothers nursed;
> When from their full and genial hearts an Irish feeling burst!
> The English monarchs strive in vain, by law and force and bribe,
> To win from Irish thoughts and ways his 'more than Irish' tribe;
> For still they clung to fosterage, to Breitheamh, cloak, and bard;
> What king dare say to Geraldine, 'your Irish wife discard'?[10]

In his historical essays Davis returned to this theme. The adoption of English names meant that the 'members of the Celtic race here are immensely greater than at first appears', he wrote; moreover 'even the Saxon and Norman colonists . . . melted down into the Irish, and adopted all their ways and language'.[11] In his study of James II's Irish parliament Davis lamented the land settlement which contained 'no provision for the families of those adventurers, who however guilty when they came into the country, had been in it for from thirty to forty years, and had time and some citizenship in their favour'.[12] Even the Wexford rebellion of 1798 could be fitted into this pattern; the rebels' blood was 'for the most part English and Welsh, though mixed with the Danish and Gaelic, yet they are Irish in thought and feeling'.[13]

Davis was fully justified in his belief that any racial purity that might have existed in Ireland was lost in the intermingling of peoples and nations since the Gaelic conquest; yet there was an air of self-defensiveness in his pleas for the 'Milesian, the Dane, the Norman, the Welshman, the Scotchman, and the Saxon', to 'combine, regardless of their blood';[14] and, despite his love of things Gaelic, he could never bring himself to admire or approve of seventeenth and eighteenth century Gaelic poetry because of its racial and religious character.[15]

Davis wished to apply racial concepts to Anglo-Irish relations, but not to relationships within Ireland itself; he wanted to erect linguistic and cultural barriers between Ireland and England, and at the same time use those same weapons to break down barriers between the descendants of Englishmen and Irishmen now dwelling in Ireland. What was an obstacle in one context must become an open door in another. From his starting point of cultural distinctiveness, therefore, Davis arrived at the conclusion that Irishness was the product, not of race, but of environment; and only by accepting that the uniqueness of the Irishman was the product of the uniqueness of Ireland (more particularly of Celtic but not Catholic, Ireland) could a truly united nation be achieved.

In retrospect, Davis's hopes of a culturally distinct, yet harmonious nation seems impossible of achievement; but the young men who were inspired by his warmth, enthusiasm and heartfelt love of country did not deem it so. One of his disciples, Charles Gavan Duffy, a Northern Irish Catholic, confessed how his nationalism 'of the school of Roger O'Moore' (sic) caused him to 'burn with desire to set up again the Celtic race and the Catholic church'; but, under Davis's influence, he abandoned his bitterness for a comprehensive nationalism based on the uniting of all description of Irishmen.[16] When a young Catholic, John O'Leary, first came into contact with Davis's ideas he 'went through a process analogous to what certain classes of Christian call 'conversion".'[17] What these young men – nicknamed 'Young Irelanders' by an English journalist who likened them to the Young England group in the Tories[18] – lacked in numbers, they more than made up for in enthusiasm; and they sought to spread the gospel of nationalism, not through revolutionary conspiracy (although they professed to admire the men of '98), nor through monster meetings (although Davis was, from 1840, a supporter of O'Connell and repeal), but by educating the Irish people that they might be free. The Young Irelanders wanted to create an educated and informed public opinion, the only moral force, Davis asserted, 'in which I have any faith'.[19] Their means were the newspaper press; reading rooms; and a 'library of Ireland' consisting of cheaply priced books within the means of more humble pockets.

The suggestion of founding a newspaper was originally made by Gavan Duffy who had a journalistic background and experience. The paper would be a weekly which Duffy, John Blake Dillon (a well-to-do Catholic graduate of Trinity College) and Davis would own and write. In the event Duffy became the sole proprietor, while Davis and Dillon helped manage the paper. The choice of title – the *Nation* – was

Davis's; and on 15 October 1842 it was launched.[20] Its declared aim
was to 'create and foster a public opinion in Ireland, and make it racy
of the soil'; and while its creators were aware of the criticism that they
might be expecting too much from a newspaper, they were confident
that a newspaper was 'the only conductor to the mind of Ireland.
Periodicals and books make no considerable impression, because they
have no considerable circulation. Speeches are more effective; but we
include them among the materials of journalism. O'Connell the orator
is as much the food of the Press as O'Connell the writer. And it is
undeniable that the journals, with all their means and appliances, were,
and are, and are to be for many a day, the stimulating power in Ireland'.
Newspapers, they were confident, exercised a 'slow and silent' power,
acting 'on the masses as the wind, which we do not see, moves the
dust, which we do see'. A newspaper was 'the shorter and surer road to
the popular mind'; it was also a means of tapping the 'young intellect
of the country'. Many a student 'pent among books, has his mind full
of benevolent thoughts for his country . . . Such men will find a fitting
vehicle in the *Nation*'. A legion of writers was more formidable than 'a
thousand men all clad in steel'.[21]

The young patriots seemed justified in their optimism, for the
Nation enjoyed an unprecedented success, with a circulation of over
10,000 by 1843 and a readership estimated at over a quarter of a
million.[22] It even penetrated the rural districts, and, according to Davis,
delighted the country people.[23] Davis knew that literacy was the key
to success in moulding the kind of informed public opinion that he
believed essential for nationalist movement;[24] and before the *Nation*
was launched, education and literacy were on the increase in Ireland.
The Hedge Schools were the main source of primary education for the
upper sections of the peasantry; and they were supplemented by a
Roman Catholic educational system run by religious orders, small in
scale and largely confined to the cities and larger towns before 1845.
The State, acting on the widely held assumption that education — of
the proper sort — might be a means of countering political disaffection,
intervened in 1831 through a National Education Board to promote,
control and largely finance primary education. Within two years almost
800 schools with over 100,000 pupils had been established within the
State system or had been brought within it. By 1845 there were over
four thousand schools and over one hundred thousand pupils; and
these schools inspired anther spurt of denominational schools, founded
by the Catholic and Anglican churches to counter 'godless' state
schools, and catering for 150,000 children by 1845. In 1841 national

illiteracy had fallen to 51 per cent, and in 1845 to 45 per cent. These were impressive figures by contemporary European standards; Ireland's poverty and destitution contrasted with her increasing literacy, with all the temptations and possibilities this held for political education.[25]

Davis was a fervent supporter of education; but only of education of a particular kind: 'educate that you may be free'. He approved strongly of a school system that taught Irish children all the glories of their past, and filled their heads with Irish language and literature; but he denounced State schools for their hostility to specifically Irish books, and for their practice of teaching exclusively through the medium of English. If this was 'modernization' then Davis was as much against it as O'Connell was for it. Moreover, Irish children were taught to think of themselves as English, and to learn respect for their superiors and acceptance of their place in society. Any compromising material was carefully examined and, if considered unsuitable, was discarded; thus a second edition of a schools' reading book omitted Thomas Campbell's poems 'The Harper' and 'The Downfall of Poland', and Sir Walter Scott's 'Breathes there a man with soul so dead'. If Ireland could be properly integrated into the United Kingdom through the medium of her educational system, then integrated she would be.[26]

It was this process of 'denationalization' that Davis and his fellow enthusiasts sought to check and reverse. Of course, they were not alone in their determination to do so; no amount of careful revision of State-school textbooks could eradicate the personal and powerful impact of nationally minded teachers in the classrooms. But the Young Irelanders embarked on a concerted campaign which profoundly influenced not only Irish nationalism, but also the relationship between literature and nationalism in Ireland. They sought to make Irish literature subordinate to Irish nationalism, and to use it to promote and foster a sense of nationality among the people. The common people could be the core of Irish nationhood – were the core of Irish nationhood – if only they were allowed to articulate their innate patriotism. 'Knowledge and organization must set Ireland free', Davis wrote, 'and make her prosperous'; 'we want a brave, modest, laborious, and instructed people'.[27] The Young Irelanders urged the establishment of 'repeal reading rooms' in the parishes of Ireland, so that the Repeal Association would become the 'schoolmaster to the people of Ireland'; every village would have a reading room, inspected by an appointee of the Repeal Association's 'reading room committee', and Davis hoped that Protestant and Catholic clergy, as a literate group, would act as patrons of the rooms. The rooms would contain all the necessities for study and thought on 'all subjects ranging from mathematics to music', and would be filled by young men who had abjured such loose and unproductive habits as cards, tobacco and dissipation.[28] Earnest Irishmen would abjure laziness and cultivate their minds, and all for the cause of Ireland. O'Connell had some reservations about the scheme, but he knew that illiteracy was a barrier to the political democracy that he aspired to create in Ireland, and he was persuaded to release funds for the reading rooms.[29]

The provision of places to read was one aspect of Davis's attempted national regeneration; another was to provide appropriate materials for reading and here again Germany offered an example. If all the offices of Prussia were abolished tomorrow, her colleges and schools levelled, her troops disarmed and disbanded, she could within six months regain her whole range of civil and military institutions, and she could do so because of her knowledge. Ignorance made a country weak and poor; education and knowledge were central to the country's aspirations to self-government. Yet there were ten counties in Ireland without a single bookseller in them; 'we blush for the fact'.[30] Worse still, the connection with England meant that the publications of the 'Useful Knowledge Society' telling 'every man how stockings were wove, how many drunkards were taken up per hour in Southwark, how the geese were plucked from which the author got his pens' – all the whole 'horde of Benthamy' – descended upon Ireland. Therefore 'to give to the country a National Library, exact enough for the wisest, high enough for the purest, and cheap enough for all readers, appears the object of "The Library of Ireland" '.[31]

The Library of Ireland was the Irish forerunner of the Left Book Club. It was modelled on the shilling volumes of Lord Brougham and sought to inculcate the habit of reading among the people by offering a fresh volume every two months over a period of two years. The first book in the series was McNevin's *History of the Irish Volunteers*, published in 1845, and followed by Charles Gavan Duffy's *The Ballad Poetry of Ireland* and John Mitchel's *Life of Aodh O'Neill*.[32] There was a history of the American revolution; collections of songs and ballads; and a history of the confederation of Kilkenny. History was a particularly popular source for the library and, as Gavan Duffy put it, Irish history was 'ransacked' for examples of public spirit and public service, and warnings against national sins and transgressions, 'for it is mad and wicked to extinguish the light history throws on the past as to extingish a beacon on the rocks where a navy may founder'.[33]

The library of Ireland was central to the Young Irelanders' purpose, that literature was a means of teaching nationalism and national self-awareness. Inevitably, the nationalistic aspect of such literature dominated and shaped its artistic content. The *Nation's* poems, ballads and stories were charged with feeling rather than style, and gave the impression that the life of an Irish literary man was one of sensations rather than thoughts. 'Patriot hearts' beat strongly, 'Saxon yokes' were overthrown (or, more commonly, 'o'erthrown'), green banners were unfurled, and 'cold clay' enwrapped the limbs of Irish chieftains "gainst England battling'.[34] Davis's energy and commitment to his cause were indefatigable; not only language and literature, but paintings could be used for nationalistic ends; a list of subjects 'for historical paintings' included 'the landing of the Milesians', 'the first landing of the Danes', 'Shane O'Neill at Elizabeth's court', 'The Dungannon convention', 'Tone, Emmett, and Keogh in the Rathfarnam Garden', 'The Clare hustings — proposal of O'Connell' and, last but by no means least 'Conciliation: Orange and Green'.[35] Ancient tombs were to be preserved; a national theatre established; native Irish names of historical men and places revived. The latter caused particular difficulty; according to Gavan Duffy the first appearance of Gaelic patronyms aroused 'consternation'.[36]

All these deeds and works were for the good of Ireland, for the revival of Irish national consciousness, and, above all, for the subject suggested by Davis as appropriate for an historical painting: conciliation, Orange and Green. But, despite the increasing literacy in Ireland, despite John Blake Dillon's cry of joy at discovering twenty-three subscriptions to the *Nation* in the village of Ballaghadreen in Co. Roscommon,[37] the strength of the Repeal movement lay in Dublin. O'Connell's mass meetings made an uneven impact throughout the country, least of all in Ulster, and less effectively also in the west; Connaught's political awakening had to await the coming of the Land League in 1879, and the very Anglicization that Davis and his followers deplored.[38] The backbone of the Repeal Association was the politically aware middle class, mainly Roman Catholic, who stimulated and organized the movement; and this middle class was convinced that the British Government was hostile to the Catholic church and to the Irish people, to 'our religion, our race, and our name'. These people, seeking to make Catholic emancipation a reality, readily identified their concerns with 'national' issues. Even local Dublin politics were coloured in this way: the question of municipal reform and the corporation's agitation for increased powers drew comparisons with England where corporations, nationalists alleged, already possessed the powers that

Dublin now claimed.[39]

Nevertheless, a professional and articulate middle class, and one possessed of grievances, was material for political agitation, especially since they possessed a genuine pride in Irish historical traditions. But the desire of the Catholic middle classes for advancement, their sense of grievance and inferiority to their English counterparts, sprang as much from a desire to benefit from the British connection as to modify it. And this was exactly the kind of reasoning that led O'Connell to launch his repeal campaign in the first place. Few Irishmen were in official positions; government patronage was denied them; they suffered, they believed, from the disadvantages of second-class citizenship based on their nationality and religion; non-Irishmen were appointed to top Irish judicial positions.[40] Repeal, therefore, was mixed with a strong dash of what the Young Irelanders referred to disparagingly as 'place-hunting'.[41] O'Connell fully accepted this, for he was at bottom concerned with the well-being of the individual, not the rights of the group. Repeal was to O'Connell what separatism was to Tone: a means of advancing Irishmen in the modern world, of removing restraints on their natural abilities and aptitudes, especially the restraints imposed on Catholic Irishmen by their religion.

And herein lay the central problem for Davis and his followers: the kind of inequalities which existed in Ireland gave the lie to Davis's belief that a united, comprehensive Irish nationality could be constructed despite, and in opposition to, the forces that were shaping modern Ireland. It made no sense to maintain that such matters could be set aside, for this presupposed either that Irishmen were very different from Englishmen in their desires and needs (for better social status, jobs, opportunities), which was, to say the least, not proven; or that equality already existed between Catholic and Protestant in Ireland, that the 'common name of Irishman' applied in real social, economic and, perhaps most important, psychological terms. 'They're gone, they're gone, those Penal Days', declared Davis emphatically, 'all creeds are equal in our isle'.[42] But some creeds were more equal than others in early nineteenth century Ireland; as Sir Robert Peel, no friend of the repealers or Young Ireland, declared:

What is the advantage to the Roman Catholics of having removed their legal disabilities, if somehow or other they are constantly met by a preferable claim on the part of Protestants, and if they do not practically reap the advantage of their nominal equality as to civil privilege.[43]

The truth was that Peel, who was perhaps the most hated politician among O'Connell's supporters, understood the aspirations of Catholic Irishmen more profoundly than any Young Irelander: and to most repealers in the 1840s their struggle was essentially one to achieve for Irish Catholics their proper place for themselves and their religion in a country in which they were the majority, and in which they were making good their right to be regarded as the Irish people.

Davis was, in a sense, asking Irish society to stand still, perhaps even to go into reverse, and retreat from modernization and 'Anglicanism'. While O'Connell was perfectly capable of calling on Irish history as evidence for the prosecution, as proof that Irishmen were brave, noble creatures whose rights had been filched from them by settlers and Englishmen, he stood firmly in the modern world, and was concerned with the present, not the past. But Davis wished to recapture the past, and, moreover, to reformulate it in his own image. This meant making light of religious and political differences amongst Irishmen; and religion was to Davis entirely a matter of private conscience. But to middle-class Dublin repealers the interests of their church and of their country coincided; and it is difficult to see how matters could have otherwise stood. The religious divisions of Ireland were not primarily rooted in clashes of private religious belief (though anti-Catholicism and anti-Protestantism for their own sake were certainly to be found), but in the results of the political/religious divisions of Ireland's past which had left Protestants, a minority in Ireland, with a firm and apparently unyielding grip on the management of the country, and with a decided sense of superiority. O'Connell and his supporters had a lively sense of Irish history; but it was not the kind of history that Davis sought to teach them.[44]

The repeal reading rooms were, to Davis, a means of creating a national public opinion that would work as much to the advantage of Protestants as Catholics; by fostering a non-sectarian and secular public they would guarantee Ireland against a 'Browne and McHale government'.[45] Such a public would stand as a model of comprehensive nationalism that Davis hoped would triumph in Ireland; but it also stood for something much deeper, something that Davis would never have admittedly publicly, and scarcely dared admit privately: a barrier against a Roman Catholic ascendancy. For Davis feared the overthrow of Protestant leadership in Ireland, and believed, with the Presbyterian radical William Drennan, that while the Catholics may save themselves, it was the Protestants must save the nation.[46] Davis wanted the Protestants to play a major role in a repeal Ireland,

and he always kept alive the hope that he could win back the Protestants, more especially the Anglo-Irish gentry, to the national cause. His aristocratic Protestant colleague, William Smith O'Brien, was another who fervently sought to rally Protestants in the defence of Ireland's interests, and thereby their own.[47]

The views of these Young Irelanders were hardly likely to endear them to O'Connell and his Roman Catholic supporters. O'Connell was in sympathy with the idea of a comprehensive Irish nationality; but it was galling for him to listen to insinuations that, as he wrote to Davis, 'you and other Protestants were "pioneering" the way to power for men who would establish any sort of Catholic ascendancy'.[48] And Davis, for his part, showed a marked lack of insight into the Catholic mind when he dismissed anyone who stood for a separate Catholic educational system as a bigot. His views of education led to a direct clash with O'Connell and the Catholic hierarchy over the question of university education in 1845. The Government sought to provide university education in a way that would reconcile the Catholic conscience with the State endowment of a specifically Catholic denominational university. A sum of £100,000 was voted for the establishment of Queen's Colleges at Galway, Cork and Belfast, where no religious tests would apply, and where Chairs in theology would be endowed by private benefactors. Not all the Catholic hierarchy found this unacceptable; some believed that with additional safeguards on certain subjects the colleges should be given a trial. But Archbishop MacHale of Tuam would have nothing to do with the scheme; and O'Connell, though not so concerned about the issues involved, felt that he should give McHale his support, since McHale had played a vital part in the successful launching of the repeal movement after its slow start in 1840. McHale described the new colleges as 'a penal and revolting measure', and an attempt to 'bribe Catholic youths into an abandonment of their religion'. O'Connell's son, John, denounced the proposal as 'an abominable attempt to undermine religion and morality in Ireland'.[49]

Such Catholic fury was, of course, provoking to the Young Irelanders. Davis remonstrated with John O'Connell, warning him that 'in any country the principle of combined education of its youth be thought a good principle, but in Ireland, whose peculiar curse was relgious dissensions, that principle was invaluable'. Davis was prepared to consider reasonable safeguards for 'Catholic youths'; but at a meeting of the Repeal Association on 26 May 1845 Daniel O'Connell denounced Peel's University Bill, 'as a Catholic, and for the Catholics of

Ireland'. A bitter exchange followed. A Mr Conway declared that St. Paul was a Roman Catholic, or, at any rate 'no friend of masked infidelity, of mixed education'. Davis declared that he had 'not more than a few words to say in reply to the useful, judicious, and spiritual speech of my old college friend, my very Catholic friend, Mr. Conway', whereupon O'Connell intervened: 'it is no crime to be a Catholic I hope?' When Davis sought to correct that impression, O'Connell replied mercilessly that 'the sneer with which you used the word would lead to the inference'. Davis later speculated on the possibility that O'Connell had hoped to drive the advocates of non-sectarian education from the Repeal Association; but Davis's death in September 1845, and the genuine affection that he inspired among all sorts of repealers, softened the animosity between Young and 'old' Ireland.[50]

The Irish nationalist movement, however, was not divided into two rigid and mutually uncomprehending camps, Catholic and Protestant, Repealers and Young Irelanders. Young Ireland included Catholics among its founder members; and one Catholic supporter, Thomas MacNevin, approved of Protestant leadership of Catholic Ireland, referring to the example of Belgium, where a 'protestant administration was chosen freely by a Catholic people'.[51] Yet there was a certain counting of heads, an ever-present suspicion that political algebra could not be neglected even by the most well-meaning of men. O'Connell once jibed that Young Ireland could attract the support of only two priests;[52] and the fact that he would make such an observation was more important than its truth or falsehood. O'Connell welcomed the presence in his association of leading Protestants such as Henry Grattan Jnr, and when he was imprisoned in 1844 he approved of Smith O'Brien as his temporary replacement;[53] but the adherence of these token Protestants could not compensate for the bitter hostility of the bulk of the Protestant people of Ireland. The landlords, in particular, upon whom Young Ireland depended for the Protestant leadership of a Catholic country, had a longstanding grievance against O'Connellism, which, during the emancipation campaign, had challenged and beaten them on their own ground, and had shown that landlords would have to fight for their traditional role as guides of public opinion at election time.[54]

A rupture between Young Ireland and O'Connell might have been occasioned by their dispute over denominational education; and O'Connell's sympathy for a federal rearrangement of the United Kingdom in 1844 had brought the wrath of one of his young critics about his head, with Gavan Duffy warning that such a settlement must lead the Irish aristocracy 'still to turn their eyes to London as the scene of their ambition', and to follow 'English manners, feelings, and prejudices and establish a centre of action apart from their native country'.[55] In 1845 O'Connell was accused of betraying the memory of the Dungannon Clubs by allowing five Irish MPs to accept posts as junior ministers in a Whig government.[56] But the breach came, not over these differences, but on account of one of the least likely and, at the time, most abstract of political and moral questions: the principle of the use of force to achieve independence. Force was never further away from the Irish political scene than it was in 1846 when O'Connell made it a point of issue which must make or break his relationship with Young Ireland. When, in 1843, O'Connell called off his monster meeting at Clontarf under threat of government military action, the *Nation* remarked that 'the man who dares to adopt any policy not sanctioned by O'Connell will deserve the deepest execration'; nothing but 'evil to those they love, and ruin to themselves, will come of violence'. 'Organization, union and order', with 'peace, vigour and patience' were the watchwords of Young Ireland; and although the *Nation*'s poetry rang with battle cries and heroic deeds and affirmed that the 'soldier's life's the life for me/A Soldier's death, so Ireland's free' it generally added the rider that

Yet, 'tis not strength and 'tis not steel
Alone can make the English reel;
But wisdom, working day by day
Till comes the time for passion's sway

Wolfe Tone was held up for admiration, for 'a better ruler for Ireland never lived'; but in June 1844 a resolution in the Repeal Association that 'they seek success in the present struggle solely by moral and legal means and without the spilling of blood or the infliction of injury on any man' was proposed by Thomas MacNevin and seconded by Smith O'Brien.[57] In November 1845 John Mitchel, perhaps the most extreme nationalist in the Ireland of his day, and a lapsed Ulster Protestant Dissenter, wrote an article in the *Nation* concerning tactics for ambushing troops which could be promulgated to Repeal wardens; when O'Connell protested, Mitchel explained that there was 'no need, no pretext for concern': Ireland's regeneration could be achieved through moral force, and the tongue and the press. Only if there were any attempt to destroy these organs, to 'meet opinion with coercion', would there be call for 'such terrible methods of resistance'.[58]

It was this conditional clause concerning violence which the Young Irelanders always inserted in their pronouncements on the subject that O'Connell seized upon to discipline his over-enthusiastic supporters. In July 1846 he demanded an absolute and unqualified declaration from a Repeal Association meeting that no political objective justified the use of violence; repeal and the union could and ought to be attained by the same means that achieved Catholic emancipation. John Mitchel protested that he could not concur in the 'abstract and unsound principle that no political rights ought, at any time, or under any circumstances, or by any people, to be sought for with an armed sword'; but O'Connell must have an unequivocal answer; and he put obedience to his resolution 'both in theory and in practice' to the assembly, and had it carried with one dissentient, Thomas Francis Meagher.[59]

Here the subject, for the moment, rested; but Gavan Duffy composed a leading article in the *Nation* a few days later pointing out, shrewdly enough, that, while the *Nation*'s pronouncements on rebellion and resistance in Ireland's past tended 'remotely' to the end of Ireland's righting her wrongs 'in battle line', they went 'not one whit beyond what was spoken by the orators of the movement at Mullaghmast dinners, and in Lismore declarations, and Mallow defiances'. Repeal reading rooms and the library of Ireland, he went on, were hardly weapons of physical warfare; but he objected to the timing of the resolution on physical force. At present the possibilities of a deal with the Whig ministry raised the danger of 'treachery and corruption', and whereas no one thought that the Irish people were prepared to raise arms against a Whig ministry, still 'the policy of presenting ourselves to our old, relentless, hereditary enemy, bound hand and foot, by a renunciation for ever, under all circumstances, of the last resource of oppressed nations, does not seem politic or manly'. O'Connell's rejoinder was both prompt and final: 'The advocacy of physical force doctrine renders it impossible for those who stand upon the constitution of the Association itself to co-operate with those who will not adhere to the constitution. This is a subject that does not admit of any species of compromise'. Smith O'Brien retorted that the doctrine that in no circumstances could there be a resort to force for the attainment of political aims was one to which he could not submit, for how else was the constitution of 1782 won; he agreed that it would be madness to appeal to arms under present circumstances. But O'Connell would not allow the Young Irelanders that loophole: once admit that the use of force was justifiable in principle and the whole Repeal Association was in danger. To this John Mitchel replied that only the Protestants could save the nation, and since he was a Protestant, a 'Saxon Irishman from the north', then to drive out his kind by 'needless tests' could 'perpetuate the degradation both of yourselves and them'. Meagher, while also admitting that a resort to arms at present would be madness ('there might be a riot in the street, there would be no revolution in the country') insisted that, 'be it for the defence, or be it for the assertion, of a nation's liberty I look upon the sword as a sacred weapon'. At this John O'Connell insisted that Meagher quit the meeting; and the Young Irelanders as a whole did so.[60]

O'Connell's decision to make the use of force a proof of loyalty to his leadership was partly personal. It was hard for a man of his long years of unquestioned pre-eminence to put up with the critical or, worse still, patronising, commentary of the Young Irelanders upon his every word and deed; and his warning that 'I do not accept the services of any man who does not agree with me both in theory and in practice' has a disagreeable note of personal rule about it. But the friction between O'Connell and the young men whom he so brutally expelled in 1846 was not merely the result of a generational difference, or differences of opinion about religious education, co-operation with English ministers, or the morality of physical force. It was the product of a fundamental clash between two views, not only of nationalism, but of the nature of politics. O'Connell was a master of the art of wielding political power, and it was his object to use such power as he could to win concessions for his 'people of Ireland'; as he himself admitted, while he always desired Ireland's liberty, he desired also the 'preservation of her people'. 'We and others differ in theory from Mr O'Connell', declared the *Nation*, 'as to the relative value of national liberty and individual life. We think scarcely any amount of the latter equivalent to the former. Mr O'Connell thinks each priceless'.[61] The Young Irelanders knew nothing of the art of politics, despised the gains that could be won by tactical manouvering,[62] and above all, could not follow O'Connell's theory of political power to its logical conclusion: the conclusion that the Roman Catholics, as the Irish people and the majority, must in the last analysis make their will prevail, and their power felt in Ireland. The Irish nation of Young Ireland was at once more comprehensive and more abstract; it was more comprehensive because it was abstract. It was to be realized not by politics but by cultural regeneration; it was to find its salvation, not in a modern industrial state, but in those parts of Ireland which had remained, as Davis put it, 'faithful and romantic'.[63] The Young Irelanders, describing themselves rather improbably as 'of the plebian order',[64] looked to the 'lower classes' for the hope of the future; and the concept of the Irish peasant, who typified all that was best and noble in the Irish character, indeed all that was essentially Irish, was born.

It was born, paradoxically, at a time when the Irish peasant was about to disappear in large numbers from the face of Ireland. In the winter of 1846-7 the potato crop failed totally, after a partial failure in 1845. Between 1845 and 1851 at least 800,000 people (some 1/10 of the population) died from hunger and disease. Famine and destitution were by no means unknown in Ireland before the great famine; and even the scale of the great famine was not unique when seen in the context of contemporary European experience. But the famine of 1846-7 was important for the political as well as social history of Ireland, in that it reversed the trend of a disproportionate rise in the size of the agricultural labouring class, and set in motion a trend towards its swift and unchecked fall. Before the famine these landless or near-landless elements comprised some two-thirds of the population, and outnumbered the tenant and independent farmers by four to one; by 1900 farmers outnumbered labourers. The cottiers – a kind of 'penniless entrepreneurs' who rented the means of subsistence in the form of a cabin and a potato patch and paid for them by labour – had increased rapidly in number since 1815.

These people, in effect, gambled with the means of life, depending as they did on the quality of their patch of land. Before 1830 the odds against such a gamble proving successful were slightly against the cottiers; after 1830 they were lengthening all the time, partly because the cottier was obliged through competition to take his patch of land on less favourable terms, partly because the quality of the land was declining. When the famine obliterated the land as a means of subsistence, the cottier was doomed. The casual labourer who tried to live on a piece of land already cultivated, or who sought to use the purchasing power of his earnings, was another fast growing class after 1830 which, in the famine, was hardest hit. The size of the agricultural labouring class declined rapidly. Between 1845 and 1851 the number of labourers and cottiers fell by 40 per cent; during the following 60 years it again fell by about the same proportion.[65] The farmer was the largest and most influential class in post-famine Ireland; the real 'peasant' – the labourer and the cottier – suffered not only the harsh fate of the famine, but also the indignity of witnessing his very name, peasant, being appropriated by his pre-famine employers (and, often, enemies) the tenant farmers.[66]

This social and economic catastrophe was to have profound

consequences for Irish nationalism in the latter half of the nineteenth century; but its immediate political effects were no less significant. For it destroyed the political machine that O'Connell had built up since the 1820s. O'Connell had always experienced difficulties in holding toge- ther his electoral forces, and now the famine destroyed large sections of that already fragile and fragmented body of men who could be organi- zed to vote for repealers.[67] Moreover, starvation and panic among the peasants whom O'Connell had always been able to arouse with his magnificent oratory and his shameless flattery deprived repeal of any significance; and O'Connell's death in 1847, and the subsequent lack of political direction in the Association, left a vacuum in Irish political life. It was one that the Young Irelanders, now organized in their new Irish Confederation, were strongly tempted to try to fill. They had by no means been silent on the land question in Ireland, even though it was not one of their prime concerns, any more than it had been the concern of O'Connell.[68] In the very first issue of the *Nation* they had drawn attention to the curse of the 'unnatural monstrous combination of poverty and profusion', and declared that while a 'landed aristocracy' existed 'there is neither economy in Government, nor freedom or happiness in society'.[69] A year earlier Thomas Davis had argued that proprietorship was preferable to fixity of tenure for the farmer; Ireland should adopt the system of Norway (Udalism) and establish a society based on sturdy yeomen, possessing small estates; this, he concluded, was preferable to the manufacturing town with its 'sickly faces and vicious and despairing looks'.[70]

But the Young Irelanders were obsessed with the political rather than the economic consequences of land policies; and their concern with the ends (a sturdy nation of free men) contributed to their lack of clarity about the means by which Irish society was to be trans- formed. Davis did not specify how his proprietors were to be placed on the land: 'The adoption of any particular plan for Irish tenures we think mischievous, because premature': and he took refuge in the vague and paralysing statement that land tenure should not be post- poned until the question of nationality was resolved, but neither should the national question be postponed until the question of tenure was resolved.[71] And, despite the *Nation*'s strictures on the landed aristo- cracy, Davis and his colleagues still hoped for much from the Irish landlord, if only he could be persuaded to become 'national'. The *Nation* agreed that it would support a landed aristocracy if it were conducive to happiness: 'if it be good, − let them prove it; if not − it ought not to exist'.[72] Charles Gavan Duffy claimed that all classes, landlords included, had suffered in the famine and that therefore 'nationality will gain'.[73] James Fintan Lalor, the son of a prosperous Catholic farmer in Queen's county who had become associated with the Irish Confederation in 1847, also hoped that landlords would rise to the occasion, and urged that they be given the chance to show their national allegiance. New titles should be offered to those landlords who would recognize the 'right of the Irish people'. Lalor's chief concern was not with the landless labourer and the cottier, but with the farmer whom he feared was being depressed to the inferior status of labourer; and he called upon the landlords to lay the foundations of a new social order: 'a secure and independent agricultural peasantry'. Lalor's hopes for the landlord's resumption of their natural station as national leaders was shared by John Mitchel; if they accepted Lalor's terms they would become the 'most powerful and popular aristocracy on earth'.[74]

Lalor's hopes seemed possible of fulfilment in the early part of 1847 when the Irish landlords, politically adrift after Peel's repeal of the corn laws, and the break-up of the conservative party, were growing uneasy about the Government's response to the famine, and, in particular, its belief that Ireland herself should bear responsibility for famine relief. Irish landlords were themselves falling on hard times, and were increasingly debt-encumbered and beggared;[75] and a meeting of peers, gentry and MPs of all political parties held in Dublin in January 1847 called for a rapid change in Government policy towards Ireland. But this united front was not followed by any firm declaration of remedies that might be applied; and in May 1847 another meeting of landlords and MPs failed to proceed beyond hints about what might be done if men would only combine for the good of their country.[76]

The influence of Lalor's writings, the growing distress in the country, and disenchantment with orthodox politics, drove John Mitchel in the direction of linking agrarian with political revolution: and in October 1847 he called on tenants to withold all agricultural produce for their own consumption. In December he went further, appealing to Irish peasants to arm themselves in defiance of the Government. Gavan Duffy countered this by prohibiting Mitchel from using the pages of the *Nation* to call for insurrection, whereupon Mitchel resigned from the Confederation's policy committee, and urged immediate armed action: tenant right for the Irish farmer could be secured only by 'successful intimidation, that is to say, by the determined public spirit of armed men'. The country was 'actually in a state of war – a war of "property" against poverty – a war of "law" against life'. The *Nation* and the Confederation should instruct the people in military affairs, in the theory and practice of guerilla warfare.[77]

Mitchel's assertion that, since society itself was in a state of dis-solution, it 'cried aloud to be cut up by the roots and swept away'[78] was the subject of a debate in the Irish Confederation in February 1848, following resolutions moved by Smith O'Brien declaring that an Irish parliament was to be attained by 'the combination of classes and by the force of opinion exercised in constitutional operations'. Mitchel, like the Young Irelanders in the Repeal Association meeting of 1845, claimed that, while not advocating the use of force in Ireland's 'broken and divided condition', he could not rule it out absolutely; he would 'oppose to the last any scheme of policy that would now limit out speech and action within the bounds of laws and constitutions, about which Ireland knows only this – that they were invented to enslave, starve, and plunder her'. He was weary of constitutional agita-tion: instead of 'agitate, agitate' he would say to the people 'arm, arm!' At the same time he did not recommend 'leading out a starving peasantry to be mown down in the open fields by the regular troops'; but, even if he did, there were 'far worse things going on around us than bloodshed'. To adopt the resolutions moved by Smith O'Brien would seal the fate of the Confederation, and turn it into another of the 'mock-force agitating associations that have plagued Ireland for forty years'. Mitchel's views, while not as yet incompatible with O'Brien's, were too extreme for most of the members of the Confederation, and when they were rejected Mitchel, John Martin and Devin Reilly with-drew.[79] Mitchel now founded his own newspaper, the *United Irishman*, to propagate his beliefs, 'that legal and constitutional agitation in Ireland is a delusion; that every man (except a born slave, who aspires only to beget slaves and die a slave) ought to have arms and to promote their use of them. That no good can come from an English parlia-ment'.[80]

There was a metaphysical air about all these earnest young men debating the morality of physical force while engaging on no more war-like an enterprise than founding a newspaper; and matters might have remained in this inconclusive state but for the revolution in Paris which broke out three weeks after the debate on Smith O'Brien's resolutions. The exciting spectacle of liberals, socialists, republicans, middle and lower classes combining to overthrow Louis Philippe and establish a popular Government could not pass unnoticed by these enthusiastic reformers. With Europe in ferment, Ireland could not afford to be left behind: Repealers and Confederates met to greet the events in France in 1848, as their political ancestors had greeted the events of 1789; and

Mitchel and Meagher, inspired by the example of France, now, and for the first time among Young Irelanders, raised the cry for an Irish republic, and evoked memories of '98 and 1803. The Young Irelanders had hitherto declared themselves satisfied with the return of the Irish Parliament of 1782.[81] and in February 1848 Smith O'Brien declared in Westminster that, while he did not profess disloyalty to the Queen, he did deny the dominion of the parliament of England over Ireland.[82] But with the inspiration of France before his eyes, Mitchel denounced the previous political objectives of Young Ireland: all the 'clubs, cliques and committees' were 'tending . . . to one and the same illustrious goal — *not* a return to "our ancient constitution", not a golden link, or a patchwork parliament or a College Green chapel of ease to St. Stephen's — but an Irish republic, one and indivisible'.[83] Moreover, this revived republicanism was strongly coloured with social-revolutionary implications. 'The life of a labouring man', wrote Mitchel in the *United Irishman* in May 1848, 'is exactly equal to the life of one nobleman, neither more nor less'.[84] James Fintan Lalor announced that the aim was not to repeal the union, or restore '82; 'this is not the year '82, this is the year '48. For repeal I never went into "agitation" and will not go into insurrection'. Lalor wanted 'not the constitution that Wolfe Tone died to abolish, but the constitution that Tone died to obtain — independence; full and absolute independence for this island, and for every man within this island'. He called for 'Ireland her own — Ireland her own, and all therein, from the sod to the sky. The soil of Ireland for the people of Ireland, to have and hold from God alone who gave it'. 'Not to repeal the Union, then, but the Conquest', and thus 'to found a new nation and raise up a free people, and strong as well as free, . . . based on a peasantry rooted like rocks in the soil of the land'.[85] The land was owned by the conquering race, or by traitors to the conquered race; it was occupied by the native people or (for Lalor was a Davisite) by settlers who had mingled and merged. Man had a right to the ownership of private property; but no man could claim such rights in the soil, which was the 'free and common property of all mankind, of natural right, and by the grant of God'. Since all men were equal, no man had the right to appropriate exclusively to himself any part or portion thereof of the land, except with the common consent and agreement of all other men.[86]

Such ideas were anathema to Duffy, who feared social revolution and the pitting of class against class, and creed against creed. But events were compelling the Young Irelanders, almost despite themselves, to the use of armed force. The wave of enthusiasm for the 1848 French revolution, which provoked even John O'Connell into describing the events in Paris as 'the really sublime spectacle presented to the world',[87] occasioned a united nationalist front from which, though fragile, was sufficient to entice Mitchel back into the Confederation in March 1848, and to impart a seditious and revolutionary tone to the *Nation*. In April Duffy issued a manifesto stating that, while he hoped an independent Irish parliament with a responsible Irish ministry under the crown could be established peacefully, he would not refuse to lend his support to the establishment of a republic by force if the government did not heed his call.[88] Nevertheless, it is doubtful if the Young Irelanders would have responded to Lalor's question, 'who draws first blood for Ireland?'[89] had it not been for the fact that the Government took the Young Irelanders' threats more seriously than perhaps the Young Irelanders did themselves. Mitchel was arrested and transported on a charge of treason, Duffy, Meagher, Michael Doheny and D'Arcy Magee were also taken, habeas corpus suspended, and membership of the Confederate Club declared sufficient grounds for arrest. The remaining Confederate leaders felt that they had no choice but to strike at once and, led by Smith O'Brien, they made their revolutionary gesture in July 1848.

The revolution was little more than a gesture; it had arisen from an unforeseen set of circumstances, and nothing could be further from the truth than the idea that '48 was the . . . inevitable . . . outcome of '98'.[90] Moreover, the hope that a starving peasantry would rally behind a 'top hat' rebellion[91] was a delusion, especially since the Roman Catholic clergy were almost uniformly hostile to the desperate enterprise. The 1848 rebellion was only significant in the minds of those who made it, and of the small group of men who resolved that, while they must bide their time for the moment, an opportunity would come for another blow at the tyrant England. Some of the younger rebels, like James Stephens and John O'Mahony, settled in Paris where they found kindred spirits, and could devote their time and energy to plotting and planning, while the world went on its way. The nationalist movement that O'Connell had built up, painstakingly, and against the powerful forces of Irish localism and limited horizons, was swept away by the famine, and could not be revived by political romanticism. John Mitchel comforted himself in his *Jail Journal* with the cry 'give us war in our time, O Lord'; and he urged courage on 'all you that Jacobins be . . . stand upon your rights, and do your appointed work with all your strength'.[92]

The 'appointed work' was delayed for a decade however, as Irish political life turned on the axes of land and religious questions, and local political elements reasserted themselves more strongly than ever.[93] But the failures of the 1850s — the collapse of Charles Gavan Duffy's Tenant Right league, and of the Independent Irish party, the growing sectarianism in Irish politics, the opportunism and office-seeking of some leading politicians[94] — all offered new hope for the ideologues who were strengthened in their belief that nothing good could come out of constitutionalism. Moreover, they were inspired by the conviction that history was about to repeat itself, for Anglo-French tension in 1857 over the French decision to enlarge and modernize her navy seemed to herald a return to the great days of 1797 and 1798, when the 'French were on the sea', and Ireland might be free.[95] In 1858 James Stephens, encouraged by John O'Mahony, who had discovered a strong and embittered nationalism among the famine emigrants in New York, founded in Dublin the Fenian Brotherhood to break the connection with England, and thus avenge 'black forty-seven'.

The new secret and revolutionary society founded in Peter Langan's timberyard was modelled on European conspiratorial lines, with an elaborate structure designed to frustrate police penetration; but some of its founder members, at least, were influenced more by Irish than continental political ideas. John O'Leary called on England to cease governing Ireland, 'and then I shall swear to be true to Ireland and the Queen or King of Ireland, even though that Queen or King should also happen to be Queen or King of England'.[96] Charles J. Kickham, one of the most fervent anti-parliamentarian Fenians, would also have been willing to live under a constitutional monarchy in an Ireland separated from Britain.[97] The form of government to be established in this independent Ireland — apart from the fact of its independence — was, to say the least, shadowy; O'Leary was not certain, even at the end of the nineteenth century, whether the society's chosen title, the IRB, stood for republican or for revolutionary brotherhood.[98] But the Fenians had one principle in common: the conviction that the Irish people wanted separation and that the Fenians had the incontestable and inviolable right to get it for them by force of arms — whatever the Irish people might say or think. The Irish nation had the right to independence; it would choose this right if it were in full and proper possession of its faculties; any denial of this right was illegitimate and untenable: and the Fenians were therefore justified in forcing the Irish to be free, that is, in securing for the Irish people that political status that they would choose for themselves if they only knew where their own true and best interests lay.[99]

The Fenians were inspired by men who had served their nationalistic apprenticeship with Young Ireland, and had, many of them, turned out in 1848. Some retained their literary and creative tradition: John O'Mahony had an interest in the Gaelic past, and coined the name Fenians after the 'Fianna', a military force led by Fiona MacCuchail, a warrior of Celtic legend; John O'Donovan Rossa was the founder of a Phoenix Literary Society in 1856 which was incorporated into the Fenians in 1858; Charles J. Kickham, although not concerned with Gaelic culture, hoped to create a national regeneration through patriotic poetry, and wrote some influential novels of Irish rural life.[100] But the 'official' IRB line, as laid down in the newspaper founded by James Stephens, who was essentially a man of action, was that a free Ireland would not be achieved by 'amiable and enlightened young men', still fondly imagining that 'they are surely regenerating their country, when they are pushing about in drawing room society . . . creating an Irish national literature, schools of Irish art, and things of this sort'. Such people were 'dilettante patriots, perhaps the greatest fools of all'.[101] The IRB looked for deeds, not words: 'soon or never' was the watchword.[102] Still, even men burning with desire to liberate their country found it necessary to propagate their ideas and to lay some sort of foundation for a rebellion, or at least to plant the seed in the public mind; Stephen's decision to establish a newspaper bore witness to this. But whereas Thomas Davis had founded the *Nation* to create a nationally minded public opinion, Stephens founded the *Irish People* with a different purpose in mind: as P.S. O'Hegarty put it, the Fenians were 'not, in any sense, educating the people, they were telling them';[103] and the message was that Irishmen would fall in behind an independent Government, once established by the revolutionary élite.

Moreover, James Stephens, who carried his own principles to their logical conclusion by acting as the conscience and the indisputable leader of the organization, differed from Thomas Davis in that he had no time for the upper classes, the so-called natural leaders of the political community. It must be admitted that the reverse was also true, for the upper classes had no sympathy for Fenianism; but Stephens was convinced that the true heart of Irish nationalism beat in the breasts of the common people, the men of no property. The *Irish People* was not directed at the middle classes, the professions, the landlords, or the farmers (who, it alleged, grew 'loyal as they grew fat', caring 'nothing for home, or country, or mankind, so long as their own bellies were full').[104] Kickham singled out the graziers, 'those men of bullocks' as 'about the worst men in Ireland', who had 'no sympathy

for the people'.[105] Protestants, however, fared better; for here the IRB
was at one with Davis's teaching about non-sectarian nationalism.
Protestants were too numerous to be left in the ranks of the enemy;
and Catholics were reminded that they 'had not even the courage to
complain of their wrongs till Presbyterian Ulster roused them from
their despair'.[106]

Presbyterian Ulster was, however, unlikely to respond to Fenianism's
call to arms. In 1853 their historian, James Seaton Reid, contemplated
with satisfaction the fact that Presbyterians in several of the larger
towns in Ireland had 'greatly increased in wealth'. Recent legislation
had 'immensely strengthened the popular element in the constitution
of the country'; and, 'other things being equal', a Presbyterian was
'the favourite candidate with an Ulster constituency'. And, in various
parts of Ulster, as the 'old gentry of the country have disappeared,
Presbyterians, enriched by trade, have been rapidly filling up their
places, and, in some instances, prosperous Presbyterian merchants may
be seen occupying the baronial halls of the ancient aristocracy'.[107]
Reid's analysis pointed to the occasion, not far distant, when the
Presbyterian middle classes would emerge as the leaders of the formidable Ulster unionist movement. No Presbyterian revolutionary followed in the footsteps of John Mitchel; and the Fenian movement,
though it claimed continuity with the United Irish tradition, was
deprived of that Presbyterian element that gave the United Irishmen
their powerful foothold in the north.

The Fenians, like the United men, sought to make Irish nationalism
a non-sectarian and non-clerical ideology; but they also had to work
with the grain of the country; the testimony of Dr Keane, Bishop of
Cloyne, that the people were Fenians, not because they wanted to give
up their faith, but because they hated the Fenians' enemy, England,
the enemy of their country, their creed, and the Pope,[108] must be
treated with caution, but it was a more convincing explanation than
one which depicted a people suddenly converted to non-sectarian and
conspiratorial nationalism. The Fenians made their strongest inroads
in the cities, market towns and larger villages, where dwelt the Catholic
petite bourgeoisie and artisans: clerks, publicans, shopkeepers, workers
in the building trade, shoemakers, tailors. The anti-British sentiment of
these people also provided the initial strength of Parnellism in the
1880s and 1890s, and it was fertile ground for Fenian propaganda.[109]
In the country, the Fenians originally gathered support from the
labourers and cottiers.[110] For the Fenians, although they placed greater
emphasis on the winning of independence than on any specific social

and economic reforms, and declared that any remedy for bettering the condition of Ireland that fell short of independence 'commences work at the wrong end, puts the cart before the horse', also attacked the law that 'leaves the toiler at the mercy of the *master* or landlord'.[111] Ribbon lodges in Connaught, Cavan, Longford, and Westmeath were won over to the Fenian cause.[112] But such people were, since the famine, declining in numbers and importance, and their hostility to their 'masters', the farmers, was an obstacle to any kind of widespread 'national unity' that the Fenians sought. It was always easier in Irish nationalist politics to win support by playing off one section of Irish society against another: landlords against tenants, labourers against farmers, Catholics against Protestants. But nationalist politics and 'real nationalism' were often clean different things; and any group that sought to mobilize national support had to choose between the impotence of the Davisite tradition, or the power of the O'Connellite tradition, between the aspiration to unite all social classes in the cause, or the necessity to mobilize such of them that could form a solid, homogenous, dependable backbone to a nationalist movement.

It is to the Fenians' credit as nationalists that they sought to recruit from all classes and creeds; this also, of course, largely explains their failure. In 1856 Stephens fulminated against the 'hostility of the aristocracy, the apathy of the farmers, the pig-headedness of the bourgeoisie', but praised the sound opinions of labourers, tradesmen, and the sons of peasants.[113] In 1860-63, however, a severe agricultural depression caused a decline in tillage and livestock, and the consolidation of landholdings, and gave notice to the prospering farmers that they too could feel the pinch of hardship, even though their hardship was relatively small compared with that of their social inferiors.[114] It was for these people that the Fenian newspaper, the *Irish People*, taking its cue from the *Nation*, coined the phrase 'the land for the people', for 'the land is the property of the people'. Landlordism must stand down; a peasant proprietry must be established.[115] This Fenian advance into rural Ireland must not be exaggerated; most of the farming classes remained aloof; but between 1866 and 1871 the occupation of farmer appears among lists of Fenian suspects, along with the by now familiar categories of builders, drapery workers, clerks, shopkeepers, and labourers.[116] And to this miscellaneous set of people was added soldiers, for the Fenians, in their preparation for an armed uprising, made a strong set at recruiting from the many thousands of Catholic Irishmen serving in the British army,[117] men who were already trained in the use of musket and sword. Here again, a sense of grievance and a sense of nationality

were complementary: as one Fenian recruit expressed it, 'I am an Irishman and a Fenian and will kick any . . . Scotch soldier'; 'I will fight for
Ireland, the . . . Queen is not able to support soldiers'. '. . . the service',
declared another, 'I wish the Fenians would come in and take the
barracks, I will help them, and would help them to cut every throat in
it'.[118]

Social utopia and national independence; a nation in which Catholic
and Protestant would live at one with each other; secret societies and
armed rebellion; some, at least, of these were a recipe for a clash with
the Roman Catholic church, the church whose support had proved so
invaluable to O'Connell, the church whose head, Cardinal Paul Cullen,
stated in 1864 that 'it is our duty and our interest . . . to walk in the
footsteps of the great liberator'. Cullen was a nationalist, profoundly
dissatisfied with the condition of Ireland under the rule of that 'wicked
empire', Britain, and like O'Connell, an exponent of the view that the
Irish past between the reformation and Catholic emancipation was one
of unrelieved tragedy. But whereas O'Connell had worked, wrong-
headedly but earnestly, for Ulster Protestant support, Cullen had no
time for such people: they were not Irishmen at all, they were invaders
and interlopers still, 'having received from a pedant and a bigot a great
portion of six counties unjustly confiscated from the owners'. And,
while the Fenians preached rebellion and force, Cullen condemned
such methods utterly; they would bring 'ruin and desolation' on the
people, and priests must work against men who sought to win over
simple people to political violence.[119]

The controversy between the Fenians and the Catholic church is
often regarded as one of the most significant and novel aspects of the
revolutionary tradition, linking it with Young Ireland and its similar
conflict over denominational education in 1845; and, certainly, from
the beginning, most clergymen had opposed Fenianism out of concern
for their flock, and fear of its involvement in an oath-bound society,
especially when that society involved itself in organizing the pastimes
and recreations of local young people.[120] The *Irish People* held its
tongue until clerical denunciation obliged it to answer back; but when
it did it was constrained by the loyal and orthodox Catholicism of the
rank and file; and although some members of the Brotherhood, James
Stephens, John O'Leary and T.C. Luby were influenced by continental anti-clericalism,[121] they were all men of secular background to
whom such an attitude provoked no conflict between religion and
nationalism. The man Stephens chose to answer clerical criticism –
Kickham – was a Catholic; but he was no anti-clerical. Indeed,

Kickham rejoiced in the fact that Ireland was 'as Catholic as ever', and denied that he would ever give up the old faith 'even for liberty'. Like most Irish nationalists of whatever shade or persuasion, Kickham could not conceive of any real or enduring conflict between his religion and his nationalism.[122] The problem in the 1860s was that the Catholic church − or at least its head, Cullen − was breaking the conventions of Irish politics by trying to act, not as auxiliary to nationalists, nor as guide to the people, but as driver and commander. In 1864 Cullen entered directly into politics when he helped the National Association of Ireland to campaign for disestablishment of the Church of Ireland, denominational education, and land reform. The party, tainted with 'Whiggery', failed to gather any wide support;[123] and this made the point that it was Cullen, not the IRB, who was the innovator. When the *Irish People*, through the pen of Kickham, declared that people were becoming better educated, and that they sought only the right possessed by people in other Catholic countries of 'acting according to the dictates of their own judgement in all wordly concerns', they were not initiating any startlingly new doctrine, but stating bluntly what was always assumed by Irish politicians from O'Connell onwards: that the priest had his well-defined role to play in politics, that he was an indispensable element of the nationalist movement, but that he was not the man to lay down the direction in which political development must go.[124] That was the job of the lay political leaders. The Fenians were at pains to point out that 'Catholic members of the Fenian Brotherhood are sincerely attached to their church'; and they acknowledge acceptance of Catholic doctrine on rebellion: that it could only be justifiable if tyranny were intolerable, and if rebellion had a real opportunity of success. The Fenians claimed simply that the tyranny was intolerable, and that they could succeed; Ireland had the same right to the protection of Catholic principles for her sons in their battle of right against might as had the Poles.[125]

There was therefore a vital difference between the earlier Young Ireland conflict with the Church, and the Fenian controversy of 1863-5. For Davis, in pressing for non-denominational education, was interfering in a field of social life where the Catholic church had an acknowledged right to make its voice heard, and, not only that, but to give a positive lead to the people and the politicians. No-one − except perhaps a Protestant of Davis's views − could deny that, or would deny it. But in the 1860s the Church was over-stepping the normal bounds by claiming the right to give people and politicians a political lead; that no nationalist leader could allow. Hence the conflict between the

Fenians and the Church was not one about anti-clericalism, for, as Kickham remarked, 'the charge that we are enemies of the Catholic Church is a vile calumny invented by trading politicians'.[126] It was provoked by Cullen's political adventures, and by the Fenians' own failure to enlist enough support among Irish Roman Catholics to enable them to ignore clerical assaults. Once the church recovered its sanity and its balance, its place in Irish political life could be resumed.[127]

Anyway, not all ecclesiastics shared Cullen's hatred of Fenians, a hatred based on his misconceived view that Fenianism was a manifestation of the anti-religious spirit of the European revolutionary sentiment exemplified in the Young Ireland movement, Mazzini and Garibaldi. Doubting the faith and accepting Godless colleges, he alleged, would fill Ireland with Fenians.[128] But there were priests, and bishops, who detested doubters of the faith and Godless colleges as much as Cullen did, but who did not lump them all together under the heading of Fenianism. Many of the clergy sympathized with Fenian objectives; many disliked British rule as heartily as the Fenians disliked it;[129] and one Patrick Lavelle, former professor in the Irish College in Paris, and then parish priest in Partry, lectured in February 1862 on the theme that the misgovernment of Ireland justified the right of rebellion. This was an extreme and atypical position; but a number of the bishops began to believe that the church should slacken its denunciations of the Fenians and adopt a more discreet line, at least until the movement should falter.[130]

Fenianism's place in the complicated pattern of Irish nationalism that developed between 1842 and the 1860s cannot be understood if nationalism is placed within a rigid, compartmentalized structure of 'constitutional' and 'revolutionary' modes. Fenians preached physical force methods, it was true; but armed rebellion, given their incompetent leadership, doubtful support, clerical hostility to violence, and the alert and active British Government reaction once the danger was appreciated, rendered success unlikely. When the Fenian blow was struck, in March 1867,[131] it proved to be as farcical, though more costly in human lives, than the Young Ireland affair of 1848. But this very failure, like that of the Young Irelanders, was important, in that it gave a clear and unmistakable demonstration of the futility of physical force methods in the circumstances of Britain's hold on Ireland, and the military force which she had the will and the means to deploy in support of that hold. Having failed in 1848 and 1867, and having bloodily failed in 1798, physical force patriots could be admired, but not emulated except as a last resort; and whereas O'Connell was too close in time to the men of '98 to revere their memory, contenting himself with references to the defenders of Limerick and (better still) Brian Boru, the parliamentarians of the late nineteenth century could profess their admiration of the '98 rebels, who were safely consigned to the more distant past, and of the '48 and '67 rebels, who were close in time but whose rebellions were so manifestly and ludicrously failures that any attempt to repeat them seemed, in the circumstances, out of the question. Violence did not die out in Ireland after the Fenian uprising; but it was agrarian violence in the countryside, and sectarian violence in Belfast, that appeared sporadically in late nineteenth century Irish politics, not the revolutionary political violence of the Young Irelanders and the Fenians.

One of the Fenians' greatest propaganda successes, the funeral of Terence Bellew McManus, a rebel of 1848 who died in New York, and whose procession in November 1861 attracted a turn out of thousands in Cork and Dublin, revealed their paradoxical contribution to Irish nationalism. T.C. Luby at the graveside affirmed the Fenian hope that McManus's example gave 'us faith and stern resolve to do the work for which McManus died';[132] but the Irish constabulary put the matter in a different perspective when it noted that the procession and ceremony was little more than a pious gesture to the man of '48.[133] The true significance of the episode lay somewhere between these two extremes. Such a procession would have been unthinkable and impossible 10 years earlier, and in this respect Fenian delight was justified; but to turn out for a dead hero's funeral did not mean that 8,000 people were on the point of following his example. It was easier to admire men, not for what they did, but for what they failed to do. Had they come near to achieving a non-sectarian, socially levelling Ireland the Fenians would have found themselves arrayed against the mass of the Irish people, the church, and Irish political representatives.

The chief significance of Fenianism was its contribution to the 're-nationalisation' of Ireland, or of parts of Ireland, after the collapse of nationalist politics in the great famine. The Fenians' commitment to the national cause, their hard work, their assiduous propaganda, made fewer converts than they liked to claim; but they helped direct Irish politics back into an 'England versus Ireland' framework; and this process was assisted by the British Government, which showed itself as deficient in understanding Irish public opinion as it was efficient in organizing state security. In September 1867 a Fenian rescue attempt in Manchester resulted in the shooting of a policeman; and the Fenians involved, Allen, Larkin and O'Brien, were tried, condemned to death, and publicly hanged for the murder. The defiant mood and noble bearing of the prisoners at their trial,[134] the brutal circumstances of their execution,[135] and, above all, the uncharacteristically severe response of the British, aroused public opinion in Ireland in a way that the Young Ireland and Fenian calls for rebellion had never done. As John O'Leary remarked, sardonically, it was:

> clear as the sun at noonday that the heart of the country always goes out to the man who lives and dies an unrepentant rebel. The rebel can reckon upon nothing in life; he is sure to be calumnated; he is likely to be robbed, and may even be murdered, but let him once go out of life, and he is sure of a fine funeral.[136]

Thus it was that A.M. Sullivan, editor of the *Nation*, who had turned that newspaper into an organ of constitutional nationalism, and was a man hated by the Fenians,[137] published some verses written by his brother T.D. Sullivan which under the title 'God save Ireland' became a national anthem; and 23 November became a day of annual commemoration for the Manchester martyrs, and one celebrated as much by parliamentarians as by conspirators.[138]

It might seem that the constitutionalists found the revolutionaries hanging, and made off with their clothes; at least, this is how it must have appeared to the IRB. But in fact it was perfectly possible for a constitutional nationalist to feel an instinctive response to such tragedies and to be sensitive to their impact on public opinion; and it was because they were moved by them that the constitutionalists sought to exercise their power to prevent their repetition. The making of the Manchester martyrs helped the assimilation of constitutional and revolutionary nationalism in another important aspect, for it assisted reconciliation between the church and Fenianism; as the *Dublin Review* remarked, Catholic clerical sympathy for the Manchester martyrs was 'a kind of posthumous sympathy, limited to such objects as the saying of masses for the souls of executed Fenians'. Nevertheless, it went on perceptively, 'it makes a difference . . . between the Fenian Society and the Italian Carbonari'.[139]

This it did; high masses were said for the repose of the martyrs' souls; and Cullen, although he maintained a discreet silence on the matter, privately spoke of the responsible English statesmen as 'that brood of vipers' who encouraged Garibaldi's invasion of the papal states while condemning the martyrs to death. Cullen drew the line at high masses, which he feared were being turned into public demonstrations to serve the Fenian cause, but he agreed that it was right to pray for the martyrs' souls and to say mass privately for them. Archbishop McHale of Tuam donated portraits of himself to the Fenian fair in Chicago, and assisted at high mass for the martyrs. Sympathy began to extend to the other Fenian prisoners in English jails, and an amnesty movement launched in November 1868 by Isaac Butt, a Protestant lawyer who had defended Fenians at their trials, quickly gathered momentum, and clerical support. Subscriptions were collected, and after the release of some forty-nine prisoners the amnesty committee decided to hold a nation-wide church door collection on St. Patrick's day. Cullen would not sanction this 'chapel-door' collection since it implied approval of Fenian objectives; but the amnesty movement continued its work, and received more clerical support when Dean O'Brien of Limerick drew a distinction between sympathy for amnesty and approval of violence, and gained 1,400 signatories from the clergy for a declaration that amnesty was a measure that might be recommended to the Government.[140]

A formal condemnation of Fenianism by name, made by the Vatican in 1870, probably at the instigation of the British Government rather than that of Cullen and his bishops,[141] could not disguise the fact that the Manchester martyrs and the activities of the amnesty association had 'fairly baptised'[142] Fenianism. After 1870 the church allowed its relations with Fenians to settle down, and under the leadership of Archbishop Walsh of Dublin it steered a more prudent, less abrasive, course.[143] Fenianism itself was symbolized by the Manchester martyrs, not by the anti-clerical Stephens; and the 'faith of a felon' was undoubtedly the Catholic faith, as the Fenians themselves had perhaps admitted when their recruiting agents among the Irishmen in the British army began by asking a likely man whether he was Irish and a Catholic.[144]

Moreover, Fenianism after 1867 itself began to change. The arbitrary dictatorship of Stephens had been discredited by his failure to create a successful, or even credible, rebellion in 1867, and a new body, the supreme council, was formed in February 1868 claiming to represent the Irish Republican Brotherhood. The prisoners released in March 1869 threw their support behind the council, rejecting Stephens as the sole 'Fenian chief'. This 'new Fenianism' was not doctrinally opposed to some participation in Parliamentary methods as Stephens's Fenianism had been; and the amnesty association campaign had helped to raise the nationalist temper of the country, and draw voters away from the localized politics of the 1850s: for, while the Fenians had not succeeded in raising armed rebels, they had succeeded in raising committed voters. In Tipperary in November 1869 the Fenian prisoner, O'Donovan Rossa, defeated a Catholic liberal, Heron, by 1,131 votes to 1,028. The poll was low; but the nature of the turnout was significant, for it saw the comfortable farmers at last lining up in the nationalist cause.[145] And not all local priests were hostile to the candidature of a Fenian. The reverend John Hacket made an 'exciting speech off the altar before he concluded mass' at Lisvernane, declaring that Rossa was:

> compelled to eat his food like a dog for no crime, that the prisoners might have committed an error, but they committed no crime, that it was the duty of every man to lose the last drop of his blood for his country . . . The priests did not side with the people on the last occasion (i.e. the 1867 rebellion), and they were right, because there was no chance of success . . .

He then compared O'Connell to Rossa 'in delivering the people from bondage, and W.E. Gladstone to Joshua, and prayed that W.E. Gladstone the leader of the people, like Joshua of the Israelites would lead them to liberty'.[146] It was an unlikely comparison, and one of which O'Connell and Rossa alike would have disapproved, but it pointed the way to the reconciliation of constitutional and physical force nationalism that lasted until the fall of Parnell.

The temptation to become involved in constitutional politics was increased after the foundation of the Home Government Association by Isaac Butt in 1870 which soon revealed that its aims of limited self-government were not unattractive to the bulk of the nationalist voters. As far as some Fenians were concerned, home government was preferable to the Gladstonian liberalism which had dominated the politics of Ireland in 1868. Butt's cultivation of the extreme men was made easier for him and more difficult of their refusal, by his record in the amnesty association; and at a meeting on 19 May 1870 in Bilton's Hotel, Dublin, to inaugurate the home government association, two members of the supreme council of the IRB promised that they would not obstruct his experiment.[147] It was the modest but significant beginning to a development that would, within a few years, see IRB men sitting as home rulers in the British House of Commons. Thus were created two hybrid political ideologies, more powerful when working together than they could ever have been apart: for the obverse of constitutional Fenianism was militant constitutionalism.

Notes

1. E. Norman, *History of Modern Ireland, p. 65.*
2. J.A. Price, 'Thomas Davis', in J. Voronwy Morgan (ed.), *Welsh Political and Educational Leaders in the Victorian Era* (London, 1908), pp. 353-72.
3. T. Davis, *Prose Writings* (London, n.d. (1890)), p. 3.
4. O. MacDonagh, *Ireland: the Union and its Aftermath* (London, 1977), p. 152. Davis was a child of the German (and English) romantic movements rather than the French; see W.R. Fryer, 'Romantic literature and the European age of revolutions', *Renaissance and Modern Studies*, vol. *8* (1964), pp. 53-74.
5. Sir C. Gavan Duffy, *Young Ireland: a Fragment of Irish History, 1840-45*, (Dublin, 1884 edn), pp. 110-11.
6. A. Griffith, *Thomas Davis, the Thinker and Teacher* (Dublin, 1918), pp. 82, 145, 147, 170.
7. J.S. Kelly, 'Political, intellectual and social background to the Irish literary revival to 1901', University of Cambridge D. Phil. (1971), p. 27.
8. Griffith, *Davis*, pp. 54-5, 81.
9. Ibid., p. 46.
10. T.W. Rolleston (ed.), *Thomas Davis: Selections from his Prose and Poetry* (London, 1914), p. 307.
11. Griffith, op. cit., p. 56.
12. Rolleston, op. cit., p. 46.
13. Davis, *Prose Writings*, p. 116.
14. Ibid., pp. 280-81.
15. Kelly, op. cit., p. 29, fn. 1.
16. R. Dudley Edwards, 'The contribution of Young Ireland to the development of the Irish national idea', in S. Pender (ed.), *Essays and Studies Presented to Tadgh O Donnachadha* (Cork, 1947), p. 125.
17. M. Brown, *The Politics of Irish Literature: from Thomas Davis to W.B. Yeats* (London, 1972), p. 68. See also M. Bourke, *John O'Leary: a Study in Irish Separatism* (Tralee, 1967), pp. 15-16.
18. R. Dudley Edwards, op. cit., p. 120.
19. Ibid., p. 130.
20. C. Gavan Duffy, op. cit., pp. 17-18.
21. *Nation*, 15 Oct. 1842.
22. O Tuathaigh, *Ireland Before the Famine*, p. 188.
23. Brown, op. cit., p. 67.
24. Davis, *Prose Writings*, p. 208.
25. O. MacDonagh, 'Irish famine emigration', pp. 379-80.
26. Ibid., pp. 380-82; Kelly, op. cit., pp. 9-10.
27. Davis, *Prose Works*, p. 208.
28. Ibid., pp. 209-11.
29. J.R. Hill, 'The role of Dublin in the national movement', University of Leeds, Ph.D (1973), p. 13.
30. Davis, *Prose Works*, pp. 212-15.
31. Ibid, pp. 224-6.
32. G. Duffy, *Young Ireland*, pp. 242-44, and notes to Chap. VI; Kelly, op. cit., pp. 18-21.
33. Gavan Duffy, op. cit., p. 104; T.F. O'Sullivan, *The Young Irelanders* (Tralee, 1944), pp. 71-2.
34. Kelly, op. cit., p. 22; A. Griffiths, *Davis*, pp. 30-47.
35. Griffith, op. cit., pp. 38-41; C. Barrett, 'Irish nationalism and art', *Studies*, vol. LXIV (1975), pp. 404-6.
36. Gavan Duffy, op. cit., p. 207.

37. Brown, op. cit., p. 67.

38. K.T. Hoppen 'Landlords, society and electoral politics in mid-nineteenth century Ireland', *P and P*, no. 75 (May 1977), p. 65.

39. J.R. Hill, op. cit., pp. 20ff.

40. Ibid., pp. 26. 48-9, 60, 62.

41. Ibid., pp. 62-5; R. Dunlop, *Daniel O'Connell and the Revival of National Life in Ireland* (London, 1900), p. 343.

42. Rolleston, *Davis*, p. 319.

43. K.B. Nowlan, *The Politics of Repeal* (London, 1965), pp. 14-15.

44. J. Hill, 'Nationalism and the Catholic church in the 1840s: views of Dublin repealers', *Irish Historical Studies*, XXI, no. 76, (Sept. 1975), pp. 371-95.

45. Hill, 'The role of Dublin', p. 162.

46. Beckett, *Anglo-Irish tradition*, p. 153.

47. Hill, 'Role of Dublin', pp. 213, 218.

48. Gavan Duffy, *Young Ireland*, pp. 235-6.

49. Lecky, *Leaders of Public Opinion in Ireland*, vol. *II*, pp. 281-4.

50. Gavan Duffy, op. cit., pp. 250-60; MacDowell, *Public Opinion and Government Policy in Ireland*, pp. 243ff.

51. Hill, 'Role of Dublin', pp. 213-4.

52. M. Buckley, 'John Mitchel, Ulster and Irish nationality' in *Studies*, vol. *65* (1970), pp. 30-31.

53. Denis Gwynn, 'Smith O'Brien and Young Ireland', in *Studies*, vol. *XXXVI* (1947), pp. 29-39.

54. M. Murphy, 'Repeal, popular politics, and the Catholic clergy of Cork', *JCHAS*, vol. *LXXXII* (1977) pp. 39-40; Hill, 'Role of Dublin', p. 218.

55. Lecky, op. cit., pp. 275-8; Gavan Duffy, op. cit., pp. 212-15. But not all Young Irelanders shared Duffy's misgivings: see Kee, op. cit., p. 214.

56. P.S. O'Hegarty, op. cit., pp. 230-31.

57. Ibid., pp. 114, 165, 172, 187; Rolleston, *Davis*, pp. 350-52; *Nation*, 22 Oct. 1842; C.G. Duffy, *The creed of the 'Nation'* (Dublin, 1848), pp. 5, 7.

58. O'Hegarty, op. cit., pp. 226-7.

59. Ibid., pp. 243-5.

60. Ibid., pp. 245-57; M.R. O'Connell, 'O'Connell, Young Ireland and violence', in *Thought*, vol. *52*, no. 207 (Dec. 1977), pp. 381-406.

61. O'Hegarty, p. 238.

62. For Mitchel's views on this see D.W. Leonard, 'John Mitchel, Charles Gavan Duffy and the legacy of Young Ireland', University of Sheffield Ph.D. (1975), pp. 13-14.

63. Gavan Duffy, op. cit., pp. 110-11.

64. *Nation*, 15 Oct. 1842.

65. MacDonagh, 'Irish famine emigration', op. cit., pp. 358-62; L.M. Cullen, *An economic history of Ireland since 1660* (London, 1972), pp. 117, 130-33.

66. J. Lee, 'The Ribbonmen' (Williams (ed.) *Irish secret societies*, pp. 34-5) discusses the 'quirk of semantic alchemy' which transformed the meaning of the word 'peasant' in nineteenth century Ireland.

67. Hoppen, 'Politics, the law, and the nature of the Irish electorate', op. cit., pp. 754-55.

68. For O'Connell's brief remarks on the land question see Kee, op. cit., p. 244.

69. *Nation*, 15 Oct. 1842.

70. Davis, *Prose Writings* (1890 edn.), pp. 54, 62, 72; T.P. O'Neill, 'The Irish land question, 1830-1850', in *Studies*, vol. XLIV (1955), p. 330; Kelly, op. cit., p. 26.

71. Davis, *Prose Writings*, pp. 63, 74-5.

72. *Nation*, 15 Oct. 1842.
73. Leonard, op. cit., p. 35.
74. N. Marlowe (ed.), *James Fintan Lalor: collected writings* (Dublin, 1918), pp. vi-vii, 7-42.
75. MacDonagh, op. cit., p. 363.
76. R.D. Edwards and T.D. Williams (eds.) *The great famine* (Dublin, 1956), pp. 172-3.
77. P.S. O'Hegarty, op. cit., pp. 342-3.
78. J. Mitchel, *The last conquest of Ireland (perhaps)*, (London n.d. first published Dublin, 1861), p. 153.
79. O'Hegarty, op. cit., pp. 344-48.
80. *United Irishman*, 12 Feb. 1848.
81. K.B. Nowlan, 'The meaning of repeal in Irish history', *Historical Studies*, IV (London, 1963), pp. 8-9.
82. R.D. Edwards, 'The contribution of Young Ireland to the national idea', op. cit., p. 133.
83. Mitchel, *Last Conquest*, p. 180.
84. *United Irishman*, 20 May 1848.
85. Marlowe, op. cit., pp. 48-62.
86. Ibid., pp. 84-98.
87. R.D. Edwards, in Edwards and Williams, op. cit., p. 190.
88. O'Hegarty, op. cit., pp. 366-7; Edwards and Williams, op. cit., p. 195.
89. Marlowe, op. cit., pp. 99-104.
90. T.W. Moody (ed.) *The Fenian Movement* (Cork, 1968), p. 102.
91; The phrase is R.D. Edwards's: 'Young Ireland and National idea', op. cit., p. 133.
92. John Mitchel, *Jail Journal* (London, n.d. (1854?)), pp. 98, 315.
93. T.K. Hoppen, 'Landlords, Society and electoral politics in mid-19th century Ireland', *Past and Present*, no. 75 (May 1977), pp. 62-93.
94. For a discussion of the significance of this decade in Irish nationalist politics see below, Chap. 7, p. 200.
95. R.V. Comerford, 'Anglo-French tension and the origins of Fenianism', in F.S.L. Lyons and R.A.J. Hawkins, op. cit., pp. 149-71.
96. John O'Leary, *Recollections of Fenians and Fenianism* (Irish University Press, 1968; first edition, London, 1896), p. 27.
97. R.V. Comerford, *Charles J. Kickham (1828-82); a Study in Irish Nationalism and Literature* (Dublin, 1979), p. 185.
98. T.W. Moody (ed.) *The Fenian Movement* (Cork, 1968), p. 105.
99. Kee, op. cit., pp. 304-7.
100. For Kickham see Comerford, op. cit., passim, esp. pp. 45-6 and Chap. 11. Kee, op. cit., pp. 300, 310.
101. *Irish People*, 19 Dec. 1863.
102. O'Hegarty, op. cit., p. 429-30.
103. Ibid., p. 432.
104. *Irish People*, 28 Nov. 1863, 12 Dec. 1863; 2 Jan. 1864; O'Hegarty, op cit., pp. 432, 435, 438; O'Leary, op. cit., pp. 30-32, 131, 238-9.
105. O'Leary, op. cit., pp. 43-4.
106. *Irish People*, 16 April 1864, 30 April 1864; Desmond Ryan, 'John O'Mahony', in T. Moody, op. cit., pp. 63-75; O'Leary, op. cit., pp. 202-3.
107. Reid, op. cit., pp. 516, 521-22, 589, 591-2.
108. P.J. Corish, 'Cardinal Cullen and the national association of Ireland', in *Reportorium Novum*, vol. *III*, No. i (1962), p. 17.
109. C.J. Woods, 'The general election of 1892: the Catholic clergy and the defeat of the Parnellites', in Lyons and Hawkins, op. cit., pp. 316-17.

110. K. Theodore Hoppen, 'National politics and local realities in mid-nine-teenth century Ireland' in Cosgrave and McCartney, op. cit., pp. 214-16.

111. *Irish People*, 28 Nov., 12 Dec. 1863 (my italics).

112. P. Bew, *Land and the national question* (Dublin, 1978), pp. 41-2.

113. Hoppen, op. cit., p. 216.

114. Bew op. cit., pp. 39-40; James S. Donnelly Jr., 'The Irish agricultural depression of 1859-64', in *Irish Economic and Social history*, vol. *III* (1976), pp. 33-54; Donnelly, however, discounts any connection between the depression and Fenianism.

115. *Irish people*, 30 July 1864; cf *Nation*, 24 Dec. 1842.

116. SPOI, Irish Crimes Record; Fenianism, Index of names, 1866-71 (VIIIB, W.P. 3/6, 7). See also J. O'Donovan Rossa, *Recollections* (New York, 1898), p. 200.

117. John Devoy estimated that some 80,000 men thus canvassed joined the IRB, of whom some 15,000 were soldiers: this latter figure is an exaggeration. For a scholarly appraisal of Fenian recruitment in the British army see A.J. Semple, 'Fenian infiltration of the British army in Ireland,1864-7', University of Dublin, M.Litt, (1974), especially, pp. 82-3, 161-8.

118. Ibid., pp. 185, 187; see also D. Ryan, *The phoenix flame* (London, 1937), p. 91.

119. E.D. Steele, 'Cardinal Cullen and Irish nationality', in *IHS*, vol. *xix*, No. 75 (March, 1975), pp. 239-60.

120. Comerford, op. cit., pp. 68-9.

121. Ibid., p. 73.

122. Ibid., pp. 69-74; see also T.F. O'Sullivan (ed.) *M. Ryan: Fenian Memories* (Dublin, 1945), pp. xiv, xxiii.

123. P. O'Farrell, *Ireland's English question*, pp. 95-6; E.R. Norman, *The Catholic Church and Ireland in the age of rebellion, 1859-73* (London, 1965), Chap. 4.

124. *Irish People*, 16, 24 Sept. 1864.

125. *Irish People*, 19 March 1864, 9 April 1864, 14 May 1864, 4 June 1864; see also Hegarty, op. cit., pp. 438-43.

126. O'Leary, op. cit., p. 200.

127. Comerford, op. cit., p. 74.

128. P. MacSuibhne, *Paul Cullen and his contemporaries*, vol. *I* (Naas, 1961), pp. 382-3, 386-7, 390, 397-405. vol. *IV* (1974), p. 170.

129. SPOI, 'F' papers, 5126 R lists clergy 'more or less in support of Fenianism'.

130. P.J. Corish, 'Political problems, 1850-1878', in *A History of Irish Catholicism*, vol. *V*, part iii (Dublin, 1967), pp. 8-16.

131. There was also a lesser rising in Kerry, in Feb. 1867; for a description of the Fenian rising see Kee, op. cit., Chap. 18.

132. O'Leary, op. cit., p. 167.

133. B. Mac Giolla Choille, 'Fenian documents in the State Paper Office', in *Irish Historical Studies*, vol. *16* (1966-7),pp. 258-84.

134. For the martyrs' speeches at the dock see T.M. Kettle (ed.) *Irish Orators and Oratory* (Dublin n.d.), pp. 365-71.

135. Kee, op. cit., pp. 341-43; Brown, op. cit., p. 209.

136. Brown, p. 215.

137. Two of Sullivan's political meetings were broken up by the Fenians in February 1863 (Comerford, p. 76).

138. Kee, op. cit., p. 344; Brown, op. cit., pp. 211-12; A.M. Sullivan, *New Ireland* (London, n.d. (1877?)), pp. 289-93.

139. K.B. Nowlan, 'The Fenians at home', in T.D. Williams (ed.) *Irish Secret Societies*, p. 95.

140. P.J. Corish, op. cit., pp. 36-41; D. MacCartney, 'The church and secret societies', in T.D. Williams, op. cit., p. 73.

141. Corish, op. cit., pp. 42-3 discusses the origin of the Vatican condemnation of 1870.

142. MacDonagh, *Ireland: the Union and its Aftermath*, p. 158.

143. McCartney, op. cit., pp. 75-77.

144. E.D. Steele, *Irish Land and British Politics: Tenant Right and Nationality 1865-1870* (Cambridge, 1974), p. 30.

145. Hoppen, op. cit., pp. 218-19; Lee, *Modernization of Irish Society*, pp. 118-19.

146. SPOI, 'F' papers, Constabulary report of 10 Oct. 1869, 4869 R.

147. Comerford, op. cit., pp. 119-25; D. Thornley, *Isaac Butt and home rule* (London, 1964), pp. 68, 71-3, 88-9. For a list of those at Bilton's Hotel see Sullivan, op. cit., pp. 339-41.

7 THE MAKING OF PARNELLISM AND ITS UNDOING

The Home Government Association was founded as another attempt to discover the holy grail of Irish politics: a comprehensive nationalism that corresponded to the pluralist nature of the Irish people. As always, Anglo-Irishmen were in the forefront of that search; and 1870 seemed an appropriate year to launch a political movement aimed at embracing all Irishmen who were dissatisfied with the government of their country. Roman Catholic concern over the state of affairs in Ireland was reinforced by Protestant disenchantment with the Gladstonian government's belief that justice for Ireland also meant injustice for Protestants; or so it seemed to them. The disestablishment of the church of Ireland in 1869 appears in retrospect a liberal and even a moral measure, for the Anglican church was a church of a minority of Irishmen and could not even claim to represent all Protestants. But to its children it was a bitter blow, not only to the church but to the Irish nation, for to them the church of Ireland was the national church, whatever religion the majority of the people, in their unwisdom, might profess. The opening lines of an anthem written for use in Derry Cathedral on 1 January 1871 summed up Anglican dismay at Gladstone's apostasy:

Darkly dawns the new year
On a churchless nation.[1]

Moreover, Anglicanism had in the eighteenth century been an important and, to some nationalists, an essential ingredient of national identity; and since the destruction of the Irish Parliament in 1800 the church of Ireland was the one remaining institution of national character with which Protestants could identify. Now it appeared that the national church was in danger of going the same way as the national Parliament. 'The protestants of Ireland', remarked one critic, 'had found to their cost that when the interest of the English Government is at stake, their interests are made a plaything and a bauble in the battle of party'.[2] And all this, it was claimed was the work of 'politicians who knew nothing about its wants and care less about its interests'.[3]

To add injury to insult the British prime minister was now

contemplating a measure of land reform; and conservative landlords, angry at their abandonment over the ecclesiastical issue, were in no mood to regard British Tories as their natural allies against Gladstone. Now that the liberals were threatening to undermine their position still further, there was at least a possibility that landlords might be won over to a new political movement; for what was 'justice for Ireland' after all but an imposition upon Ireland of those measures which an English statesman believed to be good for her, whether she willed it or no?[4]

Here, apparently, was the stuff out of which a revival of Protestant nationalism might be made; a nationalism not merely of a few isolated patriots like Davis or Mitchel, but a nationalism that could fulfil Davis's dream of aristocratic Protestant leadership of the Catholic masses. Isaac Butt himself was a typical member of the Protestant classes: the son of a country rector and a graduate of Trinity College Dublin, and a man, moreover, of impeccable conservative opinions. His conversion from defence of the union, whose case he had argued against Daniel O'Connell, to opposition to it was occasioned by the bearing and dignity of the Fenian prisoners of 1867 whose advocate he was, and whose interests he continued to press in the amnesty association; but his nationalism was at bottom similar to that of the founding father of Protestant patriotism, William Molyneux. Butt, like Molyneux, saw that the union, or a free Irish Parliament, though opposites, were in another sense complementary: for they arose out of the conviction that Ireland could only be well-governed by a real union of hearts and minds, or by a properly functioning representative institution which would not separate Ireland from England, but bind them together in mutual harmony. A true union or a real Irish Parliament were part and parcel of the same desirable end, the well-being of Ireland and the United Kingdom.[5]

Once Butt came to question the nature of the existing union between Great Britain and Ireland it was natural and logical for him to postulate that an Irish Parliament, subordinate in certain respects to the British Government, would provide a workable alternative; he sought 'the restoration to Ireland of that right of domestic legislation, without which Ireland can never enjoy real prosperity or peace'. Butt hoped to combine home rule for Ireland with a central governing body for the whole United Kingdom in which England and Scotland would also be represented. In domestic matters he wanted to retain an Irish House of Lords, partly to reassure the Irish aristocracy; and the Irish Parliament, 'consisting, be it always remembered, of the Queen, Lords, and Commons of Ireland, would have supreme control in Ireland, except in those matters which the Federal Constitution might specifically reserve to the Imperial Assembly'. The lord lieutenant would remain as the Queen's representative, responsible to the imperial Parliament, but acting through Irish ministers responsible to the Irish Parliament in the Canadian and Australian manner. Ireland would send 105 representatives to the imperial Parliament to vote on imperial questions, and in return she would submit, as at present, to imperial taxation, 'but only for certain definite purposes and in a certain definite manner'.[6]

The meeting at Bilton's hotel in May 1870 produced a committee to further the cause of home government which included twenty-eight Protestant conservatives, ten liberals, seventeen constitutional nationalists, and six Fenians or Fenian associates; in religio/mathematical terms the group divided into thirty-five Protestants and twenty-five Catholics. This looked like the breakthrough that had eluded previous architects of comprehensive nationalism, for not only were Protestants present, they were in the majority; and it was a cardinal principle of Protestant nationalists that they should play a leading-role in politics and government in a free Ireland. Moreover, the movement embraced revolutionary nationalists as well as constitutionalists, and by July 1870 the committee's list included such names as the Fenian sympathizer John 'amnesty' Nolan, Father Lavelle of Partry, and W.J. O'Neill Daunt, an O'Connellite.[7] But, ominously, this very broadening of the association began a process by which its boundaries quickly altered. By October 1870 Butt had to admit that the Catholics enjoyed a small majority on the committee, and that probably the liberals outnumbered the conservatives by three to two. The conservative newspaper, the *Dublin Daily Express*, which had originally welcomed the home government association as evidence that the power of the priests was waning, now decided that its judgement was faulty and called for the formation of an anti-ultramontane Irish party. The *Irish Times*, despite the fact that its editor, Major Knox, was a founder member of the association, remained well-disposed but non-committal.[8]

The home government association was from the beginning under extreme suspicion from all sides; some Catholic newspapers, like the *Dublin Evening Post* and the *Limerick Reporter*, dismissed it as a 'vile sham — a stalking horse to conceal Orange and Tory manouvres'.[9] But its greatest difficulty lay in defining what method it should adopt to further its aims. It was not a popular democratic movement like O'Connell's repeal association, at least not yet; and the question remained whether it could change its organization without altering its character. It had no central body until November 1873, when the Home Rule League superseded the Home Government Association; and it did little except keep local organizations informed of each other's activities. Above all it had no policy which might arouse popular support, for although Butt declared himself in favour of tenant right, and urged that this cause and the nationalist cause went together,[10] he had no network of local clubs or branches to spread the message into the homes and farms of rural Ireland, an area which not even O'Connell could properly arouse, or keep at a sustained level of political activity. And there was the question of the Roman Catholic church's attitude to the movement, which ranged from suspicion to outright hostility. Archbishop McHale referred to the need to restore a national legislature to Ireland, but the reason he advanced — that it would solve the question of denominational education — was not in the forefront of Butt's programme. And the only other member of the hierarchy to break his silence on the issue came out finally against the association; to the Archbishop of Cashel repeal of the union was desirable, but home rule in its present form was really a plot by Protestants, assisted by some Catholics, to discredit the church and the clergy.[11]

Herein lay the dilemma for the Protestant nationalist, and for any nationalist, Catholic or Protestant, who sought to reconcile all his countrymen in one grand movement. The truly 'national' aim — self-government, of whatever kind — could not catch fire unless it were combined with the sectional aims of denominational education or an attack on landlords. This might appear an idiosyncratic statement: were not land and education 'national' and nationalist aims? They were if the nation were regarded as co-terminous with the Roman Catholics; but there was another view: that, as the republican P.S. O'Hegarty put it, land reform was a 'sectional interest', to be deplored because it pitted one class of Irishman against another.[12]

This line of argument might appear to be contradicted by the failure of the overtly sectional party, the Catholic Union, founded in November 1872 to defend Catholic interests in Ireland and abroad. The Union was Cullen's answer to the home government association, which he viewed with deep suspicion as an Orange plot to bring back the Tories, aided and abetted by his old enemies, the revolutionaries;[13] but its inability to influence Gladstone's proposed Education Bill in March 1873 revealed its lack of muscle. Nevertheless, it would be mistaken to assume that this was proof of the lack of appeal among Catholic voters for Catholic issues; it was yet another demonstration of the principle that, while Catholic issues could be incorporated into a political movement led by the laity, they had little appeal when urged by priests on people as a single issue programme. It was not that nationalism and Catholic issues were seen as two different matters; on the contrary, it was because they were part of the same broader national question, two sides of the same coin, that they were best and most persuasively presented to the electorate by lay politicians. Priests were influential but subordinate (and influential because subordinate) but they could only challenge their traditional role at their own risk. Similarly, the land question caught fire when it was presented as part of the wider struggle against British rule in Ireland; and the most successful candidates were those who mixed home rule with a programme which included the aims of the Catholic union and land reform.[14]

The 1874 election campaign, in which the home rulers won 59 seats, illustrated the complex nature of the nationalist appeal in Ireland. In Limerick County, a Mr O'Sullivan referred to the need for the tenant farmers to get perpetuity of tenure at fair rents, and he also declared himself in favour of religious education in schools. At Westmeath P.J. Smyth emphasized the land question, and spoke in terms of Irish nationalism as a cultural and religious entity. 'The population of Ireland', he declared, was 'not an aggregate of human atoms drawn into a newly discovered country by the attractive force of gold, or virgin prairie or primieval forest − it represents an ancient and famous race, with a past and a history, with feelings, traditions, instincts all their own, with manners, habits, customs, character and religion different from their neighbours, and they cling to the idea of a distinct national identity'. At Castlebar, one of the new breed of constitutional Fenians, J. O'Connor Power, told his audience that 'when I reflect on your patriotic enthusiasms I can truly say "the west's awake" '; a parliament of landlords, he went on, could not settle the land question to satisfy the legitimate interest of the tenant who 'has a right . . . to be secured in the fruits of his labour'.[15] In the Waterford County election a meeting to select a candidate saw a resolution submitted to the chairman, pledging electors of the barony of Glenahiery 'not to vote for any MP who does not promise to give his undivided support to home rule, fixity of tenure at fair rents, denominational education', and called on the clergy 'who always stood to the people . . . to show that the enemies of the farming classes cannot triumph'.[16] At King's County the home rule candidate trusted to the 'men of Birr' to 'concur with him in the hope that Ireland would never cease to properly exert every power to make herself once more which

she was for many centuries – a nation among the nations of the earth';
and he pledged himself to associate religion and education 'notwithstanding, the evil spirit that was abroad trying to undermine their faith,
which spirit was possessed, for example, by Bismarck, the present perse-
cutor of Germany'. He also expressed his support for fixity of tenure.[17]
In Limerick, Isaac Butt's fellow MP, R. O'Shaughnessy, while affirming
his belief that the 'staunch Irish protestant is any day as worthy of the
support of Irishmen as an Irish Catholic' (in itself an interesting and
revealing phrase) confessed that 'in an age in which there are so many
interests exclusively Catholic – so many questions that I may call
sacred at stake every day in the British Parliament, and in every
assembly in the world, a people largely Catholic would do themselves
and their faith an injustice, which no Protestant city would their
religion – by not making their views plainly and without any
uncertainty heard in the house of commons'. The clergy of Limerick
had been 'true to the traditions of the Irish Catholic clergy in this
struggle'; the Catholic church of Ireland was the mother of liberty
which she had fostered 'during the long and terrible struggles which, I
trust, we are now concluding'.[18] And while Isaac Butt at Greenock
was assuring his audience that the British democracy were not enemies
of Ireland, but lovers of freedom like themselves,[19] a home ruler in
Waterford characterized the present struggle as a 'protest by his
countrymen against the Saxon laws of England as administered here; as
a protest of Ireland for the Irish and the Irish for Ireland'. Ireland was a
nation 'civilized and highly educated, when England was sunk in
barbarism'.[20]

The election campaign of 1874 revealed that the policy of home rule
could act as a rallying point for those whose motive was hostility to
British rule in Ireland, as well as those, like Butt himself, who saw in
the policy a means of opening a new and hopeful era in Anglo-Irish
relations. Home rule could be identified with the nationalist struggle;
it was not merely a modest proposal for reforming the Government of
the United Kingdom. But the calibre of the party's parliamentary
representatives hardly corresponded to the depth of feeling among the
electorate. Many of the home rulers were liberals who changed their
label when they perceived the way the electoral tide was flowing. Moreover, they had not been selected, nor had their candidature been
supported, by a well-organized electoral system: there were few official
endorsements of candidates by the home rule league; and endorsement
by the league was not regarded as in any way essential for acceptance
in the constituency. Many of the new recruits, in particular, soon

revealed that their sincerity was very much in doubt. The Fenian, John Barry, wrote to Butt immediately after the election expressing the disappointment of Irishmen both at home and abroad at the calibre of the majority of the men returned. Butt, however, had his own disappointments to ponder; for conservative home rule candidates were virtually unknown.[21]

Butt's party hung suspended between a lack of nationalist commitment among its MPs on the one hand, and a lack of staunch conservative support on the other; it was too extreme to gather the kind of Protestant sympathy that Butt had regarded as essential for its success, and yet its performance in the House of Commons soon failed to live up to the anti-British sentiments expressed by many candidates in the 1874 election. The home rulers were unprepared for the session which opened in March 1874; and Butt's first speech as leader of his group proved something of a disappointment: 'He did not at present ask the House to concede home rule to Ireland. That question remained to be discussed, and perhaps to be discussed for many years'.[22] Butt spoke with some foresight, for home rule and the principles underlying it were to occupy British time and attention for decades; but for the next 4 years it languished as a minor debating point in parliament. The conservatives were in an overwhelming majority in the House of Commons, and the home rulers remained a small and isolated group with no political leverage. Butt's respect for the British parliamentary system; his belief in the power of reason; his conviction that the innate justice of his cause must make it prevail, proved unavailing.[23] Nationalist patience began to wear thin; and Butt's declaration in April 1875 that 'the Irish party will in this matter (a coercion bill), at least, exhaust all the forms of the house to attain their just and righteous object' was taken at its word by one member, Joseph Biggar, whose speech proposing an amendment to the bill lasted 4 hours. Butt's dislike of such tactics was not shared by the home rule confederation in England, branches of which called upon the Irish party to adopt a policy 'more obstructive and factious'.[24]

It was in pursuing these tactics that the home rule MP for Meath, Charles Stewart Parnell, emerged as a significant member of the small group of 'advanced' nationalists in the party. Parnell's parliamentary attributes were his fearless and unflinching attacks on his opponents, and his readiness to use inflammatory language in the House: if it was unwise to rebel in Ireland, it soon proved to be not only practicable, but advantageous, to rebel in the British Parliament. In June 1876, in a debate on Butt's home rule motion, Sir Michael Hicks Beach commented on the strange delusion that 'home rule can have the effect of liberating the Fenian prisoners, the Manchester murderers' (No! NO!) — I regret to hear that there is any honourable member in this house who will apologize for murder'. Parnell retorted 'as publicly and as directly as I can that I do not believe, and never shall believe, that any murder was committed at Manchester'. This was the language that Irish nationalists, especially those living abroad, liked to hear; and in 1877 Parnell was elected to replace Butt as president of the home rule confederation of Great Britain.[25] To the majority of the parliamentary party, however, Parnell and his like were irresponsible, not to say dangerous, men; and it was not only Parnell's ambition and political opportunism that enabled him finally to win control of the home rule movement in 1880. Political and social developments, stretching back to the time of the famine, were providing the material out of which the most formidable political machine in modern Irish politics could be constructed.

The most important of these was the lowering, (but not the disappearance) of class tensions among the Catholic people of Ireland. The great famine had accelerated the already existing process of emigration from Ireland, and, moreover, had increased the proportion of emigrants who came from the poorer sections of the community. In 1841 the landless labourers constituted some 16.1 per cent of the total population; by 1871 the proportion had dropped to 13.8 per cent; and by 1881 the labourers were only 9.1 per cent. This meant that landless labourers were a decreasingly important factor in the development of a political movement based upon people who got their livelihood from the land; and the tension between labourers and farmers, which was such an important aspect of agrarian violence before the famine, became less commonplace, as the surviving labourers found their hardship alleviated since their services were increasingly in demand. Now a solid party base could be built on the farming classes, although of course the farmers were themselves by no means a completely homogenous group. Attempts were made to exploit the divisions between farmers and labourers; in the general election of 1885 the conservatives adopted a farm labourer as candidate on a joint labour-conservative ticket in North Cork.[26] And they never quite disappeared from sight in the home rule and agrarian organization manifestoes. The home rule candidate for mid-Cork felt obliged to mention them in 1885, declaring that 'the plot of ground which accompanies the labourers' cottages should be good land, and not what I am told some mercenary miscreants are endeavouring to pawn off upon some of the (Boards of) Guardians'.[27] In June 1900 the United Irish League's eleven points included a demand for a law providing agricultural labourers with cottages and one acre allotments.[28] As late as 1910 a priest recommended one home rule candidate as a man who had 'always acted impartially between the farmers and the labourers, and had always taken a deep interest in their welfare . . . He always did all in his power for the labourers'.[29] And at Limerick in 1900 F.J. O'Shaughnessy appealed to the farmers to 'do all in their power to help the labourers . . . The labourers had never worked on evicted farms, they had never become emergencymen'.[30]

Mr O'Shaughnessy's concern may have had something to do with the fact that an 'Irish land and labour association' had been founded in Limerick as the 'voice of labour', and was running its own candidate in the constituency.[31] References to the needs of landless men were few enough; and the home rulers were able to concentrate on the main business of representing the interests of the tenant farmer. Of course, there were gradations in wealth among the farmers, those of the west being much less happily circumstanced than the prosperous men around Cork. But the great social obstacle to the success of the Tenant Right League and the Independent Irish party of the 1850s — their inability to mobilize the Irish countryside on a clear, coherent and above all united programme — was well on the way to removal. And, despite its failure, the Tenant Right movement had demonstrated that an open, constitutional organization could be founded, distinguished from the secret, terrorist and local agrarian societies that had made uncoordinated assaults on their enemies, the tithe proctors, the farmers, and the landlords. The Tenant Right League sought legal redress for the farmers, but it was confronted with the problem of the labourers, who constituted a considerable part of the rural population but to whom it offered nothing.[32] O'Connell had been able to transcend class differences, and mobilize the labourer and the farmer in a common political cause; but O'Connell was a unique figure. Now that the farmer was the preponderant element in Irish society, a party could be based on him and on his interests that stood some chance of success. And the 1850s had also witnessed attempts to identify the farmers of Ireland as the core of the 'ancient race', who must not be permitted to 'forsake their dear birth-place/Without one struggle strong to keep The old soil where their fathers sleep'.[33]

There was another reason for the emergence of the farmers as the cohesive, rather than divisive, group in Ireland. The towns occupied a vital role as the social and economic centres of agrarian society, where farmers and townsmen came together to do their buying and selling.

Shopkeepers needed a prosperous tenantry to provide a market for the necessities and luxuries of life; thus Irish towns were overwhelmingly rural, with their economies linked closely to those of the surrounding countryside, and their prosperity depending on that of the country. George Russell noted that:

> the first thing which strikes one who travels through rural Ireland is the immense number of little shops. They are scattered along the highways and at the cross-roads; and where there are a few families together in what is called a village, the number of little shops crowded round these consumers is almost incredible. What are all these little shops doing? They are supplying the farmers with domestic requirements: with tea, sugar, flour, oil, implements, vessels, clothing, and generally with drink. Every one of them almost is a little universal provider. Every one of them has its own business organization, its relations with wholesale houses in the greater towns.[34]

Thus, town and countryside were not mutually hostile but mutually dependent; and their common interest provided another link in the chain which could bind together a united, socially harmonious nationalist movement dominated by rural Ireland.[35]

Moreover these social developments coincided with changes in the Irish electoral law which enabled the farmer to play an important role in politics in the 1870s and early 1880s. The Irish Franchise Act of 1850 provided for the settlement of the franchise upon the occupation of property to the poor law valuation of £12 in counties and £8 in the boroughs. Within 3 years 88.7 per cent of the electorate was registered on the new franchise; and a new registration procedure was introduced. The poorer sections of the previous electorate was excluded, and this uniformly chosen electorate provided the kind of electoral base that O'Connell had never enjoyed.[36] This electorate was not, therefore, the kind of half-starved rabble depicted by *Punch* on the one hand and by the Irish nationalists on the other; after 1850 rents lagged behind increases in the value of agricultural output, allowing tenants' incomes to increase at a greater rate than agricultural output itself.[37] Tenant farmers were becoming more prosperous and wanted that comfortable state of affairs to continue; and with the voting rights introduced in 1850 now taking their full effect they were in a position to exert political power and had every incentive to do so. The Independent Irish party of the 1850s enjoyed no such cohesive power base, and would probably not have had the political skills to exploit it even if the reforms of 1850 had reached an early maturation.

Political power in Ireland was based, as it was in England, on the vote and the possession of the vote; but political influence was more widely diffused; and a source of political influence in Ireland in the last quarter of the nineteenth century was the Roman Catholic church, now seeking to rediscover its traditional role following Cardinal Cullen's unsuccessful excursions into politics and his damaging encounters with the Fenians. Archibishop's McHale's hostility to the land league in 1879 was, perhaps, the last in a series of political blunders by church leaders since O'Connell's time;[38] for the church was now seeking a *rapprochement* with the nationalist public and leaders, and abandoning its Cullenite attempts to impose a clerical view upon them. The Roman Catholic church had its place, and an important one, in the pattern of Irish politics, always providing that it did not seek to distort the pattern to suit its viewpoint. In the 1880s a new episcopal leadership was emerging under Walsh and Croke, more sympathetic to nationalist aspirations, and unafraid of Mazzinianism and godlessness. The church had much to gain from a strong, popular home rule movement, as long as it did not overstep the mark as Cullen had done; and the priests could play a vital part in local political organization, as chairmen, orators, and scrutinizers of candidates, and as aids to the home rulers in their everyday political activity:[39] a role which was admirably suitable to the style of leadership which Parnell developed and perfected in the 1880s.

But Parnellism would not have been complete without that other source of influence which, while it could never dominate Irish politics, could occasionally alter the direction in which they might go: Fenianism. Isaac Butt had appreciated the value of reconciling Fenians to his home rule party, if only to anticipate any obstacle that they might place in his path; but after 1867 Fenians were searching for ways forward, not for obstacles, and it is probable that the supreme council of the IRB, established under its 1869 constitution, had majority support for mixing parliamentarianism and militarism.[40] In 1873 the supreme council, meeting in Dublin, declared that the decision of the Irish nation, as expressed by a majority of the Irish people, concerning the fit hour for fighting a war against England, was awaited.[41] This was a considerable concession to democratic methods, and contrasted with the notion held, especially by Stephens, that only the Fenians, and more particularly Stephens himself, had the right to interpret the will of the nation. Stephens' failure to interpret the entrails correctly in

1867 now provoked a revulsion against this kind of political sooth-saying; and the IRB, while awaiting more orthodox methods of divining the national will, was now willing to support every movement calculated to advance the cause of Irish independence consistent with the preservation of its own integrity. At the inaugural conference of the home rule league in 1873 two members of the supreme council, Charles Guilfoyle Doran and John O'Connor Power, proposed and had carried a motion calling for the return at the coming general election of men earnestly and truly dedicated to the national cause. Not all Fenians were prepared to contaminate their principles by playing such an active and constructive part in the parliamentary movement; but even those, like Kickham, who sought to oppose constitutional Fenianism found that they could do so most effectively by adopting constitutional means themselves, as they did when they ran the veteran nationalist, John Mitchel, successfully, for the Tipperary County constituency in 1875. And when there was a possibility of running Parnell for the seat on Mitchel's death, Kickham, while declining to support Parnell, spoke well of him; events had moved a long way since the Fenian attacks on the constitutionalist A.M. Sullivan in the 1860s.[42]

Parnell's greatest asset from constitutional Fenianism, however, lay not in Ireland but in Great Britain and America, where thousands of Catholic Irishmen had settled after the great famine, nursing a deep hostility to British rule, and to Protestants, and especially the Orange Lodges. These people believed that they were working with the grain of history, that history was on their side, and that in the end, by whatever means, 'Ireland' would triumph over 'England'.[43] For the Irishman living in Britain, Ireland was still home, and Irish politics were his politics: England had no claim on his loyalty.[44] For the Irishman who made the much more formidable journey across the Atlantic, there was a sense of loss and melancholia at leaving Ireland; but there was something more immediate and tangible as well: for, on his arrival in America, he received a hostile reception from anti-Catholic Americans, and from the Protestant Irish who sought eagerly to disassociate themselves from the impoverished newcomers. Thus it was not so much from the native Irish nationalism of Tone, O'Connell and Davis that the Irish emigrant took his politics, but from the sense of inferiority imposed upon him by his reception in America, mixed, paradoxically, with a longing for acceptance and respectability. Patrick Ford, a leading figure in Irish American politics in the 1870s and 1880s, admitted that he grew up knowing nothing about Ireland, but was shocked into a kind of national self-recognition by anti-Catholic feeling in Boston in the 1850s when he walked the streets seeking work, to be met everywhere with notices saying 'No Irish need apply'. But origins were no more important than the kind of prestige and leadership open to Irish Americans, and to the Irish in Britain, by political activity. As Michael Davitt put it, 'you want to be honoured among the elements that constitute this nation . . . You want to be regarded with the respect due you; that you may be thus looked on, and as in Ireland to remove the stain of degradation from your birth'.[45] It was a sentiment that the Irish in America, to whom it was addressed, and in Britain, responded to; and the militant parliamentarianism of Parnell suited it very well. The efforts of the Fenian, John Barry, the representative of the north of England on the supreme council of the IRB, who had built the home rule confederation of Great Britain into an efficient and powerful political machine, were largely responsible for Parnell's winning the important post of president of the home rule league in September 1877.[46]

Nevertheless, the heart of any popular and successful political movement lay in Ireland, however much Britain and America might provide aid and assistance; and Ireland was well prepared for nationalist politicization. The rural population of Ireland was better educated than ever before: between 1851 and 1911 the percentage of the population over 5 years of age which claimed to be able to read rose from 53 to 88 per cent.[47] In one county – Cork – the percentage of children attending primary school rose from 50.4 to 61.3 per cent between 1871 and 1891; the percentage of those who claimed to be able to read and write rose in the same period from 57.3 to 79.2 per cent in the county and from 70.6 to 84.1 in the city.[48] Sufficient laymen were now able to read and write and thus cope with the necessary paper work and administration involved in political organization and electioneering;[49] and a political movement could rely on mass support from a reading public which, because of its increasing prosperity, had more money available to purchase political literature. And in nationalist Ireland newspapers were, in effect, political literature. The number of newspapers and periodicals rose from 109 in 1853 to 230 in 1913;[50] and the Irish provincial press flourished; between 1900 and 1922 there were 114 provincial newspapers, of nationalist persuasion, with another twenty-eight described as 'independent', many of which were sympathetic to the nationalist cause.[51] In the days of O'Connell and Young Ireland the Dublin-based papers were the leading organs of nationalist opinion; and although the *Nation* penetrated the provinces, it did not possess the special local knowledge and intimacy that the editors and writers of the provincial newspapers enjoyed. Men like James Daly of the *Connaught Telegraph* and Tim Harrington of the *Kerry Sentinel* were not only able and talented journalists, but were local – and in some cases national – political leaders as well.[52] And they had, in the years 1879-1881, plenty to write about, as political events in Ireland became of immediate importance to the rural population. An American professor who visited Ireland in 1881 and 1882 noted:

> In a third class railway car in which there were probably twenty-five Irish farmers and labourers, I noticed that more than one half of the people read the morning papers, even those who looked the least intelligent showing a great interest in the news. I discovered the man who sat opposite me, and who was a rather ragged-looking individual, read the other side of my paper with evident interest. The violent agitation has helped on the influence of the press and set the people to reading.[53]

The 'violent agitation' to which the professor referred was the 'land-war' of 1879-82 which gave a new inspiration to the home rule party and helped Parnell to his supreme position, not only in the party but in nationalist Ireland at large. The land war was not simply an extension of agrarian secret society activity; nor was it the blind, instinctive revolt of an impoverished peasantry. It was a well-organized and sophisticated response to the vagaries of the Irish rural economy in the 1870s, which threatened the growing prosperity of the tenant farmer, a prosperity which had been a marked feature of the two decades following the Famine. Now foreign competition and a poor potato crop, especially in Connaught, shook the Irish farmer out of his confident expectation that each year would prove better than the one that went before.[54] The agricultural depression of 1879 affected different parts of the country to different degrees: in a buoyant county like Cork the chief effect was to convince the prosperous farmer that he must look to himself to prevent any serious inroads on his rising standard of living;[55] but the smallest tenantry of the west – the vanguard of the land agitation – had a thinner margin to fall back upon. There was no return to the famine conditions of 1847; but there was a genuine fear that an unacceptable period of hardship was on the way, with all the gains of the previous 20 years set quickly at nought.[56] But the important and novel aspect of the agricultural crisis was less the economic distress – for Ireland had known much worse distress before – than the response it provoked from the tenantry. The tenantry, Lord Spencer wrote, were 'sufficiently educated to read the latest political doctrines in the press which circulates among them'; and, he added, 'their social condition at home is a hundred years behind their state of political and mental culture'.[57]

Here was material ready for political action; and in 1879 a group of agrarian radicals − including Fenians and home rulers − set out to exploit it. John O'Connor Power, the former Fenian who had won his home rule seat in Mayo on an anti-landlord ticket, was one such man; his campaign manager, Matt Harris, was an O'Connellite, Fenian and now home ruler who had founded a tenants' defence association at Ballinasloe in 1876; James Daly, editor of the *Connaught Telegraph*, was an indefatigable organizer and propagandist for the movement.[58] Most celebrated of all was Michael Davitt, a Mayo man whose family had been evicted and had fled to Lancashire when he was 6 years of age. Davitt's participation in subversive movements had earned him a long spell in penal servitude; and when he was released he devoted his life to the land problem and its solution. Not all of these land agitators were of like mind about the nature of the problem to which they addressed themselves: Daly set his face against tenants owning the land for fear that this would simply render them more conservative than the landlords; Davitt believed in the national ownership of land, for 'peasant proprietorship is simply landlordism in another form'; by what right, he asked, were public funds or the public credit to be utilized for the benefit of a section of the community merely?[59] Michael O'Sullivan, a future assistant secretary of the land league, declared in June 1879 that 'before many years you'll own your own lands'.[60] Nevertheless the leaders and organizers were able to sink their differences and combine against the common foe; and the common foe was perceived to be the landlords and their alleged supporter, the British Government.

In April 1879 Davitt organized a demonstration at Irishtown, Co. Mayo, directed against a Roman Catholic priest, Canon Burke, who had threatened to evict all the tenants from a nearby estate unless they paid their arrears in rent forthwith. The meeting was attended by some seven thousand people and resolutions were passed demanding an abolition of landlordism and the immediate lowering of rent by local landlords. At a second, larger, demonstration at Westport in June, Parnell was present; and on 16 August 1879 the land league of Mayo was founded, with the object of using 'every means compatible with justice, morality and right reason' that would 'not clash defiantly with the constitution' to replace the existing landlord system with one 'in accord with the social rights and interests of our people'. Pending a satisfactory settlement of the land question the league pledged itself to expose injustices inflicted on the tenants and protect them against the landlords.[61]

Davitt, however, was not solely concerned with the land agitation, nor with an alliance with Parnell and his supporters; he sought also to weld together the 'open' and secret wings of Irish nationalism, and the Fenian involvement in parliamentary politics augured well for this ambition. Parnell, for his part, was making friendly overtures to the 'advanced' nationalists, and he met John Devoy, a prominent Irish American Fenian, in January and March 1878. Devoy was impressed with Parnell; and in October 1878 Davitt and Devoy found that their minds were moving towards the same conclusion: that an active alliance between Fenianism and Parnellite parliamentarianism was possible and desirable, an alliance that would involve Fenian support in election campaigns and Fenians sitting in the British Parliament. The supreme council of the IRB drew the line at such a deep commitment to constitutionalism; but it was agreed that individual IRB members could participate in election campaigns. Meetings were held between Parnell and Devoy early in 1879, and on 1 June Davitt was present when the 'new departure' was launched,[62] a departure which was, perhaps, not as new as it appeared, since it was the outcome of the gradual acclimitization of Fenianism to parliamentary politics that had been taking place since Butt's conference at Bilton's Hotel in 1870. No formal agreement seems to have been made in June 1879, and Parnell later repudiated Devoy's claim that agreement had been reached.[63] But Fenian support, moral, and material, was now forthcoming for Parnell's militant parliamentarianism; and the IRB also gave permission for its members to participate in agrarian agitation. In October 1879 Davitt persuaded Parnell to join with him in forming the Irish National Land League and to accept its leadership. Thus, slowly and imperfectly, was put together that strange and uneasy alliance of agrarian, constitutional, and physical force nationalism which was Parnellism.

Parnell did not owe his mastery of this hybrid movement to any deeply felt or fervent commitment to national independence for Ireland. While it appears that his lack of historical knowledge, or of pseudo-historical knowledge, which inspired so many Irish nationalists has been exaggerated,[64] his beliefs were neither profound nor passionate; and his American mother's anti-Britishness was, apparently, no more than an amusement or an embarrassment to him. He himself attributed his interest in nationalism to the Fenian activity in his native

Wicklow in 1867; but this did not stop him leading a perfectly contented life as a member of the country gentry.[65] His swift and sudden ejectment from Cambridge after a public brawl may not have improved his opinion of the English;[66] but it is doubtful if this incident alone would have produced the hero of nationalist Ireland. The explanation is probably more simple: Parnell was a member of the Anglo-Irish ruling class, and, whereas the bulk of that class was now Unionist, that did not prevent Parnell (like Jonathan Swift before him) possessing that hearty contempt for the English establishment that any well-connected Irish Protestant worth his salt was capable of harbouring. Moreover, Parnell was no deserter of his people; on the contrary he hoped, as Davis had hoped, that the landlords could be won over to the national cause: if the land question could be settled on a permanent basis then 'you would remove the great reason that now exists to prevent the large and influential class of Irish landlords falling in with the demand for self-government'.[67] Given the strong nationalist feelings among the Anglo-Irish gentry in the eighteenth century, the surprising thing is not that Parnell existed, but that there were not more Parnells; for he was but one, and the last and greatest, of a long line of Anglo-Irish nationalists, standing in the tradition of Smith O'Brien, Thomas Davis, and Isaac Butt.

Healthy contempt for Englishmen would not have been sufficient to bring Parnell to the pinnacle of political leadership in 1879-1880. For what Parnell possessed was precisely those skills which a great political leader required: if he was not very interested in Irish history, or in anybody else's history, he was familiar with a much more useful branch of knowledge – public affairs. He took a lively interest in contemporary Ireland, and especially in matters of tenant right; he was a 'good landlord', popular with his tenants, and with a record of never having evicted anyone.[68] Parnell's commitment to nationalism never went beyond a desire for the restoration of Grattan's parliament;[69] but then neither did Arthur Griffith's, and Griffith was the founder of Sinn Féin. However, he was deeply committed to gaining political power, and to the skills necessary for its attainment; and now that the social, economic, and political life of Ireland was on the brink of a great upheaval, Parnell was the right man at the right moment. He possessed an impeccable parliamentary record of anti-English, and, on occasion, crypto-Fenian speeches; he was the political leader who had caught the public eye; and the death of Isaac Butt in May 1879, and his replacement by William Shaw, a Protestant barrister from Cork, could not obscure Parnell's growing influence in the country, an influence which Parnell's assumption of the presidency of the land league only served to under-line and enhance. After the general election of March 1880 he gained the chairmanship of the Irish parliamentary party, though not without strong opposition;[70] and the next 5 years demonstrated the strengths and weaknesses of his political leadership, his political style, and his political position.

Parnell's problem was to reconcile his ambition to become a 'national' leader with his need to relate to local and sectional groups and their leaders. He had to make bargains and sometimes, as in the case of the new departure, repudiate them when the occasion arose. He had to weld his followers into a disciplined organization, and subordin-ate the land league, which had helped him to power, to the parliamen-tary party. He had to work within the constraints imposed by the many sided nature of Irish politics: the votes of the Catholic tenantry, the Irish Americans, the Fenians, the Catholic church; and he had to operate at different levels: the public meeting in the west of Ireland, the closed doors of the Irish parliamentary party, the forum of the British House of Commons, and devise appropriate responses to all these levels. Parnell's leadership was fluid, not static; and he succeeded in harnessing and leading the political and social forces of nationalist Ireland because he appeared to be the only man capable of performing that blend of functions which each of them perceived as necessary to the advancement of their cause. Without him there would be a diffu-sion of nationalist resources, and a weakening of each group's efforts. For one to succeed, all must succeed; for all to succeed, one must lead; and that leader was Parnell.

Parnell's political skills were not, of course, infallible; and their exercise proved to be an exhausting and demanding task. But he was fortunate in his charismatic personal qualities: his natural reticence of character suited admirably the enigma and ambiguity of the political predicament in which he must place himself; his aloof nature, his fine presence, attracted the admiration of men whose political ideas were far removed from his own. Moreover the growing realization by the leader of the liberals, Gladstone, that Ireland must have land reform and some measure of self-government strengthened Parnell's position, for he was selected by Gladstone as the man who could lead Ireland to peace and prosperity within the British empire. Parnell was there-fore as much an answer to the Government's hopes and fears as he was to those of his followers.[71]

In his years of power Parnell had to conciliate, and yet avoid cap-ture by, a wide and varied assortment of political groups and individuals;

hence the bewildering variety of his public pronouncements, which covered the whole spectrum of nationalist ideas. In his first election campaign in 1875 he demanded denominational education, the release of political prisoners, a land policy of fixity of tenure and fair rents, and the 'voice of the people in this country' ruling the affairs of Ireland. His expression of sympathy with the Manchester Martyrs was his passport to Fenianism goodwill, and a gesture to the instinctive response in Ireland to 'noble-hearted' dead heroes. His famous statement in Cork in 1885, 'let no man assign a ne plus ultra to the march of a nation' was a usefully vague concept of home rule. After he became president of the land league he called for 'tenant proprietory'. His speeches while on a trip to America in 1880 were more extreme than anything he had so far said, and he was attributed with the statement that 'the last link which keeps Ireland bound to England' must be broken.[72] He later denied that he had said any such thing, but at the time, when he was seeking support in the heartland of extreme nationalism, and involved in mastering the agrarian movement at home, he refrained from issuing a denial.[73] On his return from America he became involved in the turbulence caused by increasing distress in the west; but he managed to avoid too deep a commitment to agrarian violence by urging the tenants to 'keep a firm grip of your homesteads' and to use 'the strong force of public opinion to deter any unjust men amongst you . . . from bidding for such farms'. If a tenant were to bid for a farm from which another tenant had been evicted, Parnell advised a 'very much better way — a more Christian and charitable way' of restraining him than murder: he must be shunned 'as if he were a leper of old'.[74] This brought the law upon his own head, and he was prosecuted; but once again events worked to his satisfaction, for a Parnell defence fund was inaugurated with support from the moderate, and hitherto critical, newspapers, the *Freeman's Journal*, moderate home rulers, and the clergy.[75]

Between 1880 and 1882 Parnell manouvered for the subordination of the land league to the political goal of home rule, a goal which he sought to achieve by parliamentary means. He urged restraint on the land league when it was faced with the threat of government coercion in 1881, and when Gladstone passed a land act in 1881 conceding fair rent, to be assessed by arbitration, fixity of tenure where the rent was paid, and freedom for the tenant to sell his right to occupancy at market value, Parnell called for 'test cases' so that the league could assess the act's value. On 13 October 1881 he was arrested after a speech at Wexford in which he referred to the 'perfidious English enemy' and

appealed to the fighting tradition of '98 and '67 while paying tribute to the shooting ability of the Boers.[76] His imprisonment enabled him to take an extreme line on the land agitation in the knowledge that the more prosperous farmers, who were by now an increasingly influential element in the land league, would not support the idea of a 'rent strike', and neither would the Catholic clergy.[77] The autumn of 1881 saw an increase in agrarian crime which neither Parnell nor the land league leaders could control; and when Parnell and Gladstone reached agreement in April 1882, by which Parnell was to be released from gaol, coercion ended, the land act amended and tenants in arrears protected,[78] Parnell suffered criticism from more determined agrarian radicals. This might have proved a costly error of judgement; but he was saved by the murder in Phoenix Park of the newly appointed lord lieutenant, Lord Frederick Cavendish and his assistant-secretary, T.H. Burke, by a band of assassins. Parnell's sincerely expressed revulsion at the crime won him friends among moderates; his opposition to the coercion act which inevitably followed it retained his popularity among the more extreme men; and the effectiveness of the 1881 land act, which produced a general reduction in rents, was attributed to him.[79] Parnell was now able to move towards the goal of capturing the land league's organization for parliamentary politics, and in October 1882 he founded the national league to replace the declining land league. The committee of the new body was controlled by the parliamentary party; and thus was launched what Michael Davitt described as 'the investing of the fortunes and guidance of the agitation, both for national self-government and land reform, in a leader's nominal dictatorship'.[80]

Parnell's dictatorship, if such it was, was underwritten by the pledge, introduced in 1884, which committed candidates, if elected, to vote with the Irish party on all occasions when the majority decided that the party should act in unison.[81] This strengthening of party discipline came at a time of franchise reform in the United Kingdom; the Franchise Act of 1884 and the redistribution act of 1885 resulted in an increase in the size of the electorate from 4.4 per cent to 16 per cent of the population, and the reduction in representation of the boroughs. In the general election of 1885 the nationalists won eighty-five seats, seventeen of them in Ulster, and for the first time Parnell was leader of a large and united party, with a substantial foothold in the Protestant stronghold of the north. Within a short time the party which helped turn Gladstone out of office in 1885 was firmly supporting him as the British statesman who had finally pledged himself to deliver self-government to Ireland.

The complex political world in which Parnell had brought the home rule party to this level of success coloured the ideas of the movement, and influenced it even in the dark years of the 1890s when the party was broken and ineffective. For what might appear to be a simple, almost monotonous demand for home rule was in fact an emotional and highly charged set of political goals, changing in emphasis according to time and circumstance, but always offering a beckoning utopia to the Catholic people of Ireland. Whether it was land, religion, self-government, language and culture, or even simply jobs for the deserving, home rule was, apparently, the key to them all. Far from being a campaign for a limited measure of devolution, home rule was one of the most fascinating and passionate political programmes that Ireland ever evolved.

The home rule party had risen to popularity on the powerful and emotive land agitation of 1879-81; and this gave it one of its enduring themes when home rulers stood upon their own ground and confronted their potential voters. The idea that the landlords of Ireland were themselves responsible for the economic problems of the country was, by 1879, almost a truism among nationalists. Charles Gavan Duffy, the founder of the tenant right league in 1850, alleged that the 'peasantry' had a living claim on the land as the descendants of those who owned it in common with the Celtic chiefs, and who had been wrongfully deprived of their property. John Blake Dillon told a committee of the house of commons in 1865 that 'very recent . . . and very extensive confiscations' exercised 'a most important influence' on the relations between landlord and tenant; when asked if he understood by 'very recent' the seventeenth century, he replied 'any act that has an important bearing upon the present condition of the country is sufficiently recent to justify me in describing it as very recent'. Even John Gray, the proprietor and editor of the moderate *Freeman's Journal*, told an audience at Kilkenny in January 1868 that the title deeds of nearly all landlords who opposed the tenants' demands were traceable to the confiscation.[82] It is tempting to ascribe this simply to the existence of a kind of collective peasant folk memory, and to a strong feeling among the tenants that the ancient families would yet recover their forfeited estates; and there was contemporary evidence to support this, especially in the Gaelic poetry of the seventeenth and eighteenth centuries.[83] It is equally tempting to depict such notions as the inevitable result of bad landlordism, of rack renting, of mass evictions, of agrarian 'guerilla warfare'.[84] But before the land war most tenants pad their rent promptly enough; there were few evictions, rents lagged behind increases in the value of agrarian output; agrarian crime was not the endemic and widespread phenomenon described in lurid terms in the press and in parliamentary papers; tenants enjoyed security on most estates; and trouble arose not because of wicked landlords or historically minded peasants, but because tenants were enjoying low rents and wished to keep them that way. And there were tenants who were, quite simply, trouble makers.[85] Folk memories there were;[86] but they were not in themselves enough to arouse the tenantry until played upon by nationalist propagandists, working on an intelligent, newspaper-reading public, who were not slow to perceive the advantage of supporting the claim that the land belonged to the people. Had there been a community of political interest, a bond of politico-religious faith between landlord and tenant, then nationalist propaganda might have laboured in vain; but because the overwhelming majority of landlords were Protestants and Conservatives, they were susceptible to the accusation that they were the unjust benefactors of the 'transplantation of a nation'.[87] When Gladstone introduced his 1870 land bill in the House of Commons, he asserted that the existing distribution of legal property rights was the result of recent conquest, unsanctified by a subsequent community of interest between landlord and tenant. The 'old Irish ideas were never supplanted except by the rude hand of violence — by laws written on the State Book, but never entering into the heart of the Irish people'.[88]

When such ideas, with all their dire implications for landlords, were held by members of the British Government, it is hardly surprising that they quickly became an article of faith among Irish nationalists. Michael Davitt, in a speech delivered in June 1879, denounced the 'landlord garrison established by England in this country, centuries ago'; it was 'as true to the object of its foundation, and as alien to the moral instincts of our people, as when it was first expected to drive the Celtic race "to hell or Connaught". It is the bastard offspring of force and usury, the Ishmael of the social commonwealth, and every man's hand should be against what has proved itself to be the scourge of our race since it first made Ireland a land of misery and poverty'.[89] Home rulers quickly took their cue, and made hostility to the whole system of landlordism a central part of their nationalism. At Beleek, Co. Donegal, William Redmond told people that 'he was against the land-lords and for the people'[90], thus implying that the two were separate and incompatible. At Waterford a priest expressed his wish to see 'that the tenant farmers were not obliged to pay the last penny to allow absentee landlords to live in luxury in London and elsewhere. The tiller of the soil . . . had the first claim on it'; another priest was more explicit: 'There never could be peace in this country unless the landlords were well out of it'.[91] Matthew Harris at Ballinasloe promised that he would always keep before him 'the two ideas of National Independence and the total abolition of landlordism';[92] another home ruler at Gortlettra, Co. Leitrim, agreed that 'the winning of home rule was the shortest way to settle the land question', for an Irish parliament would put an end to 'evictions and land-grabbing'.[93] The landlords were described variously as 'as much foreigners today as their forefathers were 300 years ago – haters of the very soul of Ireland'; 'the heirs of confiscation', and (by the Parnellite newspaper *United Ireland*) 'the vile garrison who have so long trampled upon the necks and crushed the aspirations of the Irish people'.[94]

The home rule party under Parnell was an anti-landlord party; Parnell, himself a landlord, went along with this, partly because he could hardly resist such a popular crusade, partly because he believed that once the landlords were deprived of their land, and thereby of any sound reason for supporting the union, they would become nationally minded and take their rightful places as the nation's social and political leaders. Parnell feared a land settlement without a parliament, however, for, as he confessed to Davitt in 1879, 'land ownership and loyalty are generally inseparable with a peasantry – no way prone in any country to sacrifice much for the principle of patriotism'.[95] And so the land question was integrated with the overall drive for a national resurgence by the Irish people against all foreign tyrants. It may have been that the Parnellites were, many of them, so involved with the British parliamentary system that they were closer to the British political tradition than any modern Irish party today.[96] But this was not reflected in their speeches and writings in Ireland (nor, on occasion, in England, where one MP, F.H. O'Donnell, referred to Britain as the 'common enemy' of the tyrannized Indian and Irish people[97]). Constitutionalists the home rulers may have been; but they were also nationalists, and full-blooded nationalists at that. J. O'Connor Power, the constitutional Fenian, contributed to a *Book of Light on the Irish problem*, aimed at an English audience, and pleading for the establishment of 'an assembly of calm, just, and able men, friendly to (England) and useful to Ireland'; he argued earnestly for a federal union between Great Britain and Ireland, which he had for many years constantly supported, asking for 'such self-government as is compatible with the integrity of the United Kingdom'.[98] Only a few years previously he had declared in Castlebar

that 'he was cradled, so to speak, in hostility to English rule in Ireland, and was hostile to her rule in Ireland today'.[99]

It was hostility to England that provided the driving force behind nationalism in Ireland, a hostility based on what Maurice Healy described as 'this great racial conflict, which has been going on so long, which began in blood and suffering 700 years ago, and has continued through seven centuries of oppression and misery', a racial conflict that would, 'unless we are at length successful . . . continue to resound to the last syllable of recorded time'.[100] The idea of the two races, Celt and Saxon, locked in mortal combat, was the stock in trade of home rulers speeches;[101] *United Ireland*'s Westminster report was entitled 'Among the Saxons', and it is doubtful if the English reader of *United Ireland*, if there were any, would have derived much comfort from the fact that Gladstone's conversion to home rule in 1886 caused one nationalist poetaster to pen the line, 'Saxon was the name for Fiend'.[102] For Irish nationalists to speak in racial terms, and yet attend the British parliament, raised difficulties; but they could be surmounted by emphasizing the foreign nature of the house of commons, where 'it was no very great thing to be a member of the English parliament. They all wanted to get out of it as quickly as they could'.[103] William Redmond in Fermoy emphasized that 'there was not a single man from Parnell down to himself who did not hate the government of England with all the intensity and fervour of his heart' (cheers). When one English MP had asked in his presence why Parnellites were so irreconcilable and pleased when things went wrong for the government 'the answer returned was this: "We are irreconcilable because it is the wish of our constituents that we should so act, and because all the wealth of the world could not buy for us greater pleasure or greater satisfaction than sticking thorns in the side of the British lion" '.[104]

Hatred of British rule was central to Irish nationalists; but it had to be reconciled with the limited nature of self-government demanded by the party; and it had to be reconciled also with parliamentary politics, with votes, not weapons, with a role in the 'alien assembly' of Westminster. Racial conflict sat cheek by jowl with federalism and devolution; agrarian agitation helped send Irish MPs to London to sit, act and vote in the enemy's style and tradition.

This made Parnellism something of a highly skilled mystery, and one that even its formidable leader found difficult to practise indefinitely. In a speech in October 1885 Parnell was studiously vague. He acknowledged British fears that home rule would lead to the separation of Ireland from England; but when he considered whether or not they were justified, he took refuge in the counter-claim that 'under 85 years of Parliamentary connection with England, Ireland has become intensely disloyal and intensely disaffected'. Did this mean that a home rule Ireland would be a loyal Ireland? Parnell dare not admit as much; he could, however, ask the English people to 'trust the Irish people altogether or trust them not at all. Give with a free and open hand . . . and you may depend upon one thing, that the desire for separation, the means of winning separation, at least will not be increased or intensified'. Parnell dwelt more on the dangers of withholding self-government from Ireland than on the benefits of granting it: if it were not given then the chance would be lost of removing 'the greatest peril to the English empire'; a peril, he continued in a complex sentence, 'which if not removed will find some day, perhaps not in our time – some year, perhaps not for many years to come, but will certainly find sooner or later, an opportunity of revenging itself – to the destruction of the British empire, but the misfortune, the oppression, and the misgovernment of our country'.[105]

This was for British consumption; but home rule had to take hold of the Irish voter's imagination, had to rally him to the cause, and, most important of all, had to persuade him to turn out to the polling booth at election time. Definitions of home rule ranged from the precise ('that this country should be represented in Dublin which would legislate for Ireland and leave to the imperial parliament the power to deal with empire affairs')[106] to the imprecise (the restoration to Ireland of her 'ancient parliament');[107] and, most commonly of all, home rule was simply spoken of as 'legislative independence',[108] 'national independence',[109] or as 'filing through the last link of the chain that binds our country to the chariot wheels of England'.[110] But behind these differing interpretations there lay a common theme; that of a downtrodden and abused race about to become at last a risen people. 'There never was a moment since Strongbow made himself our first landlord', declared *United Ireland* in August 1881, 'when the hopes of this nation were so high'; 'our race has struggled on and on out of the Darksome valley towards the light. We are the heirs of all the ages that have fought the good fight after their several ways'. 'In the past', it continued, in picturesque fashion:

> nothing Irish was in fashion except Irish rack-renting, and a race of creatures was growing up who got rid of their nationality with their dinner on the passage to Holyhead. Two years of unity and courage have brought the West Briton to tremble and feel ashamed.[111]

At a nationalist demonstration at Carndonagh, Co. Donegal, in February 1885, in the presence of William O'Brien and John Redmond, the chairman, the reverend father Doherty, reminded his listeners that 'for well night three centuries Donegal has been in a deep trance', but 'the jubilant cry of a resurgent nation has roused her into life and energy, and Clan-Owen, Clan-Connel are once more to the front again in Ireland's battle'.[112] At Athlone the reverend father Rossiter compared the Irish with 'the captive Israelites of old . . . the poor Irish might sit on the banks of their lovely ruins, and gaze on their green hills and their fertile valleys, but it was always with tearful eyes and throbbing breasts, and hearts sighing for the restoration of their pilfered rights'.[113] Home rule meant the 'complete emancipation of the Irish race';[114] the vindication of Robert Emmet;[115] an emancipated nation;[116] and it was a sign of the coming times that street names in Dublin were changing; they had no longer Sackville Street 'But instead they had O'Connell Street'.[117] The emotional thrust of home rule was similar to that of O'Connell's repeal movement, when it called for 'Ireland for the Irish'. 'We need not quarrel here as to the definition of home rule', said one nationalist in 1880, 'it means the government of the country by Irishmen.[118]

It might be said, however, that the important thing after 1885 was not the demand for home rule in Ireland, but the supply of that commodity in England, for Gladstone's bill offering a variety of important domestic powers to a parliament in Dublin, with Westminster retaining direct control in all matters affecting the crown, defence, and foreign relations, was as far as any English politician would go, and a good deal further than many of them thought safe. But to the nationalist people of Ireland home rule was not merely devolution – it was not devolution at all – it was the nation at last coming into its own, the tribe of Israel entering the promised land, Ireland a nation once again. Thus this apparently limited measure of self-government was the vindication of the heroes of '98, of Emmet, of Davis, of the Manchester martyrs. It was a principle, not a set of rather limited constitutional powers; and, while home rulers did not rule out the use of force to achieve self-government, they realized that, as *United Ireland* put it, the battle must not be fought according to England's plans: 'It is not going to be a battle of breach-loading rifles against naked breasts – at least as long as the breasts *are* naked'.[119] In other words, the constitutional nationalist with a parliament in the hollow of his hand cut a much less ridiculous figure than the physical force nationalist without one; and thus home rule satisfied a party which the R.I.C. estimated in

1887 to contain 21 out of 83 listed MPs of probably Fenian persuasion, four likely to supoort Fenian designs, and two as Fenians.[120]

Nevertheless, the days of militant constitutionalism, even at the height of its success in 1886, were numbered: for once Parnell committed himself to the liberal alliance, once he accepted the 'conversion' of Gladstone to home rule in 1886, he effectively ended the independent existence of the Irish home rule party; and his political effort after 1886 was directed, not to championing militant constitutionalism, but, on the contrary, to reassuring British opinion that constitutionalism was not as militant as all that: that home rulers were men who could be trusted not to injure or threaten what Parnell now chose to call 'a solution of the long-standing dispute between the two countries . . . a final settlement'. Thus he was quick to disassociate himself from the 'plan of campaign' organized by John Dillon in 1886 on a number of Irish estates, which involved offering the landlord what the tenants considered a fair rent, and, if he refused, withholding the rents and using them to support evicted tenants.[121] Never again did Parnell become involved in agrarian agitation; and it was his resolution also, but one that he was obliged to break in the last months of his life, never to speak in Ireland again. He had, as he told an audience in Edinburgh in 1889, no longer any desire to come into contact with 'the butt-end of a policeman's musket'.[122]

Parnell desired his party not only to show a more responsible face in England; he also found it expedient to win and retain the trust of the Catholic church in Ireland, which would have no truck with the use of force, however much it disliked British rule. He was not the only Irish leader who sought to do so; at a land league meeting held in Irishtown in May 1880 Michael Davitt felt obliged to reassure his chairman (a priest) and his listeners that the movement was not a communist one for Ireland 'was essentially a Christian country'.[123] Parnell, as a Protestant, had to be even more circumspect, just as the Fenians had been when they selected a Catholic, Kickham, to plead their cause in the face of clerical criticism. Parnell, once secure in the leadership in 1882, began to build up a working relationship with the church. He purged the party of any objectionable traits, especially on questions of education, and he spoke against the Queen's colleges,[124] always a touchstone of sound nationalism in the eyes of the church. The clergy were involved more closely in selecting candidates for the party, and were accorded the right to attend county conventions for this purpose; the thirty-two conventions held in connection with the 1885 election averaged 150 laymen and fifty priests each.[125] Reciprocal compliments were exchanged: at Kildare Parnell praised 'the four able and patriotic members of the hierarchy who are now your guests, the numerous array of the clergy of your county whom I see round me' who 'offered undoubtable tokens that the union of priests and people has been cemented afresh . . . never to be broken'.[126] In 1886 four Irish archbishops, each attended by two of their suffragans, met in Dublin to prepare for the forthcoming national synod and pronounced in favour of home rule which alone 'can satisfy the wants and needs of the Irish people'.[127] This event perhaps was the high water mark of clerical influence in the party; the abandonment of the convention system for choosing candidates during the period 1886-1890 reduced direct clerical involvement, but the clergy still held that position in society which *United Ireland* and Parnell praised, where 'there is not . . . the smallest trace of the irreligious poisons which are eating into the heart of the continental churches';[128] and there is no reason to doubt that the candidates chosen after 1886 were any less acceptable than those chosen before then.[129] But this was, once more, a significant step away from Parnellism as it had been created and practised between 1877 and 1885; for the church was still a conservative element in Irish nationalism, and because Parnell enjoyed its support, it did not follow that he enjoyed the full trust of the nationalist people of Ireland, especially those with land on their minds. Thus, while the hierarchy could not like the lawlessness and boycotting of the plan of campaign, they knew full well that to enforce the Papal condemnation of it in April 1888 would profoundly damage their relations with the laity, and lose them power and influence over millions of Catholics at home and abroad.[130] In this, they were more immediately aware than Parnell of the emotions and hatreds that lay behind nationalism in Ireland. For Parnell, the lion of Liberal society, these emotions, which had helped him to power, were now something of an embarrassment.

The leaders of the plan of campaign, John Dillon and William O'Brien, were able to take a firm stand against the hierarchy, not because their nationalism and their religion were separate affairs, but — on the contrary — because they were synonymous. There was no opposition, Dillon stated in 1890, between Irishmen's religion and Irishmen's politics: 'the man who is a good Catholic is a good Nationalist':

The day is gone by and I thank God for it, when anyone can sow dissension between the religion of the Irish people and the nationality of the Irish people, which it has always been our proudest boast have been kept in harmony, bound together by links which no Government and no coercion can tear asunder. The religion and nationality of the Irish people are bound to-day by stronger bonds than ever, which no power, whether it be a Catholic bishop or a Coercion Government, will ever sunder.[131]

The very orthodoxy of nationalists' Catholicism was their strength against clerical criticism; it was the suspicion that the Fenians were not orthodox that placed them in unlooked for difficulties.

This did not necessarily make the home rulers a sectarian party;[132] after all, it was the liberal Gladstone who in 1891 described the nonconformists of Wales as 'the people of Wales'.[133] Home rulers pointed out that 'Mr. Parnell and his party worked as well for oppressed protestants as for oppressed Catholics',[134] and appealed to Protestants to recollect that some of the most celebrated Irish patriots were Protestants, 'the heroes and darlings of the Irish heart'.[135] But they also assumed, just as O'Connell had assumed, that 'faith and fatherland' were as one, that the same 'spiritual longings and national aspirations which their fathers held indivisably through ages of suffering' still survived.[136] And Protestant refusal to vote for home rule was met with blank disbelief or, at times, round abuse. Referring to the election results of 1885 *United Ireland* exclaimed:

86 to 18! This the way the Irish representation now stands. 86 men in favour of making Ireland a nation. 18 wanting to keep her a province, and a province on which they can selfishly batten.

And there was a hint of menace in its comment that, if Irish Protestants made peace with their countrymen, much would be forgotten and forgiven, but 'if things are to be otherwise, the parliament will be otherwise, and it is for the loyalists to make their choice'.[137] The *Connaught Telegraph* referred to the home rule gains in Ulster in 1885 as bringing back 'recollections of old time victories in that hallowed soil by Owen Roe O'Neill and other leaders, whose sacred "memory" will be "pious, glorious and immortal", in the hearts of their countrymen, when the name of Dutch and English cut-throats and soldiers will become amongst us by-words of mockery, which they should ever have been'.[138] In Longford Justin McCarthy, in one and the same breath, declared that he 'did not despair by any means' of having Protestant and Orange friends 'even yet on their side': the seat he had won in Derry showed that 'they were very near levelling the old walls of ascendancy in Derry', and 'the time was approaching when the city of Derry would be given to the Irish cause'.[139]

Parnell's mastery of Ireland – of all Ireland, and of all Irishmen – was never complete; but it was perhaps the best that any man could do in the circumstances; and the difficulty of running together in the same harness moderate nationalists, Fenians, the Catholic church, agrarian radicals, and parliamentary MPs, to say nothing of seeking to win, by votes or persuasion, Unionist Ireland and especially Unionist Ulster, made him turn with relief to the Liberal alliance, and abandon the tactics that had brought him to prominence and power. The defeat of 1886, after all, was far from final; and in August 1890 William O'Brien described as a 'mathematical certainty and absolute certainty:

> that the day was coming when . . . that principle of Ireland a nation would be recognised and welcomed just as warmly by the working millions of Great Britain as it was by that audience (in Ireland), and when the only wonder of Englishmen, Scotchmen, and Welshmen in future would be that it had taken seven centuries to discover the justice, the safety, and the indestructability of the principle of Irish nationality, for which Sarsfield once filled the breach at Limerick, and for which Robert Emmet died on the scaffold.[140]

Parnell did not entirely burn his boats, for in 1889 he warned that if parliamentary action were to fail 'I for one would not continue to remain for twenty-four hours longer in the house of commons at Westminster';[141] but this appeared unnecessary when Parnell's popularity reached its apogee after his trial and acquittal for complicity in the Phoenix Park murders of 1882.[142] Liberals and home rulers seemed set on a fair course, with Liberal victories in by-elections promising a sweeping triumph in the not too distant future. But the citation of Parnell as co-respondent in a divorce action which revealed publicly his long-concealed liaison with Mrs O'Shea, wife of one of his MPs, demonstrated both the power of the liberal alliance, and the distance which Parnell had travelled from Parnellism since his rise to the party leadership.

For the bitter dispute between Parnell and the bulk of his party was not only a dispute between 'moderates' and 'extremists', between clerical and secular nationalism; it was also one between those who adhered to the belief that the liberal alliance was the only way to get home rule and thus make Ireland a nation,[143] and those who wanted to chance a return to Parnellism as it had been practised in the heady years of 1877-1885. The Catholic hierarchy flung itself into the battle, and must have exercised some influence on public opinion in a country where the priesthood was accorded the indubitable right to pronounce on moral issues: and Parnell's fall was now a moral issue.[144] But its frantic behaviour was a mark, not of its confidence, but its anxiety, for it was now attempting to re-establish the principle, recently called in question, that it must not be taken for granted by the political leaders of the nation.[145] Parnell appeared to be calling on traditional anti-clerical forces, and appealing to the 'hill-side men'. But there were no anti-clerical forces of any significance to appeal to in Ireland; and Parnell was against the priests because the priests were against him. At times he seemed to advocate, not militant constitutionalism, but a direct resort to violence; but he never committed himself thus far: he only warned of the danger of driving out of the home rule movement the 'imperishable force' of Irish nationalism without which, he rightly said, 'we are broken reeds'. The furthest he would go towards physical force was to declare, darkly but ambiguously, that 'if Ireland leaves this path upon which I have set her . . . I will not for my part say that I will not accompany her further':[146] a profoundly anti-climactic statement.

In his last campaign Parnell was bent on surrendering himself, not to violence, but to those forces out of which he had constructed Parnellism on his way to the top. He called for an independent Irish party[147] and appealed to the kind of emotions that provided the driving power behind the home rule movement, and which continued to give home rule its attraction long after his death. When Patrick Pearse proclaimed Parnell a 'separatist by instinct,'[148] he was mistaken: Parnell was not a separatist by instinct, even though he was prepared to let separatists comfort themselves with the reflection that he was, ultimately, on their side. But while Parnell was not himself a separatist, the Irish nationalism that he represented was indeed separatist, not, perhaps, in its claim, but in its aspiration:[149] an aspiration based not, as Butt hoped, on a desire to achieve the best and most honourable agreement between Britain and Ireland, but on hostility to Britain and her empire. Parnell managed to persuade Irish nationalists that he was like them: that he could achieve the means to achieve freedom, and liberate Ireland from the Saxon.[150] For Irish nationalism was not militant merely, but constitutional as well; not constitutional merely, but anti-British as well.

Parnell now sought to mobilize these separatist, anti-British feelings on his own behalf;[151] but the vast majority of the nationalist electorate[152] continued to believe what he had taught them since 1886: that the means to achieve freedom, and thus to satisfy their aspirations, lay in the Liberal alliance, and that no other means were possible or, in present circumstances, desirable. This did not make them pro-British: it simply meant that they realized that Parnellism, the Parnellism of 1877-1885, offered less hope of making Ireland a nation than did the Liberals' promised home rule bill. Between 1877 and 1885 Parnellism carried Parnell to power and near-success; after 1886 Parnell disentangled himself from Parnellism with relief, and committed all to the Liberal alliance. When this alliance broke his leadership of the party in 1890, he sought to save his position by playing upon the sentiments that had helped him to power in the first place, and directing them against the Liberal alliance. But the party and the country would not follow him: they shared his emotions, but disapproved of his tactics. It was perhaps tragic, but appropriate, that in 1886 Parnell destroyed Parnellism, and in 1891 Parnellism destroyed Parnell.

Notes

1. J.C. Beckett, 'The church of Ireland: disestablishment and its aftermath', in *Confrontations*, pp. 154-5.

2. F.H. O'Donnell, *History of the Irish Parliamentary Party* (London, 2 vols., 1912), I, p. 19.

3. R.B. MacDowell, *The Church of Ireland, 1869-1969* (London, 1975), p. 50.

4. D. Thornley, *Isaac Butt and Home Rule* (London, 1964), p. 68.

5. See his argument in *The Famine in the Land* (Dublin, 1847), esp. p. 55.

6. Thornley, pp. 97-102.

7. Ibid., pp. 92-4.

8. Ibid., pp. 94-5.

9. Ibid., pp. 96-7.

10. Kee, op. cit., p. 359.

11. P.J. Corish, 'Political problems, 1860-1878' in *A History of Irish Catholicism*, vol. *V* (Dublin, 1967), pp. 48-50.

12. O'Hegarty, op. cit., p. 488.

13. Corish, op. cit., pp. 52-55.

14. Ibid., p. 58.

15. *Flag of Ireland*, 3 Jan. 1874, 10 Jan. 1874, 7 Feb. 1974.

16. *Waterford News*, 6 Feb. 1874.

17. *Leinster Reporter*, 12 Feb. 1874.

18. *Munster News and Limerick and Clare Advertiser*, 7 Feb. 1874.

19. *Flag of Ireland*, 3 Jan. 1874.

20. *Waterford News*, 6 Feb. 1874; see also the home rule ballads in G.D. Zimmerman, *Irish political street ballads and rebel songs 1798-1900* (Geneva, 1966), pp. 60-61.

21. Thornley, op. cit., Chap. V.

22. Ibid., p. 227.

23. A.M. Sullivan, *New Ireland*, pp. 396-99; I. Butt, *Irish Federalism: its meaning, its objects, and its hopes* (Dublin, 1874), p. x.

24. Thornley, pp. 255-6, 270; Sullivan, pp. 410-29.

25. Thornley, pp. 283, 291-99, 331.

26. K.T. Hoppen, 'Landlords, society and electoral politics in mid-nineteenth century Ireland', in *Past and Present*, no. 75 (May 1977), pp. 62-93; O. MacDonagh, 'Irish famine emigration', op. cit., pp. 358-9. Of course the proportion of labourers varied from place to place: in the Kanturk area of Cork labourers and farm servants were over ¼ of the total adult male population (Pamela L.R. Horn, 'The national agricultural labourers union in Ireland, 1873-9' in *Irish Historical Studies*, vol. *17* (1970-71), pp. 240-52).

27. *Cork Daily Herald*, 16 Nov. 1885.

28. F.S.L. Lyons, *The Irish Parliamentary Party, 1890-1910* (London, 1951), p. 220.

29. *Cork Examiner*, 13 Jan. 1910.

30. *Limerick Echo*, 21 Aug. 1900.

31. Ibid., 11 and 25 Sept. 1900.

32. The best discussion of the politics of the 1850s is J. Whyte, *The Independent Irish Party, 1850-59* (Oxford, 1958).

33. M. MacDermott, *The New Spirit of the Nation* (London, 1894), pp. 5-7.

34. G. Russell, *The national being: Some Thoughts on an Irish Polity* (Dublin and London, n.d. (1916?)), p. 21.

35. Lee, *Modernization of Irish Society*, pp. 97-99; S. Clark, 'The social composition of the land league', in *Irish Historical Studies*, no. 68 (Sept. 1971), pp. 447-69, and 'The political mobilization of Irish farmers', in *Canadian Review of Sociology and Anthropology*, vol. *12* (4: Part 2), 1975, pp. 483-97.

36. K.T. Hoppen, 'Politics, the law, and the nature of the Irish electorate', op. cit., pp. 774-76.

37. W.E. Vaughan, 'Landlord and tenant relations in Ireland between the famine and the land war, 1850-1878', in L.M. Cullen and T.C. Smout (eds.), *Comparative Aspects of Scottish and Irish Economic and Social History, 1660-1900* (Edinburgh, n.d. (1977), pp. 216-26).

38. Lee, op. cit., p. 77.

39. J. Whyte, 'The influence of the Catholic clergy on elections', op. cit., p. 254.

40. R.V. Comerford, *C.J. Kickham*, pp. 124-5.

41. L. O'Broin, *Revolutionary Underground: the Story of the IRB, 1858-1924* (Dublin, 1976), pp. 6-7, 11.

42. Comerford, op. cit., pp. 125-29.

43. MacDonagh, 'Irish Famine emigration', op. cit., pp. 376-7, 390-91, 442.

44. Sheridan Gilley, 'English attitudes to the Irish in England, 1780-1900', in C. Holmes (ed.), *Immigrants and Minorities in British Society* (London, 1978), pp. 81-110 esp. pp. 104-5; T.P. O'Connor, *The Parnell Movement* (London, 1886), pp. 282-3; C.C. O'Brien, *Parnell and his Party*, p. 161.

45. Thomas N. Brown, *Irish-American Nationalism, 1870-1890* (Philadelphia and New York, 1966), pp. 17-24.

46. O'Broin, op. cit., pp. 11; C.C. O'Brien, op. cit., pp. 124-5; P.S. O'Hegarty, op. cit., p. 472. When Parnell went to America in 1876 he did so in the company of John O'Conor Power of the IRB to present the president of the United States with an 'Address to the American people on the centenary of United States independence' drawn up at a meeting of advanced nationalists in Dublin organized by the local IRB under John Leary (L.O.Broin, op. cit., p. 13).

47. Lee, op. cit., p. 13.

48. J.S. Donnelly, *The Land and the People of Nineteenth Century Cork* (Dublin, 1973), pp. 248-9.

49. Whyte, 'Political influence of Catholic clergy', op. cit., p. 255.

50. Lee, op. cit., p. 13.

51. Figures abstracted from V.E. Glandon, 'Index of Irish newspapers, 1900-1922', part i, and part ii, *Eire/Ireland*, vol. *XI*, No. 4, vol. *XII*, No. 1.

52. Lee, op. cit., p. 69, 84; for some interesting comments on the political role of Irish journalists see T.H. Escott, *Masters of English Journalism* (London, 1911), pp. 315, 318-20.

53. Donnelly, op. cit., p. 249. For the influence of the press on land agitation between 1850 and 1870 see E.D. Steele, *Irish Land and British Politics*, pp. 26-7.

54. P. Bew, *Land and the National Question in Ireland*, pp. 8-14, 30-32; J.E. Pomfret, *The Struggle for Land in Ireland, 1800-1923* (New York, 1969 ed.), p. 101-3.

55. Donnelly, op. cit., pp. 6-7, 148-9, 251-56.

56. Bew, op. cit., pp. 56-8.

57. Ibid., p. 31.

58. Lee, op. cit., pp. 67-9; S. Clark, 'The social composition of the land league', *Irish Historical Studies*, vol. *XVII*, (Sept. 1971), pp. 447-69.

59. M. Davitt, *Leaves from a Prison Diary* (Irish University Press, 1972 edn.), p. 99.

60. Bew, op. cit., p. 59.

61. T.W. Moody, 'Michael Davitt, 1846-1906: a survey and an appreciation', part i, *Studies*, vol. *XXXV* (1946), pp. 199-208; M. Davitt, *The fall of feudalism in Ireland* (1904; I.U.P., 1970, edn.), pp. 160-63.

62. Comerford, op. cit., pp. 139-46; T.W. Moody, 'The new departure in Irish politics, 1878-9' in J.A. Cronne *et al* (eds.), *Essays in British and Irish history in Honour of James Eadie Todd* (London, 1949), pp. 303-33.

63. Bew, op. cit., pp. 47-9, 51-2; O'Broin, *Revolutionary Underground*, pp. 19-21.

64. F.S.I. Lyons, 'The political ideas of Parnell' in *Historical Journal*, vol. *XVI*, No. 4 (1973), pp. 749-75; F.H. O'Donnell is perhaps the chief source of the belief that Parnell was totally ignorant of Irish history; see his *History of the Irish Parliamentary party* (2 vols., London, 1910), I, pp. 278-9.

65. F.S. Lyons, *Parnell* (London, 1977), pp. 25-36.

66. Ged. Martin, 'Parnell at Cambridge: the education of an Irish nationalist', *Irish Historical Studies*, vol. *19* (1974-75), pp. 62-72.

67. Bew, op. cit., p. 62.

68. R.F. Foster, *Charles Stewart Parnell: the man and his family* (Sussex, 1976), pp. 133, 166-77.

69. Lyons, *Parnell*, pp. 348ff.

70. Estimates of the precise number of home rule members vary, mainly because of the loose party organization and the fact that some home rulers were, in fact, ordinary Liberals. The contemporary press puts the number at 63; Dr. C.C. O'Brien estimates that '61 were all, in some sense, home rulers and constituted the Irish Parliamentary party' (*Parnell and his Party*, pp. 12-13). The March meeting was attended by 43 members, with 23 supporting Parnell (ibid., p. 25).

71. Judith M. Brown, 'The role of a national leader: Gandhi, Congress and Civil disobedience, 1929-34', in D.A. Low (ed.) *Congress and the Raj* (London, 1977), pp. 133, 147, 151-9, offers interesting comments on the role of Gandhi as national leader in India on which I have drawn for this paragraph.

72. Lyons, *Parnell*, pp. 49-50, 53-76, 97-104, 110-13.

73. Bew, op. cit., p. 82 notes this point.

74. T.P. O'Connor, *The Parnell movement* (London, 1886), pp. 386-7.

75. Lyons, op. cit., pp. 139-40.

76. C.C. O'Brien, *Parnell and his Party* pp. 71-2.

77. Bew, op. cit., pp. 196-200; O'Brien, op. cit., pp. 72-4.

78. Lyons, op. cit., pp. 177-207; Bew, op. cit., pp. 194-206.

79. O'Brien, op. cit., p. 82.

80. Lyons, op. cit., pp. 209-37; O'Brien, op. cit., pp. 126-33; Pomfret, op. cit., pp. 190-91.

81. Lyons, op. cit., p. 257.
82. E.D. Steele, *Irish Land and British Politics*, p. 19.
83. O'Farrell, *Ireland's English question*, pp. 120-23; Stewart, *Narrow Ground*, pp. 122-7.
84. Pomfret, op. cit., passim.
85. Vaughan, op. cit., passim.
86. Both E.D. Steele, *Irish land and British politics*, pp. 2-4, 19, 20, 38, and J.C. Beckett, *Anglo-Irish tradition*, pp. 92-3 refer to the existence of a folk-memory, but without citing sources; Stewart, *Narrow Ground*, pp. 123-7 offers interesting evidence on this point. But the subject needs a full investigation.
87. L.M. Cullen, 'Irish nationalism', pp. 3-4, quoting J.P. Prendergast's, *The Cromwellian Settlement of Ireland* (1865).
88. C. Dewey, 'Celtic agrarian legislation and the Celtic revival: historicist implications of Gladstone's Irish and Scottish land acts, 1870-1886', in *Past and Present*, No. 64 (1974), pp. 30-70.
89. P.S. O'Hegarty, op. cit., p. 487.
90. *Donegal Independent*, 21 Nov. 1885; see also his speech in Nov. 1885 referring to 'landlord robbers' who must be 'cut down and trampled under foot' (*United Ireland*, 14 Nov. 1885).
91. *Waterford News*, 27 Nov., 4 Dec. 1885.
92. *Connaught People*, 17 Oct. 1885, 31 Oct. 1885.
93. *Roscommon Herald* 3 July 1886.
94. *United Ireland*, 19 Dec. 1885, 26 Sept. 1885, 28 Nov. 1885.
95. O'Hegarty, op. cit., p. 488.
96. A. O'Day, *The English Face of Irish Nationalism* (Dublin, 1977), passim, esp. pp. 23-4, 182-3.
97. M. Chamberlain, *Britain and India: the Interaction of Two Peoples* (Newton Abbot, 1974), p. 171.
98. A. Reid (ed.), *Ireland: a Book of Light on the Irish Problem* (London, 1886), pp. xii, 77-87.
99. *Connaught Telegraph*, 3 April 1880.
100. *Cork Daily Herald*, 24 Nov. 1885.
101. See e.g. *Wexford People*, 3 April 1880; *Cork Daily Herald*, 5 April 1880.
102. *United Ireland*, 10 July 1886.
103. *Connaught People*, 31 Oct. 1885 (speech of John Dillon).
104. *United Ireland*, 13 June 1885; see also 14 Nov. 1885 when he declared that one of the qualities required of a Parnellite MP was 'that he should hate with all his heart British rule in Ireland'. William O'Brien also spoke of Westminster as 'that foreign parliament', Ibid., 21 Feb. 1885.
105. O'Hegarty, op. cit., pp. 539-40.
106. *Wexford People*, 27 March 1880 (Mr Meldon).
107. *Donegal Independent*, 21 Nov. 1885 (W. Redmond).
108. *Wexford People*, 27 March 1880; see also *Kerry Sentinal*, 19 March 1880.
109. *Connaught People*, 31 Oct. 1885 (Matthew Harris).
110. *Cork Daily Herald*, 16 Nov. 1885; see also 24 Nov. 1885.
111. *United Ireland*, 13 Aug. 1881.
112. Ibid., 7 Feb.1885.
113. *Westmeath Independent*, 10 July 1886.
114. *Cork Daily Herald*, 24 Nov. 1885 (Mr Tanner).
115. *United Ireland*, 15 Aug. 1885.
116. *Kingstown Standard*, 28 Nov. 1885.
117. *Donegal Independent*, 12 Dec. 1885.
118. Mr J.W. Foley at New Ross: *Wexford People*, 27 Mar. 1880.
119. *United Ireland*, 8 Oct. 1881; see also 13, 20 Aug. 1881, 31 Jan. 1885, 28 Nov. 1885.

120. Bew, op. cit., p. 229.

121. Pomfret, op. cit., pp. 255-6.

122. Lyons, 'Political ideas of Parnell', op. cit., pp. 763, 767, 771, 773, fn. 69. Lyons 'John Dillon and the plan of campaign, 1886-90', in *Irish Historical Studies*, XIV (1965), pp. 313-47.

123. *Connaught Telegraph*, 8 May 1880; the chairman, for his part, referred to 'Catholic patriotic Irishtown'.

124. Lyons, *Parnell*, pp. 249-56; M. Tierney, *Croke of Cashel: the life of archbishop T.W. Croke*, 1823-1902 (Dublin, 1976), pp. 168-9.

125. Lyons, pp. 256-7.

126. *United Ireland*, 17 Oct. 1885.

127. E. Larkin, *The Roman Catholic Church and the Creation of the Modern Irish State, 1878-1886* (Dublin, 1975), pp. 362-3.

128. *United Ireland*, 13 June 1885.

129. C.C. O'Brien, *Parnell and his Party* (Oxford, 1974 edn), pp. 258-61.

130. E. Larkin, *The Roman Catholic Church in Ireland and the Fall of Parnell 1888-1891* (Liverpool, 1979), pp. xviii-xx, 17, 49-50.

131. Ibid., pp. 173-4.

132. G.O Tuathaigh, 'Nineteenth century Irish politics: the case for "normalcy" ', in *Anglo-Irish Studies*, vol. *1* (1975), pp. 71-81.

133. K.O. Morgan, 'Welsh Nationalism: the historical background', *J.C.H..*, vol. *6* (1971), p. 156.

134. *Donegal Independent*, 21 Nov. 1885 (W. Redmond); see also *Waterford News*, 20 Nov. 1885, 4 Dec. 1885 (E. Clancy, P.J. Power); *Limerick Chronicle*, 7 Nov. 1885 (Mr Abraham): *United Ireland*, 21 Nov. 1885 (Father Conlon).

135. *United Ireland*, 28 Nov. 1885 (W. O'Brien); see also *Wexford People*, 27 Mar. 1880 (Rev. Furlong); *Cork Daily Herald*, 16 Nov. 1885 (Alderman Hooper), 19 Nov. 1885 (J. Dillon). See also John Redmond, 'Irish protestants and home rule', in R.B. O'Brien (ed.), *Home rule speeches of J. Redmond* (London, 1910), pp. 26-41.

136. *United Ireland*, 13 June 1885.

137. Ibid., 12, 26 Dec. 1885.

138. *Connaught Telegraph*, 12 Dec. 1885.

139. *Longford Independent*, 10 July 1886. In Donegal the Reverend Canon Clifford declared that the Irish parliament would represent everyone, irrespective of his religion, and at the same time recommended the home rule candidate as 'not only a Catholic in name but a practical (sic) Catholic' (*Donegal Independent*, 12 Dec. 1885).

140. E. Larkin, *Roman Catholic Church and the Fall of Parnell*, p. 176.

141. Lyons, 'Political ideas of Parnell', op. cit., p. 756.

142. Kee, *Green Flag*, p. 409.

143. See e.g. Alfred Webb, *An Address to the Electors of West Waterford* (Dublin, 1891), pp. 6-7.

144. C.J. Woods, 'The general election of 1892', op. cit., p. 291.

145. Larkin, op. cit., Chaps. 5, 6.

146. Lyons, *Parnell*, pp. 532ff, 539, 545, 598.

147. Ibid., p. 503.

148. Ibid., p. 614.

149. For the important distinction between a claim and an aspiration see C.C. O'Brien in A.C. Hepburn (ed.), *The Conflict of Nationality in Modern Ireland* (London, 1980), pp. 205-6.

150. *United Ireland*, 24 Jan. 1885 (speech of William Redmond to the Young Ireland Society of Dublin, in reply to an address by John O'Leary).

151. T.D. Sullivan, *Recollections of Troubled Times in Irish Politics* (Dublin, 1905), pp. 296-7.

152. The general election of 1892 saw 9 Parnellite candidates returned against 71 anti-Parnellites (Kee, op. cit., p. 413).

8 THE BATTLE OF THREE CIVILIZATIONS

The Anglo-Irish presence in Ireland, from the twelfth century onwards, was a most significant influence on the development of a self-conscious Irish identity, and of parliamentary institutions to give this identity political expression; it was these people, essentially of English origin, who — often for their own ends — formulated and articulated Ireland's 'ancient historic rights'. Parnell was the last, and greatest, in the long line of Anglo-Irishmen who made a contribution to this tradition; the difference was that whereas his forbears, Swift and Grattan, spoke for the Protestant nation, Parnell represented, in fact if not in name, the Catholic nation. But the Anglo-Irish not only provided political precedents and precepts for Irish nationalists; they also, and especially after 1890, helped give Ireland a distinctive cultural identity, a sense of the individuality of the Irish nation, and of its peculiar linguistic, social and racial characteristics. This they did wittingly and unwittingly. Wittingly, in the attempt made by some prominent Anglo-Irishmen to identify with and save Irish culture in the hope that it would provide a common ground for Irishmen of all political persuasions; and unwittingly, by the fact that the 'colonial' dominance of Ireland stood for what came to be regarded as an alien culture, against which the Irish identity must assert itself, and which it must absorb, or itself suffer absorption. The 'battle of two civilizations'[1] was fought, not only between England and Ireland, but, and perhaps more fiercely, within Ireland; and it acquired a special intensity in the last decade of the nineteenth century with the fall of that most celebrated representative of the Anglo-Irish nationalists, Charles Stewart Parnell.

The paradox of Parnell's people — their interest in native culture, and yet their precarious position in that culture — was inherent in their own identity. As newcomers and, eventually, conquerors, they destroyed much that was native; but as Irishmen who had come to stay in Ireland they preserved and valued much that might otherwise have disappeared. But to their critics it was the destruction not the preservation that was emphasized and remembered.[2] Thus, while the Anglo-Irishmen gentlemen of the eighteenth century were exploring happily the world of Irish literature, architecture and language, and casting a warm eye on Gaelic ruins and graveyards, one of their foremost enemies, Daniel Corkery, accused then in retrospect of presiding over the destruction of Gaelic Ireland, of the whole Irish way of life which resided above all in the common people, 'the legatees of all the culture of the Gaelic ages' who were 'suffering so deeply that they sometimes cried out that God had forgotten them'.[3]

The paradox of the Anglo-Irish presence in Ireland – their role as destroyers and preservers of Gaelic Irish culture – was seen in their different and contrasting attitudes to that culture. Some, like provost Mahaffy, of Trinity College, Dublin, hated and despised it;[4] but they were not typical. The mainstream Anglo-Irish attitude fell into two broad responses. There were those, beginning with the eighteenth century antiquarians, who sought to salvage what they could of Irish culture and offer it as a contribution to the contemporary European literary and scholarly world. Grattan's Parliament was not, as least in any direct way, inspired by enthusiasm for the Celtic past, but the general glow of Irish nationalism encouraged an interest in the Gaelic tradition, and helped Protestants feel that here was something in which they could be proud: an ancient literary, social and linguistic tradition that enabled Ireland and Irishmen to hold up their heads in the world a little higher even than they were normally disposed to do. The energies released by late eighteenth century nationalism were the background to the work of Sylvester O'Halloran, whose enthusiasm led to the foundation of the Royal Irish Academy in 1785 devoted to the study of 'science, polite literature, and antiquities' and Charlotte Brooke, whose *Reliques of Irish poetry* were published in 1789, and Joseph Cooper Walker, who pursued antiquarian researches of considerable distinction.[5]

This tradition, of concerned but scholarly study of Ireland's culture, persisted throughout the nineteenth century, and the graph of its progress can be plotted on the points of various learned societies: the Gaelic Society of Dublin, 1806; the Iberno-Celtic Society, 1818; the Celtic Society, 1843; the Ossianic Society, 1853. Research was promoted, texts collated and published, local Irish history investigated.[6] In 1833 a group of young men in Trinity College Dublin founded the *Dublin University Magazine* to educate Irishmen in literary taste, and to encourage the publication of literary works dealing with Irish themes. There was much in all this that was mediocre; but a tradition that produced Sir Samuel Ferguson, a member of the Anglo-Irish professional middle classes, stood firmly upon its own merits. Ferguson sought to stimulate all Irishmen, and especially Protestants, to take an interest in the history and antiquities of Ireland in order to develop a distinctively Irish contribution to literature, and to lay the foundations of a national literature worthy of his country. His first volume of verse was published in 1867; and whatever his shortcomings as a poet, he succeeded in imparting literary merit to his poems, and strove to do much more than discover words and lines that rhymed, unflatteringly, with 'Saxon foe' or its equivalent.[7] The politics of these men of letters included the staunch Toryism of the *Dublin University Magazine* editors and the Burkeian Unionism of Ferguson.[8] But their efforts were directed towards establishing and fostering Irish literature for literature's sake, and as a sign to the cultured world that Ireland was no backwater, inhibited merely by stage-Irishmen, but a country with a literary and scholarly tradition of which it could be proud. They were not literary nationalists; but they were literary patriots. Taste and discernment, not propaganda, were what they sought to disseminate; thus they could establish their point that Irish literature was a worthy brand of learning, and something in which Irishmen could take pride. They could take pride in it because it was not only Irish, but critically meritorious. It was not meant to foster Irish nationalism, nor, above all, was it to be judged by nationalistic standards; it was meant to bring Irishmen to a sensibility of what great literature they had produced, and, if properly educated, could produce.

It is perhaps ingenuous to suggest that, in the highly politicized world of late eighteenth and nineteenth century Ireland, any branch of cultural pursuits could be wholly free from political implications. Maria Edgeworth was careful to preface her novel, Castle Rackrent, published in 1800, with a caution that it dealt, not with contemporary life in Ireland, but with a 'race' of landlords 'long extinct'[9]; and Lady Morgan, the daughter of an eminent English surgeon practising in Dublin, sought in her works to counter English and Protestant prejudice against Irish Roman Catholics.[10] But this was very different from the attitude and motive of the other major Anglo-Irish response to the native culture, literary nationalism, of which the most fervent exponents were Thomas Davis and his Young Irelanders.

Davis hoped that the Irish cultural past might be the means of enabling Irishmen to discover their common heritage, of linking contemporary Ireland with its romantic, heroic, bygone age. In so doing he and his colleagues sought to restore to Ireland self-respect and self-confidence; but this self-respect was to be based, not on Ireland's literary accomplishments, but on what literature could accomplish for Ireland. And what literature could accomplish for Ireland was the justification of Ireland's claims to a distinctive national existence. This marked Davis off from Ferguson, for although Davis was a man of taste and education, he was prepared, and willingly prepared to compromise literary standards for the sake of nationalistic effect. Davis's call was to 'educate that you may be free', and it was the goal of freedom that took precedence over all other considerations, although not to the extent that the *Nation* would give a book a bad review, simply because it disapproved of the politics of its author.[11] Feeling, he advised would-be contributors, came before style;[12] literature was didactic; and Irish culture was seen in a wholly uncritical light. It was too precious, too essential a part of the Irish identity, to be exposed to the blasts of literary critics.

Here were two ways of looking at Irish culture. The literary patriots were anxious to save and preserve the heritage, and to secure for Ireland a place in the European tradition. The literary nationalists wanted to preserve the heritage, not for primarily literary purposes, but because it might advance the cause of Irish nationality. The patriots were not necessarily nationalists; and the nationalists were not necessarily patriots, for they were interested only in promoting national, not literary, self-awareness: 'But if my country still doth bear the chain', wrote E. and A.M.Forrester in the *Songs of the Rising Nation*, 'Let them (the verses) be burnt – I've written them in vain'.[13] As the nineteenth century wore on the literary nationalists became less concerned about critical standards than even Davis had been, and more anxious to promote nationalism, and, even, the means to achieve it: Jeremiah O'Donovan Rossa's 'National and Literary Society', founded in 1856, quickly became a front for military action;[14] the pen was mightier than the sword, it seemed, in a literal sense. John O'Leary was aware that much Young Ireland literature was inferior and he disliked the idea that prose and poetry should be judged solely by reference to its political content; but he believed also that nationalism and literature could not live without each other. They were mutually dependent, for a political revolution could not succeed unless it was backed by a cultural revival:[15] and he summed up the Davisite tradition in a phrase: 'literature must be national and, nationalism must be literary'.[16] The Fenian newspaper, *The Irish People*, published poetry, albeit of inferior quality to that of the *Nation*; but its central aim was achieved, in that it handed on the Davisite idea of an indissoluble link between literature and nationalism, and strengthened the idea that Davis promoted, while never fully adhering to, that literature and violent revolutions were inseparable.

The nationalists of the Parnellite era were by no means unaware of the existence of Irish language and literature, nor did they neglect to include it in their general panacea of home rule. In 1883, W.J.O'Neill

Daunt, an admirer of Isaac Butt and later of Parnell and Biggar, deplored the 'contemptible indifference' of the Irish people to their 'ancient national language'. He accepted the need for the Irish to learn English as a 'utility' measure, for he was also an admirer of Daniel O'Connell; but he hoped that they might be, like the Welsh, bilingual. And he was disgusted by the fact that, when addressing a young man or woman in Irish, he was 'pretty sure to be met with some such answer as this, "I don't ondherstand Irish", or "I has no Irish" '.[17] The Parnellite newspaper, *United Ireland*, regularly printed reports of the activities of the Gaelic Athletic association, an organization founded in Thurles town in 1884 to revive Irish sports, and it praised Archbishop Croke for his efforts to revive what he called 'our national features'[18] : such things helped 'keep back the demoralizing and prostrating tide' which was threatening 'our chief racial characteristics'.[19] But the emphasis of the home rule movement was always on political action, with literature, language, culture relegated to second place. 'The time in which we advance from thinking to realising leaves less play to the fancy', wrote a reviewer of Denis Florence McCarthy's *Poems* in 1882. 'We can do with fewer sad poems, having destroyed much of the cause of sadness, we can even dispense with beautiful literary ornamentation, as soldiers, during a campaign, use little pipe clay and less gold lace on their coats'. Once the political battle was won, then the 'day of the gay uniforms and glittering banners returns for the soldiers'; but until then the 'occasional poetic revel' notwithstanding, the 'harsher summons of some evicting landlord or crimes act constable' were the realities of the Irish condition. 'The times', *United Ireland* observed in 1889, 'are highly unfavourable for the cultivation of the intellectual faculties of Irishmen, save in the direction of devising means of resisting naked tyranny'. Once the political crisis was resolved, wrote Justin McCarthy in 1890, 'the minds of Irish men and women will begin to settle down, and the lecture halls, the studies and the studios will be opened again'.[20] National culture would follow naturally upon the achievement of national independence.

It was ironic that the politically absorbed home rule movement, led by the profoundly political and non-literary Parnell, should have precipitated what subsequently became known as the Irish literary revival; but the political convulsions that followed the fall of Parnell were not confined to the members and followers of his party. Parnell down, and then Parnell dead, became a literary figure. It was not only the heroic style of the 'lost leader' that helped inspire those like William Butler Yeats, who saw Ireland as 'like soft wax for years to come';[21] it was the fact that politics, and especially the political bargaining that dominated the home rule movement's tactics, had manifestly exhausted their potential for national regeneration, at least for the time being. This is not to say that Irishmen 'turned away from politics'. They did not, as their capacity for hard and bitter political wrangling demonstrated in the decade after the Parnell split. It was rather that the kind of curb, or check, that the politicians placed on literary activity was now removed: since the defeat of the second Home Rule Bill in 1893 by the House of Lords indicated that independence was as far away as ever, there could be no excuse for postponing all other activities – cultural, literary, artistic – until the day of freedom dawned.

The literary revival, however, was not one that embraced, or even interested, the mass of the Irish people, Catholic or Protestant. Parnellism was a mass movement, attracting the support of voters and non-voters alike in the great crusade, for land reform, for self-government; literary Parnellism was different. It was essentially an affair of the intellectuals, for there was no substantial middle class outside Belfast and Dublin to sustain a literary movement which aspired to creative standards, as distinct from the homely nationalist verse and writings of the Young Ireland school. The Catholic tenant farmer, the core of the political world of nationalist Ireland, knew what he liked and liked what he knew. Nevertheless, the literary revival, however much it began and remained a minority affair, did have a contribution to make to the Irish nationalist tradition; and even those who played no part in it, or who remained suspiciously aloof from it, or even highly critical of it, were to live in an Ireland which the movement helped shape.

For the Irish revival, although it was a literary revival, was not merely literary: had it been, then it would have produced fine works of art, but exercised little influence on the political development of Ireland. The literary revival, and the whole awareness of Irish art, culture, language, were inspired by a concern that the Irish identity was in danger of erosion, perhaps even disappearance. The Young Irelanders and the Fenians had felt this as well, for the crisis of identity in nineteenth century Ireland was a cyclical one, reflecting the growing Anglicization of the country, the disappearance of traditional ways of life, of the Gaelic tongue, and the industrialization of the north-eastern part of Ulster. All this appeared less important when political activity crowded such considerations from the stage in the 1880s; but now that the politics seemed of importance mainly to the politicians, it was natural for people to examine more closely what it was that politics should be advancing or preserving. Moreover, since Parnell was depicted as the victim of the Liberal alliance and of British Nonconformity, it was natural for Parnellites to extend their argument that English influence, having destroyed their leader, was destructive of all that was worthy in Ireland. 'The blight is upon us all of English manners and English sway', complained *United Ireland* in 1891: 'Our painters form their style from the morbid and decrepit Academy on the Thames; Swinburnian phrases fill the heads of our best versifiers to the exclusion of native thought, and "the dainty trick of Tennyson" seizes upon their souls'.[22] Irish writers who wrote for an English audience were contaminated by English ideas, just as Parnell's fall revealed that Irish nationalists had become contaminated by their close contact with English politicians. The anti-Parnellites had sold out to Englishmen, had grown weak and de-nationalised by their long sojourn in Westminster; similarly, Irish writers whose eyes were fixed on London, not Dublin, had grown corrupt and effete, losing contact with their Irish environment, and their work had declined in vigour and quality.

This was all very well; but Irish writers might be forgiven for inquiring the whereabouts of the audience in Ireland that they were supposed to write for. On the face of it, such an audience existed; Ireland in the late nineteenth century was a more literate society, with only 18% of the population totally illiterate in 1891.[23] But literacy itself was no guarantee of a responsive audience. A desire to read, as well as the ability to do so, was an essential part of an appreciative audience; a desire to read good books, as distinct from nationalist propaganda, was even more essential. And there was the attitude of the Roman Catholic church, always suspicious of 'bad books and bad newspapers', the reading of which, Archbishop Logue of Armagh confessed, might weaken the faith even of an educated man like himself.[24] The tastes of the reading public. as distinct from those of the leaders of the literary movement, were to reveal the narrow base on which the revival was launched, and the contradictions inherent in it.

All this, however, was mercifully veiled from the literary enthusiasts of the 1890s. In December 1891 Yeats, with T.W.Rolleston, a former editor of the *Dublin University Review*, founded the Irish Literary Society of London; in August 1892 the National Literary Society began in Dublin, with the assistance of John O'Leary. Their object was to promote the study of the legends, folk-lore and literature or Ireland, and to evolve a sense of Irish identity, and one that would reflect and recognise the pluralist nature of Irish society.[25] Yeats was a profound admirer of Sir Samuel Ferguson, whom he described as 'the greatest poet Ireland has produced, because the most central and most Celtic'.[26]

Rolleston had been attracted to Irish themes by the Protestant Irishman Standish O'Grady, who, though a Unionist in politics, and a man highly suspicious of Irish, and of any, democracy, popularized the heroic age of Irish history, and introduced the figure of Cuchulainn into nationalist folk-memory. O'Grady was denounced for his Unionism in the 1880s, the decade which saw the publication of four of his major works (including *Cuchulainn: an Epic*); but now he was accorded a hero's welcome.[27] Since the emphasis was on Irish literature, not Irish politics, people like O'Grady could live down their Unionism – or so it seemed at the time. Thus the literary movement would be inclusive; and Davis's dream of a common Irish tradition, embracing Irishmen of all origins and persuasions, could be realized.

But the literary movement with its aspirations of an inclusive Irish culture was soon to meet the challenge of political considerations more complex than those which had occasioned the Parnell split. For it still had to resolve the questions that the Young Irelanders had left unanswered in the 1840s: the questions concerning the purpose of a national literature, the standards by which it should be judged, and, most difficult of all, the relationship between the Yeatsian idea of a national literature, choosing Irish themes (which Yeats did) and the idea that the only true national literature was that which found expression through the medium of the Irish language. Should the literature of Ireland content itself with purely nationalistic ends? Could there be an Irish literature that was not written in Irish? Was it not a contradiction, amounting to humbug, for Celtic enthusiasts to harbour a profound distrust for everything English, and yet to write in the medium of English, to, as it were, burn everything except that most persuasive influence of all, her tongue? It was these problems and possibilities that quickly destroyed any neat symmetry of political decline paralleled by cultural revival: for, just as the political crisis of 1891 gave an impetus to the literary movement, so the literary movement helped shape and release new political forces that threatened Yeats' hope of an imaginative Irish literature tailored for a critical yet appreciative audience, that would enable Ireland to make a distinctive contribution to the common European cultural heritage.

The .dilemmas confronting the Yeatsian concept of a national literature were inherent in the circumstances in which it came into being. If the fall of Parnell was a judgement on Ireland for allowing herself to become too closely entangled with English influences, then the literary movement that sprang from that event was, from its inception, obliged to define its attitude to England; and, by definition, it must adopt an anti-English tone. Thus any attempt to place the movement in a European cultural context was inhibited by its original inspiration, that of destroying English influence in Ireland; for English literature, was, after all, an important part of the European tradition. *United Ireland* claimed that 'Cockney influence and Cockney ways' were destructive of literary talent;[28] but this piece of wilfully blind prejudice could not disguise the wealth of literary achievements in the English language.

Nevertheless, there were those who persisted in asking the awkward question: was it possible to resist the erosion of the Irish identity, and yet resist it through the medium of the language of the English, the conquerors, who were held responsible for the disappearance of the identity? There were those who believed that it was not possible to compromise their national identity, and yet save it, and who took their cue from Archbishop Croke of Cashel who, in 1884, denounced England's 'accents, her vicious literature, her music, her dances, and her manifold mannerisms' which, like her 'fantastic field sports' were 'not racy of the soil, but rather alien, on the contrary to it, as are, for the most part, the men and woman who first imported and still continued to patronise them'.[29] What if, as Croke alleged, the English language were to be considered part of England's 'masher habits'? For after all the literary enthusiasts had already downgraded Ireland's national poet, Thomas Moore, as irretrievably Anglicized[30], and the 'Gaels' were in the future to mete out the same treatment to Swift, Goldsmith, Maria Edgeworth and Shaw.[31] The distinction between Irish writers who were sturdily Irish and those who were not might, perhaps, be drawn without recourse to some absolute standard; it might be a matter of opinion. But an absolute standard was at hand: the Irish language itself, which might be revived, not out of philological interest, nor as a companion to English, but as spoken, living language, peculiar to the Irish people, expressing, as Davis declared, their true national genius, and acting as the essential test of Irish nationality.

An interest in the Gaelic language was by no means new in late nineteenth century Ireland. Irish material had been printed in the *Nation* in the 1860s; a weekly journal, the *Shamrock*, did the same from 1867. The Society for the Preservation of the Irish Language, founded in 1876, had sought to revive Irish as a spoken language, and had published a weekly journal, and books of lessons in Irish.[32] But the SPIL, though influential as a pressure group — one of its successes was in the field of examination arrangements — never enjoyed any wide popular appeal; and it was ruined by dissension, for in 1880 some young men broke away to found the Gaelic Union, a body which they hoped would encourage the language among native Irish speakers.[33] But the Gaelic movement, if such it can be called, made no significant contribution because it lacked any strong political motivation or political opportunity and thus made no impression on a highly politically minded public. The home rule party and the agragarian agitation were more urgent than early Irish texts of lesson books. And, in any case, the men who sought to promote the language were concerned with its practical value, its usefulness in educating the Irish speakers in the Gaeltachts; they accepted bilingualism, and harboured no desire to turn back the tide of Anglicization or to replace English with Irish. On the contrary, they were anxious lest the general use of Irish in Ireland would be 'injurious to commercial interest'.[34]

The failure of normal politics in 1892 however, presented the Gaelic enthusiasts with an opportunity to state their case; but, more important, the case was now found to be different. For it was — whatever the protestations of the founders of the Gaelic League in 1893 — a political case, and the most ambitious and far-reaching of all political cases: the preservation and advancement of a national identity based solely on the Gaelic cultural and linguistic heritage. The three most significant figures in the new movement were Father Eugene O'Growney, Professor of Irish at Maynooth; Eoin MacNeill, a Roman Catholic from Co. Antrim, who first suggested the formation of a new organization to take the Irish language to the people; and Douglas Hyde, the son of a Church of Ireland rector from Sligo, who grew up in Roscommon, learnt Irish from the country people there, and who transferred his allegiance from the SPIL, to the Gaelic Union, the Irish Literary Society of London and then to the National Literary Society in Dublin, both of which he founded with Yeats.[35]

This threesome, in composition, reflected the pluralist nature of Irish society, at least in part: the northern Catholic MacNeill, as it were, balanced by the southern Protestant Hyde. A nothern Protestant was conspicuously absent; but, in any case, it was soon made clear by Hyde that such an article was not particularly welcome. Hyde was the most influential leader of the three simply because he was a born propagandist. In a lecture delivered to the National Literary Society in November 1892 entitled 'the necessity for de-Anglicizing Ireland' he gave the new movement a resounding inaugural. His propagandist skills were displayed from the start, with his emphasis on the urgency of the need to halt the decay of the language and to prevent the final and irrevocable loss of Ireland's cultural tradition. 'We must bring pressure upon our politicians not to snuff it out by their tacit discouragement because they do not happen themselves to understand it'. Politicians, then, were to come into the picture; but that raised the question of why politicians should trouble themselves with what was supposedly a non-political movement. Here was the nub of the matter: and it was one concerned, indeed obsessed with politics. Because, Hyde told his listeners, 'in Anglicizing ourselves wholesale we have thrown away with a light heart the best claim which we have upon the world's recognition of us as a separate nationality. What did Mazzini say? What do the *Spectator* and the *Saturday Review* harp on? That we ought to be content as an integral part of the United Kingdom because we have lost the notes of nationality, our very language and customs'.

It was at best ingenious, at worst dishonest, for Hyde to claim as he did when he was made first president of the Gaelic League in 1893 that the new organization was not to be indentified with any particular group or allegiance. This was true in the narrowest sense: the League was not attached to the home rule or Unionist parties; but it was untrue in any important political sense, for the whole tenor of Hyde's argument was that Irish nationalism stood or fell by its cultural identity; an identity, moreover, that did not include, and could not be shared by, what he called the 'aliens' of north-east Ulster, who had broken the continuity of the Irishness of Ireland. There 'the Gaelic race was expelled and the land planted with aliens, whom our dear mother, Erin, assimilative as she is, has hitherto found it difficult to absorb'. The Celtic race was about to recover possession of its country; it must also recover its Celtic characteristics, and it could do so only by striving to cultivate 'everything that is most racial, most smacking of the soil, most Gaelic, most Irish, because of this little admixture of Saxon blood in the north-east corner this island is and will ever remain Celtic at the core'.[36]

The driving force behind the Gaelic revival was nationalism, for it was nationalism that rescued the language from mere antiquarianism to become a powerful political force. It was more than a political force; it was a moral crusade, for Hyde implied that it was a species of national apostasy not to fight for the revival of the language, and he also implied that the Gaelic way of life was superior to that of the non-Gaelic. Hyde, it must be said, had good reason to adopt this dangerous tone. For the low status of Irish, the feeling that to speak Irish was to speak an inferior tongue, could not be denied. Frank O'Connor often spoke 'with a mixture of wonder and horror, of the Cork slums of his youth when an old man, too foolish or senile to conceal his knowledge of the language, was followed round by a pack of louts shouting "Irish!

Irish!" '.[37] Hyde sought to restore a much needed pride in the language, and to do so he did not scruple to employ the most political means to hand. He singled out the Irish parliamentary party for attack: they had attempted to create a nationality with one hand, and destroy with the other the very thing that made for a differentiated nationality. He used a form of blackmail, warning people that if they were not actively for the language, then they must be counted against it. And if they were against it they were the tools of England, West Britons, not true Irishmen — and yet not even Englishmen: for the English were so racially distinct that the non-Irish Irishman was an unhappy creature, stranded in a no-man's land between two distinct cultures, two distinct nations.[38]

Hyde also possessed a sound grasp of the methods of political persuasion:[39] as he declared in his 1892 oration, 'nothing less than a house-to-house visitation and exhortation of the people themselves will do, something — though with a very different purpose — analogous to the procedure that James Stephens adopted throughout Ireland when he found her like a corpse on the dissecting table'.[40] Hyde sought to spread his propaganda, not through classical texts — for these would remain closed to the mass of the people whom he wished to reach — but through the more popular media. Reports of Gaelic League activities would be circulated through the press; public lectures arranged.[41] And not only would the language be advanced. Irish sport, music, names, clothes, all must be brought back to everyday use. And an attack must be mounted on their English counterparts: only in this way could the Irish cease to be 'a nation of imitators'.[42]

It might seem strange to number Hyde, the Anglo-Irishman, among the foremost exponents of cultural Gaelic nationalism; but Hyde was not the first of his kind to take an interest in native culture. The difference was that whereas Charlotte Brooke and her father studied Irish, and, in the case of the former, mastered it, Hyde sought to use it to destroy that English culture of which he was a product. Yet there is a line of continuity from the Brookes, through Davis, to Hyde. They all represented that 'colonial' element which sought to preserve, not destroy, the culture that they found in Ireland; Davis and Hyde differed from the Brookes and Henry Flood in that they believed that the only way to save Irish culture was to destroy English culture. The Brookes stood between, and also within, two civilizations; but if these two civilizations were embattled, as they now appeared to be, then it was necessary to take one side or the other. Hyde simply chose the side that he believed in, and demonstrated once more that the Anglo-Irishman as nationalist often presented a much more formidable and full-blooded appearance than the Roman Catholic whose national identity was all of a piece.

The Gaelic movement was not to achieve the ambitious goals set for it by Hyde and his companions in 1892. Its identification of the problem of the Anglicization of Ireland was defective, for the decline of Gaelic Ireland was only one, though to Gaelic enthusiasts the most important, aspect of the immense changes that followed in the wake of the great famine. Economic and social rehabilitation of the Gaelic-speaking areas was necessary to arrest this decline,[43] and this would have required an expensive and sustained programme of the kind that the Gaelic League did not envisage. The league grew slowly, but the Gaeltacht continued to diminish. And it was difficult to sustain the early enthusiasm, for the Gaelic tongue was not an easy one to acquire: the large sales of Father O'Growney's first book of Irish grammar were not repeated for the more advanced second and third volumes.[44] After 4 years of work only 43 branches of the league had been formed; by 1904 there were nearly 600 branches, and the league claimed successes, in its campaign for bi-lingualism in Irish-speaking areas, and in the decision of the National University of Ireland, established in 1908, to include Irish as a compulsory matriculation subject. It remained the culture and interest of a minority, albeit an earnest and intelligent minority.[45] But no nationalist could afford to ignore it, or show indffference to its cause without appearing as something of a traitor to his country. More important, the movement which owed so much to the Anglo-Irishman Hyde helped foster the conditions which rendered it all the more difficult for Hyde's people to come to terms with Irish Ireland.

Ulster Protestants were, by 1905, going their own way in any event, as the establishment of the Ulster Unionist Council in 1905 indicated; but even the Anglo-Irishmen who had helped launch the Gaelic movement and the literary revival, who sought to identify with Irish Ireland, were quickly placed on the defensive. For the debate continued on the issue of whether or not Irish thought, ideas, and belief could find proper and full expression through the the the medium of the English language. Hyde was prepared to accept Anglo-Irish literature as a step on the road to the de-Anglicization of Ireland; but there were those who held that this amounted to a contradictory and even fatal policy. To keep out English influence it was necessary to use only Irish books and journals; and Eoin MacNeill, in particular, warned against the dangers of 'lying in wait for the latest piece of Gaelic lore dug out by the philologists, to dress it up in an alien garb, and turn it into third-rate English poetry'. To MacNeill, Trinity College Dublin was the one successful instrument for the English conquest of the Irish mind; and in his outline history of Ireland written for the official handbook of the Irish Free State, MacNeill devoted merely a couple of short paragraphs to the 18th century, allocating more space to early Ireland. Whereas Yeats hoped to use Irish themes through the medium of English, and thus make his distinctively Irish contribution to European culture, MacNeill was convinced that the Gaelic language had already made such a contribution: the whole technique of the poetry of modern nations was Irish or at least Celtic in origin; the ryhming stanza had reached its highest perfection of form in Gaelic; the beauty of early Irish poetry was as 'distinct from ordinary language as the heavens are from the earth'; and so Ireland had pioneered the emergence of national literatures. Irish speech was superior to English; and in speaking their own language the 'Irish show a range of speech, a diversity of usage, a play of rhetoric, a power of delicacy of diction certainly not excelled even by the educated classes in speaking English'.[46] Yeats's Anglo-Irish literature was therefore an offshoot of English literature, and 'Irish only to a certain extent'.[47]

The Gaelic league and the literary revival had both set out to check the spread of Anglicization and modernization; but by the end of the 1890s they were at the parting of the ways. To become a true Irishman, the Gaelic League asserted, required the de-Anglicization of oneself;[48] but Yeats could hardly do this without abandoning his purpose of developing an Irish contribution to literary taste and standards. In the end Yeats, despite his championing of Irish nationalists, and his anti-English posturing, was a literary patriot, not a literary nationalist. MacNeill, with his belief in the Celtic origins of European literature, managed to be both. Yeats wanted nationalism to act as the stalking horse of literature; but there were those who, while accepting the need to work through the medium of English, as Yeats did, wanted to use literature as the stalking horse of nationalism, as Davis had done. Here again cracks began to appear in the movement which had set out to establish Irish cultural unity. Yeats was highly critical of Charles Gavan Duffy's description of Davis as a great poet; such judgement produced a 'barren enthusiasm for the second hand'.[49] But the difference separating Yeats and the Davisites was one of principle, not only of taste, for whereas Yeats applied critical standards to propaganda, Gavan Duffy applied propagandist standards to criticism.[50]

Yeats's literary patriotism was, therefore, under attack from two contrasting, yet in ways similar movements, both of which owed their inspiration to the Davisite tradition of art for the sake of nationality. The Gaelic League was not, of course, neglectful of art for art's sake; no organization which included a scholar who devoted much of his time and effort to the short syllable which followed the liquid l, n and r, and its effect on the consonant could stand accused of being merely propagandist.[51] But the League as a whole was fundamentally concerned with Irish cultural nationalism, not merely with Irish culture. MacNeill's concern for consonants did not obscure his commitment to the belief that the true basis of the Irish nation was to be found in the remote Gaelic past; and although he despised Hyde's concept of race, believing that a nation was a 'brother-hood of adoption as well as of blood'[52] he gave short shrift to the Protestant eighteenth century, declaring that its nationalists were false models for nationalists of his day. A political change without a cultural revolution was worthless; and the only worthwhile cultural revolution that Ireland could make was to recover its Gaelic past and rediscover its Gaelic traditions.

The political and propagandist nature of the Gaelic movement soon caused it to shed its early rank and file Protestant supporters – and there were some[53] – and become a nationalist body in fact if not in name. And it took the honesty and intellectual clarity of D.P.Moran, a journalist who had worked for the Gaelic magazine *An Claidheamh Soluis* and for the *New Ireland Review*, and who in 1900 founded the *Leader*, to bring Gaelic enthusiasts face to face with the logic of their principles. To Moran 'the foundation of Ireland is the Gael, and the Gael must be the element that absorbs. On no other basis can an Irish nation be reared that would not topple over by force of the very ridicule that it would beget'.[54] Moran differed from the more conventional Gaelic enthusiasts in that he had no time for the peasant, but put his faith in the middle classes whose education and social position, though now misdirected towards things English, could be directed towards self-reliance, self respect, and nationalism of the Irish Ireland kind. Moran placed before the league a problem which most of its members preferred to gloss over. In theory Protestants who took the trouble could learn Gaelic just as effectively as Catholics, for the numerous and spectacular failures among Catholics, ranging from Arthur Griffith to Michael Collins, to master the tongue (and the spectacular success of the non-Catholic Sean O'Casey) revealed that Gaelic was no respecter of persons. But the difficulty was to be found in the motives for learning or simply trying and failing to learn the language: for how congenial would non-Catholics find the exercise of learning Gaelic if they were regarded as alien Saxons, or informed that the eighteenth century was an unrelieved tragedy for the real Ireland? What kind of company would they think they were keeping when they discovered that Gaelic was the natural tongue of the Catholic, even when he could not speak it, but was not the tongue of the Protestant, even when he could?[55]

Moran has been criticised for his alleged 'racism'[56]; but his real purpose was to spell out, regardless of cant and humbug, the principles which others accepted but preferred not to examine too closely. Moran denied that he was running a Catholic journal, or that he was maintaining that no one but a Catholic could be an Irishman. But, he retorted, 'when we look out on Ireland we see that those who believe or may be immediately induced to believe, in Ireland a nation are, as a matter of fact, Catholics'. 'In the main non-Catholic Ireland looks upon itself as British and as Anglo-Irish', he alleged; and those non-Catholics who would like to throw in their lot with the Irish nation 'must recognize that the Irish nation is *de facto* a Catholic nation'.[57] Moran had the unpleasant knack of stating clearly and unequivocally the direction in which the Gaelic movement was heading, and its implications for the 'English who happened to be born in Ireland';[58] any racial undertones were ones that he recognized, not ones that he invented.

Here was a serious and sustained attack on the personalities as well as the precepts of the Anglo-Irish part of the literary revival, based on the idea that 'the great connecting link between us and the real Ireland is the Gaelic tongue'.[59] But Yeats and his followers were subjected to the second, major threat to their aspirations: the belief that literature in English was a perfectly acceptable part of the Irish tradition, provided it contributed to the national regeneration of Ireland; and if it so contributed, then it was to be freed from all other critical standards. This threat was most clearly seen in the controversies aroused by the creation of the Irish literary theatre and the attempt to build a 'Celtic and Irish school of dramatic literature' which would present to an 'uncorrupted and imaginative audience', the 'deeper thoughts and emotions of Ireland'. Such a drama would ignore divisive political questions, and would show that Ireland was 'not the home of buffoonery and of easy sentiment . . . but the home of an ancient idealism'. Yeats was the leading figure in this new venture, and he gathered round him some able and colourful collaborators: Lady Gregory, George Moore, and Edward Martyn. Lady Gregory was of Anglo-Irish and landed family with estates in Co. Galway; Moore was a lapsed Catholic of landed background, who made a considerable reputation as a novelist; Martyn was a Catholic landlord who lived near Lady Gregory's house, Coole Park, and who harboured a deep dislike of English materialism, and a love of

his native countryside. Despite the varied religious origins of its founders, however, the inspiration of the theatre was Anglo-Irish.[60]

The first plays of the literary theatre were produced in May 1899;
and from then until 1907 the theatre was seldom free from public controversy, and controversy of a particular kind. Its critics took it to task
on a number of grounds: Yeats's play *The Countess Cathleen*, which
depicted Irish peasants selling their souls for gold in a famine winter,
was attacked as anti-Christian and anti-Catholic; and some students
from the Catholic University College protested in the theatre and in the
press against an art 'which offers as a type of our people the loathesome
brood of apostates'.[61] J.M.Synge's play *In the Shadow of the Glen*, produced in 1903, dealing with the theme of the loveless marriage of a
young woman to an old man, and the young woman's decision to break
with social convention and escape with a tramp to face a hard, but
more honest, life, aroused the fury of those, like Arther Griffith, who
considered the play as non-Irish, of Greek origin, and as a slur on Irishwomen who were 'the most virtuous in the world'. The most furious
storm was reserved for Synge's *The Playboy of the Western World* in
1907. Synge's play was set in the west of Ireland, and was, he insisted,
based on a story which he had heard about a son who boasted of mur-
dering his father and was taken as a local hero, until his father returned
to set him down. The competition of two women for Christy Mahon,
the would-be parricide, and the reference to Irishwomen's shifts,
amongst other equally frank scenes from Irish peasant life, were denounced as a slur on Irish chastity, morality and girlhood.[62] That face-
to-face confrontation between a playwright and his audience which
Yeats believed encouraged 'feed-back'[63] turned out to be rather more
lively than he anticipated: the first performance of the play was howled
down in the third act and disruption continued for a week.

It is tempting to dismiss these unedifying scenes as the reaction of
'stultifying pressures of a self-righteous and intolerant society';[64] but
the hostility to the *Countess Cathleen*, at least, must be seen as an
understandable sensitivity of a predominantly Roman Catholic audience to what amounted to a fairly cavalier treatment of their religion
by a Protestant set.[65] More sinister for Yeats and his purpose was the
criticism of their work on nationalist grounds; for it was here that Yeats
found himself at the parting of the ways: his view of art was incompatible with that of the Davisites who believed that art must feed and
succour nationalism if it was to have any justification at all. As Yeats
himself put it, 'Nationalist Ireland at that time was torn with every
kind of political passion and prejudice, wanting, in so far as it wanted

any literature at all, Nationalist propaganda disguised as literature'.[66] When allowance is made for Yeats' natural disgust at his opponents' willingness to sacrifice art for nationalism, his complaint went to the heart of the matter. F.H.O'Donnell, a former member of the Irish parliamentary party, and a would-be leader of the home rulers, posed the question that was in most nationalists' minds: 'How is it to help the national cause?'[67] A national theatre, which was essentially the product of literary patriotism, was, according to its critics, to be a nationalist theatre, the handmaiden of literary nationalism. Thus it was traitorous to talk about peasant girls' shifts because Ireland was all too frequently the butt of foreign humour. Irish literature could not be developed without reference to the battle of two civilizations raging around it; as Alice Milligan, the daughter of a Belfast Unionist family who had become a nationalist and now displayed all the enthusiasms of the convert, wrote 'It must be in the thick of the fight, and if brought apart from it and commanded to declare spiritual gospels to an awaiting word, the silence will come at last'.[68] Yeats replied that such criticism betrayed ignorance; the ignorance of the politician who would 'reject every idea which is not of immediate service to his cause'. Griffith retorted that if the theatre would be judged solely on grounds of its art, then it should adopt the name of Art Theatre and abandon its misleading title of Irish National Theatre.[69]

Inevitably, in such a heated controversy, both sides did less than justice to each other's point of view. Yeats believed that Ireland could hold up her head higher in the world of art if she had something of quality and lasting value to offer that world; Griffith believed that Ireland's head hung so low that all energy and creativity must be directed towards raising it. As Yeats himself put it, in a cooler moment, the kind of literary effort embodied in, for example, the poems published in *The Spirit of the Nation*, were of 'practical and political, not of literary importance'.[70] A generation which is constantly exhorted to direct its efforts and creative talents to 'relevant' subjects will, perhaps, better understand both Griffith's point of view, and Yeats' inability to accept it. And not only Yeats: for James Joyce commented on the Theatre's production of a Gaelic League play that 'a nation which never advanced so far as a miracle play affords no literary model to the artist, and he must look abroad'.[71] Yeats fell in with Joyce's comment when he looked back on his literary theatre as 'the failure of our first attempt to create a modern Irish literature'. Ireland had proved after all that she was not like soft wax for years to come.[72]

This is not to be wondered at. The very phrase 'like soft wax' betrays its author's essentially literary and artistic assessment of an island peopled by ordinary, rather conservative and highly politically-minded men and women. Yeats' hope of a distinctive Irish literary contribution made a limited impression on the Irish Catholic tenant farmers who were still the political and social substance of Ireland. Such people were reared on the Davis tradition of literature as political education; as *United Ireland* put it in 1892, commenting on Yeats' speech at the inaugural meeting of the Irish Literary Theatre, 'Mr Yeats . . . declared that the means in this matter were nobler and better that the end; but, let us not put too much faith in books. Thomas Davis was as fond of literature, qua literature, as any man, but when he wrote for Ireland it was not the book he was thinking of but what the book might do'.[73]

What had the books done in the Ireland that Yeats believed would be like soft wax for years to come? The generation of Irishmen who were the products of an improved educational system and flourishing local and national press, were not fed a cultural diet that would fit them for the role that Yeats envisaged: that of an 'uncorrupted and imaginative audience, trained to listen by its passion for oratory'.[74] The passion for oratory certainly existed; and Irishmen made highly enthusiastic, keen and perceptive political audiences. They were nobody's fool. But while they and their newspapers were alert to the possibilities of politics, their interest in cultural matters was slight. And when the Dublin press developed a heightened concern for literature and art after 1891, it was a concern inspired by the political possibilities of art, not by the artistic possibilities offered by the failure of politics. The fall of Parnell increased the awareness of the need for an Irish national cultural regeneration, and produced a ferment of ideas and suggestions; but the prime concern was for a culture that would check the encroachment of the Saxon; and while such a concern might promote artistic merit, there was no guarantee that artistic merit would prevail if nationalism were found to be at odds with art.

The strength of the Davisite tradition was that it catered for the tastes of its mass audience, and at the same time served the needs of nationalism: thus again catering for the needs of its audience. Davisism was to be found where it was most effective: not among the handful of writers and directors of the Yeatsian school, but in the minds of the Irish tenant farmers and urban middle classes whose staple diet before the literary revival was Davisite[75], and who remained substantially unaffected by the literary movement. Michael MacDonagh listed as his four 'most companionable' books which were 'closest to Irish thoughts and affections' John Mitchel's *Jail Journal*; *The Spirit of the Nation*; Charles Joseph Kickham's *Knocknagow*, and William O'Brien's *When we were Boys*: in these books were seen 'Ireland – Nationalist Ireland – plain'.[76] In 1884 J. Pope Hennessy investigated the reading matter of the Irish through the testimony of a trout fisher in County Cork. His witness was told by a priest that the Catholic Young Men's Societies ('our civic academies of Nationality') were stocked with Davisite literature, with the most popular works including the Abbé MacGeoghegan's *History of Ireland from the Earliest Times*, and John Mitchel's continuation of it; D'Arcy McGee's *History of Ireland*; Gavan Duffy's *Young Ireland* and *Four Years of Irish History*; A.M.Sullivan's *Story of Ireland*; Madden's *Lives of the United Irishmen*; Wolfe Tone's *Memoirs*; and Mitchel's *Jail Journal*.[77] In another county a countryman was observed buying *The Brian Boru Song Book* and the *Harp of Tara Song Book*, of which Pope Hennessy remarked that there was not a parish in Ireland in which some of its songs were not heard. This was, perhaps, not pure Davisite literature, since it was produced for commercial purposes; but another popular work, *Penny Readings for the Irish People*, included extracts from the Young Irelanders as well as political speeches by Burke, Grattan, Meagher and O'Connell. Its author, Henry Giles, introduced his selection by declaring that 'The meanest man lingers under the shadow of piles which tell him that his fathers were not slaves. He toils in the fields with structures before him through which echoes (sic) the voice of centuries – to his heart the voice of soldiers, of scholars, and of saints'. Pope Hennessy described this literature as 'more truly popular than any literature of the kind in Europe'; and he speculated, whether it had 'any interest for the politician'.[78]

His speculation was justified; for the political content of such literature was high. A typical example was the work of A.M.Sullivan, editor of the *Nation* after Gavan Duffy's departure for Australia in 1858. Sullivan's popular text, *The Story of Ireland*, first published in 1867, was written for young people as 'an effort to interest the young in the subject of Irish history, and attract them to its study'; to do, as he put it, what had been well done for the youth of England by numerous writers: convince them that Ireland's history 'is no wild, dreary, and uninviting monotony of internecine slaughter, but an entertaining and instructive narrative of stirring events, abounding with episodes, thrilling, glorious, and beautiful'. Sullivan was a Davisite; instructional history was what he wanted to present, for instructional history was needed for the younger generation that was now rapidly approaching manhood, with its 'cares, duties, responsibilities . . . they will be the men on whom Ireland must depend. They will make her future. They will guide her destinies. They will guard her honour. They will defend her life'. To the service of the 'Irish Nation of the Future' he devoted his book, confident that 'my young friends will not fail to read aright the lesson which is taught by "The Story of 'Ireland' ".[79]

The lesson of Irish history, as Sullivan saw it, was the breaking of Irish unity after Clontarf by the invitation of Dermot MacMurrough to the foreigners. The Norman colony thus established was 'a perpetual and self-acting mechanism for the gradual reduction of Ireland'; and when the colonists themselves seemed in danger of being conquered by Irish manners, laws and language, the king in London inevitably took measures to check that 'dreaded evil'. Then came the reformation, inspired by Henry VIII, a 'creature of mere animal passions'; England quickly succumbed to it, not through a change of religious conviction, but for wholly worldly advantage: 'Their model of policy was Judas Iscariot, who sold our land for thirty pieces of silver'. But although Irish chieftains submitted to Henry, their clans did not; and if the English nominee to the clan leadership renounced his allegiance to the crown, he was promptly deposed — an 'artful system . . . copied in all its craft and cruelty by the British in India centuries afterwards'.[80]

And so the story of Ireland unfolded. English kings were deceitful and vicious; Irish chiefs were honourable and true, and if they were not, they were soon disowned by their people. Always an Irish chieftain, like Hugh O'Neill, would arise to continue the battle against the foreign foe, dedicating his life to the liberation of his native land. Sullivan's narrative was often interspersed with Davisite poetry, excelling Irish virtues and exposing English vices; and the message was unmistakably clear: the Irish were a chosen people, always surviving the most determined and horrific assaults of the Saxons. The plantation of Ulster, the expulsion of the native Irish race, was thwarted because 'God did not more signally preserve His chosen people of the Old Law than He has preserved the Irish nation in captivity and in exile. They have not melted away, as the calculations of the evictors anticipated. They have not become fused or transformed by time or change'. The 1641 rising, with its atrocities, were dismissed as 'monstrous fictions'; 'the people were joyful'. As Gavan Duffy's poem, 'The muster of the North' put it:

'Joy! joy! the day is come at last the day of hope and pride,
And, see! our crackling bonfires light old Bann's rejoicing tide!
And gladsome bell and bugle horn, from Newry's captured tow'rs.
Hark! how they tell the Saxon swine, this land is ours — is *ours*!'

The Cromwellian conquest of Ireland was summed up in a chapter title: 'The agony of a nation'; the seige of Athlone in the Williamite wars was exhorted to give young Irishmen the heart to 'remember the authentic annals of Ireland' which recorded 'a scene of heroism' similar to that of the Horations at the bridge. And at Limerick the nation was betrayed, and 'trampled under foot by the "Protestant Interest" yelling for more plunder and more persecutions'.[81]

Sullivan, like most writers in the Davisite tradition, disagreed with the Gaelic leaguers in that he admired the Protestant patriots of the eighteenth century, who at last opened their eyes to the reality of English oppressions, only to be again betrayed. England once more broke faith with Ireland; Ireland was provoked into revolt; and Wexford rose, led by Father Murphy and other priests whose names 'should ever be remembered by Irishmen when tempters whisper that the voice of the Catholic pastor, raised in worry or restraint is the utterance of one who cannot feel for, who would not die for, the flock he desires to serve'. After the '98 rebellion the parliament of Ireland was extinguished and an independent country degraded into a province: 'Ireland as a nation was extinguished'. With the great famine, the Irish as a race nearly went the same way, as the English press gloated over the 'anticipated extirpation of the Irish race'. But Ireland was fated not to die; and although Sullivan could not approve of the 'insensate' attempt at a rising in 1867, he praised the virtue, patriotism, and Christianity of some of the Fenian leaders: 'Their last words were of God and Ireland'. And when Sullivan took his story of Ireland up to recent times, the land acts, the home rule bills, all provided proof of his contention that 'there is a god in Israel'.[82]

Sullivan's mixture of historical fact and fiction, of poetry and prose culled from writers like Moore, Davis and Gavan Duffy, his conviction that the Irish would triumph over all adversity, and move on to their 'great purpose' was the kind of literature that his, and succeeding generation of Irish nationalists were reared on; Eamon de Valera was perhaps its most celebrated exponent.[83] The histories written by Abbé Mac-Geoghegan, Mitchel and D'Arcy McGee were of exactly similar kind, even down to the detailed refutation of the massacres of 1641;[84] and McGee's publisher remarked that 'A nation with such a strange history must have some great work yet to do in the world. Except the Jews, no people has so suffered without dying'. This was the stuff of the home rule movement and of the nationalist movement that succeeded home rule. It was embodied in almost every speech, pamphlet, newspaper editorial and poem.[85] It also had its less sombre side, which found expression on the stage, where the contrast with the Irish Literary Theatre was, perhaps, rather noticeable. John Denvir, a Fenian, who with his companions 'got our inspiration from the teaching of Young Ireland', formed a theatrical group whose entertainment was called 'Terence's fireside; or the Irish peasant at home'. It consisted of 'Irish national songs and harmonized choruses, interspersed with stories such as might be told around an Irish fireside'.

The prologue to the entertainment was characteristic of the whole, and it revealed that the Irish peasant at home was not quite of the John Synge variety:

> Sons of green Erin, we greet you this night!
> And you, too, her daughters — how welcome the sight!
> We come here before you, a minstrel band,
> To carol the lays of our native land.

The 'harmonized choruses' included 'Killarney' (words by Falconer, music by Balfe); and when the backdrop showing the lakes was raised, it disclosed a typical peasant's homestead, complete with turf fire, and adorned with 'the usual pious and patriotic pictures to such an interior'. This was Terence's fireside. In the miscellaneous part of the show there was — there had to be — a 'rattling Irish jig' by one Joseph Ward and one Barry Aylmer, 'the latter being of somewhat slight figure, made a bouncing Irish coleen'; and the entertainment concluded with 'Phil Foley's Frolics' by one John McArdle who was, as Denvir pointed out, perhaps unnecessarily, 'fond of alliteration'. This company, calling themselves the 'Emerald Minstrels' were apparently in great demand, and their services were 'always cheerfully given for Catholic, National and charitable objects'.[86] Their flamboyance and national fervour were only rivalled by that of Robert Brennan, later to become a guerilla fighter with the IRA, whose troup, dressed as negro minstrels, in long dark pants with white shirts covered by green sashes, marched on to the stage carrying tin pikes. Their chorus was as evocative of Wexford as were their pikes, for it consisted of 'an English translation of the "Marsellaise" ', punctuated at appropriate moments with the pikes levelled in the 'charge' position.[87]

There is no record of any of these sterling performances being subjected to the kind of interruptions that accompanied the 'Playboy' or the 'Countess Cathleen'; if this was art — and who was to say it was not — then it was indeed Davisite, it was art, not for art's sake, but for propaganda. Obviously the Reverend O'Hickey's complaint that 'the coon and the stage Irishman have not wholly disappeared'[88] was not without foundation; but Irish nationalism was sentimental, and had room for the stage Irishman, however much such spectacles disturbed the slumbers of the puritanical Gaelic Leaguers or the aesthetic browns of the literary patriots.

Popular nationalist literature of this kind deserves serious study, however, for it showed a contradiction, or confusion, which was central to the mainstream nationalist movement. For while home rulers and their supporters believed in an Irish race (which they never clearly defined, but always assumed was the Catholic and Celtic people of Ireland) they also accepted the idea of an Irish nation (which included, whether the liked it or not, the Irish Protestants). They did not always make the distinction as clearly as this, for they were popular politicians, not political theorists; but such was the general assumption underlying their ideas. Thus William O'Brien, one of the most anti-sectarian of Irish nationalists, spoke of 'our venerable and ancient race', of a 'Celtic race ruled by its spiritual instincts'; but he also referred to nationalism's 'heart equally large and equally warm for protestant and a Catholic'; yet at the same time he denounced landlords as 'foreigners in race and language and sympathy'.[89] R. Barry O'Brien referred to that part of Ireland which 'though Hibernian enough in temperament, is still, to some extent, separated from the rest not only by race, but by feeling and history'.[90] The Gaelic leaguers were exclusive nationalists: to qualify as a member of the nation the Irishman must also be a member of the 'distinct and wholly superior'[91] Gaelic race; the Ireland of the Davisites was 'Anglo-Ireland' even though 'they called it in perfect good faith Ireland'.[92] But this presupposed that anything non-Gaelic was non-national; whereas the overwhelming evidence was that Irish nationalism was the product of that very Davisite literature that the Gaels and the literary patriots, for their different reasons, despised. The popular nationalist movement was neither fully exclusive, like the Gaelic League and the Gaelic Athletic Association, nor was it inclusive, like the Yeatsian Anglo-Irish literary movement. It was, so to say, exclusively inclusive: it postulated, in a superficial way, the idea of an Irish nation; but it drew its inspiration from the notion of the rising Catholic and Celtic race, and its everyday reading, education, and song bore witness to the grip which this romantic concept had on the minds of the nationalist people.[93]

In a sense, therefore, the battle in Ireland in the last decade of the nineteenth century, and the first decade of the twentieth, was not one between two 'civilizations', but between three; between the Gaelic league idea of Irish Ireland; the Anglo-Irish idea of Celtic literature; and, perhaps in the middle of these mighty opposites, the Davisite idea of a 'racy of the soil' literature, in the English language, but catering for the tastes of the nationally minded mass reading public. The Davisite tradition was the enemy of the other two, for it accepted the fact that the bulk of the Irish people must have their reading matter in the English tongue (at least until the day dawned when they mastered, as Davis himself hoped they would, the Irish languange), and postulated that literature must serve politics. And, despite the works of high artistic merit produced by the Anglo-Irish school, and the achievements of the Gaelic leaguers in making the language a vital issue of the day, and of succeeding years as well, it cannot be denied that the Davisites triumphed, a triumph symbolized by the appointment of Charles Gavan Duffy as first president of the Irish Literary Society.[94] They triumphed because they coincided with the tastes and intellectual capabilities of a sentimental, stubbornly nationalist, reading public. This public, mainly rural, or urban but with rural roots, loved the image of themselves that they found in the poems of, for example, Padraic Colum as much as they hated the image of themselves portrayed in the Countess Cathleen or the Playboy. It was easy for Yeats to dismiss them contemptuously as 'Paudeens';[95] but it would be truer to see them as sensitive, conservative people who held a deep affection for their locality[96], an affection perfectly illustrated in C.J. Kickhams's novel Knocknagow, when Mat the Thrasher gazed on:

> the thatched roof of the hamlet . . . And , strange to say,
> those old mud walls and thatched roofs roused him as nothing
> else could. His breast heaved, as with glistening eyes,
> and that soft plaintive smile of his, he uttered the words
> 'For the credit of the little village' in a tone of deepest
> tenderness.[97]

This was the sentimental side of Irish nationalism; but Kickham also caught the sense of betrayal of the noble Irishry (and pride in their military prowess) in his portrayal of the eviction of Tom Hogan. 'O father', exclaims his daughter 'Don't you see what's after happening? Let us go away'.

> 'What's afther happening?' he asked, with another vacant stare on
> the crowd around him. 'Where's Jemmy?' he exclaimed suddenly,
> as his eye caught sight of the fixed bayonets and red uniforms

behind him, 'Where is Jemmy? Jemmy is the boy that wouldn't let any wan lay a hand on me'.

And where *is* Jemmy?

He clutches his musket at the command to 'charge!' and his shout — clear and thrilling as when the ball was struck to the goal and Knocknagow had won — mingles with the wild hurrah that rises even above the cannon's roar. The general, surrounded by his staff, watches anxiously for what is to follow. The result of the battle hangs upon that charge. For a moment the bayonets flash in the hot sun, as they rush through the storm of iron hail that tears through their ranks; and then friend and foe are lost in a thick white cloud, and the thunder is hushed. And, as the white cloud rolls away, the general's eyes flash fire, as, rising himself in his stirrups, he shouts — 'Magnificent Tipperary!'

The day is won! England is victorious!

There is hot Tipperary blood gushing out upon the thirsty plain; and where the fight was deadliest, Jemmy Hogan lies mangled and bleeding. But there is one company of his regiment which has not shared in the glories of that famous victory. It is drawn up with fixed bayonets before his father's door at old Knocknagow; while the house in which Jemmy Hogan was born is being levelled with the ground!

Magnificent Tipperary!

Tom Hogan looks wildly around him now. He is startled by a loud crashing sound that seemed to come from the yard. It was the first crush of the crowbar through the wall of the dear old home. And it went right through Tom Hogan's heart, and broke it!'[98]

To the realism of Synge, therefore, was opposed the sentimentality of Kickham; a very different kind of art, certainly, but one that the contemporary audience preferred to recognize and respond to. It would be fruitless to compare the two schools and their portrayal of the life and ways of rural Ireland; for the popularity and influence of the Kickham/Colum school lay in its depicting a way of life that people *wanted* to regard as authentic and truthful — the 'heroism of little people'.[99] They felt at home with it; they found it congenial and satisfying. Modern Irish audiences can laugh at the *Playboy*; but perhaps the people who reacted violently against it were too close, less convinced of their superiority to the Irish countryman, less self-consciously liberated from their rural roots, to respond to the play as if it were a kitchen comedy (which it is not).[100]

And, since Irish nationalism was concerned, not only with advancing the material well-being of the Catholic people of Ireland, but also with instilling into them a sense of self-respect and pride, a pride not primarily in their religion, but in their whole way of life of which their religion was an essential part, then the Davisite tradition was likely to triumph. Both Yeats, with his search for an ideal society (which he hoped to find in Sligo in an Irish mystical order located in a ruined castle in Loch Key)[101], and the Gaelic leaguers, with their notions of a return to a pre-seventeenth century idyll, were confounded by the popularity of a form of literature that told the Irish rural dweller, not only what he wanted to hear, but what he believed in his heart to be true: that the Irishman combined in his nature a set of unique virtues: piety, loyalty, tenacity, love of his hand, love of country, concern for his family and friends – all more recognizable than Yeats' belief that the peasant was the preserver of an ancient and mystical world view, which the complexity of modern life had obliterated.[102] All this Davis had told them in the 1840s; all this the Fenians had told them in the 1860s; all this the Home rulers had told them in the 1870s and 1880s; all this Arthur Griffith and his new journal *Sinn Fein*[103], told them again in the early twentieth century.

Griffith could hardly do otherwise. English was the medium through which nationalist Ireland became a political reality. English language publications carried the gospel even to the most remote parts of the country; Irish nationalist songs, in English, were the political small change of the public; 'The harp that once', 'The west's awake', 'The Peeler and the goat', and not Gaelic laments were the songs of the 'rising nation'.[104] Anglicization, far from destroying nationalist Ireland, made possible its creation.

Notes

1. The phrase is D.P.Moran's; see *The Philosophy of Irish Ireland* (Dublin n.d. [1950?]), Chap. VI.

2. L.M.Cullen, 'The Hidden Ireland: reassessment of a concept', in *Studia Hibernica*, No. 9 (1969), pp. 7-47, esp. pp. 24-7.

3. Ibid., pp. 7-8; see also L.J. McCaffrey, 'Daniel Corkery and Irish cultural nationalism' in *Eire/Ireland*, I (Spring 1973), pp. 35-41.

4. For Mahaffy see T. de Vere White, *The Anglo-Irish* (London, 1972), Chap. XV.

5. W. Hayes, 'Nationalism in Ireland: a case study' in *Thought*, vol. XLVI, No. 181 (Summer, 1971), pp. 165-98, esp. pp. 182-3; J. C. Beckett, *Anglo-Irish Tradition*, pp. 134-5.

6. Dewey. 'Celtic agrarian legislation and the Celtic revival', op. cit., pp. 43-5;

O'Hegarty, op. cit., pp. 14-15.

7. Beckett, op. cit., pp. 135-9; E. Boyd, *Ireland's Literary Renaissance* (Dublin, 1968), pp. 20-25; Robert O'Driscoll, 'Ferguson and the idea of an Irish national literature', in *Eire/Ireland*, VI (Spring, 1971), pp. 82-95.

8. R. O'Driscoll, *An Ascendancy of the Heart: Ferguson and the beginnings of Irish literature in Ireland* (Dublin, 1976), pp. 38-42.

9. S. Gwynn, *Irish Literature and Drama in the English Language: a Short History* (London, 1936), p. 53; see also M. Butler, *Maria Edgeworth: a Literary Biography* (Oxford, 1972), pp. 359-60 for Miss Edgeworth's fear that the book would be resented by the Irish themselves, especially if the limited vision and mistaken loyalty of Thady were not taken ironically, and his picture of the Rackrents accepted as an up to date description of the Irish gentry.

10. Beckett, op. cit., p. 141.

11. This provoked O'Connell's displeasure; Lecky, *Leaders of Public Opinion*, II, p. 293.

12. J. S. Kelly, 'Intellectual and social background to the Irish literary revival', pp. 21-22.

13. *Songs of the Rising Nation* (Glasgow and London, 1869), dedication.

14. Kelly, p. 31.

15. M. Bourke, *John O'Leary*, pp. 184-5.

16. M. Harmon (ed,), *Fenians and Fenianism*, p. 57.

17. W. J. O'Neill Daunt, *A Life Spent for Ireland*, pp. 385, 391.

18. F. S. L. Lyons, *Culture and Anarchy in Ireland*, pp. 39-40; O'Hegarty, op. cit., pp. 611-12.

19. *United Ireland*, 3 Jan. 1885; see also W. O'Brien, *Irish ideas* (London, 1893), pp. 47-77.

20. J. S. Kelly, 'The fall of Parnell and the rise of Irish literature: an investigation', in *Anglo-Irish Studies*, vol. II (1976), pp. 1-23.

21. Ibid., p. 13; W. I. Thompson, *The Imagination of an Insurrection: Dublin Easter, 1916* (London, 1967), pp. 31-2; F. S. L. Lyons, 'The Parnell theme in literature', in A. Carpenter, (ed.), *Place, Personality and the Irish Writer* (Gerrard's Cross, 1977), pp. 74-5.

22. Kelly, op. cit. p. 13.

23. Kelly, 'Intellectual and social background', p. 39.

24. E. Larkin, *The Roman Catholic Church and the Fall of Parnell*, p. 270.

25. Lyons, *Culture and Anarchy*, p. 38.

26. Beckett, *Anglo-Irish Tradition*, p. 139.

27. Lyons, op. cit., pp. 33-5; Boyd, op. cit., pp. 26-54, 113-15.

28. Kelly, 'The fall of Parnell', op. cit., p. 12.

29. O'Hegarty, op. cit., p. 612; David Greene, 'Michael Cusack and the rise of the GAA' in C. C. O'Brien (ed.) *The Shaping of Modern Ireland*, pp. 74-84.

30. Kelly, 'Intellectual and social background', p. 54.

31. D. Corkery, *Synge and Anglo-Irish Literature* (Dublin, 1931), pp. 3, 6-7.

32. O'Hegarty, op. cit., pp. 614-5; J. J. Doyle, *David Comyn: a Pioneer of the Irish Language Movement* (Cork, 1926), pp. 3, 7, 22-25.

33. T. O hAilin. 'Irish revival movements' in B. O Cuív (ed.), *A View of the Irish Language* (Dublin, 1969), pp. 91-100.

34. Kelly, 'Intellectual and social background', pp. 126-7.

35. David Greene, 'The founding of the Gaelic League' in S. O Tuama, *The Gaelic League Idea* (Cork and Dublin, 1972), pp. 9-19.

36. O'Hegarty, op. cit., pp. 617-19.

37. M. Sheehy (ed) *Michael/Frank: Studies in Frank O'Connor* (London and Dublin, 1969), p. 138; see also M. E. L. Butler, *Two schools: a Contrast* (Gaelic League pamphlets, No. 2).

38. Kelly, 'Intellectual and social background', pp. 196-213.

39. S. Gwynn, *Irish Literature and Drama*, p. 131: 'his main energy was thrown into propaganda, for which he disclosed absolute genius'.

40. O'Hegarty, op. cit., p. 618.

41. Lyons, *Ireland Since the Famine*, p. 224; Kelly, 'Intellectual and social background', pp. 200-201.

42. Lyons, *Culture and Anarchy*, pp. 41-2.

43. Green, op. cit., p. 19.

44. R. P. Davis, *Arthur Griffith and non-violent Sinn Fein* (Dublin, 1979), p. 9.

45. Lyons, *Culture and Anarchy*, pp. 44-5; M. J. Waters, 'Peasants and emigrants: considerations of the Gaelic League as a social movement', in D. J. Casey and R. E. Rhodes, *Views of the Irish Peasantry* 1800-1916 (Conn., 1977), p. 162.

46. F. X. Martin and F. J. Byrne (eds.), *The Scholar Revolutionary*, pp. 81-2, 89, 93.

47. Kelly, 'Intellectual and social background', p. 226.

48. See the Gaelic League pamphlets, the Rev. Patrick Forde *The Irish Language Movement: its Philosophy* (No. 21), and the Rev. M. P. Hickey, *The Irish Language Movement: its Genesis, Growth and Progress* (No. 29).

49. Kelly, op. cit., p. 244; P. L. Marcus, *Yeats and the Beginning of the Irish Renaissance* (New York 1970), pp. 7-12.

50. C.G. Duffy, *The Revival of Irish Literature* (London, 1894), pp. 18, 21, 26, 31-2.

51. Martin and Byrne, op. cit., p. 8.

52. Ibid., p. 83.

53. Kevin B. Nowlan, 'The Gaelic league and other national movements' in S. O Tuama, op. cit., pp. 44-5.

54. D. P. Moran, *The Philosophy of Irish Ireland*, p. 37.

55. For the Gaelic/Catholic connection see Lyons, *Culture and Anarchy*, p. 80.

56. E. Norman, *A History of Modern Ireland*, p. 222.

57. *Leader*, 27 April, 27 July, 10 August 1901.

58. O'Hegarty, op. cit., pp. 624-5.

59. B. Inglis, 'Moran of the *Leader* and Ryan of the *Peasant*' in C. C. O'Brien, op. cit., pp. 108-23; see also M. P. O'Hickey, *The True National Idea* (1898).

60. Lyons, *Culture and Anarchy*, pp. 47-9; Gwynn, *Irish literature and Drama*, Chap. IX.

61. Lyons, op. cit., pp. 50-51; Gwynn, op. cit., p. 153.

62. Lyons, op. cit., pp. 50-51, 66-69.

63. Kelly, 'Intellectual and social background', p. 307.

64. R. J. Loftus, *Nationalism in Modern Anglo-Irish Poetry* (Madison and Milwaukee, 1964), p. 9.

65. This point is also made, fairly, I think, in P. C. Power, *A Literary History of Ireland*, p. 162.

66. Gwynn, op. cit., p. 153.

67. Kelly, op. cit., p. 324.

68. Ibid., p. 351.

69. Lyons, op. cit., pp. 67-8; Thompson, op. cit., pp. 68-71.

70. Gwynn, op. cit., pp. 141.

71. Thompson, op. cit., p. 60.

72. Kelly, *The Fall of Parnell*, op. cit., p. 20.

73. Ibid., p. 21.

74. Kelly, 'Intellectual and social background', p. 306.

75. Lecky, *Leaders of Public Opinion in Ireland*, II, p. 293: 'The old doggerel rhymes; the fantastic prophecies, the tales of legendary highwaymen or dubious martyrs which had once been the popular reading of the people were largely replaced by the tales and ballads of the 'Nation', and by a crowd of little books on Irish history of biography which issued from the marvellously prolific pens of

the young writers'.

76. M. MacDonagh, *The Life of William O'Brien* (London, 1928), pp. 26-7.

77. More surprisingly, it also included Lecky's *History of Ireland in the Eighteenth Century*.

78. J. Pope Hennessy, 'What do the Irish read', in *Nineteenth Century*, vol. 15 (June, 1884), pp. 920-32.

79. A. M. Sullivan, *The Story of Ireland*, preface.

80. Ibid., pp. 103, 119, 138, 151, 165, 211, 216.

81. Ibid., pp. 343, 356, 358, 387, 448, 472.

82. Pp., 495, 503, 519, 532, 564, 581, 615, 616.

83. De Valera recollected that 'the first Irish history I read was O'Sullivan's (sic) *Story of Ireland*' (M. C. Bromage, 'Image of nationhood' in *Eire/Ireland*, vol. III, (Autumn, 1968); p. 13. Apparently the book converted even Winston Churchill – for a time – to Irish nationalism (C. C. O'Brien, *Shaping of Modern Ireland* p. 166).

84. Abbé MacGeoghegan, *History of Ireland: from the Earliest Times to the Treaty of Limerick* (Dublin, 1844 edn); J. Mitchel, *History of Ireland: from the Treaty of Limerick to the Present Time* (2 vols., Dublin, 1869); T. D'Arcy McGee, *A Popular History of Ireland* (2 vols. New York, 1864). See esp. MacGeoghegan, pp. 564-8; McGee, pp. 106-7; Mitchel accounted in the same way for the burning of Protestants at Scullabogue in 1798 (vol. II, p. 7).

85. For ballads see G. D. Zimmerman, op. cit., pp. 60-86.

86. John Denvir, *Life Story of an Old Rebel* (Dublin, 1910), pp. 115-22.

87. R. Brennan, *Allegiance* (Dublin, 1950), pp. 4-5.

88. Revd., M. P. Hickey, *The Irish Language Movement*.

89. W. O'Brien, *Irish Ideas*, pp. 1, 4-5, 21, 23, 27. at the same time he denied any 'two races' theory (p. 116).

90. R. B. O'Brien, *The Home Rulers Manual* (London, 1890), pp. 71-2, 92.

91. Forde, *The Irish Language Movement*.

92. Lyons, *Ireland Since the Famine*, p. 237: O'Hegarty, op. cit., p. 624.

93. T. D. Sullivan's heroic ballad-poem, 'God save Ireland' spoke of the Manchester martyrs meeting the 'vengeful tyrant', face to face 'with the courage of their race'; John Dillon, at a martyrs commemoration in 1909 declared that 'to us Irish Catholics the greatest Catholic question in the world is the emancipation of the ancient Catholic race of Ireland' (N.L.I., Manchester Martyrs press cuttings volume, 1891-1912, *Freeman*, 27 Sept., 1909). Other home rulers frequently referred to the race and of course the very notion of 'Irish Americans' presupposed the existence of a race: in 1886 a 'Convention of the Irish race' was held in Chicago (Irish press agency pamphlets, No.3, London, 1886) and another in Dublin in 1896 (MacDonagh, op. cit., p. 151). For an interesting example of the juxtaposition of 'exclusiveness' and 'inclusiveness' see A. M. Sullivan, *et al.*, *Irish Readings* (2 vols., Dublin, 1904), where an analysis of Molyneux's *Case* precedes a poem by the Revd. P. M. Furlong "The Priests of 98", on the theme of 'Erin's noblest martyr-sons' (pp. 103-7, 108-12).

94. Boyd, op. cit., pp. 83-93.

95. Loftus, op. cit., p. 14.

96. It is perhaps worth noting, in passing, that one of the chief effects of the Gaelic Athletic Association was to promote county loyalty as much and perhaps more than country loyalty (J. A. Murphy, 'Identity change in the Republic of Ireland' in *Études Irlandaises*, vol. 5 (1976), pp. 149-50; Comerford, op. cit., p. 186).

97. Comerford op. cit; I am grateful to Dr. Comerford's biography of Kickham for bringing this valuable novel to my attention, and to Mr. John Cronin for his analysis of it in *The Anglo-Irish Novel, vol. I, The Nineteenth Century* (Belfast,

1980), pp. 99-113.
   98. Kickham, *Knocknagow* (Dublin, 1979 ed), pp. 514-15. Even Corkery approved of Knocknagow (*Synge*, pp. 23, 25).
   99. Loftus, op. cit., p. 191: for Colum generally see Loftus, pp. 14-15 and Chap. 7.
   100. For the Playboy see R. O'Driscoll. *Theatre and Nationalism in Twentieth Century Ireland* (London, 1971), pp. 123-5.
   101. Lyons, *Culture and Anarchy*, p. 49.
   102. Kelly, 'Intellectual and social background', pp. 246-70; Thompson, op. cit., 45-6, 51; G. W. L. Telfer, − 'Yeats' idea of the Gael' (Yeats Centenary papers, No. IV, Dolmen Press, 1965), pp. 93-4; Lady Gregory, *Ideals in Ireland* (London, 1901), pp. 95, 102.
   103. Much of Colum's early verse was first published in *Sinn Féin* (Loftus, op. cit., p. 15).
   104. K. T. Hoppen, in Cosgrove and McCartney, op. cit., pp. 224-6; M. Wall, 'The decline of the Irish language' in Ó Cuív, op. cit., pp. 88-90.

9 WHAT HOME RULE STOOD FOR, 1891-1918

The fall of Parnell had encouraged a surge of national introspection in Ireland which bore fruit in the literary revival of the 1890s; the purely political side of Irish life appeared sterile and bitter by comparison. The general election of 1892 witnessed scenes and speeches which appeared to bear out all the Protestant and unionist accusation that nationalists were unfit for power, and were under the thumb of the Roman Catholic church. The *Dublin Evening Herald* spoke of 'pulpit intimidation', warning that it was inadvisable to 'supercede British tyranny by tyranny of another sort': 'we want a nation of men with minds and votes of their own'.[1] Meanwhile priests went out of their way to emphasize that 'religion is the nurse, the centre and the source of nationality'; the priesthood was with the people, came from the people, and not from 'any shoneen landlords or tithe proctors either or priest hunters'; the 'grand old cause of faith and fatherland' was being sustained in the elections.[2] The Parnellites responded with accusations that their opponents were traitors, 'prepared to sell their chieftain' for what they regarded as a home rule victory.[3] *United Ireland* complained that 'all over the country . . . Catholic clergymen are using their influence as clergymen not as citizens, to intimidate and frighten the people'.[4]

Yet there was a certain air of unreality about these charges and counter-charges. Nationalist Ireland was still synonymous with Catholic Ireland; John Redmond and his Parnellites were by no means anti-clerical, for, a *United Ireland* declared, 'we have never desired that Catholic priests should be driven out of politics, but undoubtedly we have desired that they should be forced to take their position as mere citizens like other men'.[5] And it might be said that the Parnellite complaint against the church was, at bottom, that it had turned on them: clerical interference was resented, not because it was wrong in principle, but because it was exercised on their opponents' behalf. As one anti-Parnellite candidate remarked astutely, 'Parnell never insulted an Irish priest, and in the National priesthood he recognized one of the most powerful bulwarks against landlord oppression and one of the strongest forces in the national movement'.[6] More important than the priest in politics debate was the principle which Parnell had sought to emphasize in his struggle to remain leader of nationalist Ireland:

whether or not as he put it, home rule candidates were prepared 'to take dictation from an Englishman'.[7] It was disagreement about English influence, not about the Catholic character of Irish nationalism, that underlay the divisions of the 1890s. This was obscured by the extravagant language of the Parnellites, who, on the death of their chief in October 1891, keened, 'They have killed him. Under God today we do solemnly believe that they have killed him. Murdered he has been, as certainly as if the gang of conspirators had surrounded him and hacked him to pieces'. 'Shall Ireland exact no punishment for this fatal perfidy', *United Ireland* demanded? But even this lament did not omit the central political issue: 'English Liberalism' was the altar on which Parnell had been 'sacrificed by Irishmen'.[8]

Once Parnell's funeral was over, his followers met in Dublin and issued a manifesto, signed by every one of the twenty-eight members then present, and published in the press. It repudiated the policy of the Liberal alliance and declared for independent opposition; they would be independent nationalists, and would 'still believe in the future of Ireland as a nation; and they would still protest that it was not by taking orders from an English minister that Ireland's future could be saved, protected and secured'.[9] The Parnellites maintained that the home rule bill of 1893 (which was broadly similar to that of 1886) was inferior to the previous bill; it could not be taken as a satisfactory settlement of the nationalist issue: 'The word "provisional" has, so to speak been stamped in red ink across every page of this Bill', John Redmond remarked,[10] ignoring the fact that most Irish nationalists regarded any home rule bill made in England as provisional. The anti-Parnellites accused their critics of a blind devotion to the cult of Parnell's personality.[11] The Parnellites seemed justified by events, for when Gladstone's Home Rule Bill was rejected by the House of Lords he accepted the defeat; he did not resign or campaign in the country. And his successor, Lord Rosebery, in 1894 publicly shelved the policy of home rule. But, bereft of Liberal allies, the anti-Parnellites floundered in the House of Commons; and their nine-man party made no mark on the march of events.[12]

There seemed, indeed, no end to the fissiparous tendencies of the home rule movement. After Parnell's fall Justin McCarthy was elected chairman of the Irish parliamentary party. He was a cautious and popular man, but without the personal authority of Parnell; and he was unable to control the party's lieutenants, John Dillon and T.M. Healy, who were now suddenly freed from the heavy hand of their former general. Dillon and Healy were very able men, with a substantial following among the rank and file; but whereas Dillon wished to out-Herod Herod, and keep the party under firm central control, Healy, like many of the clergy, sought a diffusion of power to the constituencies. When he was expelled from the National Federation, established in 1891 to replace the Parnellite National league, he founded in 1897 a new national organization, the People's Rights Association.[13] Healy's new body was more clerically flavoured than Dillon's, though many of the clergy stood by the Dillonites. More serious was the spectacle of endless quarrelling and faction fighting which threatened to deprive home rule of its vitality and popular appeal, its emotional and patriotic content. Home rule was in danger of fulfilling C.J. Kickham's description of constitutional nationalism: 'two patriots to one plate — each seeming in mortal terror lest his competitor should get a single spoonful in advance of him'.[14]

This danger was increased by the fact that none of the competing patriots — Redmondite, Dillonite or Healyite — could harness the energies of revolutionary enthusiasm to the constitutional movement in the way that Parnell had done. This was all the more alarming in a decade when young men were already turning to literary and debating societies and thus threatening to turn the home rulers into the party of the older generation. Parnell had contrived to direct the energies of Fenians and ex-Fenians, of Irish Americans and British home rule leaguers into the parliamentary movement, a task made easier by the fact that most physical force men objected to constitutionalism, not on principle, but on grounds of its uselessness in gaining Irish freedom. Parnell demonstrated that parliamentarianism need not be feeble or disgraceful — especially when there lurked behind it a militant agrarian movement. Redmond and his followers had stood fast by their chief, but they were not in a position to show that they could achieve anything tangible by their loyalty; and the Irish Republican Brotherhood now sought to reverse the Parnellite process, and absorb Parnellites into its ranks.[15] This they failed to do; but their attempt emphasized the point that the energy and appeal of militant constitutionalism were exhausted.

The home rule movement was also under threat from the forces of British and Irish — and more particularly Ulster-unionism, in its 'moral' and 'physical force' character. After the first Home Rule Bill of 1886, the Conservatives came to office convinced that they could undermine, and perhaps even destroy, Irish nationalism by removing the social discontent that they perceived underlay it. One of the chief bulwarks of the home rulers was land, so the Conservatives made it their particular concern to provide a settlement of the land problem, a policy which set them on the course of abolishing landlordism altogether. And, despite the shortcomings of the Land Act which they passed in 1891, their acceptance of land purchase was a step in the direction of peasant proprietorship, and therefore a real threat — or so it seemed — to home rule's popular appeal.[16]

The unionist threat of physical force was, in the 1890s, less apparent than it was to become immediately before the great war. But the blunt unionist declaration made at a great demonstration held in Belfast in June 1892, 'we will not have home rule', meant that they would not have it in any part of Ireland; and in 1893 the leader of the Ulster unionist members in the House of Commons, Colonel Edward Saunderson, member for north Armagh, helped establish an Ulster Defence Union which collected money and prepared the ground for resistance to the Liberals and their nationalist allies.[17] It is possible that Parnell in 1889, with his immense prestige both in Ireland and Great Britain, might have been able to push through home rule for all Ireland over the heads of unionist opposition; but the delay during the 1890s, and the inability of nationalists to unite themselves, let alone the whole of Ireland, was not convincing evidence of the future prospects of success for the home rule movement.

Here, then, were three great difficulties confronting the home rulers after Parnell: they had to recapture the emotional and deeply felt appeal of nationalism, especially of revolutionary nationalism, without sacrificing their own character; they had to ensure that the Conservative policy of 'killing home rule with kindness' did not work; and they had to seek to bridge the political/religious divide in Ireland, which Parnell had been able to ignore, but which any future nationalist leader would be well advised to consider. The problem was further complicated by the possibility that not all of these ideals might be compatible. This daunting task would have taxed the most imaginative and dedicated Irish leader; but with nationalist Ireland now divided into three mutually hostile home rule factions, not to mention the Irish Republican Brotherhood, and displaying a rigidity of thinking, the prospects for success were not bright. Yet Irish politics were to experience a period of introspection and reappraisal that might have changed the face of the home rule movement and offered new avenues of approach to these complex questions as the party emerged, reunited, into the twentieth century.

The revival of politics came, not from the home rulers, and certainly not from the IRB, but from the fringe literary/nationalist groups which had become disillusioned by the unedifying behaviour of the politicians. In 1896 the council of the Young Ireland League – a body formed in 1891 to foster Irish culture and political ideas, and including John O'Leary, W.B. Yeats, Arthur Griffith and Michael Cusack – proposed a national celebration to mark the centenary of the 1798 rebellion. In 1897 a committee was set up to manage the preparations, and its chairman declared that the committee should be restricted to people in sympathy with the principles of the United Irishmen. The first public meeting of the new body was held at the city hall, Dublin, with the Fenian John O'Leary, in the chair. O'Leary generously appealed for help from all parties without consideration of sectarian or political partisanship, and he gained the support of Redmond and Dillon. But the management of the centenary celebrations was still firmly in the hands of IRB men, and, inevitably, nationalists managed to fall out over the great event that was supposed to unite them; and it was left to William O'Brien to point out the dangers of allowing the physical force people to monopolize the occasion.[18]

O'Brien's instincts were sound; any nationalist movement that turned its back on the heroic dead, on the patriotic tradition of self-sacrifice, could not capture and hold the imagination of the people. And soon the home rulers began to take their cues in the old, Parnellite style. In January 1898 John Dillon set the scene with a speech in Co. Sligo, in which he praised the men of '98, who sent trained soldiers flying before them; (he ignored the uncomfortable presence of the local Irish Catholic militia); and he added that 'today, if the circumstances permitted of it, and if the forces were anything like equal, there are 100,000 men in Ireland who would be glad to follow in their footsteps'. The memories of the patriots of '98 were dear to Irishmen 'as they were to the hearts of Irishmen one hundred years ago, when men fought and died to uphold them'. 'We today are in heart as great rebels as they were'. Despite famine, landlordism, and British rule, 'here you are today, the old race in the old soil'. Dillon, however, despite his appeal to the ideas of the '98 rebels, was careful to emphasize that 'times are changed, and the weapons and machinery of warfare are changed, and I am afraid that nowadays, when rifles carry two miles, a pike would not come near enough to take an effective part in battle . . . Times have changed, and the methods of carrying on the struggle for the liberty of Ireland must be changed in accordance with the times (hear, hear)'.[19]

Dillon's appeal to nationalists 'whether it be a man who does not believe in constitutional methods or whether he be a member of parliament, a constitutionalist or an anti-constitutionalist, let him, if he is an

Irish nationalist, come into this movement and join us' was another attempt to resurrect the traditional Parnellite alliance of all nationally minded men under the umbrella of home rule. Inevitably, this involved home rulers in some dangerous language. In August 1898, at the climax of the celebrations, Dillon praised Wolfe Tone in terms which implied that he should not only be remembered, but emulated: 'I recommend to all of you to study his life, his writings, and his teachings, they are a precious inheritance to the Irish people, and one which, if studied and acted upon, will, in my judgement, be the best guidance to the patriot's part'. *United Ireland* commented that if the youth of Ireland would honour Tone, 'they must follow as best they can the path he tracked out for them'; if they could not be the terror of England, at least they could fashion their lives after Tone and his 'devotion' 'self-sacrifice' and 'courage'.[20] In January 1898 Tim Harrington declared that 'no one here is afraid to speak of "98" ', and urged young men not only to celebrate, but to organize, not only to join clubs, but to emulate the rebels 'in example of united action, in the sacrifice of liberty, and, if necessary, of life, in the vindication of the sacred cause of national freedom'.[21] Even the *Freeman's Journal*, that model of constitutional and conservative nationalism, was moved to speak of sacrifice in terms that Patrick Pearse was soon to use: 'From the blood of patriots, patriots are inspired', it wrote in July 1898; 'wherever the blood of a martyr of '98 fell upon Irish earth, there today the creed of Irish nationality is living and indestructible.'[22]

The parliamentarians always ended their peroration by expressing their confidence that such sacrifice would – or at least might – not be necessary: the Irishmen of today, declared the *Freeman's Journal*, 'have only need to stretch forth their hands' to secure liberty.[23] *United Ireland* agreed that by their force of moral qualities, hatred of oppression, resource for resistance, memory of the past, the people of Ireland had 'forged their way from despair and paralysis to the very verge of National self-government'.[24] This was all very well; but it depended on the home rulers producing results, as Parnell seemed likely to produce in 1886 and 1889, otherwise there was a danger that the orators might be taken at their word by the young men whom they were urging to emulate Wolfe Tone. Fortunately for the parliamentarians, the IRB was in no position to take advantage of the home rulers' weaknesses, or to make anything practical out of the fervour aroused by the parades, meetings, unveiling of monuments and plaques, and visits to battlefields and patriot graves. Nevertheless, as Frederick Allen, a veteran member of the IRB put it, referring to a speech by John Redmond, 'there was not a single word . . . that could offend the most extreme man';[25] and historians who seek the origins of the 1916 rising must look, not only at the Gaelic league or the literary revival, but the celebrations of 1798.[26]

Parliamentarians had of course no intention of making young men sacrifice their lives for Ireland; 1798 was far enough away to be admired from the safety of distance; and it was necessary for home rulers to refresh their nationalism from the springs of the heroic past in order to sustain their momentum in the far from heroic present. They spoke daggers, but used none; and William O'Brien, whose anxiety that the celebrations should not be captured by the physical-force nationalists alone had pushed Dillon into a more positive role than he had wished to assume, was satisfied that, if no good had come out of the affair, at least evil had been averted[27] – or so it seemed at the time. But constitutional participation in the revolutionary tradition was only one part of any home rule resurgence, as O'Brien knew full well. What was needed was not only sentiment, but a firm and attractive political programme and a nation-wide organization to present it to the people. The programme and organization that had turned the home rule party of Isaac Butt into a great national crusade had been the land war and the land league of 1879-82. Now, nearly 20 years later, O'Brien, who had played a leading part in bringing to the public notice distress and the fear of distress in the west of Ireland, hoped again to turn to the west and push the Dublin based political groups into a more radical and more dynamic posture. Since 1895 O'Brien had been living in Mayo, and his attention was drawn to problems created by the giving over of a great part of the country to large cattle ranchers, and the crowding of the numerous tenants into inadequate and barren lands. As O'Brien put it, 'To look over the fences of the famine-stricken village and see the rich green solitudes which might yield full and plenty spread out at the very doorsteps of the ragged and hungry peasants, was to fill a stranger with a sacred rage and make it an unshirkable duty to strive towards undoing the unnatural divorce between the people and the land'.[28] But the Parnellite collapse of 1891 had followed the demise of the plan of campaign, which left the tenants bereft of any means to defend their interests or to check the acceleration of arable to pasture agriculture.[29]

So far the only party which seemed interested in the social and economic plight of the poorer areas of Ireland was the British Conservative party in Westminster, with its plans for rehabilitation of the 'congested districts' (areas where the rateable value was less than 30/-

per head of the population). There were such districts in nine western counties, from Donegal to Kerry, and these were divided into 'two classes, namely the poor and the destitute'. It was to their relief that much of the funds of the disestablished church of Ireland was directed, and harbours built, fisheries encouraged, and agricultural methods improved.[30] But these efforts, and the work of unofficial bodies like Sir Horace Plunkett's Irish Agricultural Organization Society, while they helped improve the standard of farming, did little to check the growth of pasture and the decline of tillage. O'Brien's aim was to arouse the west to help itself, and thus put new life into Irish politics. He had no illusions about the enormity of his task, for the better-off farmers had other interests besides those of helping their lesser brethren.

In 1895 agitation was aroused against the holder of a farm on the earl of Lucan's estate which was held on grazing tenancies. Two local priests, Father Biggin and Father O'Toole, called for united action against large graziers; and at a public meeting held in Kileena, at which William O'Brien was present, the government was urged to give compulsory powers to the congested districts board for the purchase of grazing farms in areas where the tenants needed more land. In 1897 O'Brien began organizing, extending the scope of the movement, and seeking the support and interest of the party leaders; and he appealed to Dillon to play the role of Parnell, and build up a 'great accumulation of national strength' to transplant the people 'from their starvation plots to the abundant green patrimony around them'.[31] But Dillon preferred to concentrate on the political possibilities at Westminster, which required 'close and steady attendance in the House'.[32]

O'Brien, however, was convinced that the western movement — confined as it yet was to the poor smallholders who were the most determined opponents of the wealthy graziers — could provide the nucleus for a renewal of nationalist strength similar to that which had brought Parnell to his supreme position in 1885. In January 1898, inspired by the '98 celebration, he launched a new organization at Westport, the United Irish League. The name of the new association was a compromise: the Parnellite Tim Harrington had suggested 'reviving the society of United Irishmen' on the grounds that it would 'catch the extreme men and so long as it remained an open organization would command general respect'; but O'Brien feared that the name and associations would 'rather frighten the clergy' and so the United Irish League was chosen.[33] The United Irish League would regroup the scattered forces of nationalism — clerical, revolutionary, constitutional, and possibly even add Protestants to the cause, and set free the tiger of militant constitutionalism, once again firmly ridden by the leader of the Irish parliamentary party.

John Dillon attended the Westport meeting of 16 January 1898; but he was unenthusiastic about the league and its prospects. It might be suppressed by the Government; it was untried and untested; and enthusiasm was no substitute for experience.[34] The danger of Dillon's viewpoint was that the home rulers would be a bureaucratic machine, heavy-handed and oppressive, and would fail to make the best use of the nationalist enthusiasm generated by the '98 celebrations and the new western agrarian movement. On the other hand, O'Brien revealed a naivety about his United Irish League and its possibilities for the parliamentarians: 1898 was not 1879, and the battle against graziers was one only confined to Connaught and a few countries of the south west.[35] Still, the possibilities inherent in a revival of the old slogan 'the land for the people' could not lightly be set aside;[36] and the home rule leaders were now under pressure to take serious account of the movement, and to contrast their endless quarrelling with the enthusiasm and popularity of the United Irish League. On 13 February 1899 talks were opened for the reunion of the party; and after some complex negotiations Dillon was able to outline a programme almost identical to that of the Parnellites in the 1892 election. All Irish nationalists were to combine as one party, independent of English parties, to secure home rule as embodied in the bills of 1886 and 1893; and the party was to fight on the old lines of redress of grievances, especially those concerned with land, labour, taxation and education. As a gesture of reconciliation, the anti-Parnellites supported the election of a Parnellite, John Redmond, to the chair. At a national convention in June 1900 the UIL was declared the sole official organization of the nationalist party, with power vested in the branches, and the divisional, provincial and national directories of the league. Redmond was elected president of the league; and the '98 celebrations, followed closely by the formation of the UIL and its incorporation in the whole parliamentary movement, seemed to augur well for the renewal of Parnellism in Ireland.[37]

It is tempting to blame Dillon, in particular, for the failure of the new militant constitutionalist movement launched in 1900; but the problem was more complex. Dillon was an unimaginative politician; but his greatest critic, O'Brien, was perhaps all too easily carried away by the forces of his own imagination, and saw possibilities of political opportunity where none really existed. For whereas Parnell had grown up with, and then attempted to grow out of, the land league of 1879,

Dillon and Redmond had grown up long before the agrarian agitation of 1898; and the old, long established parliamentary party was now grafted to a new, inexperienced agrarian organization.[38] But even this was less important than the fact that the strategy of the parliamentary party was essentially the same as that of 1886: a total and absolute reliance on the return to power of the British Liberal party. Parnell had declined to play any part in the plan of campaign, even at the risk of forfeiting support in Ireland; now the unfortunate home rulers found themselves, at one and the same time, depending on the Liberal party for home rule, undergoing imprisonment for involvement in the agrarian agitation,[39] and representing the anti-British temperament of Ireland by making violent speeches in favour of the Boers in the struggle with the British, assuring their listeners that as one speaker put it, 'if he were in a position to place in the hands of every man a Mauser rifle, and if he could provide a few "long Toms" (cheers) – it would not be talking constitutionalism he would be'.[40] As well as all this, the home rulers had extended their umbrella to cover the revival of cultural nationalism in Ireland. In the House of Commons in 1901 Tom O'Donnell, member for West Kerry, rose and spoke in Irish; when the Speaker asked him to be seated John Redmond raised the whole issue of a member being allowed to 'speak in his own native language'. This incident, one member asserted, 'gave more publicity to the new movement for the revival of the Irish language than any single happening in our time'.[41] This was, perhaps an exaggeration; but the United Irish League included among its eleven points 'the preservation of the Gaelic language'.[42] This owed much to William O'Brien who once declared that 'lost were the nation which should forget that the sacred passion of nationality . . . has its origin deep in the recesses of the past, among the old associations of which the Gaelic League is the very living voice and soul'.[43]

There seemed, in short, no end to the national causes that home rule could stand for; the danger was, as T.P. O'Connor warned the party, that 'we do not want thunderclaps in Ireland to arrest English attention, it is arrested already'.[44] But Redmond had his own difficulties with his supporters at home. In March 1900 he stated in Parliament that the Irish people 'will receive with gratification the announcement that Her Majesty has directed that for the future the shamrock shall be worn by Irish regiments on March 17th to commemorate the gallantry of Irish soldiers in South Africa' – a compliment which drew from William O'Brien the sharp retort that the queen was 'a lady who comes to typify all that is most hateful in English rule'.[45]

The home rulers of Redmond's day still faced the dilemma that had pursued them since 1886, one that was implicit in the policy of leading a nationalist movement from London. They were torn between the need to appear reasonable, perhaps even loyal, in the British Parliament, and yet satisfy their own voters in Ireland; and they were also aware of the other major problem arising from their tactical position: the fact that they must work hard to maintain Irish nationalist enthusiasm for the cause of home rule at a time when its realization appeared as far away as ever. At one moment the home rulers were seeking to keep up with nationalism in Ireland; at another, they were anxiously endeavouring to ensure that it did not lose its sharp edge of conviction. And this dilemma was perfectly illustrated in their divided attitude to the settlement of the Irish land question, following a public proposal in the summer of 1902 by an Irish landlord, Shawe-Taylor, that a conference should be called of landlords and tenants to settle the land problem by direct negotiation. This offer was not as surprising as it appeared: landlordism in Ireland was fast becoming a diminishing asset for political as well as economic reasons. Landlord control over their estates had been weakened by land legislation, and the 1898 establishment of elective county councils destroyed their control over local government. In December 1902 a conference of landlord and tenant representatives met, presided over by Lord Dunraven, and the formula agreed was accepted by the chief secretary, George Wyndham, as the basis of a new Land Purchase Act. The act was defective in certain respects, and had to be adjusted in 1909; but it established land purchase as the final solution of the land problem, the question that had been at the forefront of nationalist politics for a generation. And by the early 1920s nearly two thirds of Ireland's total area of land had ceased to be the property of the landlords.[46]

This, however, was not to the liking of all nationalists. Some, like Davitt and Dillon, thought that the landlords had done only too well out of the bargain; and Dillon's dislike of landlordism pursued them beyond the economic grave. They could never change their politics, he alleged; and the land bill was owed 'not to the goodwill of English ministers or Irish landlords but to the agitation of the United Irish League'. The idea held in some quarters — and this was a shaft aimed at William O'Brien — that the conciliation process could be extended into the political sphere was impossible; the landlords had only agreed to land purchase because coercion had been about to 'topple down about their ears . . . I am so far sceptical that I have no faith in the doctrine of conciliation'.[47]

But there was another, deeper, reason behind Dillon's concern: the

fear that the land question, which had rallied the Roman Catholic
tenantry of Ireland behind the home rule movement, which had helped
give it popular appeal under Parnell, might, if settled, fatally undermine home rule itself. As Lord Bryce wrote to A.V. Dicey in 1905,
'when they have the land, much of the steam will be out of the boiler
. . . That home rule will come in our time seems unlikely'.[48] Dillon
shared their belief; the land 'trouble', he declared, 'is a weapon in
nationalist hands and . . . to settle it finally would be to risk home rule,
which otherwise *must* come'. And he spoke darkly of a 'deep laid plot
to capture Ireland out of the hands of the national party'.[49]

Dillon was simplistic in his analysis of the nature of Irish nationalism. For the land question was never simply an economic one, although
it had obviously economic appeal for the astute farmers of Ireland. It
was also an expression of nationalist sentiment, appealing to the emotions, reviving or creating notions of a dispossessed people, long
deprived of their rightful property, but now marching along the road to
final victory. As one MP put it at a UIL meeting in 1900, the principal
planks in the UIL platform were 'Ireland for the Irish and the land for
the people'.[50] The 'people' did not include the farm labourers or the
working classes of Dublin or Cork or Limerick; but the slogan corresponded to the distribution of political power in Ireland, and that was
what mattered. Now that the land had been gained for the people, then
'Ireland for the Irish' remained to be achieved; and the destruction of
the economic power of the landlords, that 'British garrison', far from
undermining the demand for self-government, only opened the way to
its realization. The unionist landlords were very far from politically
finished, as they were seen to show in their fervent and well-organized
opposition to the third Home Rule Bill; but they were still quite un-
reconciled to their former tenants, and were fair game for nationalist
rhetoric. Anti-landlord feeling was strong enough to enable one candidate in the general election of 1906 to denounce the 'landlord class,
the ascendancy class',[51] just as they had been denounced in every
election since 1874.

The reason why a settlement of the land question could not 'de-
nationalise' Ireland was partly because there were vigorous groups
working to keep nationalism alive — the Gaelic League, Sinn Féin —
but mainly because Ireland still stood in the relationship to England
that had inspired and shaped her nationalism in the first place. Ireland
was a small island in the shadow of a large and influential one; but,
thanks to the Protestant nationalists of the eighteenth century, she
had inherited a tradition of separate institutional development, an idea

of a corporate national existence. After 1800 Ireland lost her separate institutions of government, except for Dublin Castle, and this style of executive signalled that Ireland was not to be treated as just another member of the United Kingdom body politic. Why was she not to be thus treated? Here, for Roman Catholics, was the crux of the matter. For while they were the majority in Ireland, the 'Irish people', they remained a minority in the United Kingdom as a whole; and they were subject, at one and the same time, to the veto also of the non-Catholic Irish minority. Thus their majority status in Ireland was not recognized, and this in a century which saw the inexorable advance of democratic politics almost everywhere in western Europe.

Irish nationalists were the majority, and their sense of the assurance of power enabled them, on frequent occasions, to display generosity towards the Protestant minority. But they were frustrated by the insistence in England – an insistence shared by Liberals and Conservative alike – that their advance to power must await the verdict of the British majority; they were even warned on occasion that it must await the verdict of the Irish Protestant minority, especially after 1892, of the Protestants in Ulster. Thus Irish Roman Catholics, despite their triumphs in the fields of education, local government, and now land purchase, were still denied that final restoration of Ireland's separate corporate existence signifying their status as the Irish nation. The precise nature of that independent corporate existence was not the important issue; what the Irish Parliament could or could not do, what there was left for it to do after a decade of conservative Unionism which followed a century of British social and economic reforms, was irrelevant. For Irish Roman Catholics were as rigidly held to their majority/minority status in 1906 as they had been in 1800; and until that problem was resolved, and resolved to their satisfaction, then home rule would not lose its vitality. It was this peculiar status, not the presence of Fenian graves, that meant that 'Ireland, unfree, shall never be at peace'.[52] And if the home rulers could, at last, translate the goal of national self-realization, of pride, dignity, sentimentality, frustrated self-respect and self-regard, into some form of native Irish institution, as the Irish Protestants of the eighteenth century had done, then nationalist Ireland would not desert them.

The French observer, Louis Paul-Dubois, analyzed what he called the 'national and anti-English spirit' in early twentieth century Ireland; and he pointed out its contradictions. Irish hatred of England was a complex feeling: 'Irishmen are never tired of anathematising the "pirate Empire", that "Empire of Hell" to which the Presbyterian Mitchel dedicated the three hundred pages of hatred which go to make up his *Jail Journal*. Nevertheless a large portion of the British Empire is administered by Irishmen, who are either members of the Indian Civil Service, or leading politicians in Canada or Australia'. And, while in the Boer war 'the honour of the British army was saved . . . by Irish soldiers', the Irish were throughout the war aggressively pro-Boer, with the newly-elected county councils in 1898 voting addresses of congratulations to president Kruger. Hatred of England still existed in Ireland, despite the fact that Irish 'mercenaries' accepted the 'Saxon shilling' either in a spirit of adventure or because work was scarce; but Irish hatred of the English people was 'not very common, or, perhaps, one can more justly say, is not very deep'. What was general and deep was a spirit of hostility and aversion for England as a sovereign power, for English law and the English Government. Ireland 'is full of rancour for the past, and of distrust for the future, and she cherishes the hope and the ambition of revenge'. This disloyalty was largely because of a hundred years of British policy which 'produced the Clearances, the Great Famine, and Emigration'. Thus anti-English feeling found expression in delight over Boer victories, while at the same time Irishmen felt pride in the fighting prowess of their soldiers 'in a cause which was not her cause'. The fact that Irish disloyalty was punctuated by outbreaks of loyalty — by the Corporation of Dublin in 1900 voting an address to the sovereign; by the lord mayor in 1903, after voting against an address, giving an official welcome to the British fleet; by some nationalists drinking the king's health at private functions, but refusing to do so in public; by military bands being hissed in Phoenix Park while children ran alongside a regimental band in the streets 'in the greatest delight, like so many Parisian *badauds*' — simply proved that human nature 'has its weaknesses, and that in Ireland, as elsewhere, a man must adjust himself to certain conventions and social necessities if he is to live at all'.[53]

Paul-Dubois's interpretation of Irish nationalist sentiment was mirrored in the reaction of nationalists to two important British and Irish public celebrations in 1902 and 1903. In August 1902 Edward VII was crowned, and Irish nationalist representatives met in Dublin at the city hall, with John Redmond presiding, to explain their refusal to take any part in the coronation celebrations. The Irish parliamentary party, Redmond declared, had assembled 'to place once more upon record the protest of our people against the usurpation of the government of Ireland by the English parliament'; and he denied the 'moral or legal or constitutional right of the English parliament to legislate for

Ireland'. Since 1800 Ireland had been governed, in effect, like a crown colony, with certain empty forms and pretences of constitutionalism; and under English rule 'millions of our people have died by artificial (sic) famines, and hundreds of thousands of homes have been levelled by the crowbar brigade'. 'Fraud, robbery and murder have characterized the English usurpation of our country'; and the Irish submitted to this English usurpation of the government only 'because we have no adequate means for successful resistance; but we loath English rule, and we will take no part in the jubilation of the coronation'.[54]

Irish nationalists, however, were anxious to draw a distinction between hostility to the crown as a symbol of the British constitution, and personal courtesy to the king; and when Edward VII visited Ireland in July 1903, the *Freeman's Journal* found no reason to anticipate anything other than the cordial welcome which Dublin gave to the sovereign: 'Dublin led the country, spoke for the country, by defining the National position of a hearty, a courteous, but unofficial, reception'.[55] But Dublin's friendly reception for the king did not prevent it, two months later, from playing host to a large and impressive demonstration, organized by a committee under John O'Leary's presidency, celebrating the centenary of the death of Robert Emmet, perhaps, after Tone, the most popular of Irish martyred heroes. The same *Freeman's Journal* which approved of the king's reception reflected proudly that Emmet's memory did not dim, but 'seems to grow brighter as the years roll on'. Emmet represented 'with unmistakable clearness and boldness, the lofty and uncompromising spirit of Irish nationality' which made his memory a vital force amongst the people today; and it was fitting that 'the people of our time should show that his memory is still dear to them, and that on the centenary of his execution they should gather together to pay honour to that hallowed memory and resolve one and all to do everything possible to hasten the day when his epitaph can be written.'

On 20 September the celebrations took place; and, as the *Freeman's Journal* remarked, 'Dublin did it well'. Thousands of people gathered, coming from all parts of the country, using special trains to take them to the scene of the great event. Most Dublin trades bodies took part in the procession; bands, banners, emblems, were on display; and the participants marched past the scenes identified with Emmet's career. The National Foresters, the GAA and the Gaelic League were present, and also the Boys Brigades, 'their presence giving pledge of fidelity to the national cause when the young lads will have grown to man's estate'. But there was no crêpe; there were no flags flying at half mast;

for 'it was not a dead cause that was being celebrated, but a cause resurgent'. Emmet taught Ireland that she must persevere, even under the most discouraging circumstances; Emmet died both wisely and well: for 'the blood of the martyrs, it is said, is the soul of the Church; and the blood of Emmet, as it flowed in Thomas Street a hundred years ago, had fructified in many a young Irish mind since, at home and abroad, to the glory and the credit and the practical benefit of Ireland'. Thus it was that thousands came to Dublin 'where a century ago the English rulers of the land exacted from Emmet the sacrifice of his life as the penalty of his devotion to his native land'; and, once there, they were treated to a short, but pointed, address by the Fenian John O'Leary, who warned his listeners that:

We are not here to talk. Emmet desired that his epitaph should not be written till his country was free, and I hold that the best way we can do honour to his memory is to strive with might and main to bring about the time when the epitaph can be written. I have nothing more to say, but I and all of you have very much to do.[56]

'National and anti-English' sentiment was alive and well in Ireland in the new century; the question facing the Irish parliamentary party was whether or not it could remain what it had been since 1880, the main, if not the sole, political repository of national sentiment: 'national unity' to the party meant, quite simply, that they controlled, organized, spoke for and bargained on behalf of, the Irish people. There were, to be sure, a few signs that new men were coming forward with a claim to represent the true nationalist spirit; and at a by-election in North Leitrim in 1908 Sinn Féin polled 1,157 votes against 3,103 for the parliamentary party. But this reasonably impressive performance was vitiated by the fact that the Sinn Féin candidate was a former home ruler who had left the party because of dissatisfaction with its recent performance; and Sinn Féin had not the financial means to act as a major political party, or even to run a viable daily newspaper. Sinn Féin clubs and societies were small in size and numbered at most 150 between 1908 and 1910.[57]

Catholic Ireland, therefore, remained a one party nation; but the parliamentary party had always to seek for ways to ensure that its control over the nation was embedded in secure institutional foundations. The taking over of the United Irish League was one example of its ability to swallow up possible rival organizations; but the party was always on the lookout for any new sources of political power that could give expression to the deep nationalist sentiments of twentieth century Ireland, and that, equally important, could offer a new infusion of blood to the party's ageing veins. So far the solid strength of the party had come from Dublin and the south and west of Ireland; but now a new political development took place that was to have important consequences, not only for the party, but for Irish nationalism and modern Irish history: the political mobilization of Catholic Ulster.

The north of Ireland had been the centre of Irish political activity in the last decade of the eighteenth century, when Presbyterian radicals made Belfast the intellectual and reforming capital of Ireland. And both the Orange Order and the unionists used Ulster as the pivot of their opposition to home rule and the advancement of the Roman Catholics to power. But so far Catholic Ulster had played little or no part in Irish politics; as John Martin remarked to John Mitchel, this was not because of their lack of commitment to the nationalist cause, for 'Ulster Catholics seem to be even more universally nationalist than those of the other provinces'. Their political immobility lay in their attitude, for, Martin went on, 'they feel the political ascendancy of the Protestants pressing more closely upon them . . . The Ulster Catholics, therefore, born and bred in practical Helotism, though very Irish and patriotic at heart, and in mind, are very cautious and timid politicians'.[58] This prudence made any central organization of the Ulster Catholics a difficult and unrewarding task; and, therefore, nineteenth-century Irish nationalism bore no imprint of Ulster Catholics.

All this was changed by the emergence of the Ancient Order of Hibernians, an organization which was founded in the mid-nineteenth century to protect the interests of Irish Catholics abroad, and especially in America. The AOH was a mixture of friendly society and defender of Irish Catholic interests; and one area of Ireland in which those interests needed defending was Ulster, where the general and inexorable advance of Catholics to power under the Union did not take place. Catholics were kept out of jobs in the urban areas of the north east, especially in Belfast, where the Belfast corporation and the port authorities gave preference to Protestants.[59] Home rule was attractive to such people because, as R. Barry O'Brien put it, it would 'reverse the condition of things';[60] but meanwhile they needed an association for mutual aid and advancement, and to give expression to their hatred for their enemies, the Orangemen. Its symbols were the exact reverse of those of the Orange Order: instead of William of Orange there appeared on AOH banners Rory O'More; in place of the Union flag stood Erin with her harp.

But despite its obvious attractions for Ulster Catholics, the AOH owed its success to the work of an Ulster member of the Irish parliamentary party, Joseph Devlin, who perceived the opportunities it offered for providing a local base for the party, corresponding to that offered by the United Irish League in the southern and western parts of Ireland. From this solid base tentacles could be stretched to other urban centres of Ireland where the UIL could not expect to enjoy the same appeal or support. Devlin had to contend with the hostility of some members of the party to his efforts, and also with that of the Archbishop of Armagh and other members of the hierarchy; but his energy and administrative ability were indefatigable; and, moreover, he brought membership, money and enthusiasm to the party at a time when its subscriptions were falling alarmingly. Leading nationalist politicians, including Dillon, William Redmond, and Thomas Kettle, became members of the AOH. AOH representation at National Conventions rose from twenty-four in 1903 to 417 in 1909 out of a total number of about 2,500 to 3,000 delegates.[61] And the AOH's growth in membership was given unintentional encouragement by Lloyd George's National Insurance Act of 1911, which provided for the administration of benefit through existing private organizations. The AOH seized the chance of recruiting members through its insurance activity, and by 1914 it had about one quarter of the insurable Catholic population among its membership.[62] It was no coincidence that John Dillon publicly praised the AOH in December 1910 as 'a body of men for whom, I confess, I have the greatest regard'.[63]

Not every nationalist, however, shared Dillon's regard for the AOH. Tim Harrington wrote to Redmond in August 1907 warning him that the AOH programme was 'in direct opposition to our policy of uniting all creeds and classes of Irishmen and though at present they are all right and giving us good services the day of decision and dissension will come'.[64] Patrick Pearse, ever mindful of the Protestant contribution to Irish nationalist thinking, deplored the fact that 'the driving force of the official Nationalists shall be supplied by an organization of which no Protestant, however good a patriot, can be a member'.[65] Yet the man most responsible for the expansion of the AOH, Joseph Devlin, was no mere 'ghetto boss', and certainly no hater of Ulster Protestants. He was a sincerely liberal man, with a deep affection for all the working-class people of Belfast, whatever their political beliefs. 'I ask no man to support me on religious grounds', he stated in 1906; and he was fond of quoting Thomas Davis:

> Then let the Orange my lily be
> Thy badge, my papist brother;
> The Orange for you
> The green for me
> And we for one another.[66]

Probably Devlin did not pause to consider the implications of what he was doing; possibly he did not think that it mattered all that much, since his impressive and well-earned record as a good constituency MP, caring for all the electors in his division, whether or not they voted for him, spoke for itself.[67] Above all, he was a practical politician, immensely loyal to the Irish parliamentary party, whose job it was to organize the Catholic vote in Ulster,[68] and who carried out that job as best he could. In 1906, after all, he had won West Belfast for the party after an interval of 14 years;[69] such a man, with his political skills, could not be disregarded by nationalist leaders.

Devlin mobilized the Ulster Catholics, more especially the urban Catholics, and the less well-off men in the countryside,[70] behind the banner of the home rule movement. Thus home rule added yet another element, with yet another perspective, to its cause: the perspective of the Ulster Catholic, whose dislike of 'England' was far surpassed by his hatred of Protestants, and especially Orangemen.[71] Irish nationalism had always found difficulty in incorporating non-Catholics comfortably into its ranks, partly because nationalism in Ireland was not only concerned with self-government, but was given widespread appeal by its campaign for a transfer of power from the Protestants to the Roman Catholics, and partly because the nationalist view of Irish history was not one likely to find favour with non-Catholics, especially when it was accompanied with a veiled warning that it might be hard for some Irish Catholics to 'forget the "blood-stained" past'.[72]

Nevertheless, home rule speakers were still able to point out, quite rightly, that a Catholic county like Clare would vote for a Protestant home ruler, Jeremiah Jordan, without asking what religion he professed, 'so long as they knew he loved Ireland'.[73] The problem with the political mobilization of Ulster nationalism was not only its more sectarian character, but also the fact that it transferred the centre of the whole Anglo-Irish controversy to the cockpit of the north of Ireland. This tendency was reinforced by the organization of the Ulster Unionists in their own body, the Ulster Unionist Council, in 1905, and the increasing tendency of British and Irish Unionists to focus the opposition to home rule on the claims and rights of the Ulster Protestants. The overall constitutional issue of the relationship that Ireland could or should hold to England, and such safeguards for the Protestant minority that any modification of that relationship might involve, was becoming transformed into the relationship between England and part (the south and west) of Ireland, and, paralleling that, the special treatment that Ulster Protestants could claim in any settlement of the problem. Thus the Ulster nationalists were organized as an important and effective force only a few years before they were regarded as a dispensable element in any overall Irish constitutional agreement. It might fairly be said of them, therefore, that if accusations that they sectarianized Irish nationalism have some foundation, it is equally true that Irish nationalism, through its willingness to use, and then compromise with, and finally abandon Ulster Catholics, further sectarianized Ulster nationalism.

The idea of an 'olive branch in Ireland' floated by William O'Brien after the successful land conference of 1903, and seeking to settle the political question by 'conference plus business'[74] as the social and economic issues of land ownership had been settled, was not one that the parliamentary party felt able to take up. It is doubtful if the same method could have been applied to the home rule issue, for neither British nor Irish unionists were prepared to give up the game as yet; but, in any case, the home rulers remained convinced that their best hope lay in making the liberal alliance work for them as it had so nearly done in 1886 and 1891. In Ireland they devoted their efforts to maintaining 'national unity', using whatever methods came to hand, including the UIL and then the AOH; in England, they bided their time in the hope that events would fall their way again. And in 1910 their patience and vigilance seemed to be justified: a long-threatened clash between the Liberal Government and the House of Lords came to a head when the Liberal budget was rejected by the lords in 1909. A general election was now inevitable; and Redmond was able to exact a public assurance from Asquith that home rule would be included in the government's election programme. Nationalist good fortune continued, for in two elections in January and December 1910 the home rulers emerged holding a strong position in the House of Commons, and no Liberal Government could survive without their consent; nor, however, could the nationalists survive without the consent of the Liberals. In August 1911 the House of Lords, after a bitter struggle, surrendered its power of veto: it could delay a bill for 2 years, but at the end of that time the bill would become law. And the home rulers' campaign song of 1910 seemed to be vindicated:

We tread the land that bore us,
The green flag flutters o'er us,
The friends we've tried are by our side,
And our hated foes before us.[75]

The Government of Ireland Bill of 1912 was in some respects less generous than the earlier home rule measures; and the Irish parliamentary party would probably have sought to enlarge its scope once it came into effect.[76] But like all the home rule bills it was a symbol as much as a piece of administrative and political reform: as John Redmond and Stephen Gwynn put it, it was 'an act of restitution – not a new departure'; for 'Ireland had a parliament, of antiquity almost as great as that of England, and possessing larger powers than are claimed under home rule'. Home rule was a 'national right', an 'historical legal title'.[77] The fate of the Irish Councils Bill of 1907, which proposed to give to Ireland a partly nominated, but mainly elected council with control over eight departments of the Irish administration, subject to the lord lieutenant's veto, was a sharp reminder to the home rulers that they must invest any settlement that England seemed willing to make with a certain nationalist mystique, or suffer the consequences.[78] It may well have been, as T.P. O'Connor wittily observed, that 'devolution is the Latin for home rule';[79] but home rule was the Irish for independence, and the search for home rule was the search for Ireland a nation, for the writing of Emmet's epitaph, and for the fulfilment of the last will and testament of countless Irish patriots and martyrs ranging from Rory O'More to Parnell.

But now that the search seemed to have come to an end; now that the holy grail had been discovered; now that the promised land was, at long last, to be entered; did home rule still stand for these emotive symbols? Might not a new opportunity be offered for a concept of nationalism that spoke, not in terms of conflict, but in terms of reconciliation? Isaac Butt had regarded federalism and home rule as the best possible and most honourable settlement, one that could substitute for a false Union a real bond between Great Britain and Ireland; might not the time have come for a revival of this sentiment, for a new concept of home rule that, as Redmond remarked in 1912, would 'put an end once and for all to the wretched ill-will, suspicion, and disaffection that have existed in Ireland' and turn her into 'a happy and prosperous country, with a united, loyal and contented people'. In 1886 Redmond had declared at Melbourne that 'as a nationalist, I do not regard as entirely palatable the idea that for ever and a day Ireland's voice should be excluded from the councils of an empire which the genius and valour of her sons have done so much to build up, and of which she is to remain a part'.[80] Now that home rule seemed to be assured, the time for a 'union of hearts' had, perhaps, come.

The idea of a union of hearts had always been implicit in the home rule movement, although home rulers were, in the main, careful to reserve it for British rather than Irish consumption in the 1880s. 'Powerful England has nothing to fear from granting impoverished Ireland home rule, but everything to gain', promised *United Ireland* in July 1886; 'The Union which is now maintained by force would thus be strengthened by the bonds of mutual confidence and friendship'.[81] A colour supplement showed Parnell and ranks of green clad soldiers grounding arms under a flag of truce, while Gladstone emerged from the redcoats carrying a white flag inscribed 'Home Rule. Abolition of landlordism'.[82] But the expression of friendship and amity were, on the whole, guarded; and the cryptic comment by *United Ireland* in June 1886, 'it must be Cromwell, or an honest shake hands',[83] was as far as the Parnell movement was prepared to go, at least in Ireland.

But Redmond now sought to give a more dynamic meaning to the concept, to make it not merely a form of assurance to England that she was doing the right and sensible thing in Ireland at last, but a positive Irish commitment to the welfare of Britain, the Union and the Empire. And the argument was now carried into the heart of nationalist Ireland. In Co. Clare in 1913 William Redmond told his audience that:

> thirty years have seen the grievances of Ireland removed one by one, and today sees the representatives of Ireland in the face of the outstretched hand of friendship from Great Britain no longer bitter, but ready and willing on the basis of the Home Rule Bill to enter the future on terms of friendship and goodwill for all time with the people of England, Scotland and Wales, and the whole Empire.[84]

And the union of hearts was not only one between Great Britain and Ireland. Redmond now made the clearest, most unequivocal statement of nationalist Ireland's commitment to a United Irish nation. 'Ireland for us', he affirmed, 'is one entity. It is one land . . . Some of the most glorious chapters connected with our national struggle have been associated with Ulster — aye, and with the protestants of Ulster — and I believe here today, as a Catholic Irishman, notwithstanding all the bitterness of the past, that I am as proud of Derry as of Limerick.' 'Our ideal', he continued:

in the movement is a self-governing Ireland of the future, when all her sons, of all races and creeds, within her shores will bring their tribute, great or small, to the great total of national enterprise, national statesmanship, and national happiness.

Within the Irish nation, however, there was 'room for diversities of the treatment of government and administration'.[85]

This noble rhetoric hardly corresponded to the state of either British or Irish public opinion in the years before the outbreak of the Great war. The Parliamentary party had revealed how ruthless it could be in its determination to preserve 'national unity' even amongst Catholic Ireland, let alone anywhere else, when hired bands of AOH 'security' men were used to intimidate Sinn Féin, Irish Labour,[86] and William O'Brien's attempts to speak at a National Convention in 1909 where, as O'Brien aptly put it, 'the melodious accent of Belfast . . . reigned wherever a delegate was to be hit on the head or a speaker guillotined'.[87] The melodious accent of Belfast was not peculiar to the AOH, as Protestants revealed when they retaliated with 'confetti' (steel discs punched out of plates by riveters in the shipyards) on Catholics following an AOH attack on some Protestant Sunday-school children.[88] Moreover, Protestants were unlikely to respond to Redmond's appeal that they be accepted as an equal part of the nation, when their whole argument against home rule was based on their denial that there was an Irish nation in the first place,[89] and on a claim, not for a position in Ireland equal with Roman Catholics, but for a superior one; a claim which the Ulster Protestants, for their part, were prepared to make good with armed force if necessary.

British unionists also denied that there was such a phenomenon as a separate Irish nationality; indeed, the whole purpose of the constructive unionism of the last decade of the nineteenth century and the first 5 years of the twentieth was based on the assumption that Irish nationalism was at bottom a protest against bad government, rather than a desire for self-government. Irish nationalism was both; but because the bad government was English, self-government was necessary.[90] When the British unionists found that all their efforts had left nationalist Ireland unmoved and resurgent, and when they lost their final constitutional check on home rule with the reform of the House of Lords, they were ready to encourage Ulster unionists in their preparation for armed resistance to the Liberal government. Patriots, they held, would frustrate the knavish tricks of politicians. The politicians, for their part,hardly seemed to know what to do. Irish nationalist leaders were warned, as early as February 1912, that 'the government held themselves free to make such changes as fresh evidence of facts, or the pressure of British opinion, may render expedient'; and if some special treatment of Ulster counties became necessary, 'the government will be ready to recognise the necessity whether by amendment of the bill or by not passing it under the provisions of the parliament act'.[91] Redmond would have found it almost impossible to resist such a compromise which William Redmond hinted at in his 1913 speech in Co. Clare; but no moves were made in this direction. And the Liberal Government virtually forfeited its authority in the Curragh crisis of March 1914, when a cavalry brigadier, Sir Hubert Gough, went to London and exacted a pledge from the Secretary of State for war that the Government had no intention of using the army to 'crush political opposition to the policy or principles of the home rule bill'.[92]

Certainly, the idea of the legitimate use of force by the Government was at variance with the notion of a union of hearts in Ireland; but Redmond's inclination to leave any initiative towards compromise in the hands of the Liberals was equally ill advised. The union of hearts might have made sense if backed up by O'Brien's policy of 'conference plus business', though it is doubtful if the confident and aggressive Ulster Protestants would have troubled themselves to attend, and the southern Irish unionists were exerting their considerable influence in British political circles to thwart any attempts at compromise. But the idea of depending on the Liberal alliance at all costs was also at variance with the union of hearts; and, moreover, as the Liberal government began to falter in the face of unionist opposition, the union of hearts began to look less convincing in nationalist Ireland. That the idea had originally some currency was noticed by John Dillon, who remarked in the spring of 1912 that a national convention, which he had feared would 'very seriously injure the whole situation', turned out to be 'in splendid form', with an overwhelming feeling 'of *enthusiastic* acceptance of the Bill and a whole hearted desire to make peace with England without any reserves. I confess that I have myself been taken by surprise with the universality of this feeling'.[93] But as militant unionism gathered strength in 1913, some Irish nationalists decided that the time had come to follow the example of the north, and in November 1913, under the inspiration of the Gaelic scholar, Eoin MacNeill, the Irish

Volunteers were inaugurated. Enthusiasts were inclined to exaggerate both the numbers and influence of the Volunteers: up to the end of 1913 the membership was only about 1,850. By July 1914 it stood at 160,000;[94] but the enthusiasm for military life was easier to arouse than to sustain; and the Irish Volunteers perhaps found the experience similar to that of their eighteenth century counterparts whose 'cloud-cap't grenadies and . . . gorgeous infantry' dissolved 'apace as the summer approaches'.[95] Redmond, moreover, was still determined to maintain the parliamentary party's unrelenting grip on all nationalist organizations, large or small; and in June 1914 he stated publicly that either he must control the Volunteers or take steps that would split the movement. The provisional committee of the Volunteers yielded; and Redmond gained formal control of the movement. But the committee resented his dictation;[96] and the dangers involved in drilling and arming were revealed when, following a confrontation with some Volunteers carrying rifles which had been landed at Howth, a group of Scottish Borderers fired on a crowd of civilians who had been jeering at them and hurling stones and bottles. Thirty-eight people were wounded and three subsequently died;[97] and the union of hearts seemed about to perish in a fusillade fired by British soldiers.

It was saved, and then given a new and dynamic phase, by the European war in August 1914. On the outbreak of war the home rule MP Thomas Kettle, was in Belgium buying guns for the Irish Volunteers. He witnessed at first hand the 'Prussian' crushing of that country; and by November 1914 he was in the Dublin Fusiliers, addressing recruiting meetings in Ireland, and declaring that 'Britain, Russia, France enter this war purged of their sins of past domination'.[98] His response was characteristic; and it was not only the British who were purged of their sins of domination, for Redmond urged the British Government to withdraw its forces from Ireland leave her defence to her 'armed sons, and for this purpose armed Nationalist Catholics in the south will be only too glad to join arms with the armed Protestant Ulstermen of the North'.[99] True, the reaffirmed brotherhood of Irishmen experienced some difficult moments, especially when Redmond forced the Government to stop prevaricating and place the home rule bill on the statute book, albeit with a promise not to put it into effect until an amending bill had been taken in the winter session. Ulster and British unionists reacted with furious hostility; but at least Sir James Craig, the Ulster unionist leader, agreed that 'we will do our best under the circumstances for the army and the country'. And the exciting scenes in the commons, when the home rule bill received the royal assent, and a green Irish flag bearing a golden harp was waved on the floor of the house to the accompaniment of a chorus (led by a Labour member) of 'God save the King', seemed an appropriate climax to the old struggle, and a favourable augury for the new.[100]

The union of hearts could be realized because Ireland now 'enjoyed' home rule, and because the tensions and stresses invoked by home rule could be minimized and finally vanquished by the common cause and the shared experience of fighting in the greatest war that mankind had ever known. Thousands of Irishmen from north and south, not to mention Irishmen resident in Great Britain, joined the colours, and by April 1916 there were 150,000 Irishmen on active service, of whom two thirds had joined the forces since the war started. Among them were some prominent nationalist MPs, including John Redmond's brother and son, Thomas Kettle, Stephen Gwynn, and J.L. Esmonde;[101] and Redmond abandoned his earlier caution,[102] and set his approval on enlistment by declaring in a speech at Woodenbridge, Co. Wicklow, that the Irish Volunteers should not merely defend Ireland, but should go 'wherever the firing line extends'.[103] Redmond now elevated the union of hearts into an almost mystical significance: on a visit to the front in November 1915 he noted that in the Royal Irish Rifles the 'Belfast men and the southern and western men . . . were the best of comrades and of friends', and that the Ulster Division and the Dublin Fusiliers were 'like true comrades and brother Irishmen'. 'I pray God', he went on:

> that whenever a battalion of the Irish Brigade goes into action there may be a battalion of the Ulster Division alongside of them. I need not point out the moral to you. That is the way to end the unhappiness and the discords and the confusion of Ireland. Let Irishmen come together in the trenches and spill their blood together and I say there is no power on earth that when they come home can induce them to turn as enemies one upon another.[104]

And, in an introduction to a short survey of the Irish regiments in the war, written by Michael MacDonagh and published early in 1916, Redmond argued that once home rule reached the statute book 'Ireland had once a charter of rights and liberties of her own to defend, and, like Botha's South Africa, her plighted word to make good. The war:

> by a most fortunate conjunction united in a common cause the defence of England against a mighty danger and the defence of principles for which Ireland, to be true to herself, must ever be

ready to raise her voice or draw her sword. Besides her honour and her interest — her interest, always the last thing to move her, but now happily involved in the same cause — human Freedom, Justice, Pity, and the cry of the small nationality crushed under the despots heel appealed to her . . . Her sons, fighting for her honour and her interest, are fighting for these things too. It is for these things — Honour, Justice, Freedom, Pity — she will stand in the new place of influence she is winning in the world's councils. There, acting with and through her sister democracies, Canada, Australia, New Zealand, South Africa, and Great Britain . . . her spirit will help to bend the British Empire to a mission of new significance for humanity.

Redmond listed tributes to the gallantry and piety of Irish troops which came from the mouths of New Zealanders, Australians, Englishmen, Protestant Irishmen and Scotsmen. This gallantry, he wrote, was essential to verify and substantiate Ireland's claim to nationhood; for, like Patrick Pearse, he believed that 'no people can be said to have rightly proved their nationhood and their power to maintain it until they have demonstrated their military powers; and though Irish blood has reddened the earth of every continent, never until now have we as a people set a national army in the field . . . It is heroic deeds entering into their traditions that give life to nations — that is the recompense of those who die to perform them'.[105]

The idea of a blood sacrifice for Ireland, however, was one that might be realized on other fields than Flanders; and the mystical concept of a union of hearts, sealed in the red wine of the battlefields, was, between 1916 and 1918, supplanted by the idea of 'ourselves alone', of the 'right Rose Tree' watered by 'our own red blood'.[106] The Easter Rising of 1916 at first appeared to vindicate and strengthen Redmond's union of hearts, for the unpopularity of the rebels, the feeling that they had stabbed Ireland in the back, was widespread.[107] But the executions which followed the surrender of the rebels ensured that, as Stephen Gwynn put it, 'nothing could have prevented the halo of martyrdom from attaching itself to those who died by the law for the sake of Irish freedom: the tradition was too deeply ingrained in Irish history'.[108] This is not surprising; it was, after all, a tradition that the parliamentarians had themselves been nourishing and preserving since the 1880s, and which they had helped to maintain in the celebrations of the '98 rebellion and the annual pilgrimage to the shrines erected to the memory of the Manchester Martyrs. All this had not seemed to matter — had not mattered — when nationalist Ireland was firmly in the grip of the constitutionalists; but now that the war was prising that grip loose, Ireland must either fall under the 'tyranny of the dead',[109] or she must be rescued by new political leaders, a new political movement that could capture the tradition of self-sacrifice and bloodshed.

The new political movement was waiting in the wings; meanwhile Redmond's idea of the union of hearts was further damaged by the two sets of people whom it was intended to embrace. The heartstrings of at least a few British unionists had indeed been softened by the Irish response to the war, and Walter Long, one of the most intransigent opponents of home rule, now admitted that Ireland had 'created a new claim for herself upon the affection, the gratitude, and respect of the people of the Empire'.[110] But British official dislike of, and even hostility, to nationalist Ireland was revealed in a series of slights and snubs offered to nationalist requests that southern Irish troops be grouped in a special 'Irish brigade', for which, Redmond noted, the Irish 'have got an historical liking'.[111] Redmond, in February 1916, was moved to complain about the meagre references in official accounts to the bravery of the Irish troops who landed on 'V' beach and Suvla in Gallipoli; and he had constantly to refute rumours and threats that conscription would be introduced into Ireland.[112] Indeed, the whole conscription controversy was symptomatic of the failure of British people and politicians to understand the Irish psychology. Irishmen by the thousand volunteered to fight in the British army, for that was in the Irish tradition of military service, and it was a free man's privilege; but to be compelled to fight for Britain was a very different matter, for it was incompatible with the Irishman's concept of his nationhood,[113] and it smacked of the English determination to 'drive Ireland'.[114] When the British Government, in the dark days of March 1918, equipped itself with powers to introduce conscription in Ireland by order in council, it showed its utter ignorance of the way in which the Irish people thought about the war. Britain's reaction was quite natural; for she had to put the war effort first, and sensitivity to Irish feelings seemed to be something of a luxury. But the incompatibility of the British and Irish concepts of the war effort had also been revealed when, in May 1915, Asquith invited the opposition unionists to join in a coalition government. This made good sense to the Government and to British public opinion; and Asquith invited not only Bonar Law and Carson to join the Government, but also offered a post to Redmond. For Redmond to have accepted such a position would have been to fly in the face of Irish nationalist practice since Parnell; and when Carson and Law accepted – and they could hardly refuse – the effort to strengthen the prosecution of the war in England temporarily weakened its prosecution in Ireland, where the bishop of Killaloe wrote of a 'great revulsion' of feeling in the country',[115] and recruiting dropped from 6,000 in April-May 1915 to 3,000 in May-June, and remained at the lower figure for several months until Redmond managed to raise it again.[116]

For a union of hearts could not be based merely on a new constitution for Ireland; it could only succeed if it grew out of a genuine respect for and understanding of the different traditions in the British Isles, an understanding that might be forged in the common dangers and sufferings of the trenches, but might not survive the political atmosphere back home. William Redmond asked in March 1917 why it was that, 'when British soldiers and Irish soldiers are suffering and dying side by side, this eternal quarrel should go on'.[117] The answer was that Irish politics and Anglo-Irish relations could not be settled in the trenches: they could be settled only in parliament, in conference, or in the country, where the old divisions were as strong as ever. Some Irish Unionists, like Colonel Sir William Hutcheson Poe, responded instinctively to Redmond's appeal which 'did more to compose our differences, to unite all Irishmen in a bond of friendship and good will, than could have been accomplished by years of agitation or by a conference, however well-intentioned it might be';[118] but Sir Edward Carson caught the mood of many southern, and all northern unionists, when he affirmed at Coleraine that 'we are not going to abate one jot or tittle of our opposition to home rule, and when you come back from serving your country, you will be just as determined as you will find us at home'.[119] Southern Irish and Ulster unionist intransigence did not have to wait until the end of the war for a demonstration of its strength and determination; the southern unionists were instrumental in wrecking the negotiations which Lloyd George conducted between the various Irish groups between May and July 1916; and the Ulster unionists blocked every attempt to reach a compromise — a compromise now supported by some leading southern unionists, who realized that some terms must be made with nationalist Ireland — in an Irish convention called by Lloyd George in July 1917.[120]

John Redmond's inability to make home rule a reality, to establish some kind of separate government in Ireland, even at the price of partition, was fatal to his cause. Redmond had claimed that Irishmen were sacrificing themselves for freedom; but freedom was as far away in 1918 as it had been in 1914, and the whole concept of home rule, with its emotional symbolism, with its associations of Irish dignity, freedom, and nationhood, was now seen to be a trick, a chimera, almost an insult to the nation. The home rulers had lost an ideology, and not yet found a role, for the union of hearts was also in ruins, and the withdrawal of the parliamentary party from Westminster over conscription amounted to a denial of its long standing conviction that Ireland's battles could best be fought at the outpost of Westminster, acting in concert with a strong nationalist garrison at home. But to stay at Westminster would, in 1918, mean the forfeiture of the Irish garrison's support and enthusiasm; and John Dillon's earlier desperate plunge towards neo-Parnellism in 1916, when he shocked the House of Commons by praising the insurgents who were, he insisted, not murderers, but men who had fought a clean fight and a brave fight, and 'it would have been a damned good thing for you if your soldiers were able to put up as good a fight as did these men in Dublin', only antagonized English opinion without making any significant impression on opinion at home. Dillon's view now was that the party must adopt the pre-1886 Parnellite tactics of independent parliamentary opposition, for, however unpopular this might make the party at Westminster, it was the only means of retaining support in Ireland.[121]

Home rule had stood for independence and 'A nation once again'; but Redmond from 1912, and especially from September 1914, had transformed its image: and now it stood for devolution and a wider British patriotism, if not a share in British imperialism. This might not have proved unsuccessful if all had gone well during the war; but the rising and the conscription crisis had drained home rule of its association with what the *Clare Champion* called 'Ireland a nation, with no boundaries to its onward march';[122] and the party was obliged to contest a series of by-elections in 1917, and then a general election in 1918, with no emotional appeal to give power to its slogans. The party's record in these by-elections was by no means one of unmitigated disaster, even though Redmond himself took the first of its reverses as evidence that the party was in irretrievable decline;[123] but what was ominous was the party's loss of confidence, its muted voice, its lack of conviction that it represented the authentic voice of Irish nationalism. In South Longford the home rulers fell back on a plea to the electorate not to 'abandon the old leaders and the old methods to suit the whims of a lot of political will o' the wisps'; a united and determined people could achieve 'a broad and generous measure of self government' by the old tried and trusted methods. And, apart from this timid, watered down programme, the party had nothing to offer except its record of material achievement for Ireland: land legislation, social reform, educational improvement.[124]

The party's problem was not that Parnellism had lost its appeal, but that the party had ceased to convince the people that they stood for Parnellism: as William O'Brien remarked:

> 'Constitutionalism' in a country whose grievance is that it possess no constitution is an historical humbug. Parnell built up his movement, not by railing at Fenianism in the spirit of a professor of Constitutional history, but by incorporating its tremendous forces in his ranks and acknowledging no criterium (sic) of the rectitude of his political action, be it 'constitutional' or 'unconstitutional' except whether it was, in the circumstances, the best thing to be done for Ireland.[125]

Moreover, even if the party could rely on the loyalties of its older voters, it had, after the 1918 representation of the people act, to win over the new voters, two-thirds of whom would be voting for the first time.[126] Deprived of its ideology, confronted by an unknown class of voters, the home rulers desperately sought to give their wartime themes a nationalist tinge; and at Fennybank, Co. Waterford, Father O'Loughran praised captain William Redmond who 'acted with chivalry like his uncle, Major Redmond, and T.M. Kettle and went to the blood plains of France and fought as Sarsfield did, and did his part not alone to free Ireland, but the Poles in Poland, and all the down-trodden peoples of the twentieth century'.[127]

But the essence of the party's difficulty in 1918 was its defensive strategy; and this led it into paths that Parnellism never trod. 'We would get all that we required and all that would be good for us',[128] declared William Redmond, a statement that stood in direct contradiction to the idea of setting no boundaries to the march of a nation. And it is difficult to imagine home rulers of the 1880s and 1890s saying (though they may well have privately admitted) that:

> in a matter which closely affects the life and interests of the race, let me say that even the most enobling ideals, the most patriotic outbursts, and the highest aspirations are no more than rash, suicidal folly if they are not carefully balanced with practical commonsense.[129]

The party's common-sense nationalism, its timid language, its lack of new ideas, forced it back upon the last refuge of the declining political party: its past record. Few parties, in elections, dwell on their record, but prefer to exploit the error of their opponents; but the home rulers had nothing much to exploit, for its opponents, Sinn Féin, were as yet an unknown quantity. Thus they claimed instead that Ireland, under 40 years of parliamentarianism, had gained substantial material benefits and sound reforms; and they expressed the hope that home rule would continue to bring the people advantages of this kind: 'better houses, higher wages, and shorter hours . . . cleanliness, health and beauty'.[130] At Islandeady, Co. Sligo, one unfortunate candidate was driven to take his stand upon his good service rendered to the community by his saving of the Castlebar bacon factory.[131]

All these claims could not be denied; but the bulk of the nationalist people of Ireland in 1918 were not concerned about cleanliness, health and beauty, nor even about the Castlebar bacon factory; they were concerned with resurgent nationalism, with the debate on Anglo-Irish relations, with the sense of betrayal provoked by British policy during the war. 'I am a rebel against British rule in Ireland', declared William Redmond in Co. Waterford; but, he added, 'I want to go to the house of commons where Parnell and Redmond went to fight British rule in Ireland. I want to rebel there in the only place where it is practicable to have a rebellion'.[132]

This was, indeed, the pivot of Parnellite strategy; and William Redmond here struck a note that few of his followers were able to strike in their election addresses. But even William Redmond erred in spelling out the message too explicitly, too honestly, too timidly. In what William O'Brien, certainly no extremist, called 'an hour of National shame',[133] the Buttite style [134] which Redmond had adopted in the confident expectation that home rule was imminent could not be shaken off by the Irish parliamentary party; but the mantle of Parnellism was now to fall on the shoulders of Sinn Féin, and make a significant contribution to the character of the coming revolution.

Notes

1. *Dublin Evening Herald*, 1, 4 July 1892.
2. *Carlow Nationalist and Leinster Times*, 18, 25 June 1892, 2, 9 July 1892. See also 16 July 1892, speech of Mr Eugene Green at Coolrain, 'He knew that the day that Irish priests and Irish people ceased to work hand in hand Ireland was a ruined Ireland (hear hear). The priests were always the guides of their flock, and they kept nationality alive in their midst (loud cheers)'.
3. Redmond at Waterford, *Waterford Mirror*, 30 June 1892.
4. *United Ireland*, 9 July 1892; see also 23, 30 July. For the 1892 election see C.J. Woods, op. cit., pp. 291-319.

5. Ibid., 9 July 1892.
6. *Carlow Nationalist and Leinster Times*, 13 July 1895.
7. *United Ireland*, 23 July 1892.
8. F.H. O'Donnell, *History of the Irish Parliamentary Party*, vol. *II*, p. 332.
9. F.S.L. Lyons, *The Irish Parliamentary Party, 1890-1910*, p. 29.
10. O'Donnell, op. cit., p. 337.
11. Lyons, op. cit., p. 31.
12. Ibid., p. 30.
13. Ibid., pp. 40-67.
14. Comerford, op. cit., p. 49.
15. L. O Broin, *Revolutionary Underground*, p. 48.
16. For 'constructive unionism' see L.P. Curtis, *Coercion and Conciliation in Ireland, 1880-1892: a Study in Conservative Unionism* (Princeton, 1963).
17. P.J. Buckland, *Irish unionism II: Ulster Unionism and the Origins of Northern Ireland, 1886-1922* (Dublin, 1973), p. 17.
18. P. Bull, 'The reconstruction of the Irish parliamentary party, 1895-1903', University of Cambridge D.Phil. (1972), pp. 93-104.
19. *United Ireland*, 15 Jan. 1898.
20. Ibid., 20 Aug. 1898.
21. Ibid., 29 Jan. 1898.
22. *Freeman's Journal*, 25 July, 16 Aug. 1898.
23. Ibid., 25 July 1898.
24. *United Ireland*, 6 Aug. 1898.
25. O Broin, op. cit., p. 75.
26. See W. O'Brien, '*Who Fears to Speak of Ninety-eight*' (Dublin, 1898) p. 31; 'The patriotic excitation which will prevail in Ireland during the year '98 will supply just the atmosphere in which hot-blooded young Irishmen and even a good many cool-headed ones might well begin to reconsider their opinions as to the efficacy of Parliamentary methods in the present circumstances of Ireland'.
27. Bull, op. cit., pp. 189-90.
28. Lyons, *The Irish Parliamentary Party*, pp. 69-70.
29. Donnelly, *The Land and the People of Nineteenth Century Cork*, pp. 374-5.
30. Beckett, *Modern Ireland*, pp. 408-9.
31. Lyons, *The Irish parliamentary party*, p. 70; Bull, op. cit., pp. 115-18.
32. Lyons, *John Dillon: a Biography* (London, 1968), p. 197.
33. Bull, op. cit., pp. 122-3.
34. Lyons, op. cit., pp. 70-74.
35. For the distribution and strength of the UIL see Bull, op. cit., pp. 200-205.
36. M. MacDonagh, *The Life of William O'Brien, the Irish Nationalist* (London, 1928), p. 148.
37. Lyons, op. cit., pp. 74-83, 95-6; Bull, op. cit., pp. 345-6.
38. For a criticism of the way in which the UIL became a 'political machine in an organization which no longer spontaneously expressed the social purpose which had been responsible for its creation' see Strauss, op. cit., pp. 211-14.
39. Lyons, op. cit., pp. 98-9; Lyons, *John Dillon*, pp. 223-27.
40. *Kilkenny Journal*, 29 Sept. 1900; see also *Limerick Echo*, 21 Aug. 1900 (John O'Brien), *Sligo Champion*, 29 Sept. 1900 (Fr John O'Grady).
41. J. Boland, *Irishman's Day* (London, n.d. (1944?)), pp. 124-8).
42. Lyons, *The Irish Parliamentary Party*, p. 219.
43. Martin and Byrne, *The Scholar Revolutionary*, pp. 77-8; Kelly, 'Intellectual and social background', pp. 216-17. See also speech by John Redmond in Westport, in 1901. 'There is a great movement on foot for the revival of the Gaelic language – a movement that has my entire sympathy (S. O Tuama, op. cit., p. 50).

44. Lyons, *John Dillon*, p. 226; Bull, op. cit., p. 354.

45. Joseph V. O'Brien, *William O'Brien and the Course of Irish Politics* (California, 1976), pp. 120-21.

46. MacDonagh, *William O'Brien*, Chap. X: Donnelly, *Land and People of Nineteenth Century Cork*, p. 384.

47. Lyons, *The Irish Parliamentary Party*, pp. 101-4; Lyons, *Dillon*, pp. 228-33.

48. R.V. O'Brien, op. cit., p. 168.

49. Lyons, *Dillon*, pp. 233-4.

50. *Kilkenny Journal*, 29 Sept. 1900 (Mr McDermott).

51. *Irish News*, 9 Jan. 1906 (Mr Doogan, candidate for East Tyrone).

52. R. Dudley Edwards, *Patrick Pearse: the Triumph of Failure* (London, 1977), p. 237. Pearse spoke these words at the graveside of the Fenian O'Donovan Rossa, in August 1915.

53. L. Paul-Dubois, *Contemporary Ireland* (Dublin, 1908), pp. 166-79.

54. J.E. Redmond, *Ireland and the Coronation: why Ireland is Discontented* (UIL of Great Britain pamphlets, No. 2 (1902).

55. *Freeman's Journal*, 22 July 1903; see also M.A. Banks, *Edward Blake: Irish Nationalist* (Toronto, 1957), p. 249, for the Queen's visit to Ireland in 1900.

56. Ibid., 19 and 21 September 1903; see also *'Robert Emmet in Poetry'* (N.L.I. IR 92 E 43, Vol. I) for the 1903 celebrations and earlier celebrations in 1878.

57. Lyons, *Ireland Since the Famine*, p. 254.

58. P.A. Sillard, *Life and Letters of John Martin* (Dublin, 1893), pp. 244-5.

59. A.C. Hepburn, 'The Ancient Order of Hibernians in Irish politics, 1905-14', in *Cithara*, vol. *X* (1971), pp. 5-18.

60. R.B. O'Brien, *The Home Rulers Manual* (London, 1890), p. 181.

61. M.T. Foy, 'The AOH: an Irish politico-religious pressure group, 1884-1975' (Queen's University of Belfast, M.A. 1976), pp. 77-79.

62. Hepburn, op. cit., pp. 10-12.

63. *Connaught Telegraph*, 17 Dec. 1910; for further evidence of Dillon's unqualified support for the AOH see Foy, op. cit., pp. 124-9.

64. J.V. O'Brien, *William O'Brien*, p. 180.

65. Foy, op. cit., p. 145.

66. *Irish News*, 8 and 15 Jan. 1906; see also his call for 'a cheer for Orange and Green' and 'the union of democratic brotherhood' (*Derry Journal*, 22 Jan. 1906).

67. He had, in any case, played a leading part in destroying the Catholic Association, a body founded by Bishop Henry, Bishop of Down and Connor, to put forward Catholic candidates in local elections in Belfast after the reform of local government there in 1896 (Foy, op. cit., p. 45).

68. Foy, op. cit., pp. 45-6.

69. Hepburn, op. cit., p. 7.

70. Ibid., p. 14.

71. Hepburn, op. cit., p. 14.

72. Speech of the secretary of the North Mayo National executive of the UIL *Connaught Telegraph*, 10 Dec. 1910. See also Dillon, ibid., 17 Dec. 1910.

73. See speech of William Redmond in Cork, *Cork Examiner*, 13 Jan. 1910; J.C. Lardner in North Monaghan, *Fermanagh Herald*, 15 Jan. 1910; Thomas Kettle, East Tyrone, ibid., 29 Jan. 1910; T. Toal, in the *Anglo-Celt*, 8 Jan. 1910; J.J. McGlad, *Derry Journal*, 10 Jan. 1906.

74. MacDonagh, *William O'Brien*, pp. 185-90; O'Brien, *An Olive Branch in Ireland and its History* (London, 1910).

75. *Connaught Telegraph*, 26 Nov. 1910.

76. Lyons, *Dillon*, p. 327.

77. S. Gwynn, *The case for home rule* (preface by Redmond), Dublin, 1911, pp. viii, 5.

78. Lyons, *Ireland Since the Famine*, pp. 260-62; R.B. O'Brien (ed.), *Home Rule Speeches of John Redmond* (London, 1910), pp. 242-3.

79. MacDonagh, *William O'Brien*, p. 170.

80. D. Gwynn, *Life of John Redmond* (London, 1932), pp. 52, 55, 202.

81. *United Ireland*, 3 July 1886.

82. Ibid., 13 March 1886.

83. Ibid., 19 June 1886; in 1893 in the house of commons one home ruler stated that the bill would 'be, at all events *in our time*, a *final settlement* of the Irish question' (A.V. Dicey, *A Leap in the Dark* (London, 1911), p. 112).

84. D. Fitzpatrick, *Politics and Irish life*, 1913-1921 (Dublin, 1977), pp. 92-3.

85. Gwynn, *Redmond*, p. 220.

86. Hepburn, op. cit., pp. 13-14.

87. MacDonagh, op. cit., pp. 182-3.

88. P.J. Buckland, *Irish Unionism* II, pp. 54-5.

89. D.W. Miller, *Queen's Rebels*, pp. 130-31.

90. R.B. O'Brien, *Home Rule Speeches*, pp. 237-40.

91. Lyons, *Dillon*, pp. 328-9.

92. Ibid., p. 348.

93. Ibid., p. 328; Patrick Pearse welcomed the Home Rule bill (Thompson, *Imagination of an Insurrection*, p. 88).

94. Lyons, p. 350.

95. Bartlett and Hayton, op. cit., pp. 114-15.

96. Lyons, op. cit., pp. 350-51.

97. Kee, *Green Flag*, pp. 509-11.

98. R. McHugh, 'Thomas Kettle and Francis Sheehy-Skeffington' in C.C. O'Brien (ed.) *The Shaping of Modern Ireland*, pp. 124-39.

99. Boland, *Irishman's day*, p. 106.

100. Stewart, *Ulster Crisis*, pp. 17-18, 232-35.

101. Boland, *Irishman's day*, p. 104; at least 100,000 Catholics from Ireland served in the British army during the war, and about 70,000 Protestants (E. Rumpf and A.C. Hepburn, *Nationalism and Socialism in Twentieth Century Ireland* (Liverpool, 1977), p. 18).

102. F.X. Martin, *The Irish Volunteers, 1913-15* (Dublin, 1963), pp. 146-8.

103. Lyons, *Ireland Since the Famine*, pp. 328-9.

104. *Account of a Visit to the Front by J.E. Redmond, M.P. in November 1915: with a speech Delivered by Mr. Redmond on 23 November 1915* (London, 1915).

105. M. MacDonagh, *The Irish at the Front* (London, 1916), pp. 1-14.

106. W.B. Yeats, *The Rose Tree*.

107. Lyons, *Dillon*, pp. 371-3.

108. S. Gwynn, *John Redmond's Last Years* (London, 1919), pp. 228-9.

109. Beckett, *Making of Modern Ireland*, p. 441.

110. Gwynn, *Redmond's Last Years*, p. 216.

111. J.E. Redmond, *Ireland and the War: Speeches Delivered at Dublin and Kilkenny, 25 Sept. and 18 Oct. 1914* (Dublin, 1914), p. 4; Gwynn, op. cit., pp. 160-80.

112. Redmond, op. cit., 10-11; Gwynn, op. cit., pp. 196-7, 208-9; Kee, op. cit., pp. 524-5; S. Parnell Kerr, *What the Irish Regiments Have Done* (London, 1916), p. 23.

113. Lyons, *Culture and Anarchy*, p. 18; Father F. Shaw, 'The canon of Irish history: a challenge' in *Studies*, vol. *LXI* (1972), pp. 143-4, 149-50.

114. Gwynn, op. cit., p. 212.

115. Kee, op. cit., p. 528.
116. Gwynn, op. cit., p. 192.
117. Ibid., p. 251; see also p. 245.
118. Ibid., p. 145.
119. Ibid., p. 147.
120. Lyons, *Ireland Since the Famine*, pp. 378-9, 384-5; Buckland, *Irish Unionism* I, Chaps. III and IV.
121. Lyons, *Dillon*, pp. 380-83; *Ireland Since the Famine*, p. 378.
122. 16 June, 1917.
123. Lyons, *Ireland Since the Famine*, pp. 382-3.
124. *Longford Independent*, 28 April 1917, 5 May 1917.
125. O'Brien, op. cit., pp. 55-6.
126. Murphy, *Ireland in the Twentieth Century*, pp. 4-5.
127. *Munster Express*, 14 Dec. 1918; see also the speech of the home ruler at Tulla, Co. Clare, *Clare Champion*, 30 June 1917.
128. *Munster Express*, 14 Dec. 1918.
129. Mr. T. Scanlon, *Sligo Champion*, 30 Nov. 1918.
130. Joseph Devlin, *Irish News*, 9 Dec. 1918; see also J.T. Donovan, *Donegal Vindicator*, 22 Nov. 1918; Monsignor Ryan, *The Nationalist* (Clonmel) 27 Nov. 1918; and leader in the *Connaught Telegraph*, 16 Nov. 1918.
131. Mr. M. Hughes, *Connaught Telegraph*, 14 Dec. 1918.
132. *Munster Express*, 14 Dec. 1918.
133. O'Brien, *The Downfall of Parliamentarianism* (Dublin, 1918), p. 56.
134. See: e.g. Redmond to Dillon, 21 Feb. 1917: 'the principle and policy purused since *1873*: the principle of an Irish Parliament loyally within the Empire, and the policy of pursuing that end by constitutional and parliamentary methods' (Lyons, *Dillon*, p. 410; my italics); cf. his statement in 1907 that armed force 'would be absolutely justifiable if it were possible' (R.B. O'Brien (ed.), *Home rule speeches*, p. 237).

10 NATIONALISM, SOCIALISM AND THE IRISH REVOLUTION

The Easter Rising of 1916, which marked the beginning of the end of the union of hearts, signalled the beginning also of the 'Irish revolution' which ended the union between Great Britain and Ireland and established two Irish states in its place. Yet the party which overthrew the home rulers in the 1918 general election, and which represented the political wing of the revolution, was in many respects an unlikely candidate for the political canonization which the name Sinn Féin was to receive from twentieth century nationalists. Sinn Féin was a product of the Irish literary movement of the last decade of the nineteenth century, and its founders, Arthur Griffith and William Rooney, were enthusiastic about the Gaelic movement and the Irish Ireland idea; they also admired the Davisite tradition in Irish literature and made it clear that they belonged to the school of literary nationalists, rather than to the school of literary patriots. Their admiration for both the Gaelic and the Davisite traditions sprang from a belief that Irish nationalism must have a special native character as well as a political objective. Their political objective was at worst vague, and at best archaic: for Rooney it was 'an Irish state governed by Irishmen for the benefit of the Irish people';[1] for Griffith it was a revival of the idea underlying Grattan's parliament, with one king as a link between two sister kingdoms.[2] And the means by which these objectives were to be obtained were by no means clear. Griffith, for his part, refused at first to recognize that his was a political movement at all; he preferred to regard it as a 'national movement', and when Sinn Féin first assumed an organizational form in October 1900, it was on Griffith's lines of a loose federation of advanced nationalist societies, with 'the utmost liberty of action' in working for an independent Ireland by cultural, economic or military means.[3]

But the significance of Griffith's and Rooney's ideas did not lie in their political aspirations; it lay in their attempt to give substance to Irish nationalism, to supply it with a cultural and economic programme that would carry the country into the new century, and give it a purpose and a meaning when freedom was finally achieved. Griffith was at first more concerned to emphasize the Davisite ideal of a comprehensive nation than the Gaelic league ideal of an exclusive Irish

Ireland race: 'Unionists,' he remarked, 'are our countrymen. This country is as much their as ours. William and James are as dead as Julius Caesar. We are all Irishmen, and this is the twentieth century'.[4] Swift and Grattan were his heroes, and he was anxious to acknowledge the non-Gaelic contribution made to the Irish nationalist tradition, as the choice of name for his newspaper, the *United Irishman*, implied.[5] But he could be touchy about sectarian issues, as his rebuttal of Protestant objections to the *ne temere* papal decree of 1907 revealed;[6] and he grew more enthusiastic about the Gaelic movement and the central place of the Gaelic language in Irish nationality, declaring in 1913 that without the language 'there will never be seen again, on this planet, an independent Irish nation, or indeed an Irish nation of any kind'.[7] The nation and the race were, for Griffith as for so many Irish nationalists, confused: and he warned in 1912 that, no matter what happened about the Home Rule Bill, 'it did not alter the objective or the ideals of the Nation which was born in Tara and had a birthright that could never be bartered'.[8] Rooney was more forthright: Those who, as he put it, 'think it "clawss" to commingle with the Britishers must be rigidly ostracised'.[9]

Both Rooney and Griffith emphasized the Gaelic cultural tradition because it was part of a wider idea of self-sufficiency, a barrier to Anglicization, a defence against a physically stronger neighbour, a guarantee of Ireland's place in the world.[10] But Griffith was no Celtic dreamer, hoping that Ireland would be a kind of rural arcadia in a naughty modern industrial world; for not only Irish literature and language, but Irish industries must be protected and secured if the nation were to be saved. A merely agricultural country could not develop the commerce necessary for the nation's well-being, and tariff barriers and protection and encouragement for home industries were as much part of the nation's needs as art and literature. Between the individual and humanity there stood 'a great fact, the nation'. The individual was dependent on the nation for his security, maintenance, culture, hence human civilization depended for its future on the existence of individual nations. The task of economics was therefore to strengthen and preserve the nation. Economics and nationality were, to Griffith, inextricably entwined.[11] Griffith was convinced of the inherent superiority of the Celtic races over the Saxon; and national power through rapid industrial advance appeared to him the 'unavoidable acid test of such Celtic pre-eminence'.[12] The idea of cultural and economic self-reliance was embodied in the name given to the movement in November 1905 by Maire Butler, a Gaelic leaguer: Sinn Féin, 'ourselves'.[13]

Such a movement, whatever its defects, might contain the seeds of a revolutionary body; it certainly did not, in its early form, assume the form of a successful political party: for such an organizational form would have been anathema to Griffith and his followers, who had set their faces against the tactics, as well as the ideas, of the home rule party. The 'Cumann na nGaedheal', as the movement was first called in 1900, allowed any existing body which accepted it and its constitution to be eligible for application as a branch; and the Cumann contented itself with laying down broad principles of policy, leaving the various clubs and societies to apply these principles in their own way. For the Dungannon Clubs, this meant separatism and a republic; for Griffith and his 'National Council' it meant the monarchical idea; and Griffith himself did not deny that home rule might be acceptable, if it were improved on. The clubs and societies that constituted this loose movement were earnest, self-educating, 'a sober and sparsely smoking movement . . . and rather puritanical';[14] and their impossibly high standards of behaviour were not those calculated to recommend themselves to the bulk of the people of Ireland, or of anywhere else for that matter: 'The only way to be a perfect Irishman', wrote the Protestant Sinn Féiner, Robert Lynd, 'is to do your best to become a perfect man'.[15]

How was this perfection to be attained? How was Sinn Féin to translate its ideals into action? One of the main complaints levelled against the home rulers by Sinn Féin was its policy of attending Westminster in the sure expectation that only thus could self-government be wrung out of the British. And at a meeting of Cumann na nGaedheal in October 1902, Arthur Griffith responded to a motion put by the Cork Celtic Literary Society that the Irish in America should withdraw support from the parliamentarians by proposing an amendment criticizing the Westminster-centred tactics of the home rulers. Such a course was, he alleged, costly, barren and useless, for the centre of the Irish struggle should be at home, not in London; and he urged as an alternative the withdrawal of all assistance from 'a degrading and demoralising policy' and the substitution of 'the policy of the Hungarian deputies in 1861 . . . refusing to attend the British parliament or to recognise its right to legislate for Ireland'. Instead Irish representatives should remain at home 'to help in promoting Ireland's interests and to aid in guarding its national rights'.[16]

This was the first public suggestion of what became known as Griffith's 'Hungarian policy'. Griffith professed admiration for the Hungarian physical force patriot, Louis Kossuth; and Kossuth, after the failure of the 1848-9 revolution, had acknowledged that war against Austria was impossible in the foreseeable future, and had turned to the support of passive resistance. Griffith did not oppose force on principle; no Irish nationalist of his day did; but he preferred civil disobedience and non-violence, and between January and July 1904 he published articles on the Ausgleich, drawing parallels between Ireland in the twentieth century and Hungary in the nineteenth. He quoted Francis Deak's dictum that the constitution of 1848 was the de jure constitution of Hungary, and suggested that Ireland could likewise secure the restoration of her constitution by adopting Deak's methods of absention from the imperial parliament and refusal to pay taxes or in any other way to co-operate with the imperial authorities. The act of union between Great Britain and Ireland could not be repealed, Griffith alleged, because it had no foundation in legality, just as the claim of the Austrians to legislate for Hungary had no basis in legality. The Hungarian passive resistance struggle ended in the Ausgleich of 1867, by which Austria and Hungary became two separate political entities linked by the emperor; and Griffith saw the resemblance between England and Ireland in 1782, with their respective Parliaments linked by the crown of England.[17]

Griffith had discovered a middle way between constitutionalism and physical force or, rather, a way of combining the best elements of both; but his analysis suffered from two defects in the Irish context that prevented it from making any headway in real political terms. It was, after all, taken from what must have been to most Irish people a rather obscure and exotic central European analogy. Griffith noted, but did not take as his inspiration, the native examples of abstentionism, or of the advocacy of abstentionism, made by Thomas Davis and Daniel O'Connell; he completely ignored Parnell.[18] O'Connell's and Parnell's suggestions were hardly serious but at least they related to the familiar language and images of Irish politics. Griffith, however, preferred the Hungarian model because it had proved successful without recourse to arms,[19] but he was vulnerable to the gibe that he and his policy were rather fanciful impracticabilities, the pipe dream of what D.P. Moran dubbed the 'green Hungarian band'.[20] The second defect of Griffith's Hungarian model was more serious, at least after 1910. For with the return of a Liberal Government to power, dependent on Irish nationalist votes for its very existence, the policy of parliamentarianism, which Griffith had derided, seemed now on the point of fruition. Sinn Féin remained, to use the expression of the home ruler, T.M. Kettle, 'a *gamin* of the cities';[21] and its political and electoral appeal in Ireland was virtually non-existent.

In revolutionary terms, however, Sinn Féin might appear to have something to offer; for here its very defects might become virtues. If it was the idea of a minority, then so be it; for revolutions were made by dedicated minorities, working against the tide, and Sinn Féin could pose as the 'national conscience of Ireland . . . determined, virile, idealistic'.[22] Individual Sinn Féiners certainly possessed the single-mindedness of revolutionaries; any man, wrote a member of the Dungannon clubs, who joined England's 'army, navy or police force takes his stand in the camp of the garrison; he is a traitor to his country, and an enemy of his people'.[23] A Sinn Féin pamphleteer, writing on the same subject, fulminated against an incident described in Lieutenant William Grattan's *Adventures of the Connaught Rangers*, published in 1847, when, in the pensinsular war:

> General Mackinnon inspecting one day the Connacht Rangers . . . found to his amazement the kit bag of one of the soldiers – Darby Rooney – Darby being the English for Diarmuid – quite empty, and asked to what squad he belonged . . . Darby Rooney understood about as much English as enabled him to get over a parade tolerably, but a conversation such as the General was about to hold with him was beyond his capacity, and he began to feel a bit confused at the prospect of a tete-a-tete with his General. 'Squidha, squadha, caddersha, vourneen' said he, turning to the orderly sergeant, Pat Gaffney, who did not himself speak the English language as correctly as Lindley Murray. 'Whist, ye bostoon', said Gaffney, 'and don't make a baste of yourself before the Gineral'. 'Why', said General Mackinnon, 'I believe he did not understand me'. 'No, sir', replied Gaffney, 'he don't know what your honour manes'.[24]

This amusing and affectionate recollection, however, inspired no humour in the pamphleteer; on the contrary, it 'reveals how low indeed our country had fallen . . . when one of their number used that native speech of an Irish soldier, his petty officer, who himself knew no other properly, reproved him in the face of an army as *making a beast of himself* . . . Surely no race had ever fallen so low as this'. Small wonder that T.M. Kettle likened Sinn Féin to 'that affinity of Goethe's who "carried her nose with as divine a tilt as if there never had been a sin committed in the world" '.[25]

'Humanity', Kettle went on, 'on the whole accepts the second best';[26] and he was right for the period before the Great war. Sinn

Féin's difficulty lay in the fact that its politics appeared impracticable, and yet its dedication and its idealism did not tempt the Sinn Féin leadership, nor its small and diminishing rank and file, to plan an armed uprising, or hazard all on a daring exploit. Irish freedom, wrote one Sinn Féiner in a preface to Griffith's edition of the poems and ballads of William Rooney, would be won by the same methods as American, Greek and Belgian freedom 'but it would be folly to invite a pitched battle yet'.[27] Thus Sinn Féin, without either electoral support on the one hand, or the desire to plunge Ireland into futile and useless violence on the other, remained a weak and shadowy rival to the home rulers; only if events took some unexpectedly favourable turn would they ever have a chance of displacing their political opponents, and representing the strong nationalist feeling in Ireland that the parliamentarians had based their success on since the 1880s.

If there was any hope of breaking the parliamentary party's monopoly of Irish political life, or revolutionizing Irish society, before the great war, it seemed to lie not with the nationalists at all, but with the Irish labour movement. The political and social importance of Irish labour could hardly have been predicted before the twentieth century. Outside north-east Ulster Ireland was barely industrialized beyond the small-scale industries typical of a predominantly agricultural country, and Irish trade unions were confined to small groups of craftsmen. Ireland lacked a tradition of militant, independent union organization, and Irish unions were affiliated to their British counterparts, holding no separate Irish trades union congress until 1894. And, like British trade unions, Irish unions were content to work within the existing economic system, and harboured no intentions of challenging the social or political order.[28] But some important changes were made under the inspiration of James Larkin, who succeeded in organizing a dockers' strike in Belfast, and in founding in 1909 the first large unskilled Irish trade union, the Irish Transport and General Workers, which struggled for existence against the hostility both of Irish employers, and of British based unions which opposed the establishment of separate Irish unions as 'perpetrating national rivalries and race hatreds'.[29]

This was an important new departure; but it is doubtful if Ireland would have made any significant contribution to socialist thought, and to the relationship between socialism and nationalism, had it not been for the intervention of James Connolly, the son of an Irish immigrant family in Scotland, who was active in working class politics in Edinburgh before coming to Ireland in 1896 as organizer of the Dublin Socialist Club. Connolly quickly revealed his belief that socialism and nationalist politics were inextricably entwined by founding the Irish Socialist Republican Party[30] with the object of establishing a socialist state 'based upon the public ownership by the Irish people of the land, and instruments of production, distribution and exchange'. But frustration with his lack of progress in Ireland persuaded him to emigrate to the United States of America, from whence he returned in 1910 to organize the Socialist Party of Ireland, with branches in Cork and Belfast, and to take up residence in Belfast as Ulster district secretary of the Irish Transport and General Workers Union. It was from this power base that Connolly sought to realize his hope of transforming capitalist society, and of using the apparatus of the modern state to carry out this transformation: 'The conquest by the Social democracy of political power in Parliament'.[31]

But to talk in terms of taking power in the state and capturing its institutions was, in Irish terms, to introduce the problem that was central to Connolly's writings: for in Ireland the state was not yet established, political institutions of the parliamentary kind did not exist, and Ireland was subject to the control of a larger and more powerful state. From the moment that Connolly began to think seriously about Ireland's social and economic future, he came up against her political present — the question of self-government, of the Anglo-Irish relationship, of Irish nationalism. And this brought him to consider the nature of Irish nationalism, the complexion of an Irish state, and the various political and religious groups in Ireland whose vested interests must be considered, and either rejected or reconciled to the new order.

Irish socialism had to reconcile its internationalist aspirations with the political realities in Ireland, a country with a long and firmly rooted nationalist tradition, a tradition in which Roman Catholicism played a key, if not a central, role. In one sense Connolly was well-fitted to consider this problem: he was a socialist and yet a devout Catholic; he was an internationalist who felt within himself and recognized in others the sentiments of nationalism. He defended the Catholic faith and the institution of marriage against accusations that socialism was inimical to both.[32] And he argued that some Roman Catholic doctrine was as radical in its implications for the ownership and control of property as any socialist thinking.[33]

Connolly maintained that since Ireland was part of the British capitalist system, then Irish political independence was an essential preliminary to the realization of the socialist republic of Ireland: 'The interests of labour all the world over are identical ... but it is also true that each country had better work out its own salvation on the lines most congenial to its own people'. The 'national and racial characteristics of the English and Irish people are different', he wrote:

> Their political history and traditions are antagonistic, the economic development of the one is not on a par with the other, and, finally, although they have been in the closest contact for seven hundred years, yet the Celtic Irishman is today as much of an insolute (sic) problem to even the most friendly English as on the day when the two countries were first joined in unholy wedlock.[34]

Connolly fully accepted the orthodox Irish nationalist version of Irish history since the coming of the Normans; more, he reinforced it. The 'invasion' was 'characterised by every kind of treachery, outrage, and indiscriminate massacre of the Irish'.[35] Pre-Norman Ireland was a kind of primitive socialist utopia, with the Irish people knowing nothing of absolute property in land; and whereas such 'primitive communism' had almost entirely disappeared before the dawn of history, in Ireland 'the system formed part of a well-defined social organization of a nation of scholars and students, recognized by Chief and Tanist, Brehon and Bard, as the inspiring principle of their collective life'. This social structure was destroyed by feudalism, the individualistic English system; and 'as it triumphed, we are reaping the fruits today in the industrial disputes, the agricultural depressions, the poorhouses, and other such glorious institutions of church and state as we are permitted the luxury of enjoying in common with our fellow subjects in this "integral portion of the British empire" '. The Irish middle class which rose to political leadership in the nineteenth century simply adopted English ways, English commercial beliefs and practices, and wished only to transfer the seat of government from London to Dublin; thus to the sin of accepting a social system 'abhorrent to the best traditions of a Celtic people, they next abandoned as impossible the realisation of national independence'.[36]

Some aspects of Connolly's nationalist beliefs appeared scarcely reconcilable with his socialism, at least on the surface. His antipathy towards England was reminiscent of that of the home rulers whom he professed to despise; for example, his use of the term 'Cockneys' as a derogatory description of the English was precisely that employed by the Parnellite newspaper *United Ireland* in 1891.[37] His praise of the bourgeois political movement, Sinn Féin, appears at variance with Griffith's furious hostility to the 'new Unionism' on the grounds that wage demands pushed up prices. And his warm approval of the Gaelic

League was at odds with his belief in international socialism and in an international language, even if he was able to account for it by his conviction that 'nations which submit to conquest or races which abandon their language in favour of those of an oppressor do so, not because of altruistic motives, or because of a love of the brotherhood of man, but from a slavish and cringing spirit. From a spirit which cannot exist side by side with the revolutionary idea'.[38]

Such inconsistencies, however, were more apparent than real. For, as Connolly himself explained, 'it is only when socialism is brought down from the clouds and is shown to have a direct bearing upon the political life of each country . . . and to have a message bearing upon the political problems of the day, it is only then that socialism has an opportunity of developing from being the cult of the few to become the faith of the many'.[39] Socialism sought the transfer of the means of production from the hands of private owners to those of public bodies directly responsible to the entire country. Socialism sought to strengthen popular action on all public bodies. Representative bodies in Ireland would express the public will more directly than bodies resident in England, for an Irish republic 'would then be the natural depository of popular power; the weapon of popular emancipation the only power which would show in the full light of day all these class antagonisms and lines of economic demarcation now obscured by the mists of bourgeois patriotism'. Hence, 'inspired by another ideal, conducted by reason not tradition, following a different course', socialist republicanism 'arrives at the same conclusion as the most irreconcilable nationalist'. The bonds which held England to Ireland must be broken; the friends of republican socialism were those who 'would not hesitate to follow the standard of liberty, to consecrate their lives in its service even should it lead to the terrible arbitration of the sword'.[40]

The 'arbitration of the sword' was to lead Connolly directly to the Easter rising in 1916; but, as his writings clearly show, this was neither mere opportunism, nor a surrender to bourgeois nationalism. The creation of the nation state was a precondition for, or part of, the creation of a democratic polity, and the struggle for national independence and thus for the destruction of imperial, super-national autocracies, had, after all, the support of Karl Marx, who spent as much time at meetings commemorating Polish or Irish freedom battles as he did supporting strikes. Socialists admired Mazzini as much as they hated Bismarck, (despite Bismarck's important social reforms).[41] A nation that was fragmented, not yet politically a nation, needed nationalism as the path to progress; but the nationalism of already established states, like Britain, was a different matter, for this took the form of reactionary chauvinism. Nationalism in Ireland was the essential foundation for social and economic progress, and an Irish revolution must therefore be both nationalist and socialist; a not impossible concept, for the Mexican revolution managed to fuse the two.[42] Nationalism to Connolly, as to many nineteenth and twentieth century socialists, was not an end in itself, but a means of creating a fuller, more dignified way of life for the downtrodden, the weak, and the deprived. Connolly, therefore, does not stand apart from, or marginal to, the socialist tradition of Europe, but is central to it.

But the very people whose rights Connolly professed to defend were, in north east Ulster, themselves deeply divided on sectarian, and indeed nationalist lines. He himself recognized the dilemma when he admitted that 'according to all socialist theories . . . being the most developed industrially', Ulster 'ought to be the quarter in which class lines of cleavage politically and industrially, should be the most pronounced and class rebellion the most common'. Connolly ascribed the failure of socialism to take root in north east Ulster to the 'devilish ingenuity of the master class' and to the fact that the 'Orange working class' had been 'reared up among a people whose conditions of servitude were more slavish than their own' — the Roman Catholics. The working classes in Catholic Ireland, however, were 'rebels in spirit and democratic in feeling because for hundreds of years they have found no class as lowly paid or as hardly treated as themselves'. Ulster's political passions were an 'atavistic survival of a dark and ignorant past'; yet in the same breath Connolly remarked that the Irish socialist movement could only be served 'by a party indigenous to the soil'[43] — and such a party was likely to possess at least some atavistic features. Connolly's double standards were revealed also in his description of his reactions to a twelfth of July Orange parade. Viewing the procession as a 'Teague' (his own expression) he found 'some parts of it beautiful, some of it ludicrous and some of it exceedingly disheartening'. The regalia was often beautiful; the juxtaposition of lyrics like 'Jesus, lover of my soul' with 'Dolly's Brae' was ludicrous; and the failure of Ulster's working class to recognize that their true interests lay with their Catholic breathren was disheartening. All this was justifiable enough; but Connolly, who accepted the authenticity of Irish nationalism, was quick to deny any such characteristic to Ulster unionism. His desire to put into correct perspective the distorted Orange version of Irish history since the plantation of Ulster was commendable; but it was not accompanied by any attempt to critically assess the nationalist version of the same story.[44]

This was because Connolly saw nationalism as a vehicle of progress, and unionism as the tool of reaction; and when he abandoned any hope that his socialist revolution would come from Ulster – a realistic appreciation in view of the unionist enlistment of the Belfast Protestant working class against the Home Rule Bill of 1912 – it was to Dublin that he turned to seek the spirit of proletarian rebellion. The Irish Catholic worker, unlike his Protestant counterpart, was 'a good democrat and a revolutionist, though he knew nothing of the fine spun theories of democracy and revolution'.[45] The social and economic condition of Dublin in 1912 was certainly a breeding ground for trade union and socialist activity. Unemployment was high – perhaps 20 per cent – wages were low, and slum conditions rife.[46] In 1911 industrial unrest came to Dublin, and James Larkin was involved in dockers', carters', coal men's and railwaymen's disputes. The following year the ITGWU managed to bargain successfully for better wages; and in 1913 Larkin gained pay rises for the dockers, and brought the agricultural labourers from the surrounding countryside into his union. But when he took on the Dublin United Tramways Company he met with stern opposition from William Martin Murphy, magnate, Irish nationalist and newspaper owner. The strike that followed in August 1913 spread, and the atmosphere of bitterness and violence increased as the winter approached, with hardship facing the thousands of men out of work. Mob violence broke out, as the police handled the strikers roughly; and out of the violence emerged a working-class organization, the Irish Citizen Army, founded by an ex-regular army captain, J.R. White, small in numbers, but offering a potential weapon for James Connolly to bring about the political revolution that would clear the way to a socialist Ireland.[47]

This marked the beginning of the enlistment of elements of the Dublin working classes in a separatist nationalist movement. When the annual commemoration procession of the Manchester Martyrs took place in November 1913, the ITGWU dominated it with the largest contingent.[48] The awakening of labour, the growth of trade union power, the developing self-awareness of working men under the tutelage of Larkin and Connolly, the frustration, humiliation and violence of the strike of 1913, all created a new force on the Irish political scene, and one, moreover, that might be placed in the vanguard of the nationalist cause. 'There is', remarked a writer in the *Worker's Republic*, 'the great tradition of love and hatred, love for Ireland and hatred for her enemies

∴ . . There is the inborn craving for vengeance over seven centuries of insult and rapine and wrong'.[49] But not all members of the working class shared this apocalyptic vision. The Irish TUC and Labour party, founded in 1912, was aware of the importance of Ulster as an industrial base, and stood aloof from the connections which Connolly sought to make between the working class organizations and nationalism.[50] Connolly's question to the Ulster labour leader, William Wallace, when he was in disagreement with him in 1911 over the relationship between nationalism and socialism, 'why sacrifice Ireland for a part of Belfast?'[51] was more important than the answer, for it revealed that a day of reckoning with the Protestant working classes must come. Indeed Connolly appears to have sought such a day when, on the occasion of Winston Churchill's visit to Belfast in 1914, he called for a 'firm application of force to establish, once for all, the right of public meeting in Ulster';[52] and he had no qualms about insisting that, in the end, the Protestant working class and small farmers belonged to the Irish nation and to the labour movement, and if they did not accept these two propositions, then they must, none the less, bow to the will of the Catholic majority.[53]

Still, a section at least of the working classes of Dublin were willing to regard national independence as a step on the road to social regeneration; and to this working class movement before the war was added an older revolutionary body with a much longer pedigree than that of the Citizen Army. Of course, a pedigree was no guarantee of revolutionary fervour, and indeed the Irish Republican Brotherhood was at the beginning of the century an ageing and uninspiring organization, talking of revolution but not preparing for it, and awaiting the propitious moment which, however, under a clause in the constitution of 1873, must be postponed until the decision of the Irish nation, as expressed by the majority of the Irish people, was made manifest.[54] To adhere to this clause was, on the face of it, to postpone the hour of rebellion indefinitely; and the IRB was described by the police in the summer of 1905 as 'very dormant', short of funds and with an apathetic rank and file.[55]

But a new, younger, and more sanguine generation of republicans emerged under the tutelage of Tom Clarke, a veteran Fenian who had undergone 15 years' imprisonment for his part in a dynamiting campaign. Clarke's importance lay not only in his willingness to help the militant republicans, Bulmer Hobson, Denis McCullough and Sean MacDermott, to positions of power; more significant was his long life of selfless devotion to his cause — a devotion that began when he was merely a boy who resolved to dedicate his life 'to the overthrow of the system which was reducing his country to a desert and his race to extinction'.[56] This referred to the events of the famine years of 1847-49, which Clarke, of course, did not experience, but the folk memory of which he absorbed. For here was the fundamental strength of the republican tradition: it was simple, even simplistic; it had a strong sense of the 'dead generations' who had tried and failed, but failed (in their view) gloriously to free Ireland by force of arms; it was uncompromising, standing, as Hobson put it, 'for the Irish Republic, because we see that no compromise with England, no repeal of the union, no concession of home rule or devolution will satisfy the national aspirations of the Irish people';[57] and, above all, it was prepared to try again, to strike a blow at England when the opportunity should present itself.[58]

This resolution was important because, at last, it coincided with the new spirit that was sweeping Ireland in the wake of the Ulster unionists' determination to resist the imposition of home rule by force of arms. The establishment of the Irish Volunteers was the first major breakthrough for the separatists, for it offered a body of men, not yet armed, and certainly not yet ready to go beyond 'defence' into 'defiance',[59] but a body of men who might at some future date form the nucleus of an army of the Irish republic. It was for this reason that the IRB threw its secret influence behind Eoin MacNeill in November 1913 when the Volunteers were founded. Bulmer Hobson was a member of the provisional committee of the volunteers, and when the movement split in 1914, with the bulk of the volunteers supporting Redmond's stand on nationalist Ireland's attitude to the war, Hobson became general secretary of the anti-Redmond remnant.[60] In the autumn of 1914 the IRB committed itself to a rising during the war; and its infiltration of the anti-Redmond volunteers was complete when Thomas MacDonagh became director of training, Joseph Plunkett director of military operations, and Patrick Pearse director of military organization. IRB men were now probably in a majority on the general council of the volunteers.[61]

The presence of MacDonagh, Plunkett and Pearse in the inner council of the IRB, and their role in planning the Easter Rising, links that enterprise with the literary movement of the 1890s: and some have seen the rising as 'almost as much a monument to the Irish Literary Renaissance as to the Irish Volunteers'.[62] In his old age Yeats speculated:

Did that play of mine send out
Certain men the English shot

Pearse, Plunkett and MacDonagh were all inspired by the movement to play a part in revolutionary politics, and they were moved by a nationalism that transcended self, by a sense of drama, by a vision of their part in a heroic act:

Wild and perilous holy things
Flaming with a martyr's sword
And the joy that laughs and sings
Where a foe must be withstood.[63]

It was but a short step for them to translate their ideals into military action. MacDonagh and Plunkett were absorbed by the study of military tactics, and studied the art of street fighting;[64] and MacDonagh spoke for the literary men of action when he declared that 'a man who is a mere author is nothing . . . I am going to live things that I have before imagined'.[65]

But the literary movement alone was not the inspiration behind the 1916 rising; for whereas Pearse, MacDonagh and Plunkett might talk in terms of translating literature into life, they also stood, as the IRB itself stood, for a much older tradition than that embodied in the plays, poems and books of the 1890s. They stood, as MacDonagh claimed at his trial, for what they saw as an unbroken tradition of revolt against English rule. The Irish volunteer of 1915 was 'the heir to Irish Nationality handed down from revolt to revolt since the alien plunderers came here 750 years ago'.[66] Sean MacDermott, addressing members of the IRB in Kerry in 1914, affirmed that:

Nationalism as known to Tone and Emmet is almost dead in the country and a spurious substitute, as taught by the Irish Parliamentary Party, exists. The generation now growing old is the most decadent generation nationally since the Norman invasion, and the Irish patriotic spirit will die forever unless a blood sacrifice is made in the next few years. The spark of nationality left is the result of the sacrifice of the Manchester Martyrs nearly half a century ago, and it will be necessary for some of us to offer ourselves as martyrs if nothing better can be done to preserve the Irish national spirit and hand it down unsullied to future generations.[67]

'Life springs from death', announced Pearse at the funeral of the veteran Fenian O'Donovan Rossa in 1915, 'and from the graves of these patriot men and women spring living nations'.[68]

The Easter Rising was, therefore, inspired not only by literary nationalism, but by the Fenian idea of striking a military blow at the enemy, a disabling blow that would show the British and the world that the present generation of nationalists could rebel in such a way that 'the event would take an authentic place in historic succession to earlier efforts to achieve freedom'.[69] The rising was more militarily successful than it has been given credit for: the fiascos of 1848 and 1867 were not repeated, for the rebels held out against a modern, fully equipped army for a whole week, and fought with resolution and determination. And they might have posed more serious problems, not only in Dublin but also in the country, had they possessed more military acumen.[70] But their unexpectedly successful performance gave the rising a propaganda value beyond its military achievements. The rising was on a sufficient scale, and of sufficient duration, to set aside notions that it was a mere riot, or an 1848 affray in the widow McCormack's cabbage patch. However, the political choice facing Irishmen after the rising was not as stark as has been maintained. It was not a simple choice of accepting or rejecting it,[71] though some, like the parliamentarians, rejected it, and some, like the guerilla leader Tom Barry, then serving with the British army in Mesopotamia, welcomed it as a sudden and necessary reminder of Ireland's unbroken tradition of armed struggle for her nationhood.[72] As usual in Irish political terms, the choices were: for physical force; against physical force; or – usually the most prudent course, if one were seriously interested in political success – both for *and* against physical force: this last requiring a carefully balanced ambiguity of language that Sinn Féin was soon to master.

The language had to be chosen all the more carefully because of the undeniable heroics of the rebels, because 1916 was neither a fiasco, like 1848 and 1867, nor was it a safely long dead episode like 1798. But in other respects the rising cleared up a few political ambiguities, for it was distinguished from earlier rebellions and insurrections by the character of its participants: whereas the rebellions of 1798 and 1848 were rebellions of the Anglo-Irish, the work of the Anglo-Irish in revolt against the English part of their inheritance, and whereas 1867 had incurred the wrath of the Roman Catholic church, 1916 was essentially a rebellion by members of the Catholic nation, the Irish properly so called, for the Catholic nation, and one that did not incur the odium of the hierarchy.

The devout Catholicism of the leaders and men of 1916, from Connolly to Pearse, was one of the most striking aspects of their personalities. And it was not only that they were all Catholics, who, with the exception of Tom Clarke, made their peace with the church;[73] they also thought in terms of the special nature of the Irish Catholic people who, as MacDonagh put it, were, like the Jews, a people who bore much and suffered much for their religion, harbouring a 'black passion' of anger for centuries of English persecution.[74] 'I am old-fashioned enough to be both a Catholic and a Nationalist', wrote Pearse in 1913.[75] And the steadfast belief of Irishmen in their religious convictions was 'one of the main strands of the long-tormented chronicle of Ireland's history'.[76] People who had suffered in God's cause could, happily, expect to partake in a large share of God's glory: 'the soul of the enslaved and broken nation may conceivably be a more splendid thing than the soul of a great free nation'.[77]

This is not to imply that the men of 1916 were in any respect religious bigots; sectarianism played no part in their thinking, and Pearse, for his part, had reacted angrily when confronted with the suggestion that the people of Ireland were divided into 'Palesmen' and 'Gaels'.[78] But, like so many Irish nationalist thinkers, they never properly worked out what they meant by the Irish nation. It is clear from Pearse's writings that sometimes he meant Catholics and Protestants, and sometimes he meant simply the 'Gaelic', and, by implication, Catholic people. When MacDonagh spoke of 'our lyric poetry' and 'our oratory' he meant 'the ideal always held by the Gaelic race that once dominated Europe — now held by the heir and successor of that race, here, the Irish'.[79] Connolly, anyway, had written off Belfast and its Protestant working men a long time ago when they stood out stubbornly against his nationalist socialism. The Catholicism and nationalism of the 1916 leaders fitted neatly together, and avoided any nagging doubts and ambiguities about the pedigree and identity of the Irish nation.[80]

Any remaining sources of friction between nationalism and religion were weakened by the Roman Catholic hierarchy's muted response to the rising. The very secrecy and suddenness of the event meant that the hierarchy was unable to prepare its position, and to make the kind of considered statement that it had made on Fenianism. Individual bishops condemned the rising; but by the time the hierarchy as a whole was in a position to issue a rejoinder, the executions of the 1916 leaders had caused much public sympathy to swing towards the rebels, and the church — in its traditional role as guide, not driver — knew better than to jeopardize its influence by clashing head on with public opinion. In any case, some bishops were by no means satisfied with the parliamentary party's record since 1914, and while they could not of course condone the violence of the rising, some of them felt that it had, on balance, done more for the nationalist cause, and for the advancement of home rule, than any event since the outbreak of the war.[81] Some members of the lower clergy were in outright sympathy with the rebels, and Father Fahy of Belvedere College confirmed for John Dillon the story of priests in the General Post Office hearing the confessions of all the garrison.[82]

The fact that the leaders and men of 1916 were Catholics did not, of course, mean that the Easter Rising was a rising against Protestants: Patrick Pearse's proclamation of the republic guaranteed civil and religious liberty to all its citizens, and promised the pursuit of the happiness and prosperity of the whole nation 'oblivious of the differences carefully fostered by an alien government, which have divided a minority from the majority in the past'.[83] The rising was not a rising against Protestants; but it was a rising without Protestants, or at least without Protestants playing the kind of leading role that they had played in 1798 and 1848. Constance Georgina Gore-Booth, Countess Markievicz, held a commission in the Citizen Army and took part in the fighting in Dublin; Roger Casement tried, unsuccessfully, to recruit men from amongst Irish prisoners of war in Germany to fight the British, and then went back to Ireland in a German submarine to attempt to stop the rising 'and then face the fate I knew must be mine'.[84] But although the Anglo-Irish were not without their representative in 1916, the difference was that whereas they had (as Yeats wrote of The O'Rahilly), 'helped to wind the clock', and whereas one or two of them had 'come to hear it strike',[85] they did not themselves plan and execute the blow that was struck. Nationalist Ireland had, at last, found its own leaders. It was true that the ideology of the Easter Rising was in large part of Anglo-Irish creation: the idea of a comprehensive Irish nationality propounded by Pearse was the ideal of Thomas Davis; the idea of a separate Ireland belonged to Tone; the concept of an Ireland, not free merely but Gaelic as well was Pearse's vision, but it was the Anglo-Irishman, Douglas Hyde, who inspired the Irish Ireland movement in the 1890s and gave Gaelic revivalism its initial impetus; and the declaration in 1916 of 'the right of the people of Ireland to the ownership of Ireland', while it reflected the influence of James Connolly, echoed the writings of James Fintan Lalor, who belonged to

Pearse's catalogue of Irish heroes — the rest being Protestants, Emmet, Tone, Davis and John Mitchel, whose 'holy hatred' of England also inspired Pearse to his supreme sacrifice.[86]

In ideological terms, therefore, 1916 was no new creation but was little more than a summary of the ideas and beliefs of past Anglo-Irish and Irish Protestants in revolt. But in terms of its planning, leadership, and above all its nationalist/Catholic apotheosis, it was a significant turning point in the history of Irish nationalism. For nationalist and Catholic Ireland found that at last it could stand on its own feet: no longer did it need Protestants to provide the leadership that in the nineteenth century, after O'Connell, it was incapable of providing for itself.[87] The Anglo-Irish absence might be accounted for by the 'devotional revolution' of the last half of the nineteenth century, by the newly formed fervour of the Catholic people of Ireland and their growing alienation from Protestants; it might be ascribed to the sectarian influences of the AOH in the Irish parliamentary party after 1900, to what one historian has called the 'era of clericalism'.[88] But the explanation is not primarily a religious one; it is a political and social explanation. Ireland under the Union had undergone a silent but irreversible transfer of power from Protestants to Catholics, in landholding, in local government, in education. With the exception of Ulster, Irish Catholics were, by 1914, virtually running their own country in all but the final legislative and executive processes. Between 1870 and 1890 the parliamentary movement was led by the Protestants Butt and Parnell; from 1891 it was led by Catholics, Redmond and Dillon. The Irish revolutionary movement in 1798, 1848 and, to a large extent 1867 was inspired and led by Protestants, Tone, Smith O'Brien, Stephens; when it became important again, in 1914-16, it was led almost exclusively by Catholics, Pearse, MacDonagh, MacDermott, Connolly. The most prominent, and, in 1913, most powerful republican leader, the Protestant Bulmer Hobson, opposed the rising, supporting Eoin MacNeill in his stand against Pearse; he was arrested by his opponents in the IRB military council, played no part in the rising, and never again returned to Irish political life.[89] By the twentieth century Catholic Ireland was reaping the fruits of 100 years of concessions: her people were now educated enough, able enough, and, above all, possessed of sufficient self-confidence and self-esteem to produce their own leaders, constitutional and revolutionary. Nationalist Ireland was ready for political power and independence in 1914. But for British and Irish and Ulster unionist opposition to home rule she would have obtained it by an act of the British parliament; that opposition gave an opportunity for revolutionaries to attempt to take power in a very different way. But it was the Union which, by enabling the Catholic nation to regain its feet after the degradation of the eighteenth century, made possible the Catholic leadership of the new Ireland. And, even while the generation of 1916 was in rebellion against the nature of the union, against the kind of society which it had produced, it remained none the less the product of the political and social transformation that the union had brought about.

When Pearse and Connolly struck their blow for Irish freedom in 1916, they were both aware of the virtual impossibility of success; but the IRB and Connolly believed in 'the event creating the forces to complete it';[90] traditional nineteenth century revolutionaries themselves, they sought to set in motion a train of events in which the people, inspired by their example, would rise up almost spontaneously and overthrow their oppressors. But the rising, although it began seriously to undermine the position of the parliamentary party, was, after all, the work of influential, but minority, groups in Ireland: poets, conspirators and socialists. Poets and conspirators provided much of the stuff of Irish nationalist sentiment, constitutional as well as anti-constitutional; socialists were a new and rather more disturbing element. The rebels in the Citizen army and the Irish volunteers who turned out in 1916 were mainly working men, with strong assistance from the commercial middle class. Farmers were conspicuously absent, though some small farmers and labourers were involved in the uprising in Galway.[91] It seemed that Connolly's hope of a union between 'Irish workers who toiled as ordinary day labourers', and 'those other workers whose toil was upon the intellectual plain'[92] might come to something, for Pearse, Joseph Plunkett, Eamon Kent and Sean MacDermott were all sympathetic to the cause of labour. But the dangers inherent in a combination of rebels, intellectuals and the proletariat might not prove to the liking of the tenant farmers of rural Ireland; and the countryside, though it had in 1916 lost the initiative to Dublin, could not for ever be ignored by anyone engaged in the serious pursuit of political power in Ireland.

For the growing problems of the parliamentarians, their loss of ground to their political opponents, Sinn Féin, did not mean that the political geography of Ireland had been altered out of all recognition. Intellectuals and socialists might rebel, but political power must still be sought wherever it could be found, and the Irish electorate was the reservoir of power, a reservoir that must be tapped if the initiative given to Sinn Féin by 1916 were to be seized and exploited. For the next 3 years, therefore, the primacy of politics was reasserted; and 1916 marked, not the beginning, but the end of a period of revolutionary activity that stretched back to the formation of the Ulster Volunteers in 1912. The rising was, of course, venerated; the martyred dead extolled. But the politicians who were now emerging as the leaders of nationalist Ireland, like their predecessors in the parliamentary party, sought to consign the rising to a place among the other venerable Irish insurrections – 1798, 1848, 1867 – as episodes to be admired, turned into political capital, but not to be repeated save in extremis. The rising had taken place, it was a fact, an event that Irishmen must respond to; but the response that politicians sought was to accept it as a noble and necessary sacrifice for Irish freedom, but to reject any suggestion that it must be emulated, or new martyrs created. Ireland had martyrs enough to help Sinn Féin to power; or so the leaders of Sinn Féin hoped.

'It is to the Sinn Féin party that Ireland must now look to mould the future of her people' wrote William O'Brien in September 1916.[93] However, the Sinn Féin party after the rising did not seem fit to launch itself on the popular reaction to the executions of the rebel leaders. It was still a small and apparently insignificant party, further weakened by the imprisonment of Griffith and other Sinn Féiners who were mistakenly supposed by the British to be implicated in the plot, and weakened even more by the almost mandatory splits within the party. Its first breakthrough came with its by-election success in Roscommon in February 1917; but this was the work of local Sinn Féiners, and it was the prelude, not to a sense of unity and purpose, but to a bitter rivalry between the victorious candidate, Count Plunkett (father of the executed 1916 rebel) and Arthur Griffith, who, although he supported Plunkett on the platform, was appalled at his posing as a kind of national saviour who could brook no rival or equal. Moreover, Sinn Féin was plagued by its origins as a movement that kept separatist bodies in touch with one another, but had no central unity as a political party. When finally a measure of unity was achieved in April 1917, the compromise adopted was the 'Mansion House Committee'[94] which was to act as co-ordinator to the various Sinn Féin organizations. This expedient proved more successful than might have seemed possible; its loose and flexible nature corresponded to the diversity of opinion within Sinn Féin over what kind of independence was desirable, and how best it could be achieved.[95]

The revival of political activity after 1916 was assisted by the fragmented and scattered physical force groups. The IRB was still a small elite, even though it possessed the ability to infiltrate political organizations, as it later did with Sinn Féin. The Irish Citizen Army had never numbered above two hundred, and it had been destroyed in the fighting in 1916. The Irish Volunteers, with a membership of about 15,000 men before the rising, was more significant, but it too had lost its directing force, at least for the time being, with hundreds of its members interned in Great Britain. Most important of all, the mood of the people and of the politicians was not in favour of taking on the British army for a second round: the rising had not freed Ireland, nor had it brought freedom nearer.[96]

In the spring and early summer of 1917 Sinn Féin spread rapidly through the country, mainly because of the activity and enthusiasm of local members, often released Volunteers, and of Griffith's untiring propaganda. In July 1917 the RIC Inspector General reported that 166 clubs with a membership of about 11,000 had been noted by the police. A month later the membership had doubled and the number of clubs trebled. And just as Sinn Féin began to make progress as a popular political movement, the surviving heroes of Easter week were released and returned to Ireland amid scenes of great public rejoicing. Eamon de Valera quickly overcame his soldier's aversion to politics, and the new mood of Volunteer participation in the hurly burly of elections was signalled by his appearance in the East Clare by-election of July 1917, clad in his Volunteer uniform.

Uniformed he may have been; but Sinn Féin was, potentially, too valuable a political means to power to be set aside in favour of another armed struggle. And de Valera's campaign soon demonstrated the new political role that he, a man of 1916, was anxious to play. He stressed the Catholic nature of his nationalism, for it was 'in Bruree, listening to the sermons that were given by their patriotic priests in the red chapel of St. Munchin, that he first learned what an Irishman's duty was. Religion and patriotism were combined'. When he and his men went out in Easter week — men who were true Irishmen and good Catholics — some people tried to put down their movement as anti-clerical, but he stood there and said, as he said in Bruree, that 'they regarded their first duty was to God, and their second to their country'. He urged the electors not to be afraid of him and his party — they were 'sane, reasonable men'. He left his audience in no doubt that, as far as he was concerned, Sinn Féin stood for the principles of Easter week, for separation, for a Gaelic Ireland, for an Irish republic, for the 'tricolour . . . and not for the Union Jack'. But he also made it clear that he and the party did not stand for the methods of the men of

1916. Like the home rulers before him, de Valera did not rule out the use of force 'if a favourable or feasible opportunity came'; and, like the home rulers, he quickly qualified this by declaring that 'unfortunately, the robber was stronger than they were at the present moment'. Easter week had been necessary to arouse the nation from its torpor, to revive the spirit of independence, and win the people back to their national faith; but 'Easter week had achieved its object. Another Easter week would be a superfluity'. And, again like the home rulers, de Valera likened the vote to 'the crack of a rifle in proclaiming your desire for freedom'.[97]

Much of this must have sounded familiar to the generation brought up under the shadow of Parnell. Here again was faith and fatherland, the enlisting of local clergy in a political campaign, the insistence that votes would prove as effective, indeed more effective, than bullets in winning independence. These parallels were not merely accidental, for de Valera not only spoke the language of Parnellism, he went out of his way to stress the continuity of Sinn Féin in the Irish nationalist tradition. Sinn Féin, he proclaimed at Ennis, were the 'logical followers of Parnell'; the Irish parliamentary party were not.[98] At Roscommon, in February 1917, Count Plunkett's campaign had been fought on the same themes, Laurence Ginnell reminding the electors that Plunkett 'had many claims on the people, not the least of which was that he was one of the four men upon whom the head of the Catholic church had conferred the highest honour that could be given to a layman, and the Count had been a supporter of Parnell from start to finish'.[99]

Sinn Féin's desire to stress the continuity of its ideas reflected the fact that the solid support of Irish nationalism — the farmers, shopkeepers and employers, the local priests, the clerks and officials who had served the parliamentarians, the newspapermen — all had to be placated and enlisted if the party were to succeed in its attempt to supplant the home rulers.[100] All these groups and individuals were familiar to a long-established pattern of political behaviour and rhetoric. The loyal speeches of Redmond in 1914 and 1915 were replaced by the anti-British sentiments of 1916 and 1917; but this represented a return to the older tradition of nationalism, not a radical departure from it. The emergence of de Valera as president of Sinn Féin in October 1917 was a measure of the strength of republicanism in the party; but the constitutional goal agreed upon, after much discussion, bore the marks of compromise: Sinn Féin aimed at winning a republic, and, once that had been achieved, the people could decide what form of government they wanted.[101] This also was reminiscent of the home rulers' tactics;

for 'home rule' was an aspiration, and once home rule had been attained, the people could move towards any form of government they considered appropriate. Moreover, the use of the term 'republic' probably meant, to the public, simply another word for independence, just as home rule could stand for independence in the heady days of 1886 and 1912.[102] The growing acclimatization of Sinn Féin to the nationalist tradition was reflected in Arthur Griffith's newspaper *Nationality* in 1917-1918. For whereas Griffith in 1904 had offered to the public the unfamiliar and foreign example of Hungary, combined with contempt for O'Connell, and no mention even of Parnell, now he asserted that 'The election of O'Connell for Clare was the first Sinn Féin election in Ireland', and agreed that Parnell had forced 'the clear issue between Provincialism and Nationalism. He succeeded in 1885, when he swept out of the Irish representation every Whig compromiser'.[103]

Traditional nationalist themes were further developed in the general election of 1918. 'Sinn Féin was God's truth', declared a speaker in Clerihan, Co. Tipperary, 'and God's truth was on the side of Sinn Féin'. John Dillon was 'in favour of the secularisation of the schools of Ireland. He wanted to hurl the priests out of the schools'.[104] Dillon was also singled out for criticism on the grounds that 'he . . . the Catholic leader of a Catholic people, so he claimed, had on a public platform grossly insulted a man whom all Irishmen should love and thank . . . Father O'Flanagan, the man who manned the breach when Ireland was leaderless'. And the electors were urged to 'show him how they regarded an insult to the clergy'.[105] In Wexford the Reverend M. O'Byrne, while not claiming that Sinn Féiners were 'models of every virtue and the pillars of Irish Catholicity', none the less ventured to say that 'the men who knelt on the filthy floors of cattle boats reciting the Rosary as they were borne into exile' were not likely to teach the 'unholy doctrine' or to overthrow the church in Ireland.[106]

The widespread support of the Catholic church for Sinn Féin would not have been forthcoming for a movement that sought either to transform Irish society radically, or to use physical force to achieve its ends. One Sinn Féin councillor in Clonmel promised that in an independent republic open competition in education would 'leave the highest position in the country open to the humblest individual who had merit';[107] but this was about as far as Sinn Féin's social radicalism went. 'The struggle in which Ireland was now engaged was the question of national liberty, and should not be confused with any question of socialism, red ruin and revolution', one speaker warned.[108] In March 1918 de Valera had made it abundantly clear that Sinn Féin was not a 'class movement'.

A Labour movement was a class movement; but Sinn Féin was a national movement which could embrace all classes for the good of all. Sinn Féin aimed at the 'uplifting of the entire nation', an absolute raising of all classes 'which may be done and leave their relative levels and the relative equilibrium undisturbed'. A class movement disturbed this 'internal equilibrium', but a national one would raise the 'centre of gravity of the entire nation'. Increasing prosperity for the nation as a whole ought to mean increased prosperity for the worker.[109] The election was an election for Ireland's freedom, remarked a secretary of a Sinn Féin club in December 1918 'and nothing else should stand in the way'.[110]

When it came to the methods by which Ireland's freedom should be achieved, the old Parnellite and home rule tactic of standing for and against physical force was once more deployed. Ireland's past heroes – from Tone to the Fenians – were enlisted in support of the party; and, as P.S. O'Hegarty remarked, 'what was sold to the electorate, what they voted on, was not Sinn Féin, not the republic, but Easter Week'.[111] But it was the memory of Easter week, and not the methods of Easter week, that were held up for approval. The use of force was mentioned, but only as a last resort if the Sinn Féin policy of parliamentary abstention and an appeal to the Peace Conference at Versailles for recognition of Ireland's right to nationhood were to prove insufficient – which of course it would not.[112] The claims of the parliamentarians that to get Irish independence, separation, or a republic, Ireland must be prepared to fight,[113] were set aside as scurrilous propaganda.[114] 'Sinn Féin', wrote Robert Lynd in 1919, 'accepts the tradition of physical force in the past, though it does not advocate it in the present'; if it objected to physical force, it was because it objected to failure.[115] It was almost an exact repetition of Dillon's sentiments in the '98 celebrations, and of Redmond's before home rule seemed at last a reality in 1912-14.

The central issue in the 1918 election has been described by one historian as 'about deference', about the tone of the debate with England.[116] But the tone was debated in traditional language, accompanied by traditional postures, traditional loyalties, with Sinn Féin claiming that, far from forsaking the methods of the past, it was returning to them, to the true and essential nature of the Irish demand which John Redmond's recent leadership had vitiated.[117] Sinn Féin candidates, sought to emphasize that it was they who had inherited Parnell's mantle, that they stood for Parnell's dictum that no man had the right to set bounds to the onward march of a new nation.[118] And on another important issue Sinn Féin had little to offer in 1918. The Ulster question was virtually ignored, though de Valera was prepared to go further than any home ruler, or indeed an Irish nationalist, had gone when he remarked in July 1917 that he 'did not believe in mincing matters, and if Ulster stood in the way of the attainment of Irish freedom, Ulster should be coerced. Their natural political enemies were Unionists'.[119]

The revival — or, more accurately, survival — of traditionalist and conservative forces in Irish politics, after the dangers of 1916, was encouraged by the non-political stance of Irish labour following the high water-mark of its revolutionary commitment in the rising. This was partly because no leader of Connolly's prestige or ability emerged from the ranks of the Citizen Army such as had now, in the person of de Valera and others, come from the Irish Volunteers;[120] and partly because labour was deeply divided over the attitude it should adopt to the struggle for Irish independence. Labour's task was a perplexing one, for it had to define its role in a country where the key political issue was, as Connolly had by 1914 acknowledged, the nationalist question; and its response was to avoid any strong commitment to either nationalism or socialism. The movement was divided between those who could not shake off their tradition as part of a pan-British labour movement, and those who believed that labour must come to terms with the likelihood of an independent Ireland under new leadership.[121] Connolly had opted for the radical path. Labour leaders after 1916 were more cautious, but also more anxious than he ever was to prevent the labour movement from splitting. Thus, while in 1918 labour planned to develop an independent political party 'erect, free' to secure representation on all local and national public elective bodies, it also outlined a strategy of non-attendance at the British House of Commons. Negotiations with Sinn Féin to explore possible grounds of co-operation looked likely to precipitate a division in the party's leadership; and it was probably a relief for the beleagured labour men when they finally decided not to contest the election at all.[122]

Connolly had stressed the political power that labour must strive to achieve if it were ever to radically transform Irish society; and there were those in 1918 who believed that the working man would vote for his own candidates if he got the chance, especially since Sinn Féin's economic policy amounted to little more than a vague promise of a 'living wage' for the labourers of Ireland.[123] But the argument that labour should concentrate on the industrial environment, while waiting for the time when an excursion into the political field might be more promising, was fundamentally a sound one. In 1918 the Irish working class, perhaps, in a sense, following the Connolly of 1916, was more concerned with nationalism than with socialism. Connolly had warned that, to have any chance of success in Ireland, or in any other country, a labour movement must adapt itself to the nature of the country, to the political traditions of the people. Labour after Connolly had failed to do that; and the Irish labour leaders, wrote Sean O'Casey – no lover of Arthur Griffith and Sinn Féin – were all 'painfully ignorant of their country's history, language and literature . . . Persecution has deepened our sympathy with our Irish origin, and the Irish Labour leadership, sooner or later, will be forced to realize that they must become Irish if they expect to win the confidence and support of the Irish working class'.[124] Labour's abstention from the electoral contest of 1918 was the final proof of the soundness of Connolly's judgement in the nationalist Ireland of his day.

For the new electorate of 1918, which greatly augmented the old, pre-Reform Act electorate, was as nationalistic as old Ireland had been; any chance that things might prove otherwise was undermined by the clumsiness of British policy from the spring of 1918 to the general election in December. But now that Sinn Féin had won the victory, they were faced with the necessity of exhibiting what one contemporary called 'Parnell's skill in the use of "constitutional" weapons, as well as his daring in utilising "unconstitutional" ones'.[125] The dualism inherent in Sinn Féin, as in any successful nationalist movement in Ireland, was shown in their words and deeds during the first session of Dáil Éireann on 21 January 1919. Parliamentary methods, modelled closely on Westminster, were used;[126] but the Dáil also declared that the Irish republic had been proclaimed on Easter Monday 'by the Irish Republican Army, acting on behalf of the Irish people'; and it ratified the establishment of the republic and pledged itself to make this declaration effective 'by every means' at its command. But there was no declaration of war on England, no promise that these means should encompass those which the volunteers used in 1916. Instead the Dáil, following Griffith's teaching, declared that the elected representatives of the Irish people alone had 'power to make laws binding on the people of Ireland, and that the Irish Parliament is the only parliament to which the people will give its allegiance'.[127]

The difficulty facing the elected representatives of the Irish people was that some members of the republican movement were only prepared to accept passive resistance 'until by active resistance they could end the foreign government of Ireland'.[128] To sit in Dublin, to try to establish a rival administration to the British, was of considerable propaganda value but it would only ultimately prove successful if it brought the British Government to terms with Sinn Féin, as the same tactics had brought Francis Joseph to terms with Deak in 1867. Moreover, there remained the further difficulty of deciding what course of action to adopt if the British Government should adopt a firm line with Sinn Féin, arresting its leaders, harassing them, proclaiming their institutions. Sinn Féin might find itself meekly accepting suppression in order that the policy of passive resistance should not be compromised in any way.

The truth of the matter was that Arthur Griffith and his disciples needed a Gladstone in 1919, just as Parnell had needed one in the days of the land war, of the home rule struggle, of the plan of campaign. Griffith and de Valera must have visible proof of the efficacy of constitutional methods, be they abstentionist or not.[129] Instead they got a British cabinet minister remarking tritely that 'nothing would annoy the Irish more than the conviction that they were not absorbing the minds of the people of Great Britain'.[130] This was all the more dangerous since there were those in the Volunteers who were alarmed lest political methods should eclipse military tactics altogether. In September 1918 the Volunteer journal *An tÓglach* had looked forward with satisfaction to the prospect of coercing the civilian population when it warned that:

Martial Law will be proclaimed *on both sides*. The military authorities of the Irish republic will become the persons to whom *all* Irish Republicans, whether combatants or not, must look for light and leading . . . political methods will be practically suspended, and schemes for 'passive resistance', based on the theory of normal conditions, must prove unworkable . . . Every Volunteer officer must contemplate the possibility of finding himself called upon to act as the chief military authority of his district.[131]

But now the physical force men saw their opportunity of exercising arbitrary force slipping away from them. 'The position is intolerable', Michael Collins complained in May 1919, 'the policy now seems to be to squeeze out any one who is tainted with strong fighting ideas or I should say I suppose ideas of the utility of fighting'. Collins feared that, with too many 'of the bargaining type' among the Dáil ministers 'official Sinn Féin is inclined to be ever less militant and ever more political and theoretical'.[132] One volunteer, Dan Breen, later to earn a reputation as a gunman, declared that 'the volunteers are in great danger of becoming merely a political adjunct to the Sinn Féin organization'.[133] And the decision of Collins and individual volunteers to push ahead strongly with physical force methods was aimed as much at outflanking the politicians as it was at driving the British out of Ireland.

The physical-force men were, not for the first time, assisted by British Government policy. The Government showed no inclination to seek a settlement with Sinn Féin, and its home rule measure, introduced in 1920, was too limited to prove in any way attractive to the Irish political leaders, and was accompanied by the stigma of partition. Moreover, as the parliamentarians had warned in the 1918 election campaign, the absence of any significant Irish nationalist contingent in the British house of commons left the way clear for the British Government to push ahead with its plans, and for the Ulster unionists to amend the bill in their favour on some points of detail.

When clashes between the volunteers – now generally styled the Irish Republican Army – and the crown forces increased in the years 1919 and 1920, the Dáil was in no position to act as any kind of controlling body. It met only rarely; its 'government departments' were shadowy affairs; and the IRA resented any attempt by the minister of defence, Cathal Brugha, to impose on them an oath of allegiance to the Dáil.[134] Yet without it the armed struggle would have appeared much less of a 'liberation' war, and more of a sporadic terrorist campaign. Nationalists had not voted for the application of the physical force policy in 1918, and had indeed been assured that no recourse to violence would be necessary; and there were ample signs, especially in the early phases of the struggle, of the public's disapproval of the ruthlessness and callousness of the republican forces.[135] Not surprisingly, farmers could show resentment at the prospect of IRA men being 'billeted' on their farms, and had it not been for the British Government's expedient of handing the enforcement of law and order over to the ill-disciplined 'Black and Tan' recruits to the RIC, and to the brave but reckless Auxiliary division, public sympathy for the peace-keeping authorities might have been retained, or, at any rate, forfeited less easily; even as matters stood, Ernie O'Malley's 2nd southern division admitted in August 1921 that for 12 months the IRA had been 'steadily losing its grip of the towns and villages'.[136] One member of the Dáil protested publicly about the IRA's campaign of violence, and many were privately uneasy;[137] but the Dáil did not come out and collectively condemn the physical force men. De Valera, in particular, knew that once the shooting had started, Sinn Féin must not allow the British to drive a wedge between the political and physical force wings of the nationalist movement; and he kept up the fiction that the Dáil was in some way in control of the IRA, with the minister of defence 'of course, in close association with the voluntary military forces which are the foundation of the national army'.[138] In April 1921 the Dáil at last accepted official responsibility for IRA operations;[139] and this shadowy and belated 'control' of the IRA by the Dáil, however tenuous, gave the military struggle some semblance of association with the political movement, and prevented it from degenerating entirely into a conflict between an irresponsible armed body, the IRA, and the crown forces. In later years some members of the IRA were wont to twit the politicians about the way in which the gunmen had beaten the British army while the Dáil did little or nothing; but, by giving tacit, and then active, approval to the military wing of the movement, the Dáil invested the IRA with a legitimacy that it could not otherwise have claimed, and in the end the Dáil did more for the IRA, and for the fight for freedom, than its detractors ever allowed.

The fighting in Ireland in 1919-1921 was a conflict that neither the IRA nor the crown forces could win; but the IRA's success in maintaining an army, however small and however depleted, in the field made it imperative for the British Government to seek some compromise with its opponents before taking the stern measures that would bring the struggle to an end. In July 1921 a truce was arranged as a preliminary to talks, correspondence and the negotiations for an Anglo-Irish settlement. But the Irish struggle did not have only military and diplomatic significance; it also exercised a profound influence on the ideology of Irish nationalism, and especially on the ideology of Irish republicanism. For not only was the conflict seen in retrospect as the 'four glorious years',[140] when the IRA became (in their own eyes) the personification of the Fianna, hardly able to see themselves 'for the legends built up around us',[141] it was also, many of the IRA claimed, a war that they had won. They had won it, they boasted, without the trammels of civilian control, and by their own efforts. The less heroic aspects of the troubles — the shooting of civilians as spies by the IRA, the killing of innocent civilians caught up in cross fire, the murder of elderly and inoffensive people on the flimsiest of grounds — were all conveniently forgotten, and episodes such as Tom Barry's brilliantly executed ambush at Crossbarry celebrated.[142] This is not surprising; armies prefer to recall their heroic deeds rather than their disgraceful episodes; but the IRA's campaign of 1919-21, and its apparent success, gave political violence a new lease of life in Ireland, and this political violence was not the kind of conflict envisaged by Meagher of the

Sword or Patrick Pearse. The IRA could hardly have operated other than they did during the troubles, for any attempt at a formal military engagement with the British army would have been a disastrous failure; but as the war progressed, and brutalities became commonplace, the notion that almost any kind of killing was justified providing it aided the 'cause' gathered momentum. Previous Irish insurrections, from 1798 to 1867, had ended in defeat or almost ludicrous failure; and 1916, though certainly not a fiasco, had been swiftly crushed by the British. Now, in the present, a protest in arms had been made; violence, no matter how ruthless or callous had been justified by apparent success; and Irish nationalist appeals to the 'hillside men' were no longer a safe rhetorical device, made in the secure knowledge that, as Sean O'Casey's pedlar, Seumas Shields, put it 'there wasn't a gun in the country; I've a different opinion now when there's nothin' but guns in the country'.[143] There was no atmosphere of violence in Ireland in 1918, but an atmosphere of politics; and the symbolic nature of the worship of dead heroes was shown in a criticism made by the *Cork Examiner* in November 1918 when the authorities suppressed a Manchester Martyrs commemoration parade. 'It is twenty five years since a military proclamation prevented the holding of this annual demonstration in Cork', it commented, and 'during all these years no reason was ever forthcoming for its suppression, the fixture being invariably marked with unfailing good order and respect for its object'.[144] The Sinn Féiners of 1918 were, so to say, political animals, not bold Fenian men. But by 1921, after years of violence and terror, traditional Irish nationalist reverence for the physical force men was less safe than it had been since 1870; and the problem of reconciling the methods by which freedom had been achieved with the long-established democratic tradition in Ireland was to prove a difficult, and at times almost intractable one, for the new State.

The struggle for independence had other significant effects on Irish nationalism. Sinn Féin won its electoral victory in 1918 on the issue of Anglo-Irish relations, with 'separatism' replacing 'home rule' as the formula for freedom. The compromise agreed on — that Sinn Féin aimed at securing the international recognition of Ireland as an independent republic, while leaving the Irish people free to choose their own form of government — did not, as an admirer of James Connolly, Desmond Greaves wrote, 'necessarily involve complete separation'.[145] But when the military wing began to assert itself in 1919, when people like Collins feared that they had gone too far in condoning political methods, the republic became, for the IRA, the goal for which they were fighting, and the goal for which Sinn Féin and the people were struggling – or should be struggling, whether they wanted to or not. The casualties among the IRA, the heroic deeds, the fasts, hunger strikes, deaths in prison, death 'on the hillside or in quicklime near a barrack-wall',[146] all created a host of martyrs for the cause, so that the republic attained an almost mystical quality; and the conviction, amounting almost to a quasi-religious belief, grew that Irishmen could live under 'no other law'. These were the words of Liam Lynch, commander of the 2nd North Cork Brigade of the IRA, who, once he became converted to republicanism, would speak on no other subject.[147] 'The Republic of Ireland *is* and *will be*' proclaimed *an t'Oglach*;[148] and the oath which Cathal Brugha administered to the Dáil deputies and the IRA in August 1919, obliging its recipients to 'support and defend the Irish Republic and the Government of the Irish Republic, which is Dáil Eireann, against all enemies' placed Irish nationalism ever more tightly into the strait-jacket of republicanism. From now on nationalism and republicanism became almost synonymous; or, rather, republicans claimed that they were synonymous, and were quick to place anyone who disagreed with them in the category of traitor to their country and to the men who died for Ireland.

This narrowing down of the horizons of nationalism was compounded by the impact of the struggle on relations between nationalists and unionists. Sinn Féin, and the Irish Volunteers when they were originally founded in 1913, more than any other nationalist organizations stressed that their ideal was a free Ireland irrespective of religious dissensions; but during the Irish troubles this ideal became more difficult to sustain. The IRA itself was, one of its members admitted, 'a force almost entirely Catholic';[149] and when Ulster unionists began asserting their authority in the new state of Northern Ireland, and when Protestants attacked Catholics in their homes, in the streets, and at work in the worsening atmosphere of 1921-22, the IRA quickly slipped into the role of defender of Catholics against Protestants, and as attackers of Protestant 'Carsonia' (as they liked to refer to Northern Ireland). Ulster and its Protestant inhabitants became a military objective with 'flanks' that might be turned by offensive action.[150] And not only were Ulster Protestants regarded as enemies; Counties Clare and Cork were areas where Protestants were particularly subject to attack, and murders of Protestant farmers were frequent: one Cork farmer wrote sadly of twenty of 'my own dear friends – all protestants – who were shot or had to leave or were preparing to leave'.[151] Previous Irish insurrections, of 1848, 1867 and 1916, had not included attacks on Protestants; and whereas 1798 had witnessed much sectarian conflict, this was mitigated by the fact that Protestants were in the ranks of the rebels, and Catholics in the ranks of the militia. But after 1921 Irish republicanism was more firmly identified than ever it had been with Catholicism, and the very name 'IRA' signified to Protestants a dangerous and cruel enemy. It was an ironic and tragic, though not perhaps unpredictable, end to the high ideals of Tone, Mitchel, Stephens and Pearse.

Sinn Féin underwent a similar transformation, almost without realising it. When it sought to resist conscription in March 1918 it enlisted the help of the Roman Catholic bishops who responded with an appeal, not only to the rights of the 'Irish nation', but, more specifically, to the 'Holy Mother of God, who shielded our people in the days of their greatest trials'. 'Our people' probably excluded the Protestants, who were the inflictors of these 'trials'; and, to clear up any ambiguiity, the bishops also called upon the heads of families to have the Rosary recited every evening 'with the intention of protecting the spiritual and temporal welfare of our beloved country'. As Sinn Féin's first historian, and prominent supporter of its cause, R. M. Henry, remarked, many Sinn Féiners deplored this development, as the Bishops' manifesto 'seemed to rule out of existence the section of Irish Nationalists who belonged to the protestant faith and to identify a national question with a particular creed'.[152] It was true, as Henry went on to point out, that criticism of Sinn Féin's sectarianism came strangely from the mouths of Ulster unionists, who 4 years earlier induced the Protestant churchs in Ulster to pass official resolutions against home rule; but if Sinn Féin were to retain any vestige of its claim to be the party of the whole Irish nation, it had to weigh its words and deeds carefully. This it failed to do, and in 1920, under provocation from the riots in Belfast and the threat of a sectarian State in Ulster, the Dáil seemed to accept Protestants as its enemies by voting for a boycott of Belfast goods. This action was strongly urged by Arthur Griffith himself.[153] The modern apostle of Davisite comprehensive nationalism had become the advocate of a sectarian boycott; and there was justification in P.S. O'Hegarty's accusation that the boycott 'denied the whole principle upon which separatists of every generation had claimed for the country – independence' and amounted to 'a blind and suicidal contribution to the general hate . . . an utterly shameful episode in the history of Sinn Féin'.[154]

But Sinn Féin had only succumbed to the dualism endemic in Irish nationalist thinking: thus Aodh de Blacam (Hugh Blackham) accepted that Protestant Irishmen's possession of wealth and skill made them 'valuable citizens', and yet hoped that 'Sinn Féin Ireland', 'this ancient but renascent Catholic nation' would form 'the world's working model of a modern Catholic state'.[155] And there was another aspect to the national struggle that was to contribute to the evolution of Irish republican thinking after independence. De Blacam in his account of *What Sinn Féin stands for* described the Irish question as 'largely a class question'; but he quickly laid this Marxist spectre to rest by explaining that 'the nationalist tradition is resident chiefly in the proletariat, while the landed aristocracy (what there is of it) the capitalists and the bureaucracy, are predominantly anti-Irish'.[156] The class struggle in Ireland was a nationalist struggle; therefore the only class which stood in the way of freedom was the class which stood for the Union. Michael Collins accepted this version of class relations in Ireland when he declared that attacks on landlords could only be justified if they were part of the higher national cause: 'Were it not for this the killing of landlords would have been murder'.[157] Collins objected to the 'democratic programme', a social and economic plan for the new Ireland drawn up by Labour, and adopted — after some important revisions which removed its most radical statements — by Dáil Éireann in 1919, on the grounds that such things obscured the main objective, which was to get the British out of Ireland.[158] The IRA, it was true, was from a lower social scale than the Dáil deputies;[159] but militant Irish nationalism had, since the Fenians, drawn many of its recruits from the men of no property; and the lack of social and economic objectives of the IRA was seen in the fact that the west of Ireland, the most disturbed part of the country in the 1880s and 1890s, was among the quietest areas during the troubles.[160] And when agrarian unrest seemed likely to recur, with smallholders and labourers seizing the opportunity to indulge in landgrabbing, the IRA was quick to add its authority to the decision of the Sinn Féin courts that such action was illegal.[161] Irish republicanism, therefore, was further shorn of the socialistic character that Connolly had hoped to give it in his writings and by his participation in the 1916 rising.[162] Not until 1934 did republican army theoreticians begin seriously to question the whole basis of class relations in Ireland, and seek — unsuccessfully — to lead Irish republicanism out of the narrowly nationalistic ideology that it acquired during the war of independence.

The treaty negotiations, the Anglo-Irish settlement of December 1921, and the civil war which followed were governed by the developments in Irish nationalism that had taken place since Sinn Féin's electoral victory in 1918. The intensification of republicanism meant that the Irish delegation to the treaty negotiations in London was placed in the position of attempting to achieve two aims: to seek out and modify as best they could the real and practical offer of dominion status, with certain safeguards, made by the British Government; and to defend the integrity of the ethereal republic, already established in 1916 and ratified by Dáil Eireann in 1919. This raised the question of whether or not there could be, as Michael Collins maintained, a 'path to freedom', or, as the republican intransigents held, only a retreat from freedom if anything less than the republic were accepted by the Irish. If the republic of Ireland was a living entity, and if Irishmen could live under no other law, there could be no paths leading anywhere except away from the already existing republic. This was what de Valera meant when he accused the signatories of the treaty of 'subverting the republic', and when he declared at the end of the treaty debate that he would do everything in his power 'to see this established republic is not disestablished'.[163] Liam Mellowes denounced the Irish Free State, established by the treaty of 1921, as 'not Irish, because the people of Ireland established a republic'.[164]

Mellowes held that the Irish declaration of independence in 1919 was the announcement of the republic, not a mandate to proceed towards one; but he also knew that his constituents who elected him deputy for County Galway in the uncontested elections of May 1921 were tired of the conflict and dreaded a renewal of war. Mellowes held that this made the treaty a species of 'coercion act' since Lloyd George had offered it with the threat of 'immediate and terrible war' if it were not accepted by the Irish plenipotentiaries; and he denied that England was in any position to make good its threat.[165] Mellowes was anxious to explain away his constitutents' fears; and this raised the question of how the IRA, for its part, would react to public opinion if public opinion showed itself to be in favour of accepting the Anglo-Irish treaty. At the conclusion of the treaty debate in the Dáil Richard Mulcahy, minister for defence in the new provisional government, stated that the army would remain 'the army of the republic', by which he meant the Government which Arthur Griffith was leading, of which Mulcahy was minister, and which was maintaining the republic until the people had voted for or against the Free State.[166] But once again the impact of the war of independence was felt. For not only were many of the IRA units not Mulcahy's to command, having been created under local initiative in 1918 and 1919,[167] they were often reluctant to accept civilian control, partly because they were committed to the republic, and partly because they had enjoyed the prestige and power which grew out of the barrels of their guns. As Sean Moylan boasted in the Dáil:

> My men were ready to fight for the republic against England; they were promised that the army of the republic would be kept in being . . . During the war, my word went in north Cork. In any terms that could be applied to me today, my word goes yet . . .[168]

The suspicion of and hostility to civilian control was summed up in the words of Rory O'Connor, director of engineering in the old IRA and now a leader of the anti-treaty faction. When he was asked if there was any government in Ireland to which he gave his allegiance he answered 'No', and when his interviewer speculated 'Do we take it we are going to have a military dictatorship?', O'Connor replied brusquely 'You can take it that way if you like'.[169]

The actions and pronouncements of IRA men and Dáil deputies in 1921 and 1922 were not, of course, inspired by idealism alone. Personal rivalries, like that between Cathal Brugha and Michael Collins, were present to further embitter differences; and it is likely that many Dáil deputies voted and spoke as they did because they were anxious to secure their place in the republican version of the history of Ireland that was yet to be written.[170] Many of those who supported the treaty claimed that they did so, not because it gave Ireland her rightful place among the nations of the earth, but because it held out the possibility of moving on, as Griffith put it, 'in peace and comfort to the ultimate goal'.[171] There was little attempt to defend dominion status and membership of the commonwealth on the 'union of hearts' ideas propounded by John Redmond in the last years of the home rule movement. Instead, Parnell was quoted — no man can set bounds to the march of a nation —[172] and appropriately quoted. For the separatist feeling that lay behind home rule lay also behind dominion status, and was based on the very same principles: that, as Darrell Figgis put it in his short explanation of the Irish constitution, 'Ireland is an ancient nation and a mother-country in her own right', possessing 'an intricate, if uncompleted, national polity when the neighbouring island was peopled by distinct and scattered populations of conquerors'.[173] So strong was this sentiment that the original constitution, produced by the provisional government in May 1922, was rejected by the British on the grounds that it was incompatible with the whole concept of dominion status;[174] and de Valera's 'document No. 2', his plan of 'external association', was a similar attempt to accommodate Ireland's separate, distinct status with the monarchical commonwealth, but without compromising republican unity.[175] The difference between the pro- and anti-treaty political groups was one of means, not ends. The question which confronted them in 1922 was similar to that which had confronted the home rulers from the 1880s: how to reconcile Irish nationalism's deep conviction about the unique nature of the race with the fact of British propinquity and British power.

There was another problem which arose out of the notion that the Irish were a distinct race; and that was the question of how that race could reconcile its version of history with the version, also widely accepted by nationalists, that Ireland was inhabited by a nation which included what Darrell Figgis called 'the breed of Molyneux' which 'political differences have divided . . . from the ancient race'.[176] Dominion status might conceivably prove acceptable to the Anglo-Irish, with their imperial outlook on life; but the Ulster Protestants, who were generally included in the Irish nationalist concept of the Protestant part of the nation, were still, by the terms of the treaty, excluded from the jurisdiction of the Irish Free State. The provision in the settlement for a boundary commission to examine the border between Northern Ireland and the South 'in accordance with the wishes of the inhabitants, so far as may be compatible with economic and geographic conditions'[177] was held up as promising an end to partition in the near future; but Irish nationalist politics during the treaty negotiations, and after the settlement, were dominated by the question of the right road to republicanism.[178] There were no representatives of the Roman Catholics of Northern Ireland at the treaty negotiations; no Joseph Devlin to put their case. The power of the AOH in the early twentieth century had been broken with the fall of the home rule party that gave it birth: Sinn Féin did not need the AOH, and was, in any case, ideologically hostile to it. It was one of the supreme ironies of modern Irish nationalism that the rise of Sinn Féin, with its firm support in the south of Ireland, and its early commitment to a comprehensive Irish nation, should have undermined the basis of northern Catholic power, and helped the Ulster unionists to establish their grip over 'those districts which they could control'.[179] Yet this undermining of Northern Catholic nationalism was not, in the years 1919-1921, accompanied by any deep or clear insight into the ideas and power structures of Ulster unionism; and the new government of Northern Ireland contemplated with equanimity the prospect of Sinn Féin's divisions over the republican issue, and the Free State's slide into civil war in 1922.

The coming of civil war in the south of Ireland was not an inevitable process; the provisional government and the anti-treaty politicians made strenuous attempts to reach some sort of agreement to preserve 'national unity'. In May 1922 they produced a pact, which provided that the next election (itself a referendum on the treaty) should be contested by a national coalition of Sinn Féin candidates, with the number of candidates allocated to each side according to their existing strength in the Dáil. In the government to be assembled after the election, four out of the nine ministers would be chosen from the minority party, the anti-treatyites. It was a compromise that would have prevented, as the anti-treaty faction intended, any real expression of the electorate's views; but Collins at the last minute decided that such an arrangement could not work, since he and his colleagues had accepted a constitution in accordance with the treaty, setting the Irish Free State firmly within the framework of the British empire.[180] 'National unity' was further compromized by Labour's decision to put forward candidates in the 1922 election. Labour had lent its support, moral and practical, to the struggle for independence; but now it offered its own issues to the public with a programme of moderate social reform, and was rewarded with the return of seventeen out of eighteen candidates. Some of their success may have been because, in the worsening political atmosphere of the treaty dispute, they were regarded as a moderating influence; some votes came from old supporters of the Irish parliamentary party who had not yet found their new political home; and Labour failed to maintain its challenge in the election of 1923, when only fourteen out of forty-three candidates were returned.[181] But Labour had at least demonstrated that voters in Ireland could be presented with a choice other than that arising from splits in the predominant nationalist movement, be it home rule or Sinn Féin.

The civil war which broke out in June 1922 sealed the differences between pro- and anti-treaty groups, and added the finishing touches to the Irish political profile that had been developing since 1918. Anti-treaty accusation that the Free State government had acted at the dictation of the British further embittered political divisions, and made republicans ever more secure in their convictions that they, and they alone, represented the true spirit of Irish nationalism.[182] And because the pro-treaty supporters included men of property, whose demand for the enforcement of law and order could be construed as part of their concern for their earthly goods, the republicans countered with the old Wolfe Tone claim that the 'men of no property' were the only true reservoirs of republicanism. Not all anti-treatyites were men with nothing to lose; not all Free-Staters were men with something to lose.[183] But it was easy to build on the myth that, as Liam Mellowes put it, 'We are back to Tone – and it is just as well –relying on the men of no property. The stake in the country people were never with the republic; they will always be against it until it wins'.[184] This, however, was no prelude to social revolution; for references to the men of no property were essentially political judgements couched in social terms; but they prepared the way for the populist image that the anti-treaty-ites adopted when they returned to political methods in the 1920s.

Some doubted whether Ireland could maintain the essentially democratic and political nature of her society. When Countess Markievicz declared, somewhat incongruously, that she stood for 'James Connolly's ideal of a workers' republic', a county schoolmaster, the deputy for Sligo, pleaded:

> Give us Dominion Home Rule, give us Repeal of the Union, give us anything that will stamp us as white men and women, but for Heaven's sake don't give us a Central American Republic.[185]

The fear that war and the prospect of civil war would, as the deputy quaintly put it, encourage men to 'settle their quarrels with Webleys instead of their fists', seemed a very real one; for not only were local IRA men maintaining their grip on their areas, they were, as defeat came ever closer in the first half of 1923, more convinced that their allegiance was and should be, not to the real Irish people, but to the abstract, idealized nation that inhabited the abstract, idealized republic of Ireland. 'By now', wrote Sean O'Faolain:

> I was the mad mole who thought he had made Mont Blanc. I was the mouse in the wainscotting of the Vatican who believed that he told the Pope every night what His Holiness must tell the world every morning. I was Ireland, the guardian of her faith, the one solitary man who would keep the Republican symbol alive, keep the last lamp glowing before the last icon, even if everybody else denied or forgot the gospel that had inspired us all from 1916 onwards. I firmly believed in the dogma that had by now become the last redoubt of the minority's resistance to the majority; that the people have no right to do wrong. Like all idealists, I was fast becoming heartless, humourless and pitiless.[186]

'A true revolutionary movement in Ireland', Parnell had confessed to an

American journalist in 1888, 'should, in my opinion, partake of both a constitutional and an illegal character';[187] but the question facing Sinn Féin in 1919, as it had faced Parnell in 1888, was that of finding the most appropriate, and least dangerous, mixture of the two. After the violence and sacrifice of 1916, Sinn Féin had hoped to build a firm political foundation on the embers of Easter, only to find that Michael Collins, Dan Breen, and other Volunteers were resolved to fan the embers back into flame, and reassert the primacy of physical force. Thus in 1920 a new period of revolutionary activity began, one that led to the destruction, not only of the Union with Britain, but to the 'national unity' that Sinn Féin had temporarily achieved in 1917. By 1923 Ireland was more deeply divided politically than at any time in her fragmented history. The existence of pro- and anti-treaty groups, regular and 'irregular' armies, 'men of no property' and the 'stake in the country' people, not to mention unionists (northern and south-ern), northern Ireland nationalists, and partition, all revealed how flimsy and transient the national movement represented by Sinn Féin really was. Not even the 'southern part of Ireland/Three-quarters of a nation once again' could claim the political allegiance of all of its citizens. Nationalism had not united the nation nor the three-quarters of a nation; time would tell if the experience of statehood in Ireland could succeed where the promise of statehood had failed so spectacularly.

NATIONAL MOVEMENT = FLIMSY / UNUNITED

Notes

1. S. MacManus, *William Rooney* (Dublin, 1909), p. 75.

2. R. Davis, *Arthur Griffith and Non-Violent Sinn Féin* (Dublin, 1974), pp. 10, 21-22, 113.

3. Ibid., p. 17.

4. N. Breen, 'Concepts of Ireland: a study of four Irish nationalists in the period 1891-1916' (M.A., University College, Cork, 1973), p. 13.

5. Davis, op. cit., p. 108.

6. Ibid., p. 57; the 'ne temere' decree extracted from the parents of a mixed marriage an undertaking that the children of the union would be raised in the Catholic faith.

7. Breen, op. cit., p. 46-7.

8. A. Griffith, *The Home Rule Bill Examined* (Dublin, 1912).

9. MacManus, op. cit., p. 265.

10. Breen, op. cit., p. 13.

11. A. Griffith, *The Resurrection of Hungary* (Dublin, 1918 ed.), p. xxi.

12. Lyons, *Ireland Since the Famine*, pp. 244-6, 249-51; Davis, op. cit., pp. 128-36, 144.

13. Lyons, op. cit., p. 252.

14. P.S. O'Hegarty, *Ireland under the Union*, pp. 639-40.

15. R. Lynd, *The Ethics of Sinn Féin* (Dublin, n.d. 1919?).

16. O'Hegarty, op. cit., p. 641-2.

17. Davis, op. cit., pp. 18, 21-22, 113; Griffith, op. cit., pp. xxii-xxiii, 2-6, 16-34, 82-91.

18. Lyons, op. cit., p. 248; Griffith, op. cit., pp. 91-5.

19. O'Hegarty, op. cit., pp. 642-3, where Griffith extols the Hungarian victory; Griffith, op. cit., p. 34.

20. D. McCartney, 'The political use of history in the work of Arthur Griffith' in *Journal of Contemporary History*, vol. *8*, No. 1 (Jan. 1973), p. 12.

21. T.M. Kettle, 'A note on Sinn Féin in Ireland', in *North American Review*, vol. *CLXXVII* (Jan. 1908), p. 55.

22. S. MacManus, 'Sinn Féin', in *North American Review*, vol. *CLXXXV* (Aug. 1907), p. 825.

23. Dungannon Club, publications, No. 1, 'Irishmen and the English army'.

24. National Council publications, No. 7, 'Ireland and the British army', p. 13; the full context of the incident is in Gratten, op. cit., vol. *I*, pp. 168-9.

25. T.M. Kettle, 'A note on Sinn Féin', p. 46.

26. Ibid., p. 52.

27. Patrick Bradley, preface to *Poems and ballads of William Rooney*, (Dublin, n.d.), p. xlv.

28. F.S.L. Lyons, *Ireland Since the Famine*, pp. 267-70.

29. P. Beresford Ellis, *James Connolly: Selected Writings* (London, 1973).pp. 9-19.

30. For Connolly's place in organizing the ISRP's part in the 1798 celebrations see William O'Brien, *Forth the Banners Go*, (Dublin, 1969), Chap. 2.

31. Lyons, op. cit., p. 272; Beresford Ellis, op. cit., pp. 9-19.

32. O. Dudley Edwards and B. Ransome (eds.), *James Connolly: Selected Political Writings* (London, 1973), pp. 101-2.

33. Ibid., pp. 88-9.

34. Ibid., pp. 189-90.

35. Ibid., p. 64.

36. Ibid., pp. 171-77.

37. Ibid., p. 177; S. Kelly, 'The fall of Parnell', in *Anglo-Irish Studies*, p. 12.

38. Dudley Edwards and Ransome, op. cit., pp. 217-19.

39. Ibid., p. 152.

40. Beresford Ellis, op. cit., pp. 127-8; C. Desmond Greaves, *The life and Times of James Connolly* (London, 1961), pp. 180-81.

41. E. Kamenka, 'Political nationalism: the evolution of an idea' in *Nationalism: the Nature and Evolution of an Idea*, (Canberra, 1972), pp. 15-18.

42. Ibid., p. 18.

43. Dudley Edwards and Ransome, op. cit., pp. 143-50; for Connolly's reasons for this argument see Beresford Ellis, op. cit., p. 242.

44. For a critique of Connolly's thought, and especially his attitude to Ulster Protestants, see C.C. O'Brien, *States of Ireland* (London, 1972), p. 90-99.

45. P. Beresford Ellis, op. cit., p. 267.

46. For a vivid description of these conditions see E. Larkin, *James Larkin* (London, 1965), pp. 41-7.

47. Lyons, op. cit., pp. 275-84; C. Desmond Graves, op. cit., Chap. 17; Larkin, op. cit., pp. 120-58.

48. Greaves, op. cit., p. 265.

49. P. O'Farrell, *Ireland's English Question*, p. 264.

50. Rumpf and Hepburn, *Nationalism and Socialism in Twentieth Century Ireland*, pp. 12-13.

51. Greaves, op. cit., p. 210.

52. Beresford Ellis, op. cit., p. 269.

53. C.C. O'Brien, op. cit., p. 98; Larkin's view was similar; see E. Larkin, op. cit., pp. 179-80.

54. L. O Broin, *Revolutionary Underground*, pp. 6-7.
55. Ibid., p. 129; O Broin estimates the strength of the IRB as 1,660 members in Ireland and 367 in Great Britain in 1912.
56. L.N. Le Roux, *Tom Clarke and the Irish Freedom Movement*, (Dublin, 1936), pp. 10-13.
57. B. Hobson, *The Creed of the Republic*, Dungannon Club pamphlet, n.d.
58. For the shifts in power in the IRB between 1907 and 1914 see K.B. Nowlan, 'Tom Clarke, MacDermott and the IRB' in F.X. Martin (ed.), *Leaders and Men of the Easter Rising: Dublin 1916* (London, 1967), pp. 109-21; Lyons, op. cit., pp. 313-17; O Broin, op. cit., pp. 141-5.
59. The motto of the volunteers was 'defence not defiance'; see O'Hegarty, op. cit., pp. 670-71.
60. Hobson, however, lost much influence in the inner circles of the RIRB because he urged that the Irish Volunteers acquiesce in Redmond's demand that they accept his nominees on the provisional committee. The Volunteer split in 1914 over Redmond's position on the war went seventeen to one in Redmond's favour (O Broin, op. cit., p. 159).
61. Lyons, op. cit., p. 329. The general council of the Irish Volunteers consisted of one representative from each of the 32 counties and one from each of nine cities and towns. The central executive was a president and eight other members selected by annual convention of the Volunteers from candidates resident within ten miles of Dublin. It was the real power in the Volunteers.
62. M. Tierney, 'A prophet of mystic nationalism: AE' in *Studies*, vol. *26*, (1937), p. 576.
63. Lyons, op. cit., p. 334; Lyons, *Culture and Anarchy*, pp. 86-7. For MacDonagh see Thompson, op. cit., pp. 126-31, and for the Plunkett see pp. 131-9. See also R.J. Loftus, *Nationalism in Modern Anglo-Irish Poetry* (Wisconsin, 1964), Chap. 6.
64. Lyons, *Ireland Since the Famine*, p. 330.
65. N. Breen, 'Concepts of Ireland', p. 135.
66. Ibid., p. 136-7; see also E.W. and A.W. Parks, *Thomas MacDonagh: the Man, the Patriot, the Writer* (University of Georgia, Athens, 1967), p. 69.
67. J. Anthony Gaughan, *Austin Stack: Portrait of a Separatist* (Dublin, 1977), pp. 34-5.
68. P. Pearse, *Political Writings and Speeches* (Dublin, 1966 ed.), p. 137. For an analysis of the idea of blood sacrifice see G.F. Dalton, 'The tradition of blood sacrifice to the goddess Éire', in *Studies*, vol. *63* (1974), pp. 343-54.
69. Major F.O'Donoghue, quoted in F.X. Martin, 'The 1916 rising – a coup d'état or a "bloody protest"?', in *Studia Hibernica*, vol. *8* (1968), p. 110.
70. Ibid., pp. 125-31: C. Townshend, 'The Irish Republican Army and the development of guerilla warfare, 1916-1921', in *E.H.R.*, vol. *94* (1979), p. 320.
71. O'Farrell, *Ireland's English Question*, p. 277.
72. Thompson, op. cit., p. 105; see also F.X. Martin, '1916 – myth, fact, and mystery', in *Studia Hibernica*, vol. *7* (1967), pp. 8-39.
73. D.W. Miller, *Church, State and Nation in Ireland, 1891-1921*, (Dublin, 1973), p. 340; F.X. Martin, in *Studia Hibernica*, vol. *7*, pp. 114-17.
74. Breen, op. cit., pp. 118-19.
75. Pearse, op. cit., pp. 176-77.
76. Breen, op. cit., p. 60.
77. Loftus, op. cit., p. 145.
78. Pearse, op. cit., pp. 103-7; see also p. 189 for his comments on the AOH.
79. Loftus, op. cit., pp. 145-6.
80. For an exploration of this theme see P. O'Farrell, op. cit., pp. 266-8.
81. F.X. Martin, '1916 – myth, fact, and mystery', pp. 112-14; J.H. Whyte, '1916 – revolution and religion' in F.X. Martin (ed.), *Leaders and Men*, Chap. 17;

D. MacCartney, 'The churches and secret societies', in T. Desmond Williams (ed.), *Irish Secret Societies*, p. 77.

82. Lyons, *Dillon*, p. 371.

83. Full text in Curtis and MacDowell, *Irish Historical Documents*, pp. 317-18.

84. R. McHugh, 'Casement and German help' in Martin, *Leaders and Men*, p. 183. For Markievicz see E. Coxhead, *Daughters of Erin* (London, 1965), and A. Marreco, *The Rebel Countess* (London, 1967). Erskine Childers also helped to 'wind the clock' of the rising by assisting in the Howth gun running in 1914.

85. P. Costello, *The Heart Grown Brutal*, p. 88; the O'Rahilly was one of the pioneers of the Irish volunteers; he helped organize the Howth gun running, and joined the rebels in the GPO, where he was killed.

86. Pearse, *Political Writings*, pp. 53-7, 364-71.

87. Beckett, *Anglo-Irish Tradition*, p. 114.

88. Strauss, *Irish Nationalism*, Chap. xxi.

89. Martin, '1916 – myth, fact and mystery', pp. 87-9.

90. C. Desmond Greaves, op. cit., p. 304.

91. S.V. Larsen and O. Snoddy, '1916 – a workingman's revolution', in *Social Studies*, vol. *2*, No. 4 (Aug-Sept. 1973), pp. 377-98.

92. Ibid., p. 391.

93. J.V. O'Brien, *William O'Brien*, p. 223.

94. So-called because the Sinn Féin convention that produced it was held in the mansion house, Dublin.

95. M. Laffan, 'the unification of Sinn Féin in 1917', in *Irish Historical Studies*, vol. *17* (1970-71), pp. 353-79.

96. R.M. Henry, *The Evolution of Sinn Féin*, (Dublin and London, 1920), p. 225.

97. *Clare Champion*, 30 June, 7 July, 14 July 1917; see also D.W. Miller, *Church, State and Nation*, p. 392; F.X. Martin, *et al.*, *Scholar Revolutionary*, p. 193 for de Valera's anxiety to persuade Eoin MacNeill to campaign in Clare, because 'the clergy are with MacNeill and they are a powerful force'.

98. *Clare Champion*, 7 July 1917; see also the leader in the *Champion*, 30 June 1917, which claimed that Parnell, had he been alive, would not stand by while other small nations got their independence, and would recognize that the day had come when Ireland's 'claim for full and complete independence could not be denied'.

99. *Longford Independent*, 3 Feb. 1917.

100. D. Fitzpatrick, *Politics and Irish Life*, pp. 233, 267; Miller, op. cit., p. 391.

101. P. Pyne, 'The politics of parliamentary abstention: Ireland's four Sinn Féin parties, 1905-1926', in *Journal of Commonwealth and Comparative Politics*, vol. *12* (1974), pp. 206-27.

102. As Laffan suggests, loc. cit., p. 377; see also P.S. O'Hegarty, *The Victory of Sinn Féin* (Dublin, 1924), p. 91: 'Adhesion to Sinn Féin in 1918 no more committed Ireland to consider nothing but independence than adhesion to Parnell in 1885 committed Ireland to consider nothing but Home Rule'.

103. *Nationality*, 7 July 1917, 9 Feb. 1918.

104. *The Nationalist* (Clonmel), 30 Nov. 1918.

105. *Donegal Vindicator*, 6 Dec. 1918: Father O'Flanagan was vice-president of Sinn Féin and one of its most active members. See also *Waterford News*, 22 March 1918 for a similar attack on Joseph Devlin.

106. *Wexford People*, 11 Dec. 1918.

107. *The Nationalist*, 23 Nov. 1918.

108. Ibid., 30 Nov. 1918; see also *Galway Vindicator*, 7 Dec. 1918 (Revd. M. Hayes).

109. *Waterford News*, 22 March 1918.

110. *Kerry News*, 20 Nov. 1918, (Mr Guerin).

111. O'Hegarty, op. cit., pp. 724-5; *The Victory of Sinn Féin*, (Dublin, 1924), p. 31.

112. See e.g. *The Nationalist*, 23 Nov. 1918 (Mr Morrisey) and 4 Dec. 1918, (Mr Cooney); *Anglo-Celt* (Cavan), 30 Nov. 1918; *Wexford People*, 4 Dec. 1918 (Dr Ryan); *Kerry News*, 4 Dec. 1918 (Mr Browne); *Cork Examiner*, 19 Nov. 1918 (Mr Walsh).

113. See e.g. *Connaught Telegraph*, 30 Nov. 1918 (Mr Scanlon); *Kerry News* 25 Nov. 1918 (Mr O'Donnell); *Donegal Vindicator*, 13 Dec. 1918 (Mr O'Donovan).

114. But Cathal Brugha made explicit reference to the possible need to fight for independence (*Waterford News*, 22 Nov., 13 Dec. 1918).

115. *Ireland — a Nation* (London, 1919), p. 55.

116. J. Lee, op. cit., p. 162.

117. *The Nationalist*, 30 Nov. 1918 (Mr O'Boyle).

118. *Sligo Champion*, 30 Nov. 1918 (Mr Osborne): *Wexford People*, 4 Dec. 1918 (Dr Ryan); *Galway Vindicator*, 7 Dec. 1918 (Revd. M. Hayes); *Waterford News*, 22 Nov. 1918 (Mr Kenny).

119. *Clare Champion*, 21 July 1917 (speech made in Dublin). By 1921, however, de Valera had come to oppose coercion of Northern Ireland (C.C. O'Brien, op. cit., p. 295).

120. A. Mitchell, *Labour in Irish Politics, 1890-1939*, (Dublin, 1974), pp. 71-2.

121. For Irish and international socialist reaction to Connolly's participation in the 1916 rising, see S. Levenson, *James Connolly* (London, 1973), pp. 327-8.

122. B. Farrell, *The Founding of Dáil Eireann: Parliament and Nation Building*, (Dublin, 1971), Chap. 3.

123. See e.g. *Galway Vindicator*, 7 Dec. 1918 (Revd. M. Hayes).

124. Mitchell, op. cit., p. 102.

125. W. O'Brien, *The Downfall of Parliamentarianism*, p. 56.

126. Farrell, op. cit., p. 51; see also *The Irish Parliamentary Tradition*, pp. 208-11.

127. Text in Curtis and MacDowell, op. cit., pp. 318-19.

128. P.T. Daly of the IRB (Davis, op. cit., p. 24).

129. See R.M. Henry, op. cit., p. 284: 'The means at the disposal of Sinn Féin at present hardly seem adequate to accomplish their object'.

130. D.G. Boyce, *Englishmen and Irish Troubles* (London, 1972), p. 43; the cabinet minister was Winston Churchill.

131. F. O'Donoghue, *No Other Law* (Dublin, 1954), p. 23.

132. M. Forester, *Michael Collins — the Lost Leader* (London, 1971), p. 104.

133. C. Townshend, 'the IRA and the development of guerilla warfare, 1916-1921', op. cit., p. 320.

134. J.A. Murphy, *Ireland in the Twentieth Century*, (Dublin, 1975), pp. 14-15.

135. R. Kee, *The Green Flag*, pp. 632-33, 657, 663.

136. Townshend, op. cit., pp. 327-9.

137. Murphy, op. cit., p. 13.

138. T.E. Hachey, *Britain and Irish Separatism: from the Fenians to the Free State* (Chicago, 1977), p. 269; Kee, op. cit., pp. 660-61.

139. Boyce, op. cit., p. 92.

140. The title chosen by Frank Gallagher for his account of the troubles.

141. Kee, op. cit., pp. 708-9.

142. Ibid., pp. 702-3.

143. *The Shadow of a Gunman* (1923).

144. *Cork Examiner*, 25 Nov. 1918.

145. C. Desmond Greaves, *Liam Mellowes and the Irish revolution*, (London, 1971), p. 139 fn 2.

146. Roger McHugh, 'The rising', in R. O'Driscoll (ed.), *Theatre and Nationalism in Twentieth Century Ireland*, (London, 1971), p. 105; see also J.A. Gaughan, op. cit., pp. 156-7.

147. F. O'Donoghue, op. cit., pp. 10-12, 40.

148. Townshend, 'Development of guerilla warfare', p. 336.

149. O'Donoghue, op. cit., p. 55; he adds 'and in the main devout'.

150. Townshend, op. cit., p. 340.

151. Buckland, *Irish Unionism One*, pp. 213-17.

152. Henry, *Evolution of Sinn Féin*. pp. 261-2.

153. P.S. O'Hegarty, *The Victory of Sinn Féin*, pp. 51-2; M. Wall, 'Partition: the Ulster question', in T.D. Williams, (ed.), *The Irish Struggle*, pp. 86-7.

154. O'Hegarty, op. cit., p. 53.

155. A. de Blacam, *What Sinn Féin Stands For* (Dublin, n.d. [1921?]), pp. xvi, 219, 225.

156. Ibid., p. 107.

157. M. Collins, *The Path to Freedom* (Dublin, 1922), p. 57.

158. B. Farrell, *The Founding of Dáil Éireann*, pp. 57-61; A. Mitchell, *Labour in Irish Politics*, pp. 107-110.

159. Fitzpatrick, *Politics and Irish Life*, Chap. 6; 'The geography of Irish nationalism, 1910-21', in *Past and Present*, vol. *78* (Feb. 1978), pp. 113-44, esp. p. 114.

160. Strauss, op. cit., p. 265; Rumpf and Hepburn, op. cit., pp. 50-57.

161. Fitzpatrick, *Politics and Irish Life*, p. 282; Murphy, op. cit., p. 10; W. Alison Phillips, *The Revolution in Ireland* (London, 1923), pp. 180-81.

162. P. Lynch, 'The social revolution that never was', in T. Desmond Williams (ed.), *The Irish Struggle*, p. 49.

163. Curtis and MacDowell, op. cit., p. 328.

164. C. Desmond Greaves, op. cit., p. 278.

165. Ibid.

166. Murphy, op. cit., p. 45.

167. Townshend, 'Development of guerilla warfare', p. 332.

168. Desmond Williams, *The Irish Struggle*, p. 122.

169. Kee, op. cit., p. 733.

170. See P.S. O'Hegarty's strictures, *The Victory of Sinn Féin*, Chap. xvi.

171. Curtis and McDowell, op. cit., p. 330.

172. By Griffith, ibid.

173. D. Figgis, *The Irish Constitution Explained* (Dublin, 1922), pp. 7-8.

174. Boyce, op. cit., pp. 174-78.

175. A.C. Hepburn, *The Conflict of Nationality in Modern Ireland*, pp. 121-3.

176. Figgis, op. cit., pp. 8-9.

177. Curtis and McDowell, op. cit., p. 324.

178. M. Wall, op. cit., pp. 87-88.

179. D.W. Miller, *Queen's Rebels*, pp. 122-29.

180. Lyons, *Ireland Since the Famine*, pp. 455-57.

181. Rumpf and Hepburn, op. cit., p. 25; Mitchell, op. cit., pp. 117-22; 153-62. Labour had already contested local elections in 1920. (Ibid. pp. 122-29).

182. C. Desmond Greaves, op. cit., pp. 345-6; M. Forester, op. cit., p. 322.

183. A. Mitchell, op. cit., p. 167.

184. Desmond Williams, op. cit., p. 50.

185. C. Desmond Greaves, op. cit., pp. 276-77.

186. Ruth Dudley Edwards, *Patrick Pearse: the Triumph of Failure* (London, 1977), pp. 327-8.

187. Quoted in E.D. Steele, 'Ireland for the Irish', *History*, vol. *57*, (1972), p. 247.

STATE AND NATION IN MODERN IRELAND

> Had de Valera eaten Parnell's heart
> No loose-lipped demagogue had won the day,
> No civil rancour torn the land apart.
> Had Cosgrave eaten Parnell's heart, the land's
> Imagination had been satisfied . . .

W. B. Yeat's lines[1], written in 1935 in the middle of what was perhaps the most turbulent decade in Irish politics since independence, expressed his disappointment at the quality of life in the new Ireland that he, like other literary men, held himself in part, at least, responsible for bringing to birth in the 1916 rising. Cheap patriotism, demagoguery, internecine quarrels, threats to law and order and, above all, the absence of any great, heroic figure who could, by his nobility and inspiration, dominate the Irish people, provoked in Yeats a revulsion of feeling, a sense almost of betrayal. National freedom had proved an aesthetic disappointment; the drab, anti-intellectual atmosphere of the country disgusted him; the high hopes embodied in nationalism seemed to have evaporated; and the outlook for the new state, after only a few years of its existence, seemed bleak and unpromising.

The outlook from the political point of view appeared scarcely more optimistic: 'In Ireland in 1922', declared Kevin O'Higgins, minister for justice in the free state government 'there was no state and no organised forces . . . . No police force was functioning through the country, no system of justice was operating, the whole wheels of administration hung idle, battered out of recognition by the clash of rival jurisdictions'.[2] Putting these statements, that of the poet and of the practical man of affairs, together, it seemed that Ireland lacked two essentials if she were to make a success of freedom, and not succumb to her enemies' slanders that she was a banana republic, or, what was worse in the eyes of many, a banana non-republic: she lacked any kind of firm, solid administrative and political base; and she did not possess the necessary charisma to gather to her the loyalty, the affection and the respect of all her citizens.

Certainly the new regime was confronted with problems and difficulties arising both from the nature of the revolution that brought it into being, and from the nationalist ideology that inspired that revolution in the first place. From the beginning the Irish Free State was plagued by doubts about its legal foundation, for the anti-treaty members of the Dáil refused to accept allegiance to any authority other than the second Dáil, elected in 1921, and remaining the sovereign authority of the Irish republic; in their eyes there could be no third Dáil, nor any succeeding Dáils, no legitimate government, no Irish Free State. The thirty-two county republic, founded in the Easter rising, was the only legal government under which Irishmen could live; as Mary MacSwiney, the 'sea-green incorruptible' republican, put it in 1924, 'all the citizens of Ireland today are legal citizens of the Republic; some are loyal, some disloyal, but all owe the same allegiance even if all do not now pay it'.[3]

There was an implied threat here directed towards those who were 'disloyal' citizens of the republic; for if they were disloyal, then perhaps they could be made loyal by what Miss MacSwiney called the 'Army and Government of the republic'. That army had waged war for a year in an effort to defend the republic; and when in 24 May 1923 the IRA chief of staff, Frank Aiken, ordered republicans to cease fire, he ordered them also to 'dump arms', not to surrender them, for their arms would be necessary in the future when an opportunity of over-throwing the illegitimate Free State regime again presented itself:[4] it was the duty of the army to 'stand by as the situation develops'.[5] It seemed, indeed, as if the new State could not even rely on its own forces; for in 1924, under threat of a reduction in the Free State army, culminating in the demobilisation of nearly 2,000 officers, the Govern-ment was presented with an ultimatum demanding the removal of the army council, the suspension of demobilization, and a more speedy move towards the republic. The Government managed to suppress the mutiny, but only at the cost of the resignation of two ministers and three senior members of the army council.[6]

The Free State's lack of full legitimacy, the threat of violence against its disloyal citizens, and its brush with its own armed forces hardly augered well for the political stability of Ireland. And the Government was also vulnerable to the charge that it had let down the nation by its failure over the border; for not only had the Treaty Settlement of 1921 accepted partition, de facto if not de jure, the boundary commission which reported in 1925 confirmed the existing arrangements with only slight changes proposed on either side of the frontier. Here was another betrayal of the ideals of the men of 1916, which the 1924 army muti-neers attempted to exploit when they complained about the Govern-ment's failure to realise the ideals of Michael Collins, who had taken 'drastic action' against the enemies of both the independence and the

unity of the country.[7] There was an element of hypocrisy in such crit-
icisms, for no-one had as yet produced any suggestions that might result
in the digesting of 800, 000 Protestants without the diluting of Irish
Catholic identity; but the emotional issue of Irish unity was not one to
be lightly set aside, and no future Government of Ireland dare refrain
from making the appropriate responses to the issue of the 'indivisible
island'.

The Irish revolution was fast assuming the character of the most
unstable of all revolutions: it was incomplete. It was incomplete in that
Ireland was not wholly 'free', it was not united, and it had not realised
the ideals of its founding fathers. Moreover, although the revolution
had not been made for material reasons, although James Connelly's
concern for social justice was pushed into the background, the poverty
and hardship which was the lot of many of the new state's citizens
raised yet another issue. Irish nationalists, from Tone and O'Connell,
through Davis to Pearse, had maintained that a free Ireland could
support a much larger population that a subject Ireland; a free Ireland
would be a prosperous country, a self-sufficing one; yet the Irish
economy still depended upon the export of cattle and the import of
manufactures, and she was unable to live off her own home grown
food. Here again the ideals of Irish patriots were, apparently, in danger
of being compromised.[8]

And there was another, less tangible, grievance that could be held
against the Irish free state, one that Yeats touched on in his poem: one
that referred, not to the content of the government, nor to the substance of its legislation, but to its style. Political style in Ireland was a
vital ingredient of success at national level, especially in a predominantly rural country where politics, speeches, elections, provided much
of the colour and entertainment of life. But not even the Free State
Government's greatest admirers could maintain truthfully that it
possessed the gift of inspiring political excitement. W. T. Cosgrave and
his ministers built up an impressive record in home and foreign affairs:
they sought to establish the rule of law based on the rule of the
majority; their budgets were balanced; private enterprise was allowed to
flow freely;[9] and between 1924 and 1932 the Government pressed for
a new legal and practical definition of dominion status, playing their
part in the evolution of the statute of Westminster of 1931, which acknowledged co-equality between Britain and the dominions, and the
right of dominion parliaments to repeal or amend Westminster legislation affecting them.[10]

But these solid and impressive achievements were not the stuff of

Irish nationalism, which was always more of a bundle of sentiments than a logical array of facts. And the doubts concerning the nationalist sentiments of the Free State Government were only increased by the belief that it was 'controlled', as one critic put it, 'by Unionists and Freemasons'.[11] If such people defended the Free State, if the Government of Northern Ireland found it a congenial neighbour, then its nationalist credentials must be in doubt. Did freedom amount to nothing more than 'normalcy' in administration and green-painted pillar boxes? But if it amounted to more than that, if the revolution were to be taken up and moved forward again, the question of means was no less important than the question of ends. For Yeats's desire for the satisfaction of the land's imagination might not be reconcilable with O'Higgins's belief in the need for the State to establish a sound institutional base.

There were those among the political and military groups which had opposed the treaty who still refused to accept any kind of constitutional activity, on the grounds that to do so would compromise further the already compromised republic of 1916. In the general election of 1923 the republicans, under the name 'Sinn Féin' won 44 seats, but refused to take their seats in a 'usurping legislature'; and when the policy of abstention, now applied to an Irish instead of a British legislature, proved unpopular with the electorate, the military wing of the republican movement, the IRA, took this as further proof of the futility of any kind of political methods.[12] But for those who, like de Valera, sought power to gain their ends, the policies of abstention and physical force held little attraction. For the new Irish State was one firmly founded on the democratic principle, and no Irish political leader, no Irish politician who aspired to be a leader, could ignore the long-established parliamentary tradition of his country. From the time of O'Connell mass political activity in Ireland was associated with democratic procedures, and the union with Britain further cemented the relationship between politics and parliamentarianism; but the establishment of the Irish Free State was perhaps the most important step in the process by which Ireland escaped the adventures of a banana republic. For the first time since 1800 the Irish electorate was conscious of electing, not simply a party to go to Westminster and coax reforms out of a foreign Government, not merely a party to sit in the Dáil and defy that foreign Government, but a party that would itself form a Government if it were accorded a majority of seats. The apparatus of the State, the civil service, the army, the police, were all at its disposal if it were prepared to use them in a responsible manner. Whatever abstentionists and IRA men said or thought, the State would continue to be governed: the first ten years of statehood under Cosgrave's cautious but firm political tutelage had demonstrated that. Whether the opposition politicians cared to try for the governance of the country, or preferred to sit on the sidelines and await the second coming of the republic, it was becoming clear that, as de Valera himself put it, 'there must be somebody in charge to keep order in the community'.[13] The reality of statehood was about to exercise an important and lasting influence on the idealism of Irish republicanism.

From 1923 de Valera was pondering on the roads to freedom that republicans might reasonably follow without selling the pass on their principles. The second Dáil was not the sticking point for him, as he acknowledged in a draft letter to Mary MacSwiney; if the oath of allegiance were removed, then 'the question of going in or remaining out would be a matter purely of tactics and expediency . . . I have always been afraid of our people seeing principles where they really do not exist'.[14] De Valera was still not prepared to admit the legitimacy of the Free State legislature: but he saw that it had a de facto existence simply because most Irish people recognised it as their parliament; and he knew that the de jure position of the republic could not be maintained indefinitely if Sinn Féin were to exercise any kind of political influence in the land. The desire for constitutional purity among members of the de jure republican Dáil led the party into abstruse discussion about the legitimacy of those members elected since 1920; and members who claimed to represent constituencies from which they had subsequestly been ejected by the electorate raised further complications.[15] In November and December 1925 de Valera sought to modify the abstentionist policy; and in January 1926 he announced that he was prepared to enter the Free State Parliament if there was no oath to be taken. To do otherwise, he warned in May 1926, would be to place republicans in the same category as French monarchists, unable to resist the 'authority which every de facto controlling power acquires by prescription and the lapse of time'.[16]

The Sinn Féin party organisation was still controlled by the most committed republicans, to whom the policy of non-recognition of the Free State legislature was a cardinal article of faith; and, after de Valera had called upon all his political ingenuity to reconcile his position on entry into the Dáil with the republican principle of non-recognition,[17] he acknowledged that, if he and his followers were not to spend the rest of their political – and probably their natural – lives arguing about their principles, they must break with Sinn Féin. De Valera was a politician who sought compromise when all others had recognised that the day for compromise had passed, as his 'document No. 2' and his agreement to the electoral pact of 1922 demonstrated; indeed, his belief in his ability to find new formulas that would reconcile the irreconcilable was inexhaustible, and his compromises became a positive hindrance to compromise. But he had learned much after the harrowing and frustrating years of 1922 to 1926; and now he was prepared to break with Sinn Féin, stop wasting time, and take up the suggestion of one of his ablest leiutenants, Sean Lemass, to found a new party, Fianna Fáil.[18] Lemass's advice soon proved sound and realistic. In the 1927 general election de Valera's new party won 44 seats, while Sinn Féin was reduced to five; and the resolutions passed at a Sinn Féin 'republican government' meeting in April 1928 must have removed any lingering doubts. In one fell swoop the 'government' condemned those deputies who had reneged on the republic in 1922 and 1927, repudiated all acts of the government of Northern Ireland, denied the right of the 'king of England' to confer the title 'earl of Ulster' on his son, called on the 'race' to renew its allegiance to the Government of the republic, and ended with a rhetorical flourish, congratulating the 'peoples of Egypt, Arabia and India on their determination to assert their absolute independence of the arch-enemy of human liberty'.[19] It was magnificent, but it was also rigidly orthodox, and it was, as de Valera had earlier acknowledged, not politics.

The founding of Fianna Fáil, however, did not mean that Irish politics turned away finally from the old questions raised by the issue of physical force, its place in Irish nationalism, its role in the origins of the state. After the assassination of Kevin O'Higgins in July 1927, the Cosgrave Government responded with legislation, part of which would have required candidates for election to the Dáil to take the oath of allegiance, and which would therefore have driven Fianna Fáil out of elective politics altogether. De Valera had no option but to enter the fray, and take the oath, describing it as an 'empty formula'.[20] But his party in the Dáil was not prepared to deny its roots as the descendants of the men of 1916 and of the war of independence and the civil war. In March 1928 Sean Lemass defined Fianna Fáil as a 'slightly constitutional party . . . perhaps open to the definition of a constitutional party, but before anything we are a republican party . . . Our object is to establish a Republican Government in Ireland. If that can be done by the present methods we have, we will be very pleased, but if not, we would not confine ourselves to them'.[21] In 1929 de Valera conceded that those who continued in the IRA could claim 'exactly the same continuity that we claimed up to 1925'[22], that is the legitimacy which devolved on the men who remained true to the republic, and who opposed what de Valera called the *coup d'etat* of the summer of 1922. CONSTITUTIONALISM + REVOLUTIONARY TRAITS

For de Valera's rise to power saw — for the last time in the mainstream of Irish politics — a clear link between the constitutional and revolutionary streams of Irish nationalism. Fianna Fáil members marched with the IRA and Sinn Féin in the same parades to Wolfe Tone's grave in Bodenstown; at election times IRA men supported Fianna Fail's candidates, even to the point of intimidating their opponents; and 1932 witnessed the election slogan of 'release the prisoners' fulfilled, when de Valera set free jailed republicans, and removed Cosgrave's security legislation. De Valera, once in office, maintained contact with the IRA army council about the possibility of future co-operation.[23] It was hard to see how a truly republican party could set its face against its old comrades in arms, many of whom were, after all, the heroes of the fight for freedom; and all Irish nationalists had to tread warily when it came to defining their attitude to the physical force movement.

Once again, however, statehood, government, brought about an adjustment of traditional nationalist and republican attitudes. To the surprise of many of the Fianna Fáil deputies, the Cosgrave Government accepted the rules of the constitutional game, and quietly turned over power to their opponents;[24] and de Valera responded in kind when he made no political dismissals of civil servants, even though he complained that his party's advent to office was handicapped by unsympathetic administrators.[25] But more significant was the way in which Fianna Fáil's experience as a governing party obliged it to confront the problem of law and order in the state, and the legitimate source of force in a democratic community. 'There is no way today in which the arms of any section of the people can be used from the point of view of general national defence except under the control of the duly elected government', he stated in 1934; and he praised the police force which, like the army, was 'largely recruited from former comrades of the IRA — those who took one side when it divided'. De Valera acknowledged the 'difficult work' which they had to do when they were sent out unarmed and often amongst a hostile people: and he confessed that 'as far as we are able to know . . . these officers have loyally served us. We came into office and we got service . . . because these men realised that we are not a partisan government'.[26]

In 1936 de Valera was even more emphatic about the way in which the existence of a popular democratic community must necessarily diminish the place of force in national life. Any party or group could put its policies before the people confident in the knowledge that if they secured a majority they would be entrusted with the machinery of government. 'That being so', he urged, 'what possible excuse is there for any section seeking to secure power by force?'.[27] In 1922 de Valera had ruminated on the conflict of principle between 'majority rule on the one hand and the inalienability of the national sovereignty on the other';[28] but now he warned of the danger of any group having the intention of trying to subject the majority to their will; and he promised that the Government would do all it could to 'see that no military organisations are built up here except those which are responsible to the representatives of the people'. No authority save that of the State had the right to take the life of a citizen for any cause; and he pleaded with the young men of the country 'not to be led away by the glamour attached to the name IRA'. The IRA had, he argued, won its respect by acting as the army of the people, under the authority and Government of the people.[29] This was a dubious interpretation, for the IRA had commenced its campaign of violence in 1919, as Pearse had begun his rising in 1916, without any popular authority whatsoever; but de Valera justified his stand by explaining that physical force was valid in the past because it was the only alternative to looking vainly for a majority in an 'alien parliament' where Irish representatives were out-numbered six to one. Now that the Irish majority had its voice, and could make it heard clearly and unequivocally, matters were on a different footing altogether.[30]

But Fianna Fáil had to contend with the IRA, which stated in 1932 that 'until the republic of Ireland is freed from foreign aggression and can function freely, the necessity for an Irish Republican Army will continue';[31] and the glamour of the military life had by no means lost its attraction for the youth of Ireland, nor could it while nationalists continued to pay homage to the graves of dead Fenians, and praise the efforts of more recent revolutionaries, dead or alive. Irish nationalism thrived on the glamour of the physical force tradition; and it would have been political suicide for any party which now denied that tradition, or sought to obliterate it from the national memory. De Valera's Government did neither. It set out to satisfy Irish martial ardour and love of its violent traditions by political means. It awarded pensions to anti-treatyites, thus integrating the heroes further into the legitimacy of the state: the state could use its resources to attract loyalty to itself, for there was nothing dishonourable about accepting recognition from the republican party. In 1934 the Government set up the volunteer militia, providing a safety value for military-minded people. And when, inevitably, he came into conflict with the IRA, de Valera was careful not to create new martyrs. He allowed the IRA to discredit itself in clashes with Eoin O'Duffy's Blueshirts, an organisation modelled on Mussolini's private army, and consisting of ex-Free State army members aroused by the fear of partisanship on the part of Fianna Fáil's government; then he turned his attention to the IRA itself, declaring it illegal in 1936, and banning the annual Bodenstown march, while sending its chief of staff to prison.[32] The vindication of de Valera's methods was seen in 1940, when Brian O'Higgins, a volunteer who had fought in the general post office in 1916, attempted to identify some IRA men who planted a bomb in Coventry which killed and injured innocent bystanders, with the Manchester Martyrs.[33] It was a shrewd comparison, and one that might have won public approval; but de Valera ensured that the State kept its authority as the only legitimate wielder of force by protesting against the death penalty passed on the Coventry bombers, while warning the nation of the dangers of IRA activity in a time of European war when 'small nations throughout Europe are devoting all their efforts to strengthening national unity'.[34]

Ireland was now, for the first time, presented with two traditions of violence: a legitimate one, stretching from Tone, through the Fenians, to the men of 1916 and 1919-23; and an illegitimate one, dating from the period when, in de Valera's eyes, a truly 'national' Government had taken power in 1932, and had, moreover, taken power through a democratic election.[35] Of course, other parties had won elections in Ireland in the recent past, only to be told that their victory was irrelevant because it betrayed the Irish nation. But Fianna Fáil was the republican party; the republic was the true national goal of the Irish nation; and de Valera set out to demonstrate that the national goal could be reached by constitutional means. This meant not only must he pursue that goal while in office, but its pursuit must be given that anti-British edge, that nationalist fervour that would assuage republican sentiment, except perhaps among those whose thoughts were still occupied with the legitimacy of the second Dáil. It was essential, in short for de Valera to revive the old, tried and trusted policy of militant constitutionalism: for in that way only could militancy be made constitutional.

Fianna Fáil's election campaign of 1932, therefore, was of a full-blooded nationalist hue. The old issue of the land for the people was revived, and Cosgrave's Cumann na nGaedheal's Government was accused of continuing the old British policy of turning the land into a prairie producing cheap beef.[36] Fianna Fáil was 'out to diffuse ownership', said de Valera in Cork, 'they want to distribute the land and have happy homesteads where they had herd's houses'; but he was careful not to disturb the conservative elements in Irish society too much, for he promised that Fianna Fáil's policies contained 'nothing that interfered with the rights of private property'.[37] The full force of Fianna Fáil's attack was directed against Britain, and combined Griffith's economics with promises of a refusal to pay the land annuities owing to Britain as a result of the land purchase policies of the late nineteenth and early twentieth centuries. De Valera also promised to 'resume the march towards an independent republic';[38] but, again, he was careful not to frighten his opponents unnecessarily: the aim of all Irish nationalists, he remarked, was 'the complete independence of a united Ireland. That aim is not inconsistent with a certain voluntary association with Britain and the States of the British commonwealth'.[39] From this belief he had not wavered since 1921; and it was to be the guiding star of his political life until Ireland was taken out of the commonwealth by his political opponents in 1949.

De Valera struck familiar notes, not only in the policies he presented to the public, but in the style of his campaign. Any fears that Fianna Fáil were godless Fenians were quickly dispelled by the spectacle of their leader interrupting his speech in Tulla, co. Clare, at the sounding of the Angelus Bell, blessing himself, and silently saying the Angelus prayer 'the crowd reverently following his example'.[40] The party, in a public advertisement in the press, announced that it fully accepted 'responsibility for governing in accordance with the principles enunciated in the encyclical of Pope Pius XI on "the social order" ';[41] and although de Valera told the electorate in Dublin that his ideal was 'the ideal of Thomas Davis' and denied that his intention was to make any test of citizenship on religious grounds, he reminded his listeners that 'the majority of the people of Ireland are Catholic, and we believe in Catholic principles. And as the majority are Catholics, it is right and natural that the principles to be applied by us will be principles consistent with Catholicity'.[42] This, of course, was the complete opposite of the teachings of Davis and Tone, not to mention the Fenians; but de Valera knew his Ireland, and knew that, while godless Fenians were likely to run into difficulties, godly Fenians usually fared much better. And, of course, no nationalist campaign could be fought as a party political campaign: like the home rulers, like Sinn Féin, de Valera claimed that his party stood for the nation, for national unity. Fianna Fáil was a national movement, not a mere party; and the *Irish Press*, de Valera's newspaper, recalling the 'bitter and barren strife' that followed the

Parnellite split, emphasised the need for the reunion of nationalist forces behind a truly national leader.[43]

Between 1932 and 1939 de Valera's adminstration fulfilled the constitutional part of its programme, even if economic self-sufficiency remained something of a receding goal. At the top of de Valera's shopping list was the oath of allegiance taken by the Dáil deputies and officers of government; and in 1937 a new Irish consitution, 'republican in everything but name', all but reversed the verdict of the Anglo-Irish treaty of 1921. The doctrine of popular sovereignty was embodied in the first article, which declared that 'the Irish nation hereby affirms its inalienable, indefeasible, and sovereign right to choose its own form of government, to determine its relations with other nations, and to develop its life, political, economic and cultural, in accordance with its own genius and traditions'. Ireland was a 'sovereign, independent, democratic state', ran article five; and the state's independence was emphasised by a separate Irish flag (green, white and orange) and by the inauguration of the office of president to guard the constitution.[44] But just as exhilarating was the experience of economic nationalism, for here were more tangible concerns, here was the ancient nation fighting for its life, aided by a traditional nationalistic images: the old claim that Ireland under the union had been over-taxed and must be compensated;[45] and the still older claim that 'during the first five centuries' of the struggle against the invader 'everything was taken from the Irish people'[46], and so there could be no money 'owing' to England for the purchase of land that was by right the property of the Irish people. De Valera had set himself to fulfil Fintan Lalor's dictum, and undo not only the union, but the conquest. And when the Fine Gael party denounced the retention of land annuities and the constitutional changes as violations of national honour, they were routed with the counter claim that Fianna Fáil was fighting for national liberty, the right of a small nation to free itself from imperial ties, and was nonetheless being thwarted by Fine Gael's siding with the enemy.[47]

Between 1932 and 1938 the Anglo-Irish war was fought all over again, only this time the weapons were propaganda and economic sanction, not bombs and bullets: diplomacy was to de Valera a continuation of warfare by other means. But his victory was one tempered by the recognition that, in the end, economic independence must give way to economic interdependence, and that Ireland could not be a country of 'boundless wheatlands', but must satisfy herself with a plan for 650,000 acres: an unpleasant intrusion of statistics into an idealistic programme.[48] However, de Valera's nationalism struck a blow, not only at the Anglo-Irish relationship, but at the intransigent republicans within Ireland who, in their own words, continued their 'weary march . . . the same sad, proud story — a funeral procession, a graveside gathering' until death gave them 'release or until Ireland is free'.[49] De Valera demonstrated that an Irish Government could itself make a new thrust towards Irish freedom; and once again the apparatus of the state enabled the state to further stabilise itself, and to win over the loyalty, or at least the compliance, of its former enemies: for the removal of oath of allegiance opened the way for those outside the Dáil to 'come in'.[50] And the more the British Government upbraided the Irish for renegeing on their financial obligation, or threatening the stability of Anglo-Irish relations, the more did Fianna Fáil appear loyal to the separatist ideal. Above all, de Valera's new constitution would, he promised the people, be 'Irish from top to bottom';[51] and such a constitution, given by the people to themselves, true to the separatist ideal, must lay to rest the idea that any government of Ireland that did not derive its authority from the second Dáil was a usurping regime. The patriot army could hardly claim to fight for a free Ireland if Ireland — or — and this was a difficulty — most of Ireland was already free: in such an Ireland the patriots themselves were the enemies of freedom. In 1948 Sean Lemass, who twenty years before had described Fianna Fáil as a slightly constitutional party, and who had hinted at other means if republicans could not achieve their aims peacefully, now answered a heckler in Limerick, who demanded to know why 'political prisoners' were detained by the state, that 'there is no-one in prison today to whom that description applies except those convicted of murder or attempted murder. The government is bound to, and will, protect the lives of the Irish people'.[52]

The final vindication of Irish sovereignty came in the Second World war, when de Valera's vigilance, aided by luck, and the fact that Northern Ireland provided the allies with sufficient facilities for naval defence, enabled Ireland to maintain her neutrality in the face of often hostile criticism not only from Britain, but from her erstwhile special friend, the United States. Irish neutrality proved that Ireland was indeed a sovereign independent state, capable of pursuing her own course, whatever her powerful neighbour might wish; and de Valera's dignified response to Winston Churchill's condemnation of his Government for its 'frolic with the German and later with the Japanese representatives to their hearts' content' set the seal on his record as a great national leader.[53] When in 1949 a coalition government severed the last link with the commonwealth and made Ireland's republican status formal[54], the anti-climactic nature of the transaction arose not only from Fianna Fáil's lukewarm response, not only from the fact that many southern Irish citizens were alarmed at the implications of the move for Irish people living in Great Britain[55], but from the clear evidence provided in the war that Ireland was, beyond cavil, a sovereign nation.

It was de Valera's defence of Irish sovereignty at all points that was his special political skill; and this defence was couched in terms that appealed to the sentiments and aspirations of most of the Irish nationalist people. De Valera appealed to the sense of pride and moral virtue of a small, conquered, oppressed but never servile and never absorbed nation. Like O'Connell, who told his people that they were the finest peasantry in all Europe; like Parnell, who defended the dignity of the Irishman in the house of commons, de Valera went down to his constituents in County Clare and addressed them simply as 'men of Clare, worthy descendants of Claremen who fought under Brian Boru'.[56] Like the Fenian Charles James Kickham he had an idealised vision of Irish society: an Ireland of small farms, of a God fearing, manly peasantry; a frugal Ireland, turning its back on materialism; the Ireland 'we dreamed of would be the home of a people who valued material wealth only as the basis of a right living, of a people who were satisfied with frugal comfort and devoted their leisure to the things of the spirit'.[57] It was Knocknagow made manifest;[58] and, even if the bulk of the Irish people had never any real intention of accepting this vision as their national destiny, it was comforting to know that a great national leader could articulate such sentiments, and tell the world what Irishmen were really like, even if most of them were not really like that at all.

This nationalist ideal was shared by de Valera's bitter opponent in the treaty split, Michael Collins, who, like de Valera, stood for:

an Irish civilisation based on the people and embodying and maintaining the things — their habits, ways of thought, customs — that make them different — the sort of life I was brought up in . . . Once, years ago, a crowd of us were going along the Shepherds Bush Road when out of a lane came a chap with a donkey — just the sort of donkey and just the sort of cart that they have at home. He came out quite suddenly and we all cheered him. Nobody who had not been an exile will understand me, but I stand for that.[59]

Here, once more, and expressed less poetically, but more movingly, was the stuff of nineteenth and twentieth century romantic nationalism, whose essence lay in an ideal of agrarian, homely, Catholic society. But such a society could hardly accommodate north east Ulster; nor did it. Michael Collins denounced the north east for having 'lost all its native distinctiveness. It has become merely an inferior Lancashire. Who would visit Belfast or Lisburn or Lurgan to see the Irish people at home?'.[60] Collins had included Lurgan, one of the most Irish towns in Ireland, in his general condemnation of Ulster; but de Valera's attitude, though it differed from Collins' in approach, was essentially similar. De Valera simply ignored modern Ulster; 'The area that Ireland has lost', he complained in 1933,

> contains many of her holiest and most famous places. There is Armagh, the See of St. Patrick; Downpatrick, his burial place, where lies also the body of Brian who drove out the Danish invaders; Bangor, the site of one of the greatest of Ireland's ancient schools; Derry of St. Columcille; Tyrone of the O'Neills; MacArt's Fort, where Wolfe Tone swore to work for Irish freedom; Belfast, the birthplace of the Irish Republican movement.[61]

Fortunately for this vision of Ireland, rural, pious and Catholic, the Anglo-Irish treaty of 1921 confirmed the partition of the country, and in so doing set aside the awkward issues raised by Collins and de Valera in their nationalist credo. For the twenty-six county Irish state held out at least the possibility of maintaining that Ireland, the real Ireland, the essential Ireland, corresponded in some degree to the nationalist vision of what it was, or should be. De Valera's government, in particular, made it clear that, while all respect would be paid to Protestant suscep- tibilities, the Irish people 'ever firm in their allegiance to our ancestral faith and unswerving even to death in their devotion to the See of Peter, constituted 'a Catholic nation'.[62] The Protestant minority were, formally at least, fairly treated; no religious discrimination of any sig- nificant kind was ever encouraged by the state;[63] the contrast with Northern Ireland was marked.[64] Nevertheless, de Valera's pronounce- ments, and above all his constitution of 1937, which attempted to incorporate Catholic social principles into the everyday life of the people[65] seemed to indicate that it was the Government's intention to turn its part of Ireland into a homogeneous Catholic state. What was more, the small and vulnerable Protestant minority could hardly do anything to frustrate such an intention even if it had plucked up the nerve to do so. The State, in this important area of national life, once more came to the aid of the nation. It was too tempting a prospect for Irish bishops, and Roman Catholic pressure groups such as the Dublin Institute of Catholic Sociology and the Christus Rex society (not to mention the more fervent bodies such as Maria Duce, which wanted the state formally to recognise the Catholic church as the one true church) to ignore.[66] The State defined their area of operation; that coincided, roughly, with accessible Roman Catholic Ireland; and Government and pressure groups thought increasingly in terms of what they could achieve in the state and nation that they had inherited from the British, rather than what they might have been faced with had they inherited a united Ireland. Daniel O'Connell, who had resurrected the seventeenth century idea of the Irish Catholic nation, and who combined religious toleration with the conviction that, in the end, the Protestant minority would, as he put it, 'melt' into the nation[67], was vindicated. Despite their repeated and vociferous protests against partition, the boundaries of the minds of Irish politicians, churchmen, and socially active laymen, had shrunk with the boundaries of the state. De Valera's 'Eire' (Ireland) of the twenty-six counties was becoming more of a reality than he could ever have forseen.

This growth of a homogeneous state was more important in the everyday lives of most of its citizens, to whom to be Irish was, as a matter of common fact, to be Catholic, than was the idea of a Gaelic nation, of Ireland not free merely, but Gaelic as well. Fianna Fáil made a particular effort to identify itself with the ideals of the Gaelic movement; and article seven of the programme for which it sought a mandate in 1932 pledged the party to 'endeavour by systematic effort to preserve the Irish language and make it again the spoken language of the people'.[68] What this meant in practice was explained in the department of education's notes for teachers, who were instructed not only to teach the Irish language, but to 'restore, as far as is practicable, the characteristically Gaelic turn of mind and way of looking at life'. This was all the more vital in 'these modern days of foreign penetration by newspaper, book and cinema'; and to combat this danger of Ireland becoming 'a hybrid people' (sic) the Gaelic attitude, encompassing 'a high spirituality, a vivid awareness of the presence of God, and a deep spirit of resignation to His will' must be instilled. The example held up before teachers and pupils was Patrick Pearse, 'one of the noblest characters in Irish history'.[69] A Gaelic League pamphlet, published in 1937, put the issue more bluntly: 'English came, Irish went. If Irish is to come, English must go'. Irish or English? That was the choice, 'the desperate choice', that the Irish people must make some day.[70]

But this was precisely the choice that the Irish people refused to make. The Irish language survived among a few thousand people along the western coast; would-be Irish speakers went there to benefit from the experience of mingling with those Irishmen whose native tongue Gaelic really was; but English remained the everyday speech of home and work. The 819 branches of the Gaelic League of 1922 withered away rapidly to 139 in 1924.[71] The State was, in this most central aspect of Irish nationalism, modifying the nature of the ideology that inspired its birth. The very establishment of an Irish State created the widespread belief that such an act, by itself, ensured the preservation of the Gaelic League idea. As Michael Collins put it, now that Ireland was free 'we can fill our minds with Gaelic ideas, and our lives with Gaelic customs, until there is no room for any other'.[72]. The task was, by implication, completed now that the state was a reality. And the Gaelic League, that most effective pressure group, was the victim of its own political influence: by helping to inspire political freedom it left the state with no really effective critic;[73] an English administration, and perhaps even John Redmond's home rulers, would have been much more vulnerable to the shafts fired by Irish Irelanders, and more likely to respond to them. The Gaeltacht withered away; and the voices raised in protest were few and ineffective. And when governments made efforts to preserve the Gaeltachts, to inject new social and economic life into them, they only succeeded in further undermining their unique character. The relief of these 'congested areas' meant loss of population; the setting up of small industries led to the introduction of English speakers; and Gaelic speakers often left for new employment when they had received sufficient training to equip them for a future in English-speaking areas.[74]

As the life of the state lengthened, and its perspectives and priorities altered accordingly, Sinn Féin's economic precepts as much as its cultural beliefs were modified; and the economic nationalism of the 1930s was, by the end of the third decade of the state's existence, seen to be insufficient to meet the needs of its citizens. Protectionist policies and the development of home industries were by no means unsuccessful; but the industrial economy still depended on imported fuel, machinery, and raw materials, and home industries were on too small a scale to develop proper export outlets. Even the tillage policy was disappointing, and the cattle trade reasserted itself after the coal-cattle pact with Britain in 1935.[75] The war further blighted the Irish economy. Ireland's supplies were now threatened, many raw materials were almost completely cut off, and there was a heavy fall in industrial production and employment, with a corresponding rise in emigration. Even Irish agriculture failed to profit from war-time conditions; and shortage and rationing were part of the wartime experience in Ireland as in Britain. After the war the economy remained stagnant, and emigration continued; and it was becoming clear to many in Fianna Fáil, and in other political parties, that economic nationalism must give way to national economics.

The worst economic crisis since the foundation of the new State in 1922[76] was a major factor in the fall of the Fine Gael, Clann na Poblachta and Labour coalition government which had defeated Fianna Fáil in the 1948 election. Clann na Poblachta, a new party founded in 1946, but one based on the republican activists of the inter-war period, had risen rapidly in the public estimation on a policy of republicanism and social and economic reform;[77] its colourful and gifted leader, Sean MacBride, son of Maud Gonne, pursued de Valera relentlessly in 1948 on his alleged statement that '45/- a week is an adequate family wage in a Christian country'.[78] Wages, social security, education, work, were the issues that Clann put to the electorate; and it pointed out that 'no real progress can be made (on partition) unless and until we create economic conditions and social security services here that will at least approximate those available in the six counties since the advent of the British labour government'. Having covered this flank, Clann proceeded to demolish any slander that it might be socialist, or even communistic; its intention, MacBride stressed, was 'to give practical effect rather than lip service' to the papal encyclicals.[79] 'The high cost of living' declared also the Fine Gael leader, General Richard Mulcahy, 'is the pressing problem of the day'.[80]

Unfortunately for the coalition it did little about the pressing problems of the day; it collapsed in 1951, and retrieved office in 1954, only to fall from grace again in 1957. In the 1957 election, the Fianna Fáil counter-attack was fought with the new weapons that had been wielded so effectively by the coalition parties in 1948. It was perhaps to be expected that Sean Lemass, an able and experienced minister in the department of industry and commerce in the 1930s, would stress economic policy and the need to get the concerted support of the leaders of farmers, workers and industrialists for a comprehensive plan of campaign.[81] But now even Eamon de Valera found himself on the platform in Drogheda warning the electorate that the coalition wanted them 'to forget that the real issue is how the country is to be rescued from the serious economic position in which it now finds itself'.[82] It was the cost of living in Ireland, not the cost of dying for Ireland, that now engrossed his thoughts; and in his victory speech in March he called for 'one great and combined effort', not to end partition, but to end the country's economic ills.[83] The *Cork Examiner*, a Fine-Gael orientated newspaper, and the Fianna Fáil organ, the *Irish Press*, were at one in recognising that, as the *Examiner* put it, 'The new generation is thinking in terms of bread and butter, and of more comfortable existence' than the older generation; John Citizen was not worried about national records of the past.[84] Or, as the *Press* put it rather less crudely, the vision today was 'of an ancient nation' fully able to meet the demands of modern life'.[85]

Fianna Fáil's concentration on social and economic issues was justified at the polls, for the party took office with its highest ever total of Dáil seats — 78 — and de Valera formed his eighth and last administration. His Government still included many of the old guard: Dr James Ryan, Sean MacEntee, Frank Aiken, and of course Lemass himself. But not only were there new men as well, Jack Lynch, Neil Blaney, Charles Haughey, Donough O'Malley, Kevin Boland and Dr Patrick Hillary:[86] one member at least of the older generation, Lemass, showed that not all old republicans lived for the past. Lemass showed the importance of political control of the machinery of administration; for he gave life and vigour to the economic proposals contained in a report prepared by Dr T.K. Whitaker, the secretary of the department of finance, which drew attention to the failures of 25 years of self-government: the backwardness of agriculture, the stagnation of industry, the decline in population, emigration, the lack of public capital, and the lack of intelligent direction of public capital. The remedy he suggested was for the State to spend money on modernising agriculture and industry, to solicit for foreign capital by tax concessions and other facilities, and to abandon the old Sinn Féin policy of protection for its own sake. Ireland would before long find herself participating in some way in the European economic community, and 'it must now be recognised that protection can no longer be relied upon as an automatic weapon of defence'. The initial cost of the new plan was high: but taking a risk was a necessary part of economic expansion.[87] Lemass took up the Whitaker report, and used his power and skills to hurry along the civil servants, dispel gloom and defeatism, and convince workers and employers of the need for planning.[88] He was helped by the general economic climate of the 1960s; and the return in 1965 of the problem of an adverse balance of payments, together with inflation and disappointing agricultural performance showed that the 'economic miracle' was by no means accomplished for all time.[89] But Lemass showed that he could not only replace de Valera in 1959, but keep the party in office in 1961 and then lead it to an impressive victory in 1965.[90] The departure from active politics of the last great leader of nationalist Ireland, and his replacement by the talented, but much less striking figure of Lemass, was a sign, not of the failure of self-government in the twenty-six counties, but of its success. Ireland, it seemed, no longer needed the great man, the Yeatsian Parnellite figure, the larger than life hero.[91]

The party which de Valera led into the second half of the twentieth century presided over, and benefited from, social change in Ireland since independence, social change that made the idea of an Ireland 'all west coast' an ever-receding vision. In 1926, the year of Fianna Fáil's foundation, over half a million of the population were engaged in agriculture, and many of the rest in economic activity closely related to agriculture; by 1970 the proportion of the rural to urban population was 4 to 3, and the number of persons engaged in industry was 264,000 one-third of them in the building and service type industries, mining and turf, and two-thirds in manufacturing. One person in four of the population lived in Dublin and its environment:[92] if Ireland still had no north east corner, it had a considerable east coast to compensate.[93] This might have undermined Fianna Fáil, which started out with the image of the party for the underprivileged, the 'men with the seatless trousers'[94]. Fine Gael had stood for law and order, respectability and a return to normal political life, and it naturally gathered support from those who had something to lose: the business class, former unionists, large farmers.[95] But even before the Second World war Fianna Fáil, while retaining its radical and populist image, while relying on the votes of the labourer, the small farmer, the clerks, was already assuming the appearance of a respectable party; and after the era of planning and economic advance which Fianna Fáil inaugurated in 1957, the party naturally attracted the men of property, the business men who appreciated a sound administration when they saw one. Fianna Fáil managed to be both a nationist party, emphasising the traditional virtues of rural Ireland, while all the time modernising that society, if not out of existence, then out of the dominant place which it had occupied in Irish nationalist politics since the days of the land war.[96] Fine Gael, for its part, was revitalised by young recruits who sought to ensure that the new prosperous Ireland of the 1960s did not lose sight of the idea of social justice; and even the Labour party began to offer itself as a socialist party; but its representation was still confined to the Dublin area, and to places with large numbers of rural labourers; and it made no significant mark, except as a potential partner in a coalition with Fine Gael.[97]

The distribution of support for the main political parties, and the disappearance of the smaller sectional parties such as the Farmers' party (representing relatively wealthy farmers) and Clann na Talmhan (a small farmers' party), and of the independents who were such such a feature of the pre-1948 electoral contests[98], was further evidence of the homogeneity of life in the republic of Ireland. Representatives of sectional interests found a home in the major parties; men of no property voted for the same party as men of much property; the excitement of campaigns like that fought by Clann na Poblachta, with its rousing speeches and its torchlight processions, so reminiscent of Irish elections since the great days of Parnell, had given way to modern publicity methods, political packaging and the American-style campaign fought by Lemass's successor, Jack Lynch, in 1969.[99] Irish politics now revolved around the three major parties, each with its own social base, to be sure, but each competing for the votes which might reasonably be accorded to any party that promised to handle social and economic issues more effectively than its rival.[100] Fianna Fáil was able to claim, convincingly, that Protestants were numbered among its voters, having lost their original adherence to Fine Gael as the least republican, most respectable choice confronting them in the new Ireland; for Fine Gael had, after all, been one of the parties responsible for inaugurating the formal declaration of a republic in 1949. Thus there were no significant class politics, no sectarian politics, no racial politics, but simply Irish politics and Irish − southern Irish − issues. The only troublesome reminder of turbulent times was the reappearance of Sinn Féin, the political wing of the IRA, in the March 1957 election. It won four seats, polling 66,000 first preference votes; but its doctrinaire refusal to take its seats at the Dáil quickly cost it the support that it won, and it made no mark on the political scene.[101] Moreover, despite their ritual condemnation of partition, no members of the major political parties ever considered offering themselves as candidates in Northern Ireland elections, as Michael Collins and de Valera had done when Sinn Féin was in the ascendant in 1918-1922. The occasional practice of subsidising the campaigns of Northern Ireland nationalists was soon discontinued;[102] and nationalist M.P.s in the north made only a few sporadic and half-hearted gestures of taking their troubles south rather than sitting in, or simply abstaining from, Stormont.[103] The southern Irish electorate was engrossed in its own concerns; its parties' policies and activities were constrianed by the boundary of the state; and the homogeneity of the twenty-six county state was thus further reinforced by its political life, thought and practice.

All this was encouraged by the settlement of the outstanding constitutional issues in the period 1932-49, the issues that had deeply divided the State's leaders and men since the civil war. The questions surrounding the oath of allegiance, the governor-general, the status of the Free State, and the rest of those fine but deep points of dispute were cleared up, one by one, by Fianna Fáil and by the coalition Government of 1948. Thus the state settled its 'first order' issues, those concerning its constitution, the very basis of its political existence; and, these settled, 'second order' considerations of social and economic reform, jobs, wages, houses, could be accommodated within the framework of the State's normal political order. The distribution of goods and rewards was by no means an uncontroversial matter, especially in a time of economic recession; but − unless that recession became a disastrous economic collapse − it was a matter that could be resolved within the framework of political bargaining, and political give and take.

The border was still an issue; but it was not, in the 1950s and 1960s, an issue that divided the southern Irish nation, which appeared more and more satisfied with its 'three quarter' status. An IRA cross-border campaign in 1956 caused a tremor, and the wave of popular sympathy for the death of two IRA men − Sean South and Fergal O'Hanlon − in a raid on Brookeborough barracks[104] seemed to indicate that the land's imagination, to borrow Yeats's phrase, had not, as far as partition went, been satisfied. Apparently the public's disapproval of illegal organisations only extended to their actions against the southern Irish state, and was suspended when those actions involved attacks on life and property in the north. But the revulsion of Fianna Fáil against its physical-force republican roots was convincingly demonstrated in the 1957 election when, in so far as public order was an issue at all, Fianna Fáil and Fine Gael vied with each other in competing for the image of the anti-terrorist party. The Taoiseach, J.A. Costello, accused the opposition of complacency in its attitude to the IRA in the years 1951-54[105], while de Valera attacked the coalition Government for its equivocal attitude to violence.[106] Fianna Fáil, Sean MacEntee declared, did not tolerate any illegal organisation; they had dealt with them before, and when they left office in 1948 there was peace in the land. The question arose over whose policy would prevail in a MacBride−Costello coalition: 'would it mean more raids for this country and more lives lost. Would it mean greater numbers of British troops than ever before poured into the six counties? Or were we . . . going to be brought again to the brink of civil war?'[107] Force was no solution to partition, de Valera told foreign correspondants in Dublin after his victory at the polls; the only armed force in the country was that of the State 'otherwise you are facing anarchy'. Sinn Féin abstentionist M.P.s were 'living in the past . . . trying to do something that we did in 1924 and . . . forgetting that conditions have completely changed. The reasons for abstention do not exist today'.[108]

It might be supposed, however, that the new look, 'spick and span' republic[109] of the 1960s was a State in grave danger of losing any specifically Irish identity, and becoming just another off-shoot of the predominant culture of the British Isles: in short, that the experience of statehood bore out Douglas Hyde's and Patrick Pearse's dire predictions about 'West Britonism'. It was certainly true that fewer people seemed to be searching for a 'core' identity, for an essential mark of national, or even racial distinction. The strident Gaelic tone of the 1930s, with its repetition of Moran's idea of a racially distinctive Gaelic type[110], was less often heard, even though Gaelic enthusiasts were wont, like An tAthair Tomas O Fiaich, to repeat Michael Collins's unforgiving phrase that 'we can only keep out the enemy and all other enemies by completing the task'.[111] But most people, while sympathetic towards the language, and wishing to see it survive, were not prepared to go beyond a passive acceptance of its role in defining Irish nationality, nor to work for Pearse's idea of bilingualism as a prelude to monolingualism.[112] Fewer people maintained that, as Michael Matthews put it:

> we'd be a nation sooner
> If we bumped off every crooner
> And danced sets around Tom Moore in College Green.[113]

Catholicism was still one of the essential ingredients of Irishness; but the idea that the church should work towards turning Ireland into a model Catholic State was gradually relaxed and, in the 1960s, virtually abandoned.[114]

But these important changes in the southern Irish national consciousness did not mean that the 'bargaining, incrementalist and particularist political style'[115], and the decline of the ideals of the Catholic and Gaelic rebels of 1916, were in danger of depriving Irishmen of any sense of nationality altogether. For the experience of living in a sovereign State, with its own institutions, local and central, its own police and armed forces, its own political parties, legislation, and pressure groups, its own educational system, its peculiar religion, its 'culture of the small community'[116], proved a more integrating force in Irish nationalism than Gaelic leaguers or Maria Duce enthusiasts could ever have imagined. The dwindling Protestant minority in the new state, and the growth of the Roman Catholic majority from 92.6 in 1926 to 94.9 in 1961[117] meant that a southern Irishman in work, the public house, the train, was less and less likely to meet someone different from himself. Nor would he have needed to worry overmuch if he had; for the Protestant minority had no special political point of view, no desire to trouble the majority with complaints or grievances. It was easier to accept the majority culture, and more congenial, as well as prudent, to live down Yeats's arrogant claim that 'we are no petty people'. By the end of the first half-century of the state's existence the dualism that had been a central feature of life and culture in the south of Ireland since the twelfth century had all but disappeared; and, as James Joyce's Leopold Bloom put it, the nation was 'the same people living in the same place'.[118] Thus, to the idea of Irish nationality embodied in the phrase 'the Irish, properly so-called', to the myth of the endless struggle for freedom against the Saxon, was added a final essential ingredient of nationalism in Ireland: the experience of statehood. In the end, the despised parliamentarians had, in a sense, been vindicated: the restoration of her parliament was indeed indispensable if Ireland were to be 'a nation once again'.

But the nature of twenty-six county nationalism left the republic face to face with the failure of triumph. For it was all too easy to forget that the Irish 'nation', and the State which most of its citizens referred to as 'Ireland', was three-quarters of the whole, and that the remaining one quarter, while formally part of the nation, and sharing the same island, was very different in character from its southern brethren. Not only had Ulster Protestants rejected the concept of Irish nationalism, and remained determined to be masters in their own areas;[119] Ulster Catholics themselves had, until the rise of Joseph Devlin and the AOH, occupied a subordinate position in the nationalist movement. Devlin had advanced their influence in the years 1906-1914, only to find himself obliged to urge upon his people the sacrifice of partition in the 1916 negotiations; and the Sinn Féin/Parliamentary split in the 1918 general election further divided Ulster Catholics' political strength. After the 1920 Government of Ireland Act, Northern Ireland Catholics had to redefine their political position, both in the new State, and in relation to the 'National' state in the south. Individual Catholics, and some of their representatives at a local and unofficial level, were by no means utterly opposed to seeking a working relationship with the Government of Northern Ireland;[120] but the nationalist party refused to recognise the existence of the State, and expressed their refusal by abstention from the Northern Ireland Parliament between 1921 and 1927 and after 1932, resuming regular attendance only after 1945.[121] The Government of William Cosgrave hoped to push the Northern Ireland Catholics into fuller participation in the life of the state, and in 1925 he justified his failure to protect them by making provisions in the boundary commission agreement on the grounds that 'the minority should have the only real security, which is . . . to be sought only in neighbourly feeling'. He refused to allow a delegation of Northern Ireland nationalists to present a petition opposing the agreement, and consoled himself with the thought that 'the Free state will lose nothing. It will gain good will'.[122] De Valera showed a more active concern to reopen the controversy, declaring in 1932 that the 'area cut off was not determined on any principle of right or justice. It was gerrymandering pure and simple'.[123] But no-one in southern governing circles was prepared to jeopardise Irish sovereignty for Irish unity, as de Valera revealed in the second world war when he rejected Churchill's overtures for reopening the partition question in return for Irish participation on Britain's side.[124]

Anti-partition propaganda, such as that waged by an all-party campaign after 1949, was as futile as it was rancorous, for not only did it offer to the unionist Government in Northern Ireland a useful slogan to prevent their followers breaking ranks, and voting for a rival party such as Northern Ireland Labour[125], it made life in the six counties even less comfortable for Catholics without any way advancing the cause of unification. Moreover, southern economic policy in the 1930s worked to the disadvantage of Northern Ireland trade, and the Northern Ireland Government was obliged to ask the British cabinet for special protective measures against Free State imports into the United Kingdom. The 1938 Anglo-Irish agreement, which ended the economic war, required Sir James Craig to subordinate Ulster to imperial interests;[126] and in the post-war world southern and Northern Ireland, far from developing complementary economies, which might work to each other's advantage, remained in competition, with both seeking for the best advantage in the British market. And whether the unionist administration and the unionist middle-class leadership of the province were regarded as a fraud upon the working classes (Catholic and Protestant) of Northern Ireland, or as a justifiable, if in some respects unsavoury, defence of beleaguered Protestant interests, it was clear that, as de Valera admitted in 1957, the question of partition was one best left alone for the time being.

This, however, represented an essentially negative attitude; there was still little sign of a positive concept of Irish nationalism that would go beyond merely including the Protestants of Ulster in the nation, whether they accepted that status or not, while excluding them from the race. Irish nationalists in the home rule era and after bore no ill-will towards Ulster Protestants; but their understanding of their minority in the north was so incomplete that they could only emphasise the short-lived Presbyterian radical/nationalists of 1798, or dangle the figures of Wolfe Tone and John Mitchel before their unsympathetic eyes. Not until the premiership of Sean Lemass was any positive attempt made to regard Protestant traditions as, in themselves, legitimate;[127] and this only exposed the poverty of nationalist thinking about the border in the previous 50 years, since Lemass had to devise a specific Northern Ireland policy, thus emphasising the point that, if Northern Ireland were not exactly a matter of foreign affairs, neither was it a domestic concern of the Irish nation, as anti-partitionists had always claimed.

The three-quarter nation had, in fact, parted company mentally as well as physically from the other quarter by the time of the 1949 proclamation of a republic, if not earlier: the experience of statehood was indeed rendering Northern Ireland and her problems a foreign rather than a home office question.[128] But it might be supposed that, since Northern Ireland was also a State, she might undergo the same experience; for, to add to her statehood was the undeniable and enduring fact of her unique regional qualities: her special community relations problems; her significant industrial character; the distinctions that existed between her people (Catholic and Protestant) and their religious counterparts in the south. It might be urged that in their way of life, their preoccupation with each other, their mutual occupation of a small, yet in many ways distinct, territory[129], Ulster Catholics and Protestants might find that, in the end, their State would help them to develop a sense of community, out of which might grow a form of local Ulster patriotism, from which might emerge a sense of national identity, and then possibly even an Ulster nationalism. In this way the state might build up 'diffuse' support that did not depend merely on the dispensation of specific benefits or rewards, but on a more long-term, general attachment that could survive temporary setbacks.[130]

The problem in evolving this kind of sentiment was that nationalism is the attribute not of nations, but of nationalists.[131] Sinn Féin had created nationalist unity, only to discover that, while it was able to free Ireland, it could not thereby create a united nation; and the discordant voices that were heard in southern Ireland after 1922 were only slowly and gradually stilled – and never completely stilled – by the modifying influence of sovereign statehood. The State was able to blend nationalist myth with its everyday operation and activity, to such an extent that, after 1949, few Irishmen born before that date were even aware of the fact that they had been born British subjects and citizens of the British commonwealth. And even fewer Protestants had any kind of contact with their once proud and powerful unionism.

For the Northern Ireland State to undergo such a transformation it needed a certain pattern of administration and a nationalist myth, thus enabling statehood to build nationhood. But it possessed, or found itself able to evolve, neither. There was no nationalist myth among the Protestant majority, no propaganda pointing to Cuchulainn as (for example) the founder of the nation, no tradition of a long struggle for national self-determination. Ulster Protestants certainly possessed an 'integrative myth'; but it was one inimical to the creation of an Ulster nation, for it included a deep suspicion of 'popery' and Roman Catholicism, both on theological and political grounds, and it involved a strong sense of 'loyalty' to Britain as the most effective way to prevent incorporation in a Catholic dominated Ireland.[132] Moreover, the apparatus of the state was used by successive unionist Governments to ensure that the Catholic minority was kept in its place, and unionist control of the police forces only increased the Roman Catholic awareness that this was indeed, as Sir James Craig remarked in an unguarded moment, 'a Protestant parliament for a Protestant state'.[133] The Unionist Government's acceptance that Catholics had 'their' districts, and its practice of confining loyal processions and symbols to Protestant districts, was a recognition that Northern Ireland consisted of various regions in which dwelt members of one 'side' or the other.[134]

It had taken nationalists in the south several decades to settle the question of allegiance to the state, and construct national unity out of the fragmentation of 1922. The diffuse support accorded to the state after 1939 was by no means inevitable; but the sense of nationality founded by the O'Connellite tradition, based on the Catholic religion and the historical experiences held to flow from possession of that religion, allied to a nationalist myth, and, most important of all, cemented together by the experience of statehood, enabled southern Ireland to accept that a nation was the same people living in the same place, and it might be added, under the same Government. Northern Ireland had no sense of nationality, no nationalist myth, and no unifying experience of statehood. In so far as an Ulster nationalism emerged at all, it was a purely Protestant, and never very convincing phenomenon;[135] indeed, the presence of Ulster flags in the 1970s might well have been a reflection of their cheapness, compared to the cost of the union flags normally waved by loyalists on commemorative occasions.[136] Stormont was the symbol of the defiance of Irish Catholic nationalism, not a symbol of Ulster Protestant nationalism. Moreover, since Ulster political leaders made the very existence of the parliament, of the state itself, an issue, Northern Ireland politics were again encouraged – if they need any encouragement – never to get beyond the 'first order' issues and into the less divisive 'second order' issues. When 'second order' issues were, apparently, the stuff of politics, the nationalist, religious and constitutional questions were never out of sight. The Ulster unionist Government was believed to be against the introduction of increased family allowances into Northern Ireland for fear that they might benefit Catholics, with their larger families;[137] and some members of the working-class Protestant community in the second half of the 1960s were convinced that 'Liberal' unionist socio-economic policies were deliberately channelling resources away from them to Catholics, as part of the overall strategy of 'appeasement'.[138]

It was this new unionist policy of 'appeasement' that seemed to promise political change in Northern Ireland. The retirement from the premiership of Lord Brookeborough in 1963, and the new style of political leadership of his successor, Terence O'Neill, was paralleled by an attempt on the part of Roman Catholics to rearrange the order of political priorities. Nationalist politicians in Ulster may have been united in their resentment of the border, but they had little else in common. They had no modern electoral machinery, no coherent strategy on the day-to-day managing of nationalist affairs, and were, like the unionists, divided by the often conflicting interests of the eastern part of the province, particularly the Belfast urban area, and the west of the River Bann, where rural constituencies prevailed.[139] In order to avoid the splitting of the Catholic vote they were obliged to make an electoral pact in the 1950s with Sinn Féin, whereby the nationists contested only Stormont seats, and left Westminster elections free for Sinn Féin candidates. But the middle-class leaders who emerged in the 1960s were impatient, both with the stagnant nature of nationalist politics, and with the continuing burden of discrimination practised against them by the state. The first significant change in Catholic political outlook came in 1964 when a 'political study group', National Unity, founded in 1959, arranged a convention of nationalist representatives to consider the idea of reunification by consent, and a new strategy of concentration on social and economic issues instead of the principle of the constitution. The nationalist party leader, Eddie McAteer, was hostile to the ambitions of the new movement, and when it did constitute itself the National Democratic Party in 1965 it made no impression on the electorate. But it had put forward the idea of a secular, progressive party, based on Catholics but not making its appeal exclusively to them.[140]

Catholic politics were by the mid-1960s moving into a more comprehensive, less nationalistic, and yet more militant phase. The founding of the Northern Ireland Civil Rights Association in 1967 was a sign that Northern Ireland Catholics had, for the time being at least, abandoned their old-style nationalist politics for a concentration on major Catholic grievances: and Catholic impatience with Terence O'Neill's modest reformism was increased by the nationalist party's abandonment of their old-style political ineffectiveness, based on the policy of boycott, for a new-style political ineffectiveness based on a policy of official opposition in Stormont.[141] The NICRA tacitly, and in some cases more openly, recognised the constitutional position of Northern Ireland; but their demands for reform, and their tactics of direct action, were perceived by many unionists, and especially the Protestant working classes, as a threat both to Protestant social and economic interests and to the stability of Northern Ireland itself.[142] Reformist unionism was essentially middle class and it found its base in the unionist party melting away as marches and demonstrations resulted in violence, with the very agents of the State's protection and security, the police and the special constabulary, subjected to British and international criticism.

But, apart from the practical difficulties of making a unionist government an instrument of change, O'Neill's idea of a Northern Ireland sense of community, which he believed was essential for the State's survival[143], was bedevilled by the same kind of ambivalence that was characteristic of Irish nationalism. For O'Neill, like the home rulers, like Sinn Féin, and like Sinn Féin's successors, Fine Gael and Fianna Fáil, spoke of 'our people', meaning, not the Roman Catholic and Protestant communities as a whole, but the community of which he was an ornament. And, like them, he expressed confidence that, if treated properly, the minority would behave just like the majority, or, as O'Neill himself put it in an unfortunate turn of phrase, they would 'live like Protestants'.[144] Moreover, again like the nationalists, he found it impossible to account for the behaviour of his own supporters; unionism, after all, covered the same wide social spectrum that nationalism did, and the unionist administrations of the past had always found it imperative to work hard at the task of preventing their rank and file from threatening unionist unity. This they managed to do by concentrating on the one great issue of the border;[145] but the task of accommodating the grievances of the minority, and assuaging the fears of the majority, even if it had been undertaken in a more vigorous and imaginative manner, would have proved beyond the capabilities of any traditionally sectarian party. Protestant unity was broken on the issue of civil rights, which destroyed the hegemony that the unionist party had enjoyed for 50 years, and produced a variety of unionist splinter groups and parties, including a strong, self-consciously working class, but still Protestant and loyalist, movement in the urban areas.[146] By contrast, Roman Catholics in their adversity discovered not only a sense of common purpose and action, but a modern political party, the Social Democratic and Labour party, founded in August 1970, and endowed with a coherent organisation and set of policies on a wide variety of issues. The SDLP did not speak for all Catholics in the province; but it had supplanted the old nationalist party and Sinn Féin, and it moved from constitutional opposition, through a difficult and harrowing period of abstentionism, to the new and far-reaching aim of participation in a power-sharing government of Northern Ireland.[147]

It might seem, therefore, that the Catholic role of political participation, allied to the willingness of some unionists to accept power-sharing, might provide the basis of the kind of co-operation that could lead to a new, non-sectarian state. But, as well as enduring the destructive effect of the provisional IRA campaign, begun in 1970 and continued with increasing ferocity during the last years of Stormont and the period of direct rule after the fall of Stormont in 1972, the new power-sharing administration of 1974 suffered from the inability to present itself as a 'national' government. This difficulty in turn sprang from the fact that Ulster politics, unlike southern Irish politics, had never been cast in a 'national' role. No one in Ulster thought of the province or its people as a nation: Ulster unionists saw themselves as a Protestant community, the 'loyal' element in Ireland, and gave no more than passive acquiescence to the idea, held by some in Britain, that there were 'two nations' in Ireland, as different from each other as any two nations in the world.[148] Ulster nationalists were nationalists of Ireland, seeing themselves as part of the Catholic Irish nation; and when they abandoned this cross-border nationalism for internal reform and de facto recognition of the State of Northern Ireland, they were asked by the British Government to participate in nation-building, in power-sharing with many of their major civil rights grievances still outstanding, and without that most essential part of any State's apparatus placed in the new executive's hands: the legal use of force.[149] By 1939 southern Governments had managed to persuade their people that they had the right to use force, and a rightful monopoly of its use; by 1974 the Government of Northern Ireland still had not established that right, and, since security was reserved to Westminster, would not be given the opportunity to establish it. Yet the experience of southern Ireland had shown how essential was the possession of full State powers in all departments of government and administration, if nation-building were to have any chance of success.

But even if the power-sharing executive had been endowed with the full range of governmental functions, it would still have had to overcome two formidable obstacles: the suspicion among many Protestants, especially among the working classes, that power-sharing unionism was yet another betrayal of loyal interests by weak unionist political leaders; and the unnatural nature of a power-sharing government that rested upon no long-established or well-defined political tradition. It had taken nationalist leaders in southern Ireland years of patient endeavour to construct 'national unity' in nineteenth and early twentieth century Ireland, and a long period of effort to reconstruct that concept in the new Irish sovereign state. Unionist and SDLP politicians had no myth of 'national unity' to draw upon, no proper State apparatus to manipulate, and, above all, no time to develop either of these essentials of nation-building before they were confronted with a British general election that was, in effect, a referendum on the Sunningdale power-sharing agreement, and one that augured badly for its future.[150] In May 1974 a loyalist workers' strike quickly gathered support from all sections of the Protestant community, and not only brought down the executive, but revealed how dependent it was on the British Government for its preservation.[151] The contrast with the Free State was instructive: had William Cosgrave called upon the British Government, and British troops, to suppress anti-treaty activity in 1922, the Free State would have perished in ignominy.

Power-sharing in Northern Ireland was not only confronted with these internal complexities, it had also to contend with the vacillations of the Dublin Government, which was suddenly brought face to face with the contradictions of its political assumptions and its 50 years of statehood. The nationalist tradition required Dublin to recognise that, as the Taoiseach Jack Lynch put it in August 1969, 'the reunification of the national territory can provide the only permanent solution for the problem',[152] and there were some prominent members of his Government who were prepared to resurrect the idea of achieving this 'reunification' by force of arms.[153] The activities of the provisional IRA in the north struck some early sympathetic response, especially in the border areas, for the romantic notion of the 'boys of the column' lingered, until press and television exposure of violence deprived them of most of the romanticism that they still possessed.[154]

The Council of Ireland, a body established by the Sunningdale agreement on the lines of the 1920 council to discuss matters of common concern, was pressed upon the official unionist leader, Brian Faulkner, by Dublin and the SDLP as the price of their co-operation. But, despite continual assurances by southern leaders that, as Lynch put it, 'any Irishman is an Irishman' and that Protestants 'need have no fear in a country whose sovereignty they would share, and in whose councils they would have a strong voice, of any interference with their religious and civil liberties'[155], southern Ireland was simply not prepared to take the steps necessary to fundamentally modify, let alone dispel, the attitudes and assumptions fostered by 50 years of national independence.[156] Their limited understanding of Northern Ireland's problems revealed one of the most significant developments in modern Irish politics: the parochialism of the three-quarter nation, its limited horizons, and its dangerous desire to combine nationalist rhetoric with an unwillingness to pay the full price of national unity.

For the stuff of politics in the south of Ireland remained local concerns, local problems, or, as her politicians would have claimed, 'national' concerns, 'national' problems, such as rates, jobs, employment, prices and the managing of the nation's resources.[157] Occasional concessions to the 'unity' question, such as the deletion of the special position of the Roman Catholic church from the constitution, were insignificant when set beside the preoccupations of the modern sovereign state; the revolt of a million taxpayers against the excessive demands of the Irish inland revenue was perceived as a greater threat to the government of the Fianna Fáil leader, Charles Haughey, than the revolt of a million Protestants against Irish unification. In so far as the Ulster crisis — especially the IRA hunger strike deadlock — impinged on the 1981 general election in the Republic, it emphasized that, while some politicians and sections of the electorate had a northern Ireland posture, they had (after thirteen years of turmoil in the north) no Northern Ireland policy. And the question asked by one Irish historian: 'Had a homogeneous twenty-six county sovereign state developed to the point where it no longer wished to consider the radically disturbing implications of a union of Catholic, Protestant and Dissenter',[158] remains, for good or ill, a rhetorical one.

Notes

1. From 'Parnell's funeral' (1935).

2. K.O'Higgins, *Three years Hard Labour: an Address to the Irish Society of Oxford*, 31 October, 1924.

3. M. MacSwiney, *Where We Stand Now: the Truth About the Republic*, (March, 1924).

4. F. Munger, *The Legitimacy of Opposition: the Change of Government in Ireland in 1932*, (London, 1975), p. 8.

5. Columban na banban, *Lecture on the Ethics of the Irish Revolution* (Sinn Féin Ard Comhairle, March, 1924).

6. Munger, op. cit., pp.29-32. Lyons, *Ireland Since the Famine*, pp. 482-5.

7. Munger, p. 29; for Sinn Féin protests see J.A. Gaughan, op. cit., pp. 249-50.

8. J. Meenan, *The Irish Economy Since 1922*, (Liverpool, 1970), pp. 270-75, 332.

9. W.K. Hancock, *Survey of British Commonwealth Affairs*, vol. *i*, *Problems of Nationality* (London, 1937), pp. 323-4.

10. D.W. Harkness, *The Restless Dominion* (London, 1969), passim.

11. *Irish Press*, 5 Feb. 1932 (Mr Brady in Blackrock, Co. Dublin).

12. Munger, op. cit., pp. 8-9; J.A. Murphy, 'The new IRA, 1925-62', in T.D. Williams (ed.), *Irish Secret Societies*, pp. 150-65; Rumpf and Hepburn, op. cit., pp. 89-92.

13. Munger, p. 22. For the continuity of the Irish administration, and a brief discussion of the British legacy see B. Chubb, 'Fifty years of Irish administration' in O. Dudley Edwards and F. Pyle, op. cit., pp. 182-90.

14. T.P. O'Neill, 'In search of a political path: Irish republicanism, 1922 to 1927', in *Historical Studies*, x (1976), p. 157.

15. Ibid, p. 159; Gaughan, op. cit., pp. 326-33.

16. O'Neill, op. cit., pp. 161-2.

17. Ibid., pp. 163-9.

18. Ibid., p. 170.

19. Gaughan, op. cit., pp. 262-3.

20. Munger, op. cit., p. 9; Murphy, op. cit., pp. 67-71.

21. Munger, p. 22.

22. T.P. Coogan, *The IRA* (London, 1970), pp. 56-9.

23. J.A. Murphy, 'The new IRA, 1925-62', op. cit., pp. 153-4.

24. Munger, pp. 11-12.

25. Ibid., pp. 26-7.

26. Eamon de Valera, *The Way to Peace* (Dublin, 1934).

27. De Valera, *National Discipline and Majority Rule*, (Fianna Fáil pamphlet, No. 1, 1936).

28. Murphy, *Ireland in the Twentieth Century*, p. 50.

29. *National Discipline*.

30. Ibid.

31. 'Oglach', *Oglach na nEireann* (Dublin, 1932), see also *Governmental Policy and Constitution of Oglach na nEireann, adopted by the General Army Convention*, March, 1934 (Dublin, n.d.).

32. Murphy, 'New IRA', pp. 156-7.

33. B. O'Higgins, *Martyrs for Ireland: the Story of MacCormick and Barnes* (Dublin, 1940).

34. B. Share, *The Emergency: Neutral Ireland, 1939-45*, (Dublin, 1978), p. 81; Earl of Longford and T.P. O'Neill, *Eamon de Valera* (London, 1970), pp. 359-60.

35. Fianna Fáil's *National Policy*, (May 1926) only ruled out the use of force

on practical grounds: force was impossible while 'an elected native government under contract with the enemy to maintain his overlordship stands in the way with a native army at its command', (p.6), though perhaps the use of the word 'native' foreshadowed the later position (1936), when de Valera declared that the army of the state was a 'parliamentary army in theory and in practice' (*National Discipline*). In that same pamphlet de Valera stated that the use of the name 'IRA' by any non-state, illegal bodies was a 'usurpation'.

36. *Irish Press*, 3 Feb. 1932.

37. Ibid., 1 Feb., 12 Feb. 1932.

38. Fianna Fáil, *A National Policy*, p. 25.

39. *Irish Press*, 18 Feb. 1932.

40. Ibid., 9 Feb. 1932.

41. Ibid., 16 Feb. 1932.

42. Ibid.

43. Ibid., 15 Feb., 16 Feb. 1932; see also leader in first issue of *Irish Press*, 5 Sept. 1931.

44. Harkness, 'England's Irish question' in C. Cook and G. Peele (eds.), *The Politics of Reappraisal, 1918-1939*, (London, 1975), pp. 39-63; and 'Mr. de Valera's dominion' in *Journal of Commonwealth Political Studies*, vol. *viii* (1970), pp. 206-28; Lyons, *Ireland Since the Famine*, pp. 513, 533-36.

45. Hancock, op. cit., p. 349.

46. De Valera, 'opening speech of Athlone broadcasting station', 6 Feb. 1933, *Recent Speeches and Broadcasts* (Dublin, 1938), p. 50.

47. Murphy, *Ireland in Twentieth Century*, p. 78; Rumpf and Hepburn, op. cit., pp. 115-16.

48. Hancock, op. cit., p. 367.

49. Gaughan, op. cit., pp. 311-13 (oration delivered at Austin Stack's grave, June 1929).

50. *Irish Press*, 6 Feb. 1932 (Mr Fahy).

51. Hancock, op. cit., p. 377.

52. *Irish Independent*, 13 Jan. 1948.

53. Murphy, *Ireland in the Twentieth Century*, pp. 106-7.

54. For the political background to this see M. Manning, *Irish Political Parties* (Dublin, 1972), pp. 101-6.

55. N. Mansergh, *Survey of British Commonwealth Affairs: Problems of Wartime Co-operation and Post-War Change 1939-1952*, (London, 1958), pp. 287-88.

56. Mary C. Bromage, 'Image of nationhood' in *Eire/Ireland*, vol. *III*, No. iii (Autumn, 1968), p. 25.

57. Costello, *The Heart Grown Brutal*, p. 189.

58. Comerford, *Kickham*, pp. 210-11.

59. Costello, op. cit., p. 188.

60. *The Path to Freedom*, p. 123.

61. *Recent Speeches and Broadcasts*, pp. 60-61.

62. Ibid., p. 29; J.H. Whyte, *Church and State in Modern Ireland*, (Dublin, 1971 edn.), p.48.

63. Whyte, pp. 42-6 discusses the only *cause celebre* in this area, the case of Miss Dunbar-Harrison's appointment as librarian in Co. Mayo, in 1930. For de Valera's condemnation of a later incident, the boycott of Protestants by Catholics in Fethard on Sea, Co. Wexford, in 1957, see Whyte, pp. 322-4.

64. For a balanced and sensitive treatment of the minority see Jack White, *Minority Report, the Protestant Community in the Irish Republic*, (Dublin, 1975), pp. 91-182.

65. Lyons, *Ireland Since the Famine*, pp. 540-42.

66. Whyte, op. cit., pp. 158-65, 179-93.

67. E.D. Steele, 'Gladstone, Irish violence and conciliation', op. cit., pp. 258-9.
68. Munger, op. cit., p. 16.
69. R. Dudley Edwards, *Patrick Pearse*, pp. 340-41.
70. Gaelic League pamphlet, *Irish Literature*, by 'Torna' (Dublin, n.d. (1937?)).
71. Brendan S. Mac Aodha, 'Was this a social revolution', in S. O Tuama (ed.), *The Gaelic League Idea*, p. 29.
72. *The Path of Freedom*, p. 27.
73. B.S. Mac Aodha, op. cit., pp. 29-30.
74. C.O. Danachair, 'The Gaeltacht', in B Ó Cuív, *View of the Irish Language*, p. 120.
75. Murphy, *Ireland in the Twentieth Century*, pp. 85-7; Hancock, op. cit., pp. 347-68.
76. J.J. Lee, 'Sean Lemass', in *Ireland, 1945-1970*, (Dublin, 1979), p. 16.
77. J.A. Murphy, 'The Irish party system, 1938-51', in K.B. Nowlan (ed.), *Ireland in the War Years and After* (Dublin, 1969), pp. 158-62.
78. *Irish Independent*, 21 Jan. 1948.
79. Ibid., 24 Jan. 1948.
80. Ibid., 26 Jan. 1948.
81. *Cork Examiner*, 16 Feb. 1957.
82. Ibid., 27 Feb. 1957.
83. Ibid., 8 March 1957; see also *Irish Press*, 1 March 1957.
84. Ibid., 22 Feb., 2 March 1957.
85. *Irish Press*, 4 March 1957.
86. Manning, *Irish Political Parties*, pp. 50-53.
87. Lyons, op. cit., pp. 618-20; Longford and O'Neill, *Eamon de Valera*, p. 329.
88. Lee, op. cit., pp. 16-21.
89. Lyons, op. cit., pp. 622-3.
90. Lee, op. cit., p. 18; J.A. Murphy, ' "Put them out!" Parties and elections, 1948-69', in Lee, op. cit., pp. 4-6.
91. For contemporary references to de Valera as the 'new Parnell' see D. Gwynn, *de Valera*, (London, 1933), p. 255; S. O Faolain, *The Life Story of Eamon de Valera*, (Dublin, 1933), pp. 9, 53.
92. Meenan, op. cit., pp. 280-81; see also B. Chubb, *The Government and Politics of Ireland*, (London, 1974 edn.), appendix A.
93. T. Garvin, The destiny of the soldiers: tradition and modernity in the politics of de Valera's Ireland', in *Political Studies*, vol. *XXVI*, No. 3, (Sept. 1978), p. 347.
94. J.A. Murphy, 'Put them out', op. cit., p. 10.
95. M. Gallagher, *Electoral Support for Irish Political Parties, 1927-1973*, (London, 1976), pp. 29-32.
96. Garvin, op. cit., passim; Murphy, 'The Irish party system, 1938-51', op cit., pp. 150-51; Murphy, 'Put them out', op. cit., pp. 5-11.
97. Murphy, 'Put them out', pp. 7-8, 12-13.
98. Gallagher, op. cit., pp. 46-69; Murphy, 'Put them out', p. 12.
99. Murphy, 'The Irish party system', op. cit., p. 151.
100. Chubb, op. cit., pp. 77-87; Gallagher, op. cit., pp. 69-70.
101. Rumpf and Hepburn, op. cit., p. 153.
102. Ibid., p. 185.
103. Indeed, it was Sean Lemass who suggested that the Nationalists become the official parliamentary opposition in Stormont in 1965, (P. Bew, P. Gibbon and H. Patterson, *The State in Northern Ireland, 1921-1972*, (Manchester, 1979), p. 164).
104. Murphy, 'The new IRA', op. cit., pp. 160-63.
105. *Cork Examiner*, 16 Feb. 1957.

106. *Irish Press*, 2 March 1957.

107. Ibid., 4 March 1957.

108. *Cork Examiner*, 9 March 1957.

109. The phrase is F.S.L. Lyons's (*Ireland Since the Famine*, p. 672).

110. It would be tedious to recite the numerous examples of this mode of thought, but see E. Larkin, 'A reconsideration: Daniel Corkery and his ideas on cultural nationalism', in *Éire/Ireland*, vol. *VIII*, i (Spring, 1973), pp. 42-51. R.J. Loftus, *Nationalism in Modern Anglo-Irish Poetry*, pp. 236-45. And for a typical contemporary account, J. Hanley, *The National Ideal*, (Dublin, 1931), pp. 9, 37-8, 63, 130, 216.

111. Ó Cuív, op. cit., p. 111.

112. J.A. Murphy, 'Identity change in the republic of Ireland', in *Études Irlandaises*, vol. *5* (1976), pp. 148-9.

113. B. Share, *The Emergency*, pp. 142-3.

114. Whyte, *Church and State in Modern Ireland*, Chap. xi.

115. T. Garvin, 'Nationalist elites, Irish voters and Irish political development: a comparative perspective', in *Economic and Social Review*, vol. *8*, No. 3 (1976-77), p. 184; see also M. Bax, *Harpstrings and Confessions: Machine Style politics in the Irish Republic* (Amsterdam, 1976), esp. pp. 45-53.

116. Jack White, op. cit., p. 192.

117. J. Whyte, *Church and State*, p. 3.

118. Mary C. Bromage, 'Image of nationhood', op. cit., p. 20.

119. For an excellent analysis of Ulster Protestants' rejection of the nationalist idea see D.W. Millar, *Queen's Rebels*, passim, esp. pp. 64-86.

120. Bew, *et al*, pp. 67-8; Buckland, *The Factory of Grievances: devolved government in Northern Ireland, 1921-39*, (Dublin, 1979), pp. 72-3.

121. I. MacAllister and S. Nelson, 'Modern developments in the Northern Ireland party system', in *Parliamentary Affairs*, vol. *32* (1978-9), pp. 298-9.

122. A. Mitchell, op. cit., p. 212.

123. *Recent Speeches and Broadcasts*, pp. 13-14.

124. Murphy, *Ireland in the Twentieth Century*, p. 101.

125. Bew, *et al.*, op. cit., pp. 124-5.

126. Buckland, op. cit., pp. 73-77, 110-16.

127. Lee, 'Sean Lemass', pp. 22-3.

128. The spectacle of an Orange banner with an Irish language device was taken notice of officially in Summer 1970, by the Department of external affairs (C.C. O'Brien, *States of Ireland*, p. 75).

129. For an illuminating analysis of this see R. Harris, *Prejudice and Tolerance in Ulster* (Manchester, 1972).

130. Miller, op. cit., p. 130.

131. D. Fitzpatrick, 'The geography of Irish nationalism', op. cit., p. 113.

132. F. Wright, 'Protestant ideology and politics in Ulster', in *European Journal of Sociology*, vol. *14* (1973), pp. 213-80.

133. Buckland, op. cit., p. 72.

134. Miller, op. cit., pp. 137-8.

135. Ibid., pp. 53-4.

136. As suggested by Wright, op. cit., p. 237, fn 51.

137. D.P. Barritt and C.F. Carter, *The Northern Ireland Problem: a Study in Group Relations*, (London, 1962), pp. 110-11; for other examples see D. Birrell and A. Murie, *Policy and government in Northern Ireland: Lessons of devolution* (Dublin, 1980), pp. 250-51, 284-5.

138. Wright, op. cit., p. 276.

139. For the geographical and political variations between east and west Ulster see I. MacAllister, 'Territorial differentiation and party development in Northern

Ireland', University of Strathclyde, Centre for the study of public policy, paper no. 66 (1980); Buckland, op. cit., p. 33; Bew *et al.*, op. cit., pp. 164-5.

140. I. McAllister, 'Political opposition in Northern Ireland: the National Democratic Party, 1965-1970', in *Economic and Social Review*, vol. 6, No. 3, (1975), pp. 353-66.

141. Bew, *et al.*, op. cit., p. 169.

142. Miller, op. cit., pp. 141-3; Wright, op. cit., pp. 272-77.

143. Wright, op. cit., p. 271.

144. O'Brien, op. cit., p. 170.

145. For some examples see I. Budge and C. O'Leary, 'Permanent supremacy and perpetual opposition: the parliament in Northern Ireland, 1921-72', in A.F. Eldridge (ed.), *Legislatures in Plural Societies* (Indiana, 1977) pp. 172-3.

146. For a useful analysis and list see McAllister and Nelson, op. cit., pp. 279-316.

147. McAllister, 'political parties and social change in Ulster: the case of the SDLP' in *Social Studies*, vol. 5, No. i, (1976), pp. 75-89; *The Northern Ireland Social Democratic and Labour party*, (London, 1977).

148. Miller, op. cit., p. 112; P.J. Buckland, *James Craig*, (Dublin, 1980), p. 19.

149. Miller, op. cit., pp. 163-4.

150. Anti-Sunningdale candidates in the election polled 51.1 per cent of the votes cast and won eleven of the twelve Northern Ireland seats in Westminster; the combined votes of the executive parties (Unionist, Alliance and SDLP) amounted to only 38.6 per cent, (I. McAllister, 'The legitimacy of opposition: the collapse of the 1974 Northern Ireland executive', in *Eire/Ireland*, vol. *XII*, No. 4 (1977), pp. 36-7).

151. Miller, op. cit., p. 164; McAllister, op. cit., pp. 37-40.

152. J. Lynch, *Speeches and Statements on Irish Unity, Northern Ireland, and Anglo-Irish Relations, August 1969-October 1971* (Dublin, 1978), p. 3.

153. O'Brien, op. cit., pp. 208-16.

154. Murphy, 'Identity change in the republic of Ireland', op. cit., p. 152.

155. Lynch, op. cit., pp. 28, 31.

156. For the impact of these on Sunningdale see McAllister, 'The legitimacy of opposition', op. cit., pp. 34-6.

157. See e.g., the *Irish Times*' comment on the 1973 general election in the republic, 1 and 3 March 1973.

158. Murphy, *Ireland in the Twentieth Century*, p. 171; for a valuable analysis of southern Irish attitudes in the 1960s see Garret Fitzgerald, *Towards a New Ireland*, (Dublin, 1972), esp. pp. 19-20, 45-6, 53-4, 94-5.

CONCLUSION: IRELAND AND NATIONALISM

The strength and endurance of the nationalist tradition in Ireland gives that country its distinctive place in the history of the British Isles. Wales and Scotland possessed as strong, and in many respects more deep-rooted, sentiments of nationality; Scotland had the additional advantage of an existence as a united, distinct kingdom for hundreds of years, while Ireland was a fragmented polity. Yet it was Ireland that most strongly resisted English colonization in the sixteenth and seventeenth centuries, which enjoyed a separate, if subordinate legislature in the eighteenth century, when Scotland was united with England, and which, when modern politics began to develop in the mid-nineteenth century, sent to Westminster not Liberals, but, in their place, Irish nationalists of varying shades and hues. Ireland alone developed a significant physical force tradition; yet in the eighteenth century it was Scotland which, for 50 years, remained the most rebellious part of the British Isles. Wales retained her linguistic identity longer and more effectively than Ireland; yet it was in Ireland that a strong cultural nationalist movement rose, which did not lose its momentum, but strongly influenced separatist nationalism in the early twentieth century. And it was Ireland alone that broke away from the United Kingdom and evolved a completely independent sovereign status. Irish nationalism is, in a word, (and using that word in the vulgar, popular sense) 'Irish': paradoxical, self-contradictory and guided by its own internal logic.

The historian, faced with these contradictions, might seek solace, possibly even explanation, in the general laws of social science: if Ireland and Irish nationalism were subjected to the rigorous methodology of the social sciences, instead of the very imprecise and discrete analysis offered here, the short sharp shock might bring Irish nationalism to its senses. And, thus stabilized, Ireland might conform, or be made to conform, to the rules of the game, instead of pursuing her own wayward path.

Since it is accepted medical practice to subject a recalcitrant patient to the latest cure prescribed by experts, the theory of modernization might first be applied. Modernization has been defined as 'the complex of social changes which accompany the transformation of an agricultural society into one dominated by, or in the shadow of, factory

375

industry'. Modernization erodes traditional social structures, and its effect is 'uneven', 'hitting' different territories at different times. In a primitive society there is generally a highly developed structure in which each individual occupies a clearly ascribed role regulating his relationships to every other member; but in a modern, complex society, with a wide variety of individuals playing different roles, relationships are 'ephemeral, non-repetitive, and optional'. Thus 'communication, the symbols, language (in the literal or in the extended sense) that is employed, become crucial'. Since the individual's essence is no longer simply his social position, he must carry his identity with him: his 'culture' becomes his identity; and classification of men by culture is the classification of nationality. Thus men become concerned about the 'ethnic rubric' under which they survive. Moreover, since literacy is the minimal requirement for effective membership of a modernizing society, only a nation-size educational system can command the resources to produce universal literacy. The nation therefore becomes the minimal political unity in the modern world. And this is reinforced by the fact that the products of the educational system are generally mobile within the linguistic frontiers corresponding to it, but not mobile across these frontiers.

The particular nation which an individual calls his own is decided by the uneven effects of modernization: thus a territory whose inhabitants enjoy the fruits of modernization will be resented by those members of a territory who are suffering only its dislocative effects. If this resentment can find expression in some easily identifiable differentiation — skin colour, deep rooted or religiously sanctioned custom — then their lot will be even worse, and their resentment can be expressed in a 'national' way. Their own intellectual class will perceive that, first of all they are not welcome in the ranks of the more affluent territories because of their special cultural characteristics; and, secondly, that they can best prosper by monopolizing the desirable posts in the new nation which is in the process of formation. The nation is distinguished from other loyalty evoking groups (the tribe, the kin, the clan) by its mass nature and by the definition of its membership by 'culture'.[1]

This theory of the origins of nationalism can conveniently be set beside two different, but closely related, theses, both involving the idea of uneven modernization. The uneven spread of development means that some people suffer by this process; the backward country, like Ireland, is confronted with the blind process of capitalist metropolitan-centred development and will be crushed into 'some kind of prolonged colonialism' unless it fights back, and resists. The basis of this resistance is not class, but nationality, for it is in nationality that the 'ancient social formations' found their fault lines.[2] A second theory, that of 'internal colonization', is also founded on the idea of the 'core' region, inhabited by the ethnic group which dominates its own region and the development that takes place in the peripheral regions. The peripheral regions find their economies shaped by their need to meet the demands of the core region; Ireland, for example, developed a one-sided dependence on a subordinate agricultural economy based on the supply of cattle to industrial Britain. The failure of this cattle-based economy in the 1870s helps explain the initial emergence of Irish nationalism as a mass electoral phenomenon, for trade unions or a labour party could not penetrate this kind of economy. Nationalism was therefore a political response to 'internal colonisation'; and the ethnic identity of the periphery provides a basis for the movement of resistance. Regional inequality and ethnic identity, in Ireland, created nationalism.[3]

It would be inappropriate here to discuss the defects of these theories in explaining the general phenomenon of nationalism;[4] but their application to the case of Ireland requires investigation. The theory of internal colonization might account, in part, for the rise of the home rule movement of the late nineteenth century: the economic depression which struck Ireland in the 1870s caused a lowering of prices for Irish agricultural exports, and the success of the home rulers was based, in large degree, on the rise of the land league in the west. But Irish nationalism pre-dated this crisis: the Fenians were active from the 1850s onwards, and Isaac Butt founded his home government association before 1879. It could be argued their neither the Fenians nor the early home rulers succeeded in mobilizing the masses for nationalism, whereas Parnell did after 1879; but here again it is important to point out that O'Connell did succeed in (to use Dr W.J. Argyle's well-chosen word) mustering[5] mass support for repeal of the union. Repeal of the union might be dismissed as not a truly 'national' demand; but the radical nationalism of Sinn Féin cannot be thus dismissed, and this was a mass movement and one that bore no relationship to the cattle trade. Nationalism in Ireland flourished after the land question was settled in 1903, and settled in favour of the periphery 'ethnic' group.[6]

The theory that nationalism was the response to the blind process of capitalist metropolitan-centred development may now be considered; and, here again, some symptoms in the patient correspond to the diagnosis. James Connolly believed that Ireland must free herself from the stranglehold of English capitalism; the Irish question was a social question; and the progress of the fight for national liberty must 'keep pace with the progress of the struggle for liberty of the most subject class in that nation'.[7] Certainly the ranks of militant Irish nationalism were most often filled from the lower orders, farm labourers, urban workers, and the like; but the solid core of Irish nationalism from the mid-nineteenth century onwards was the Irish tenant farmer, a conservative, yet tenaciously nationalist, class. And Michael Collins, who came from a humble background, condemned the killing of landlords as murder, *unless* it was done as an act of national liberation, not as an act of the oppressed member of a class against his *economic* oppressor. Then there was the difficulty, that Connolly himself never solved, of comprehending the unwillingness of the Belfast 'oppressed' classes to participate in the nationalist movement. It was, and is, fashionable to ascribe this to a form of 'false consciousness' induced by the Belfast bourgeoisie, who used religious differences to divide the working class from itself; but the introduction of the question of religion further increases the difficulty of applying this thesis to Ireland; and, furthermore, the thesis fails to explain why Arthur Griffith, the founder of Sinn Féin, looked, not to the workers or farm labourers for the salvation of the nation from the Saxon, but to the very business classes who were, presumably, benefiting most from the status quo. William Martin Murphy, the Dublin Catholic and nationalist capitalist, was as guilty of the oppression of the workers as was any English capitalist; and he was eager to call in the AOH to break strikes and demonstrations in the interest of 'national unity'.

Gellner's theory of modernization offers a partial, but defective, explanation of nationalism. In particular, his belief in the defection of the periphery's intellectual class from allegiance to the centre because they are not welcome in the more affluent society, and their consequent desire to monopolize the best jobs in the new nation which is in the process of formation, finds some reflection in the Irish experience. Anti-Irish feeling in Victorian Britain ran high, coupled as it often was with anti-Catholic sentiment;[8] and the home rulers, at least, could look forward to a utopia of job-holding in the new Ireland that they could not contemplate in Britain. But, again, exceptions arise: many Anglo-Irishmen of the elite sections of society were able to pursue very successful careers in Britain and in the empire, but that did not prevent some leading members of this group from embracing nationalism. These men might be dismissed as not truly representative of the nation; but, while many home-rule Catholics looked forward to, and indeed already practised, jobbery, the Sinn Féin purists of the early twentieth century did not become nationalists to secure their material position in an independent Ireland: on the contrary, they despized the brokerage and place hunting of the parliamentarians, and often sacrificed already promising careers in teaching, and university work, to free their country. O'Connellism was strongly influenced by the desire to create opportunities for able members of the Irish middle and professional classes; but Davisites became nationalists in order to frustrate the sordid materialism of the age, and Davisites were drawn almost solely from the intellectuals. In any case, O'Connell himself was willing to forego repeal of the union if his professional men were allowed to prosper within its framework.

The exceptions to the diagnosis offered by the theorists of modernization and its impact do not, of course, render these theories completely useless. Indeed, they help the historian to understand more fully certain turning points or episodes in the evolution of the subject which he is considering. But the theories do not explain why, for example, Wales reacted to modernization by turning, not to nationalism, but to radicalism and then socialism; why Wales sought, not self-government nor separation, but equal treatment with the core region.[9] They do not account for the enduring appeal and popularity of the idea, not only of nationality in Ireland, but of the nation state;[10] of the restoration of Ireland's legislative independence. Nor do these theories explain the varied, and often highly contradictory, nature of Irish nationalism: its confusion of beliefs, ranging from democratic theory to jacobinism, from constitutionalism to revolution, from comprehensive nationality to sectarianism, from French republicanism and enlightenment to the 'seminarist gallantry of Trent',[11] from Marxism to near-fascism. Anyway, nationalists were individuals, and their beliefs and actions were often influenced by their personal experiences: Michael Collins was, as he himself put it, of plain Irish stock whose principles are burnt into them; Austen Stack followed, almost fatalistically, in his Fenian father's footsteps;[12] Liam Mellowes read a copy of Bulmer Hobson's *Irish Freedom* and promptly joined Na Fianna Eireann, a militant nationalist youth movement;[13] Liam Lynch was inspired by a desire to avenge the martyred dead of 1916;[14] Thomas Davis by his hatred of modernization and Yankeeism; Charles Gavan Duffy, originally, by his dislike of Davis's religion; and one anonymous politician in Mayo by his observation when:

I was but a little child with my book going to school, and by the house there I saw the (land) agent. He took the unfortunate tenant and thrun him in the road, and I saw the man's wife come out crying and the agent's wife thrun her in the channel, and when I saw that, though I was but a child, I swore I'd be a Nationalist. I swore by heaven, and I swore by hell and all the rivers that run through there.[15]

Theories of nationalism of the social scientific type do not take account of the multiple and varied nature of human experience, of the rich variety of the nationalist tradition in Ireland. They are rather like the cartography of the ancient or medieval world, which corresponds in some respects to a modern map: as one moves the traced outline over the modern map, one recognizes a river here and a contour there; but while some features are recognizable enough, many are widely distorted, still more are omitted altogether, and all suffer from a lack of fine detail, of the minutiae that render the whole intelligible.

So, of course, does this book; for a general survey cannot provide a satisfactory map of such a complex and crowded landscape as Irish nationalism. But it is hoped that this general survey might offer a coherent and comprehensive map that researchers can fill in, and of course alter, by the historical equivalent of ordnance survey work. And the main guidelines, it is argued, are the investigation and uncovering of the dual inheritance of Irish history, of the 'interaction between different cultures',[16] that takes its origin many hundreds of years ago in the arrival in Ireland of the first Englishmen; the impact of British policy in Ireland; and the social change that took place in Ireland under the union, social change that was influenced in important ways by British legislation.

The Anglo-Irish, as they later came to be called, both Catholic and Protestant, were not merely crafty and greedy adventurers, but men who had special reasons for showing a degree of political and constitutional sophistication more advanced than that of the Gaelic population. They were both English and Irish, English by blood or birth and Irish by geographical circumstances, and their attitude to their former country, England, and their adopted country, Ireland, was to say the least, ambivalent. They were never far from home; yet they were also at home; and they developed a complex range of reactions to both their homelands. For England they felt affection and regard, and they gloried in the nobility of their origins; but they were able to reconcile that sentiment with pride in their new homeland. As the seventeenth century Old English author, John Lynch, put it:

> As seeds transplanted from their native climate to a foreign soil
> change their nature and qualities, and imbibe the properties of the
> new land in which they are planted and grow to maturity, so when
> the colonist fixes his home and embarks his hopes, and sees his
> children growing around him under a foreign sky, the land of his
> adoption becomes more dear to him than the mother country.[17]

By the beginning of the early modern period Ireland was a hotch-
potch of races and cultures; but although there was, as might be expected, much cultural, linguistic and social interchange, a political distinction, based on national origin, remained.[18] After the reformation the
national distinction became identified with religion; and English government policy forced the Old English into the arms of the native Irish,
and with the willing assistance of the new English, and the somewhat
more qualified support of the Ulster Scots, encompassed the ruin of
both.

From the beginning of the eighteenth century it became more and
more possible for the victorious new English to think of themselves as
the Irish nation. Like John Lynch, they imbibed the properties of the
new land, and rejected with indignation the name of Anglo-Irish; but
their concept of nationality suffered from one overwhelming defect:
they were a minority in Ireland, and if the Roman Catholic majority
ever managed to reassert itself, their claims to be the people of Ireland
would appear absurd. The only way in which they could maintain their
claims would be by incorporating the Roman Catholics, or those of
them whose trading and commercial talents had brought them position
in the community, into the nation, providing leadership and tutelage
in such a way as to defend themselves against the encroachments of an
age of reform, political, then economic and social. But not only prejudice stood in the way of such an identification of interests; Protestant
power, won in the seventeenth century, might not survive the rise of a
Roman Catholic democracy. It might be saved, however, if the Irish
Protestant minority relied upon the British Protestant majority for
defence and support. Thus the Roman Catholics were divided, not only
from their Protestant minority, but from the British Protestant
majority; and any loyalty the Catholics may have felt towards the
crown — and such loyalty was felt by the Roman Catholic hierarchy
and influential laity in the time of the French revolution — was soon
dissipated by the recognition that the Roman Catholics had majority
status in Ireland, but minority status in the United Kingdom; and,
moreover, their Protestant minority was able to rely on the British to

defend privileges that seemed more appropriate to a majority in Ireland as well: local power, landed monopoly, and an established church — and, above all, a sense of superiority, of being the masters in the new Ireland as in the old.

The mainstream of Irish nationalism, therefore, involved mounting an attack not only on England, the alleged originator of Ireland's ills, but on the Protestant minority in Ireland, who sheltered behind the British Protestants' skirts. This attack — from the time of O'Connell to that of Redmond — was not of course upon Protestants as such; it was upon Protestant power and privilege, on the Protestant's refusal to accept the inevitable fact that the Roman Catholics were the majority, the Irish people, and must eventually have their way in Ireland. Many nationalists saw their campaign as a species of religious crusade; but most regarded it as the assertion by a downtrodden and dispossessed people of their right to be masters in their own house. British reforms in the nineteenth century could not undermine this sentiment, for such reforms were not, in the eyes of nationalists, reforms at all: they were simply something on account, a down payment for all the wrongs done by England (and by her Protestant lackeys) in the past. It was because material advancement, in the professions, in public life, in land ownership, in local government, and a strong sense of historical wrong went hand in hand in Ireland that nationalism lost none of its momentum.

This sense of English perfidy and enmity was not, of course, plucked from nowhere: it took great leaders like O'Connell, a strong nationalist propaganda machine, pamphlets, street ballads and the press to spread it; it took strenuous political organization, by O'Connell, by Parnell, by Sinn Féin to channel it into politically powerful directions; it required nationalists to work hard to collect and use a wide and varied set of local groups and organizations — the peasant secret societies, the tenant farmers clubs, the land league, the AOH — and mobilize their hostility to their Protestant oppressors and to their oppressors' champion and defender, England. Above all, it required ingenuity and insight to disarm the mutual resentment which existed between Roman Catholics, between farmers and labourers, between employers and workers, and to forge a 'national unity' that could give power, as well as shape, to nationalist ambitions.

It must be admitted that nationalists had plenty of scope for their work. English policy decisions, or the lack of them, provided material for the nationalist belief that nothing but indifference, neglect, or downright hostility was to be expected from Britain. The Fitzwilliam episode in 1795; the failure to carry emancipation with union in 1800;

the state's support of the landlord and the tithe proctor in the early nineteenth century; the Government's strong rearguard action against Catholic emancipation; above all, the great famine, with its harrowing memories and dreadful consequences for millions of Irish people, all acted as a 'trigger'[19] to Irish nationalism, giving it the impetus it needed, often when it seemed on the point of decline. Similarly, the series of judgements, or mis-judgements made by the British between 1912 and 1919 helped Sinn Féin to an unexpected victory. It is impossible to understand the rise of Parnellism, with its bitter anti-English sentiment, without appreciating the depth of feeling aroused by the execution of the Manchester martyrs in 1867, and its place in the whole catechism of 'English misgovernment' since the union.

The Roman Catholic nation constituted a self-conscious minority in the United Kingdom; and it was not possible to reform that self-consciousness into oblivion. A large, culturally, politically and economically advanced country existed side by side with a small, culturally, politically and economically retarded (or, to use a less pejorative phrase, less developed) country. Such a union must produce tensions; and it is not surprising that these tensions were, at different times, of a cultural, political and economic kind. They might have been dispelled, or their severity lessened, had Ireland shared fully in the undoubted advantages offered her by participation in the United Kingdom; but by the mid-nineteenth century it was obvious that the union had failed: it had not made Ireland prosperous; it had not offered her Roman Catholic majority any advantages; it had regarded, with apparent lack of unconcern, the great famine; and, when by the last quarter of the nineteenth century it had begun in earnest to hand Ireland over to the Irish, it was threatening, not less, but more, to assimilate her culturally, to destroy the Gaelic and Irish tradition.

This line of argument is open to at least one important objection: that the Roman Catholic sense of national identity, forged in the seventeenth century, and recovered, after its temporary disappearance in the Ireland of the Protestant ascendancy, in the early nineteenth, need not have taken the specific form of demanding an Irish parliament and government. After all, the Roman Catholics might have pressed their claims as a Whig, Radical or Liberal group in Westminster; they might have constructed a cultural movement within Ireland that could set aside any notions of statehood, and make Ireland 'Irish' from within. But there are two reasons why nationalism, the desire for statehood for the nation in its own homeland, won the day. Firstly, England was seen as the rock in the path of 'Ireland for the Irish': she was the

Protestant and British entity that backed the Protestant minority in its defence of its privileges; she ensured that the Irish majority remained a minority, culturally, politically and economically.[20] But as well as this Ireland had a tradition of parliamentary government, of her own constitution, of her own symbol of nationhood. And here again the presence of the Anglo-Irish was of vital importance; for it was the Anglo-Irish who developed and maintained parliamentary institutions in Ireland, and who, moreover, were the first to assert Ireland's constitutional rights in the middle ages. Of course, it would be naive to pretend that they did this solely, or even mainly, for the good of Ireland. They did it mainly, but not exclusively, for the good of themselves; but their peculiar predicament — Irishmen who were conscious of their British cultural heritage[21] — meant that they never stopped talking and thinking about their legal, constitutional and national rights. Their very vulnerability, their heightened perception of the nature of the Anglo-Irish relationship, gave them an almost unhealthy obsession with political and constitutional theory. *They* had to define their relationship to both England *and* Ireland: and their nationalism of the eighteenth century — 'triggered off' by insensitive British government policy and the economic grievance of the old colonial system — provoked them into establishing the legislative independence of Ireland, and thus providing a model that most Irish nationalists could emulate and aspire to.

The Irish Parliament, therefore, had both a material and a symbolic importance in the eyes of nineteenth century nationalists. It would give them the opportunity and the means to carry out the reforms that would make them the masters in Ireland; and even when Westminster had carried out many of those reforms by 1900, and apparently deprived self-government of its meaning, the strength of Irish nationalism, demonstrated in the 1903 Emmet celebrations, showed that, if home rule was, as Gladstone held, a debt by man owed to God, it was to Irish nationalists a debt owed by God to man. For it was the sign that the indomitable Irishry had indeed dragged themselves from the famine pits of 1847[22] to the national self-respect whose outward and inward sign was the restoration to their country of its native parliament.

But there was another important issue here: where would the Protestant minority find a home, or a political role, in this self-governing nation whose constitutional rights they had founded? And herein lay the contradiction of modern Irish nationalism: for the political theory of nationalism, from Grattan, through Tone, to Davis (who were the inspiration of repeal and home rule, republicanism, and cultural nationalism respectively), stressed the comprehensive nature of nationalism, its need to incorporate all Irishmen within its bounds, its inclusiveness, its non-sectarianism; but the popular appeal of nationalism, its emotional attraction, its sentiment, were derived, not from this ideology, but from a myth, a view of the past that was accepted whether it was true or false.[23] This view of the past was exclusive, describing the struggle of the Irish race, or, as some called it, the 'real nation', to free itself from the wrongs and oppressions of the English *and* of the English and Scottish colonists. And it was enduring: it was expressed in the speeches of O'Connell, of the home rulers, of Sinn Féin. Aodh de Blacam in 1921 referred contemptuously to the 'foreign Ascendancy whose feet were on the necks of the Gaels';[24] a learned academic in 1973 declared that the 'main function of the National University of Ireland . . . has been and will be to build the Irish nation. A large part of the task is rebuilding: the recovery of the almost obliterated spirit and traditions in which our country lived and developed up to the disasters of the seventeenth century';[25] and the modern Dublin poet Richard Webber wrote of the flight of the wild geese, after which:

The island of Ireland recedes and dims and dies
To a dream of dreams for more than two hundred years.[26]

If learned, gifted and privileged men thought this, there was little chance that the less favoured members of the 'race' would think otherwise.

They could hardly think otherwise when they were, in any event, surrounded with the view of Irish history illustrated above. Of course the rank and file, as well as the leaders, of Irish nationalism were aware of Grattan, Tone and Davis; but these were mere names, and their theories were only partially and imperfectly grasped. It might be said that popular nationalism derived its symbols − harps, '98 pikes, the old Parliament House on College Green, *'Erin go Brah'*, the green, white and gold flag − from its Protestants, but its substance from a much deeper and more influential source. That source was the teaching at every level of a Catholic Irishman's life − his home, school, places of work and leisure, place of worship, the press, the penny song books − of the myth of the persecuted but now risen nation. Its foes were the English Government and those Protestant Irishmen (*most* Protestant Irishmen) who stood in the path of progress. This process of political socialization[27] was more lasting, and seemed more relevant to everyday experience, than the political theory of a comprehensive Irish nation, even though that theory was never quite abandoned. Michael Collins reputedly 'studied' Davis, but his principles were burnt into him; de Valera paid tribute to the priests who had helped make a nationalist and a true Irishman out of him; and it was Dan Breen's schoolteacher who set him on the path that led to the ambush of two RIC men at Soloheadbeg in 1919.[28] Hostility to the English and to their 'garrison' was woven into Irish Catholic society, just as hatred and suspicion of Catholics was woven into the day-to-day life of Ulster Protestants. Ideas of a comprehensive Irish nationalism could not compete with this; and although Protestants fairly bristled with prejudice, none the less words and expressions like Saxon, Gall, or West Briton were scarcely welcoming signs to the Protestant members of the nation. Even John Mitchel, surely the most committed hater of England that Irish nationalism ever produced, paused, and wondered what kind of movement he was trying to lead, and where it might take him. 'The Anglo-Irish and Scottish Ulstermen', he warned, 'have now far too old a title to be questioned: they were a hardy race, and fought stoutly for the pleasant valleys they dwell in . . . A deep enough root these planters have struck into the soil of Ulster, and it would now be ill-striving to unplant them'.[29]

This helps explain the contradictory nature of Irish nationalism. Its political theory advocated the incorporation of all Irishmen, whatever their origin, within the Irish nation; but its popular appeal, and its organizational strength, lay not in nationalist philosophy but in a process of political socialization, begun under O'Connell and continued into the twentieth century, and founded upon an historical myth. This myth of the fall and rise of the Irish nation in the end took on an independent existence of its own, outliving and outlasting any material reforms offered to the nation by the British, inspiring home rulers and Sinn Féiners, Fine Gael and Fianna Fáil, and going some way towards holding together a people composed of different social and economic groups, bedevilled by localism, and divided by civil war. It took 50 years of sovereign statehood to reconcile the myth with reality, and make Ireland a truly homogenous twenty-six county nation. But in this nation the descendants of the men who made the greatest contribution to Irish nationalist political theory had to accept the majority myth. It was not, perhaps, too heavy a burden to shoulder, or too large a price to pay for the privilege of living in the new Ireland; most minorities (such as that in Northern Ireland) have had much more to bear.[30] And it was not only Catholic Ireland that refused to accept Anglo-Irish nationalist ideology, or accepted it only on Catholic Ireland's own terms; Protestant Ulster rejected the ideology outright, as traitorous to the good old cause which triumphed at the battle of the Boyne.

The problem with Ireland was that she encompassed a plural socity that did not and could not see itself as plural. The racial self-consciousness of the Gaels was rivalled by the sense of distinctiveness of the Catholic Anglo-Irish. The distinctiveness of the Old English was surpassed by the religious exclusiveness of the new English. The Ulster Protestant concept of the 'public band' – a body of men bound together in mutual trust for the purpose of community defence –[31] automatically excluded any Roman Catholic participants. The nationalist idea of the race,[32] of the 'real nation' excluded all but the most enthusiastic and thick-skinned Irish Protestants, and worried even Thomas Davis and John Mitchel. And this exclusiveness was a consequence of the colonial period in Irish history, which brought to Ireland layers of peoples, strongly self-conscious of their national or religious distinction from the majority of the inhabitants.

The colonial period of Irish history came to an end in the third decade of the seventeenth century,[33] and there followed a struggle for power, precipitated by the crisis of crown and parliament in Great Britain. This struggle was one, not only between native and colonist, but within these groups, for the Catholic Old English colonists were ranged against the Protestant new English. The Williamite victory in 1690 enabled the Protestants to establish the claim that theirs was the kingdom of Ireland, and to lay the foundations of modern Irish nationalism. But the impact of the French revolution, the romantic era, and the rise of democracy in Ireland challenged and finally overthrew this Protestant claim, and replaced it with the idea that the Roman Catholics were the Irish people.

At the same time, few Irish nationalists denied that the Protestants were in some sense part of the Irish nation; but because of the heterogeneous nature of Irish society, its temptation to lapse into fragmentation and localism, nationalist politicians had to strive to create and maintain a core of national unity. This obliged them to stress, not the pluralism of Ireland, but the homogeneous nature of those Irishmen whose loyalty and support were essential to the realization of their political programme. Thus the pluralism of Irish society, in a country where nationalist politics came to dominate all aspects of life, was the very factor that prevented any practical or lasting acknowledgement of the pluralism of Irish society.

This difficulty confronted eighteenth century Protestant nationalists as well as nineteenth century Catholic nationalists. When all was said and done — said by Grattan and his like, and done by the United Irishmen and their like — a man, and especially a politician, had to stand by his own people. His own people were defined, not by ideologists like Grattan or Davis, but by the conflict between majority and minority in Ireland, a conflict given its emotional thrust by a particular view of Irish history. In this view of history, 'Irishness' was identified with nationalism:[34] thus the spectacle of John Denvir and his Emerald Boys, or Robert Brennan and his tin pikes, was considered genuinely 'Irish', while the social life of the Lagan Valley was dismissed as a poor imitation of Lancashire; and people who had lived in Ireland for generations were dismissed as intruders. A 'colonial' view of Irish history, totally inappropriate to nineteenth century Ireland, and highly divisive in its implications, was widely propagated and readily accepted as authentic.

Ireland after the seventeenth century was not a colony, but a sister-kingdom and then, after 1800, an integral part of the British polity, inextricably linked with British politics, and, as always, exposed to British cultural influence. This made Irish political, social and economic development a concern of England in the way that the affairs of a remote dependency were not.[35] England insisted on regulating the course of nationalism in Ireland from the late eighteenth century onwards; and this process of regulation enabled nationalism to develop and mature in a parliamentary and constitutional manner, although in the end it played into the hands of the physical force movement. It also enabled and encouraged a silent transfer of power to take place over most of Ireland, while in the end giving statutory recognition to the emergence of a particularist movement in north-east Ulster.

The English presence in and near Ireland did not make Irish nationalism 'worse' or 'better'; but, in a real sense, it made it possible. Ireland's political tradition, unlike that of, for example, France, had no independent existence, no clear-cut line of development. English constitutional reforms and the English language enabled nationalist Ireland to realize itself as a cultural and political entity over most of the country, fending off or containing the challenge of, on the cultural front, Irish Irelanders and Anglo-Irish literary patriots, and, on the political front, Irish unionists and the revolutionary minority. Irish nationalism, therefore, was not peculiarly 'Irish'; on the contrary, its many paradoxes and self-contradictions arise from the close and permanent relationship between Ireland and her neighbour. And Ireland's dominant political tradition, like most aspects of her life, bears the ineradicable influence of England.

Notes

1. These paragraphs are based on a lucid and convenient summary provided in D.W. Millar, *Queen's Rebels*, pp. 46-9, on my reading of F. Gellner, *Thought and Change*, (London, 1964), and on articles kindly supplied to me by A.W. Orridge, of the University of Birmingham: 'Explanations of Irish nationalism: a review and some suggestions', originally published in the *Journal of the Conflict Research Society*, vol. *1*, Part i, (1977), pp. 29-57, 'Uneven development and nationalism', (1978), and 'Structural preconditions and triggering factors in the development of European sub-state nationalism'.

2. Orridge, 'Uneven development', pp. 3-18.

3. Ibid, pp. 3-18; 'Explanations of Irish nationalism', pp. 40-41. M. Hechter, *Internal Colonialism: the Celtic Fringe in British National Development, 1536-1966*, (London, 1975), esp. pp. 4-5, 270-73.

4. For which see Orridge, 'Uneven development' and 'Structural preconditions', and E. Page, *'Michael Hechter's Internal Colonial Thesis: some Theoretical and Methodological Problems'*, University of Strathclyde, Centre for the study of public policy paper No. 9 (1977).

5. W.J. Argyle, 'Size and scale as factors in the development of nationalist movements', in A.D. Smith (ed.), *Nationalist Movements* (London, 1976), p. 47. As Argyle remarks, the word means both to 'show or display' and 'to collect or assemble'.

6. Orridge discusses these points in 'Explanations', pp. 41-2.

7. Ibid., p. 33.

8. For which see L.P. Curtis, *Anglo-Saxons and Celts*, (New York, 1968) and *Apes and Angels: The Irishman in Victorian Caricature* (Newton Abbot, 1971); see also P. O'Farrell, *England and Ireland since 1800* (London, 1975), Chaps. 2 and 3.

9. For an explanation of which, see K.O. Morgan, 'Welsh nationalism: the historical background' in *Journal of Contemporary History*, vol. *6* (1971), pp. 153-72; Glanmor Williams, *Religion, Language and Nationality in Wales*, (Cardiff, 1979), pp. 144-5.

10. Orridge, 'Uneven development', p. 21, discusses this point in a general context.

11. O. MacDonagh, *Ireland: the Union and its Aftermath*, (London, 1977), p. 58.

12. Gaughan, op. cit., pp. 10-13.

13. Greaves, *Liam Mellowes*, p. 39.

14. O'Donoghue, op. cit., p. 8.

15. Costello, *The Heart Grown Brutal*, p. 34.

16. MacDonagh, 'Irish famine emigration', op. cit., p. 446.

17. Lynch, *Cambrensis Eversus*, I, p. 233.

18. For a stimulating modern essay on medieval national identity in Ireland see A. Cosgrove 'Hiberniores Ipsis Hibernis', in A. Cosgrove and D. McCartney (eds.), *Studies in Irish History Presented to R. Dudley Edwards* (Dublin, 1979), pp. 1-14.

19. Orridge, 'Structural preconditions' discusses the 'triggering factors' in European nationalism.

20. This was one of the arguments used to persuade Irish Protestants to give up their parliament: see *Arguments For and Against an Union Between Great*

Britain and Ireland Considered (Dublin, 1799), p. 26: 'The Catholics would lose the advantage of the argument of numbers, which they at present enjoy, and the Constitution of the Empire would agree with the theory'.

21. For a stimulating and elegant explanation of the Anglo-Irish mind see J.C. Beckett, *The Anglo-Irish Tradition* (London, 1976)

22. The phrase is Joseph Lee's (*Modernisation of Irish society*, p. 168).

23. For a brief but illuminating discussion of the role of myth in nation-building see R.H.C. Davis, *The Normans and Their Myth* (London, 1976), esp. pp. 15-16.

24. *What Sinn Féin Stands For*, p. 32.

25. J.J. Horgan, president of U.C.D., in foreword to Martin and Byrne, *The Scholar Revolutionary*.

26. N. Vance, 'Celts, Carthaginians and constitutions', p. 2.

27. My attention was drawn to this consideration by F. Wright, 'Protestant ideology', op. cit., pp. 217-18; for political socialization see *International Encyclopedia of the Social Sciences*, vols. *13-14*, (New York and London, 1968), p. 551.

28. L.M. Cullen, 'Irish nationalism', p. 23.

29. T.W. Moody, *Thomas Davis* (Dublin, 1945), p. 55, fn 93.

30. H. Jackson, *The two Irelands: the Problem of the Double Minority*, (Minority Rights Group, Report No. 2, 1972), pp. 17-21.

31. Miller, op. cit., passim, esp. pp. 21-6, 95-7.

32. F. Hertz, *Nationality in History and Politics* (London, 1944); p. 53: 'Race sentiment consists in the belief in a deep, natural hereditary diversity not changeable by education and assimilation, while national sentiment assumes merely historical and social differences which can be modified by society'.

33. I use the term 'colonial' in the older, and historically valid, sense, meaning 'a settlement of the subjects of a state beyond its frontiers' (*Encyclopedia of the Social Sciences*, vol. *III*, New York, 1967 edn., p. 653). After 1641 there was no such major settlement of British subjects in Ireland, for the Cromwellian period saw no great influx of New English, and the Cromwellian victory proved, in the end, to be a victory for the Old Protestants. Of course, the term 'colonial' may be used in a much wider sense: the Stormont government has been referred to as colonial; so has the direct rule system now in use in Northern Ireland. Some would regard all Ireland as in some sense a British colony, in economic terms. Likewise, some would regard Britain as a 'colony' of the United States. But this is to deprive the expression of any accurate usage, and indeed of any value at all.

34. For the Irishness of Orangeism see Zimmerman, op. cit., pp. 295-305.

35. W.B. Hodgson (trans.), *Count Cavour on Ireland*, (London, 1868), passim, esp. pp. 29, 62, 72-3, 93; see also *Arguments For and Against an Union Between Great Britain and Ireland Considered*, esp. pp. 29-32.

EPILOGUE: HISTORY, POLITICS AND NATIONALISM

The beginning of the last decade of the twentieth century is an appropriate time to take stock of Irish nationalism and its place in Irish historical scholarship. The doctrine of nationalism, which after the Second World War appeared to be a discredited and outmoded concept in both western and eastern Europe, has returned as a central force in political mobilization. Even in the European Community, as it moves towards an ever closer integration, nationalist and separatist groups and peoples renew their demands for some form of political or cultural recognition. And in eastern and central Europe, the Soviet Union, which appeared to have vindicated the claim that class superseded nationality in the historical process, finds itself embattled with hitherto dormant or suppressed groups, with its Russian heartland threatening to secede — a shock as great as an English declaration of intent to secede from the United Kingdom. Yet as recently as 1962 Professor Howard Warrender told a class of students in the Queen's University, Belfast that Europe had undergone the trauma of nationalism (as he called it), lamenting the fact that the so-called Third World seemed to be about to experience what Europe had abandoned.

Nationalism presents particular problems to the historian of Ireland because he or she is immediately aware of an engagement with a very immediate past. This is not unique: a Hungarian scholar, György Csepeli, remarked that in his country the situation

> is basically unfavourable for the analytical investigation of social phenomena and especially for research into national awareness, because of the passions ... and historical cataclysms traced back, justly or unjustly, to disturbances in national feeling and consciousness.[1]

The Irish equivalent of these 'disturbances' has not prevented a whole generation of Irish academics from seeking to subject nationalism to the rigorous and objective investigations of modern scholarship. Irish nationalism was given a kind of historical equivalent of the scientific examination of the Turin Shroud: its social and economic basis was laid bare; its battles with localism and provincialism explained; and its historians' failure to explore parallels with other parts of the British Isles

391

deplored. Above all, the idea that there was something special about Irish history, some especially tragic story of death, rebirth, and an eternal struggle against the foreigner, was dismissed as a wholly inappropriate context within which to place the history of Ireland: nationalist historiography was the root of the problem; and, furthermore, it was misleading to write the history of a 'nation' anyway, since the lines of development were never as clearcut as that term would imply. 'Ireland' was not a distinct political entity, and it was anachronistic to regard it as such: there was, for example, no 'Anglo–Irish' conflict in the Middle Ages, no demand for 'home rule' which lasted from the fifteenth century until the twentieth.[2]

This non-national approach to the history of Ireland had profound implications for the history of Irish nationalism, for it challenged the whole basis on which Irish nationalism, as a political idea, was founded — the idea that there was an historic people, a community whose national consciousness could be traced down the ages, and whose struggle to survive is the central theme of Irish history. Moreover, this anti-national historiography had on its side the idea that it was engaged in the de-mythologizing of the Irish past. History, claimed one of the finest of modern Irish scholars, need not be 'the death of us', because

> if 'history' is here used as meaning the past itself, it can well be argued that the consequences of long-standing bitterness and violence will destroy us. But if 'history' is used in its proper sense of a continuing, probing, critical search for truth about the past, my argument would be that it is not Irish history but Irish mythology that has been ruinous to us and may prove even more lethal. History is a matter of facing the facts of the Irish past, however painful some of them may be; mythology is a way of refusing to face the historical facts. The study of history not only enlarges truth about our past, but opens the mind to the reception of ever new accessions of truth.[3]

But even as Professor T.W. Moody proclaimed the virtues of historical truth, he was forced to admit that, whereas 'Irish history has made great and unprecedented advances during the past forty years ... the effect on the public mind appears to be disappointingly slow'. The 'mental war of liberation' was an endless and at times agonizing process.[4] This view — a mixture of certainty about the task of the historian, and doubt about the achievement of history — prevailed in the 1970s and 1980s. But by the end of the 1980s some leading Irish historians were driven to wonder why their collective efforts at what was known as 'revisionism' had failed to have any discernible impact on Irish public opinion and, in particular, on the Northern Ireland crisis. But their assumptions — that history was concerned with challenging Irish political myths, and Irish nationalist myths — were themselves undergoing a challenge. This came mainly from various political figures, and thus could be regarded as a kind of vindication of the new Irish history in the first place, which was bound to challenge political orthodoxies. But the question about the direction and motives of Irish historical scholarship was put in passionate, honest and academic form by Dr Brendan Bradshaw when he asked for an Irish history, and especially an Irish nationalist *and Unionist* history, which did not seek, as he put it, to make the modern Irish community 'aliens in their own land', cut off from their past, a past characterized as one of 'achievements and sufferings'.[5] This raised another question which Professor Moody had regarded as resolved: whether or not there could be such a discipline as 'value-free history', a history in which the search for the 'truth' was unequivocal; where, indeed, there was 'truth' to be discovered.

This is a discussion relevant to the writing of any kind of history; and there is no clear answer, in the historians' craft, to the question of what constitutes 'truth'. The notion that 'revisionist' history was especially prominent in Ireland, or in Irish nationalism, is misleading; all history is revisionist, since new generations of scholars will challenge older gener-ations, and will unearth new material to support that challenge. Without this process — the lifeblood of history —, history could cease to exist. No history is value-free, for the historian is a product of his own time and circumstances, and what he writes, indeed what he chooses to write about, reflects the preoccupations of the age. The question, then, is not one of 'truth' and 'revisionism', but the more mundane (but very important) one of whether Irish nationalism has in some sense been given shallow or inadequate historical treatment: that historians of Irish nationalism have in some respects been found wanting in what Dr Brad-shaw rightly identifies as two of the main tools of historical scholarship, empathy and imagination.[6]

The historian of nationalism in Ireland, if he is to make anything out of his subject, cannot help but be aware of the longevity of national identity; and he must not be lulled into the mechanical, social–scientific explanation of nationalism which sees it as 'beginning' with the French Revolution in 1789, and developing as a response to 'modernization' and the 'uneven spread of capitalism', or some such phenomenon. The historian of nationalism in Ireland needs to explore his subject in the recognition that — as Dr Bradshaw rightly argues — the forging of Irish (and for that matter English, Welsh and Scottish) identities was a gradual process, and therefore a complex one. The idea of an Irish/ Catholic identity is as old as the sixteenth and seventeenth centuries, and was rediscovered, not invented, by Daniel O'Connell in the early nineteenth century. The concept of Ireland as a distinct political entity was one that Henry Grattan and the Patriots accepted when they made the case for the constitution of 1782. The idea of the constitution of 1782 was one used by home rulers from the 1870s, and by Sinn Fein in 1918. It was easier to say 'this is where we are going', when there were precedents which could guide political behaviour: an important and influential argument in all political societies, from the English love of continuity, to the Baltic States' rediscovery of their pre-Soviet independence, to the Armenian or Ukrainian 'parliaments', where such institutions, weak as they might be, at least gave people a sense of continuity and precedent.

Irish nationalism was the product of a long, and slow, historical process, one which the various groups and communities of peoples in Ireland involved themselves in, and contributed to. It had a cultural dimension in the general sense of the experience of living in Ireland, of living in that country with its specificity and its particularity. Ireland was, and remained until the last two decades, a predominantly rural and religious country; and these values were of central importance in the development of her society and in any attempt to evolve a sense of Irishness. They imposed mental horizons on all her people (that mixture of Protestant, Catholic and Dissenter), and a relationship between landlord and tenant, out of which Irish politics were forged. But nationalism was also a debate about which of these groups should wield political authority in Ireland; and the wielding of that authority affected, or was affected by, relations with Ireland's large and powerful neighbour, England. It was a debate therefore that especially exercised those whose relations with the Irish majority (Gaelic, later Catholic) and with England were of central and inescapable significance for their security and even survival as a people. Thus the leading proponents of the idea of a particular Irish constitutional past, one in which the rights of Ireland were enshrined, were the Old English and the Anglo–Irish. It was they — Catholic Old English, Protestant Anglo–Irish — who had to come to terms with their domicile in Ireland, and their identification with the English Crown, and who in the process applied their minds to constitutional and political theory. In the nineteenth century the Anglo–Irish struck out on yet another path in their quest for a place in Irish history and society when they became the leading figures in the making of cultural nationalism, advocates of the idea of a liberal and pluralist Ireland which should encompass the 'Gael', the 'Norman', the 'Dane', and all the rest of the heterogeneous Irish people. This was not necessarily because they were more enlightened than the bulk of their fellow-countrymen (though many of them were). It was because they sought a role in Ireland, one which would guarantee them not only security, but leadership of a Catholic nation — even of a Catholic democratic nation.

This mentality was brilliantly, if arrogantly, expressed by John Eglinton in his collection of *Anglo–Irish Essays*, published in 1917,[7] and taken from what he himself described as 'various defunct Irish magazines and newspapers and from a booklet of which the remaining copies contributed their little flame to the conflagrations in Dublin during Easter Week of 1916'.[8] Eglinton wanted to remind what he called 'Irish Ireland' that the 'Anglo–Irishman' was still there — but altered.

> More than a hundred years, in which he has assisted at the progress of democratic ideals in Ireland, have taught him tolerance, have infected his Protestant eudaemonism with a melancholy scepticism, have mitigated his unsuspecting selfishness and caused him many misgivings as he conned the records of the past, and have bound him by new and inextricable ties to the ancient population of this island.

This process had 'improved him out of all recognition as the descendant of the old rollicking Irishman of the eighteenth century'; the Anglo–Irishman accepted 'as a good European the connection with Great Britain and yet feels himself to be far more distinct from the Anglo–Saxon than he is from the mere Irishman'.[9]

The Anglo–Irishman, then, was a cosmopolitan; yet he had 'made a present to the Mere Irish of the stand which we made for our liberties in the eighteenth century'. Moreover, he had contributed to the intellectual life of Ireland 'by never pressing to a conclusion the Protestant and Roman Catholic controversy'; 'we live amicably together, those of us who are Catholics being as little capable of starting an Inquisition as our Protestants of starting a Salvation Army'.[10] To this 'race' destiny entrusted 'the task of unifying and governing Ireland as clearly as to the Anglo-Norman race it committed the task of unifying and governing England'. But this task had been frustrated by the 'premature introduction of democratic ideals into Ireland at the time of the French Revolution', and the country's 'natural rulers' had to look on while 'England made what bargain she could with the subject race'. And so the 'modern

Irishman' was deprived of his rightful position as leader of the 'Celtic nationality' when it 'woke up into the democratic era'. The Anglo–Irish, deprived of their right to rule, helped England govern her colonies; but there were not enough posts to go round. Pitt made one of England's bitterest enemies when he neglected to answer a request for an appointment from Wolfe Tone. Under these conditions 'we often, in fact, became bad citizens':

> our sons and daughters chafe at our provincial atmosphere, amaze us by their petulant outbreaks, and set up as rebels.... Wherever there has been any ferment of revolutionary ideas ... it will usually be found that one of us has been mixing himself with action lest he should wither by despair.[11]

Eglinton's analysis must not of course be taken at its face value; but it contained important grains of truth, for it made the point that a minority — social, political and intellectual — played an important role in the making of Irish national, and nationalist, identity. This was because at various times the Old English and Anglo–Irish minority faced a crisis in their existence, and sought to resolve it by constitutional and, from the 1880s, cultural means. This series of crises, or the recurring crisis, perhaps, enabled these people — the Old English recusant, Patrick Darcy, in 1641, the Anglo–Irish Protestant, Henry Grattan, in 1782, Isaac Butt and Charles Stewart Parnell in the 1870s and 1880s — to claim the rights of the Irish parliament and nation from medieval times, and to assert the rights of Irishmen on the same footing as Englishmen. It also provoked some Anglo–Irishmen, as Eglinton put it, to take 'from the Mere Irishman all his terms and traditions', and chant 'the sorrows of Kathleen ni Houlihan in strains "more Irish" than anything in the ancient language of the country'. This aspect of the literary movement, he believed, 'ended in bloodshed in Easter Week'.[12]

Modern Irish nationalism owed much to the Old English and the Anglo–Irish, with their concern to establish the distinctiveness of Ireland in institutional and later cultural terms. But the Ulster Presbyterian, in turn, had a significant contribution to make to the nationalist tradition. It was, after all, in Antrim and Down that the ideas of Wolfe Tone — of a secular, democratic and radical Ireland — were protested in arms. But here again the specific, historical nature of the tradition must be emphasized. The Presbyterians of the 1790s harboured a suspicion of popery; they anticipated that all European reactionary movements and ideas — including popery — would be abolished by the

French Revolution. They were in a local numerical majority, and were the better able to ignore the dark dangers of the Catholic masses — dangers which obsessed even their most enlightened leader, William Drennan. But they believed that they could guide the politics of the Catholic majority, and oblige it to accept the Presbyterian idea of Liberty. They were, as they saw it, Watchmen in Sion. But when their idea of Liberty was shattered in the bloodshed and defeat of the 1798 rebellion — a rebellion which jolted Ireland back into a kind of historical memory of past conflicts and disasters, both Catholic and Protestant — then they came to acknowledge that Liberty might have a better guardian than an independent Ireland — that indeed its best guardian was the United Kingdom, established in the wake of revolution in 1800.

The Roman Catholic, in the end, became the repository of Irish nationalist thinking, both Anglo–Irish and Presbyterian. If nationalism were to be equated with majority rule and democracy, then, as O'Connell told the Roman Catholics, they were the 'Irish nation'. Roman Catholics were able to use this reservoir of Old English, Anglo–Irish and Presbyterian ideas the more effectively to advance their claims that, on the one hand, they were part of a pluralist political tradition (with Tone, Thomas Davis and the like as their guides), and, on the other, that they were a homogeneous Catholic people, and, ultimately, state. This ambiguity was both useful and dangerous. It enabled nationalism to present a liberal face to the world, but it encouraged nationalists to ignore the deep divisions amongst the rest of the Irish people, divisions which in the nineteenth century caused Anglicans and Presbyterians to close ranks against the common foe, as they had done in their great crisis of 1689-90.

The siege of Derry is a useful reminder that, in Ireland, politics and history are not far apart; that, on the contrary, the issues raised in these apparently far-off conflicts are still, some of them, unresolved, as Ireland, north and south, moves towards European integration by 1992. The connection between politics and history involves the Irish historian in a self-consciousness about his work in a way that English historians find unusual or even exaggerated. Dr Brendan Bradshaw's challenge to what he regarded as the new orthodoxy deplored the sceptical, anti-nationalist thrust (as he saw it) of modern Irish historical writing: for example, in its glossing over some of the worst wrongs inflicted on the Roman Catholics, from the massacres of the sixteenth and seventeenth centuries to the Great Famine of the mid-nineteenth century. He did not ask for the writing of uncritical, unhistorical or propagandist work, but he wanted historians to recognize that there was a tragic Irish past, one which was not experienced by other peoples in the British Isles. Modern Ireland was shaped by heroic suffering and endurance, by a trauma which could not or should not be forgotten.[13]

Certainly modern scholars have sought to get behind such ideas as the 'suffering' and 'heroism' of the nationalist people of Ireland. They have tried to discover who it was that suffered, and which sections of the people appeared to derive benefits from the sufferings of others: for example, in the Great Famine, where the decline of the labourers and cottiers opened the way for tenant farmers to consolidate their holdings and move into an era of real, if uneasy, prosperity. Such scholars have challenged the idea of a pantheon of Irish nationalist heroes, from Tone to Pearse, leading their people to the light. They have explored the doubts and frailties of the rebels whose deeds were held up as exemplary. The Fenians — usually regarded as the living embodiment of the 'otherness' of Ireland, and the torch-bearers of Irish separatism — have been shown as a middle-class would-be intelligentsia, who were not averse to playing cricket and whose main activity seemed to be planning social outings.[14] The Gaelic movement likewise was subjected to acute social analysis,[15] and the question asked here was what 'causes the transformation of a small-scale forum of intellectuals into a significant socio-political movement'? The answer was not so much a protest against 'English civilization' in Ireland but rather the very nature of Irish nationalism itself. 'There is a tendency of political nationalism to ossify into a bureaucratic oligarchy, remote from the community it purportedly serves.' This imposed a dictatorship on the young by the old, and thus

> The rising young nationalist intelligentsia, already disillusioned by the divisiveness of political nationalism, now perceives itself to be excluded from power and status in the community.... At this time in its isolation the intelligentsia seeking a vocational outlet is increasingly attracted to the dynamic integral vision of cultural nationalism, as reformulated by its political intellectuals. For this offers both a return to roots in the historical community and a modernising alternative to the worn-out legislative panaceas of political nationalism.[16]

The making of the revolutionary generation of 1916-23 was subject to the test of modern political sociology, with revolutionary nationalism revealed, not as some perpetually renewed historical force, handed down from generation to generation, but, on the contrary, as a revolt against one generation by another.[17] 'The children of the artisan, the shopkeeper, the small farmer, the civil servant, the business manager or the officer had no guarantee of inheriting their fathers' position in society.' Frustration, created by a mismatch between education and available employment, was not unique to Ireland in shaping pre-1914 radicalisms.[18] One of the most perceptive students of modern Irish nationalism threw down another gauntlet when he declared that:

> The Irish publican who advocated first Home Rule, then the Republic, in order to secure his clerk's stipend on the Old Age Pensions Committee, was as much a nationalist as Padraic Pearse, who had himself shot in order to secure his place in Irish history. Both Pearse and the publican sought benefits for themselves but also participated in collective actions designed to benefit their country.[19]

And the doyens of the Irish revolution, Patrick Pearse and James Connolly, were subjected to keen and revealing scrutiny, and exposed not as modernizers, but as traditional nationalists whose 'socialism' or 'radicalism' was but a veneer on their instinctive political thinking.[20]

Some aspects of this historical revolution were not free from the danger that, in asking important and searching questions about power in Irish society, they stood rather too far apart from the political culture of Ireland; that indeed they did not 'empathize' sufficiently with the Irish past. At the same time, it is important to qualify Dr Bradshaw's concept of a kind of 'communal mind' linking the 'Irish people' across the centuries.[21] One of the articles cited by Dr Bradshaw to illustrate the trauma of Irish history (which it does, at least in part) also warns the historian against the too easy acceptance of the idea of an unchanging *mentalité*. Tom Bartlett establishes the point that Roman Catholic tenants in the eighteenth century moved from acceptance of, and even affection for, their Protestant landlords to a rejection of their earlier deference.[22] Yet it must be acknowledged that the deep religious/political divisions in Irish society were an enduring and recurring factor (though in different forms at different times) in the making of modern Irish identity.

For there was certainly a danger that, in adopting a too-rational approach to the Irish past, modern historians might leave the reader rather up in the air: if the violence and confrontation were only myths, then what was all the fuss about? The trauma of the 1641 massacres of Protestants by Catholics, of the Cromwellian onslaught, of the Famine in 1847, of the violence that characterized the foundation of the two states of modern Ireland in 1921, must not be disregarded. Indeed, the failure to acknowledge the sustained Republican assaults on Northern Ireland in the early years of the state is at the root of the unwillingness of many modern commentators to allow that Ulster Unionists had much to fear from Irish nationalists. These insecurities and fears require empathetic examination.

Nevertheless, the value of modern scholarship was that it explored the complexity and diversity of Irish society, and the relationship between different groups of people as they became involved in the cause of nationalism. The tensions between farmer and labourer (as well as landlord and tenant), between businessman and worker (as well as Catholic and Protestant), while they must not be exaggerated, posed problems for Irish nationalist (and for that matter Unionist) leaders. One of the main problems for nineteenth-century nationalists was to resolve what every nationalist movement disguised: 'The almost total irrelevance of constitutional questions to the basic things of life.'[23] The provincialism and localism of Irish society were explored in the work of Theodore Hoppen, whose research altered the whole perception of what 'Irish society' meant, and gave the lie to the idea of a collective, spontaneous nationalist movement.[24] Paul Bew explained how power was sought in rural Ireland, and demonstrated that historians were mistaken when they declared that John Redmond was 'out of touch' with Irish nationalism as a result of his parliamentary role; the real problem lay in the fact that he was all too closely in touch with it and its uncritical assumption of what it meant by the 'Irish nation'.[25] Tom Garvin uncovered the life of urban nationalist Ireland, the Ireland of the Roman Catholic lower middle classes. If the Fenians, Land Leaguers, Home Rulers and Sinn Feiners were thus revealed as men of less than heroic stature, they were also shown to be political leaders whose approach to organizing and creating popular political movements, risings and nation-states deserved serious and sustained political analysis, instead of facile admiration.

The argument of 'revisionism' versus 'counter revisionism', of the 'morality' of revisionism, loses its value if it becomes a political one, one of for or against the 'nation'. It is more constructive simply to acknowledge that there is no such thing as 'value-free' history, no 'scientific' history, but that all history books are informed by what might be called a 'tone', or flavour, or style, which, however, does not preclude serious scholarly investigation. It is important in the history of Irish nationalism to uncover the reasons why Ireland developed a grievance culture. And there can be no doubt that this requires empathy.[26] But the claim that Irish historians ought to mediate between themselves and their people, or administer to the Irish in Britain, or the like, is to ask history to do more than it can possibly accomplish. People have their own history, and they will probably keep it. The only thing the historian can hope to do is to understand what it was that turned flawed men into gods and heroes in the first place. What kind of culture made them; how did they respond to it; how did they seek to mould it in new ways, how far did they succumb to old notions; how did the culture define and redefine itself and its leaders? The study of Eamon de Valera by Owen Dudley Edwards recreates the central role of religion in the politics of nationalist Ireland's greatest modern leader: the ritual of political priest and congregation in the celebration of a national tradition, as de Valera engaged with his people in their special view of the world (and the flesh and the devil).[27] It would be unfortunate if, in the search for answers to these, and other, questions, the credentials of historians were to be examined in some pseudo-ethnic light.[28]

The study of Irish nationalism needs an agenda, and the essential items on an agenda must include a consideration of the regional differences which distinguish nationalism, and render the creation of a nation-state so difficult. In particular, nationalism in the north of Ireland needs a much deeper treatment than it has so far received. This is perhaps not surprising, since it was primarily a southern phenomenon, and its great modern leaders, Tone, O'Connell, Parnell, Pearse and de Valera were all from southern Ireland. But the idea of a republic — secular, radical and democratic — gained most support from the Presbyterians of the north in the 1790s; and the strength of Catholic nationalism in contemporary Ireland lies in the northern areas. Here are contradictions and paradoxes sufficient to attract attention, and they require special treatment of Ulster. When in 1883 Parnell and his supporters spoke of the 'invasion' of Ulster they betrayed a sense of difference, and suggested that the north was some kind of alien territory. But these themes — of Presbyterian radical nationalism and Catholic home rule nationalism — require a deeper treatment than they are usually afforded. Presbyterians were not all radical republicans in 1798; Roman Catholics voted Liberal (those who had a vote) for most of the nineteenth century; and Presbyterians ceased to be radical in the course of that century (while not yet becoming affiliated to the mainly Anglican Conservatives).

Nationalists in the north were slow to organize in the home rule era, and slower still to react to the political movements that were transforming the political landscape of the rest of Ireland, particularly the Land League and the Land War. They did not produce adequate political leadership, they relied upon external leaders and reacted, rather than shaped, events. They were obliged to send different signals, both to southern nationalists, and to northern Protestants, which were reflected in their tendency to choose Protestant home rulers (few in number, it need hardly be said) as candidates for election, especially in the key county of Ulster, Co. Tyrone. Nationalists were here in a majority, but Protestants were numerous and had the advantage of the balance of property and political influence.

Northern nationalism followed a different course in the home rule crisis of 1912-14 and its aftermath. The northern nationalists were less concerned with Anglo–Irish relations, or the niceties of dominion status as against home rule as against the republic, than were southern nationalists. Like the Unionists of the north they were obsessed with their local predicament; and nationalism, either home rule or Sinn Féin, was attractive, not just because of its constitutional possibilities, but because of its promise of casting down those who deserved to be cast down: politics and political organizations were judged by their impact on Protestants. As one local priest put it in 1912, referring to the Catholic nationalist organization, the Ancient Order of Hibernians (AOH), he never 'had any suspicions' about the Order, 'when he saw the virulence of the Unionist onslaught against the AOH, it must be good'.[29] While southern nationalists were obsessed with sovereignty, those in the north were concerned with partition: hence the northern participation in the Irish Convention of 1917-18 which seemed to offer the possibility of some kind of alternative — a convention generally dismissed as irrelevant by southern nationalists.

The history of northern nationalism since 1921 has differed even more markedly from that of the south. The partition of Ireland placed the Roman Catholics in a permanent minority position, and one to which the minority was slow to accommodate. They were now in the Northern Ireland state, but they were uncertain about whether to adjust to the fact, and thus abandon their aspirations towards a reunited Ireland, or deny the new state their allegiance, and thus marginalize themselves further. Their predicament was compounded by the ambivalent attitude of southern nationalists to Northern Ireland and to the Roman Catholic minority. This ambivalence has been explored in a well-written and sustained critique of Irish nationalism, exposing its mixture of bafflement, complacency and distaste for northern politics.[30] The whole question of the northern Protestant and Catholic predicament has been used to explore what nationalists in their day barely troubled themselves to address: their concept of the 'Irish nation' and the means which they proposed to use to maintain, or reconstruct, what they liked to call 'national unity'.

This had a profound effect on northern nationalism. While the south proceeded to assert its sovereignty, culminating in the state's neutrality in the Second World War, and its declaration of a republic in 1949, northern nationalists were unable to develop a political strategy appropriate to their predicament. This would have been difficult whatever the general context, but their failure to do so pushed them into taking refuge behind the institutional structures of the Catholic church in the north — its clubs, societies, schools — with attempts to 'borrow into' certain aspects of Irish nationalism, such as the Gaelic language and Gaelic sports. The northern troubles which came to a head in 1969 have attracted much attention, as might be expected, but there is a serious lack of continuity in exploring the early days of the northern state, the nationalist response to the state, its history within the state, and the crisis of politics of the late 1960s. Northern Ireland has been part of the United Kingdom throughout its existence; and the politics of the minority has involved an appeal to Liberal and Labour elements in Great Britain, as in 1945 when the election of a Labour government helped create a nationalist revival in the north, and an anti-partition campaign.[31] The reactive tendency of northern nationalism is important, for its minority position has obliged it to review events in Dublin and London, as much as Belfast.

This parallel between nationalist reaction in 1945 and the civil rights movement of 1964 (following the election of the third post-war Labour government) raises a neglected aspect of northern nationalism. The lack of research on northern nationalism before 1964 is inhibiting; the need for a continuous study is obvious, for if Ulster Unionism were to be studied in isolation from its historical background, then the defects of such an approach would be clearly exposed. Yet northern nationalism has had no such treatment. Instead it has been subjected to a rather polemical discussion on the issue of the deductions which might properly be made from Northern Ireland elections in the 1960s. Christopher Hewitt has argued from this data that the trend in the 1960s was not — as writers on the Civil Rights movement have argued — away from traditional nationalism, but, on the contrary, towards nationalism; and that nationalism was not successfully challenged by leftist politics in the 1960s: 'To conclude, all indicators of nationalist sentiment among Catholics show an increase in the period just before NICRA became active.'[32] But this was before Civil Rights offered a more modern alternative. Steve Bruce, in his study of Paisleyism, suggests that there is a need for more research here, because while

> perhaps some parts of the civil rights movement were genuinely, rather than tactically assimilationist [i.e. to the United Kingdom state] ... the speed with which many of its leaders shifted to more traditional nationalist and republican positions suggests that a large part of the movement was always ultimately interested in dismantling Northern Ireland.

This he stresses

> does not rule out the possibility that some civil rights activists began as assimilationists and then abandoned their commitment to an Ulster solution when they saw the Unionist government alternating reformism with repression. But the tentative and tenuous nature of their commitment to an Ulster solution should not be overlooked.[33]

These are tentative suggestions, and must remain so while so much basic research needs to be done. So far historians have left the field to political sociologists, anthropologists and the like, whose research, while certainly valuable,[34] lacks an historical approach, and leaves the discussion of northern nationalism bereft of its essential roots in the past. The experience, the total cultural, personal, as well as political, experience, of the Catholic minority needs exploration. Its marginalization in Ulster began long before 1921, let alone 1969; its particular political perspective was well expressed by Bishop McHugh of Derry who, when he protested against Sinn Féin foisting Eoin MacNeill (an Ulster candidate with a southern allegiance) on Derry City in 1918, remarked that 'in Derry we cannot forget that we are Catholics. To be a party to any action that would lose the seat would be very unCatholic.'[35]

The study of Irish nationalism rarely invites a highly conceptual or theoretical debate. It has not necessarily suffered because of this, for the specificity of Ireland — in the early modern period a sort of kingdom and a sort of colony; in the eighteenth century a kingdom and a dependent state; in the nineteenth century a part of the United Kingdom with a separate administration — renders it a not particularly suitable laboratory for direct comparisons or generalizations. But one part of the Irish political tradition — Ulster Unionism — has, paradoxically, raised a theoretical dimension that must be addressed, and one that provokes reflection on the concept of nationalism itself.

The Northern 'troubles' have, again, provided an occasion for academic speculation about what constitutes 'nationality': nationalism, or — an increasingly popular expression — 'ethnicity'. The Protestant majority of the north has been described as constituting a nation: it has a sense of the past, a sense of common identity, a distinctive region in which to live, a clear and unmistakable desire to define itself against its Irish Catholic political opponents. The 'troubles', in this view, are not a conflict between two groups of people. 'They are a conflict between two nationalistic ideologies.'[36] Social scientists have defined Ulster Unionism as a form of 'ethnic identity', a vague and unsatisfactory term, borrowed from anthropology, and now given a political and social meaning as

> a principle of recruitment to group membership which stresses a shared social or cultural identity, which is frequently combined with an oppositional stance relative to other ethnic groups. In other words, membership of an ethnic group offers a definition of 'us' *and* a characterisation of 'them'. As such, ethnicity can either be the source of conflict or the cultural or ideological idiom in which conflict is pursued; it can also, of course, be a source of social solidarity.[37]

If the Ulster Unionists constitute an ethnic group, then it might be argued that they are not a nation, but a sub-group of nation;[38] but others have insisted that Ulster Unionists are an 'ethnic nation', that is, a people whose sense of the past, and participation in a communal identity, has made them so distinct from the other inhabitants of the island that they are indeed a separate nation, whose state was founded amidst violence and disorder in 1921.[39]

The difficulty with this line of argument is that the Ulster Unionists did not claim to be a nation, even at a time when, in the late nineteenth and early twentieth centuries, it would have suited them to do so — when the idea of the nation-state and national self-determination were fast becoming political orthodoxies. Ulster Unionists might have been expected to judge it expedient to move with the trends, and thus pose problems for Gladstone, Asquith and Lloyd George. Yet in the 1880s and 1890s they still spoke of themselves as Irish. The Reverend James Cregan of Belfast admitted, at the 1892 Ulster Unionist Convention, that he 'never felt prouder of being an Irishman than I did on Friday June 17th.' 'I'm an Irishman — born in Loyal Belfast' a 'New Loyal Song against Home Rule' began, warning that 'Old Ireland's fate' would be ruined by home rule.[40] Ulster Unionists denied that nationalism could be a principle of political action; they asserted that the conflict was one between 'loyal' and 'disloyal' Ireland. Even as late as 1925 the Unionist *Northern Whig*, provoked by the Irish Free State's intention of setting up a separate medical profession, declared that

> When Ulster declined to join the South in separating from Great Britain it did not surrender its title as part of Ireland, nor renounce its share in those Irish traditions in art, in learning, in arms, in song, in sport and in science that were worth preserving in a united form.[41]

And one of the ablest of contemporary Unionist political thinkers has written that:

> Only if one is an Irish nationalist is there something intrinsically incompatible (an identity crisis) if one drinks Guinness, loves to holiday in Donegal or Killarney, supports an all-Ireland rugby team in Dublin, recognises that one is 'Irish', and yet at the same time is a committed Unionist.[42]

This debate, however problematical in its use of terms like 'ethnic' and 'nation', had at least the merit of making historians and political scientists self-conscious about the subject of nationalism and national identity. In particular, it directed their attention to the indices of nationalism, not only those that were normally listed in any such discussion — language, race, religion — but the historical experience that moulded a varied set of people (in the Unionist case, Anglicans, Presbyterians, Methodists, and a whole host of small sects) into a 'Protestant people'. Moreover, it challenged the idea, held by some, that Ulster Unionists lacked a 'cultural dimension' that Irish nationalism possessed — ignoring the firm location of this Irish nationalist dimension in the Anglo–Irish, rather than Catholic Irish, tradition. Ulster Protestants at least possessed a culture in the sense defined by Hugh Kearney: 'life-styles, customs, religion and attitudes to the past.'[43]

This academic debate had, of course, political overtones. Political activists explored the traditions of the northern Protestants and produced a lively, if unhistorical, literature, relating to the idea of an Ulster nation, or, in more relaxed fashion, a whole Ulster community, distinct from that of the rest of Ireland, and embracing all the people of the province, Catholic and Protestant alike. Ulster formed a 'Scots–Irish cultural province'; when the Presbyterians came to the north in the seventeenth century, then, as one of their historians wrote, 'they were only returning to their own lands like emigrants returning home again'. The language of Ulster was a unique blend of Gaelic and Scottish Lallans, and both linguistic traditions were 'under threat by the combined influences of British and Irish nationalisms'. Sir Samuel Ferguson was the real father of Ulster culture because his nationality encompassed 'both a British and an Irish sentiment, in which the common denominator was Ulster'. Cuchulainn was not the champion of Patrick Pearse and the men of 1916, but the champion of 'Ulster, legendary defender of Ulster's boundaries against the "men of Ireland"'.[44]

But if Ulster Protestants and Catholics were engaged in exploring what held them together, as well as what pushed them apart, the same cannot be said for the rest of Ireland. While nationalism in the north remained disputed territory between the Social Democratic and Labour Party and the Provisional Sinn Féin party (the political wing of the Provisional IRA), nationalism in the south presented a more unusual spectacle. This was the apparent discrepancy between the nationalist style in which its political elite sometimes conducted its politics, and the total lack of concern of the electorate and public opinion on constitutional matters. As in 1981, politics in the south of Ireland were dominated by local concerns, local issues — or, more properly, in the context of a sovereign state, 'national' concerns and national issues.[45] The revolt of the tax-payer was of more immediate concern than the revolt of the IRA. Yet the head of the Fianna Fáil elite, in a press conference with British journalists in the November 1982 election, could declare that 'I can only take one foreigner at a time', and in an official statement his party branded the Duke of Norfolk as a 'trained British spy'.[46] The idea of the 'natural unity' of the country remained unchallenged. Even the most avowedly pluralist of Irish party leaders, Dr Garret Fitzgerald, insisted that the unity of Irishmen was destroyed by partition; that partition had divided Irishmen, rather than been caused by Irishmen's pre-existing divisions.[47] The rejection of a reform of the Republic of Ireland's anti-abortion laws in a referendum in which the Roman Catholic church played a significant role was a clear denial of the natural unity of Ireland and of the concept of a pluralist Irish society.[48]

When eventually nationalism did take stock of itself, in the New Ireland Forum launched in May 1983 and lasting until February 1984, it only revealed its inability to advance beyond the ground rules laid down in the preceding fifty, one hundred, or perhaps several hundred years. The Forum comprised an impressive and distinguished assembly of lay and clerical leaders, representing the constitutional nationalist tradition. It held numerous sessions, collected written and verbal submissions, and visited the north to meet groups 'representative of a wide range of opinion'.[49] But its conclusions were entirely traditional, if not predictable. The root of the problem lay in the constitutional arrangements devised by Britain in 1920 'which resulted in the arbitrary division of Ireland'. The 1920 Government of Ireland Act was a denial of the 'democratically expressed wishes of the Irish people'. The Act was the direct consequence of Ulster Unionist violence, or the threat of violence, which convinced nationalists that they too were entitled to use violence.[50] What history had done wrong, history could only put right by undoing history: by the creation once again of a unitary Irish state 'by agreement and consent, embracing the whole island of Ireland and providing irrevocable guarantees for the protection and preservation of both the unionist and nationalist identities'.[51] But a unitary state was exactly what Unionists felt could not provide any such guarantee. And the southern state's rejection of any change in its attitude to abortion law reform and divorce[52] seemed to suggest that the new Ireland would be very much like the old — only rather larger.

The Forum glossed over another aspect of the nation's problems, that of the Roman Catholic minority in the north, whose experience was so different from that of the south, and who would in a very real sense constitute yet another all-Ireland minority in a united Ireland, joining the northern and southern Protestants in that unwelcome status. Territorial integrity in the face of political disunity none the less remained the southern goal, as the Anglo–Irish Agreement of 1985 indicated. This Agreement was not a takeover bid for the North, nor was it another notch in the tally stick of the Provisional IRA as they marched through blood to freedom. It was an effort to protect constitutional nationalism from falling to Sinn Féin as the latter rose to prominence in the wake of the hunger strikes of 1981.[53] Sinn Féin claimed to be the legitimate successor of the founding fathers of the republic — not of the state that really existed and exists in Ireland, but of the state that should have existed, and would be recreated in the future. The 'Northern nationalist' (*sic*), Gerry Adams wrote, 'looks at the 26 counties and is not impressed. From the perspective of an Irish person in a British state — a dispossessed and disadvantaged person — the 26 county state looks pretty sick, in political life even more so.' Leinster House, the Irish Parliament, was the preserve 'by and large, of unprincipled careerists'. And Sinn Féin was now taking steps to reverse the 'counter revolution' of 1919-23.[54]

In these circumstances it was perhaps unrealistic, though undoubtedly for Unionists highly desirable, for the Irish Republic to abandon its claims to the north, claims made in the 1937 constitution's articles 2 and 3. There was nothing, wrote Mr Justice Donal Barrington, a judge of the High Court, 'in articles 2 and 3 of the Constitution ... to inhibit the Government in its quest for an interim solution, provided that the aim of ultimate national unity is preserved' — which was precisely the claim that Ulster Unionists disputed, and the fear that they held most deeply. Barrington added, disarmingly, that 'in the interval, we must all try to keep the peace'.[55]

Yet this formal nationalist claim, repeated and renewed in each generation since 1937, and regarded now as inviolable, was not accompanied by any significant or sustained public interest in such matters. General elections revealed the public's declining nationalism, or rather its declining interest in actively promoting the national cause. The overwhelming support in the south for the Anglo–Irish Agreement almost certainly reflected, not a desire to push the Unionists of the north into an all-Ireland state, but the uncertainty of the whole southern political world about unification; it represented the belief in the principle of unification, the distaste for northern and especially IRA violence, the willingness to allow for 'interim' solutions (interim being a term of infinite flexibility), and the need to have as much to do with the north as appeared respectable, and as little to do with it as possible, given the north's potential for destabilizing the whole island of Ireland. Recent opinion polls seemed to indicate that the general public did not share the political establishment's convictions about the territorial integrity of the island. A survey in 1987 found in its sample that only 56 per cent of the people in the Republic considered the Irish nation to consist of thirty-two counties (down from 63 per cent in 1983), with 38 per cent opting for the twenty-six counties as the extent of the Irish nation (up from 34 per cent in 1983); only 33 per cent of those questioned considered the people of Northern Ireland unambiguously Irish (down from 41 per cent in 1983), with 42 per cent of the sample considering the people of Northern Ireland both Irish and British (up from 39 per cent in 1983); a 15 per cent minority considered the Northern Irish people to be unambiguously British. On the question of reunification, 67 per cent of the 1987 survey hoped for reunification (down from 76 per cent in 1983), with 19 per cent not wanting unification. About half of those questioned believed that the north would never be reunited with the rest of Ireland.[56]

Southern Irish nationalism, then, remains uncertain about its ideals and goals as it approaches the twenty-first century. It still holds to the idea of the essential territorial unity of Ireland; yet the general public of the south apparently do not regard this as any kind of constitutional imperative, and frequently reveal fear and distaste for Northern Irish political violence (and sympathy for its victims). The political parties hold to their nationalist goals; yet are careful not to present their electorate with stark choices that might not win votes. Ambiguity is enshrined in the 1985 Anglo–Irish Agreement as much as in the 1921 Anglo–Irish Treaty, or the 1938 Anglo–Irish Agreements, where southern perspectives were apparently reconciled with a certain pragmatism about the north, even a feeling that, when all is said and done, Ireland is still Ireland, as de Valera put it, without the north. Irish nationalists have always regarded the Protestant as an Irishman, but one with a difference; yet a difference that cannot be politically acknowledged lest the idea of 'one nation' be compromised. The southern state has developed its own special kind of politics, small-scale, based on family and personal ties; even the modern state is based upon that political style. But the stability of the southern state and the ever more homogeneous nature of its population, have inhibited its leaders from appreciating the morbid suspicions and anxieties of the north. They have found it hard to understand the fears of a million Protestants, and can hardly even grasp the depth of disaffection of the northern Roman Catholics.

Irish nationalism in the 1990s seems, as always, on the verge of change, and yet committed to staying the same. In its most virulent and assertive form it is the preserve of Northern nationalists (or most of them), of the Irish political establishment and some of the Irish literary establishment. A book dedicated to exploring the 'Irish mind', published in 1985, opened with an onslaught on English influence in Ireland, denouncing Disraeli's and Charles Kingsley's 'colonial characterisation of the Irish', and deploring the fact that Catholic, Protestant and Dissenter had 'over time come to espouse some of the intellectual, or rather anti-intellectual, prejudices of their historical opponents'. 'Master and slave' was the relation of the 'Irish' to the 'English', and 'the slave's image of himself is precisely that — an image. His speech is taken from him not only by the master but by himself . . . he is a slave because he identifies with servile discourse'. The 'colonial image of the master had been adopted by a considerable section of our population', and Ireland's leading poet, Seamus Heaney, stood 'exposed to the cultures of coloniser and colonised, Catholic and Protestant, Gael and Saxon'.[57]

This cultural Anglophobia is, probably, more self-maiming than other-maiming. And there is another kind of nationalism — or, more precisely, sense of nationality — that informs the mass of the southern Irish people, one that has little to do with the Anglophobia of the literary elite, and is unlikely to be challenged by 'revisionist historians', in their wonderment at the lack of impact of their work on the public at large. It is what Professor John A. Murphy defined as 'a sense of nationality (pietas towards the past, commitment to the present, hope for the future)' which 'is an integral and essential part of the outlook of the common Irishman whose life style ... is of necessity bounded by domestic horizons'.[58] There is, on the face of it, nothing in this uncomplicated sense of nationality at all malevolent towards Ulster Unionists, or dismissive of their background and traditions. It is the kind of sentiment that Ian Adamson and those like him are seeking to create in the north: popular, democratic, homely. But it still suffers from the old disability of all Irish nationalisms in that it represents a homogeneous Catholic people. Yet when Irish nationalism is seen in historical perspective, it is surely the creation of an interplay and tension between what Edmund Curtis (a nationalist after his fashion and a Protestant) called 'the balance between the three dominant creeds of Ireland ... the primary factor in modern Irish history'.[59]

Notes

1. György Csepeli, *Structures and Contents of Hungarian National Identity* (Frankfurt, 1989), p. 9.

2. See e.g. Steven G. Ellis, 'Nationalist historiography and the English and Gaelic worlds in the late Middle Ages', in *IHS*, vol. xxv, no. 97 (1986), pp. 1-18; Hugh Kearney, *The British Isles: A History of Four Nations* (Cambridge, 1989).

3. T.W. Moody, 'Irish history and Irish mythology', in *Hermathena*, nos. CXXIV-CXXVII (1978-9), pp. 7-24.

4. Ibid., p. 23; for another example see R.F. Foster, 'History and the Irish Question', in *TRHS*, 5th series, vol. 33 (1983), p. 192.

5. Brendan Bradshaw, 'Nationalism and historical scholarship in modern Ireland', in *IHS*, vol. xxvi, no. 104 (1989), pp. 329-51.

6. Ibid., p. 350.

7. J. Eglinton, *Anglo-Irish Essays* (London and Dublin, 1917).

8. Ibid., p. 3.

9. Ibid., pp. 3-4.

10. Ibid., p. 5.

11. Ibid., pp. 6, 7, 8.

12. Ibid., p. 9.

13. Bradshaw, op. cit., pp. 338-40.

14. R.V. Comerford, *The Fenians in Context: Irish Politics and Society, 1848-82* (Dublin, 1985).

15. John Hutchinson, 'Cultural nationalism, elite mobility and nation-building: communitarian politics in modern Ireland', in *British Journal of Sociology*, vol. 38

(1987), pp. 482-500; *The Dynamics of Cultural Nationalism: The Gaelic Revival and the Creation of the Irish Nation State* (London, 1987).

16. Hutchinson, op cit., p. 498.

17. Tom Garvin, *Nationalist Revolutionaries in Ireland, 1858-1928* (Oxford, 1987); 'Great hatred, little room: social background and political sentiment among revolutionary activists in Ireland, 1879-1923', in D.G. Boyce (ed.), *The Revolution in Ireland, 1879-1923* (London, 1988), pp. 91-114.

18. Garvin, op cit., pp. 93, 95.

19. David FitzPatrick, 'The geography of Irish nationalism, 1910-1921', in *P. and P.*, no. 78 (1978), p. 113.

20. Ruth Dudley Edwards, *Patrick Pearse: The Triumph of Failure* (London, 1977); Austen Morgan, *James Connolly: A Political Biography* (Manchester, 1989).

21. What he calls 'national consciousness' or 'communal memory' (pp. 341, 344).

22. Tom Bartlett, 'An end to moral economy: the Irish militia disturbances of 1793', in *P. and P.*, no. 99 (1983), pp. 41-64.

23. Comerford, op. cit., p. 21.

24. K.T. Hoppen, *Elections, Politics and Society in Ireland, 1832-1885* (Oxford, 1984); see also his *Ireland Since 1800: Conflict and Conformity* (London, 1989).

25. P. Bew, *Conflict and Conciliation in Ireland, 1890-1910: Parnellites and Radical Agrarians* (Oxford, 1987), p. 210.

26. Examples of empathy which yet remain critical are given by Dr Bradshaw on pages 343-4, fn. 43, op. cit.

27. Owen Dudley Edwards, *Eamon de Valera* (Cardiff, 1988).

28. Which seems to be the implication of Dr Bradshaw's point in his refutation of what he sees as such an approach in Steven Ellis's article (Bradshaw, op. cit., pp. 332-3; Ellis, op. cit., p. 4, fn. 14).

29. John B. Dooher, 'Tyrone nationalism and the question of partition, 1910-1925' (M. Phil., University of Ulster, 1986), p. 70; Mr Dooher's thesis is one of the few serious scholarly studies of Northern nationalism.

30. Clare O'Halloran, *Partition and the Limits of Irish Nationalism: An Ideology under Stress* (Dublin, 1987).

31. Bob Purdie, 'The Irish Anti-Partition League, South Armagh and the abstentionist tactic, 1945-58', in *Irish Political Studies*, vol. 1 (1986), pp. 67-77.

32. C. Hewitt, 'Catholic grievances, Catholic nationalism and violence in Northern Ireland during the Civil Rights period: a reconsideration', in *British Journal of Sociology*, vol. 32 (1981), pp. 362-80. The complete list of articles and counter-articles is given in the bibliography.

33. Steve Bruce, *God Save Ulster: The Religion and Politics of Paisleyism* (Oxford, 1986), p. 266.

34. See for example the interesting essay by Graham McFarlane, ' "It's not as simple as that": the expression of the Catholic and Protestant boundary in Northern Irish rural communities', in Anthony P. Cohen (ed.) *Symbolising Boundaries: Identity and Diversity in British Cultures* (Manchester, 1986), pp. 88-104.

35. Dooher, op. cit., p. 255.

36. D.G. Pringle, *One Island, Two Nations? A Political Geographical Analysis of the National Conflict in Ireland* (Research Studies Press Ltd, Letchworth, Hertfordshire, 1985), p. 24.

37. Richard Jenkins, 'Northern Ireland: in what sense "religions" in conflict?', in Richard Jenkins, Hastings Donnan and Graham McFarlane, *The Sectarian Divide in Northern Ireland Today* (Royal Anthropological Institute of Great Britain and Ireland, Occasional Paper no. 41, 1986), p. 4.

38. Bruce, op. cit., p. 258.

39. B.A. Follis, 'The establishment of Northern Ireland, 1920-1925' (Ph.D., Queen's University of Belfast, 1990).

40. D.G. Boyce, 'Marginal Britons: the Irish', in Robert Colls and Philip Dodd (eds), *Englishness: Politics and Culture, 1880-1920* (London, 1986), pp. 232-3.

41. Dennis Kennedy, *The Widening Gulf: Northern Attitudes to the Independent Irish State, 1919-1949* (Belfast, 1988), p. 230.

42. Arthur Aughey, *Under Siege: Ulster Unionism and the Anglo-Irish Agreement* (London, 1989), p. 16.

43. Hugh Kearney, op. cit., p. 4.

44. Ian Adamson, *The Identity of Ulster: The Land, the Language and the People* (Belfast, 1982), pp. ix, xi, 12, 78-9, 108, 116.

45. As I remarked in the first edition of *Nationalism in Ireland* (1982), p. 369.

46. Bruce Arnold, *What Kind of Country: Modern Irish Politics, 1968-1983* (London, 1984), p. 204.

47. *The Times*, 21 May 1982.

48. Clare O'Halloran, op. cit., pp. 193-4; Bruce Arnold, op. cit., pp. 217-18.

49. *New Ireland Forum Report* (Dublin, 1984), p. 3.

50. Ibid., pp. 5, 7-8.

51. Ibid., p. 19.

52. As Charles Haughey put it, 'we need apologise to nobody about the character or performance of our State, and we do not intend to do so' (Clare O'Halloran, op. cit., p. 207).

53. At an election held in November 1982 Sinn Féin won one third of the nationalist vote in the North.

54. Gerry Adams, *The Politics of Irish Freedom* (Bandon, Kerry, 1986), pp. 37, 38, 160.

55. Donal Barrington, 'The North and the Constitution', in Brian Farrell (ed.), *De Valera's Constitution and Ours* (Dublin, 1988), p. 73.

56. Gearóid Ó Tuathaigh, 'The Irish nation-state in the Constitution', in Farrell, op. cit., p. 58.

57. Richard Kearney (ed.), *The Irish Mind: Exploring Intellectual Traditions* (Dublin, 1985), pp. 7-8, 12.

58. John A. Murphy, 'Further reflections on Irish nationalism', in *Crane Bag*, vol. 2, nos. 1 and 2 (1978), p. 307.

59. Edmund Curtis, *A History of Ireland* (1939; London, 1961 edn), p. 399.

EPILOGUE: CONTEMPORARY IRELAND: NATIONALIST AND POST-NATIONALIST?

I

On the morning of 31 August 1994 the Provisional IRA declared a 'complete cessation of military operations' to take effect from midnight. Two days previously the president of Sinn Féin, Gerry Adams, put it to the IRA that it was his 'considered position' that 'Irish nationalism, if properly mobilised and focused at home and abroad, now has sufficient political confidence, insight and support to bring about the changes which are essential for a lasting peace'. On the day of the IRA ceasefire he told cheering crowds outside Sinn Féin headquarters that 'the struggle is not over; it is in a new phase'.[1] This 'new phase' poses challenges as profound to the people of southern Ireland as it does to those in the north; if this were to be an historic moment, then the clock would strike on both sides of the border.

Unionists felt a sense of relief pervaded by fear: the spectacle of the Irish Taoiseach Albert Reynolds, the leader of the constitutional nationalist party, the SDLP, John Hume and Gerry Adams clasping hands in Dublin could be taken as indicating that the Irish nationalist project had indeed entered a new phase. Albert Reynolds' observation on television that his own party, Fianna Fáil, had after all taken root in a militant Republican movement in the Irish civil war of 1922–3 might be taken as comforting in one context – for it showed that militant Republicanism could, in the end, produce a moderate, pragmatic and decent leader like himself. But it might equally indicate that from such unpromising beginnings there could grow a political movement that could take power in Ireland, and that Sinn Féin was only at the beginning of a long trail that would at least take it to the heart of the Irish nationalist pantheon; and this could hardly bode well for Unionists and the Union.

These remarkable and dramatic moves, followed by talk of a peace process, of 'bits of the jigsaw falling into place', and then six weeks later, by a Loyalist paramilitary ceasefire, must provoke reflections on the character of nationalism in Ireland, that most adaptable political phenomenon. The expression 'nationalism in Ireland' is perhaps more appropriate than Irish nationalism, for this book has demonstrated the differences that have evolved between nationalism in the north of Ireland, and its counterpart in the south; differences which provoked one

414

articulate Sinn Féin representative, Danny Morrison, to declare in 1988, in response to the question, 'In terms of a political solution, what about those who don't want a united Ireland?':

> Tell us. People of the 26 counties that don't want the Six Counties, let us know. If they're telling us to f...k off, telling us they're happy with the state they've got and f...k 1916, then tell us. Because, if they don't want us then I would have to look again at the situation.... If they think they've got an Irish nation inside the 26 counties, they should build a wall and lock us out.[2]

Morrison's bewilderment was shared by others. The years of Charles Haughey's political ascendancy were remarkable for his ability to combine and even reconcile traditional nationalist rhetoric, calls for the British to end the Unionist veto on unification, and a reaffirmation of the nation's need to hold on to its nationalist interpretation of its past, with a fine understanding of the limited appeal of such rhetoric to the Irish electorate. In September 1982, for example, in a speech on the 'Renewed Political Struggle in Ireland', Haughey reiterated Theobald Wolfe Tone's claim that Ireland's divisions 'arose directly from British rule', but denounced the very means by which Tone sought Irish freedom – the use of force – and concluded that Fianna Fáil sought 'genuine reconciliation based on justice, mutual respect, and democracy between every inhabitant of this island'.[3] When beside this is set the spectacle of Margaret Thatcher, a declared supporter of the Union, placing her name on the 1985 Anglo–Irish Agreement that most Unionists perceived as compromising the Union with Britain, then the notion that the 1980s were a period when ideological politics flourished must be treated with caution.

It is an oversimplification, therefore, to present the change of political leadership in southern Ireland and the United Kingdom, from Thatcher/Haughey to Major/Reynolds, as some kind of fundamental shift in the Anglo–Irish relationship, and therefore in Northern Ireland policy. Albert Reynolds was perfectly capable of satisfying his more nationally minded Fianna Fáil supporters. On 1 April 1933 he reaffirmed his commitment to articles 2 and 3 of the 1937 Irish constitution laying claim to Northern Ireland in a speech which the *Irish Times* declared was 'unbearably complacent and historically inaccurate'.[4] As far as the United Kingdom was concerned, the Union seemed as safe under John Major as it had been under the self-professed Unionist, Margaret Thatcher. But the central guiding principle of Anglo–Irish relations was still that laid down by the Anglo-Irish Agreement of 1985: that the London and Dublin governments, for all their occasional and sometimes frequent disagreements, were committed to working for good relations with each other, and would not jeopardize these for the Unionists or the nationalists in the North. If Ulster was British, it was British with a difference; if Ulster was still Irish, then too that was a claim made with some qualification. A public opinion poll in southern Ireland, taken in November 1993, indicated that 51 per cent of the Irish electorate would vote to change articles 2 and 3 of the Irish constitution; that 41 per cent wanted them rewritten as an aspiration; that 21 per cent didn't know; and that 28 per cent wanted to retain them. A similar poll two years previously indicated that 58 per cent wanted to retain the articles. In 1992 the percentage wishing to retain them was 41.[5] Clearly, then, national aspirations in the south of Ireland were in a process of change, and the hope that the people of the south might yet be induced to coerce, or approve of, the coercion of the Unionists in the North was a fading dream of Republican orthodoxy.

Not that Republican orthodoxy, in its purity, had ever claimed to wish to coerce the protestants of Ireland; on the contrary, it was a Republican tradition, constantly restated, that what distinguished it from other forms of Irish nationalism was precisely its desire to replace the divisions between Protestant, Catholic and Dissenter with the common name of Irishman. But the problem was that those to whom this tradition most appealed in recent decades were the kind of people whose outlook and grievances most fuelled sectarian conflict. The IRA war since 1970 pushed Republicanism further down the road to a divisive rather than a unifying political ideology. And since Republicanism took an insurrectionary form, it naturally accepted that the few had the right to dominate and, if need be, coerce the many, be they dissident nationalists, 'Free Staters', or the million Protestants of the North – the majority had no right to be wrong. This gave militant Republicanism, in the form of the Provisional IRA, and its political wing, Sinn Féin, a certain strength; and armed struggle creates its own inner securities, as the certainty of ultimate victory is fuelled by the joy of battle in the present. But from the late 1980s there were signs that Northern Republicanism was at least taking stock of its own political predicament. It had failed to break out of its traditional areas into a more general support; its share of the vote stood stubbornly at 10 per cent; the Roman Catholic people whose protection it invoked as a justification for its existence were suffering increasingly from attack at the hands of loyalist paramilitaries; and it stood in danger of appearing to be neither more nor less than a manifestation of inner-city social and economic deprivation. This seemed appropriate material for sociological analysis on the one hand, police surveillance on the other, and not the wider political canvas on which any settlement of the Troubles must be painted.

It is not all that surprising then that the Sinn Féin leader, Gerry Adams, should find it possible to renew talks with John Hume, talks which had taken place in the aftermath of the Anglo–Irish Agreement, and then been broken off. The two leaders met again on 10 April 1993, not having met for discussions in two years. The SDLP continued to show its ability – which it shares with the old Home Rule party that dominated Irish politics between 1886 and 1918 – to adjust itself to changing circumstances, even to exhibit traces of Republicanism without compromising its constitutional nationalism, to almost dazzle with its kaleidoscopic image and, above all, to appear indispensable to British governments as they searched for an Irish settlement. In October 1992 John Hume described Northern Ireland as an 'unnatural political entity', irreformable in normal democratic terms. In May 1993 his agreed statement with Gerry Adams used the Sinn Féin language to claim the right to self-determination for the Irish people 'as a whole', though with the qualification that this must be on an agreed basis between Unionists and Nationalists. A leading Sinn Féiner, Mitchel McLaughlin, saw the need for 'the next three or four generations to arrive at political arrangements which would allow those of a Unionist tradition to live in an Irish democracy and with nationalism, without being compelled to be part of that nationalism.'[6] But he did not explain why Unionists should exchange what they regard as the certainty of their survival as a community in the United Kingdom for the uncertainty of their survival in an 'Irish democracy'.

In August 1994, in Co. Wicklow (Parnell's home ground) a conciliatory John Hume could nevertheless complain about Unionists' inability or unwillingness to stand on their own two feet, instead of clinging to Great Britain[7] – which was the equivalent of Unionists' irritation at nationalists for wanting to do just that, and stand up on their legs as a 'nation' when they were manifestly proclaiming a myth. Hume was capable of turning the Republican saint, Theobald Wolfe Tone, against Gerry Adams in their discussions, when Hume argued that Sinn Féin ought to abandon its role as a sect, and become a political party, with a more positive approach to Unionism.[8]

Above all, Hume, like Parnell, remained at the centre of the political process, for he was perceived (at least by most politicians in Britain and southern Ireland) as the man who could deliver a settlement. This, however, only served all the more to convince Unionists that, as one of their number put it following a speech by the Northern Ireland Secretary, Sir Patrick Mayhew, in Bangor, Co. Down in March 1993, 'it seems to Unionists that John Hume has an absolute veto over any progress in the province'.[9]

And yet progress was made. It was becoming clearer in 1992 and 1993 that most, if not all, parties to the political conflict were seeking a way out of the deadlock that had characterized Northern Ireland policy and politics since the collapse of the so-called Brooke–Mayhew talks which were initiated in May 1990.[10] These talks, called after the two Northern Ireland secretaries who had steered them through to their unsuccessful conclusion, Peter Brooke and Sir Patrick Mayhew, identified three 'strands': the achievement of devolved government for Northern Ireland; North–South relations; and Irish–United Kingdom relations, though 'nothing is agreed until everything is agreed'. The talks seemed only to reveal the gap between Unionism and Nationalism. But the Official Unionists had gone to Dublin to meet representatives of the Irish government (which the Democratic Unionists refused to do), and the Ulster Unionists clearly accepted power-sharing and an Irish dimension. The SDLP produced its 'European' formula, which was that there should be a six-man Northern Ireland executive commission, including one representative from the European community, one from Dublin and one from London.[11] The Brooke–Mayhew talks collapsed in November 1992, revealing that for Unionists, the Irish state's claim to the north was a major obstacle to progress, and that nationalists seemed less committed to a united Ireland, but deeply committed to some kind of joint authority rule by Dublin and London.

If the SDLP was open to the accusation that it exercised too much influence with Dublin, and perhaps also with London, then it could at least reply that it was a party whose leadership showed a variety of political skills, and a relentless search for initiatives. Although an overworked word, initiative seemed a more acceptable alternative to succumbing to the despair that periodically engulfed Northern Ireland as fresh waves of atrocity followed relentlessly one upon the other. It seemed that by 1992 there were significant movements in the subterranean politics of Republicanism; perhaps a little more of the concealed part of the iceberg was inching its way to the surface. In February 1992 Sinn Féin published a discussion paper, *Towards a Lasting Peace in Ireland*, which acknowledged that Unionist fears must be addressed, rather than dismissed, and accepted that a British 'withdrawal' must be an agreed one, not the consequence of a military defeat. Both London and Dublin must be involved in this agreed withdrawal.[12] This amounted to an acknowledgement that Sinn Féin recognized the legitimacy of the Irish government, which was a long step from its aspiration in the early 1980s to 'take power in Ireland' and overthrow the 'illegitimate' southern regime. This had another effect, in that it would in the passage of no great time, enable the Irish government to assert its moral authority over Sinn Féin, and move it closer to a new realism. For if the Irish government was indeed legitimate, and spoke for most people in the whole island of Ireland, then it was hard for Sinn Féin to ignore its wishes, or flout its advice.

In March 1993 the IRA managed to create a wave of revulsion comparable to that which followed its bombing of a Remembrance Day parade in Enniskillen in November 1987. On 20 March a three-year-old boy was killed, and 56 people injured by a bomb in Warrington; on 25 March a twelve-year-old boy died of injuries received in the blast. British reaction to this outrage was matched only by that in southern Ireland, when president Mary Robinson's presence at the memorial service disassociated southern Ireland from Republican violence which claimed to be working for the nationalist goal of a thirty-two county Ireland. On 28 March up to 20,000 people attended a peace rally in Dublin,[13] and not even Sinn Féin's shrewd attempt to persuade the protestors to condemn 'British state violence' as being on a par with that of the IRA could quite enable Republicanism to recover from the propaganda setback.

The Republican war was by no means undermined by this crime; but it took place against a background of the British government's greater flexibility on the Union, initiated by Peter Brooke's claim in November 1990 that Britain had no economic or strategic interest in Northern Ireland. In December 1992 Sir Patrick Mayhew stated that Britain was neutral on the issue of Northern Ireland's position in the United Kingdom, and though he later qualified this by explaining that Britain was 'not neutral in defending the right of Northern Ireland people to democratic self-determination',[14] it was clear that a pattern of thinking had been established that could offer an opening to militant, as well as constitutional, nationalism. The Irish government for its part, built upon this when Albert Reynolds stated in the Dáil on 1 April 1993 that 'any attempt in a political vacuum to walk away from constitutional republicanism would be a very dangerous exercise and would most certainly provide a new recruiting platform for terrorism.'[15] Republicanism was now described as having a 'constitutional' character: Sinn Féin, by this reckoning, was not the 'political' but rather the 'constitutional' wing of the Provisional IRA. In April 1993 John Hume and Gerry Adams renewed their political dialogue, and on 24 April they issued a joint statement that:

> Everyone has a solemn duty to change the political climate away from conflict and towards a process of national reconciliation which sees the peaceful accommodation of the differences between the people of Britain and Ireland and the Irish people themselves.

This was followed by a complex statement that 'the Irish people as a whole have a right to national self-determination. This is a view shared by a majority of the people of this island, though not by all its people', adding the rider that 'we are mindful that not all the people of Ireland share that view or agree on how to give meaningful expression to it.'[16] This was a statement for nationalists, by nationalists, and meant to overcome the disagreements that divided nationalists: the phrase 'we do not disguise the different views held by our own parties' on how to give 'meaningful expression' to the aspiration of the declaration was less an acknowledgement of disagreement, and more of a move towards seeking a common nationalist ground. But the Hume–Adams talks, however alarming to Unionists, and possibly to the Dublin and London governments, helped move the two governments forward.

A new IRA outrage on 23 October 1993, when ten people including a child were killed in the Protestant Shankill Road seemed to set the stage for yet another setback to peace, followed as it was a week later by a loyalist reprisal in Greysteel, Co. Londonderry. But on 27 October 1993 the Irish foreign minister, Dick Spring, set out six democratic principles for peace, which he attributed to Hume's efforts: that the people of Ireland, north and south, should freely determine their future; that this could be expressed in new structures arising out of the three-stranded relationship; that there could be no change in Northern Ireland's status without freely given majority consent; this could be witheld; the consent principle could be written into the Irish constitution; and that a place would be available at the conference table for Sinn Féin, once the IRA had renounced violence.[17]

The way was paved for the discussions between British and Irish officials that led to the Downing Street Declaration of 15 December 1993 (see appendix). This declaration was not a settlement, nor did it contain any detailed proposals for the future of Northern Ireland. What it sought to do was affirm the Dublin–London axis, with each side giving a little in order to encourage the beginnings of a peace process. The most important part of the document, from the nationalist point of view, was the reiteration of the principle that Britain had no selfish strategic or economic interest in Ireland. This placed Sinn Féin, in particular, in an awkward position. They were now in effect being told that, in pushing the door to open the way to the British leaving Ireland, they were pushing an already open door – open as far as the British, though not of course the Ulster Unionists, were concerned. Republican violence, far from pushing the British out of Northern Ireland, was keeping them in – rather as if the door were a revolving one, in that the harder you pushed it, the more likely it was simply to propel you around to where you started in the first place. The Downing Street Declaration was welcomed by all parties in Great Britain and southern Ireland, and given a guarded degree of acceptance by the leader of the Ulster Unionists, James Moly-neux, and an enthusiastic endorsement by the Alliance Party. It was denounced as a sell-out by the Reverend Ian Paisley, leader of the Democratic Unionists. But the key response from nationalists must come from Sinn Féin.

Sinn Féin had to ransack its full vocabulary of opaque political language to find an appropriate response to the Downing Street Declaration. It procrastinated, demanding 'clarification' of the document. It postponed a full discussion until its annual Árd Fheis in February 1994, when Gerry Adams accepted it as a fundamental shift in policy, but added that it was riddled with contradictions and confusion. He demanded clarification on Britain's long-term intentions in Ireland, and urged Britain to persuade Unionists that their future lay in a united Ireland. Shortly afterwards, Adams embarked on a tour of the United States, where he appeared on various platforms and media programmes urging Britain to grasp the historic opportunity and issue a new unequivocal and all-inclusive 'proposition for peace'. Were such a proposition to be made, he would personally undertake to persuade the IRA to make a definitive ceasefire and end the violence.[18] The IRA called a ceasefire between 6 and 8 April to encourage a 'clarification' of the issues, probably in the hope of exploiting disagreement in London and Dublin about the best strategy to pursue. Republicans were shocked when London and Dublin criticized the ceasefire as wholly inadequate, and called for a permanent end to violence. Adams now tried again. He had on 31 March asked for clarification of the Declaration in three areas: certain tactical matters; conflicts in interpretation; and the 'processes envisaged in it'. He was rebuffed on 7 April,[19] but on 13 May Sinn Féin returned with a written list of questions, forwarded to the Irish government for transmission to London. On 19 May the British government replied, confirming that a referendum would be used to determine the wishes of the people of Northern Ireland, but saying that most of the questions were 'to some extent invitations to negotiate', and this was unacceptable unless violence ended. On 30 May the Sinn Féin spokesman, Martin McGuinness, described the answers as a 'small step in the slowly moving peace process', and Gerry Adams declared himself satisfied with the reply.[24] In a conference in Letterkenny on 24 July Sinn Féin stated that the Declaration was a 'step' in the peace process, but unacceptable in its present form as it did not deal 'adequately with some of the core issues' and contained 'negative and contradictory elements'. In particular, Sinn Féin was concerned about the Unionist 'veto'.[21]

The British and Irish governments were having their own differences over the process, in particular disagreeing about the Irish state's claim to the North in articles 2 and 3 of its constitution, with the Irish government refusing to repeal these, and the British arguing that, unless steps were taken to do so, the British could not bring the Unionists along with the peace process.[22] Nevertheless, the Letterkenny declaration angered both governments, as did Sinn Féin's refusal to renounce violence. Once again, the authority of the two governments, working in concert, and in particular the Irish government's growing authority over nationalists in Northern Ireland, pushed the process along. When the IRA finally declared its ceasefire on 31 August, it described the Downing Street Declaration as 'not a solution, nor was it presented as such by its authors. A solution will only be found as a result of inclusive negotiations'.[23]

II

The outcome of this process, now begun, cannot yet be foreseen. But the events of the last three or four years must now be reviewed against the changing character of nationalism in Ireland.

The contrast between nationalism in the north of Ireland, and that in the south, though it may be exaggerated, is undeniable. But it would be more accurate to say that southern nationalism has not so much declined (as the literary and political critics of post-nationalist Ireland, Dublin 4, would have it, in their fury at the influence of that suburb on the Irish mind), than that it has, yet again, successfully redefined itself. Just as nationalism in the nineteenth century moved from the essentially Catholic character given to it by Daniel O'Connell, to the broader, more liberal ideology of Young Ireland, to the militant constitutionalism of Parnell, to the Gaelic and literary movements with their emphasis on cultural enhancement, to the independent Irish state's quest for sovereignty and nationhood, and then to the idea of neutrality as the crowning achievement of the nation – so, once again, contemporary Ireland is redefining itself in the context of the European Union, which John Hume sought to invoke in his attempts to broaden the basis of his brand of nationalism. Irish politicians proclaimed themselves 'good Europeans' though it is claimed by some that their deeds do not necessarily match their words.[24] The European Union enabled Ireland, a small country, to exercise influence and catch the attention of the world in ways reminiscent of her early experience in the United Nations (and, earlier still in the League of Nations). Even the Eurovision Song Contest had a role to play. Moreover, the vigour and freshness of Ireland's youth culture, however far it departed from the Gaelic League's concept of what Irish culture was, drew not only attention, but money to the country. Ireland also portrayed herself as a key actor in attracting and sending aid to third world countries, though not without much exaggeration, and a certain sanctimoniousness at her own sad predicament as a 'post-colonial' nation – a conceit which did not escape some timely and trenchant criticism.[25]

All this showed that Irish identity was still secure in a changing world. This process was not without stress, seen in such episodes as the 1983 abortion referendum, when the perfectly just opposition to the amendment seemed at times to take on the character of moral superiority, not to say hypocrisy;[26] and the anguish of sections of the Dublin intelligentsia at the 'colonial' influence still exercised in Ireland by English culture. Resistance to change was clearly a powerful influence, that the new liberal-pluralist image of Ireland could not disguise. But it could be argued that contemporary Ireland was in the way of uncoupling nationalism as an ideology from a sense of national identity. Ideology has been defined in many ways, and its definition would require at least a chapter to itself, but a working model is provided by Kenneth Minogue, who describes it as follows:

> Ideology is thus an attempt to solve the problem of political conflict by a kind of amalgamation of the state and civil society in terms of a single, supposedly natural identity.[27]

This is of course, the essence of the Irish nationalism that triumphed, only to divide against itself, from 1916 to 1923, and which Sinn Féin and the IRA stand for today. This has been dressed up in what one astute observer calls the 'folksy language' of Gerry Adams, who denies that Sinn Féin stands for a narrow definition of Irish nationality, and puts the problem down to the refusal of Unionists to 'accept that they're Irish[28] –

which is a repetition of the fundamental refusal of nineteenth-century Irish nationalism, both political and cultural, to allow for any other than their definition of what 'Irishness' was. Indeed, one of the chief characteristics of Adams' nationalism is – oddly enough, for one regarded by Unionists as a cruel and implacable enemy – sentimentality. Adams waxes nostalgically about holidays in the west of Ireland, when he was young, and writes lovingly of the Falls Road district of Belfast where he grew up.[29] The search for an Ireland that existed 'when I was young' is, of course, the hallmark of the cultural and then political nationalists who plotted and fought to create an Ireland in their image at the turn of the century. The Gaelic League and Irish Republicanism were driven by nostalgia for a lost youth and, again, sentimentality is a mode of feeling rather than thought, and one that bears down heavily on those who do not fit into the world that it seeks to resurrect.

Southern Ireland still possesses individuals and groups who would seek to amalgamate state and society in a 'natural identity'. But it is safe to say that a sense of national identity, shorn of this ideological dimension, has advanced at the expense of the more exclusivist ideological nationalism of the late nineteenth and first half of the twentieth century. This can be illustrated in a brief examination of the role that sport plays in Irish people's thinking about themselves and their nation.[30]

In the late nineteenth century sport was placed on a more organized basis than ever before, with leagues formed, rules standardized, and supporters' clubs established.[31] With sport given a higher profile, it was unable to steer clear of political implications, especially if one sport or another was defined as a 'national' game. Thus in 1884 English games were denounced as 'fantastic field sports' by Archbishop Croke of Cashel, as 'not racy of the soil'. The place of sport in the national identity developed in importance in the twentieth century, as the growth of the mass media, especially television, enhanced sporting victories and linked them to a mass audience. A people who saw itself as dominated by a large neighbour, as for example, Wales is by England, could take satisfaction in a game (rugby) that – usually – they could win. Success on the sporting field was followed by increased interest in, and commitment to, a sport which enhanced the strength of the national team, and further built up its relationship to the nation.

Thus, in the 1990s, the Irish football team, following an unusual degree of success in international competitions, easily became a focus of attention for not only its faithful followers, but for the people of the Republic as a whole. The Irish team's success in winning a place in the final rounds of the World Cup was given further publicity because the finals were held in the United States of America, where the Irish team would naturally be the centre of media attention. Success brought financial rewards not only to the team, but to their country, in the form of sponsorship, sales of souvenirs and the like. The good conduct of the Irish fans contrasted with the sigh of relief emitted in Britain when the English team failed to qualify for the final rounds, and thus left the Foreign Office free from the embarrassing difficulty of explaining soccer hooliganism to yet another foreign audience. The fact that most of the Irish players were of English or Scottish birth, with unmistakably mainland accents, mattered not at all. The fact that the manager of the Irish football team, Jack Charlton, was the nearest approximation to an ethnic Englishman, was not at issue. 'He has created a labouring team for a labouring race', declared one fan. 'There's no problem about that. He's made them proud to be Irish'.[32] The modern Irish nation is hardly a 'labouring race', but, again, myth came to the aid of national identity, and comfort was found in a certain kind of harmless self-esteem.

Pride in Irishness could, and did, extend from the most English game to the Anglo-American pop culture of the 1980s and 1990s. In the political sphere, it could send thousands of young people out to work in continental Europe, and enable Ireland to accept a comfortable role in European Union affairs. This is not to say that the Irish state was any less determined to defend its interests; on the contrary, it showed a shrewd assessment of how to combine the national interest with the process of closer European union, with Europe as the source of financial input. But the new national identity was not based on the 'fear of the other' that characterized Irish nationalism at various important phases in its history.

This has not had any appreciable impact on Northern Ireland Unionism. Unionism feared what it saw as the aggressive claim of the Irish state to the north, and its fundamental character as a Catholic state, professing Catholic social and moral values, and with the capacity to absorb all other groups. As John Fulton has observed, 'Protestant solidarity exists in Northern Ireland because protestant polity is under threat, and a part of that threat is monopoly catholicism ... such a threat is real, and ... Northern protestants would lose a number of their liberties in a united Ireland, unless monopoly catholicism in Ireland was ended and the church leadership modified its political–religious beliefs and strategy'.[33] In fact, the liberal–pluralist mood in the Republic is more confident than Unionists appreciate; and the younger generation has lost the awe of the bishops that the older generation felt. But this works in some degree against reconciliation, because the very confidence of the liberal–pluralist mood has induced a complacency in contemporary

Ireland, and an unwillingness to examine protestant fears more closely –
though one of the important concessions made by the Irish government
in the Downing Street Declaration was a promise by the Taoiseach to
Unionists that his government would

> examine with his colleagues any elements in the democratic life and
> organisation of the Irish state that can be represented to the Irish
> Government in the course of political dialogue as a real and substan-
> tial threat to their way of life and ethos, or that can be represented as
> not being fully consistent with a modern democratic and pluralist
> society, and undertakes to examine any possible ways of removing
> such obstacles.

The concept of a post-nationalist Ireland must not be pressed too far.
Two recent episodes reveal that the drive for sentimentality could catch
at least some sections of the public. The state's muted response to the
seventy-fifth anniversary of the 1916 Easter Rising was challenged by an
unofficial 'happening' in Dublin, in which

> a group of citizens, led by artist Robert Ballagh and frustrated at the
> government's failure to organise a more splendid celebration, held its
> own festival in central Dublin. Thousands of families took part, as did
> poets, musicians, face-painters, and so on. RTE's six o'clock news
> reported the event for thirty-two seconds as its final item; and the
> camera focused not on the crowd of families, but on the presence of
> Sinn Féin president, Gerry Adams MP.

This media reaction to the event was described, with perhaps uncon-
scious irony, by its advocate Declan Kiberd as 'bizarre'.[34] It was followed
a few years later by an extraordinary outburst of sentimentality over a
book purported to have been written by a genuine witness of the Great
Irish Famine of 1847. This 'famine diary' was given wide publicity in
respected journals and newspapers, and proved to be a best-seller.[35] But
its impact on northern nationalism was minimalist, if indeed it had any
impact at all.

These episodes revealed that nationalism in the south of Ireland could
still strike up a response; but it could no longer drive the political life of
the Republic. In the north, and especially in Republican circles, folksy
self-regard could take a less ephemeral form. The contrast between the
nationalism of the south, and the deeply rooted ideology of the Republican movement in the north, is almost too obvious to require discussion.

But two points need to be made. It is certain that the bulk of Northern Ireland nationalists are as alarmed by the IRA manifestation of the nationalist creed as are those in the south. This can be dismissed as the natural response of the growing sector of society that encompasses middle class, professional Catholics who have advanced themselves during a quarter of a century of direct rule[36] – rather like those Catholics who, in southern Ireland, underwent a similar experience under the Union, and who voted for John Redmond and, later, Fine Gael. And the strength of nationalist opinion cannot be gauged fully until a referendum is held on questions of a constitutional settlement. But the party led by John Hume, who now appears to be himself moving towards a modified nationalism, has not and will not endorse the cult of violence, and the sense of moral superiority that – paradoxically – it induces in its perpetrators and supporters.[37] IRA violence is undoubtedly fuelled by injustice, deprivation and harassment by the forces of the state in Northern Ireland,[38] but its secure place in a strand of the Irish nationalist tradition legitimizes, sustains and even enobles IRA activities, including some of its worst outrages.[39]

But the overall impression that Northern Ireland nationalists give at the present time is one of confusion. Nationalists have, since the nineteenth century, claimed that Unionists have no clear sense of who they are; that their stubborn refusal to accept their 'true' Irish identity renders them pathetic leftovers from a long past imperial age. But it is equally true to say that Roman Catholics in the north have no clear sense of who they are, and of where they want to go. Despite Gerry Adams' clear and unmistakable sentimentality, allied to his wish that the British government 'join the persuaders', and cajole Unionists into a united Ireland (expressed in his first address to the 'Forum for Peace and Reconciliation' which opened in Dublin under official Irish government auspices in October 1994), most Northern Ireland Catholics do not see their way as clearly as does Mr Adams. To be fair, Adams' request to the British government is no different from that of Irish Nationalists in 1914 and 1918 and 1921. But it seems safe to say that most nationalists in the north cannot so easily identify with the symbols of Irish nationalism to which Sinn Féin and the IRA remain firmly attached. 1916 does not mean as much to northern Catholics as Sinn Féin would want it to mean. It is hard to generalise, but a recent series of interviews with Roman Catholics reveal not certainty, but confusion. Most, however, take their politics from their surroundings, some declaring that, for example, they vote Sinn Féin because they 'stand up' for us, while others in Republican areas feel only disgust with politics in general.[40] Nationalism has been fragmented by the fact that the Northern Ireland Unionist state has not existed since 1972, and Roman Catholics no longer have the sense of community solidarity created in the political crisis of that state and the Catholic people in 1968–72. Some watch with cynicism the way in which the Roman Catholic middle class has grown and prospered over the last twenty-five years; others cling to a sense of victimhood, even in a time when British governments have shown more partiality for nationalists than unionists.[41] Many feel alienated by what they see as southern Irish indifference, even hostility, towards them; some even admit that they feel that the south is not 'their' country and that they do not feel at home when they go to the country that their ideology claims is their own.[42] Some even acknowledge that they have no idea where west Donegal or Waterford are.[43] Only the most myopic Republicanism can put this down to the impact of 'British Imperialism', and some, like Gerry Adams, do.[44] But it is safe to say that Northern Catholics agree that they can never go back to the days of Unionist political supremacy, and some regard the IRA as an organization that should retain its weapons and structure 'just in case. The Catholic community cannot ever leave itself defenceless again'.[45]

Neither Protestants nor Catholics in the north form the ideologically solid communities that they at first sight appear to constitute. Ideologues like to see them as national, community, or (a vague and unsatisfactory term) 'ethnic' groups. But these are what might be called 'imagined communities': that is, varied and heterogeneous people, divided by experience, class, lifestyles, hopes and fears, and looking to two 'parent' nations, the British and the Irish, who show no strong desire to embrace their progeny. In time of trial, as in 1968–72 for the Roman Catholic people, and 1974 and 1985 for the Protestant people, the imagined communities take on something of a reality, with solidarity replacing division; and there is no doubt that if the British government acceded to Gerry Adams' request and joined the persuaders, Unionist solidarity would re-emerge, as would nationalist solidarity in similar circumstances of stress and danger. If the Dublin government's 'Forum for Peace and Reconciliation' is to move beyond the discussion of nationalist platitudes that the 1984 Nationalist Forum adhered to, then it must address these issues, as the British government must address them in its own, different, context.

Over the last 25 years, the two states of Ireland have undergone revolutions of a sort. In the south, there has been a peaceful and gradual, but escalating revolution, loosening the grip of the Roman Catholic Church and the Irish political élite (especially the Fianna Fáil party), and challenging the authoritarianism of Irish political culture. In the north, the monopolistic grip of Ulster Unionism and the place of Northern Ireland in the United Kingdom was challenged by both political and militaristic means. These are not incompatible revolutions, but they are very different revolutions. Both depended upon a fundamental shift of opinion amongst significant groups of people; but the liberal–pluralist southern revolution contrasts with the communal–nationalist northern revolution. The southern revolution was helped, if not driven, by the decline in nationalist solidarity; the northern revolution was driven, if not always helped, by the development of a sense of nationalist solidarity arising from the speical conditions in which the Roman Catholic minority existed. The southern revolution was made at home; the northern revolution was inspired by local conditions, but the changes wrought in the North since 1972 were largely the direct result of British government intervention. In the south, power still found its own level; in the north, power was brokered by the British government, using its superior military and economic force, for however indifferent the British state appeared to be from time to time, it never lost its grip on the northern predicament. It is clear, then, that the two revolutions have not converged, but may well be moving in quite separate directions.

Contemporary Ireland, then, stands at a crossroads in its history. In one sense, convergence and divergence are the story of Ireland, and it is this story that any new institutional arrangements must in some sense articulate. The Anglo–Irish 'framework document' which has been some two years in the making was two years in the making precisely because it sought to accommodate traditions that have hitherto appeared irreconcilable, and of course may yet be irreconcilable. It proposed the creation of closer cross-border links, including the establishment of institutions with executive powers. This reflected the implications of the Downing Street Declaration's reiteration of the statement that Britain has 'no selfish strategic or economic interest in Northern Ireland' and that Northern Ireland is no longer regarded as *de jure* part of the United Kingdom.[46] It may be, then, that Northern Ireland is entering, or has already entered a post-Union phase, or at least a post-Unionist phase, in that it will remain within the United Kingdom, but without its ideological underpinning that sustained its identity between 1921 and 1972. It remains to be seen whether the arguably post-nationalist mood of public opinion in southern Ireland, and the highly nationalist mood of at any rate a section of the Roman Catholic people of the north can themselves be accommodated in a constitutional settlement: the insertion of such phases as an 'agreed Ireland' and the democratic rights of the majority in Northern Ireland are steps in that direction, combined as they are with cross-border institutions. Irish nationalism has so often confounded itself through its mixture of pluralist rhetoric and sectarian activity that it may yet stumble over its own past, and lose sight of Unionist fears yet again. Its present, and understandable, desire to keep Sinn Féin on the constitutional path may cause it to do what it has, again, done in the past: place its own 'national unity' before the unity of the nation. What Dr Conor Cruise O'Brien calls its 'ancestral voices' may yet provoke modern Ireland to cock its ear more readily to the Northern Ireland nationalist agenda, whatever its frequently expressed reservations about the Nationalism of Sinn Féin and the IRA.[47] But much hard bargaining lies ahead; and this bargaining will be deeply influenced by the continuation, or otherwise, of the ceasefire, which in its own way is a dynamic part of the process, and an integral part of the making of a settlement. Most of the people of Northern Ireland will be influenced by A. J. P. Taylor's dictum that 'jaw jaw is better than war war', and will thus direct their thoughts closer towards compromise – but not surrender. But the outcome, for the nationalist as well as the Unionist, project is uncertain. For, as Eugene Kamenka has remarked,

> Despite the claims of nationalism, a country has not one history but many histories, not one future but many futures. Some may seem unlikely; more of them will be unpredictably contingent.[48]

Notes

1. *Keesings Contemporary Archives* (1994), p. 40149. Hereafter referred to as *KCA*.
2. Henry Patterson, *The Politics of Illusion: Republicanism and Socialism in Modern Ireland* (London, 1989), p. 206.
3. Martin Mansergh (ed.), *The Spirit of the Nation: The Speeches and Statements of C.J. Haughey, 1957–1986* (Cork and Dublin, 1986), pp. 672–3.
4. Paul Bew and Gordon Gillespie, *Northern Ireland: A Chronology of the Troubles, 1968–1993* (Dublin, 1993), pp. 293–5.
5. Fergal Cochrane, 'Any Takers? The isolation of Northern Ireland', in *Political Studies*, vol. xlii (1994), pp. 378–95, at p. 392.
6. Fionnuala O'Connor, *In Search of a State: Catholics in Northern Ireland* (Belfast, 1993), pp. 343–4. For the 'Republicanism' of the SDLP see p. 94.
7. Speech at the Parnell Summer School, Rathdrum, Co. Wicklow, August 1994.
8. Paul Arthur, 'The Anglo-Irish Joint Declaration: towards a lasting

peace?', in *Government and Opposition*, vol. 29, no. 2 (Spring, 1994), pp. 218–30, at p. 225.

9. Bew and Gillespie, *Chronology*, p. 290.

10. For a summary of these see Paul Arthur, 'The Brooke Initiative' in *Irish Political Studies*, vol. 7 (1992), pp. 111–15, and 'The Mayhew Talks, 1992', in *IPS*, vol. 8 (1993), pp. 138–43.

11. Bew and Gillespie, *Chronology*, pp. 277–8.

12. Paul Arthur, 'Anglo-Irish Joint Declaration', in *Government and Opposition*, vol. 29, no. 2, p. 226.

13. Bew and Gillespie, *Chronology*, pp. 292–4.

14. Ibid., pp. 289–90.

15. Ibid., p. 294.

16. Ibid., p. 298.

17. Arthur, 'Anglo-Irish Joint Declaration', in *Government and Opposition*, vol. 29, no. 2, p. 227.

18. *KCA*, 1994, pp. 39878, 39976–7.

19. Ibid., pp. 39976–7.

20. Ibid., p. 40026.

21. Ibid., p. 40115.

22. Ibid., p. 40115.

23. Ibid., p. 40149.

24. See the symposium in *Studies* (Dublin), vol. 78, no. 311 (Autumn, 1989).

25. Liam Kennedy, 'Modern Ireland: Post Colonial Society or Post Colonial Pretensions', in *Irish Review*, no. 13 (Winter, 1992–3), pp. 107–21.

26. J.P. O'Carroll, 'Bishops, Knights – and Pawns? Traditional thought and the Irish abortion referendum debate of 1983', in *IPS*, vol. 6 (1991), pp. 53–71.

27. Kenneth Minogue, 'Ideology after the collapse of Communism', in *Political Studies*, vol. xli (1993), pp. 9–20, at p. 12.

28. Fionnuala O'Connor, *In Search of a State*, pp. 245–8, 345–6.

29. See Gerry Adams, *Falls Memories* (Kerry, 1982) for a fine example of the sentimentality.

30. For a discussion of this see Michael Holmes, 'Symbols of National Identity and Sport: the case of the Irish Football Team', in *IPS*, vol. 9 (1992), pp. 91–8.

31. Keith Robbins, *Nineteenth-Century Britain: England, Scotland, and Wales. The Making of a Nation* (Oxford, 1987), ch. 6.

32. *Sunday Times*, 1 July 1990, p. 11.

33. John Fulton, *The Tragedy of Belief: Division, Politics and Religion in Ireland* (Clarendon Press, Oxford, 1991), p. 229. See also Desmond Smith, 'The Dissolution of the Irish Republic: A step on the way to peace', in *Studies*, vol. 83, no. 329 (Spring, 1994), p. 59: 'When it comes to understanding the deep suspicions that exist in the Northern community we in the south have not always proved good listeners.'

34. Declan Kiberd, 'The Elephant of Revolutionary Forgetfulness', in Máirín Ní Dhonnchadha and Theo Dorgan (eds), *Revising the Rising*, (Derry, 1991), p. 4.

35. Jim Jackson, 'Famine Diary: the making of a Best Seller', in *Irish Review*, no. 11 (Winter 1991–2), pp. 1–8.

36. David McKitterick, 'Catholics find a middle-class oasis in Belfast', in *Independent*, 11 January 1991, p. 8. Fionnuala O'Connor, *In Search of a State*, ch. 2.

37. See Seamus Murphy, S.J., 'I don't support the IRA, But ... Semantic and Psychological Ambivalence', in *Studies*, vol. 82, no. 327 (Autumn, 1993), pp. 276–86.

38. Jennifer Todd, 'Northern Ireland Nationalist Political Culture', in *IPS*, vol. 5 (1990) pp. 31–44.

39. Sean Kinsella, 'The Cult of Violence in the Revolutionary Tradition in Ireland', in *Studies*, vol. 83, no. 329 (Spring, 1994), pp. 20–9.

40. Fionnuala O'Connor, *In Search of a State*, ch. 3.

41. Ibid., pp. 150–1.

42. Ibid., pp. 236–41.

43. Ibid., p. 248.

44. Ibid., p. 246–8.

45. Ibid., p. 378.

46. Fergal Cochrane, 'Any Takers?', in *Political Studies*, vol. xlii, p. 387.

47. C.C. O'Brien, *Ancestral Voices* (Dublin, 1994).

48. Eugene Kamenka, 'Nationalism: Ambiguous Legacies and Contingent Futures', in *Political Studies*, vol. xli (1993), pp. 78–92, at p. 92.

APPENDIX: THE DOWNING STREET DECLARATION , 15 DECEMBER 1993

The Taoiseach, Mr Albert Reynolds TD, and the Prime Minister, the Rt Hon John Major MP, acknowledge that the most urgent and important issue facing the people of Ireland, North and South, and the British and Irish governments together is to remove the causes of conflict, to overcome the legacy of history and to heal the divisions which have resulted, recognising that the absence of a lasting and satisfactory settlement of relationships between the peoples of both islands has contributed to continuing tragedy and suffering.

They believe that the development of an agreed framework for peace, which has been discussed between them since early last year, and which is based on a number of key principles articulated by the two governments over the past 20 years, together with the adaptation of other widely accepted principles, provides the starting point of a peace process designed to culminate in a political settlement.

The Taoiseach and the Prime Minister are convinced of the inestimable value, to both their peoples, and particularly for the next generation, of healing divisions in Ireland and of ending a conflict which has been so manifestly to the detriment of all.

Both recognise that the ending of divisions can come about only through the agreement and co-operation of the people, North and South, representing both traditions in Ireland.

They therefore make a solemn commitment to promote co-operation at all levels on the basis of the fundamental principles, undertakings, obligations under international agreements, to which they have jointly committed themselves, and the guarantees which each government has given and now reaffirms, including Northern Ireland's statutory constitutional guarantee.

It is their aim to foster agreement and reconciliation, leading to a new political framework founded on consent and encompassing arrangements within Northern Ireland, for the whole island and between these islands. They also consider that the development of Europe will, of itself, require new approaches to serve interests common to both parts of the island of Ireland, and to Ireland and the United Kingdom as partners in the European Union.

The Prime Minister, on behalf of the British Government, reaffirms that they will uphold the democratic wish of a greater number of the people of Northern Ireland on the issue of whether they prefer to support the Union or a sovereign united Ireland.

On this basis, he reiterates, on behalf of the British Government, that they have no selfish strategic or economic interest in Northern Ireland.

Their primary interest is to see peace, stability and reconciliation established by agreement among all the people who inhabit the island, and they will work together with the Irish Government to achieve such an agreement, which will embrace the totality of relationships.

The role of the British Government will be to encourage, facilitate and enable the achievement of such agreement over a period through a process of dialogue and co-operation based on full respect for the rights and identities of both traditions in Ireland.

They accept that such agreement may, as of right, take the form of agreed structures for the island as a whole, including a united Ireland achieved by peaceful means on the following basis.

The British Government agree that it is for the people of the island of Ireland alone, by agreement between the two parts respectively, to exercise their right of self-determination on the basis of consent, freely and concurrently given, North and South, to bring about a united Ireland, if that is their wish.

They reaffirm as a binding obligation that they will for their part, introduce the necessary legislation to give effect to this, or equally to any measure of agreement on future relationships in Ireland which the people living in Ireland may themselves freely so determine without external impediment.

They believe that the people of Britain would wish, in friendship to all sides, to enable the people of Ireland to reach agreement on how they may live together in harmony and in partnership, with respect for their diverse traditions, and with full recognition of the special links and the unique relationship which exists between the peoples of Britain and Ireland.

The Taoiseach, on behalf of the Irish Government, considers that the lessons of Irish history, and especially of Northern Ireland, show that stability and well-being will not be found under any political system which is refused allegiance or rejected on grounds of identity by a significant minority of those governed by it. For this reason, it would be wrong to attempt to impose a united Ireland, in the absence of the freely given consent of a majority of the people of Northern Ireland.

He accepts, on behalf of the Irish Government, that the democratic right of self-determination by the people of Ireland as a whole must be achieved and exercised with and subject to the agreement and consent of a majority of the people of Northern Ireland and must, consistent with justice and equity, respect the democratic dignity and the civil rights and religious liberties of both communities, including:

▫ the right of free political thought;

▫ the right to freedom and expression of religion;

▫ the right to pursue democratically national and political aspirations;

▫ the right to seek constitutional change by peaceful and legitimate means;

▫ the right to live wherever one chooses without hindrance;

▫ the right to equal opportunity in all social and economic activity, regardless of class, creed, sex or colour.

These would be reflected in any future political and constitutional arrangements emerging from a new and more broadly based agreement.

The Taoiseach, however, recognises the genuine difficulties and barriers to building relationships of trust either within or beyond Northern Ireland, from which both traditions suffer. He will work to create a new era of trust, in which suspicion of the motives or actions of others is removed on the part of either community.

He considers that the future of the island depends on the nature of the relationship between the two main traditions that inhabit it. Every effort must be made to build a new sense of trust between these communities.

In recognition of the fears of the Unionist community and as a token of his willingness to make a personal contribution to the building up of that necessary trust, the Taoiseach will examine with his colleagues any elements in the democratic life and organisation of the Irish state that can be represented to the Irish Government in the course of political dialogue as a real and substantial threat to their way of life and ethos, or that can be represented as not being fully consistent with a modern democratic and pluralist society, and undertakes to examine any possible ways of removing such obstacles.

Such an examination would of course have due regard to the desire to preserve those inherited values that are largely shared throughout the island or that belong to the cultural and historical roots of the people of this island in all their diversity.

The Taoiseach hopes that over time a meeting of hearts and minds will develop, which will bring all the people of Ireland together, and will work towards that objective, but he pledges in the meantime that as result of the efforts that will be made to build mutual confidence no Northern Unionist should ever have to fear in future that this ideal will be pursued either by threat or coercion.

Both governments accept that Irish unity would be achieved only by those who favour this outcome persuading those who do not, peacefully and without coercion or violence, and that, if in the future a majority of the people of Northern Ireland are so persuaded, both governments will support and give legislation effect to their wish.

But, not withstanding the solemn affirmation by both governments in the Anglo-Irish Agreement that any change in the status of Northern Ireland would only come about with the consent of a majority of the people of Northern Ireland, the Taoiseach also recognises the continuing uncertainties and misgivings which dominate so much of Northern Unionist attitudes towards the rest of Ireland.

He believes that we stand at a stage of our history when the genuine feelings of all traditions in the North must be recognised and acknowledged. He appeals to both traditions at this time to grasp the opportunity for a fresh start and a new beginning, which could hold such promise for all our lives and the generations to come.

He asks the people of Northern Ireland to look on the people of the Republic as friends, who share their grief and shame over all the suffering of the last quarter of a century, and who want to develop the best possible relationship with them, a relationship in which trust and new understanding can flourish and grow.

The Taoiseach also acknowledges the presence in the constitution of the Republic of elements which are deeply resented by Northern Unionists, but which at the same time reflect hopes and ideals which lie deep in the hearts of many Irish men and women North and South. But as we move towards a new era of understanding in which new relationships of trust may grow and bring peace to the island of Ireland, the Taoiseach believes that the time has come to consider together how best the hopes and identities of all can be expressed in more balanced ways, which no longer engender division and the lack of trust to which he has referred.

He confirms that, in the event of an overall settlement, the Irish Government will, as part of a balanced constitutional accommodation, put forward and support proposals for change in the Irish constitution which would fully reflect the principle of consent in Northern Ireland.

The Taoiseach recognises the need to engage in dialogue which would address with honesty and integrity the fears of all traditions. But that dialogue, both within the North and between the people and their representatives of both parts of Ireland, must be entered into with an acknowledgement that the future security and welfare of the people of the island will depend on an open, frank and balanced approach to all the problems which for too long have caused division.

The British and Irish governments will seek, along with the Northern Ireland constitutional parties through a process of political dialogue, to create institutions and structures which, while respecting the diversity of the people of Ireland, would enable them to work together in all areas of common interest. This will help over a period to build the trust necessary to end past divisions, leading to an agreed and peaceful future. Such structures would, of course, include institutional recognition of the special links that exist between the peoples of Britain and Ireland as part of the totality of relationships, while taking account of newly-forged links with the rest of Europe.

The British and Irish governments reiterate that the achievement of peace must involve a permanent end to the use of, or support for, paramilitary violence. They confirm that, in these circumstances, democratically mandated parties which establish a commitment to exclusively peaceful methods and which have shown that they abide by the democratic process, are free to participate fully in democratic politics and to join in dialogue in due course between the Governments and the political parties on the way ahead.

The Irish Government would make their own arrangements within their jurisdiction to enable democratic parties to consult together and share in dialogue about the political future. The Taoiseach's intention is that these arrangements could include the establishment, in consultation with other parties, of a Forum for Peace and Reconciliation to make recommendations on ways in which agreement and trust between both traditions in Ireland can be promoted and established.

The Taoiseach and the Prime Minister are determined to build on the fervent wish of both their peoples to see old fears and animosities replaced by a climate of peace. They believe the framework they have set out offers the people of Ireland, North and South, whatever their tradition, the basis to agree that from bow on their differences can be negotiated and resolved exclusively by peaceful political means. They appeal to all concerned to grasp the opportunity for a new departure. That step would compromise no position or principle, nor prejudice the future for either community. On the contrary, it would be an incomparable gain for all.

It would break decisively the cycle of violence and the intolerable suffering it entails for the people of these islands, particularly for both communities in Northern Ireland. It would allow the process of economic and social cooperation on the island to realise its full potential for prosperity and mutual understanding. It would transform the prospect for building on the progress already made in the talks process, involving the two governments and the constitutional parties in Northern Ireland.

The Taoiseach and the Prime Minister believe that these arrangements offer an opportunity to lay the foundations for a more peaceful and harmonious future devoid of the violence and bitter divisions which have scarred the past generation. They commit themselves and their Governments to continue to work together, unremittingly, towards that objective.

1: Political Geography of Ireland: Present County Divisions

Source: R. Dudley Edwards (1973) *An Atlas of Irish History* (Methuen and Co. London), p. 14. Maps drawn by W.H. Bromage.

2: **The Irish Parliament**

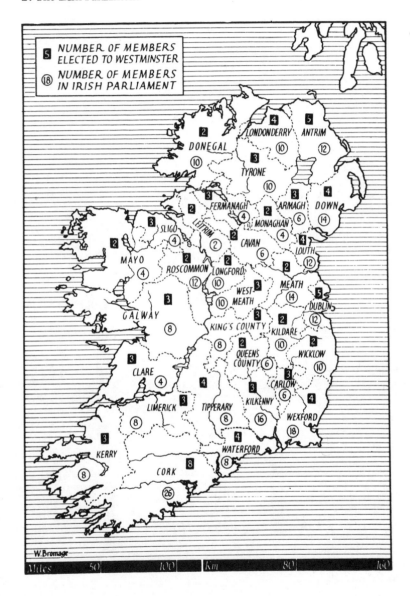

NUMBER OF MEMBERS ELECTED TO WESTMINSTER

NUMBER OF MEMBERS IN IRISH PARLIAMENT

Source: R. Dudley Edwards (1973), p. 95.

3: Religious Affiliations

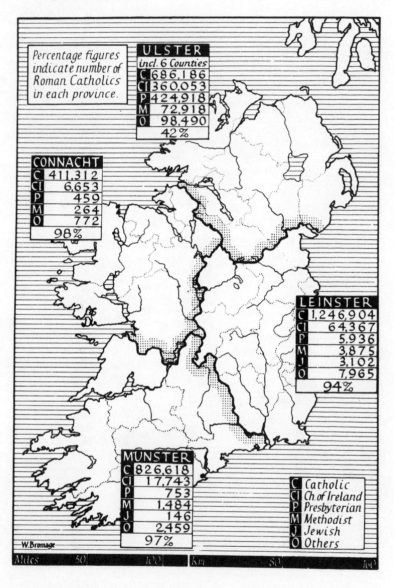

Percentage figures indicate number of Roman Catholics in each province.

ULSTER incl. 6 Counties
C	686,186
CI	360,053
P	424,918
M	72,918
O	98,490
	42%

CONNACHT
C	411,312
CI	6,653
P	459
M	264
O	772
	98%

LEINSTER
C	1,246,904
CI	64,367
P	5,936
M	3,875
J	3,102
O	7,965
	94%

MUNSTER
C	826,618
CI	17,743
P	753
M	1,484
J	146
O	2,459
	97%

C	Catholic
CI	Ch. of Ireland
P	Presbyterian
M	Methodist
J	Jewish
O	Others

W.Bromage

| Miles | 50 | 100 | Km | 80 | 160 |

Source: R. Dudley Edwards (1973), p. 128.

4: Cromwellian Land Distribution

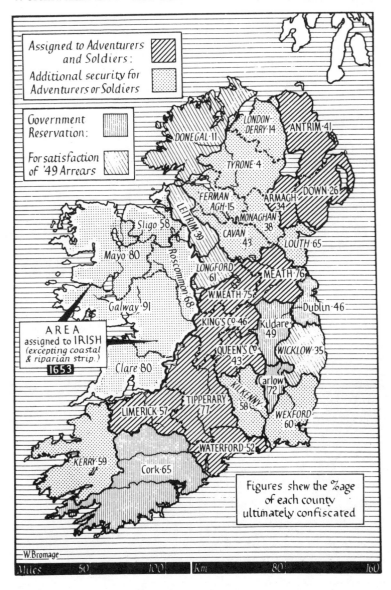

Assigned to Adventurers and Soldiers:

Additional security for Adventurers or Soldiers

Government Reservation:

For satisfaction of '49 Arrears

DONEGAL·11

LONDON-DERRY·14

ANTRIM·41

TYRONE·4

DOWN·26

FERMAN AGH·15

ARMAGH·34

MONAGHAN·38

LEITRIM·39

Sligo·58

CAVAN·43

LOUTH·65

Mayo·80

Roscommon·68

LONGFORD·61

MEATH·76

Galway·91

W.MEATH·75

Dublin·46

AREA assigned to IRISH (excepting coastal & riparian strip.) **1653**

KING'S C°·46

Kildare·49

QUEEN'S C°·43

WICKLOW·35

Clare·80

Carlow·72

LIMERICK·57

TIPPERARY·77

KILKENNY·58

WEXFORD·60

WATERFORD·52

KERRY·59

Cork·65

Figures shew the %age of each county ultimately confiscated

W.Bromage

Miles   50   100   Km   80   160

Source: R. Dudley Edwards (1973), p. 164.

5: Irish Speakers: 1851-1971

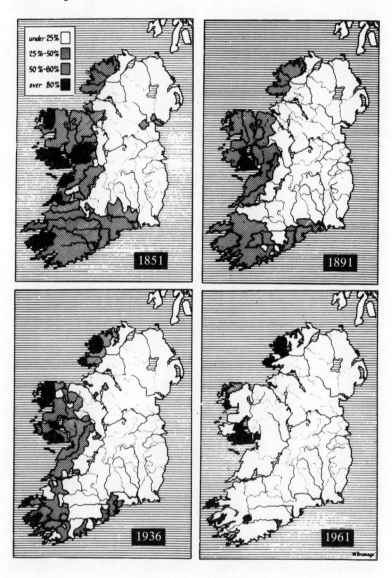

Source: R. Dudley Edwards (1973), p. 230.

BIBLIOGRAPHY

1. Theory of Nationalism

Coban, A. *The Nation State and National Self-Determination* (London, 1969).

Deutsch, K.W. *Nationalism and Social Communication* (MIT Press, Cambridge, Mass., 1966 edn.).

Elviken, A. 'The genesis of Norwegian nationalism', *JMH*, vol. *III* (1931), pp. 365-91.

Encyclopedia of the Social Sciences, vol. *III* (New York, 1967 edn.), p. 653.

Field, G.C. *Political Theory* (London, 1965 ed.).

Gellner, E. *Thought and Change* (London, 1964).

Ginsberg, M. *Nationalism: a Reappraisal* (Leeds, 1961).

Hayes, C.J.H. *The Historical Evolution of Modern Nationalism* (New York 1948).

——, *Nationalism: a Religion* (New York, 1960).

Hechter, M. *Internal Colonialism: the Celtic Fringe in British National Development, 1536-1966* (London, 1975).

Hertz, F. *Nationality in History and Politics* (London, 1944).

Hobsbawm, E. 'Some reflections on nationalism', in Nossiter, T.J., Hanson, A.H., and Rokkan, S., (eds.), *Imagination and Precision in the Social Sciences* (London, 1972).

International Encyclopedia of the Social Sciences, vol. *11* (New York and London, 1968), 'Nationalism'.

International Encyclopedia, vols. *13* and *14*, 'Political socialization'.

Kamenka, E., (ed.) *Nationalism: the Nature and Evolution of an Idea* (Canberra, 1973).

Kedourie, E. *Nationalism* (London, 1960).

Kohn, H. *The Idea of Nationalism* (New York, 1945).

——, *Nationalism: its Meaning and History* (Princeton, 1955).

——, *Prophets and Peoples* (New York, 1957).

Minogue, K. *Nationalism* (London, 1967).

Moody, T.W. (ed.), *Nationality and the Pursuit of National Independence* (Belfast, 1978).

Namier, L.B. 'Nationality and history', in *Avenues of History* (London, 1952).

Obolensky, D. 'Nationalism in eastern Europe in the middle ages', in

TRHS, vol. *27* (1972) pp. 1-16.

Orridge, A.W. *Uneven Development and Nationalism* (University of Birmingham, 1978).

——, *Structural Preconditions and Triggering Factors in the Development of European Sub-State Nationalism* (Political Studies Association paper, 1979).

Page, E. *Michael Hechter's Internal Colonial Thesis: Some Theoretical and methodological Problems* (University of Strathclyde, 1977).

Reading, H.F. *A Dictionary of the Social Sciences* (London, 1977).

Renan, E. 'What is a nation', in *The Poetry of the Celtic Races and other Studies of Ernest Renan*, Translated by W.G. Hutchinson (London, n.d., [1896?]).

Seton-Watson, H. *Nationalism: Old and New* (Sydney, 1965).

——, 'Unsatisfied nationalism', in *JCH*, vol. *6* (1977), p. 3-14.

Shafer, B.C. *Nationalism: Interpreters and Interpretations* (New York and London, 1963 edn.).

Shea, W.R., and King-Farlow, J. (eds.) *Contemporary Issues in Political Philosophy* (New York, 1976).

Smith, A.D.S. *Nationalist Movements* (London, 1976).

——, *Nationalism in the Twentieth Century* (London, 1979).

Snyder, L.L. *Race: a History of Modern Ethnic Theories* (New York and Toronto, 1939).

2. General Works on Irish History and Irish Nationalism, and Works Covering More Than One Period

Ball, J.T. *Historical Review of the Legislative Systems Operative in Ireland, from the Invasion of Henry II to the Union* (London, 1888).

Beckett, J.C. *A Short History of Ireland* (London, 1979 edn.).

——, *The Making of Modern Ireland, 1603-1923* (London, 1966 edn.).

——, *Confrontations: Studies in Irish History* (London, 1972).

——, *The Anglo-Irish Tradition* (London, 1976).

Birch, A.H. *Political Integration and Disintegration in the British Isles* (London, 1977).

Cavour, Count Camillo, *Count Cavour on Ireland*, Translated W.B. Hodgson (London, 1868).

Cullen, L. *Anglo-Irish trade, 1660-1800* (Manchester, 1968).

——, *An Economic History of Ireland since 1660* (London, 1972).

Cullen, L.M. and Smout, T.C. (eds.), *Comparative Aspects of Scottish and Irish Economic and Social History* (Edinburgh, n.d., 1977).

Cullen, L.M. 'The cultural basis of Irish nationalism', unpublished seminar paper delivered at Gregynog Hall, University of Wales, 1979.

Curtis, E., and MacDowell, L.B. *Irish Historical Documents, 1172-1922* (London, 1977 edn.).

De Paor, L. 'Cultural pluralism', *Studies*, vol. *67* (Spring-Summer, 1978), pp. 77-87.

Evans, E.E. *The Personality of Ireland: Habitat, Heritage and History* (Cambridge, 1973).

Farrell, B. (ed.) *The Irish Parliamentary Tradition* (Dublin, 1973).

Flower, R. *The Irish Tradition* (Oxford, 1947).

Green, Alice Stopford *The Irish National Tradition* (Dublin, 1921).

——, *Irish Nationality* (London, 1929).

Gwynn, S. *Irish Literature and Drama in the English Language : a Short History* (London, 1936).

Hayes, W. 'Nationalism in Ireland: a case study', *Thought*, vol. *XLVI* (1971), pp. 165-98.

Hepburn, A.C. *The Conflict of Nationality in Modern Ireland* (London, 1980).

Kee, R. *The Green Flag: a History of Irish Nationalism* (London, 1972 edn).

Lyons, F.S.L. *Ireland Since the Famine* (London, 1971).

—— and Hawkins, R.A.J. (eds.), *Ireland Under the Union: Varieties of Tension* (London, 1979).

MacDonagh, O. *Ireland: the Union and its Aftermath* (London, 1977).

Madden, R.R. *History of Irish Periodical Literature from the end of the Seventeenth Century to the Middle of the Nineteenth Century* (New York, 1968 edn.).

Mansergh, N. *The Irish Question, 1840-1921* (London, 1965 edn.).

Miller, D.W. *Queen's rebels: Ulster Loyalism in Historical Perspective* (Dublin, 1978).

Murphy, J.A. 'Priests and people in modern Irish history', *Christus Rex*, vol. *23* (1969), pp. 235-59.

Norman, E. *A History of Modern Ireland* (London, 1973).

O'Brien, C.C. *States of Ireland* (London, 1972).

O'Brien, R.B. *Studies in Irish History, 1649-1775* (Dublin, 1903).

O'Farrell, P. *Ireland's English Question: Anglo-Irish Relations, 1534-1970* (London, 1971).

——, *England and Ireland Since 1800* (London, 1975).

——, 'Millenialism, Messianism and utopianism in Irish history', *Anglo-Irish Studies*, vol. *II* (1976), pp. 45-68.

O'Hegarty, P.S. *A History of Ireland Under the Union* (London, 1952).

Orridge, A.W. 'Explanations of Irish nationalism: a review and some suggestions', *Journal of the Conflict Research Society*, vol. *I*, (1977), pp. 29-57.

Phillips, W.A. *History of the Church of Ireland* (3 Vols., Oxford, 1933-4).

Shaw, Revd. F. 'The canon of Irish history: a challenge', *Studies*, vol. *LXI* (1972), pp. 113-53.

Stewart, A.T.Q. *The narrow Ground: Aspects of Ulster, 1603-1969* (London, 1977).

Strauss, E. *Irish Nationalism and British Democracy* (London, 1951).

Walker, B.M. *Parliamentary Election Results in Ireland, 1901-1922* (Dublin, 1978).

Zimmermann, G.D. *Irish Political Street Ballads and Rebel Songs, 1780-1900* (Geneva, 1966).

3. From the Beginnings to 1689

Bagwell, R. *Ireland Under the Tudors* (3 vols., London, 1963 edn.)

——, *Ireland Under the Stuarts* (3 vols., London, 1963 edn.).

Barnard, T.C. 'Planters and policies in Cromwellian Ireland, *Past and Present*, No. *LXI* (1973), pp. 31-69.

——, *Cromwellian Ireland: English Government and Reform in Ireland, 1649-1660* (London, 1975).

Binchy, D.A. *Celtic and Anglo-Saxon Kingship* (Oxford, 1970).

Bossy, J. 'The counter-reformation and the people of Catholic Ireland, 1596-1641', in *Historical Studies*, vol. *VIII* (Dublin, 1971).

Bottigheimer, K.S. *English Money and Irish Land* (Oxford, 1971).

——, 'Kingdom and colony: Ireland in the westward enterprise, 1536-1660', in Andrews, K.R. *et al.*, (eds.), *The Westward Enterprise: English Activities in Ireland, the Atlantic and America, 1480-1650* (Liverpool, 1978).

Bradshaw, B. 'The opposition to the ecclesiastical legislation in the Irish reformation parliament', *Irish Historical Studies*, vol. *XVI* (1969), pp. 285-303.

——, 'Cromwellian reform and the origins of the Kildare rebellion, 1533-4', in *TRHS*, 5th series, vol. *27* (1977), pp. 69-93.

——, 'The Elizabethans and the Irish', *Studies*, vol. *66* (1977), pp. 38-50.

——, 'Sword, word and strategy in the reformation in Ireland', *His-*

torical Journal, vol. *21* (1978), pp. 475-502.

——, 'Native reaction to the westward enterprise: a case study in Gaelic ideology', in Andrews *et al.*, *The Westward Enterprise*, pp. 65-80.

——, *The Irish Constitutional Revolution of the Sixteenth Century* (Cambridge, 1979).

Bryan, D. *Gerald Fitzgerald, the Great Earl of Kildare* (Dublin, 1933).

Byrne, F.J. *Rise of the Ui Néill and the High Kingship of Ireland* (Dublin 1970).

——, *Irish Kings and High Kings* (London, 1973).

Calendar of State Papers, Ireland, 1633-47 (London, 1901).

Canny, N.P. 'Hugh O'Neill, Earl of Tyrone, and the changing face of Gaelic Ulster', *Studia Hibernica*, vol. *X* (1970), pp. 7-35.

——, The ideology of English colonisation: from England to America', *William and Mary Quarterly*, 3rd series, vol. *XXX* (1973), pp. 575-98.

——, *The Elizabethan Conquest of Ireland: a Pattern Established, 1565-1576* (Sussex, 1976).

——, 'Dominant minorities: English settlers in Ireland and Virginia, 1550-1650', in Hepburn, A.C. (ed.), *Minorities in History* (London, 1978).

Clarke, A. 'The policies of the Old English in parliament, 1640-41', in *Historical Studies*, V (London, 1965).

——, *The Old English in Ireland, 1625-1642* (London, 1966).

——, 'Ireland and the general crisis', *Past and Present*, vol. *48* (1970), pp. 79-99.

——, 'Colonial identity in early seventeenth century Ireland', in *Historical Studies*, XI (Belfast, 1978).

Corish, P.J. 'The origins of Catholic nationalism', in Corish, P.J. (ed.), *A History of Irish Catholicism*, vol. *III*, parts 7 and 8 (Dublin, 1968).

Cosgrove, A. 'The Gaelic resurgence and the Geraldine supremacy, 1400-1534' in Moody T.W., and Martin, F.X. (eds.), *The Course of Irish History* (Dublin, 1967).

——, 'Hiberniores ipsis Hibernis' in Cosgrove A. and McCartney, D., (eds.), *Studies in Irish History Presented to R. Dudley Edwards* (Dublin, 1979).

Curtis, E. *A History of Medieval Ireland from 1086 to 1513* (London, 1973 edn.).

Darcy, P. *An Argument Delivered by P. Darcy, Esquire* (Dublin, 1764 edn.).

Davies, J. *Discoverie of the True Causes Why Ireland was Never Entirely Subdued* (I.U.P., 1969 edn.).

Davis, R.H.C. *The Normans and Their Myth* (London, 1976).

De Paor, L. *Early Christian Ireland* (London, 1960).

Dillon, M. *The Cycles of the Kings* (Oxford, 1946).

——, *Early Irish Society* (Dublin, 1963 edn.).

——, and Chadwick, N. *The Celtic Realms* (London, 1973 edn.).

Dudley Edwards, R. 'The Cromwellian persecution and the Catholic church in Ireland', in *Blessed Oliver Plunkett, Historical Studies* (Dublin, 1937).

——, 'Anglo-Norman relations with Connaught', *Irish Historical Studies*, vol. *I* (1938), pp. 135-53.

——, 'Ireland, Elizabeth and the counter-reformation' in Bindoff., S.T., *et al.*, (eds.), *Elizabethan Government and Society* (London, 1961).

——, *Church and State in Tudor Ireland* (Dublin, 1935).

——, *Ireland in the Age of the Tudors* (London, 1977).

——, 'The Irish Catholics and the Puritan revolution', in Franciscan Fathers (ed.), *Father Luke Wadding: Commemorative Volume* (Dublin, 1957).

Ellis, P.B. *Hell or Connaught: the Cromwellian Colonization of Ireland, 1652-1660* (London, 1975).

——, *The Boyne Water* (London, 1976).

Ellis, S.G. 'Tudor policy and the Kildare ascendancy in the lordship of Ireland, 1496-1534', in *Irish Historical Studies*, vol. *XX* (1977), pp. 235-71.

Fitzgerald, B. *The Geraldines* (London, 1951).

Frame, R. 'Power and society in the lordship of Ireland, 1272-1377', in *Past and Present* No. 76 (1977), pp. 3-33.

Gilbert, Sir John T. *Contemporary History of Affairs in Ireland from 1641 to 1652* (3 vols., Dublin, 1879-80).

——, *History of the Irish Confederation and the War in Ireland, 1641-1649* (7 vols., Dublin, 1882-91).

——, *A Jacobite Narrative of the War in Ireland, 1688-91* (First published 1892; Irish University Press, Dublin, 1971).

Hand, G.T., 'The status of the native Irish in the lordship of Ireland, 1272-1331', in *Irish Jurist* (1966), pp. 93-115.

——, 'The forgotten statutes of Kilkenny', *Irish Jurist* (1966), pp. 299-312.

——, *English Law in Ireland, 1290-1324* (Cambridge, 1967).

Hayes-McCoy, G.A., 'Gaelic society in Ireland in the late sixteenth century' in *Historical Studies*, IV (London, 1963).

Hynes, M.J., *The Mission of Rinuccini, Nuncio Extraordinary to Ireland, 1645-49* (Dublin, 1932).

Irish Manuscripts Commission, *Wadding Papers* (ed. B. Jennings), (Dublin, 1954).

Jones, F.M. 'the counter-reformation', in *History of Irish Catholicism*, vol. *III* parts 2 and 3 (Dublin, 1967).

Judson, A. *Life of Edmund Spenser* (Baltimore, 1945).

Kearney, H.F. 'Ecclesiastical politics and the counter-reformation in Ireland, 1618-48', in *Journal of Ecclesiastical History*, vol. *XI* (1960), pp. 202-12.

——, 'The political background to English mercantilism, 1695-1700', in *Economic History Review*, 2nd series, vol. *XI* (1959), p. 484-96.

——, *Strafford in Ireland, 1633-41* (Manchester, 1959).

Kelleher, J.V., 'Early Irish history and pseudo history', in *Studia Hibernica*, vol. *III* (1963), pp. 113-27.

Knott, E. and Murphy, G., *Early Irish literature* (London, 1966).

Lennon, C., 'Richard Stanihurst (1547-1618) and Old English identity', *Irish Historical Studies*, vol. *XXI* (1978), pp. 121-43.

Lindley, K. 'The impact of the 1641 rebellion upon England and Wales', in *Irish Historical Studies*, vol. *XVIII* (1972), pp. 143-76.

Lowe, J. 'Charles I and the confederation of Kilkenny, 1643-49', in *Irish Historical Studies*, vol. *XIV* (1964), pp. 1-19.

Lydon, J. *Ireland in the Later Middle Ages* (Dublin, 1973).

Lydon, J.F. 'The Bruce invasion of Ireland', in *Historical Studies*, IV (London, 1963).

——, *The Lordship of Ireland in the Middle Ages* (Dublin, 1972).

Lynch, J. *Cambrensis eversus* (3 vols., Dublin, 1848-51).

Mac Curtain, M. *Tudor and Stuart Ireland* (Dublin, 1972).

MacErlean, Revd. J.C., (ed.), *The Poems of David O Bruadair* (3 vols., London, 1910-17).

MacNeill, E. *Celtic Ireland* (Dublin, 1921).

Martin, F.X. 'The first Normans in Munster', in *JCHAS*, vol. *LXXVI* (1971), pp. 48-71.

Meehan, C.P. *The Confederation of Kilkenny* (Dublin, 1882).

Millett, B. 'Survival and reorganization, 1605-95', in *History of Irish Catholicism*, vol. *III* parts 7 and 8 (Dublin, 1968).

Moody, T.W. 'The treatment of the native population under the scheme for the plantation of Ulster', in *Irish Historical Studies*, vol. *I* (1938), p. 59-63.

——, 'The history of Poynings' Law: part I, 1494-1615', in *Irish Historical Studies*, vol. *II* (1941), pp. 415-24.

——, *et al.*, (eds.), *New History of Ireland, vol. III, Early Modern Ireland, 1534-1691* (Oxford, 1976).

Mooney, C. 'The first impact of the reformation', in *History of Irish Catholicism*, vol. *III* parts 2 and 3 (Dublin, 1967).

Moran, P.F. *Spicilegium Ossoriense* (3 vols., Dublin, 1874-84).

Morley, H. (ed.), *Ireland under Elizabeth and James I* (London, 1890).

Morres, H.R. Lord Mountmorres, *History of the Principal Transactions of the Irish Parliament from the year of 1634 to 1666* (2 vols., IUP, 1971 edn.).

Murphy, J.A. 'The expulsion of the Irish from Cork in 1644', in *JCHAS*, vol. *LXIX* (1964), pp. 123-31.

——, 'Inchiquin's change of religion', Ibid., vol. *LXXII* (1967), pp. 58-68.

——, 'The politics of the Munster protestants, 1641-49', Ibid., vol. *LXXVI* (1971), pp. 1-20.

Murray, R.H. *Revolutionary Ireland and its Settlement* (London, 1911).

Nicholls, K. *Gaelic and Gaelicised Ireland in the Middle Ages* (Dublin, 1972).

O'Brien, Fr S. *Studies in Honour of Michael O Cleirigh* (Dublin, 1944).

O Corrain, D. *Ireland Before the Normans* (Dublin, 1972).

Ó Cuív, B. 'Literary creation and Irish historical tradition', in *British Academy Proceedings*, vol. *XLIX* (1963), pp. 233-62.

O'Doherty, J.F. 'The Anglo-Norman invasion, 1167-71', in *Irish Historical Studies*, vol. *I* (1938), pp. 154-7.

O Lochlainn, C. *Irish Men of Learning* (Dublin, 1947).

——, *Irish Chiefs and Leaders* (Dublin, 1960).

Orpen, G.H. *Ireland under the Normans* (4 vols.; vols. *I* and *II*, Oxford, 1911; Vols. *III* and *IV*, Oxford, 1920).

O'Rahilly (T.F.) *Early Irish History and Mythology* (Dublin, 1946).

Otway-Ruthven, A.J. 'The native Irish and English law in Medieval Ireland', in *Irish Historical Studies*, vol. *VII* (1950), pp. 1-16.

——, 'The character of the Norman settlement in Ireland' in *Historical Studies*, V (1965).

——, *History of Medieval Ireland* (London, 1968).

Perceval-Maxwell, M. *Scottish migration to Ulster in the Reign of James I* (London, 1973).

——, 'the rising of 1641 and the depositions', in *Irish Historical Studies*, vol. *XXI* (1978), p. 144-67.

Petty, W. *The Political Anatomy of Ireland* (first published 1691; IUP, 1970).

Powell, T.G.E. *The Celts* (London, 1958).

Quinn, D.B. 'Edward Walsh's "conjectures" ', in *Irish Historical Studies*, vol. *V* (1947), pp. 303-22.

Quinn, D.B., 'The Munster Plantation: problems and opportunities' in *JCHAS*, vol. *71* (1966), pp. 19-40.

——, *The Elizabethans and the Irish* (Ithaca, New York, 1966).

Raftery, J. (ed.), *The Celts* (Cork, 1964).

Richardson, H.G. and Sayles, G.O. *The Irish Parliament in the Middle Ages* (Philadelphia, 1964 edn.).

Ronan, M.V. *The Reformation in Ireland under Elizabeth, 1558-1580* (London, 1930).

Ryan, J. (ed.), *Essays and Studies Presented to Eoin MacNeill* (Dublin, 1940).

Sayles, G.O., 'The rebellious first earl of Desmond', in Watt J.A. and Martin, F.X. (eds.), *Medieval Studies Presented to Aubrey Gwynn, S.J.* (Dublin, 1961).

Sheehy, M., *When the Normans Came to Ireland* (Cork, 1975).

Silke, J.J., *Kinsale: Spanish Intervention in Ireland at the End of the Elizabethan Wars* (Liverpool, 1970).

Simms, J.G., *Jacobite Ireland, 1685-91* (London, 1969).

Todhunter, J. *Patrick Sarsfield* (London, 1895).

Warren, W.L. 'John in Ireland, 1185', in P.J. Jupp and J. Bossy (eds.), *Essays Presented to Michael Roberts* (Belfast, 1976).

Watt, J. *The Church and the Two Nations in Medieval Ireland* (Cambridge, 1970).

White, D.G. 'The reign of Edward VI in Ireland', in *Irish Historical Studies*, vol. *XIV* (1965), pp. 197-211.

Wilson, P. *The Beginnings of Modern Ireland* (London, 1912).

4. 1690-1800

Akenson, D.H. and Crawford, W.H. *Local Poets and Social History: James Orr, Bard of Ballycarry* (Belfast, 1977).

Arguments For and Against an Union between Great Britain and Ireland Considered (Dublin, 1799).

Baratariana: a Select Collection of Fugitive Political Pieces Published During the Administration of Lord Townshend in Ireland (3rd edn., Dublin, 1777).

Barrington, Sir J. *Rise and Fall of the Irish Nation* (Dublin, 1853 edn.).

Bartlett, T. and Hayton, D.W. (eds.), *Penal Era and Golden Age: Essays in Irish History, 1690-1800* (Belfast, 1979).

Bolton, G.C. *The Passing of the Irish Act of Union* (London, 1966).

Bromwich, R.S. *The Continuity of the Gaelic Tradition in Eighteenth*

Century Ireland (Yorkshire Celtic Studies, IV, 1947-8).

Brooke, H. *Essay on the Antient and Modern State of Ireland* (Dublin, 1760).

Burns, R.E. 'The Irish penal code and some of its historians' in *Review of Politics* vol. *XXI* (1959), pp. 276-99.

——, 'The Irish Popery laws', in *Review of Politics* (1962), pp. 485-508.

——, 'The Catholic relief act in Ireland, 1778', in *Church History*, vol. *XXXII* (1963), pp. 181-206.

Butterfield, H. *George III, Lord North and the People, 1779-80* (London, 1949).

Calkin, H.L. 'For and against an union' in *Eire/Ireland*, vol. *XIII*, (1978), pp. 22-33.

Chart, D.A. *The Drennan Letters* (Belfast, 1931).

Clark, J.C.D., 'Whig tactics and parliamentary precedent: the English management of Irish politics, 1754-1756', in *Historical Journal*, vol. *21* (1978), pp. 275-301.

Cloney, T. *A Personal Narrative of Those transactions in the Co Wexford in which the Author was Engaged during the Awful Period of 1798* ... (Dublin, 1832).

Coughlan, R.J. *Napper Tandy* (Dublin, 1976).

Craig, M.J. *The Volunteer Earl* (London, 1947).

Cullen, L.M. 'The hidden Ireland: reassessment of a concept' in *Studia Hibernica* vol. *9* (1969), pp. 7-47.

Curran, J.P. *The Speeches* (Dublin, 1845).

Davis, H. (ed.), *The Prose Works of Swift*: vol. *II, Bickerstaff Papers* (Oxford, 1939); vol. *IX, Irish Tracts, 1720-23 and Sermons* (Oxford, 1948); vol. *X, The Drapier's Letters and Other Works, 1724-25* (Oxford, 1941); *Irish Tracts, 1728-33* (Oxford, 1955).

Debates in the House of Commons of Ireland on a Motion Whether the King's Most Excellent Majesty and the Lords and Commons of Ireland, are the Only Power Competent to Bind or Enact Laws in this Kingdom (Dublin, 1780).

De Latocnaye, C. *A Frenchman's Walk through Ireland, 1796-7* (Translated by J. Stevenson, Belfast and Dublin, 1917).

Derry, J.W. *Castlereagh* (London, 1976).

Donnelly, J.S. Jnr., 'The Rightboy movement', in *Studia Hibernica*, vols. *XVII-XVIII* (1977-8), pp. 120-202.

Dunlop, R., *Henry Grattan* (London, 1889).

Elliott, M. 'The origins and transformation of early Irish republicanism' in *International Review of Social History*, vol. *XXIII* (1978), pp. 405-28.

Ferguson, O.W. *Jonathan Swift and Ireland* (Urbana, Illinois, 1962).

Froude, J.A. *The English in Ireland in the Eighteenth Century* (3 vols., London, 1887 edn.).

Gibbon, P. 'The origins of the Orange Order and the United Irishmen', in *Economy and Society*, vol. *I* (1972), pp. 134-63.

Gilbert, Sir J.T. *Documents Relating to Ireland, 1795-1804* (Irish University Press edn., 1970).

Grattan, H. *Speeches . . . in the Irish and Imperial Parliament, Edited by his Son* (4 vols., London, 1822).

——, *Memoirs of the Life and Times of the Right Hon. Henry Grattan by his Son* (5 vols., Dublin, 1837-46).

Gwynn, S., *Henry Grattan and his times* (London, 1939).

Hardy, F. *Memoirs of the Political and Private Life of James Caulfield, Earl of Charlemont* (2 vols., London, 1812).

Hayes, R. *The Last Invasion of Ireland: When Connacht Rose* (Dublin, 1937).

Hobson, B. (ed.), *Letters of Wolfe Tone* (Dublin, n.d.).

Jacob, R. *The Rise of the United Irishmen, 1791-4* (London, 1937).

Jones, W.T. *A Letter to the Societies of United Irishmen in the Town of Belfast . . . to Reassure Protestants that the Catholics will make no Attempt to Inquire into Past Land Titles* (Dublin, 1792).

Kearney, H.F. 'The political background to English mercantilism, 1695-1700', in *Economic History Review*, 2nd series, vol. *XI* (1958-9), pp. 484-96.

Kelly, P. 'British and Irish politics in 1785', in *English Historical Review*, vol. *90* (1975), pp. 536-63.

King, R.A. *Swift in Ireland* (London, 1903).

King, W. *The State of the Protestants Under the Late King James's Government* (Dublin, 1730 edn.).

Landa, L. *Swift and the Church of Ireland* (Oxford, 1954).

Lecky, W.E.H. *History of Ireland in the Eighteenth Century* (5 vols., London, 1892).

Lucas, C. *The Political Constitutions of Great Britain and Ireland Asserted and Vindicated* (London, 1751).

Luce, A.A. and Jessop, T.E. *The Works of George Berkeley, Bishop of Cloyne* (vol. *VI*, London, 1953).

MacAonghusa, P. and O Reagain, L. *The Best of Tone* (Cork, 1972).

McCracken, J.L. 'The conflict between the Irish administration and parliament', in *Irish Historical Studies*, vol. *III* (1942-3), pp. 159-79.

——, 'Irish parliamentary elections, 1727-68', in *Irish Historical Studies*, vol. *V* (1946-7), pp. 209-30.

MacDermot, F. *Theobald Wolfe Tone: A Biographical Study* (London, 1939).

MacDowell, R.B. 'United Irish plans for parliamentary reform, 1793', in *Irish Historical Studies*, vol. *III* (1942-3), pp. 39-59.

——, *Irish Public Opinion, 1750-1800* (London, 1944).

——, *Ireland in the Age of Imperialism and Revolution, 1760-1800* (Oxford, 1979).

MacNeven, W.J. *Pieces of Irish History* (New York, 1907).

Madden, R.R. *The United Irishmen, their Lives and Times* (7 vols.; revised edn., 4 vols., Dublin, 1857-60).

Malcolmson, A.P.W. *John Foster: The Politics of the Anglo-Irish Ascendancy* (Oxford, 1978).

Molyneux, W. *The Case of Ireland's Being Bound by Acts of Parliament in England, Stated* (Dublin, 1698).

Moran, P.F. *Spicilegium Ossoriense* (3rd series, Dublin, 1884).

Nicholson, H. *The Desire to Please: A Study of Hamilton Rowan and the United Irishmen* (London, 1943).

Moore, T. *Life and Death of Lord Edward Fitzgerald* (2 vols., London, 1832).

Murphy, J.A. 'The support of the Catholic clergy in Ireland, 1750-1850', in *Historical Studies* (1965).

Musgrave, Sir R. *Memoirs of the Rebellions in Ireland: From the Arrival of the English* (2 vols., Dublin, 1802).

O'Connell, M.R. *Irish Politics and Social Conflict in the Age of the American Revolution* (Philadelphia, 1965).

O'Connor, T.M. 'The conflict between Flood and Grattan, 1782-3', in H.A. Cronne, T.W. Moody and D.B. Quinn (eds.), *Essays in British and Irish History in Honour of J. Eadie Todd* (London, 1949).

Ó Cuív, B. 'The wearing of the green', in *Studia Hibernica*, vols. *17-18* (1977-8), pp. 107-19.

Pakenham, T. *The Year of Liberty* (London, 1969).

Palmer, R.R. *The Age of the Democratic Revolution* (2 vols., Princeton, 1959-64).

Parsons, Sir L. *Observations on the Bequest of Henry Flood Esq to T.C.D.: With a Defence of the Ancient History of Ireland* (Dublin, 1795).

Powell, T.J. 'The background to the Wexford rebellion, 1790-98', in *Irish Economic and Social History*, vol. *II* (1975), pp. 61-3.

Robbins, C. *The Eighteenth Century Commonwealthman* (Cambridge, Mass., 1959).

Rogers, P. *The Irish Volunteers and Catholic Emancipation, 1778-93*

(London, 1934).

Ronan, M.V. *Insurgent Wicklow* (Dublin, 1948).

Sheridan, T. *A History and the Relation, or a Discovery of the True Causes of why Ireland was Never Entirely Subdued* (Dublin, 1733).

Simms, J.G. *The Williamite Confiscation in Ireland, 1690-1703* (London, 1956).

—— 'Irish Catholics and the parliamentary franchise, 1692-1728', in *Irish Historical Studies*, vol. *XII* (1960-61), pp. 28-37.

—— *Colonial Nationalism, 1698-1776: Molyneux's The Case of Ireland ... Stated* (Cork, 1976).

Stewart, A.T.Q. ' "A stable unseen power": Dr William Drennan and the Origins of the United Irishmen', in P.J. Jupp and J. Bossy (eds.), *Essays Presented to Michael Roberts* (Belfast, 1976).

The Proceedings of the Honourable House of Commons of Ireland in Rejecting the Altered Money Bill on Dec. 17, 1753, Vindicated (Dublin, 1754).

The State of the Question in Relation to the Alteration of the Money Bill Humbly Submitted to the Friends of Ireland (Dublin, 1753).

Tone, Theobald Wolfe *Life, Written by Himself and Extracted from His Journals* (London, 1831 edn.).

Vance, N. 'Celts, Carthiginians and constitutions: Anglo-Irish literary relations, 1780-1820', paper read at the second Anglo-Irish history conference, Swansea, 1979.

Wall, M. 'The rise of a Catholic middle class in eighteenth century Ireland' in *Irish Historical Studies*, vol. *XI* (1958-9), pp. 91-115.

——, *The Penal Laws, 1691-1760* (Dundalk, 1961).

——, 'The United Irish movement', in *Historical Studies*, (London, 1965).

——, 'The Whiteboys' in T.D. Williams (ed.), *Secret Societies in Ireland* (Dublin, 1973).

5. 1800-1870

Barrett, C. 'Irish nationalism and art' in *Studies*, vol. *LXIV* (1975), pp. 393-409.

Beames, M.R. 'Rural conflict in pre-famine Ireland: peasant assassinations in Tipperary, 1837-47', in *Past and Present*, No. 81 (1978), pp. 75-91.

Bourke, M. *John O'Leary: A Study in Irish Separatism* (Tralee, 1967).

Bowen, D. *The Protestant Crusade in Ireland, 1800-1870* (Dublin, 1978).

Brown, M. *The Politics of Irish Literature* (London, 1972).

Buckley, M. 'Attitudes to nationality in four nineteenth century nationalists', in *Journal of the Cork Archaelogical and Historical Society*, vol. *78* (1973), pp. 27-34, 109-16; vol. *79* (1974), pp. 129-36.

——, 'John Mitchel, Ulster, and Irish nationality', in *Studies*, vol. LXV (1976), pp. 30-44.

Butler, M. *Maria Edgeworth: A Literary Biography* (Oxford, 1972).

Butt, I. *The Famine in the Land* (Dublin, 1847).

Carleton, W. *Traits and Stories of the Irish Peasantry* (2 vols., London, 1843).

Clarke, R. 'Relations between O'Connell and Young Ireland', in *Irish Historical Studies*, vol. *III* (1942), pp. 18-31.

Comerford, R.V. *Charles J. Kickham (1828-82) A Study in Irish Nationalism and Literature* (Dublin, 1979).

Corish, Fr. P.J. 'Cardinal Cullen and the national association of Ireland', in *Reportorium Novum*, vol. *III* (1962), pp. 13-61.

——, 'Political problems, 1860-1878', in *A history of Irish Catholicism*, vol. *V*, parts 2 and 3 (Dublin, 1967).

Cronin, J. *The Anglo-Irish Novel, Vol. I, the Nineteenth Century* (Belfast, 1980).

D'Alton, I. 'A contrast in crises: southern Irish protestantism, 1820-43', in A.C. Hepburn (ed.), *Minorities in History* (London, 1978).

Davis, T. *Address Read Before the Historical Society, Dublin on 26 June 1840* (Dublin, 1840).

——, *Letters of a Protestant, on Repeal* (ed. T.F. Meagher, Dublin, 1847).

——, *The Patriot Parliament of 1689* (ed. with an intro. by C.G. Duffy, London, 1893).

——, *Prose Writings: Essays on Ireland* (London, 1890).

——, *Essays and Poems* (London, 1914 edn.).

Desmond Williams, T. and Dudley Edwards, R. (eds.), *The Great Famine: Studies in Irish History, 1845-52* (Dublin, 1956).

Devoy, J. *Recollections of an Irish Rebel* (Irish University Press, 1969 edn.).

Donnelly, J.S. 'The Irish agricultural depression of 1859-64', in *Irish Economic and Social History Journal*, vol. *III* (1976), pp. 33-54.

Dowling, P.J. *The Hedge Schools of Ireland* (London, 1935).

Dudley Edwards, R. 'The contribution of Young Ireland to the Irish national idea', in S. Pender (ed.), *Féilscribhinn Torna: Essays Presented to Tadhg ua Donnchadha* (Cork, 1947).

Dudley Edwards, R. *Daniel O'Connell and His World* (London, 1975).

Duffy, Charles Gavan *The Ballad Poetry of Ireland* (Dublin, 1845).

——, *The Creed of the Nation* (Dublin, 1848).

——, *Young Ireland: A Fragment of Irish History, 1840-45* (Dublin, 1884 edn.).

Dunlop, R. *Daniel O'Connell and the Revival of National Life in Ireland* (London, 1960).

Flanagan, T. *The Irish Novelists, 1800-1850* (New York, 1959).

Forrester, E. and A.M. *Songs of the Rising Nation* (Glasgow and London, 1869).

Freeman, T.W. *Pre-famine Ireland: A Study in Historical Geography* (Manchester, 1957).

Fryer, W.R. 'Romantic literature in the European age of revolution', in *Renaissance and Modern Studies*, vol. *VIII* (1964), pp. 53-74.

Gleeson, D. 'Father Kenyon and Young Ireland' in *Studies*, vol. *XXXV* (1946), pp. 99-110.

Godkin, J. *Education in Ireland: Its History, Institutions, Systems Statistics and Progress* (London, and Dublin, 1862).

Goldstrom, J.M. *The Social Content of Education, 1808-1870: A Study of the Working Class Reader in England and Ireland* (IUP, 1972).

Griffith, A. (ed.), *Thomas Davis, the Thinker and Teacher* (Dublin, 1918).

Gwynn, D.R. *Daniel O'Connell* (London, 1947).

——, 'William Smith O'Brien' in *Studies*, vol. *XXXV* (1946), pp. 448-58; vol. *XXXVI* (1947), pp. 29-39, 129-40; vol. *XXXVII* (1948), pp. 7-17, 149-60.

——, 'Father John Kenyon and Young Ireland', in *Irish Ecclesiastical Record*, vol. *LXXI* (1951), pp. 226-43.

Gwynn, S. *Thomas Moore* (London, 1905).

Harmon, M. *Fenians and Fenianism* (Naas, 1968).

Hill, J.R. 'Nationalism and the Catholic church in the 1840s: views of Dublin repealers', in *Irish Historical Studies*, vol. *XIX* (1975), pp. 371-95.

Hoppen, K.T. 'Landlords, society and electoral politics in mid-nineteenth century Ireland', in *Past and Present*, No. *75* (1977), pp. 62-93.

——, 'Politics, the law, and the nature of the Irish electorate, 1832-1850', in *EHR*, vol. *92* (1977), pp. 746-76.

——, 'National politics and local realities in mid-nineteenth century Ireland', in Cosgrove and McCartney, op. cit.

Ireland and O'Connell: A Historical Sketch of the Condition of the Irish People Before the Commencement of Mr O'Connell's Public Career (Edinburgh, 1835).

Johnson, J.H. 'The two "Irelands" at the beginning of the nineteenth century', in Glasscock, R.E. and Stephens, (eds.), *Irish Geographical Studies* (Belfast, 1970).

Jupp, P.J. 'Irish parliamentary elections and the influence of the Catholic vote, 1801-20', in *Historical Journal*, vol. *X* (1967), pp. 183-96.

Kennedy, B.A. 'Sharman Crawford's federal sheme for Ireland', in H.A. Cronne *et al.*, *Essays in British and Irish History in Honour of J.E. Todd* (London, 1949).

Kettle, T.M. (ed.), *Irish Orators and Oratory* (Dublin, n.d.).

Kickham, C.J. *Knocknagow* (Dublin, 1873; 1979 edn.).

Larkin, E. 'The devotional revolution in Ireland, 1850-75', in *American Historical Review*, vol. 77 (1972), pp. 625-52.

Lecky, W.E.H. *Leaders of Public Opinion in Ireland, Vol. II, Daniel O'Connell* (London, 1912 edn.).

Lee, J. 'The Ribbonmen', in T.D. Williams (ed.), *Secret Societies in Ireland*.

Lees, L.H. and Modell, J. 'The Irish countryman urbanized: a comparative perspective on the famine emigration', in *Journal of Urban History*, vol. *III* (1977), pp. 391-408.

Lewis, G.C. *On Local and National Disturbances in Ireland and on the Irish Church Question* (London, 1836).

Lowe, W.J. 'The Lancashire Irish and the Catholic church, 1846-71: the social dimension', in *Irish Historical Studies*, vol. *XX* (1976), pp. 129-55.

Lucas, E. (ed.), *Life of F. Lucas* (London, 1861).

McCaffrey, L.J. *Daniel O'Connell and the Repeal Year* (Lexington, 1966).

MacDonagh, O. 'The politicization of the Irish Catholic bishops, 1800-1850', in *Historical Journal*, vol. *XVIII* (1975), pp. 37-53.

——, 'The Irish famine emigration to the United States', in *Perspectives in American History*, vol. *X* (1976), pp. 357-446.

MacDowell, R.B. *Public Opinion and Government Policy in Ireland, 1800-1846* (London, 1952).

——, *Social Life in Ireland, 1800-1845* (Dublin, 1957).

McGee, T. D'Arcy *A Popular History of Ireland to the Emancipation of the Catholics* (2 vols. New York, 1864).

MacGeoghegan, Abbe *History of Ireland from the Earliest Times to the*

Treaty of Limerick (Dublin, 1844 edn.).

Mac Giolla Choille, B. 'Fenian documents in the State Paper Office', in *Irish Historical Studies*, vol. *XVI* (1966-7), pp. 258-84.

MacGrath, K.M. 'Writers in the *Nation*, 1842-45', in *Irish Historical Studies*, vol. *VI* (1949), pp. 189-223.

MacIntyre, A. *The Liberator: Daniel O'Connell and the Irish Party, 1830-47 (London, 1965)*.

MacManus, M.J. (ed.), *Thomas Davis and Young Ireland* (Dublin, 1945).

MacNevin, T. (eds.), *Speeches of the Rt Hon. Richard Lalor Sheil* (Dublin, 1845).

MacSuibhne, Fr, P. *Paul Cullen and his Contemporaries* (6 vols, Naas, 1961-77).

Marlowe, N. (ed.), *James Fintan Lalor: Selected Writings* (Dublin, 1918).

Miller, D.W. 'Irish Catholicism and the great famine', in *Journal of Social History*, vol. *IX* (1975), pp. 81-98.

Mitchel, J. *Jail Journal* (Dublin, 1913 edn.).

——, *An Ulsterman for Ireland* (Dublin, 1917 edn.).

——, *The Last Conquest of Ireland (Perhaps)* (Dublin, 1861).

——, *An Apology for the British Government in Ireland* (Dublin, 1960).

——, *History of Ireland: From the Treaty of Limerick to the Present Time* (2 vols, Dublin, 1869).

Moody, T.W. *Thomas Davis, 1814-45* (Dublin, 1945).

——, 'Irish American nationalism', in *IHS*, vol. *XV* (1967), pp. 438-45.

——, (ed.), *The Fenian Movement* (Cork, 1968).

Murphy, M. 'Repeal, popular politics and the Catholic clergy of Cork, 1840-50', in *JCHAS*, vol. *LXXXII* (1977), pp. 39-48.

Norman, E.R. *The Catholic Church and Ireland in the Age of Rebellion, 1859-73* (London, 1965).

Nowlan, K.B. 'The meaning of repeal in Irish history', in *Historical Studies, IV* (London, 1963).

——, *The Politics of Repeal: A Study in the Relations Between Great Britain and Ireland, 1841-50* (London, 1965).

——, *Charles Gavan Duffy and the Repeal Movement* (Dublin, 1963).

O'Brien, W. 'Was Fenianism ever formidable', in *Contemporary Review*, vol. *LXX* (1897), pp. 680-93.

O Broin, L. *Charles Gavan Duffy* (Dublin, 1967).

O Buachalla, B. 'A speech in Irish on repeal', in *Studia Hibernica*, vol. *X* (1970), pp. 84-94.

O'Connell, D. *A Memoir on Ireland, Native and Saxon* (Dublin, 1843; 1970 edn.).

O'Connell, J. (ed.), *Life and Speeches of Daniel O'Connell* (Dublin, 1846).

——, *The Select Speeches of Daniel O'Connell, MP* (Dublin, 1865).

O'Connell, M.R. 'O'Connell, Young Ireland and violence', in *Thought*, vol. *LII* (1977), pp. 381-406.

——, 'Daniel O'Connell and religious freedom', Ibid., vol. *L* (1975), pp. 176-87.

——, (ed.), *The Correspondence of Daniel O'Connell* (vols. *I, III* and *IV* only, Dublin, 1972-77).

O'Leary, J. *Recollections of Fenians and Fenianism* (2 vols, London, 1896; IUP, 1968 edn.).

O'Mahony, J. *Chief of the Comeraghs – A John O'Mahony Anthology* (ed. J. Maher, Mullinahone, 1957).

O'Neill, T.P. 'The Irish land question, 1830-50', in *Studies*, vol. *XLIV* (1955), pp. 325-36.

——, 'James Fintan Lalor: economic and political ideas', in *Irish Ecclesiastical Record*, 5th series, vol. *LXXIV* (1956), pp. 398-409.

O'Neill Daunt, W.J. *A Life Spent for Ireland* (IUP, 1972 edn.).

O'Sullivan, T.F. *The Young Irelanders* (Tralee, 1944).

——, (ed.), *Mark Ryan: Fenian Memories* (Dublin, 1945).

O Tuathaigh, G. 'Gaelic Ireland, popular politics and Daniel O'Connell', in *Galway Archaeological and Historical Society Journal*, vol. *34* (1974-5), pp. 21-34.

——, *Ireland Before the Famine, 1798-1848* (Dublin, 1972).

Pender, S. 'Luby, Kenyon and the MacManus funeral', in *JCHAS*, vol. *LVI* (1951), pp. 52-65.

Pigott, R. *Recollections of an Irish National Journalist* (Dublin, 1882).

Price, J.A. 'Thomas Davis', in J. Vyrnwy Morgan (ed.), *Welsh Political and Educational Leaders in the Victorian Era* (London, 1908).

Repeal Essays: Prize Essays on the Repeal of the Union (Dublin, 1845).

Repeal: Ballads and Songs (British Library): *A New Song on Repeal; The Speedy Repeal; Ireland for the Irish; The Liberator; The Ass and the Orangeman's Daughter.*

Reid, J.S. *History of the Presbyterian Church in Ireland*, vol. *III*, 2nd edn., London, 1853).

Reynolds, J.A. *The Catholic Emancipation Crisis in Ireland, 1923-29* (New Haven, 1954).

Roche, Kennedy 'The relations of the Catholic church and the state in England and Ireland, 1800-52', in *Historical Studies, III* (London and Cork, 1961).

Rolleston, T.W. (ed.), *Thomas Davis: Selections from His Prose and Poetry* (London, 1914).

Rossa, Jeremiah O'Donovan *Recollections* (New York, 1898).

Ryan, D. *The Phoenix Flame* (London, 1937).

——, *The Fenian Chief: A Biography of James Stephens* (Dublin, 1967).

Savage, J. *'98 and '48: The Modern Revolutionary History and Literature of Ireland* (New York, 1884).

Sillard, P.A. *Life of John Martin* (Dublin, 1894).

Steele, E.D. *Irish Land and British Politics: Tenant Right and Nationality, 1865-1870* (Cambridge, 1974).

——, 'Cardinal Cullen and Irish nationality', in *Irish Historical Studies*, vol. *XIX* (1975), pp. 239-60.

——, 'Gladstone, Irish violence and conciliation' in Cosgrove and MacCartney, op. cit.,

Sullivan, A.M. *The Story of Ireland* (Dublin, 1867).

Sullivan, T.D. *Recollections of Troubled times in Irish Politics* (Dublin, 1905).

Tierney, M. (ed.), *Daniel O'Connell: Nine Centenary Essays* (Dublin, 1949).

Ward, B. *The Eve of Catholic Emancipation* (London, 1911-12).

Whyte, J.H. 'The influence of the Catholic clergy on elections in nineteenth century Ireland', in *EHR*, vol. *LXXV* (1960), pp. 239-59.

——, 'Landlord influence at elections in Ireland, 1760-1885', ibid., vol. *LXXV* (1965), pp. 740-60.

——, *The Independent Irish Party, 1850-59* (Oxford, 1958).

——, 'Fresh light on archibishop Cullen and the tenant league', in *Irish Ecclesiastical Record*, 5th series, vol. *XCIX* (1963), pp. 170-76.

——, 'Political problems, 1850-60', in P.J. Corish (ed.), *A History of Irish Catholicism*, vol. *V*, parts 2 and 3 (Dublin, 1967).

Wyse, T. *Historical Sketch of the Late Catholic Association of Ireland* (2 vols., London, 1839).

6. 1870-1921

Banks, M.A. *Edward Blake, Irish Nationalist* (Toronto, 1957).

Bew, P. *Land and the National Question in Ireland, 1858-1882* (Dublin, 1978).

Boland, J. *Irishman's Day: A Day in the Life of an Irish MP* (London, n.d.).

Boyd, E. *Ireland's Literary Renaissance* (Dublin, 1968 edn.).

Boyle, J.W. (ed.), *Leaders and Workers* (Cork, 1966).

Brennan, R. *Allegiance* (Dublin, 1950).

Brown, M. *The Politics of Irish Literature: From Thomas Davis to W.B. Yeats* (London, 1972).

Brown, T.N. 'The origins and character of Irish American nationalism', in *Review of Politics*, vol. *XVIII* (1956), pp. 327-58.

——, *Irish American Nationalism* (Philadelphia, 1966).

Buckland, P.J. *Irish Unionism One: The Anglo-Irish and the New Ireland, 1885-1922* (Dublin, 1972).

——, *Irish Unionism Two: Ulster Unionsim and the Origins of Northern Ireland, 1886-1922* (Dublin, 1973).

Butt, I. *Irish Federalism: Its Meaning, its Objects and its Hopes* (Dublin, 1874).

Casey, D.J. and Rhodes, R.E. *Views of the Irish Peasantry* (Hamden, Conn., 1977).

Chavasse, M. *Terence MacSwiney* (Dublin, 1961).

Clark, S. 'The social composition of the land league', in *Irish Historical Studies*, vol. *XVII*, (1971), pp. 447-69.

——, 'The political mobilization of Irish farmers', in *Canadian Review of Sociology and Anthropology*, vol. *XII* (1975), pp. 483-97.

——, 'Agrarian class conflict and collective action in nineteenth century Ireland', in *British Journal of Sociology*, vol. *XXIX* (1978), pp. 22-40.

Coffey, D. *Douglas Hyde, President of Ireland* (Dublin and Cork, 1938).

Collins, M. *The Path to Freedom* (Dublin, 1922).

Colum, P. *Arthur Griffith* (Dublin, 1959).

——, and O'Brien, E.J. *Poems of the I.R.B.* (Boston, 1916).

Comerford, M. *The First Dáil* (Dublin, 1969).

Connolly, J. *Labour in Irish History* (Dublin, 1910).

Costello, P. *The Heart Grown Brutal: The Irish Revolution in Literature from Parnell to the Death of Yeats* (Dublin, 1977).

Coxhead, E. *Daughters of Erin: Five Women of the Irish Renaissance* (London, 1965).

——, *Lady Gregory: A Literary Portrait* (London, 1961).

Curran, C.P. 'Griffith, MacNeill and Pearse', in *Studies*, vol. *LV* (1966), pp. 21-8.

Curtis, L.P. *Coercion and Conciliation in Ireland, 1886-1892: A Study in Conservative Unionism* (Princeton, 1963).

Dalton, G.F. 'The tradition of blood sacrifice to the goddess Eire', in

Studies, vol. *LXIII* (1974), pp. 343-54.

Daly, D. *The Young Douglas Hyde: The Dawn of Irish Revolution and Renaissance, 1874-1893* (Dublin, 1974).

Davis, R.P. *Arthur Griffith and Non-violent Sinn Féin* (Dublin, 1974).

Davitt, M. *The Fall of Feudalism in Ireland* (1904: IUP, 1970 edn.).

—— *Leaves From a Prison Diary* (1885; IUP, 1972 edn.).

de Blacam A. *What Sinn Féin Stands For* (Dublin, n.d. [1921?]).

Denvir, J. *Life Story of an Old Rebel* (Dublin, 1910).

Desmond Williams, T. (ed.), *The Irish Struggle, 1916-26* (London, 1966).

Devoy, J. *Recollections of an Irish Rebel* (London, 1929).

Dewey, C. 'Celtic agrarian legislation and the Celtic revival: historicist implications of Gladstone's Irish and Scottish land acts, 1870-1886', in *Past and Present*, No. 4 (1974), pp. 30-70.

Donnelly, J. *The Land and the People of Nineteenth Century Cork: The Rural Economy and the Land Question* (London, 1975).

Doyle, J.J. *David Comyn (1854-1907): A Pioneer of the Irish Language Movement* (Cork, 1926).

Dudley Edwards, O. and Pyle, F. (eds.), *1916: The Easter Rising* (London, 1968).

Dudley Edwards, O. and Ransome, B. (eds.), *James Connolly: Selected Political Writings* (London, 1973).

Dudley Edwards, R. *Patrick Pearse: The Triumph of Failure* (London, 1977).

Duffy, C.G. *The Revival of Irish Literature* (London, 1894).

Dungannon Club: Pamphlets: No. *1 Irishmen and the English Army;* R. Lynd *The Orangemen and the Nation*; B. Hobson *The Creed of the Republic*

Ellis, P.B. *James Connolly: Selected Writings* (London, 1973).

Farrell, B. *The Founding of Dáil Eireann: Parliament and Nation Building* (Dublin, 1971).

Ferguson, Lady M.C. *Sir Samuel Ferguson in the Ireland of His Day* (Edinburgh and London, 1896).

Fitzgerald, D. *Memoirs, 1913-16* (London, 1968).

Fitzpatrick, D. *Politics and Irish Life, 1913-1921* (Dublin, 1977).

——, 'The geography of Irish nationalism, 1910-1921', in *Past and Present*, No. 78 (1978), pp. 113-44.

Forester, M. *Michael Collins: The Lost Leader* (London, 1971).

Foster, R.F. *Charles Stewart Parnell: The Man and His Family* (Sussex, 1976).

Fox, R.M. *The History of the Irish Citizen Army* (Dublin, 1943).

464   Bibliography

Gaelic League Pamphlets: No. *1 The True National Idea;* No. *2 Two Schools – A Contrast;* No. *6 Irishwomen and the Home Language;* No. *10 The Reign of Humbug;* No. *21 The Irish Language Movement: Its Philosophy;* No. *24 The Threatening of a Nation;* No. *29 The Irish Language Movement: Its Genesis, Growth and Progress*
Gaughan, J.A. *Austin Stack: Portrait of a Separatist* (Dublin, 1977).
Greaves, C.D. *Life and Times of James Connolly* (London, 1961).
——, *Liam Mellows and the Irish Revolution* (London, 1971).
Gregory, Lady *Ideals in Ireland* (London, 1901).
Griffith, A. *The Resurrection of Hungary: A Parallel for Ireland* (Dublin, 1918).
——, *Poems and Ballads of William Rooney* (Dublin, 1901).
——, *The Sinn Féin Policy* (Dublin, 1906).
——, *The Home Rule Bill Examined* (Dublin, 1912).
——, *Meagher of the Sword* (Dublin, 1916).
Gwynn, D.R. *Life of John Redmond* (London, 1932).
Gwynn, S. *The Case for Home Rule Stated* (Dublin, 1911).
——, *John Redmond's Last Years* (London, 1919).
Hachey, T.E. *Britain and Irish Separatism: From the Fenians to the Free State* (Chicago, 1977).
Healy, T.M. *Letters and Leaders of My Day* (2 vols., London, 1928).
Henry R.M. *The Evolution of Sinn Féin* (Dublin, 1920).
Hepburn, A.C. 'The A.O.H. in Irish politics, 1905-14', in *Cithara*, vol. *X (1971), pp.* 5-18.
——, 'Catholics in the north of Ireland, 1850-1912: the urbanization of a minority', in Hepburn *Minorities in History*.
Horgan, J.J. *From Parnell to Pearse* (Dublin, 1948).
Horn, P.L.R. 'The national agricultural labourers' union in Ireland, 1873-9', in *Irish Historical Studies*, vol. *XVII* (1970-71), pp. 340-52.
Hurst, M. 'Ireland and the ballot act, 1872', in *Historical Journal*, vol. *VIII* (1965), pp. 326-52.
Hyde, D. *A Literary History of Ireland* (London, 1967).
Irish Press Agency: Pamphlets, 1886-7.
Kelly, J.S. 'The fall of Parnell and the rise of Irish literature: an investigation', in *Anglo-Irish Studies*, vol. *II* (1976), pp. 1-23.
Kerr, S. Parnell *What the Irish Regiments Have Done* (London, 1916).
Kettle, T.M. 'A note on Sinn Féin in Ireland', in *North American Review*, vol. *CLXXXVII* (1908), pp. 46-59.
——, *The Day's Burden* (Dublin, 1910).
Laffan, M. 'The unification of Sinn Féin in 1917', in *Irish Historical Studies*, vol. *XVII* (1971), pp. 353-79.

Larkin, E. *James Larkin: Irish Labour Leader* (London, 1965).

——, 'The Roman Catholic hierarchy and the fall of Parnell', in *Victorian Studies*, vol. *IV* (1961), pp. 315-36.

——, *The Roman Catholic Church and the Creation of the Modern Irish State, 1876-1886* (Dublin, 1975).

——, *The Roman Catholic Church in Ireland and the Fall of Parnell, 1888-91* (Liverpool, 1979).

Larson, S.V. and Snoddy, O '1916 – a workingman's revolution', in *Social Studies*, vol. *2* (1973), pp. 377-98.

Lavelle, P. *James O'Mara – A Staunch Sinn Féiner* (Dublin, 1961).

Lee, J. *The Modernization of Irish Society, 1848-1918* (Dublin, 1973).

Le Roux, N. *Tom Clarke and the Irish Freedom Movement* (Dublin, 1936).

Levenson, S. *James Connolly: A Biography* (London, 1973).

Loftus, R.J. *Nationalism in Modern Anglo-Irish Poetry* (Madison and Milwaukee, 1964).

Lynd, R. *Ireland: A Nation* (London, 1919).

Lyons, F.S.L. *The Irish Parliamentary Party, 1890-1910* (London, 1951).

——, *Parnell* (Dundalk, 1963).

——, 'John Dillon and the plan of campaign, 1886-90', in *Irish Historical Studies*, vol. *XIV* (1964-5), pp. 313-47.

——, *John Dillon: A Biography* (London, 1968).

——, 'The political ideas of Parnell', in *Historical Journal*, vol. *XVI* (1973), pp. 749-75.

——, *C.S. Parnell* (London, 1977).

——, 'The Parnell theme in Literature', in A. Carpenter (ed.), *Place, Personality and the Irish Writer* (Gerrard's Cross, 1977).

——, *Culture and Anarchy in Ireland, 1890-1939* (Oxford, 1979).

McCaffrey, L.J. 'Home rule and the general election of 1874 in Ireland', in *Irish Historical Studies*, vol. *IX* (1954), pp. 190-212.

——, 'Isaac Butt and the home rule movement: a study in conservative nationalism', in *Review of Politics*, vol. *22* (1960), pp. 72-95.

——, *The Irish Diaspora in America* (American Universities Publishers, 1976).

——, *Irish Nationalism and the American Contribution* (New York, 1976).

Macardle, D. *The Irish Republic* (London, 1968 edn.).

McCartney, D. 'The political use of history in the work of Arthur Griffith', in *Journal of Contemporary History*, vol. *8* (1973), pp. 3-19.

McCartney, D. 'The churches and secret societies', in T.D. Williams (ed.), *Irish·Secret Societies*.

MacDermott, M. *The New Spirit of the Nation* (London, 1894).

MacDonagh, M. *The Irish at the Front* (London, 1916).

——, *The Life of William O'Brien, the Irish Nationalist* (London, 1928).

MacDowell, R.B. *Alice Stopford Green: A Passionate Historian* (Dublin, 1967).

MacManus, S. 'Sinn Féin', in *North American Review*, vol. *CLXXXV* (1907), pp. 825-36.

——, *Prose Writings of William Rooney* (Dublin, 1909).

MacNeill, J. Swift *The Irish Parliament: What it Was and What it Did* (London, 1885).

Malins, E. *Yeats and the Easter Rising* (Dublin, 1965).

Mansergh, N. 'Eoin MacNeill – a re-appraisal', in *Studies*, vol. *LXIII* (1974), pp. 133-40.

Marcus, P.L. *Yeats and the Beginning of the Irish Renaissance* (New York, 1970).

Marreco, A. *The Rebel Countess: The Life and Times of Constance Markievicz* (London, 1967).

Martin, F.X. 'Eoin MacNeill on the 1916 rising', in *Irish Historical Studies*, vol. *XII* (1961), pp. 226-71.

——, *The Irish Volunteers, 1913-15* (Dublin), 1963).

——, '1916-myth, fact and mystery', in *Studia Hibernica*, vol. 7 (1967), pp. 7-126.

——, 'The 1916 rising: coup d'etat or a "bloody protest" ', in ibid., vol. 8 (1968), pp. 106-37.

——, (ed.), *Leaders and Men of the Easter Rising: Dublin, 1916* (London, 1967).

——, (with F.J. Byrne, eds.), *The Scholar Revolutionary: Eoin MacNeill, 1867-1945 and the Making of the New Ireland* (IUP, 1973).

Martin, Ged 'Parnell at Cambridge: the education of an Irish nationalist', in *Irish Historical Studies*, vol. *19* (1974-5), pp. 62-72.

Miller, D.W. 'The Roman Catholic church in Ireland, 1898-1918', in *Eire/Ireland* vol. *III* (1968), pp. 75-91.

——, *Church, State and Nation in Ireland, 1898-1921* (Dublin, 1973).

Mitchell, A. *Labour in Irish Politics, 1890-1930* (IUP, 1974).

Moody, T.W. 'The new departure in Irish politics, 1878-9', in *Essays in British and Irish History*.

——, 'Michael Davitt, 1846-1906: a survey and an appreciation', in *Studies*, vol. *XXXV* (1946): part i, pp. 199-208; part ii, pp. 325-438.

Moran, D.P. *The Philosophy of Irish Ireland* (Dublin, n.d. [1905?]).

National Council Pamphlets: A. Griffith *How Ireland is Taxed;* R. Lynd *The Ethics of Sinn Féin;* 'O' *Ireland and the British Army;* J. Sweetman *Nationality;* J. Sweetman *Liberty*

Nowlan, K.B. *The Making of 1916: Studies in the history of the Rising* (Dublin, 1969).

O'Brien, C.C. *Parnell and His Party, 1880-90* (London, 1957 edn.).

——, (ed.), *The Shaping of Modern Ireland* (London, 1960).

——, 'Passion and cunning: an essay on the politics of W.B; Yeats', in A.N. Jeffares (ed.), *In Excited Reverie* (London, 1965).

O'Brien, J.V. *William O'Brien and the Course of Irish Politics, 1881-1918* (California, 1976).

O'Brien, R.B. *Life of C.S. Parnell* (London, 1910 edn.).

——, *The Home Rulers Manual* (London, 1890).

——, *Home Rule Speeches of John Redmond* (London, 1910).

O'Brien, William *The Irish National Idea* (Cork, 1886).

——, *When we were Boys* (London, 1890).

——, *Irish Ideas* (London, 1893).

——, *Who Fears to Speak of '98* (Dublin, 1898).

——, *An Olive Branch for Ireland and its History* (London, 1910).

——, *The downfall of Parliamentarianism in Ireland: A Retrospect for the Accounting Day* (Dublin, 1918).

——, *Irish Fireside Hours* (Dublin, 1927).

O'Brien, W. and Ryan, D. (eds.), *Devoy's Post-bag, 1871-1928* (2 vols., Dublin, 1948, 1953).

O'Brien, William *Forth the Banners Go* (Dublin, 1969).

O Broin, L. *Revolutionary Underground: The Story of the I.R.B. 1858-1924* (Dublin, 1976).

O'Connor, T.P. *The Parnell Movement* (London, 1886).

——, *Memoirs of an Old Parliamentarian* (2 vols., London, 1929).

O'Day, A. *The English Face of Irish Nationalism: Parnellite Involvement in British Politics, 1880-86* (Dublin, 1977).

O'Donnell, F.H. *A History of the Irish Parliamentary Party* (2 vols., London, 1910).

O'Donoghue, F. *No Other Law* (Dublin, 1954).

——, 'The Irish Volunteers in Cork, 1913-16', in *JCHAS*, vol. 71 (1966), pp. 41-8.

O'Driscoll, R. *Theatre and Nationalism in Twentieth Century Ireland* (London, 1971).

——, 'Ferguson and the idea of an Irish national literature', in *Eire/Ireland*, vol. *VI* (1971), pp. 82-95.

——, *An Ascendancy of the Heart: Ferguson and the Beginnings of*

Modern Irish Literature in English (Dublin, 1976).

O'Grady, S. 'The last kings of Ireland', in *EHR*, vol. *IV* (1899), pp. 286-303.

O'Hegarty, P.S. *Sinn Féin: An Illumination* (Dublin, 1919)

——, *The Victory of Sinn Féin: How it Won it and How it Used it* (Dublin, 1924).

O Luing, S. 'Arthur Griffith: thoughts on a centenary', in *Studies*, vol. *LX* (1971), pp. 127-38.

O'Neil, D.J. 'D.P. Moran, and Gaelic cultural revitalization', in *Eire/Ireland*, vol. *XII* (1977), pp. 109-13.

O Tuama, S. *The Gaelic League Idea* (Cork and Dublin, 1972).

O Tuathaigh, G. 'Nineteenth Century Irish Politics: The Case for "normalcy" ', in *Anglo-Irish Studies*, vol. *I* (1975), pp. 71-81.

Parks, E.W. and A.W. (eds.), *Thomas MacDonagh: The Man, the Patriot, the Writer* (Athens, Georgia, 1967).

Paul-Dubois, L. *Contemporary Ireland* (Dublin, 1908).

Pearse, P. *Political Writings and Speeches* (Dublin, 1918; 1966 ed.).

Phillips, W.A. *The Revolution in Ireland* (London, 1923).

Pomfret, J. *The Struggle for Land in Ireland, 1880-1923* (New York, 1969 edn.).

Pope-Hennessy, J. 'What do the Irish read?', in *Nineteenth Century*, vol. *15* (1884), pp. 920-32.

Power, P.C. *A Literary History of Ireland* (Cork, 1969).

Redmond, J.E. *Historical and Political Addresses* (Dublin and London, 1898).

——, *Ireland and the Coronation: Why Ireland is Discontented* (United Irish League of Great Britain, leaflet no. 2, 1902).

——, *Ireland and the War: Speeches Delivered at Dublin and Kilkenny, 25 Sept. and 14 Oct., 1914* (Dublin, 1914).

——, *Account of a Visit to the Front* (London, 1915).

Reid, A. (ed.), *Ireland: A Book of Light on the Irish Problem* (London, 1886).

Ronsley, J. (ed.), *Myth and Reality in Irish Literature* (Waterloo, Ontario, 1977).

Russell, George. *The National Being: Some Thoughts on an Irish Polity* (Dublin, 1916).

Ryan, D. *Socialism and Nationalism: A Selection from the Writings of James Connolly* (Dublin, 1948).

Ryan, J. 'Eoin MacNeill, 1867-1945', in *Studies*, vol. *XXXIV* (1945), pp. 433-48.

Sheehy, J. *The Rediscovery of Ireland's Past* (London, 1980).

Sheehy, M. *Michael/Frank: Studies in Frank O'Connor* (London, 1969).

Sullivan, A.M. *New Ireland: Political Sketches and Personal Reminiscences* (Glasgow and London, n.d. [1882?]).

Sullivan, A.M., T.D. and D.B. *Irish Readings* (2 vols., Dublin, 1904).

Taylor, R. *Michael Collins* (London, 1968).

Telfer, G.W.L. *Yeats' Idea of the Gael* (Dublin, 1965).

Thompson, W.I. *The Imagination of an Insurrection: Dublin, Easter, 1916* (London, 1967).

Thornley, D.A. 'The Irish conservatives and home rule, 1869-73', in *Irish Historical Studies*, vol. *VI* (1959), pp. 200-22.

——, *Isaac Butt and Home Rule* (London, 1964).

Tierney, M. 'A prophet of mystic nationalism: AE', in *Studies*, vol. XXVI, (1937), pp. 568-80.

——, *Croke of Cashel: The Life of Archbishop T.W. Croke, 1823-1902* (Dublin, 1976).

Townshend, C. *The British Campaign in Ireland, 1919-21: The Development of Political and Military Policies* (London, 1975).

——, 'The IRA and the development of guerilla warfare, 1916-21', in *EHR*, vol. *94* (1979), pp. 318-45.

Webb, A. *An Address to the Electors of West Waterford* (Dublin, 1891).

White, T. de V. *The Anglo-Irish* (London, 1972).

Woods, C.J. 'The politics of cardinal McCabe, archbishop of Dublin, 1879-1885', in *Dublin Historical Record*, vol. *XXVI* (1973), pp. 101-110.

7. Since 1921

Akenson, D.H. and Fallin, J.F. 'The Irish civil war and the drafting of the Irish free state constitution', in *Eire/Ireland*, vol. *V* (1970), pp. 42-93, 28-70.

Barritt, D.P. and Carter, C.F. *The Northern Ireland Problem: A Study in Group Relations* (London, 1962).

Bax, M. *Harpstrings and Confessions: Machine Style Politics in the Irish Republic* (Amsterdam, 1976).

Beckett, J.C. 'Northern Ireland', in *Journal of Contemporary History*, vol. *6*, pp. 121-34.

Bew, P., Gibbon, P. and Patterson, H. *The State in Northern Ireland, 1921-72: Political Forces and Social Classes* (Manchester, 1979).

Birrell, D. and Murie, A. *Policy and Government in Northern Ireland: Lessons of Devolution* (Dublin, 1980).

Bromage, M. De Valera and the March of a Nation (London, 1967).

——, 'Image of nationhood', in *Eire/Ireland*, vol. *III* (1968), pp. 11-26.

Buckland, P. *The Factory of Grievances: Devolved Government in Northern Ireland, 1921-39* (Dublin, 1979).

——, *James Craig* (Dublin, 1980).

Budge, I. and O'Leary, C. 'Permanent supremacy and perpetual opposition: the parliament of Northern Ireland, 1922-72', in A. Eldridge (ed.), *Legislatures in Plural Societies* (London, 1974).

Campbell, T.J. *Fifty Years of Ulster, 1890-1940* (Belfast, 1941).

Chubb, B. *The Government and Politics of Ireland* (London, 1974).

Columban na Banban *Lectures on the Ethics of the Irish Revolution* (Sinn Féin Ard Comhairle, 1924).

Coogan, T.P. *The I.R.A.* (London, 1970).

Corkery, D. *The Hidden Ireland* (Dublin, 1925).

——, *Synge and Anglo-Irish Literature* (Cork, 1931).

——, *The Philosophy of the Gaelic League* (Dublin, n.d. [1943?]).

Cronin, S. 'Nation building and the Irish language revival movement', in *Eire/Ireland*, vol. *XIII* (1977), pp. 7-14.

Curran, J.M. 'The consolidation of the Irish revolution, 1921-33', in *University Review*, vol. *V* (Dublin, 1968), pp. 36-50.

De Valera, E. *A National Policy Outlined: Speech Delivered at the Inaugeral Meeting of Fianna Fáil, May 1926.*

——, *Recent Speeches and Broadcasts* (Dublin and Cork, 1933).

——, *The Way to Peace* (Dublin, 1934).

——, *National Discipline and Majority Rule* (Dublin, 1936).

Dudley Edwards, O. (ed.), *Conor Cruise O'Brien Introduces Ireland* (London, 1969).

Farrell, B. 'The drafting of the Irish free state constitution', in *Irish Jurist*, vol. *V* (1970), pp. 115-40; vol. *VI* (1971), pp. 111-35, 343-56.

Figgis, D. *The Irish Constitution Explained* (Dublin, 1922).

Fine Gael *Policy for a Just Society* (Dublin, 1968).

Fitzgerald, G. *Towards a New Ireland* (Dublin, 1973 edn.).

Fitzgerald, W.G. (ed.), *The Voice of Ireland: A Survey of the Race and Nation From all Angles by the Foremost Leaders at Home and Abroad* (Dublin, n.d. [1923?]).

Gaelic League *You May Revive the Gaelic League* (Dublin, n.d. [1937?]).

——, *Irish Literature* (Dublin, n.d. [1937?]).

Gallagher, F. *Fianna Fáil Pamphlet No. 2, King and Constitution* (Dublin n.d. [1926?]).

Gallagher, M. *Electoral Support for Irish Political Parties, 1927-73* (London, 1976).

——, 'Party solidarity, exclusivity, and inter-party relations in Ireland, 1922-77: the evidence of transfers' in *Economic and Social Review*, vol. *X* (1978), pp. 1-22.

Garvin, T. 'Nationalist elites, Irish voters and Irish political development: a comparative perspective', in ibid., vol. *VIII* (1977), pp. 161-84.

——, 'The destiny of the soldiers: tradition and modernity in the politics of de Valera's Ireland', in *Political Studies*, vol. *XXVI*, (1978), pp. 328-47.

Gwynn, D.R. *De Valera* (London, 1933).

Hackett, F. *The Story of the Irish Nation* (Dublin, 1924).

Hancock, W.K. *Survey of British Commonwealth Affairs, Vol. I, Problems of Nationality, 1918-1936* (London, 1937).

Hanly, J. *The National Ideal: A Practical Exposition of True Nationality Appertaining to Ireland* (Dublin, 1931).

Harkness, D.W. *The Restless Dominion* (London, 1969).

——, 'Mr de Valera's dominion', in *Journal of Commonwealth Political Studies*, vol. *VIII* (1970), pp. 206-28.

——, 'England's Irish question', in C. Cook and G. Peele (eds.), *The Politics of Reappraisal, 1918-1939* (London, 1975).

Harris, R. *Prejudice and Tolerance in Ulster: A Study of Neighbours and 'Strangers' in a Border Community* (Manchester, 1972).

Irish Republican Army *Address from the Soldiers of the Army of the Republic to Their Former Comrades in the Free State Army and the Civic Guard* (Dublin, 1922).

——, *Oglach na nEireann* (Dublin, 1932).

——, *Governmental Policy and Constitution of Oglach na nEireann Reported by the General Army Convention, March 1933* (Dublin, n.d. [1933?]).

Jackson, H. *The Two Irelands: A Dual Study of Inter-group Tensions* (London, minority rights group report No. 2, 1972).

Larkin, E. 'A reconsideration: Daniel Corkery and his ideas on cultural nationalism', in *Eire/Ireland*, vol. *VIII* (1973), pp. 42-51.

Lee, J. (ed.), *Ireland, 1945-1970* (Dublin, 1979).

Longford, Earl of and O'Neill, T.P. *Eamon de Valera* (London, 1970).

Lynch, J. *Speeches and Statements on Irish Unity, Northern Ireland, and Anglo-Irish Relations* (Dublin, 1971).

McCaffrey, L.J. 'Daniel Corkery and Irish cultural nationalism', in *Eire/Ireland* vol. *VIII* (1973), pp. 35-41.

McAllister, I. 'Political opposition in Northern Ireland: the national democratic party, 1965-70', in *Economic and Social Review*, vol. *VI* (1975), pp. 253-66.

——, 'Political parties and social cleavage in Northern Ireland', in *Social Studies*, vol. *V* (1976), pp. 75-89.

——, 'Social influences on voters and non-voters', in *Political Studies*, vol. *24* (1976), pp. 462-8.

——, *The Northern Ireland S.D.L.P.: Political Opposition in a Divided Society* (London, 1977).

——, 'The legitimacy of opposition: the collapse of the 1974 Northern Ireland executive', in *Eire/Ireland*, vol. *XII* (1977), pp. 25-42.

——, 'Modern developments in the Northern Ireland party system', in *Parliamentary Affairs*, vol. *XXXII* (1979), pp. 279-316.

——, 'Centre-periphery within Northern Ireland: a model for the development of a party system' (Paper delivered at the Economy, Territory, Identity workshop, University of Brussels, April, 1979).

——, *Territorial Differentiation and Party Development in Northern Ireland* (University of Strathclyde, 1980).

MacManus, M.J. *Eamon de Valera* (London, 1944).

MacSwiney, M. *Where We Stand Now: The Truth About the Republic* (Dublin 1924).

Mair, P. *The Break-up of the United Kingdom: The Irish Experience of Regime Channge, 1918-49* (University of Strathclyde, 1978).

Manning, M. *Irish Political Parties* (Dublin, 1972).

Mansergh, N. *Survey of British Commonwealth Affairs: Problems of Wartime Co-operation and Post War Change, 1939-52* (London, 1958).

Meenan, J. *The Irish Economy Since 1922* (Liverpool, 1970).

Munger, F. *The Legitimacy of Opposition: The Change of Government in Ireland in 1932* (University of Strathclyde, 1975).

Murphy, J.A. 'The New I.R.A., 1925-62', in T.D. Williams (ed.), *Irish Secret Societies*.

——, 'Identity change in the republic of Ireland', in *Études Irlandaises*, vol. *V* (1976), pp. 143-58.

——, *Ireland in the Twentieth Century* (Dublin, 1975).

——, *Eamon de Valera: The Politician* (Bulletin of the department of foreign affairs, Dublin, No. *872*, 1975).

——, 'Fianna Fáil: the historical perspective and the early years', in *Irish Times*, May 1976.

——, 'Taking the constitutional path', in *Irish Press*, May 1976.

Nowlan, K.B. and Williams, T.D. (eds.), *Ireland in the War Years and*

After (Dublin, 1969).

O'Brien, G. *The Four Green Fields: Irish Nationalism from the Union to the Present Day* (Dublin, 1936).

Ó Cuív, B. (ed.), *A View of the Irish Language* (Dublin, 1969).

O Faolain, S. *The Life Story of Eamon de Valera* (Dublin, 1933).

O'Higgins, B. *Martyrs for Ireland: The Story of MacCormick and Barnes* (Dublin, 1940).

O'Higgins, K. *Three Years Hard Labour* (Address to the Irish society of Oxford, 31 Oct., 1924).

O'Kelly, J.J. *Partition: Dáil Eireann Comes of Age* (Lecture delivered at Sinn Féin Headquarters, 21 Jan., 1940).

O'Leary, C. 'Ireland: the north and south', in S.E. Finer (ed.), *Adversary Politics and Electoral Reform* (London, 1975).

O'Neill, T.P. 'In search of a political path: Irish republicanism, 1922-27', in *Historical Studies, X* (1976).

Pechell, J.M. *De Valera* (London, 1939).

Power, P.F. 'Violence, consent and the Northern Ireland problem', in *Journal of Commonwealth and Comparative Politics*, vol. *14* (1976), pp. 119-40.

Pyne, P. 'The third Sinn Féin party, 1923-26', in *Economic and Social Review*, vol. *I* (1969-70), pp. 29-50, 229-58.

——, 'The politics of parliamentary abstentionism: Ireland's four Sinn Féin parties, 1923-26', in *Journal of Commonwealth and Comparative Politics*, vol. *12* (1974), pp. 206-27.

Rumpf, E. and Hepburn, A.C. *Nationalism and Socialism in Twentieth Century Ireland* (Liverpool, 1977).

Ryan, D. *Unique Dictator* (London, 1936).

Sacks, P.M. *The Donegal Mafia: An Irish Political Machine* (Yale UP, 1977).

Share, B. *The Emergency: Neutral Ireland, 1939-45* (Dublin, 1978).

Stuart, F. *Lecture on Nationality and Culture* (Sinn Féin Ard Comhairle, 1924).

White, J. *Minority Report: The Protestant Community in the Irish Republic* (Dublin, 1975).

White, T. de V. *Kevin O'Higgins* (Tralee, 1967).

Whyte, J.H. *Church and State in Modern Ireland* (Dublin, 1971).

Wright, F. 'Protestant ideology and politics in Ulster', in *European Journal of Sociology*, vol. *XIV* (1973), pp. 213-80.

8. Wales and Scotland

Butt Philip, A. *The Welsh Question: Nationalism in Welsh Politics, 1945-70* (Cardiff, 1975).
Davies, R.R. 'Colonial Wales', in *Past and Present*, No. *65* (1974), pp. 3-23.
Evans, G. *Nonviolent Nationalism* (Swansea, 1973).
Hanham, H.J. *Scottish Nationalism* (London, 1969).
Harvie, C. *Scotland and Nationalism* (London, 1977).
Jenkins, R.T. 'The development of nationalism in Wales', in *Sociological Review*, vol. *27* (1935), pp. 163-82.
Mitchison, R. 'Patriotism and national identity in eighteenth century Scotland', in *Historical Studies, XI* (Belfast, 1978).
Morgan, K.O. 'Welsh nationalism: historical background', in *Journal of Contemporary History*, vol. *6* (1971), pp. 153-71.
Williams, G. *Welsh Reformation Essays* (Cardiff, 1967).
——, *Religion, Language and Nationality in Wales* (Cardiff, 1979).

9. Newspapers

Glandon, V.E. 'Index of Irish newspapers, 1900-1922', in *Eire/Ireland*, vol. *XI* (1976), pp. 84-121; vol. *XII* (1977), p. 86-115.

Anglo-Celt (Cavan)
Ballina Herald
Bray Herald
Carlow Nationalist and Leinster Times
Clare Champion
Clare Examiner
Connaught People
Connaught Telegraph
Cork Daily Herald
Cork Examiner
Derry Journal
Donegal Independent
Donegal Vindicator
Dublin Evening Herald
Dublin Evening Post
Dublin Journal

Irish Press
Irish Times
Irish Tribune
Kerry News

Kerry Sentinel
Kilkenny Journal
Kingstown Standard
The Leader
Leinster Reporter
Limerick Chronicle
Limerick Echo
Longford Independent
Munster Express
Munster News and Limerick and Clare Advertiser
Nation

Fermanagh Herald	*Nationality*
Flag of Ireland	*The Nationalist* (Clonmel)
Freeman's Journal	*Nenagh Guardian*
Galway Vindicator	*Pilot*
Hibernian Journal	*Public Register or Freeman's*
Irish Felon	*Journal* (18th century)
Irish Independent	*Roscommon Herald*
Irish News (Belfast)	*Saunders' News Letter*
Irish People	*Sligo Champion*
Strokestown Democrat	*Waterford Mirror*
United Ireland	*Waterford News*
United Irishman	*Weekly Observer* (Newcastle West)
Volunteer's Evening Post	*Westmeath Independent*
Volunteer's Journal or Irish Herald	*Wexford People*

Volumes of press cuttings in the National Library of Ireland:
Robert Emmet in Poetry (2 vols);
Manchester Martyrs (1891-1912).

10. Theses

Barrett, R.J. 'A comparative study of imperial constitutional theory in Ireland and America in the age of the American revolution', University of Dublin, D. Phil., 1958.

Breen, N. 'Concepts of Ireland: a study of four Irish nationalists in the period, 1891-1916', University of Cork, MA, 1975.

Bull, P.J. 'The reconstruction of the Irish parliamentary party, 1895-1903: an analysis with special reference to William O'Brien', University of Cambridge, D. Phil., 1972.

Foy, M.T. 'The A.O.H.: an Irish politico-religious pressure group, 1884-1975', Queen's University of Belfast, MA, 1976.

Hill, J.R. 'The role of Dublin in the Irish national movement, 1840-1848', University of Leeds, Ph.D., 1973.

Kelly, J.S. 'The political, intellectual and social background to the Irish literary revival to 1901', University of Cambridge, D.Phil., 1971.

Leonard, D.W. 'John Mitchel, Charles Gavan Duffy, and the legacy of Young Ireland', University of Sheffield, Ph.D., 1975.

McGuire, J.L. 'Politics, opinion, and the Irish constitution, 1688-1707', National University of Ireland, MA, 1968.

Powell, T.J. 'The background to the rebellion in Co. Wexford, 1790-98',

National University of Ireland, MA, 1970.

Semple, A.J. 'Fenian infiltration of the British army in Ireland, 1864-67', University of Dublin, M.Litt., 1974.

Van der Wusten, H. 'Irish opposition to the political unity of the British Isles, 1800-1921: a study in the political geography of the processes of integration and disintegration', University of Amsterdam, Ph.D., 1977.

SUPPLEMENTARY BIBLIOGRAPHY

This bibliography includes works relating to nationalism in Ireland published since 1982, with a few earlier item‏ not included in the original bibliography.

Adams, Gerry, *The Politics of Irish Freedom* (Kerry, 1986).

Adamson, Ian, *The Identity of Ulster: The Land, the Language and the People* (Belfast, 1982).

—— , *Cruthin: The Ancient Kindred* (Belfast, 1986).

Akenson, D.H., *Small Differences: Irish Catholics and Irish Protestants, 1815-1922* (Kingston/Montreal, 1988).

Alexander, Yonah, and O'Day, Alan (eds), *Ireland's Terrorist Trauma: Interdisciplinary Perspectives* (London, 1989).

Archer, J.R., 'Necessary ambiguity: nationalism and myth in Ireland', in *Éire/Ireland*, xix, 2 (1989), pp. 23-37.

Arnold, Bruce, *What Kind of Country: Modern Irish Politics, 1968-1983* (London, 1984).

Arthur, Paul, *The Government and Politics of Northern Ireland* (London, 1983).

Atkinson, Colin B., and Atkinson, J.O., 'Sydney Owenson, Lady Morgan: Irish patriot and first professional woman writer', in *Éire/Ireland*, xv, 2 (1989), pp. 60-90.

Bartlett, Tom, 'An end to moral economy: the Irish militia disturbances of 1793', in *Past and Present*, no. 99 (1983), pp. 41-64.

Beames, M., *Peasants and Power: The Whiteboy Movements and their Control in Pre-famine Ireland* (Brighton, 1983).

Bell, Desmond, 'Acts of union: youth, sub-culture and ethnic identity amongst Protestants in Northern Ireland', in *British Journal of Sociology*, 38 (1987), pp. 158-83.

Bew, Paul, and Patterson, Henry, *Sean Lemass and the Making of Modern Ireland 1945-66* (Dublin, 1982).

Bew, Paul, *Conflict and Conciliation in Ireland, 1890-1910: Parnellites and Radical Agrarians* (Oxford, 1987).

Bew, Paul, *et al.*, *The Dynamics of Irish Politics* (London, 1989).

Birch, A.H.,*Nationalism and National Integration* (London, 1989).

Bishop, P., and Mallie, E., *The Provisional I.R.A.* (London, 1987).

Boal, Frederick W., and Douglas, H. *et al.*, *Integration and Division: Geographical Perspectives on the Northern Ireland Problem* (London, 1982).

Bowen, D., *Paul Cullen and the Shaping of Modern Irish Catholicism* (Dublin, 1983).

Bowman, John, *De Valera and the Ulster Question, 1917–1973* (Oxford, 1982).

Boyce, D.G. (ed.), *The Revolution in Ireland, 1879-1923* (London, 1988).

Boyle, Ken, and Hadden, Tom, *Ireland: A Positive Proposal* (London, 1985).

Bradshaw, B., 'Nationalism and historical scholarship in Modern Ireland', in *Irish Historical Studies*, xxvi, no. 104 (1989), pp. 329-51.

Brady, Ciaran, and Gillespie, Raymond (eds), *Natives and Newcomers: Essays on the Making of Irish Colonial Society, 1534-1641* (Dublin, 1986).

Brady, John, 'The New Ireland Forum: the search for a political solution in Northern Ireland', in *Studies*, xxiii (1984), pp. 318-23.

Brooke, Peter, *Ulster Presbyterianism: The Historical Perspective, 1610-1970* (Dublin, 1987).

Brown, Terence, *Ireland: A Social and Cultural History, 1922-1979* (London, 1981).

—— , *The Whole Protestant Community: The Making of a Historical Myth* (Derry, 1985).

—— , *Ireland's Literature: Selected Essays* (Mullingar, 1988).

Bruce, Steve, *God Save Ulster: The Religion and Politics of Paisleyism* (Oxford, 1986).

Buckley, Mary, 'Thomas Davis: a study in Nationalist philosophy' (Ph.D., University College Cork, 1980).

Bull, Philip, 'The U.I.L. and the reunion of the Irish parliamentary party, 1898-1900', in *Irish Historical Studies*, xxvi, no. 101 (1988), pp. 51-78.

Cairns, David, and Richards, Shaun, *Writing Ireland* (Manchester, 1988).

Candy, C.M., 'Popular Irish literature in the age of the Anglo–Irish literary revival: four case studies' (MA, University College Cork, 1987).

Canny, N.P., 'The formation of the Irish mind: religion, politics and Gaelic Irish literature, 1580-1750', in *Past and Present*, no. 95 (1982), pp. 91-116.

Casway, Jerrold I., *Owen Roe O'Neill and the Struggle for Catholic Ireland* (Pennsylvania, 1984).

Chenevix Trench, Charles, *The Great Dan: A Biography of Daniel O'Connell* (London, 1984).

Clarke, S., and Donnelly, J.S., Jr (eds), *Irish Peasants: Violence and Political Unrest, 1780-1914* (Manchester, 1983).

Coldrey, B.M., *Faith and Fatherland: The Christian Brothers and the Development of Irish Nationalism, 1838-1921* (Dublin, 1988).

Comerford, R.V., *The Fenians in Context: Irish Politics and Society, 1848-82* (Dublin, 1985).

Connolly, S.J., 'Catholicism in Ulster, 1800-1850', in P. Roebuck (ed.), *Plantation to Partition: Essays in Ulster History in Honour of J.L. McCracken* (Belfast, 1981), pp. 157-71.

—— , *Priests and People in Pre-famine Ireland, 1780-1845* (Dublin, 1982).

—— , *Religion and Society in Nineteenth Century Ireland* (Dublin, 1985).

Corish, Patrick J., *The Irish Catholic Experience: A Historical Survey* (Dublin, 1985).

—— (ed.), *Radicals, Rebels and Establishments* (Belfast, 1985).

Cox, W. Harvey, 'Who wants a United Ireland?', in *Government and Opposition*, xx (1985), 29-47.

Curtin, Chris, Kelly, Mary and O'Down, Liam, *Culture and Ideology in Ireland* (Galway, 1984).

Curtin, Nancy J., 'The transformation of the Society of United Irishmen into a mass-based revolutionary organization, 1794-6', in *Irish Historical Studies*, xxiv (1985), pp. 463-92.

Daly, Mary E., *The Famine in Ireland* (Dublin, 1986).

Darby, John (ed.), *Northern Ireland: The Background to the Conflict* (Belfast, 1983).

Deane, Seamus, *Celtic Revivals: Essays in Modern Irish Literature, 1880-1980* (Dublin, 1985).

—— , 'Swift and the Anglo–Irish intellect', in *Eighteenth Century Ireland*, i (1986), pp. 9-22.

Dooher, John B., 'Tyrone nationalism and the question of partition, 1910-1925' (M. Phil., University of Ulster, 1986).

Downey, J., *Them and Us: Ireland and the Northern Question, 1909-1982* (Dublin, 1983).

Doyle, David N., *Ireland, Irishmen and Revolutionary America, 1760-1820* (Dublin, 1984).

Dudley Edwards, Owen, *Eamon de Valera* (Cardiff, 1988).

Dunne, Tom, *Maria Edgeworth and the Colonial Mind* (Cork, 1984).

Drudy, P.J. (ed.), *Ireland: Land, Politics and People* (Cambridge, 1982).

Dwyer, T.R., *De Valera's Darkest Hour: In Search of National Independence, 1919-1932* (Dublin, 1982).

—— , *De Valera's Finest Hour: In Search of National Independence, 1932-1959* (Dublin, 1982).

Elliott, Marianne, *Watchmen in Sion: The Protestant Idea of Liberty* (Derry, 1985).

—— , *Wolfe Tone: Prophet of Irish Independence* (New Haven/ London, 1989).

Ellis, Stephen G., *Tudor Ireland: Crown, Community and the Conflict of Cultures* (London, 1985).

—— , 'Nationalist historiography and the English and Gaelic worlds in the later Middle Ages', in *Irish Historical Studies*, xxv, no. 97 (1986), 1-18.

Fallon, C.H., *Soul of Fire: A Biography of Mary MacSwiney* (Cork, 1986).

Fanning, Ronan, *Independent Ireland* (Dublin, 1983).

—— , *The Four-Leaved Shamrock: Electoral Politics and the National Imagination in Independent Ireland* (Dublin, 1983).

—— , 'The meaning of revisionism', in *Irish Review*, no. 4 (Spring, 1988), pp. 15-19.

Farrell, Brian, 'The unlikely marriage: de Valera, Lemass and the shaping of modern Ireland', in *Etudes Irlandaises*, x (1985), pp. 215-22.

—— , *Sean Lemass* (Dublin, 1985).

—— (ed.), *De Valera's Constitution and Ours* (Dublin, 1988).

Fennell, Desmond, 'Against revisionism', in *Irish Review*, no. 4 (Spring, 1988), pp. 20-6.

Fisk, R., *In Time of War: Ireland, Ulster and the Price of Neutrality, 1939-1945* (London, 1985).

FitzPatrick, Brendan, *Seventeenth Century Ireland: The War of Religions* (Dublin, 1988).

Flanagan, Marie Thérèse, *Irish Society, Anglo–Norman Settlers, Angevin Kingship: Interactions in Ireland in the Late Twelfth Century* (Oxford, 1989).

Follis, B.A., 'The establishment of Northern Ireland, 1920-1925' (Ph.D., Queen's University Belfast, 1990).

Ford, G.A., *The Protestant Reformation in Ireland, 1590-1641* (Frankfurt, 1985).

Foster, R.F., 'History and the Irish Question', in *Transactions of the Royal Historical Society*, 5th series, vol. 33 (1983), pp. 169-92.

—— , *Modern Ireland, 1600-1972* (Harmondsworth, 1988).

—— , *Cultural Traditions in Northern Ireland: Varieties of Irishness* (Institute of Irish Studies, Queen's University Belfast, 1989).

Frame, Robin, *English Lordship in Ireland, 1318-1361* (Oxford, 1982).

Gallagher, Michael, *Political Parties in the Republic of Ireland* (Dublin, 1985).

Garvin, Tom, 'Priests and patriots: Irish separatism and fear of the modern, 1890-1914', in *Irish Historical Studies*, xxv, no. 97 (1986), pp. 67-81.

—— , 'The anatomy of a nationalist revolution: Ireland, 1858-1928', in *Comparative Studies in Society and History*, xxviii (1986), pp. 468-501.

—— , *Nationalist Revolutionaries in Ireland, 1858-1928* (Oxford, 1987).

Geary, L.M., *The Plan of Campaign, 1886-91* (Cork, 1986).

Gillespie, Raymond, *Colonial Ulster: The Settlement of East Ulster, 1600-1641* (Cork, 1985).

Gilley, Sheridan, 'The Catholic Church and revolution in nineteenth century Ireland', in Yonah Alexander and Alan O'Day (eds), *Terrorism in Ireland* (London, 1984), pp. 121-45.

Girvan, B., 'Social change and moral politics: the Irish constitutional referendum, 1983', in *Political Studies*, xxxiv (1986), pp. 61-81.

—— , 'National identity and conflict in Northern Ireland', in B. Girvan and R. Sturm (eds), *Politics and Society in Contemporary Ireland* (Aldershot, 1986), pp. 105-34.

Glandon, Virginia E., 'Arthur Griffith and the ideal Irish state', in *Studies*, lxxiii, no. 289 (1984), pp. 26-36.

—— , *Arthur Griffith and the Advanced Nationalist Press in Ireland, 1900-1922* (New York, 1985).

Goldring, Maurice, *Faith of our Fathers: The Formation of Irish Nationalist Ideology, 1890-1920* (Dublin, 1982).

Greaves, C. Desmond, *Liam Mellowes and the Irish Revolution* (London, 1987).

Hachey, Thomas E., and McCaffrey, Laurence J. (eds), *Perspectives on Irish Nationalism* (Lexington, Kentucky, 1989).

Harkness, David, *Northern Ireland Since 1920* (Dublin, 1983).

Harp, Richard, 'The Shan Van Vocht (Belfast, 1896-1899) and Irish Nationalism', in *Éire/Ireland*, xxiv, 3 (1989), pp. 42-52.

Haslam, Richard, 'Lady Morgan's novels from 1806-1833: cultural aesthetics and national identity', in *Éire/Ireland*, xxii, 4 (1987), pp. 11-25.

Haughey, Charles J., *The Spirit of the Nation: The Speeches and Statements of Charles J. Haughey, 1951-1985*, ed. Martin Mansergh (Cork, 1986).

Hayton, David, and O'Brien, Gerard (eds), *War and Politics in Ireland, 1649-1730* (London, 1985).

Hewitt, Christopher, 'Catholic grievances, Catholic nationalism and violence in Northern Ireland during the Civil Rights period: a reconsideration', in *British Journal of Sociology*, 32 (1981), pp. 362-80.

——— , 'Discrimination in Northern Ireland: a comment', *British Journal of Sociology*, 34 (1983), pp. 446-51.

——— , 'Catholic grievances and nationalism in Northern Ireland', *British Journal of Sociology*, 36 (1985), pp. 102-5.

——— , 'Explaining violence in Northern Ireland', *British Journal of Sociology*, 38 (1987), pp. 88-93.

Hickey, John, *Religion and the Northern Ireland Problem* (Dublin, 1984).

Hill, Jacqueline R., 'National festivals, the State and the "Protestant Ascendancy" in Ireland, 1790-1828', in *Irish Historical Studies*, xxiv no. 93 (1984), pp. 30-51.

——— , 'Popery and Protestantism, civil and religious liberty: the disputed lessons of Irish history, 1690-1802', in *Past and Present*, no. 118 (1988), pp. 96-129.

Holmes, R. Finlay, 'Ulster Presbyterianism and Irish Nationalism', in Stuart Mews (ed.), *Religion and National Identity: Studies in Church History* (Oxford, 1982), pp. 535-55.

Hopkinson, Michael, *Green Against Green: The Irish Civil War* (Dublin, 1988).

Hoppen, K.T., *Elections, Politics and Society in Ireland, 1832-1885* (Oxford, 1984).

——— , *Ireland Since 1800: Conflict and Conformity* (London, 1989).

Hutchinson, John, 'Cultural nationalism, elite mobility and nation-building: communitarian politics in modern Ireland', in *British Journal of Sociology*, 38 (1987), pp. 482-500.

——— , *The Dynamics of Cultural Nationalism: The Gaelic Revival and the Creation of the Irish Nation State* (London, 1987).

Inglis, T., *Moral Monopoly: the Catholic Church in Modern Ireland* (Dublin, 1987).

Jeffrey, Keith (ed.), *The Divided Province: The Troubles in Northern*

Ireland, 1969-85 (London, 1985).

Jenkins, Richard, 'Northern Ireland: in what sense "religions" in conflict?', in Richard Jenkins, Hastings Donnan and Graham McFarlane, *The Sectarian Divide in Northern Ireland Today* (Royal Anthropological Society, Occasional paper no. 41, 1986).

Jordan, Donald, 'John O'Connor Power, Charles Stewart Parnell and the centralisation of popular politics in Ireland', in *Irish Historical Studies,* xxv, no. 97 (1986), pp. 46-66.

Kearney, Richard (ed.), *The Irish Mind: Exploring Intellectual Traditions* (Dublin, 1985).

Keenan, D.J., *The Catholic Church in Nineteenth Century Ireland* (Dublin, 1983).

Kelly, Patrick, 'A light to the blind: the voice of the dispossessed elite in the generation after the defeat at Limerick', in *Irish Historical Studies,* xxiv (1985), pp. 431-62.

Kennedy, Dennis, *The Widening Gulf: Northern Attitudes to the Independent Irish State, 1919-1949* (Belfast, 1988).

Kennedy, Liam, *Two Ulsters: A Case for Repartition* (Belfast, 1986).

Keogh, Dermot, *The Vatican, the Bishops and Irish Politics, 1919-1939* (Cambridge, 1986).

Kiberd, Declan, *Anglo–Irish Attitudes* (Derry, 1984).

—— , 'Irish literature and Irish history', in Roy F. Foster (ed.), *The Oxford Illustrated History of Ireland* (Oxford, 1989), pp. 275-337.

Knowlton, Steven R., 'The politics of John Mitchel: a reappraisal' in *Éire/Ireland,* xxii, 2 (1987), 38-55.

Kovalcheck, Kassian A., 'Catholic grievances in Northern Ireland: appraisal and judgement', in *British Journal of Sociology,* 38 (1987), pp. 76-87.

Larkin, Emmet, *The Consolidation of the Roman Catholic Church in Ireland, 1860-1870* (Dublin, 1987).

Lee, Joseph, *Ireland, 1912-1985* (Cambridge, 1989).

Leerson, Joseph T., *Mere Irish and Fiór Ghael: Studies in the Idea of Irish Nationality* (Amsterdam and Philadelphia, 1986).

Lloyd, David, *Nationalism and Minor Literature: James Clarence Mangan and the Emergence of Irish Cultural Nationalism* (London, 1987).

Loughlin, James, 'The Irish Protestant Home Rule Association and nationalist politics, 1886-93', in *Irish Historical Studies,* xxiv, no. 95 (1985), pp. 341-60.

Lydon, James (ed.), *England and Ireland in the Later Middle Ages: Essays in Honour of Joycelyn Otway-Ruthven* (Dublin, 1981).

——— , *The English in Medieval Ireland* (Dublin, 1984).

Lyons, J.B., *The Enigma of Tom Kettle: Irish Patriot, Essayist, Poet, British Soldier, 1880-1916* (Dublin, 1983).

MacCarthy-Morrogh, Michael, *The Munster Plantation: English Migration to Southern Ireland, 1538-1641* (Oxford, 1986).

MacDonagh, Oliver, *et al.* (eds), *Irish Culture and Nationalism, 1750-1950* (London, 1982).

MacDonagh, Oliver, *States of Mind: A Study of Anglo–Irish Conflict, 1780-1980* (London, 1983).

MacDonagh, Oliver, and Mandle, W.F., *Ireland and Irish–Australia: Studies in Cultural and Political History* (London, 1986).

MacDonagh, Oliver, *The Hereditary Bondsman: Daniel O'Connell, 1775-1829* (London, 1988).

——— , *The Emancipist: Daniel O'Connell, 1830-1847* (London, 1989).

MacMahon, Deirdre, *Republicans and Imperialists: Anglo–Irish Relations in the 1930s* (New Haven and London, 1984).

McMinn, J.R.B., *Against the Tide: A Calendar of the Papers of the Reverend J.M. Armour, Irish Presbyterian Minister and Home Ruler, 1869-1914* (Belfast, 1985).

Mitchell, Arthur, and O Snodaigh, Padraig, *Irish Political Documents, 1916-1949* (Dublin, 1985).

——— , *Irish Political Documents, 1869-1916* (Dublin, 1989).

Mokyr, J., *Why Ireland Starved: A Quantitative and Analytical History of the Irish Economy, 1800-1845* (London, 1983; revised edn, 1985).

Morgan, Austen, *James Connolly: A Political Biography* (Manchester, 1989).

Morgan, Hiram, 'The end of Gaelic Ulster: a thematic interpretation of events between 1534 and 1610', in *Irish Historical Studies*, xxvi, no. 101 (1988), pp. 8-32.

Moxon-Browne, E., *Nation, Class and Creed in Northern Ireland* (Aldershot, 1983).

Murphy, John A., and O'Carroll, J.P. (eds), *De Valera and His Times* (Cork, 1983).

Murphy, William M., *The Parnell Myth and Irish Politics, 1891-1956* (New York, 1986).

Murray, A.C., 'Agrarian violence and Nationalism in nineteenth century Ireland: the myth of Ribbonism', in *Irish Economic and Social History*, xiii (1986), pp. 56-73.

——— , 'Nationality and local politics in late nineteenth century

Ireland: the case of Co. Westmeath', in *Irish Historical Studies*, xxv (1986), pp. 144-58.

New History of Ireland: vol. ii, *Medieval Ireland, 1169-1534*, ed. A. Cosgrove (Oxford, 1987); vol. iv, *Eighteenth Century Ireland, 1691-1800*, ed. T.W. Moody and W.E. Vaughan (Oxford, 1986); vol. v, *Ireland Under the Union, i: 1801-70*, ed. W.E. Vaughan (Oxford, 1989).

New Ireland Forum Report (Dublin, 1984).

Newsinger, John, 'James Connolly and the Easter Rising', in *Science and Society*, xlvii (1983-4),'152-77.

Nowlan, Kevin B., and O'Connell, Maurice (eds), *Daniel O'Connell: Portrait of a Radical* (Belfast, 1984).

Nolan, William (ed.), *Tipperary: History and Society* (Dublin, 1985).

O'Brien, Conor Cruise, *God Land: Reflections on Religion and Nationalism* (Cambridge, 1988).

O'Brien, Gerard, 'The Grattan mystique', in *Eighteenth Century Ireland*, i (1986), pp. 177-94.

——— , *Anglo–Irish Politics in the Age of Grattan* (Dublin, 1987).

O Broin, Leon, *Protestant Nationalism in Revolutionary Ireland: The Stopford Connection* (Dublin, 1985).

O'Callaghan, Margaret, 'Language, nationality and cultural identity in the Irish Free State, 1922-7', in *Irish Historical Studies*, xxiv, no. 94 (1984), pp. 226-45.

O'Connor, Garry, *Sean O'Casey: A Life* (London, 1989).

O'Day, Alan, *Parnell and the First Home Rule Episode, 1884-7* (Dublin, 1986).

——— (ed.), *Reactions to Irish Nationalism* (London, 1987).

O'Donnell, Edmund, 'History lessons', in *Studies*, lxxiii (1984), pp. 265-71.

O'Ferrall, Fergus, *Catholic Emancipation: Daniel O'Connell and the Birth of Irish Democracy, 1820-30* (Dublin, 1985).

O'Flanagan, Neil, 'Dublin City in an age of war and revolution, 1914-1924' (MA, University College Dublin, 1985).

O Grada, Cormac, *The Great Irish Famine* (London, 1989).

O'Halloran, Clare, *Partition and the Limits of Irish Nationalism: An Ideology Under Stress* (Dublin, 1987).

O'Hearn, Dennis, 'Catholic grievances: comments', in *British Journal of Sociology*, 38 (1987), pp. 94-100.

——— , 'Again on discrimination in the North of Ireland: a reply to the rejoinder', *British Journal of Sociology*, 36 (1985), pp. 94-101.

O'Keefe, Timothy, 'The art and politics of the Parnell Monument', in

Éire/Ireland, xix, 1 (1984), pp. 6-25.

—— , 'The 1898 efforts to celebrate the United Irishmen: the '98 centennial', *Éire/Ireland*, xxiii, 2 (1988), pp. 51-73.

O'Malley, P., *The Uncivil Wars: Ireland Today* (Belfast, 1983).

O'Neil, Daniel J., 'The cult of self-sacrifice: the Irish experience', in *Éire/Ireland*, xxiv, 4 (1989), pp. 89-105.

O'Neil, Shane, 'The politics of culture in Ireland, 1898-1910' (D.Phil., University of Oxford, 1982).

Patterson, Henry, *The Politics of Illusion: Republicanism and Socialism in Modern Ireland* (London, 1989).

Philpin, C.H.E., (ed.), *Nationalism and Popular Protest in Ireland* (Cambridge, 1987).

Prager, J., *Building Democracy in Ireland: Political Order and Cultural Integration in a Newly Independent Nation* (Cambridge, 1986).

Princess Grace Irish Library, *Irishness in a Changing Society* (Gerard's Cross, Bucks., 1989).

Pringle, D.G., *One Island, Two Nations? A Political Geographical Analysis of the National Conflict in Ireland* (Letchworth, 1985).

Purdie, Bob, 'The Irish Anti-Partition League, South Armagh and the abstentionist tactic, 1945-58', in *Irish Political Studies*, i (1986), pp. 67-77.

—— , *Politics in the Streets: The Origins of the Civil Rights Movement in Northern Ireland* (Belfast, 1990).

Quinn, Peter A., 'Yeats and revolutionary nationalism: the centenary of '98', in *Éire/Ireland*, xv, 3 (1980), pp. 47-64.

Robinson, Philip S., *The Plantation of Ulster: British Settlement in an Irish Landscape, 1600-1670* (Dublin, 1984).

Sawyer, Roger, *Casement: The Flawed Hero* (London, 1984).

See, Katharine O'Sullivan, *First World Nationalisms: Class and Ethnic Politics in Northern Ireland and Quebec* (Chicago and London, 1986).

Simms, Katharine, *From Kings to Warlords: The Changing Political Structure of Gaelic Ireland in the Later Middle Ages* (Suffolk, 1987).

Thuente, Mary Helen, 'Violence in pre-famine Ireland: the testimony of Irish folklore', in *Irish University Review*, xv (1985), pp. 129-47.

Todd, Jennifer, 'Northern Irish nationalist political culture', in *Irish Political Studies*, 5 (1990), pp. 31-44.

Townshend, Charles, *Political Violence in Ireland: Government and Resistance Since 1848* (Oxford, 1983).

Vaughan, W.E., *Landlords and Tenants in Ireland, 1848-1904* (Dublin, 1984).

Walker, B.M., *Ulster Politics: The Formative Years, 1868-86* (Belfast, 1989).

Whelan, Kevin, 'The religious factor in the 1798 Rebellion in Co. Wexford', in Patrick O'Flanagan, Patrick Ferguson and Kevin Whelan (eds) *Rural Ireland, 1600-1900: Modernisation and Change* (Cork, 1987), pp. 62-85.

White, Barry, *John Hume: Statesman of the Troubles* (Belfast, 1984).

Whyte, John, 'How much discrimination was there under the Unionist regime 1921-1968', in T. Gallagher and J. O'Connell (eds), *Contemporary Irish Studies* (Manchester, 1983), pp. 1-35.

Williams, Martin, 'Ancient mythology and revolutionary ideology in Ireland, 1878-1916', in *Historical Journal*, xxvi, 2 (1983), pp. 307-28.

Winstanley, Michael, *Ireland and the Land Question, 1800-1922* (London, 1984).

Yeats, W.B., *Collected Letters, Vol. I, 1865-1895*, ed. John Kelly and Eric Domville (Oxford, 1986).

INDEX